FIGHTING FOR
RELIABLE EVIDENCE

FIGHTING FOR RELIABLE EVIDENCE

Judith M. Gueron
and
Howard Rolston

Russell Sage Foundation • New York

The Russell Sage Foundation

The Russell Sage Foundation, one of the oldest of America's general purpose foundations, was established in 1907 by Mrs. Margaret Olivia Sage for "the improvement of social and living conditions in the United States." The Foundation seeks to fulfill this mandate by fostering the development and dissemination of knowledge about the country's political, social, and economic problems. While the Foundation endeavors to assure the accuracy and objectivity of each book it publishes, the conclusions and interpretations in Russell Sage Foundation publications are those of the authors and not of the Foundation, its Trustees, or its staff. Publication by Russell Sage, therefore, does not imply Foundation endorsement.

Library of Congress Cataloging-in-Publication Data

Gueron, Judith M.
   Fighting for reliable evidence / Judith M. Gueron and Howard Rolston.
      pages cm
   Includes bibliographical references and index.
   ISBN 978-0-87154-493-3 (pbk. : alk. paper) — ISBN 978-1-61044-800-0 (ebook)
1. Social service—United States—Evaluation.   2. Social service—Research—United States.   3. Evaluation research (Social action programs)—United States.   I. Rolston, Howard.   II. Title.
   HV91.G87 2013
   361.973072—dc23   2013005099

RUSSELL SAGE FOUNDATION
112 East 64th Street, New York, New York 10065

10 9 8 7 6 5 4 3 2 1

CONTENTS

TABLES AND FIGURES

ABOUT THE AUTHORS

JUDITH M. GUERON is scholar in residence and President Emerita at MDRC.

HOWARD ROLSTON is principal associate at Abt associates.

PREFACE

All historians are prisoners of their own experience.
—Arthur M. Schlesinger Jr.[1]

Welfare policy in this country is unique among all areas of social policy in having had forty-five years of uninterrupted, large-scale random assignment studies that assessed the effectiveness of reform initiatives. This book tells the story of our participation in that history. It is not an impartial account. For most of these years, we were actors in the story. Judy helped to build and then led a private nonprofit company, MDRC (originally the Manpower Demonstration Research Corporation), dedicated to learning what works to improve the well-being of low-income Americans. MDRC was one of the pioneers in demonstrating the feasibility of using random assignment to assess social programs. From 1982 to 2004, Howard was a senior career civil servant in the U.S. Department of Health and Human Services with responsibilities for evaluation of state and federal welfare reform initiatives.

By the mid-1980s, when we both had become convinced of the distinctive value of random assignment, we were insiders in two of the most active organizations promoting such work. Collectively, we spent almost sixty person-years fighting to implement these studies in diverse arenas and to show that the approach, done correctly, was realistic, ethical, and uniquely able to answer certain questions. For us this was not cold history but our life's work, and our passion.

How did we come to write the book together? In 2004 each of us stepped down from the positions we held during the period focused on in this book and decided to publish our own versions of a story that had been told before but not with an insider's experience and not entirely accurately in important respects. Learning of our separate intentions, we decided to join forces, suspecting that our complementary perspectives would better illuminate what really happened. We had never jointly written anything before, but we had worked closely enough through the years to know that we shared a commitment to rigor and to putting research at the service of informing and improving policy. Since then, the growing interest in this type of research—in fields as diverse as education and economic development and on the part of people in many countries—has only reinforced our conviction of the relevance of our experiences.

This book does not pretend to be a balanced or comprehensive history of random assignment studies in the welfare reform field, a treatise or how-to volume on research methodology, a summary of what has been learned about the effectiveness of alternative welfare reform and antipoverty strategies, a history of welfare policies, an analysis of the interaction between career civil servants and appointed officials, or an assessment of whether research affects policy. We touch on all these topics. But our intent in doing so is to lay out a ground-level view of how a major government agency and a pivotal private organization made and implemented decisions. We speak in our separate voices in all but the first and last chapters, reflecting our different experiences and perspectives and passing the baton back and forth.

Our approach is chronological. But we do not march in equal detail through the years. We focus on what we know firsthand and on the major turning points in the story. We hope this deep-dive approach will give readers a flavor of the incentives, motivations, and emotions behind actions in the real world. We highlight the art, craft, risk taking, and commitment required. We describe the exhilaration we felt participating in such high-quality studies and being part of a community of people who learned from and inspired one another. We also recount the draining fight to defend this work, sometimes in the face of hostile political appointees and under assault from intimidating academic critics until the recent turnaround in support for random assignment, influenced in part by our story, as Judy describes in a coda to the book.

Two results of our insider approach bear mention up front. The first concerns our primary focus on the Department of Health and Human Services and MDRC. The former is obvious: how and why people in Washington make decisions is crucial, since the federal government partners with the states in implementing welfare policy and is a major research funder. The value of the MDRC perspective comes not from the salience of the organization per se but from what it tells about the game-changing role a private organization and its funders—particularly, in our case, the Ford Foundation—can play in the public policy process. Research costs money, and this story would have been very different if, at several critical moments, Ford had not financed MDRC's random assignment experiments. Our story would also have been very different, and might not have happened at all, without the state and local administrators we encountered in communities across the country who were willing to take political risks by testing their programs in a way that risked the discovery, for all to see, that their initiatives were failing to deliver on their promises.

The second result of our approach concerns our sources. We have drawn to the maximum extent possible on contemporary records. We benefited from access to extensive archives, and we combine internal unpublished memos, notes of phone calls and meetings, and proposals, as well as published reports and articles, often quoting from them directly to intensify the flavor of events and avoid relying mainly on decades-old memories. We also interviewed key actors for their recollections, to supplement our own.

We tell the story to help reveal the part played by luck, by people, by funders, by institutional structures, and by the evolving policy context and questions. Our hope is that our insight into the forces that nurture and hinder progress can aid others who pick up where the book leaves off to continue to develop rigorous evidence on ways to improve the social policies that affect all our lives.

Judith M. Gueron
Howard Rolston

ACKNOWLEDGMENTS AND DEDICATION

Many people over many years made this book possible. Some of them were responsible for the story itself, and the fact that it reports success in using experiments to test social policies; others directly supported our work on this volume. Those in the first category fill the pages of this book. They are the state and community officials and staff who, by participating in random assignment studies, let us redefine, expand on, and make a reality of Justice Brandeis's famous description of states as laboratories for policy experiments; the hundreds of thousands of people in the studies we describe who gave their time to answer our questions and cooperate with our protocols; the funders who supported these controversial evaluations; the small group of academics who helped us defend the methodology over the tough first twenty-five years; and our colleagues in the Department of Health and Human Services and MDRC who worked tirelessly with us to oversee and implement the studies. Successful social experiments require excellence at each step of the process; the record we recount reflects the dedication of every member of the team. Although we cannot acknowledge them all by name, our story is a tribute to each of them. More directly in preparing this book, we are grateful to the Ford, William T. Grant, and (for Howard) Annie E. Casey Foundations for their generous funding of our work. We also owe an immense debt to the many people who were kind enough to answer questions about our shared history (sometimes multiple times), and in some cases to read early drafts, as we wrestled to extract the truth out of memories and documents: Mary Jo Bane, Jo Anne Barnhart, Richard Bavier, Michael Barth, Gordon

Berlin, Susan Berresford, Dan Bloom, Barbara Blum, Thomas Brock, Prudence Brown, David Butler, Nancye Campbell, Mike Fishman, Keith Fontenot, Peter Germanis, Olivia Golden, Barbara Goldman, Robert Granger, John Greenwood, William Grinker, Gayle Hamilton, Ron Haskins, James Healy, Robinson Hollister, Wade Horn, Aletha Huston, Robert Ivry, Julie Kerksick, David Kleinberg, Virginia Knox, Karl Koerper, Frederick (Fritz) Kramer, Michael Laracy, Joan Leiman, Julia Lopez, Richard Nathan, Janice Peskin, John Petraborg, James Riccio, William Roper, Ann Segal, Robert Solow, Franklin Thomas, John Wallace, Gail Wilensky, Carl Williams, and Don Winstead. Still others kindly answered questions and provided information about the evolution of academic and government support for experiments, including Joshua Angrist, Jon Baron, Howard Bloom, David Card, Thomas Cook, Esther Duflo, David Elwood, Naomi Goldstein, David Greenberg, Jean Grossman, James Heckman, Larry Hedges, Martin Hirsch, Rebecca Maynard, Larry Orr, Judith Singer, Kathryn Stack, and Grover (Russ) Whitehurst.

Drafting the guts of a book is one task; shaping it into a story that sings is quite another. This was a particular challenge for us, with our two voices and sometimes different takes on the same events. In tackling this, we had the privilege to work with a remarkable editor, Felicity Skidmore. Her combination of vision, toughness, patience (up to a point), eloquence, and substantive knowledge vastly improved this volume. When we were struggling, she offered (and implemented!) solutions, and even made it fun. As for any remaining errors, they are wholly ours.

From Judy: I also thank Eric Wanner, president of the Russell Sage Foundation, for the opportunity as a Visiting Scholar to begin the research that led to this volume and for his and Suzanne Nichols's enthusiastic encouragement at every stage in what became a long process. At MDRC, I am particularly grateful to the exceptional librarian, Barbara Gewirtz, who, with her assistant Natalie Brant, worked tirelessly to track down sources, and to Louise London, who helped me scour the archives.

On a more personal level, I thank Henri Gueron for the hikes he took alone, for not complaining when at least half of my mind was elsewhere, and for telling me (after reading early versions of several chapters) that what I was struggling to say was worth the telling. Finally, I owe the greatest debt to the person to whom I dedicate this book, my father Albert Mitchell, who fostered the ambition and confidence that made my work at MDRC possible by telling me, for as long as I can remember, that girls, and I in particular, could do anything. Born more than 100 years ago on the Lower East Side of Manhattan, he was a fighter and an idealist. He might have been happy to hear about this methodological triumph, but he would have been proud if I could have also told him that we had been wise enough to harness it to do some good for others. I hope that in the fight for random assignment we have delivered on both fronts.

From Howard: I also thank Kathleen Flanagan and Katie Heintz at Abt Associates (where I currently work) for their encouragement and for providing very substantial time for me to work on the book. In addition, I am grateful to Ron Haskins and Isabel Sawhill, codirectors of the Center for Children and Families at the Brookings Institution, for initially providing me a home when I retired from government.

I dedicate this book to my wife, Marsha, and our son, Sean, for their patience, love, and support for my efforts.

CHAPTER 1

Introduction: The Issue, the Method, and the Story in Brief*

The federal government should follow a systematic experimentation strategy in seeking to improve the effectiveness of social action programs. . . . The process of developing new methods, trying them out, modifying them, trying them again, will have to be continuous. . . . [Otherwise] it is hard to see how we will make much progress in increasing the effectiveness of our social services.

—Alice Rivlin[1]

I was struck by the power of this novel [random assignment] technique to cut through the clouds of confusing correlations that make the inference of causality so hazardous. . . . I have never quite lost my sense of wonder at this amazing fact.

—Larry Orr[2]

How can we know whether social programs do what they are designed to do? Can that question even be answered convincingly? A simple example illustrates the problem:

The governor of a large midwestern state is under pressure. Welfare rolls are rising. Legislators are pushing for action. Armed with a report from a blue-ribbon panel, she recommends a new program with a catchy name: WoW, for

*Chapter 1 authored by Judith M. Gueron and Howard Rolston.

Working over Welfare. A year later the program is up and running, the rolls are down, and the press declares a winner. Basking in the glow, she runs for national office.

But did WoW actually bring about the change? Did it cause the rolls to go down, or were other factors at work? Take the case of Mary, a single mother who was laid off from her job, applied for welfare, and, under the new rules, was told she had to look for a job or enter a training program. Within six months, she was back at work. Since "people like her" living in that state typically took a few years to get off welfare, this sounds like a clear WoW success. But how can we be sure the new program was really responsible for what happened? Mary hated being on the dole. Perhaps the comparison with what "people like her" (as measured by her background and personal characteristics) had been doing did not really mimic her likely behavior under the previous system. Also, during this same period the job market in her area improved. So how can we determine whether Mary got a job because of WoW, or because of her drive to escape welfare, or because of the stronger economy? Furthermore, can that question really be answered with any confidence by looking at what thousands of Marys across the state had been doing without WoW? Or is this inevitably a case of "on one hand" and "on the other"?

This book describes how an approach that is akin to clinical trials in medicine solved this type of social policy problem—yielding a simple but utterly convincing answer to the question of whether a social program actually achieves its goals. A type of random selection similar to tossing a coin or running a lottery was developed under which similarly eligible people applying for a new form of welfare were randomly placed in either the new program or the prior system. This approach enabled analysts to measure and compare the outcomes of two groups that differed systematically only in their welfare program experience. What the new program achieved can be accurately estimated as the difference in outcomes between the two groups, because they were randomly selected from the same group and lived through the same shifting economic and social conditions. Both the claims of politicians and academic arguments about the "correct" interpretation of complex statistics were successfully replaced by the simple concept of a coin toss.

This book tells the story, step by step, of how this research strategy—which for much of the period was ignored or belittled by most scholars—was shown to be feasible in the rough-and-tumble real world and how it went on to win converts and influence people. We tell our tale deliberately as an action story, which indeed it is, to give readers some of the intense flavor of our struggle as it unfolded. Our story focuses on the policy issue of providing financial support while encouraging self-reliance. But our overriding purpose is much deeper. Our intent is to use our experience to draw useful lessons for people struggling to isolate the impacts of initiatives in other social policy areas, as well as researchers, government officials, funders, and interested citizens who share our belief that the development of reliable evidence is central to improving social policy and practice, whatever the specific area may be.

THE ISSUE: PROVIDING SUPPORT VERSUS ENCOURAGING SELF-RELIANCE

The basic dilemma of welfare—identified at least as far back as Tudor England, when it was first tackled legislatively in the Poor Law of 1601—is how to assist needy citizens without stimulating behavior that perpetuates poverty and dependence. The U.S. cash welfare program created by Franklin D. Roosevelt's New Deal sought to avoid this conundrum by restricting benefits to a small group of single mothers who were not expected to work: primarily poor widows who, according to the general view of the time, should stay at home and care for their children rather than be forced to go to work and put the children in orphanages. Since these were cases of hardship, not choice, the issue of work incentives did not arise. (Throughout this book, we use the word *welfare* to refer to the federal-state program that provides cash assistance to low-income families. In 1935, when cash welfare replaced the existing state mothers' pensions programs, it was called Aid to Dependent Children. Subsequently, though the welfare program always provided cash assistance in some form, the name was changed to Aid to Families with Dependent Children [AFDC] and currently Temporary Assistance for Needy Families [TANF].)

Over the next sixty years, however, reality increasingly diverged from this vision, eroding support for the program: the rolls and costs grew dramatically (particularly between 1965 and 1975); the vast majority of single mothers receiving welfare were not widows but divorced, separated, or never married; and women across the country (including single parents with very young children) were flooding into the labor force, often not by choice.[3] These changes raised questions about the equity of long-term support for one group of single mothers and whether the very design of the program was having a range of unintended side effects. These potentially included encouraging family breakup and teen pregnancy, discouraging women from earning a living, and making it easier for fathers to leave their families to avoid having to support their own children.

Once it became clear that some welfare recipients were indeed employable, the central tension epitomized in the Poor Law led to the following logical chain:

- Most people have to work for income. Welfare provides an alternative and thus reduces the incentive for people to work.
- So that only those in need receive assistance, benefits must go down as earnings go up.
- This benefit reduction rate in effect functions like a tax on individuals' earnings, further reducing the incentive for welfare recipients to take jobs.
- Since welfare benefits are financed from the taxes other members of society pay, there is always public pressure to keep program costs low by keeping benefits low and benefit reduction rates high, the latter exacerbating the negative incentives of welfare on parents' working.

The weaknesses of programs described in this way are obvious. But when they look at ways to improve them, policy makers differ, often strongly, on which objectives should be primary—cutting costs, enforcing work (even for mothers of small children?), reducing poverty, protecting children, keeping fathers in the home, or strengthening families. This disagreement is not surprising, since the choices involve often contentious trade-offs among the central value judgments of income redistribution, social justice, the roles of men and women, economic efficiency, and individual responsibility.

Important for our story, in contrast to Social Security, which was fully funded by the federal government and operated under standard, nationwide rules, the welfare program was designed as a federal-state partnership. The program was a federal entitlement, meaning that no person who satisfied the eligibility criteria could be denied benefits. The states retained substantial discretion over those criteria as well as over grant levels, however, while sharing the program cost (in varying proportions over time) with the federal government. As a result, not only the states but also the federal government would be on the hook to pay for any state decision to increase the number of beneficiaries or the level of support.

Over the ensuing years, reflecting the dramatic shift in attitudes toward single mothers and thus in the basic rationale for the program, the original New Deal welfare system was progressively replaced by a program that used various means to encourage, assist, or require an increasing share of women to seek and accept jobs as a condition for receiving cash assistance. The cycles of reform reflected battles about both the balance between competing objectives and how to achieve them and drew on emerging evidence from the experiments we describe in this book.

A major turning point came in 1956, when the federal government recognized the goal of encouraging independence by expanding AFDC to include services to help persons caring for the recipient children to "attain the maximum self-support and personal independence." In 1961 the federal government for the first time recognized the family stability goal by expanding the program to include, at state option, the unemployed parent program (AFDC-UP), under which two-parent families in which the father was employable but had become unemployed became eligible for cash support. At this point, however, AFDC program benefits were still calculated as if the program were directed solely at reducing hardship rather than also encouraging work. Thus, if recipients didn't work, they received the full cash benefit, which depended on family size. But if they started to earn, their cash benefit was reduced dollar for dollar, leaving the family no better off financially.

The War on Poverty, a part of President Lyndon B. Johnson's Great Society initiative, brought the issue of poverty to the fore. In this context, two distinguished economists from opposite ends of the political spectrum (both subsequent Nobel Prize winners) advocated a new idea: the negative income tax (NIT).[4] The negative income tax would combine the positive tax system with the welfare (cash-benefit) system, so that those above and below a given income threshold would face similar tax rate schedules. Those with no earned income would receive the maximum payment, called the guarantee. As they started earning, their guarantee would be taxed at a rate that gradually eliminated it as income rose, at which point the system would merge into the positive tax system. Central to the NIT was the idea that payments should be based on income, not a particular status (such as single parenthood), thus removing a concern about the perverse incentives on family formation and stability.

Not surprisingly, the idea of an NIT raised a firestorm of questions and concerns when it hit the arena of public debate, including concern that many households could be made worse off under an NIT than under the then-current network of income support programs. The major question for our story was how the poor would react to the change with regard to their attitude toward work. By 1967 fewer than half the states had implemented an AFDC-UP program, and even in those states the number receiving benefits was relatively low, leaving most two-parent poor families outside the system. How much less might these parents, especially fathers, work as a result of greatly expanded eligibility for cash assistance? Or would lower tax rates lead to greater work effort?

Economic theory unambiguously predicts that extending welfare to a new group will reduce their work effort. But the effect of different tax rates is ambiguous. In particular, lower tax rates are something of a two-edged sword: they clearly encourage people who are not working to take a job; but they also keep working families, who would have become ineligible under a higher tax rate, on welfare longer and thereby extend all the negative work incentives to those families. Which effect would predominate—more work by those currently on welfare or less work by those newly affected by it? Economic theory could not say, and no reliable evidence existed to answer the question.

Early in 1967, a grant application was submitted to the Office of Economic Opportunity—the federal administrative home of the War on Poverty—proposing a field test to answer these questions. The idea was to mount a field experiment to test empirical responses to a range of NIT guarantee–tax rate combinations. The experiment would be directed to the working poor—that is, two-parent families who would be eligible for cash assistance if low income were the only criterion for eligibility, the very group skeptics of unrestricted cash assistance were most concerned would work less. The really novel idea in the grant application was its methodology. It proposed to determine the effects of an NIT by selecting a population of low-income couples and using a coin toss, lottery, or similar random mechanism to allocate them either to one of a series of experimental groups, who would receive different NIT plans (that is, differing guarantee generosities or tax rates), or to a control group, who would simply continue with their lives. Although random assignment as a way of identifying cause and effect in medical clinical trials was already in use, this was the first time that a random process had been suggested as a way to test cause and effect on a large scale in relation to potential social policy reform.[5]

The initial NIT proposal was further refined and was then implemented as the New Jersey Negative Income Tax Experiment beginning in 1968. The statistical design of the experiment was the work primarily of economists at the recently created Institute for Research on Poverty at the University of Wisconsin–Madison, a research center established by the Office of Economic Opportunity. The field operations of the experiment were designed and run by Mathematica (later Mathematica Policy Research), a research firm located in Princeton, New Jersey. No operating welfare or other public program office was involved, and no social service component was tested. The experiment began with little fanfare, until the Nixon administration pushed it into the spotlight by using and misusing some of the very early results in its campaign to push a legislative welfare reform proposal that included a type of NIT for families as its centerpiece. The Nixon proposal, called the Family Assistance Plan, passed the U.S. House of Representatives in April 1969. It then went through a long series of revisions in what had become the impossible hope of making it politically palatable to both the right and the left in the Senate. No version ever passed the Senate, which killed the legislation for the last time in October 1972.

The New Jersey experiment, which finished field operations in 1972 and published its three-volume final report in 1976–1977 (Kershaw and Fair 1976; Watts and Rees 1977a, 1977b), was followed closely over the next several years by three essentially similar experiments—the most ambitious being the Seattle/Denver Income Maintenance Experiment, known as SIME/DIME—each of which used random assignment to estimate the effects of NITs of different generosities, in different environments, extending the population to single parents, and, in some cases, offering additional services designed to help recipients get work. The bottom line from the studies was that the NIT reduced rather than increased overall work effort.[6]

This whole body of research and practice—referred to collectively as the income maintenance experiments—might well have remained a relatively minor footnote in the history of U.S. social policy were it not for its legacy: first, a group of analysts (in academia, research organizations, and government agencies) who learned their craft in one or more of the income maintenance experiments, participated in important ways in many of the experiments we describe in subsequent chapters, and were fearless advocates for our cause when we needed them; second, the body of knowledge and experience about how to design and implement a random assignment experiment that these analysts brought with them and on which we were able to build; third, an important negative lesson about when and how to release findings into a politically charged atmosphere. This legacy is an invaluable part of our story.

Although Congress failed to pass an NIT, it did during these years enact changes that to this day remain key tools used by states to affect behavior: reducing tax rates for AFDC and establishing a welfare-to-work program (originally called the Work Incentive, or WIN, program) under which employable welfare recipients (a group first thought to be small but redefined upward repeatedly over the next thirty years) could be required to work, or participate in activities intended to help them get jobs, or face financial penalties. The hope was that either the assistance or the threat of the loss of benefits for noncooperation would spur people to take a job.

THE METHOD: RANDOM ASSIGNMENT IN THE CONTEXT OF A SOCIAL EXPERIMENT

The fundamental concept is familiar from medical research. We have all seen headlines like "Randomized Clinical Trial Challenges Conventional Wisdom." Whether the issue is hormone replacement therapy, colon cancer drugs, or a new heart valve, the logic is the same. Evidence from one or many clinical trials overturns long-standing practices based on observational studies or clinical experience. The randomized trial in medicine, in which a group of people with defined characteristics that make them eligible to participate in the trial are allocated at random either to one or more experimental groups, which get the test treatments, or to a control group, which gets the prevailing level of care or a placebo. The impact of the treatment is then calculated as the resulting difference in outcomes, along the relevant dimensions, between the two (or more) groups. Because, owing to random assignment, the nontreatment characteristics of the groups can be assumed not to differ in any systematic way that would affect success, any difference in outcomes can be ascribed with a known degree of statistical confidence to the treatment. All other influences on the outcomes are washed out in this calculation because they are the same for the control group and however many experimental groups there may be.

In a field or social experiment, just as in a medical trial, people are randomly placed into two (or several) groups: one (or more) involved in the program or programs being tested (the treatment or experimental group[s]);

Figure 1.1 Factors Affecting the Impacts of Welfare Reform Programs

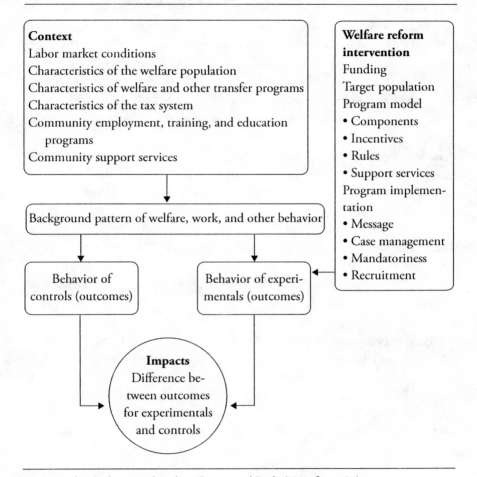

Source: Authors' adaptation based on Gueron and Pauly (1991, figure 2.1).

and one receiving no special attention (the control group). If well implemented (an extremely big "if" that we return to repeatedly in later chapters), any subsequent difference in behavior among the people in the different groups (behavior that can affect a program's benefits and costs) can be attributed to the treatment to which each group is exposed. Figure 1.1 sketches out the types of environmental or personal factors controlled for in this conceptually simple way.

An alternative way of explaining the concept of random assignment is to talk directly about the counterfactual—what would have happened without the program. There is no way to observe this directly because the program does, in fact, exist. The beauty of random assignment into otherwise identical groups is that it allows measurement of the counterfactual, which is the experience of the control group as it moves through time. If the economic environment suddenly improves, for example, it improves for the control group in exactly the same way that it improves for the treated group. The transparency of the method—no complex statistics, scant potential for researcher bias—is obvious.

This sounds wonderfully simple, and in concept it is. But as our story in subsequent chapters makes clear, how it is put into practice—how the control group is in fact insulated from the program experience; and when, in the process of enrolling for the program and beginning to be affected by it, the random assignment allocation actually takes place—is extremely complex. These issues define the exact question the evaluation will answer and where, as the experiment gets further and further integrated into ongoing program operations, the random assignment process can best be carried out without destroying either the rigor of the experiment or the operations of the program being evaluated.

Over the period covered in this book, the dimensions of experiments in this area of social policy changed in numerous ways: the background conditions, level of control, scale, and subject. They moved from tests of voluntary opportunities to those of mandatory obligations; from pilots for several hundred (and then thousands of) people to evaluations of full-scale programs involving tens of thousands; from centralized direction, funding, and leverage to a more decentralized partnership with states and localities; from tests of stand-alone programs to tests of components within the welfare system to tests of multidimensional systemwide reforms. Substantively, they expanded from welfare-to-work programs only to tests of financial work incentives, time limits on welfare, comparisons of education-first versus jobs-first approaches, child support enforcement, and a wide range of other program variants designed to change the behavior of recipients in particular ways. And they expanded beyond welfare itself to include the broader population at risk of welfare recipiency but not currently receiving assistance, as well as to nontraditional strategies such as promoting healthy marriage among low-income unmarried and married couples. The substantive issues the experiments sought to clarify were all causal questions, which changed as the results from previous experiments and other research added to the cumulative knowledge base.

As noted, many of the test programs were complex and multidimensional, and it quickly became clear that defining the "treatment" involved understanding how and whether the program was actually implemented. Reform legislation might sound simple—for example, change welfare from a system that primarily paid checks to one that also imposed work and participation obligations and penalized people who balked. But state and local staff might not be willing or able to actually implement the policy change, especially given resource constraints and competing pressures to protect particular groups. Understanding the nature, feasibility, and replicability of the reform programs—the what, how, and why questions—thus became integral to interpreting experimental results.

THE STORY IN BRIEF

When our story began, we did not imagine we were launching a forty-year adventure to test the feasibility and potential of the random assignment approach to learning. There was no overarching master plan; nor did any of us anticipate that the hurdle would keep getting higher, either because political changes would create an increasingly demanding environment or because we would seek to address more—and more complex—issues. We did not envision or prepare for the battles ahead. What we did have were questions. We started, in our relative ignorance, with no answers to even the most basic questions about different strategies to move people from welfare to work: Do they have any effect? For whom? At what cost?

Despite ignorance about what would work, the pressure was on to change welfare. As successive presidents and governors promoted highly visible and often highly controversial ways to fix what they saw as a failed system, different actors—at different times and for different reasons—sought more reliable evidence on whether the proposals would deliver on the claims. The problem was not a lack of research. There had been plenty of demonstrations, evaluations, and studies of welfare and employment and training programs, but often they had ended in unresolved arguments about methodology and credibility. To get stronger proof of effectiveness, an initially small group of people pushed to try out random assignment.

Our book focuses on a subset of the scores of experiments in which one or both of us played a direct role. Although they were by no means the only ones that followed the original, pathbreaking income-maintenance experiments, they illustrate how social experiments in the welfare area moved out of the researcher-controlled environment (testing behavioral responses with statistical designs driven largely by economic theory) into the more complex context of mainstream public agencies and became the federal standard for the evaluation of real-world programs. In the process, we tell why and how MDRC and different agencies within the U.S. Department of Health and Human Services (HHS) became committed to this approach and acted to fashion a coherent knowledge-building agenda, how people inside and outside government sparked and sustained this innovation, how the experiments were successful in answering important policy questions, and how the findings affected Federal and state policy. The rest of chapter 1 summarizes the highpoints of our story and the lessons learned.

Act One: Chapters 2 and 3

During the first act of our story, random assignment was almost an afterthought grafted onto new initiatives launched by private and public sector social entrepreneurs. The initial step was a specially funded demonstration run by community-based organizations (chapter 2). Supported Work—a project initiated by the Ford Foundation and managed by MDRC (specially created for the purpose), with funding also contributed by six federal agencies led by the Department of Labor—fit into the try-small-before-you-spend-big vision of policy making. The idea was to run a relatively small demonstration (several hundred volunteers per site) of a specific program model (structured paid jobs to help transition hard-to-employ people into the regular labor market); to randomly assign a total of 6,500 people in four very disadvantaged target groups (former prisoners, former addicts, AFDC mothers, and unemployed youth) to get the strongest possible evidence on whether the program affected key outcomes and how benefits compared with costs; and only then to recommend whether it was worthy of broader replication.

When the project started in 1974, many thought it would implode—that program operators would refuse to let an outsider running a lottery decide who could and who could not get in. Surprisingly, that did not happen. Through a combination of persuasion, flexibility on the noncore issues, and absolute rigidity on the central issue of random assignment, the team at MDRC, Mathematica Policy Research, and the Institute for Research on

Poverty—a team that included many veterans from the original New Jersey NIT experiment—was able to convince organizations to sign up. At the time, we concluded that success was the result of four circumstances: more people than could be served volunteered for the new program and study, making it relatively easy to argue that a lottery was a fair way to ration scarce opportunities; the project was tightly controlled from the center; local sites were offered millions of dollars if they agreed to play by the rules of evidence-based science; and the intentionally low profile slipped the experiment under the political and press radar.

The next step came in 1977, when the national director of the WIN program proposed creating "laboratories" in a few offices to test locally generated ideas to improve performance (chapter 3). With his sponsorship, it proved feasible to insinuate random assignment into the intake process in regular government offices without unduly disrupting operations. Although recruiting sites and putting the procedures in place took patience, skill, and obstinacy, there were no knock-down, drag-out fights. Two of the Supported Work conditions continued—the tests were voluntary, and the programs were small and largely invisible to the press and public—but there were no big bucks and no tight central control. Instead, there was a new twist: creation of programmatic and research partnerships among federal agency staff, local WIN practitioners, and evaluators, with the hope that the arrangement would lead to smarter innovations and stronger research (that is, both better questions and more support for the research requirements and findings).

Act Two: Chapters 4, 5, and 6

In the second act, experiments moved into real-world, public-private partnerships. Ronald Reagan's election in 1980 transformed welfare policy and research. All the favorable conditions from Supported Work vanished. The new administration proposed legislation that imposed new obligations on welfare recipients and significantly restricted benefit eligibility—at the same time that it dramatically shrank the federal funds available for testing programs or for policy research more generally.

But there turned out to be an unexpected saving grace in what emerged from Congress with respect to work programs: newfound flexibility for state welfare agencies to undertake state-based initiatives to move welfare recipients into work. Reeling from the cancelation of multiple studies (and after letting go 45 percent of its staff), in desperation MDRC invented a partnership-with-states paradigm that, ironically, ended up having greater relevance and policy impact than earlier experiments and became the model that flourished for the next thirty years.

This strategy (chapters 4 and 6) drew on both the WIN Laboratory vision and the 1981 federal budget bill that gave state agencies the option to change and take ownership of welfare-to-work programs. (States could require single mothers to work in return for their benefits in so-called workfare or community work experience programs and could restructure WIN, which at the time was judged ineffective in imposing a participation requirement.) MDRC's key insight was to make a reality out of the cliché that the states were laboratories. The idea was to graft experiments onto the often controversial demonstrations that emerged as governors responded enthusiastically to the opportunity to take control of WIN and, to a lesser extent, to operate community work experience programs. Instead of testing a uniform model in multiple sites (as in Supported Work), the resulting Work/Welfare demonstration used eight state-specific experiments to assess programs that reflected each state's particular values, resources, goals, and capabilities—but primarily required people to search for a job—with random assignment integrated into the helter-skelter of normal public agency operations. The initial reaction of welfare commissioners to this idea was incredulity: Is this ethical? Will it impede operations? Will it explode?

MDRC ultimately convinced administrators by making three promises. The first was to ensure that the evaluation would answer states' questions, inform their staff, improve their programs, meet high standards, avoid political minefields, not hinder performance, provide a spot in the limelight, and satisfy the then vague evaluation requirements imposed by the federal government in return for permitting states to make innovations beyond what was allowed by law. The second promise was to create a learning community for senior staff. The third was to provide real-time advice on program design.

The two additional ingredients needed to make this vision a reality were money to pay for the research and the assurance of an initially hostile Reagan administration that it would not obstruct the evaluation. In a show of creative and enabling philanthropy, the Ford Foundation put up a large challenge grant to cover half the projected cost; and federal officials (often working behind the scenes) offered significant support, including facilitating the use of matching AFDC administrative and special demonstration funds to help pay for the evaluation, with the rest coming from a few states and other foundations. The result surprised even those who proposed this departure: 28,500 people were randomly assigned in eight states, no state dropped out, and there were no palace coups or citizen revolts. The success of the Work/Welfare demonstration raised the profile of and made important allies for random assignment, not only because the project demonstrated its feasibility in a more real-world context than previous experiments but also because (aided by its timing, important findings, and aggressive communications strategy) it showed that diverse audiences could appreciate the exceptional quality of the evidence and would conclude that it had an almost unprecedented influence on policy and practice.

While MDRC was implementing the Work/Welfare demonstration, a new force for experimental evaluation began to emerge in the Department of Health and Human Services (chapter 5). The Office of the Assistant Secretary for Planning and Evaluation (ASPE) in HHS had followed the Office of Economic Opportunity in sponsoring additional income maintenance experiments, had also launched the major health insurance experiment, and had helped fund and provide waivers for the Supported Work program. But it was another HHS office, the Office of Family Assistance (OFA) in the Social Security Administration, that took on this role. With no direct experience in funding or overseeing experimental evaluations, OFA launched a series of projects, one of which resulted in the addition of two sites in the Work/Welfare demonstration. In addition, OFA quietly and indirectly funded several other states that participated in the demonstration and undertook several other experiments as well. Through these experiences, OFA staff began to understand better what was necessary to design, fund, and manage experimental research and became ever more convinced of both its unique value and its feasibility.

Act Three: Chapter 7

In 1987 a new federal thrust for experimental evaluation emerged from an unexpected quarter. The federal government had the authority to grant states waivers (through section 1115 of the Social Security Act) of most AFDC program requirements in order to try program innovations in their state. Hitherto, the Reagan administration had approved section 1115 waiver demonstrations only for projects that implemented changes in line with its policy preferences. In 1987, however, the Office of Policy Development in the White House pushed HHS to interpret this authority more flexibly, encouraging states to apply for AFDC and other waivers to implement demonstrations of their own choosing. Alarmed that this policy would drive up the federal costs of AFDC and other means-tested open-ended entitlements, the federal Office of Management and Budget conceived of and fought internally within the administration for an approach that would require states, in return for federal flexibility, to incorporate random assignment in the design of any demonstrations for which states needed waivers. The stated purpose of this requirement (termed the quid pro quo) was to include costs in their list of impacts to be measured, so that the federal government could limit its share of program expenditures to an amount extrapolated from the costs incurred by the control group. Internal battles over the decision continued for several years, during which the federal government did not uniformly require the quid pro quo for waiver requests. But HHS and the Office of Management and Budget staff continued to fight for it. As a result, in 1992—at the beginning of an explosion of state waiver requests—random assignment became the de facto as well as the de jure standard for federal welfare reform evaluations.

Act Four: Chapters 8, 9, and 10

The fourth act involved tests of full-scale programs and, in some cases, state-initiated experiments. In that spirit, between 1986 and 1990 senior officials in California and Florida, seeking reliable information but not driven by the need for waivers, invited MDRC to use random assignment for the first time to determine the effectiveness of full-scale and ongoing programs (chapter 8). The scale of these initiatives was huge in comparison with previous random assignment efforts (the California Greater Avenues for Independence study alone included 35,000 people), attracting high visibility and great antagonism in certain quarters. Some state legislators in both states tried to close down the studies and even to impose an outright ban on control group research, threatening both projects in their entirety. Both were eventually saved, but only as a result of a coalition of supporters, led by champions in the California and Florida welfare agencies and legislatures and including advocates, congressional staff, and a small number of academics.

The year 1988 saw passage of the Family Support Act, federal welfare reform legislation that included passage of the Job Opportunities and Basic Skills Training (JOBS) program (which replaced WIN with a program that extended the participation obligation to mothers with younger children; set minimum participation standards; and, like the Greater Avenues for Independence program, emphasized education). A major hypothesis underlying JOBS was that remediation of basic education deficits was central to improving employment outcomes for potential long-term AFDC recipients. Relying on the fact that the legislation could be interpreted as requiring HHS to conduct a random assignment study to evaluate at least some components of the legislation, HHS staff, jointly in the Family Support Administration (a new agency that included OFA) and ASPE, took the opportunity to initiate a competition for an impact evaluation of the new program. This became the JOBS evaluation, the contract for which MDRC won.

As with MDRC's post-1986 evaluations, the JOBS evaluation assessed large-scale, operating programs that state and local governments volunteered to put under the microscope (chapter 9). Together, HHS and MDRC designed an evaluation that was able to explore in depth the underlying basic education hypothesis of the JOBS program and, by creating stylized labor-force attachment programs that were experimentally compared with stylized human-capital development programs in head-to-head tests, greatly strengthened the findings. Since Greater Avenues for Independence became California's JOBS program, the two studies together provided even stronger evidence than either could have done alone. As MDRC was the evaluator of both, common measurement across the two studies enabled powerful syntheses of the results to emerge in later years. Finally, by the end of the 1990s, after nearly two decades of capacity building, the JOBS evaluation and its other work would again propel HHS to the forefront of federal leadership of experimental social policy research.

By the early 1990s, the credibility and prestige of the earlier random assignment studies (and by extension of the states that participated in them), and the growing evidence of the feasibility of this approach and the weakness of alternative methods, prompted the Canadian government, the state of Minnesota, and the New Hope program in Milwaukee to seek experimental evaluations of programs intended to make work pay more than welfare (chapter 10). Because these and the simultaneous JOBS evaluation assessed impacts on poverty, employment, dependency, costs, children, and other family outcomes, MDRC and its partners were able to assess the trade-offs in results (including the impacts on children) between these different strategies, producing compelling syntheses that combined results from multiple studies. Although implementing each study brought challenges, there was growing acceptance that if one wanted evidence that would both withstand the scrutiny of the research community and have an impact on policy, this was the required route.

Act Five: Chapter 11

The fifth and final act in our story began with passage of the Personal Responsibility and Work Opportunity Reconciliation Act (PRWORA) in 1996, the federal reform law that replaced AFDC with TANF. The major provisions of TANF included giving states enormous flexibility to design their programs; potentially penalizing states that did not require significant percentages of adults on welfare to participate in work activities; imposing a lifetime limit of five years on federal welfare receipt; and replacing open-ended federal matching of state dollars with a block-grant formula that did not depend on caseload size or state costs. From now on, states could expand their cash assistance programs, but the federal government would not have to share the cost of any expansion. In President Bill Clinton's famous words, TANF would "end welfare as we know it."

Important for our story, PRWORA eliminated the waiver quid pro quo, under which the government had required that states perform a random assignment evaluation in return for flexibility to test new welfare reform initiatives. Many observers were understandably concerned that this would be the end of the random assignment era. For several reasons, this turned out not to be the case. First, Senator Daniel Patrick Moynihan and key congressional staff inserted language into TANF that provided money for HHS to continue to fund studies, as well as strong authorizing language. This was critical, because the new block-grant funding scheme meant that any program evaluation costs would otherwise have to come directly out of state funds (from either their share of TANF's block-grant funds or state general revenues). Federal funding was particularly important, as many foundations either shifted to funding observational studies or stopped welfare evaluation funding altogether. Second, the Administration for Children and Families (ACF), the successor to the Family Support Administration, built on earlier lessons to create new partnerships.

ACF was able to combine the new funds with others to help finance a significant number of demonstration studies with willing states and, in a few years, to initiate multisite experiments in new employment areas of interest to states. In some instances ASPE was a partner in these new ventures. In the first years after PRWORA, the new research funds were critical in enabling ACF to support to completion a subset of the best experimental state-waiver studies. Building on these continuing waiver experiments allowed ACF to foster additional contributions to the syntheses of results.

After this initial effort not to lose the investment previously made in the waiver experiments, ACF, working with states, launched two major experimental projects aimed at addressing new questions that the policy environment of TANF—stricter work requirements and time limits—generated. The first, the Employment Retention and Advancement demonstration, went beyond programs designed to move welfare recipients into work and aimed at identifying effective strategies for helping them stay in jobs and advance in the workforce. The second project, the Hard-to-Employ demonstration, focused on finding effective approaches for helping individuals with significant work-limiting problems to be more successful in the labor market. Thus both studies examined programs that moved beyond the job search, work experience, and remediation welfare-to-work programs. ACF and the Department of Labor have continued to launch major experimental evaluations of employment interventions for low-income populations.

OVERARCHING LESSONS FOR BUILDING RELIABLE EVIDENCE

The forty-five-year experimentation with random assignment showed that this technique could be used to address most of the policy options in a wide range of conditions and, furthermore, that the distinctive quality of the evidence was often recognized and valued. This experience—which helped transform an idea that was outside the policy research mainstream into the method of choice for assessing welfare programs—provides lessons for other fields seeking similar rigor.

Our concluding chapter (chapter 12) details the many lessons from our story, including those that apply primarily to the welfare field. Here we briefly highlight the lessons that stand out for people interested in applying our experience to their particular policy area.

Methods

Embedding random assignment in real-world programs and maximizing the yield of such studies requires a blend of policy insight, technical research skills, and operational expertise. It is crucial to balance research ambition and program needs. In many areas, the two may conflict, as they did in the welfare case. Moreover, the possibility that the pattern of impacts may not match expectations based on theory or intuition needs to be kept firmly in mind. In such cases, only a transparently credible evaluation strategy will yield evidence that convinces. Finally, building knowledge step by step, by combining experimental with nonexperimental methods and synthesizing results across studies, clarifies the how and why questions left by previous studies in ways that are much more convincing in total than would be the sum of the various parts.

Program Effectiveness

Outcomes (for example, how many people took jobs) proved again and again to be poor proxies for impacts (for example, how many took jobs as a result of the program), raising challenges for program managers who seek easily obtainable standards to drive and reward positive performance. In addition, although many reforms beat the status quo, the gains were generally modest. Economic and other conditions, and personal characteristics, were the primary influences on behavior, pointing to the importance of setting realistic expectations. Finally, different policies were more or less successful in reaching different goals—saving money, reducing poverty, or reducing dependency—suggesting the likelihood of trade-offs.

A Comprehensive Body of Evidence

The power of the welfare experiments flowed from their logic, consistency of findings across multiple locations, and relevance, reflecting the independent determination of both MDRC and HHS that successive experiments be accretive (substantively and methodologically) and respond to the dynamic policy context. The paradigm of partnership with states, though forged out of necessity, had the important benefit of producing results relevant to the diverse context of the real world, rather than seeking to identify a single, most effective model. Beyond this, the central factor that sustained the uninterrupted decades of experiments we describe was the conscious creation of a community of researchers, public officials, funders, advocates, and state and federal legislative staff who recognized and valued the distinctive quality of the evidence they produced.

Advocates for experiments need to keep in mind that research evidence—no matter how reliable—is at best a relatively small element in what are usually very political policy debates. The random-assignment welfare experiments (combined, importantly, with forceful but evenhanded marketing of the results) produced uncontested findings, widespread media coverage, and a perception that the results had an unusually strong impact on policy and practice. This does not mean the findings determined policy. They did not, nor should they. But does the experience show that uncontestable findings can be weighed in the political balance? Yes.

High-quality research (experimental or not) costs money, and the welfare area benefited from four unusual conditions: long-term support by the Ford Foundation to pursue studies of little initial interest to the federal government; creation of a federal incentive (the waiver process) for states to evaluate their programs; the entitlement financing structure that allowed states to draw down matching funds for administrative functions (which provided an open-ended subsidy for state program evaluations); and continuing congressional funding for federally sponsored evaluations. Since 1996, the first three ended, making funding more centralized and vulnerable to changes in the political winds.

CHAPTER 2

They Said It Couldn't Be Done: The National Supported Work Demonstration*

We were told [random assignment] would never wash.

—Robert M. Solow[1]

Too many costly federal programs had been established and expanded without adequate information about their effectiveness. Supported Work sought to change this process: to acquire knowledge before legislators had to decide whether a demonstration should be expanded into a national program.

—MDRC Board of Directors[2]

The Supported Work project started out as a small local program offering subsidized jobs to two hard-to-employ groups (former prisoners and former addicts) in a structured environment, followed by assistance in finding an unsubsidized job. The national Supported Work demonstration, the subject of this chapter, built that concept into a successful random assignment experiment that tested the program's effectiveness for the two original target groups and two additional ones: young high school dropouts and long-term welfare mothers. Eli Ginzberg, the chairman of MDRC's board of directors, as quoted in its February 1975 press release announcing the demonstration, described

*Chapter 2 authored by Judith M. Gueron.

it thus: "Supported Work is not a charitable undertaking. It's a social invest-ment. Unless people who have had difficulties with themselves and with soci-ety are able to work, they cannot become whole. It is work that binds people to the rest of society."

This chapter tells the story of how the national Supported Work demon-stration, which was initially characterized by Ginzberg in an internal memo as "a social initiative and not a research experiment," pioneered a research method that became, arguably, its greatest legacy. Although this country had already successfully launched several path-breaking negative-income-tax (NIT) experiments using random assignment, those were researcher-con-trolled endeavors that essentially handed out money to people and sought to measure the effect of economic incentives strictly defined. Supported Work had less design control and different objectives: to find out whether a promis-ing program could be replicated for different people in diverse locations; to determine the effectiveness of the approach and the feasibility of using ran-dom assignment to do so; to show the value of a rigorous try-small-before-you-buy-big model of social policy making; and to test a new technique for the management and oversight of large-scale, private, and publicly funded research efforts.

This chapter describes how and why the Supported Work demonstration was created, why particular decisions were made, and how the project became a four-year demonstration and five-year research effort costing a total of $82.4 million. (All cost estimates in this book are in current, not constant, dollars.) I also present lessons for methods, substance, and process in several areas: Could one get defensible answers on whether social programs worked? Did the answers confirm or refute the Great Society's legacy of skepticism about the success of social programs? What insights from this project affected the management and nature of future experiments? Did having more definitive results translate into an impact on policy and practice, and, if not, why not?

THE ORIGIN OF THE SUPPORTED WORK
DEMONSTRATION

In late 1973, a consensus emerged at a number of federal agencies and the Ford Foundation on the importance of funding a major demonstration to test the potential of a specific work-experience program to address the prob-lems of people who had the most difficulty obtaining or holding regular jobs, people often deemed unemployable. Several factors contributed to this commitment. First, there had been growing national concern with the problems of central cities, as reflected in high rates of crime and drug abuse, extensive unemployment, large numbers of discouraged workers, and rapidly increasing welfare dependency. Although general policies to stimulate growth might yield some employment improvement, there appeared to be a group of people largely outside the regular economy who were at once the chief source of social disintegration and its major victims. Second, the individuals involved in creating the demonstration, mirroring the shift in public sentiment discussed in chapter 1, shared a perception of the value of work as an integrating force in people's lives. They argued that stable employment would offer people an opportunity and a reason to change.

Third, the planners of the demonstration had been close to the employment initiatives of the 1960s. They had been impressed with the potential of the programs but discouraged by the lack of reliable data on program effectiveness and the resulting widespread skepticism that the tens of billions of dollars spent on them had produced any positive results. They had also observed firsthand the prevalent roller coaster of policy development, wherein a bright idea was quickly transformed into a national program and just as rapidly discredited. They sought to demonstrate the feasibility and utility of a more cautious method. This strategy had another appeal. At a time when large-scale welfare reform was going nowhere (President Richard Nixon's Family Assistance Plan had recently died in Congress) and the federal role in employment and training had been cut back, a demonstration offered a way to generate momentum, surface promising new directions, and shift public debate.

The program called Supported Work, operating at that time on a small scale in New York City, appeared to answer all three concerns: it addressed the population of interest with an approach that stressed work; it had already been the subject of a promising pilot; and limited expansion with some kind of serious research design seemed feasible. Beyond that, by providing voluntary paid work with the mantra of converting a welfare check into a paycheck, it offered a seemingly more humane alternative to an approach bubbling up from the states (notably from Governor Ronald Reagan in California) that many viewed as punitive: mandatory unpaid "workfare," in which welfare recipients would be required to work in exchange for their benefits.[3]

The Supported Work program had both short- and long-run objectives. In the short run, local Supported Work companies offered subsidized jobs in an environment intended to attract and hold people. Although there was an attempt to mimic the realities of the workplace, several features were added to help people adjust to work and prepare for subsequent employment in the regular labor market, including peer support (working in crews with similar employees), graduated stress (supportive but gradually increasing work demands), and close supervision. But the emphasis was firmly on work, with strict limits on the time spent in services such as formal training or counseling. At the end of a year, program staff assisted participants in finding permanent, unsubsidized jobs. The longer-term hope was that participants would develop some combination of the habits, attitudes, self-worth, skills, and credentials needed to secure and hold regular jobs and thereby reduce the behaviors that had relegated them to the category of "unemployable." The combined goal was to reduce poverty and improve the quality of life for both people in the program and people living in the communities the program served.

The Entrepreneur

In 1972 the Vera Institute of Justice launched the first Supported Work program for a group of former addicts and former offenders in New York City.[4] Not long thereafter, Herbert Sturz, Vera's director, approached Mitchell (Mike) Sviridoff, vice president for national affairs at Ford, about its replication.[5] He had gone to the right person. Sviridoff, an ardent proponent of work programs and a long-term Vera funder, knew the program well and, like Sturz, was an exceptional social policy innovator and entrepreneur. With decades of experience running community development and employment initiatives in New Haven and New York City, and a foundation focus on combating poverty and racial discrimination, Sviridoff saw Supported Work's potential as a way to create jobs, provide useful public services, reduce welfare, and transform people's lives. As William Grinker, Sviridoff's protégé and self-described "spear carrier" at Ford, who went on to head MDRC, recalls, "At one point . . . I said to Mike 'What the hell is new about this? You did this 10, 15 years ago in New Haven. Work for someone, what's the big deal?' And Mike said something which I never forgot. He said: 'Timing is everything.' He . . . sensed that this concept which was not new and had been part of the war on poverty when it first began, he could sell it at that point, repackage it, and so forth, and he was right."

But Sviridoff also knew that Supported Work was expensive and complex. Preliminary results from the Vera pilot (some from a small random assignment study) showed that it could operate and have positive short-term impacts for former addicts; but they did not answer why the program worked and whether success could be replicated or sustained after participants left the program. As one Ford staffer put it: Was Vera's success derived from the Supported Work model or from factors such as the spirit and élan created by its talented staff, the way applicants were screened by the program, or the exceptional public entrepreneurship of Herbert Sturz? Sviridoff was impressed, but the 1960s experience had convinced him that the environment had changed and that Ford could no longer push for major initiatives without more convincing evidence. He therefore proposed a multisite demonstration with an active operating component.

Sviridoff's focus was on replication, capacity, and feasibility: Was the program relevant to other populations? Under what auspices would it function most effectively? What work settings offered the greatest potential? How would union officials, private employers, and different levels of government respond? Would large-scale expansion be feasible? But he also knew, as Grinker recalls, that there would have to be "a respectable research component." Just as he would use the early Vera research to make the case for a demonstration—in the face of the prevailing view that nothing works, Sviridoff would say, "Look, this is a program that works. Let's go with it and prove on a large-scale demonstration basis that programs do work"—he knew he would ultimately have to sell the demonstration's results based on some kind of convincing evidence. But what that meant was not spelled out. At a minimum, "convincing" meant good outcome data, a solid management information system, reliable cost estimates, and some yet-to-be-specified way to find out whether the program made a difference. Thus the initial vision was long on demonstration and short on research, did not specifically call for an effectiveness or impact study, and certainly did not envision random assignment, according to the memories of multiple participants in the demonstration planning. But this changed quickly, with several people claiming paternity for the transformation.

The Money
Sviridoff knew that a multisite demonstration would have a big price tag and that, though the foundation could bring prestige and unusually flexible money, it could not stake this on its own. Thus, ever the master of leverage

and strategy, and having "an uncanny ability to reach out to the best people and think in fresh ways,"[6] he mustered his and Sturz's contacts—Sturz knew the senior people in the criminal justice and drug agencies, and Sviridoff knew others in the Department of Labor (DOL) and the Department of Health, Education, and Welfare (later the Department of Health and Human Services [HHS] and referred to consistently as such in this chapter for simplicity) and assembled a rare consortium of federal partners. His first stop in October 1973 was Howard Rosen, the director of research and development in DOL's Employment and Training Administration (then the Manpower Administration), which had supported Sviridoff's work in New Haven and had been a primary early funder of the Vera program. An early account prepared for the Ford Foundation reports that "Rosen could not commit the Manpower Administration. But Sviridoff left the meeting confident that he had not wasted his time. What Rosen *didn't* say was highly significant. He didn't say that no discretionary funds were available, or that it would be necessary to wait for appropriation time. He didn't say that there were opponents of Supported Work in the higher reaches of the agency. Manpower Administration support, in short, was a sufficiently likely probability to warrant full speed ahead" (Brecher 1976, 63).

Rosen's next move was critical: briefing and paving the way for Sviridoff to meet Rosen's boss, Assistant Secretary William H. Kolberg. As Frederick (Fritz) Kramer (who worked for Rosen and became DOL's program officer for Supported Work) recalls, "After we had this meeting . . . Howard and I went to his office and he said, 'This is something that's really going to be important.' And Kolberg came in and said, 'Yes, we can find the money,' and they were both excited about doing something . . . like welfare reform that moved beyond their more traditional focus. . . . They were completely committed to that point. . . . And Kolberg got some extra money from the secretary, and this was going to be a grand plan." Kolberg became the lynchpin. He not only gave his imprimatur for funding but also put up the money immediately, personally reached out to peers, and unleashed DOL staff to help recruit federal partners.

What followed was a full court press, culminating in a whirlwind January 1974 day of Ford meetings with numerous under and assistant secretaries that Grinker describes as unlike anything he has seen before or since ("they were like maniacs putting up money"). When the dust settled, the federal agencies were on board, the money pledged, and DOL anointed their lead agency.

Of the $82.4 million total cost, the Ford Foundation's $4.3 million outlay was matched by $45.2 million from six federal partners—of which $26.9 million came from DOL and the rest from the Law Enforcement Assistance Administration in the Department of Justice, the Office of the Assistant Secretary of Planning and Evaluation and the National Institute of Drug Abuse in HHS, and the Departments of Commerce and Housing and Urban Development—and another $32.9 million from diverse sources. One component of the $32.9 million was the diversion of welfare benefits that participants would have received had they not been working and that were instead used to partially fund their Supported Work wages, prompting the program's claim to turn welfare checks into paychecks.[7] (This "diversion" was made possible by federal waivers to provisions of the Social Security Act, a process that was to play a prominent role in the random assignment story described in later chapters but that in Supported Work served a much more limited function.)[8]

Sviridoff's pitch worked because of the policy consensus described at the beginning of this chapter;[9] the win-win potential of Ford's strategy, under which each agency could buy the inclusion of the population it cared about while benefiting from the infrastructure offered by the combined funding; and the institutional goals of particular funders.[10] The result was something much larger—in scale, rigor, and visibility—than any of the participating agencies could afford on its own. Finally, Sviridoff signaled that this would be an important national effort and, in style and substance, a class act. He promised to tap an illustrious advisory committee that was headed by the prominent scholar and Washington insider Eli Ginzberg[11] and engaged the future Nobel Prize–winning economist Robert Solow to plan and oversee the evaluation, which, combined with Ford's general halo, would make this a grant to be proud of. At the more operational level, it was important that Sviridoff offered a true partnership, in which the funders would together make key project decisions.

The Early Months

The new Supported Work Advisory Committee—which, in addition to Ginzberg of Columbia University and Solow of MIT, included Richard Nathan and Gilbert Steiner of the Brookings Institution, Robert Lampman of the University of Wisconsin, and Phyllis Wallace also of MIT—delivered much more than was promised. In typical understatement, several of its members (Ginzberg, Nathan, and Solow 1984, 307) later observed that "collaboration between a foundation and several federal agencies requires an unusually high degree of cooperation among many actors, something that is extremely difficult to achieve." With no funder solely in charge and all attending its monthly meetings during the first half of 1974, the committee became the go-to place for decisions that ranged from determining the project's ambition and knowledge objectives, designing the research, defining the target groups, and balancing multiple project goals to resolving how to manage the endeavor and select subcontractors.

In playing this role, four of its members (Ginzberg, Solow, Lampman, and Steiner) brought a perspective shaped by their recent experience in preparing an issue of *The Public Interest* that assessed lessons from the Great Society. Among the conclusions they drew was the danger of making excessive claims that would trigger exaggerated expectations and the corollary value of a precisely designed and carefully researched demonstration with limited and achievable objectives. In their final paper in that volume, Ginzberg and Solow (1974, 214) urge that promises about the results from interventions be "realistic rather than extreme. A public which has been encouraged to expect great things will become impatient, critical, and alienated if the progress that is achieved falls short of the rosy promises. A wise leadership is careful to promise no more than it can feel reasonably sure it can deliver within a reasonable time." For Supported Work, this translated into a conscious management of expectations and positioning, starting from the earliest brochure: "The present approach is a limited exploration of the value of Supported Work for selected groups and is not a pre-test of a program for general welfare reform or guaranteed jobs."[12]

A second conclusion Ginzberg and Solow (1974, 215–16) reach is the value of experimentation broadly defined. "A responsible leadership will proceed with caution in areas where it lacks adequate knowledge and experience, in the expectation that second efforts at social intervention will be improved by what is learned from the initial experiments. We do not know if the idea of a frankly experimental public policy can be made politically viable. It is worth a try."

WHY RANDOM ASSIGNMENT?

During the early months, pressure mounted to go beyond Sviridoff's original vision of a demonstration with some research to a project with a major focus on research, in particular, rigorous impact research. The debate took place in the context of weak prior studies, most of which compared people's earnings before and after they entered the program (revealing gains that could well have had more to do with participants' getting jobs on their own than with the program) or used unreliable comparison groups. As Solow recalls, the decision to study effectiveness flowed directly from the designation of four distinct target groups (which itself followed directly from the multiagency funding strategy). "That decision must have been taken with the thought in mind that [the program] could work differently for one group . . . and therefore we're already talking about measuring impacts." Indeed, from the beginning the federal funders stated their interest in determining effectiveness separately for each of the four target groups.

The result was the formulation of five broad knowledge objectives to be addressed through a centralized research effort:

1.   How effective is Supported Work in increasing the long-term employment and earnings of participants and in reducing welfare dependency, criminal activities, or drug abuse?
2.   What target populations benefit most from the program?
3.   What does the program cost? To what extent does it produce valuable goods and services? How do the program's costs compare with its measurable benefits?
4.   What local conditions, administrative auspices, and implementation strategies seem to be the most conducive to success?
5.   What characteristics of the program model have the greatest impact on participant performance and behavior?

But agreement to study impacts did not mean agreement on how to estimate them. This is captured in Ginzberg's memo summarizing of the initial meeting of the advisory committee in January 1974. He began with the two points of "preliminary agreement: (a) recognition that the Supported Work demonstrations represent a social initiative, not a research experiment; and (b) affirmation of the sponsors' view that a serious effort must be made to design a reporting/evaluation approach that would enable the country to learn some useful lessons from the demonstration efforts."

The rest of his memo focused on the pros and cons of using random assignment to estimate impacts. After stating that such an approach has much to commend it, he turned to a long list of potential negatives: public relations difficulties, legal and administrative risks, diverse biases, distortions from paying controls, and difficulty in following controls over time. He also reported other concerns, including that "the odds are very strong that any social intervention will be too weak to show a clear-cut positive effect," given the very disadvantaged people in the program—a concern that came to be known as confirming the null hypothesis (the hypothesis that the program has no effects); that "the best designed and controlled social experiment can never take account of exogenous factors"; and that although "admittedly ex-post analyses have their limitations, . . . it is doubtful whether any system of evaluation can do better than use one or more gross discriminators—i.e., employment, income, absence of arrests."

This sounds strong, but it told only part of the story. Ginzberg's summaries were not minutes but an art form, crafted both to help achieve and capture consensus and to control the record. As Solow puts it in retrospect: "This was Eli writing for himself, for posterity, and putting his slant on things . . . with an eye to making a record that he would like." Reading his memo thirty-five years later, I see Ginzberg's skepticism about letting this project tip too heavily toward rigorous, "scientific" data crunching and move away from what he saw as the more important issues. As an early account puts it, "Ginzberg's position . . . was that large-scale quantitative research undertakings rarely paid off. He saw the concrete operating data emerging from the project, and close scrutiny of what was actually happening at the Supported Work demonstration sites, as a sounder basis for evaluation" (Brecher 1978, 29–30). Despite these concerns, at the next monthly meeting Ginzberg reported, "We are committed to use control groups though the question as to whether all sites must be controlled, or only some, remains moot—until later."

What prompted this turnaround? I was not at these meetings and could find no written record of this pivotal decision. Solow offers what seems a reasonable interpretation: this was not so much a reversal as a shift in forces within a committee that had been more divided than Ginzberg's January write-up suggests. Although he does not know why that decision was made, Solow thinks the pressure for random assignment came from inside the advisory committee and specifically from two "intransigent advocates," himself and Robert Lampman (who had been involved in earlier NIT experiments).

We wanted random assignment because, otherwise, how are you going to be able to say that this is the impact on ex-addicts and so on. . . . Eli was skeptical, very skeptical, but then Eli was skeptical of any kind of formalized research, and he certainly had no enthusiasm for the random assignment idea. Gil Steiner was happy with random assignment, but he was from the very beginning worried about the human subject aspects of this. For instance, we had really intense discussions of the issue . . . of how can you deny half of the people who were referred to the program . . . the treatment? And the answer always was: we're going to make the sample big enough so that we use up all the money we have on treatment, and not having a control group would not increase the size of the . . . treatment group any. That notion carried the day.[13]

Although he and Lampman were convinced by this logic—particularly because they anticipated at best small and complex effects—Solow remembers that Ginzberg and Nathan remained concerned that random assignment would evoke the horrors of human experimentation and outrage the general public.

As for the rapid shift between the two memos, Solow reflects that Ginzberg "may have recognized . . . some merit to the argument that, if you are going to try to give some sort of authoritative, respectable, defensible answers to the questions we were asking, that there was no other way or no better way to do it." Solow (1980, 8–9) also may have won him over, at least in part, with the argument he presented at the time:

We want to find out if participation in Supported Work improves the subsequent labor-market experience of participants. But, of course, the dominant influence on the later employment and wages of participants will be the later condition of the labour market, as it is affected both by the business cycle and by conditions specific to . . . [the local site]. The only way to isolate the effects of supported work from these much louder background noises is to deal statistically with differences between the experimental and control groups who are exposed to identical extraneous conditions and differ only in their status with respect to supported work. Attempts in connection with after-the-fact evaluation of other manpower programmes to construct artificial "comparison groups" have mostly failed, so the formal randomized control group seemed essential.

In the last sentence, Solow points to the key weakness of non–random assignment designs: the risk that people who choose to apply for Supported

Work or are screened by program staff would differ in some systematic, un-measured, but influential way from people in a comparison group (even a carefully matched one), with the result that comparisons of their subsequent behavior would produce a biased estimate of the program's impact. This phe-nomenon, dubbed "selection bias," has been the Achilles' heel of non–random assignment studies.

This pressure from inside the committee might alone have carried the day. But committee members were not alone. Michael Barth and John Palmer, both at HHS and fresh from writing up results from the New Jersey NIT experiment, also "had the religion on random assignment," as Barth remem-bers it. Grinker recalls that Barth (a self-described "enfant terrible" on this subject) went so far as to make random assignment a condition of the depart-ment's participation. And although it is not clear who initially pushed Aid to Families with Dependent Children (AFDC) recipients as one the four target groups, once that decision had been made, Ford wanted HHS involved. The result was an instant expansion of the demonstration's relevance beyond crime and reentry (the Vera focus) to offering the first large-scale, experimental test of a service strategy to move people from welfare to work.

The decision to use random assignment did not mean anyone was at all confident about its feasibility. Even though Supported Work was not the first social experiment, earlier efforts—the negative-income-tax, health insurance, and housing allowance demand experiments—tested variations in economic incentives: treatments that could be exactly defined by a small number of parameters (guarantee levels, tax rates, coinsurance requirements, and so on) and were tightly controlled and administered by the researchers. Until Sup-ported Work, random assignment had never been attempted in a large, mul-tisite employment demonstration and, as we wrote at the time, it was the general consensus that "it would antagonize operators and local interests to such a degree as to jeopardize the entire effort" (Gueron, Rubinger, and Walker 1976, 100).[14] Grinker and I both remember being told in 1974, at the beginning of our demonstration planning, that "asking program operators to turn people away would be like asking doctors to deny a patient a known cure. They won't do it."

Solow confirms the widespread concerns: "Everyone said [there was a real risk that random assignment would not work] . . . even inside the committee" and for at least three reasons. The first was the danger that referral agencies and program operators would be implacable in resisting it as cold-hearted, immoral, and unethical: "I thought that was a real thing. I just thought personally that you had to fight through that. There was no point in giving up because then you were giving up the ghost, but that was one danger." The next two reasons were related to the study sample: whether we could generate a big enough sample to be able to detect impacts of the expected magnitude and whether we could locate and interview the controls and experimentals for enough years to detect long-term impacts: "We had no idea how rapidly you'd lose them. If you lost half of them every six months or something, then you were dead. We realized that was a problem and nobody had the slightest notion as to how that would play out. . . . For those three reasons at least, and there may have been others . . . I was by no means sure that we would bring this off."

Looking back over the same forty years, Robinson Hollister, who had headed the federal initiative (in the Office of Economic Opportunity, later Health, Education, and Welfare, and later still Health and Human Services) that set up the first NIT experiment and later led the Supported Work impact study, draws somewhat different conclusions. In his view, those earlier experiments had been the breakthrough that showed the feasibility of experiments. Nonetheless, he (seconded by Barth) acknowledges that the Supported Work challenge was much tougher: setting up new operating programs, not just handing out money; multiple and geographically dispersed sites; the dependence on numerous agencies to refer people over many years; and the fact that members of the control group might enroll in a host of other employment and training programs (raising the question of their value as a yardstick against which to measure Supported Work's achievements). He recalls how, when he made a presentation on the study at one of the sites (Philadelphia), a local academic threatened to sue him under the Helsinki conventions for engaging in inhumane treatment.[15] So, even if the NIT experiments had blazed the trail, the community context of Supported Work—with mission-driven and politically connected local programs—made the process more controversial and the outcome highly uncertain.

THE CREATION AND ROLE OF MDRC

Memories differ on the original vision of who would run Supported Work: Sviridoff out of the Ford Foundation, DOL (though they could not accept money from Ford), or an interagency committee of federal officials. Whatever the truth, by April 1974 it had become clear that the sheer complexity of the effort made all those options unrealistic. With fifteen sites, four target groups, seven funders pushing their own agendas, and a sophisticated research plan, it is not surprising that Hollister describes the situation as "just chaos" and says that the researchers invited to bid on the study called this "the most complex research effort ever undertaken by the Feds." Nathan, having recently left senior jobs in the Office of Management and Budget and HHS, recalls advising strongly against managing it "inside the belly of the beast."

But if Supported Work could not be run by one of the funders, what options remained? In assessing alternatives, the planners sought to avoid difficulties that had undercut earlier demonstrations and they feared would be even more dangerous in a lengthy, multifunder environment—resisting political pressures, maintaining a consistent focus and design, disciplining program operators, controlling costs, assuring quality implementation of the research and program, and coordinating operational and evaluation priorities in the context of the project's overall knowledge development objectives. Grinker recalls what happened next: "There was a meeting at some point in the spring [of 1974]. . . . Everybody had agreed to put up their bucks and they said 'Now, who's going to run this?' 'Well,' Rosen said, 'we're not doing it.' and Mike [Sviridoff] said, 'Well, we're not doing it. . . . Who's going to do it?'"

Fortunately, as Ford's program officer, Grinker had anticipated this, and to be on the safe side, he had created a shell corporation.[16] Thinking back, he observes, "It was very good that we had it . . . because, when push came to shove . . . I had the corporation there. And so, you know, it was a pretty easy lift to get everybody with me . . . [especially with] this prestigious group of research scientists as the Board."[17]

The result in June 1974 was the nonprofit corporation, MDRC, with the six advisory committee members installed as its original board of directors (Ginzberg as chairman, Solow vice chairman, and Nathan secretary-treasurer), followed a few months later by Grinker's appointment as MDRC president and only five months after that by the start of program operations (see table 2.1 for the timeline).

Founding presidents often leave a lasting imprint on a company, and this was certainly true at MDRC, because a number of the core staff thirty-five years later (and two of its subsequent three presidents) had directly imbibed Grinker's technique.[18] His style was, to put it mildly, controversial. On one side was the abrasive tough guy who—through a combination of veiled threat,

Table 2.1   Timeline of the National Supported Work Demonstration and Related Events

Date	Event
January 1974	Six-member advisory committee first meets
June 1974	Creation of Manpower Demonstration Research Corporation (MDRC)
August 1974	MDRC selects Mathematica Policy Research to conduct impact and benefit-cost analysis
October 1974	Grinker becomes first president of MDRC
March 1975	Start of program operations
1975–1981	Publication of reports on implementation and impacts
1980	Publication of MDRC's summary book on Supported Work demonstration
November 1980	Ronald Reagan elected president

Source: Author's compilation.

put-down, bluff, poker face, and hanging tough—negotiated and then enforced every contract as if each penny of the funders' resources came from his own pocket. His unparalleled keep-them-guessing style left the other party at the least not knowing what to expect and at the most incensed. A few weeks into the job (I was hired in December 1974), after I had been part of such a negotiation, the lead person at one of our subcontractors asked me how I could work for that SOB. I remember thinking that Grinker was not (or was not only) the bully my questioner perceived him to be but might instead (or also) have been covering my back by playing the bad cop—so I could play the good cop and hide behind the statement that "Grinker won't budge."[19]

But there was another side to Grinker, the one that made me ask—again during those first weeks, when we were in decrepit offices dispersing millions of dollars while trying not to be the odd person out in the musical-chairs game on seats that were too few, did not match, and often had no backs— "What is it about this guy that could make such a tacky operation seem like the most important event in the country?" Through a combination of intimidation, sarcasm, and inspiration, Grinker garnered exceptional loyalty and hard work from MDRC staff, who might have feared his words but viewed him as a brilliant craftsman and original thinker, decisive and strategic leader, demanding perfectionist and tireless line-by-line reviewer, remarkable master of both the big picture and the detail, and an iconoclastic manager who rejected hierarchy. Through all this he also communicated that MDRC stood for something; we were not a hired gun. Finally, at some point down the line, we also saw the very decent and human side of the man, who cared about and sought to protect the staff. Although he was sui generis, and none of us who went on to lead MDRC even attempted to replicate his style, I did seek to maintain his deeper values and his drive for quality and integrity in all aspects of our work.

Presidents frequently leave a legacy, but boards of directors are less likely to do so. In MDRC's case, however, because the advisory committee had run the show directly for nine months before Grinker was appointed and it had morphed into MDRC's board, there was a more intimate connection. As Solow puts it, they were not just board members but founders, who, as a result "had a lot more of their own egos at stake in the organization" and a tradition of active participation in substantive decisions. Because most of the initial group remained on the board for decades, with Solow still chair even as this book goes to press, the habit of ex ante contribution on substance—versus the more typical focus on governance, finance, and ex post review—persisted. As Ginzberg wrote at the time—in words that could well have described his own deep involvement in MDRC's early activities—"The fact that the Board early recognized that it could play an active and constructive role resulted in the members being willing to make heavy commitments in time and involvement" (Gueron, Rubinger, and Walker 1976, ix).

At the beginning, MDRC's stated purpose was narrow: to coordinate and manage the operational and research activities of the Supported Work project on behalf of the sponsoring agencies. This included several distinct activities: specification of the program model and its implementation to ensure a fair test, oversight of the development and implementation of the research, resolution of conflicts in achieving these two functions, and monitoring of the overall conduct of the demonstration in a financially responsible and cost-effective manner. These responsibilities were to be carried out over three years (later extended to five) on a scale that was unprecedented in employment and training research.

But though that was the public line—no long-term or grandiose mission and certainly no particular commitment to random assignment—the founding fathers clearly had a grander vision. At the time, and speaking also for Sviridoff, most members of the advisory committee, and Rosen, Ginzberg wrote that "from the start, it was recognized by at least some of the founding fathers that if the supported work program proved successful, MDRC might sooner or later become the instrument for carrying out additional social demonstrations" (Brecher 1978, i). As Grinker puts it looking back,

> My vision for MDRC . . . came out of the antipoverty program, where I always thought that, rather than [the Office of Economic Opportunity] becoming this big multibillion-dollar agency, it should be a kind of laboratory for new ideas. . . . I never would have said this publicly at that point, [but] ideally that's what I sought for MDRC, that it would become a laboratory for testing out new antipoverty kinds of strategies. Whether that would come to pass, or not . . . depended primarily at least on how well we did with the first one. If we couldn't pull that off, obviously, nothing was going to happen.

In these years, MDRC often described itself as an intermediary corporation, reflecting its position as a bridge between the interests of many diverse parties—public and private, national and local—and described its key strengths as flexibility, speed, and independence. To ensure that they were informed and consulted and retained their share of ultimate authority and responsibility, the funders attended board meetings and were involved in all major decisions. In this role, MDRC viewed itself as neither a management consultant nor a research organization but rather some combination of the two. It did not (and still does not) operate local programs directly but subcontracted with local organizations to set up nonprofit Supported Work corporations. Similarly, after a competitive selection process, it subcontracted the Supported Work impact, benefit-cost, and statistical process studies to Mathematica Policy Research, at that time Mathematica, Inc., which in turn contracted some of the analysis to the Institute for Research on Poverty at the University of Wisconsin–Madison, a team judged to have the required broad capabilities and experience in large-scale research. The subcontracting to local programs was judged important, both in putting operations in the hands of agencies resembling potential future service deliverers and in ensuring the objectivity of MDRC managers and Mathematica Policy Research researchers.

Although MDRC did not present itself in political terms, it had a hardnosed but big-hearted tone. On one hand, the push for random assignment reflected a "just the facts, Ma'am" view of its mission. If rigor required that controls be turned away from potential benefits, so be it. On the other, Supported Work offered a voluntary paid job to extremely disadvantaged people, at a time when others were suggesting get-tough workfare mandates. Participants would be fired if they did not meet program standards, but those demands increased gradually over time. The program was cast as extending a helping hand to those willing to grasp it. But MDRC did not view itself as another do-gooder organization. Staff were told their job was not to advocate for Supported Work but to learn whether it worked. As Grinker put it in MDRC's 1977 and 1978 annual reports, we were to "reach conclusions about program effectiveness with an open mind and without a predetermined commitment to particular solutions. . . . Staff pride and morale have to hinge on the organization's capability as a manager, and not on whether a program such as Supported Work is or is not . . . effective."

Nonetheless, though we knew it was just as important to determine that a social program did not work as to learn that it did, the staff were generally liberal. Most people probably shared Ginzberg's view: "A rich society has an obligation to enable all who desire to work, even if they cannot meet competitive norms, to do so as long as their output carries the costs of the society—and possibly even if their economic contribution does not" (Finney 1974, 24). We hoped Supported Work would prove a route to achieving this. As Ginzberg, Nathan, and Solow (1984, 314–15) wrote at the end of the project, "All those involved in the Supported Work Demonstration wanted it to succeed. The board, staff, and the program operators in the field had to keep reminding themselves that it probably would not. The most important reason for the need for objectivity is that there is always pressure from the policy apparatus to come up with *something* when the true effects are likely to be small; it is often too easy to bias the results or the interpretation of results in the desired direction." Fortunately for MDRC in these formative years, we had random assignment—with its inexorable comparison of experimental versus control outcomes—to keep us honest and help us avoid the pitfalls of advocacy research.

Grinker organized MDRC in two main divisions: research and operations. Fresh from a job in New York City's welfare agency and with a doctorate in economics but no prior experience with random assignment studies, I was put in charge of the research division.[20] My initial mission was to manage the research subcontract (basically to push that the work be both of the highest possible quality and completed on time and within budget) and to oversee an in-house study of program implementation. Gary Walker, who had run the first Supported Work program for the Vera Institute, headed the operations department, with the goal of monitoring and providing technical assistance to the local programs. Grinker laid out his vision of the operations role in MDRC's 1977 annual report: "In order to function successfully, MDRC must have a thorough understanding of and ability to work well with these local operators. . . . [The operations] staff interprets the program model and research constraints on local operational flexibility; assists local operators in program development; monitors the program's progress; and recommends new MDRC policies which may be required to preserve the programmatic, contractual or research integrity of the demonstrations."

The result was an organization that differed from other research and consulting firms in having two core staffs (research and operational) that did not have distinct spheres of influence. As I have described it elsewhere, "The organization saw as an essential precondition of its success the integration of the research and operational activities to achieve its overall corporate mission: the establishment and oversight of an operating program in a manner that would optimally test its utility and replicability. This concept did not include a separate operational role per se for MDRC. Rather, the corporation measured its effectiveness by the extent to which it could avoid the disintegration and fragmentation of the program and research designs exhibited by prior research/demonstration efforts" (Gueron 1984b, 290–91).

Supported Work planners knew success would require the balancing of diverse goals. On one hand, they wanted to make the most of the rare opportunity to do a social experiment. This created pressure to seek answers to multiple important questions by adding complexity to the experiment's design. On the other, the planners sought to give the nascent local programs a chance to thrive—fearing that, if the sites were overly burdened by the random assignment process or other aspects of the research, or if they were studied too soon, the model would not get a fair test. Finally, they knew that site cooperation and buy-in would be essential to the study's success. Over the years, many of us at MDRC concluded that Grinker's vision of dual perspectives inside the company went a long way toward explaining why we may have been particularly effective in resolving these tensions and in integrating experiments into operating programs.

TESTING FEASIBILITY AND EFFECTIVENESS

Three examples illustrate how MDRC's board and staff, the funders, and the research contractors balanced operational and research perspectives in reaching key design decisions. These included choices about the operational design and a key component of the research and the effort to avoid the shortcomings of earlier evaluations.

A Demonstration and an Experiment

The first concerns Supported Work as both a demonstration and an experiment, a hybrid vision that came to dominate many of the early decisions and was embedded in Grinker's choice of our original name—the Manpower Demonstration Research Corporation. In its demonstration guise, the project sought to provide a real-world test of the administrative, legal, or other obstacles to the program's replicability. The prior decade's experience had pointed to the importance of the method of implementation and the difficulty of transplanting a particular program model from one local setting to another. Early project documents reveal that these concerns were acute: Could sites recruit and put to work these extremely disadvantaged people? Was the model too complex to be replicated? Could enough work sites be created? Could sites raise the required matching funds? The list went on and on. In its research guise, in contrast, Supported Work was a methodological innovation; for the first time on a large scale, it sought to evaluate an employment program using random assignment.

As Hollister (who became the research director of Mathematica Policy Research and principal investigator on Supported Work) notes, though Vera's program provided a useful example for replication, in contrast to his experience with the NITs, "there was really no tightly defined, *a priori* theoretical model around which an employment program for highly disadvantaged populations could be constructed" (Hollister 1984, 18). Instead, in diverse locations, independent nonprofit corporations (which more closely resembled small businesses that raised money by selling the goods and services produced by Supported Workers than social service agencies) would be charged with operating a complex, multidimensional work program.

The competing demonstration and experimental visions resulted in a tug of war for the project's soul that played out around major design decisions. To ensure the integrity of an experiment that would have to pool data from ten small programs employing an average of 165 supported workers at a time (five additional programs would operate purely as demonstrations, without random assignment, with the combined group enrolling more than 10,000 during the four years), researchers argued that the local programs had to share certain core characteristics. On the other hand, MDRC operations staff urged that, in order to function effectively, the local directors must be given flexibility to develop their programs along lines suitable for the populations employed, local conditions, and the operators' personal styles and objectives. Solow (1980, 8) sums up this tension: "You cannot run successful manpower programmes without tapping local initiative, but the scope you can allow to local initiative must be limited or the experiment, as experiment, will go down the drain."

The result was a compromise. MDRC agreed to rigidly standardize those program features that met four criteria proposed by Hollister:

1. They could be expected to produce statistically significant differences in major behavioral hypotheses.
2. They would be measurable and monitorable.
3. They would be amenable to control without unduly constraining or disrupting local operations.
4. They could be controlled in any subsequent national program.

The characteristics that met these criteria included eligibility definitions to ensure that the programs served extremely disadvantaged people in the four target groups;[21] a wage, bonus, and benefit structure designed to reflect both local wages and the gradually increasing work requirements; maximum program duration of twelve or eighteen months, depending on site; and intake procedures that specified random assignment. In each case, regulations were drafted and site selection made conditional on agreement (incorporated in formal contracts) to implement these policies. In particular, by the time local operators applied for substantial funds and were competitively selected, they knew random assignment would be used to allocate people to Supported Work or a control group.

Other program features (for example, the method for implementing peer support or graduated stress) defied uniform definition but could be controlled by detailed guidelines. Still other elements (for example, leadership and supervision) were judged to be either not amenable to rigorous control or dependent on local conditions (such as the nature of in-program work sites— ranging from painting, home insulation, renovation, and tire recapping to clerical and business services, child care, and home health care—and postprogram work opportunities) or deemed so critical to management style and administration that standardization might jeopardize operational viability (for example, assignment of workers to specific work sites and detailed personnel policies).

Explaining Success or Failure

The second example of how design decisions were made concerned the research plan. The random assignment study supported the first three knowledge goals for the Supported Work demonstration: Does the program change behavior? If so, for whom? And at what cost? But Ginzberg was not alone in pushing for the importance of the what, how, and why questions: What did the programs look like when adapted to meet local conditions and challenges? How did particular characteristics of the program, or leadership, or the environment and administrative structure affect performance and behavior? Why did some strategies work better than others? As Grinker recalls, Sviridoff (and initially Ginzberg and Steiner) considered these questions fully as important as the impact research, since lessons about program structure and management would be critical to any subsequent Supported Work expansion and could also inform the general understanding of work program design.

To address the what, how, and why issues, we adopted two research approaches. The first would be a quantitative and qualitative documentation (descriptive analysis) of program implementation conducted by MDRC staff and consultants. Through qualitative interviews, field observation, and the project's extensive management information system, we would attempt to decompose the complex black box of the local supported work programs. The second would be a statistical process analysis conducted by Mathematica Policy Research to determine how key components of the Supported Work treatment influenced in-program and postprogram performance. The analysis would use detailed individual data, from payroll time sheets and the project's management information system, and surveys of supervisors and participants. Hollister was clear that the approach was exploratory and the results uncertain.[22] I told MDRC's board (in my very first memo to them) that, since a detailed management information system was being built in any case, the additional cost of this statistical analysis seemed relatively limited. This turned out to be a big mistake.

Notably, the MDRC demonstration managers weighed and ultimately rejected the plea of Mathematica Policy Research to address these issues either by systematic variation of discrete program elements among sites or by random assignment of participants to different program features within sites. This is not the place to discuss whether that choice was a wise one. The tension between research ambition and operational realism requires a judgment call on which wise people may reasonably disagree. However, it is worth repeating the three main arguments we at MDRC made at the time, since some of the same logic explains the cautious but incremental complexity of the random assignment designs that we brought to projects described later in this book.[23]

First, we doubted that a variation at one or two small programs would provide conclusive information on its usefulness, especially given the many other uncontrolled differences among sites.[24] Second, we considered the specific suggestions to be impractical—for example, either randomly assigning people to work in crews or as single placements in host agencies or providing the identical job placement services to both controls and experimentals. Third, we were intensely concerned that excessive research demands might push the local programs too hard, thereby endangering the success of the overall operation. Our general theme was to avoid jeopardizing the ability to address the basic questions on Supported Work's efficacy, even if this meant giving up an opportunity to obtain evidence on more refined questions. In short, we had the proverbial fear that the best might be the enemy of the good.

The Experimental Design

A third example of the effort to balance operational and research perspectives concerns how the planners sought to avoid the three pitfalls that in their view had limited the conclusiveness of earlier evaluations. They felt that earlier analyses included no appropriate counterfactual, that the research sample sizes were inadequate, and that the follow-up period was too short.

The counterfactual issue was resolved by the decision on random assignment, which, for reasons just discussed, also included a decision to have a simple, two-group design. The result was a lottery in which roughly half the people who volunteered for the program were offered a Supported Work job (the experimental or program group) and the other half were offered no special activities (the control group) but remained eligible for all benefits and services existing in the general community.[25] The program's effects were measured as the difference in behavior between people in the two groups, as revealed by in-person interviews conducted periodically after people applied for the program and in subsequent years. The design was remarkably simple compared with the NIT designs. As Hollister puts it, "We knew the mistakes we made in the negative-income-tax experiments. . . . The sample design model was very complex. Brilliant modeling, but it was so complex that in the end it just caused more headaches than it was worth. So we knew there was a premium on keeping it as simple as possible."[26]

In addressing sample size and follow-up, the experiment's designers sought to ensure that, for each of the four distinct target groups, the sample would be large enough and people would be followed long enough to yield reliable conclusions on whether Supported Work did or did not work (defined somewhat differently for each group). With a sample that was too small, even if the program was actually effective the study might conclude that it made no statistically significant difference (in the language of evaluation, the study would be underpowered); if the follow-up period was too short, the study might miss impacts that emerged over time or fail to detect impact decay.

These risks were serious. From the beginning, we suspected that long-term impacts might be relatively small. Lampman had repeatedly warned that the extremely disadvantaged nature of participants increased the likelihood of confirming the null hypothesis of no impact.[27] Ginzberg, Nathan, and Solow (1984) write that, if there had been any clear-cut solutions to the problems addressed in Supported Work, they would have long since been legislated.[28] In addition, all the planners feared that the severe recession of 1974 to 1975 would limit success.[29] We also expected impacts to vary in size, and we knew that distinguishing their pattern over time—whether they were "ephemeral or enduring," as Solow (1980, 9) puts it—could be key to conclusions on the program's success and cost-effectiveness.[30] In addition, we wanted the sample to come from an adequate number of sufficiently mature sites to ensure that the findings would be representative of a variety of operating styles and local conditions and thus more relevant to a subsequent national program. The challenge was to address these issues in the context of, first, a known and fixed research budget and, second, unknown and difficult-to-predict site performance levels (including program size and no-show and turnover rates) and data collection costs (including survey costs and completion rates).

The approach we adopted was two-pronged. First, the study used what Hollister and his colleagues called a "sequential design," shorthand for a process of continual optimization under which the sample size and its allocation across sites, target groups, and time periods was not set in stone at the start but periodically reevaluated as we learned more about costs and realities on the ground. This was possible because the Supported Work sample was recruited over two and a half years (from April 1975 to July 1977). As soon as supported workers left the program, they were replaced by new enrollees.[31] Thus that Supported Work offered a temporary job, not an ongoing transfer payment or subsidy, meant that the sample build-up was continuous, constrained only by the availability of job slots.

This innovative use of a sequential design strategy was more or less explicitly repeated in studies described in subsequent chapters. As I wrote years later, establishing an experimental design

> may sound easy, but estimating the needed sample size requires understanding factors ranging from the number of people in the community who are eligible and likely to be interested in the program, the recruitment strategy, rates and duration of participation by people in the program, what (if anything) the program staff offer [to] controls, access to and participation by controls in other services, sample attrition (from the follow-up data), the temporal placement of random assignment, and the likely net impact and policy-relevant impact of the program. Some of these factors are research-based, but others require detailed negotiations with the program providers, and still others (for example, the flow of people or the cost of data collection) may be clear only after the project starts. The complexity of this interplay between sample size and program operations points to the advantage of retaining some flexibility in the research design and of continually reassessing the options as operational, research, and cost parameters become clear. (Gueron 2002, 29)

The strategy delivered on its promise. We were able to extend the Supported Work sample and follow-up from the initially projected 5,400 people in eight sites, interviewed every six or twelve months for up to twenty months after random assignment, to 6,600 individuals at ten sites, interviewed every nine months for up to thirty-six months.[32]

The second part of the solution involved two strategies to reduce the risk of evaluating a poorly implemented—and for that reason ineffective—start-up period. We delayed the introduction of random assignment for several months or more after the start of the program, and we had MDRC's operations staff provide ongoing technical assistance.[33]

Outside the System and Below the Radar

In contrast to the later generations of experiments described in subsequent chapters, the foregoing discussions are striking for what they do not say. Reflecting both our style and the times, they make almost no reference to state-level, public sector administrators. Supported Work was a relatively centralized, top-down project. Key decisions were made by MDRC, the funders, and the researchers sitting in New York City, Washington, D.C., and Princeton, New Jersey (the office of Mathematica Policy Research). Although the local sites did intersect with the mainstream public systems—for example, to get referrals, raise local funds, develop work sites, and elicit support for a waiver application—state officials had minimal input into program or evaluation design. From the 1980s perspective, this is surprising, but at the time, federal employment and training funds flowed to localities, not to states. The result, nonetheless, was a stealth strategy that had the advantage of greatly simplifying decision making and keeping the controversial random assignment process below the political radar; but there was also a disadvantage: state administrators (when they later moved into a key role) did not feel any ownership for or pay much attention to the project or its results.[34]

IMPLEMENTING THE EXPERIMENTAL DESIGN

A social experiment is uniquely powerful only if it is well implemented. For those of us conducting such studies for decades, tried and true procedures have become almost second nature. We know that for a social experiment to be successful, it is not enough for all parties to have good intentions or even to ensure that no one rigs the lottery. Although this is critical, it is only the first step in creating meaningful experimental and control groups. A study can easily be undercut if the members of the two groups are not treated appropriately down the line—for example, if they are not offered or denied the correct services over the following months or years, or if data or completion rates differ too much, or if sample members are inappropriately dropped from the analysis.[35]

But in 1974 the field was new. We did not start Supported Work with a checklist of possible threats. We crafted the "art" decision by decision, as we encountered new challenges.[36] But we did start with four powerful advantages. The people in charge at Mathematica Policy Research—David Kershaw, until his untimely death in 1979, and Robinson Hollister—had also been among the leaders of the initial negative-income-tax experiment, and they applied or adapted its lessons as potential landmines were detected.[37] The MDRC staff kept research ambition to realistic levels and communicated with the local actors in language that reassured them we were not wild-eyed fanatics who would walk them off an ivy-tower cliff. MDRC's highly engaged board brought wisdom and perspective to its new staff. Finally, those of us involved in the project shared a fervent commitment to do it right. We all knew that the value of the whole superstructure rested on our not messing up on random assignment, whatever that might entail. Since the goal of this book is to point to the lessons from our experience, rather than to write a primer on how to do a high-quality experiment, I only briefly touch on what we did to gain and sustain the cooperation of the key local administrators—the sites and referral agencies.

To do their jobs well, local Supported Work staff had to believe they were helping people. Any program intake procedure involves some form of rationing—first come first served, serving the more motivated first, allowing caseworker discretion, covering only certain neighborhoods, or limiting recruitment so no one is actually rejected. But staff vastly prefer these approaches to a random process in which they have to personally confront and turn away people they view as eligible and deserving. Yet for a social experiment to succeed, these staff must be converted. They must buy into and own the process or at least agree to cooperate fully with it. Otherwise the study is doomed, which is what we feared would happen in Supported Work.

As expected, opposition arose early. According to a June 1976 MDRC document highlighting site activities, "If there was one divisive issue that generated lingering and often bitter conflict between the sites and MDRC in the planning period, it was the research component. . . . [The local] planners considered the random assignment approach destructive. One planner said, 'You are presenting the controls with one more thing that doesn't work for them, to go along with the rest of their luck in life.'"

Yet despite this and the predictions of disaster, random assignment turned out to be largely a nonissue. As the MDRC board of directors (1980, 42–43) sums up the experience, "There was initial resistance to random assignment by some referral agencies and program operators, who felt the process was unfair to controls and necessitated too large a recruiting effort. As the demonstration progressed, however, operators became more familiar with the process, complaints diminished and eventually disappeared, and the procedure became only a minor operational annoyance."

Why was this so easy in Supported Work compared with the vitriolic opposition to later experiments? At the time, I thought the main explanation for our ability and authority to induce and discipline compliance was money: we were offering sites millions of dollars for a new program conditional on their playing by the research rules. The experiment was not an add-on to an already funded program but a tied sale, built in from the beginning. As a result, we could require some level of standardization in the program and research, could pool data across sites, and could ensure a large difference in treatment between people who were offered the program and those in the control group, who were not. As Solow (1980, 8) says, "We have found that the only practical way to maintain control over experimental conditions is to place the purse strings in the hands of the research organization. There is nothing like being the chap who pays the piper if you want to be the chap who calls the tune."

Hollister (1984, 35) emphasizes the importance of not just money but an iron will. "It is only because of MDRC's adamant refusal to concede on [random assignment], and its insistence on making it a prerequisite for continued funding at research sites, that the process was carried out successfully over such a long period of time."

Grinker, in retrospect, points to yet another factor: that the sites and assorted interest groups all viewed the program as a positive good. No hard sell was needed. This was not mandatory workfare but a voluntary program behind which local administrators could easily rally the troops.

In hindsight, given the success of later experiments that brought none of these assets to the table, I see it somewhat differently. Although it is probably true that at that time we would not have broken through without the funding, it is probably also true that we would not have succeeded if we had relied on money to buy cooperation in an otherwise offensive endeavor. And we did not do that. Instead, we made every effort to show local actors that what we were proposing was ethical and legal, to sell them on the program and on the potential value for them and participants of what might be learned, and to reduce the burden on operations. Furthermore, we took pains to explain what we were doing in language that they could understand and, we hoped, would elicit their trust. Finally, given what was at stake, we did not rely on stated commitments or good intentions but made sure that we controlled the only gate into the local Supported Work programs.

Since experimenting with humans can conjure up images of Nazi-like atrocities, our first step was to demonstrate our firm commitment to high ethical and legal standards. In training the referral agencies and the sites and in describing the project, we made a strong case for the morality of random assignment. Supported Work was a specially funded demonstration that would provide enriched services that otherwise would not exist. We were not denying people access to services to which they were entitled. We were not reducing service levels. Instead, we had the resources to enroll only a small number of those likely to be interested. The experiment increased services for one group without reducing them for another: people in the control group would retain eligibility for all other services in the community. Finally, though the program sounded like an idea that could not fail, we did not know whether it would actually help—or hurt—people. In these conditions, we argued, a lottery was fairer than other ways to allocate scarce opportunities.

But we did not think this argument eliminated our responsibility to protect people involved in the research. From the beginning, board member Gilbert Steiner worried about this issue. In addressing it, Supported Work became the first social experiment to be covered by new federal regulations on the protection of human subjects. Steiner headed an institutional review board that set up procedures to protect the rights and integrity of individuals in the demonstration. At intake, through a process of obtaining informed consent, we told applicants about the lottery and the possible risks (including being in a program with former addicts and former offenders) and informed them of both the kind of data that would be collected in surveys (in some cases on illegal activities) and the strict procedures we would be putting in place to protect confidentiality and limit access.

The second step to sell the experiment involved reducing the burden it would place on program staff, while at the same time ensuring that we left no loopholes for staff to game the system (thereby letting people they thought particularly deserving escape the lottery and go directly to a Supported Work job). In addition to the effort to balance operational and research demands, Mathematica Policy Research and MDRC developed streamlined intake procedures. After determining that applicants to the program were both eligible and acceptable (for example, not likely to be disruptive), program staff explained the lottery and then provided the Princeton staff with key identifiers used to check whether the person was already in the treatment or control group. If not, the Princeton staff immediately randomly assigned the applicant to one or the other.[38] Although some sites still complained (particularly about how random assignment complicated their ability to assemble well-balanced work crews), they rapidly concluded that their toughest challenges lay in other program areas, for example, developing sufficient work sites or raising local funds.

The third step in implementing our experimental design was to convince program operators that the research findings could make a difference in policy and future funding and that undermining random assignment or helping controls would make their programs look worse and undercut their long-term objectives. This took creative salesmanship, since at that time an assertion about the particular power of this type of research was based more on hope than on a track record of success.

LESSONS ABOUT PROGRAM AND POLICY

The Supported Work demonstration produced numerous lessons—some counterintuitive—that began to shed light on the wide range of unknowns. The effort would continue, with many a struggle, over the next thirty-five years.

Modest Success for Some

Supported Work sought to change the behavior of four diverse groups of people. From the beginning, we had expected the program to have its smallest impacts on AFDC women. Not only might they not like the stereotypically male jobs offered at some of the sites, but they were more likely than men to have competing child care responsibilities, be in poor health, have a hard time finding subsequent work, and face low monetary incentives (since they had welfare as an alternative source of income, would have their benefits cut when they got a job, and were likely to be paid less than men). Instead, they were not only the most stable and reliable workers while in the program but also the group with long-term earnings impacts after they had left, which was generally not the case for the three other, largely male groups.[39]

Although the effects for AFDC recipients were statistically significant (that is, large enough so that it is unlikely they were due to chance), were they also policy significant?[40] Were the changes large, moderate, or small? Was the program substantively successful? About two years into the study, the employment rate for those who had been in the program was 8 percentage points higher than for women in the control group (49 percent versus 41 percent); monthly earnings were 46 percent higher ($243 versus $166, averaged over people who did and did not work); and twice as many experimentals as controls had left the welfare rolls (30 percent versus 15 percent).[41] Moreover, the benefit-cost findings were encouraging. Even though the program was relatively expensive—$10,300 per person year or $8,100 per person in the AFDC group (which was in the program longest, 9.5 months on average) in 1978 dollars—Mathematica Policy Research estimated that under a wide range of assumptions the benefits to society as a whole (participants plus nonparticipants) substantially exceeded the costs. Although the study focused primarily on this social perspective, it also examined whether participants and nonparticipants (sometimes called taxpayers) separately came out ahead.[42] (The study did not present the impact on government budgets, which emerged as a key measure in later studies.) However, the positive impact on earnings did not translate into a reduction in poverty.[43] Although this was not entirely unexpected—since the low-paying jobs the women got generated immediate reductions in welfare benefits—it was nonetheless disappointing.

In 1980 when the results came out, different people viewed them differently. Some saw the glass half full. Here, for the first time, was convincing evidence that an employment program could work and be cost effective. For this extremely disadvantaged group of long-term AFDC recipients, the program beat the null hypothesis of no impact and provided a counterweight to the Great Society's legacy of skepticism. A March 2, 1980, editorial in the *New York Times* concluded that the program provided "a boost to welfare recipients, and a bargain for taxpayers." As Solow (1980, 16) puts it, "No one who cares seriously about the employment of disadvantaged groups will sneer at those results. They are not at all trivial. . . . Somehow we have to learn to make a convincing case for policy initiatives based on reasonable estimates of the probability of success and the quantitative meaning of success. If the professional policy community allows itself to promise more than it can deliver, it will end up not delivering what it promises, and eventually the promises will be disbelieved and there will be no delivery at all."

Others saw the glass half empty. Even this costly program, which to some had appeared an obvious winner, either failed or had mixed results for three of the four groups. This fit the founders' expectation that the program would probably not work for all groups, but people were disappointed that even for the AFDC group it did not do more to "solve" the problems of poverty and dependency.

Howard Rosen grappled for the right balance in a 1979 letter to Sviridoff, observing that, while he had not naively expected sensational results, it is clear that "we have not stumbled upon the Holy Grail." In MDRC's 1978 annual report, Grinker points to the limits of research:

> [Success] is in the eyes of the beholder. Some people might think that supported work is a success—that if, for example, the number of people on the welfare rolls is reduced by 10 percent, and these people work rather than collect welfare—this is success. On the other hand, if it costs more to do this, other people will say it is not worth the expense. It's how you define success, and in the end it has to do with values. . . . We will make recommendations on issues like these in the demonstrations we manage and try to provide policy makers with some options and alternatives. But, in the end, they have to make the judgments.

Since we did not start with clear expectations and had no similarly reliable data on other approaches, we were not sure how to characterize the effects and, as a result, often steered clear of adjectives, relying on the comprehensive benefit-cost analysis to provide one form of a bottom line.

The findings for the AFDC group led to what became themes in later studies: some women on welfare clearly want to work;[44] work programs can be cost effective; earnings impacts do not automatically produce poverty reductions; and the program was no panacea. Impacts were modest and, at the end of the follow-up, most people in the AFDC group were still receiving welfare and not working.

Lower Outcomes but Higher Impacts

Lurking behind this brief summary is an insight that was to reemerge repeatedly in later studies: high outcomes do not necessarily reflect high impacts. Outcomes show the status of people (for example, the percentage employed or on welfare) at some point in time; impacts show the difference between the outcomes that did occur and the outcomes that would have occurred had the people not participated in the program. In the real world, outcomes for people in a program (for example, how many are placed in jobs) are straightforward and therefore often used as performance measures, whereas impacts are hard to measure and are not available to program operators. This pushes people to ask: Do outcomes at least track impacts? Do they send the right signals and lead to correct policy conclusions? Supported Work was an early warning that in social programs the answer may be no.

Table 2.2 **Percentage Employed Some Time Between Nineteenth and Twenty-Seventh Month after Random Assignment in Supported Work**

Target group	Program group	Control group	Difference
AFDC recipients	49.1	40.6	8.5**
Former addicts	56.5	53.0	3.5
Former offenders	56.5	53.3	3.2
Youth	62.6	62.6	0.0

Source: Author's compilation based on MDRC Board of Directors (1980, tables 9-1, 9-2, 9-3, and 9-4).
**Statistically significant at the 5 percent level.

The key reason Supported Work did not work for men (that is, did not have a positive net impact) was not that men in the program did not go on to get unsubsidized jobs (in fact, men were more likely to find jobs than the AFDC women) but that men in the control group got jobs just as quickly, sometimes using other programs in the community but often on their own. Table 2.2 shows how this worked. The outcome data in column 1 provide some support for our initial (mistaken) hunch that the program would be least successful with AFDC women. Between the nineteenth and twenty-seventh months after random assignment, when almost all people had left their Supported Work jobs, the former addicts, former offenders, and youth who had been enrolled in the program were somewhat more likely than the AFDC women to be working. For example, 56.5 percent of former offenders worked at some point during these nine months, compared with only 49.1 percent of AFDC mothers (column 1). However, data for the control group (column 2) tell us that these men would have gotten jobs just about as frequently without the program, whereas the women would not have. Thus Supported Work succeeded with AFDC women not because the participants did so well (as measured by outcomes) but because the corresponding controls (without program aid) did so poorly. This result—higher impacts for the most disadvantaged—also occurred within all four target groups.

The implication was clear: anyone judging the program using typical outcome-type performance measures would have reached the incorrect conclusion that the program succeeded with the three primarily male groups as much as or more than with the AFDC women (depending on the outcome measure).[45] This phenomenon reflects Solow's point that the main influences on behavior are the economy and other background factors, not the program, and thus is just another way of highlighting the critical need for a reliable counterfactual. Because we had one (behavior of the control group over the same period), we could show trends in hours worked by controls and remind ourselves and others that the program challenge was not merely to raise outcomes but to beat the control group's outcomes (the counterfactual moving through time).

This lesson further vindicated the random assignment decision. As Hollister (1984, 41–42) puts it,

> It is easy to say that no one would be so foolish as simply to compare [outcomes for] those who had been in the program without reference to some sort of comparison group, but if Supported Work had been carried out as only a demonstration, without the added research dimension that included control groups, this sort of comparison would have been the major basis for judgments about the groups for which Supported Work was relatively most successful. Furthermore, it seems reasonable to question whether any "comparison group" constructed without recourse to random assignment really would have captured the subtleties of these trends. The problems of the "cohort phenomenon" add weight, in my view, to the doubt that methods other than random assignment would have been nearly as precise and powerful.[46]

These findings led to related themes in later studies: keep your eye on the control group, be cautious about outcome-based performance standards, and pay attention to subgroups. (In presenting conclusions in this and subsequent chapters, unless noted otherwise, we focus on those reached at the time—not what later analysts using somewhat more exacting methods might have concluded. This is particularly the case in comparison across subgroups and sites.)

LESSONS ABOUT RESEARCH METHODS

The Supported Work demonstration pioneered numerous big and small innovations in research methods. Five stand out for their influence on our story.

The Feasibility and Value of Random Assignment

Learning the feasibility of using random assignment to evaluate an operating employment program was a huge step forward. With decades of successful experience, it is tempting to be blasé, but as this chapter shows, at the time this was a revolutionary idea. This achievement permanently changed the debate about what could and should be done in employment and welfare evaluations. As Hollister (1984, 35) suggests, "Perhaps it will be easier to apply this method in future studies of employment programs since it will be possible to point to the successful implementation of it, on a large scale, in the Supported Work Demonstration."

But Supported Work also showed that the angel is in the details. The lesson was not that random assignment got a blank check but that success was possible under certain conditions—community organizations that volunteered even knowing a lottery was part of the deal, substantial funding tied to cooperation, a new and oversubscribed program, and a fly-below-the-radar strategy—and following certain procedures—skillful marketing, a central mechanism to monitor compliance, informed consent, confidentiality, and efforts to limit intrusiveness. Experiments discussed in later chapters tested anew the limits of feasibility.

Confirming the value of random assignment was also an important advance. On this score, the initial argument came from the magnitude, unpredictability, and complexity of the impacts. Given the variation across sites, groups, and time periods, by the end of the demonstration even the initially more skeptical members of MDRC's board had signed on. As Ginzberg, Nathan, and Solow (1984, 314) conclude, "Only the control group strategy—the fact that the behavior of participants could be measured against the benchmark of the behavior of a randomly chosen group exposed to exactly the same labor market and year-to-year variations in it—held promise of reliable results on a widespread or general basis." A second argument came from subsequent analyses of the Supported Work data by other researchers, which showed that alternative, nonexperimental research designs would have yielded incorrect conclusions.[47] The impact of those studies (see the Coda in this volume) also pointed to the value of the investment in creating a Supported Work public-use data file, which started what became a flourishing industry of reanalyses of experimental data.

The Feasibility of an In-Person Survey Tracking Strategy

Supported Work proved that we could use an in-person survey to track a large sample of extremely disadvantaged people for three years and collect high-quality data on sensitive issues, including criminal activities and drug use. Not only did the field interviewers succeed in meeting the target completion rates, but also analyses of sample attrition and comparisons with administrative records showed that the data did not suffer from serious bias or misreporting.[48]

The Benefits of a Rigorous Benefit-Cost Analysis

A third finding on methods concerned the pioneering benefit-cost research. There was much debate, including within our board, about the assumptions involved in benefit-cost analysis and how much weight to place on the estimates. But the rigor of the researchers' approach—which, among other things, showed how having a control group contributed to estimating the program's net cost—provided the foundation for future studies and for the claim that social programs could be investments that produce measurable returns.

Widespread Acceptance of the Experiment's Results

That the study was judged credible and trustworthy followed in part from the feasibility and value of random assignment as we implemented it. Before Supported Work, there were questions about whether one could produce reliable results and whether those results would be widely believed. After it— and despite continued academic debate about whether statistical modeling could produce equally reliable answers at lower cost and whether experiments addressed narrow and relatively unimportant issues—I do not recall anyone questioning whether the results accurately reflected the impact of the experiment (that is, had internal validity). We were helped by two types of transparency. The first was the simplicity of the method itself. Anyone could understand the basics of the analysis. There was no fancy statistical footwork. Random assignment delivered on its promise as a powerful communications tool. The second was that we expressed impacts using measures that were both relevant and comprehensible to our audience of diverse decision makers: the percentage of people working, on welfare, or in poverty; average earnings or welfare benefits; the percentage of people arrested; and the percentage of people using heroin.

But another aim of social experiments is to produce findings that would be relevant to a subsequent program serving the larger eligible population. Whether an experiment's results can be replicated depends on how typical are the participants, the operating environment, and the sites. In Supported Work we did not choose the sites or the sample at random from the universe of eligible places and people. We also started in what was, at that time, the deepest recession since the 1930s, and during a period when there were many alternative employment services provided under the Comprehensive Employment and Training Act (CETA) and the Work Incentive (WIN) program. The demonstration planners hoped that selecting ten varied sites would approximate the variety in operating experience and local conditions likely to be encountered in an expanded program, thereby increasing generalizability and reducing the risk of idiosyncratic findings. There is no way to know whether they succeeded. Although Supported Work did not solve these problems, it did confront them, and they became staples in the debate about the design and interpretation of subsequent experiments.

Learning What It Was but Not Why It Worked

By 1977 we had an answer to Sviridoff's basic demonstration question: at least at the scale attempted, Supported Work could be replicated for different groups under varied conditions. We also had a rich description of the local programs and of the strategies used to adapt the model.[49] This would obviously be useful in any subsequent expansion, but we wanted to know not only how the program operated but why it succeeded or failed. What particular characteristics of the treatment or the local environment had the greatest effect on in-program and postprogram performance and behavior? As mentioned earlier in this chapter, we used two strategies to address this: qualitative and quantitative documentation and statistical process analysis. Both produced insights and generated hypotheses, but despite a lot of talent, effort, and money, the dots led mainly to dead ends or further questions.

On the qualitative strategy, Grinker and I both recall painfully the showdown near the end of the study, when we finally had enough follow-up data to examine the relationship between site quality and postprogram impacts. Based on numerous field visits and years of detailed performance data, we at MDRC were confident we could distinguish the good sites from the weak ones and thereby identify some of the winning and losing practices. Separately, Grinker, Walker, I and others ranked the sites. Then, and only then, Mathematica Policy Research ran site-specific impacts and came back with the verdict: they found no correlation between our judgments and the experimental estimates. Looking back, I realize that this was to some extent just another version of the outcome-impact dilemma, even though we had thought we were smarter than that. We had taken a holistic view of the sites—considering the quality of leadership, program components, performance data, and what we heard from participants—but we were still wrong. We were looking at the programs and the supported workers, but we were not (and realistically could not be) considering the controls. This experience prompted some healthy humility.

But we still had an ace in the hole, or so we thought: the statistical process analysis. This sought to create what economists call a production function, a mathematical model that would relate inputs and outputs for this complex social program. Hollister remembers that from the beginning he described his attempt to link participants' individual characteristics to internal components of the program and various outcomes as exploratory; however, he argued that, if successful, the payoff would be large and that, in any event, the exceptional data on Supported Work made it worth a try.[50] Unfortunately, the analysis turned out to be both more difficult and less informative than anticipated. The construction of the huge microdata files proved expensive and time consuming, and the absence of random assignment on these variables made it difficult to determine whether the statistically significant relationships that were found represented real differences or self-selection. Also, though the data were extraordinarily detailed—as far as I know, no later experiment had such extensive data—they may still not have captured elements that were critical to program success (for example, the nature and quality of leadership and supervision; implementation of graduated stress). The conclusion of the MDRC staff and board of directors (1980, 41, 161) was that "in general, this effort was not very successful and contributed little to an understanding of the usefulness of the components of supported work. . . . This . . . indicates the extreme difficulty of doing quantitative process research on an operating program, even in a relatively controlled environment. Understanding which features of the supported work model deserve modification, expansion, or abandonment must still come largely from qualitative observation and judgment." Hollister (1984, 46) reaches a different, "mildly positive" conclusion that enough had been learned—particularly from negative findings that disproved operators' hunches—to warrant more such studies in the future.

Later chapters in this book describe how this quest to understand better why programs work and determine what works best for whom continued over the next thirty years, with some breakthroughs, notably when random assignment was used to get inside the black box of a complex social program.

LESSONS ABOUT MDRC AND ITS PARTNERS

In addition to determining the replicability and effectiveness of Supported Work, the demonstration had two further objectives: trying out a new technique for managing such endeavors and determining the value of the test-small-before-you-act-big model of social policy making.

Within a few years, the management story was viewed as a clear winner. At the beginning, as Grinker recalls, "nobody ever thought we could pull this thing off as well as we did." What had started almost by default—who else could run the project?—emerged as a virtue. Managing large-scale demonstrations and social experiments is akin to directing multiple trains speeding forward, some on parallel but others on crossing tracks. Excellence requires sustained focus. It is easy to waste money, get diverted, and not deliver the goods. The Supported Work demonstration outlived the terms of three U.S. presidents and all the assistant secretaries active in its birth, making MDRC's relative insulation a clear plus. If it had been run out of a federal agency, the changing leadership and priorities would have made it much more difficult for staff to sustain the initial vision. Barth now views this management achievement as the project's major lesson:

> It showed that you could get a consortium of federal agencies that have disparate goals and activities to work together on something. It showed you could develop something pretty new in a reasonable amount of time and get it off the ground. It showed that you could start a new organization that could have a fundamentally important impact on social policy. It's one of the good things the government did. [It's true that] without the Ford Foundation none of this would have happened, but that's philanthropy's job. The government was helpful in that it showed that it could delegate this kind of work to a non-profit entity that could be independent, which is very important.[51]

Clearly MDRC's success was not just an affirmation of structure but also reflected the talent and actions of specific people. Grinker argues that the two were connected, in that the intermediary structure enabled quality by giving people the green light to proceed in a way that might not have been possible within government. Furthermore, he points out, flexibility also came from having Ford money, which meant that "we weren't totally beholden to government. . . . We were kind of protected. We had enough money to keep working even if the feds said 'You don't know what you're doing.' So we could pretend to play hardball with them. . . . That large Ford grant was very important to us in terms of our ability to negotiate. . . . It gave us a level of independence which is very important."

Beyond its own staff, MDRC benefited from the quality of its three key partners and the relationships it had or built with them. The first was the Ford Foundation. The staff and board of MDRC were the agents that made the most of the opportunity; but the real entrepreneur, the éminence grise, was Mike Sviridoff. It was his combination of attributes—an initially grandiose vision, skill and flexibility in nurturing it to realization, willingness to use his clout or halo when needed, an appetite for institution building, and recognition of the value of flexible money—that gave us (and in particular his mentee, Grinker) the opportunity and breathing room to deliver. The Supported Work story and MDRC speak to the potential power of philanthropy. They are examples of Ford at its best. As the next chapters show, the story of philanthropic innovation was to be a play with many more acts.

The second factor was the dedication of staff in the federal agencies, in particular Howard Rosen and Fritz Kramer at DOL, who showed an intense personal commitment to Supported Work and MDRC. Grinker recalls that Rosen was always there for us when needed, but it is Kramer, his key staffer, whom Grinker singles out as invaluable in solving the myriad issues that came up when five federal agencies were channeling funds through DOL to MDRC. Rosen and Kramer, in turn, could rely on the strong backing of their boss, William Kolberg. As an early chronicler of the Supported Work story puts it, "Thus, the two essentials for effective relationships with a Federal agency were both abundantly present—a dedicated operating official in the intermediate ranks plus a hotline to the top for emergencies" (Brecher 1976, 172). In the end, as Rosen had hoped, the success of the project cast a glow on his own shop and set a new standard for work within the department, prompting subsequent experiments. As Kramer describes it, "We never had anything like this in Howard's office before. This was the shining star."

Finally, we were fortunate in selecting Mathematica Policy Research as our research subcontractor. Given our relative inexperience, their talented and dedicated team (which included a young researcher, Rebecca Maynard, who went on to be a leader in the field) deserves the lion's share of credit for the high quality of the research. Many of the design and analysis decisions set the standard for later experiments.

THE STUDY'S EFFECT ON POLICY AND PRACTICE

The value of the try-small-before-you-buy-big vision that motivated Supported Work rested on two unknowns: Could one get reliable evidence on whether a complex, operational program did or did not work? Would such evidence matter to policy makers? The project obviously cleared the first hurdle. What about the second? The demonstration's founding fathers and architects were not optimistic about the relationship between research and policy. As Ginzberg, Nathan, and Solow (1984, 312–13) write,

> Experience shows . . . that new developments and major shifts in social policy have little to do with actual advances in knowledge in the social sciences. The direction of policy responds to much deeper forces—historical commitments, political developments, ideological trends, and shifts in the balance of power among social classes. Social science does not initiate changes on such a broad scale, nor can it be used to resist a particular policy that has strong support despite social science findings suggesting that it is unlikely to succeed. . . . Thus, when it comes to major directions and redirections or policy, the record of having and using social science knowledge is not a very good one; the lag in impact . . . is usually long.

They launched the demonstration in any case, because they either thought or hoped that getting good evidence would at least figure in the equation, providing some counterweight to a values- and conjectures-only debate.

By 1982 Ginzberg and Grinker had reluctantly concluded that MDRC was successful in building knowledge but much less so in translating results into policy change, pointing to the "disheartening" failure of the federal government to act on the board's recommendation to launch a national Supported Work program for AFDC women. Reflecting on this more than a quarter century later, Grinker sees it somewhat differently. He now thinks the AFDC findings had a major impact, transforming views about moving welfare recipients into jobs and, in so doing, serving as the first link in a chain of results that led to the welfare reforms of the 1980s and 1990s. Moreover, both he and Kramer remain convinced that, but for Ronald Reagan's election in 1980, there would have been a national Supported Work program run out of DOL with special funding, along the lines of Job Corps. As Grinker sees it, they came "very close": "We were well on the road toward institutionalizing it with

Congress. . . . The legislation was drafted and Labor was going to put it in their appropriation. . . . Then Reagan came in and Congress changed and that was the end of it. They killed it. . . . Then, the second thing that killed it was MDRC's own [subsequent] research, which said this is too expensive and there are cheaper ways to do it."

My own views on whether Supported Work affected policy have also evolved. At the time—when we had no comparably reliable data on the effectiveness of alternative approaches—I shared Grinker's disappointment and pondered why, despite what I saw as the encouraging AFDC findings, the program had proved so easy to kill. I attributed this, at least in part, to a combination of the project's style and the times. Supported Work was a stealth project in two senses: MDRC kept a relatively low profile (by intent and also because we were not very savvy about dissemination), and the project was designed by elites in Washington and New York, with little input from the state and local agencies that (starting in the 1980s) increasingly shaped, funded, and ran such programs.[52] Although, as I have noted, our strategy was useful in keeping random assignment below the radar and reflected the 1970s context, it meant that key political actors who were later responsible for decisions never owned the results. Even though some of the local Supported Work programs survived the Reagan axe (one was reborn as a national franchise), and some states picked up on the idea, in general the programs lacked local allies and folded. With hindsight, a different strategy of partnership with states and localities at an earlier stage might have prompted replication under the increasingly decentralized employment and training system.[53]

Another possible weakness, I now think, was that, throughout the project and in developing a strategy for institutionalizing Supported Work, MDRC had worked most closely with DOL, the lead agency, not with HHS nor, within DOL, with the WIN program itself. When the story turned out to be as much about welfare reform as about what were then called manpower programs, it hurt that HHS was busy with other priorities and did not consider it its project. Supported Work also ran against the grain of HHS's then-current push for reforms based on cash assistance, not services, according to Barth's recollection. This focus on the manpower versus welfare systems had its state counterpart. As Barbara Blum has noted, state welfare officials did not feel connected to the Supported Work study and as a result did not use the findings as they redesigned their programs in response to the 1981 legislation (see chapter 4).

It is unclear whether either a bottom-up strategy or one focused on the WIN or AFDC programs would have been more successful than the top-down and CETA-focused approach we took, but it is clear that those of us who remained at MDRC (Grinker left in 1982) took this lack of buy-in as a lesson that helped drive our subsequent behavior. Although we had always known positive results would not and should not automatically lead to expansion, and were chary about becoming advocates of the program rather than of the research, we went away thinking we had failed to build a constituency in the then-existing systems that would be waiting for the results and primed to act on them. Determined not to repeat that, we took a more inclusive and grassroots approach in subsequent demonstrations.

As late as 2007, I wrote that "Supported Work was a beautiful study. . . . Yet it had no real impact on national or local policy" (Gueron 2007, 136). But with even more distance I now see that, for example, the generally null findings for former addicts, former offenders, and youth clearly had an immediate effect. The federal government avoided spending huge sums on ineffective employment programs. This is what the planners had hoped for when they espoused testing the program before recommending national expansion. (Although this is true, we also knew at the time that MDRC would have had trouble surviving—and launching subsequent similar studies—if we produced only negative findings.)

I now think the AFDC results also affected policy, just not in the way I had anticipated. The case for Supported Work for AFDC mothers was not undermined by the findings themselves, viewed in isolation. Had there not been a series of later experiments, it is possible that (after the highly ideological early years of the Reagan administration) the credible if modest effects might have been seen as sufficiently encouraging to warrant expansion. But I share Grinker's view that the evidence from subsequent experiments that lower-cost programs could yield comparable long-term impacts ended that.[54] If this higher-cost and harder-to-replicate program did not buy correspondingly higher returns, why go to the great trouble of expanding it? Because that was the reading of the results, and people lost track of the fact that Supported Work addressed a particularly hard-to-employ group, the program pretty much dropped off the policy screen, even as it remains part of the cumulative wisdom generated by forty years of experiments. It was the findings from the lower-cost programs—starting with the Louisville WIN Laboratory Project but particularly the later experiments—that had a major impact on welfare reform policy and practice, in both Washington and the states.

NEXT STEPS

This chapter describes how the Supported Work initiative delivered on its goals. As a result, for people in a small number of private, philanthropic, and public organizations, it put to rest two first-order questions: Can public programs increase work effort? Can one assess such programs by using experiments? But it tested a specific program under special circumstances, leaving unanswered the effectiveness of other strategies and the potential to use this powerful learning tool in different contexts.

Over the next twenty years, the random assignment approach was tested anew as later experiments pushed the envelope on all the conditions that had seemed critical to Supported Work's success. The results were fresh challenges and some name calling, as new communities and organizations had to be convinced that such studies were ethical and worth the risk and not acts of political suicide. Proponents of random assignment also had to defend their work against a chorus of academic critics who argued that the approach was not necessary or failed to address the most salient questions. The next chapter describes what was originally viewed as a small-scale test of innovative ideas but turned out to be a trial run for a new vision of experiments. At the end of that chapter, I draw some larger lessons from the 1970s, as we entered the very different world of the 1980s.

CHAPTER 3

Bridge to the 1980s: Implementing Random Assignment in Work Incentive Program Offices and Testing a Job Guarantee*

Everything that MDRC did after that was in many ways patterned on the Louisville WIN Lab. . . . It was a stepping stone. Without it, I don't think the step from Supported Work to the state Work/Welfare studies would have happened in the way it did. We had clearly gained experience in working with states and localities and in how to put random assignment in place within operating programs.

—Gordon Berlin[1]

Launching a nationwide demonstration, like [the Youth Incentive Entitlement Pilot Projects], is an exercise in politics, administration, and research.

—Richard Elmore[2]

This chapter tells the story of two initiatives that helped MDRC not only survive as an institution in the dramatically different policy and policy-research environment of the Reagan era but also continue using random assignment to learn more about program evaluation generally and the work-welfare area in particular. The first of these initiatives was the Work Incentive

*Chapter 3 authored by Judith M. Gueron.

(WIN) Laboratory Project, notably the two job-search programs implemented in the Louisville, Kentucky, WIN program office. In many ways less ambitious than Supported Work, WIN Labs took an important next step by showing that random assignment could be implemented in regular government offices to assess programs within the welfare and employment systems. Although we did not realize it at the time, this experiment served as a bridge to the state-based experiments described in later chapters, in which the technique was applied in much larger demonstrations and then to tests of full-scale reform.

The second initiative that helped prepare us for the 1980s was the Youth Incentive Entitlement Pilot Projects (YIEPP), the nation's first and only job guarantee. Passed as part of the Youth Employment and Demonstration Projects Act of 1977, which sought to address the alarming increase in youth unemployment and to find out what might work to reverse the trend, YIEPP was a massive ($240 million) demonstration of a job creation program for low-income youth (part-time during the school year, full-time in the summer). Although its evaluation did not target welfare recipients or use random assignment, YIEPP is relevant to our story for three reasons. First, we had to examine important management and feasibility issues related to running an open-ended jobs program, which proved central in later studies of welfare-to-work and workfare programs. Second, YIEPP propelled MDRC out of the protected environment of relatively small experiments into the real world of full-scale operating programs run by public agencies.[3] Third, on an institutional level, the feverish pace, political stakes, and operational and research demands built skills that would serve us well in the coming years.

THE ENTREPRENEUR AND THE
VISION FOR WIN LABS

The WIN Laboratory Project was the brainchild of Merwin Hans, the national director of the Work Incentive program. Housed within the Department of Labor but reporting to assistant secretaries in both the Departments of Labor (DOL) and Health and Human Services (HHS), WIN's goal was to move Aid to Families with Dependent Children (AFDC) recipients into jobs through a combination of employment, training, and social services and to enforce a work requirement. Hans viewed good research as essential to making this large, decentralized system (which was also dually administered at the state level) more effective and had worked with Howard Rosen (who controlled his research budget) to set up a number of important studies. Although some of these had produced useful results, Hans was not satisfied with the pace of change. As he saw it, local office staff often undermined or disregarded the research. If the findings came from demonstrations conducted outside the system, staff argued that the conditions could not be replicated in the regular operating environment; if the findings came from demonstrations conducted inside their offices but thought up by non-WIN folks, staff questioned the value of the approaches being tested and felt no stake in the studies' success. Hans compared that resistance with what occurs when a patient rejects a heart transplant: "We would get a notion of something we wanted to try; then we would find a researcher; then we would find a location . . . and then we would struggle mightily. . . . The system didn't want it. . . . The research was always a foreign body" (Leiman with Seessel 1982, 7).

To counter this and get local buy-in, Hans proposed transforming four WIN offices into ongoing R&D laboratories that would function as programmatic and research partnerships among federal agency staff, local WIN practitioners, outside experts, and evaluators. Rather than work with ideas from on high, Hans wanted local staff to develop new approaches based on their personal experience with the WIN system and welfare recipients and then work closely with outside evaluators on the study protocols and research questions. Hans thought that local staff would cooperate more enthusiastically in providing the data and implementing the design correctly if they had some ownership of the study. He also hoped this grassroots approach would produce more useful innovations, build capacity, and lead to greater take-up by the participating sites and the WIN system of any significant findings.

This far-reaching vision was typical of Hans. Looking back thirty years later, Gordon Berlin (then a young staffer who was located in Rosen's shop but worked on Hans's research projects and became the program officer for the WIN Labs project) and Fritz Kramer (DOL program officer for Supported Work) describe Hans and Rosen, both long-time senior career civil servants, as rare leaders who gave people unusual responsibility and inspired uncommon loyalty. Berlin remembers Hans as a creative genius, a terrific manager, and brilliant in working with the Hill.[4]

"He was very smart about policy and future directions. He was the one who said, 'These Carter people have it all wrong. The future is workfare. He could see it coming up through the states. He was also adept at managing a big bureaucracy. He was very agile and savvy about getting funding and building walls around his staff so they could do what they thought was right. He had working groups that consisted of the local managers from the regions, and those regional people were instructed to stay close to local state programs.

He . . . would have a hundred ideas and ninety of them were totally crazy. . . . But if you listened hard and you worked with them and you gave him back feedback and he gave you feedback, you'd come out of there with ten really smart, forward thinking, important things to do that were based on real-world experience. . . . The WIN Laboratory idea grew out of that.' "

In January 1977, DOL staff drew up a prospectus laying out the WIN Labs vision and the benefits to all parties. In return for their agreement to cooperate with the research, local offices would have new flexibility and receive special funds (only to cover the R&D activities, since regular WIN activities would continue as before) and states would be held financially harmless from any negative effects on WIN performance. The prospectus also called for an umbrella organization that would act as the department's agent and oversee the development and management of the WIN Labs and the research activities.

Shortly thereafter, Rosen and Hans asked MDRC to take on this role. As far as I can tell, the reason was twofold. MDRC had surpassed expectations in its management of the Supported Work project (becoming what William Grinker calls DOL's "poster child" for taking on difficult demonstration and research efforts), and Rosen and Kramer wanted to build a future for the organization they had helped create. As Berlin recalls, Kramer was adamant about giving the WIN Labs to MDRC: "I think part of what made MDRC successful is that it had champions inside DOL in Fritz [Kramer] and Howard [Rosen]. MDRC was not just another contractor. Fritz saw the value and he wanted the organization to thrive. That mattered immensely. . . . When . . . the WIN Lab idea [came up], it was Fritz who urged me to consider MDRC. And I think he was speaking for Howard."

The result put the company on track toward the original vision of MDRC's founding fathers. MDRC had already responded positively to a mid-1975 request from the Ford Foundation and the Department of Housing and Urban Development to oversee a demonstration of tenant-managed public housing.[5] With our agreement to take on the relatively small WIN Labs project and then several months later the massive YIEPP project, MDRC was transformed from a Supported Work company to a multiproject intermediary with management and research responsibilities for four national demonstra-

Table 3.1   Timeline of the WIN Labs and Related Events

Date	Event
Spring 1977	Department of Labor invites MDRC to oversee the WIN Labs and approves planning proposal
November 1978	Random assignment begins in Louisville study of individual job search
1980–1983	MDRC publishes findings on individual job search experiment
October 1980	Random assignment begins in Louisville study of group job search (job clubs)
January 1981	Ronald Reagan inaugurated
1981	Reagan administration begins to close down the WIN labs

Source: Author's compilation.

tion programs, a staff of some hundred people, and oversight of about $340 million in demonstration and research funds. Table 3.1 gives a timeline of events.

Although our Supported Work experience was directly relevant to many of the management challenges in WIN Labs, the vision of partnering with operating public agencies was new. Moreover, Hans extended this to the research, where he envisioned ongoing links between individual labs and local universities. MDRC followed this in three of the four sites but decided to have an in-house team, led by Barbara Goldman, conduct all aspects of the research at the fourth site, Louisville, Kentucky. (Goldman, an economist hired to oversee research for the WIN Labs project, wanted to do—not just manage—research, and we concurred that having her in this role would deepen our knowledge of WIN and issues that might arise in the other sites.) This break from our prior strategy of subcontracting the impact and cost-benefit studies (made for personnel and substantive reasons) had important repercussions (see chapter 4), providing us with in-house expertise that would serve us well in the harsh climate of the 1980s.

WHY RANDOM ASSIGNMENT?

Hans mirrored Mike Sviridoff not only in his role as social entrepreneur but also in his focus on the big picture rather than the specifics of research methodology. As Gordon Berlin recalls, Hans saw the laboratories as a way to develop and get good evidence about more effective ways to deliver services, to do so more systematically than in the past, and to have ideas percolate up from the state systems. "It's been too top down and it's time that we created a structure that let [local offices] design, develop, and conceive of ideas that would be tested." His concept was iterative: "We'd try things, we'd get feedback, we'd try some more things, we'd get feedback, etc." Just as Sviridoff wanted a demonstration but knew there had to be "convincing evidence," Hans saw the need for a "good study," but he was not distinguishing among kinds of studies.

What explains the leap from Hans's general interest in effectiveness to the decision to use random assignment? As in Supported Work, there is no written record, but later interviews suggest the following. Back in early 1977, MDRC was primarily a management company. Supported Work had taught us the hows and whys of random assignment, but we were ill equipped to judge the alternatives. As a result, as Joan Leiman (who joined MDRC in 1977 to manage the WIN labs project) recalls, "random assignment was one of the major pillars of MDRC's identity." Although as the research director I did not see myself as a single-minded zealot, Supported Work had certainly hooked me on the beauty and power of an experiment. And both Grinker and Goldman recall that this was the default setting I pushed for whenever possible. Since, in my view, it would be possible in WIN Labs, we most likely did not consider alternatives. (In other projects, including YIEPP, where we found random assignment infeasible for political, ethical, or methodological reasons, we turned to subcontractors to devise the strongest alternatives.)

As Berlin recalls, "MDRC's line was, 'If you're going to do this, do it right and use random assignment.' There was MDRC's interest in and commitment to random assignment and there was [Hans's] interest in getting new ideas and trying them out in a real-world setting. . . . Merwin never said, 'I don't want anything to do with random assignment.' He bought into it . . . but he didn't start by saying 'We're always going to do random assignment.' He didn't care about that. He trusted us [his staff]; that was our job . . . to decide what kind of research would get done. His concern had to do with other issues."

This probably was not a hard sell. Kramer was already a fan, and Berlin was familiar with experiments from a slightly earlier pioneering study of job clubs, funded by Rosen and Hans, that had implemented random assignment on a small scale to study mandatory job search within WIN, although somewhat off to the side rather than as part of the regular WIN process.[6] The result of DOL's WIN Labs decision was to use random assignment, on a far larger scale than attempted before, operating in WIN offices as part of the regular intake process.

MAKING IT HAPPEN

Selecting the sites and putting the programs and research in place proved to be no simple task. MDRC and DOL sought four diverse WIN programs in medium-sized and large cities, each committed to the laboratory concept, each serving enough people to produce reliable research findings, and each with the management capacity to simultaneously operate a lab and a regular program within the same office. It ultimately took fourteen months of intensive field work to get from concept to start-up. As Berlin recalls, it was a messy and difficult process, partly collegial and collaborative and partly selling, cajoling, and arguing, during which he, Leiman, and Goldman spent weeks on the road.

Hans gave MDRC flexibility in recruiting sites but insisted that the process be split into two parts: first select the sites, and only then discuss the research requirements. As a consequence, our recruitment message was somewhat general: sites would have an opportunity to help define the research but a responsibility to meet the as-yet undefined constraints of the design. As Leiman reported, interest was not overwhelming. "To some states, the Labs represented an attractive offer: program funds for demonstration; special status within the WIN program; the opportunity to improve services; the chance to try something new. At the same time, the project brought with it a number of unknowns: a relationship with a strong outside contractor (MDRC); uncertain problems in organization and staffing; and possible consequences for general productivity. The net result of all of these factors was a limited pool of potential sites to choose from"[7] (Leiman with Seessel 1982, 17).

The states' greatest concern was the impact on productivity. They feared the WIN Lab activities might affect their ability to meet regular WIN performance measures, thereby jeopardizing federal funding and even possibly incurring the wrath of the legislatures and the governors of their states. Reflecting on why sites volunteered, Goldman attributes a lot to individual leaders at the state level, an assessment that Berlin confirms: "Well, there was money, but not a lot. . . . Again, this was part of Merwin's charisma and kind of genius. He had a following in the states of people who really believed in him and wanted to work with him. . . . He was revered."

The first stage of the courtship ritual—identifying sites (for what was conceived of as an unlimited series of test projects) and deciding on the initial projects—took seven months, but MDRC ultimately selected four sites that it judged had the interest and capacity to do a competent job. In line with Hans's approach, sites had been given wide discretion in developing the test programs, as long as the central office and MDRC thought they would provide insights about strengthening WIN's capacity to assist single mothers get regular jobs. Leiman recalls that everyone's key concern was getting the sites to run projects that were important enough to warrant the research superstructure.

The test programs varied. As its first WIN Labs project, Denver proposed new outreach, orientation, child care, and training services for mothers with young children and, as a second project, case management services to help women hold onto jobs. Louisville came up with two strategies to get more women to look for jobs. Madison and Racine, Wisconsin (a joint site), proposed generous economic incentives to employers who offered welfare recipients higher-wage jobs. St. Louis sought better outreach to private employers through a contract with a business group supported by the small business administration.[8]

Although these ideas sound innovative, in fact they often involved only subtle changes from existing local WIN office operations. In part, the modesty of the proposals resulted from limited special funds—no one was providing the tens of millions of dollars that Supported Work sites had received—but Berlin attributes it also to the difficulty local staff had in thinking outside the box. Noting that this has been a constant problem over the years, he describes the WIN Labs tests as not quantum leaps but incremental steps.

Once the sites were selected, the next seven months were spent planning for the demonstrations, including determining the research questions and design, selling random assignment, figuring out how to insert random assignment and the informed consent process into WIN office operations, and assessing data quality and accessibility. The result was a multicomponent research strategy. To the extent possible and affordable, we would determine the success of each site's proposal using a bare-bones approach that drew on what was done in Supported Work: an effectiveness or impact study using an experimental design, a cost study, and a process analysis to understand the nature of the program and how the experience of the experimentals differed from that of the controls.[9] At the same time, the project would address two overarching questions: Did Hans's partnership vision make sense? And would embedding random assignment in WIN offices prove feasible?

Not surprisingly, winning acceptance to fit experiments into the WIN intake process took a major campaign. The objections were not to the concept of random assignment or to dividing staff into two groups and running two programs (one for experimentals and one for controls) but to the specifics of how and when to integrate random assignment into the intake process and, depending on that decision, the research and program questions it would answer.

The art in doing an experiment within an operating program, as noted in chapter 2, goes beyond technical issues, such as whether you can enforce random assignment, get good data, and do the analysis correctly. A key challenge is to make sure all the effort is worthwhile—that is, you answer important questions and make the most of the opportunity. In WIN Labs, as in Supported Work, the savvy of MDRC's operations staff (backed up by Berlin's affirming DOL's united front) was key in the struggle to transform the sites' program concepts into useful policy tests. A good example of this is the Louisville case. The local staff wanted to run job search only for those women whom they thought would benefit, by which they meant people who had recently been employed. MDRC and DOL wanted to test the model for everyone, to find out who, in fact, would participate and be helped. To do this, we needed to randomly assign the full caseload, which meant the staff would have to serve people they thought were not job ready.

In the end, the local staff agreed, and the study produced findings of great relevance to subsequent welfare reform efforts. But getting to that point in Louisville and the other sites was a fight, involving not infrequent explosive, even nasty meetings that Goldman recalls with emotion more than thirty years later:

> There must have been a lot of angst, because I remember one visit to Colorado with Karen Dixon [MDRC's site representative] . . . in which we were basically asked to leave. When we came back and told Bill [Grinker], he called up the head of the program and said, "If you ever treat my staff this way again I'm going to pull them out of the project." . . . I also remember how Joanne Hayes [another MDRC site representative] taught me how to walk out at the right time when things were blowing up. At one point, when the tension got high,

she said, "OK, I think we need to end this meeting. Barbara and I are going to lunch, goodbye." I was traumatized. . . . I said, "We're going to lose the site," and she said, "No, we're not."

Berlin agrees: "I just can't stress enough how much work was involved. This was no simple thing. It was like any other MDRC experiment. We had a huge amount to do to figure out random assignment, to convince everybody, to win them over. And I remember personally feeling like I was on the line making this happen."

Ultimately, the sites cooperated with all aspects of the research, including providing data, keeping the test programs in place for the required period, and random assignment in the three sites where it was relevant.[10] Leiman (with Seessel 1982, 40, 71) attributes this to a combination of factors:

This easy acceptance could have been due to the fact that both MDRC and the research teams took a great deal of time to make sure that program personnel understood why this particular feature of the research was important, and what it did for them. In addition, the fact that the comparison group was not a "no-service" group but a group referred to the regular WIN program, could have also served to ease acceptance. . . . Other factors that played a major role were the promise of considerable site control over the research agenda; the "live-in support" provided by MDRC itself; and, perhaps most significantly, Hans's own strong and personal backing, which included his direct personal involvement on a number of occasions.

Berlin seconds the importance of Hans's role: "I think it was basically that these laboratories are special. [We could say,] 'Merwin cares about them. It's part of our vision of how we are going to move this program forward, and we're going to use random assignment.' I think we only got there because Merwin agreed and stood behind it." Goldman notes the contribution of state and local officials who, once on board, threw their support behind key decisions.

In contrast to Supported Work, where the ten random assignment sites tested the same approach and were analyzed as a group, each WIN Lab site tested a unique treatment and thus had to have a large enough sample to stand on its own. Anticipating a combined sample of several thousand but a research and management budget that, at around $2.7 million for the four sites, was much smaller than Supported Work's, we faced severe cost constraints and had to find a lower-cost way to track people's behavior. The result was a decision, for the first time that we were aware of in a relatively large-scale welfare experiment, to make routine administrative records—rather than special surveys as in the negative-income-tax and Supported Work projects—the primary data source for the impact study.[11] We knew that this would sharply limit the number of questions we could address but figured that, if the data were available and the quality adequate, we could get good answers on the key issues.

We focused on two sources: welfare agency records, showing who got a check each month and the amount, and earnings files (not the same things as the claims files) from state unemployment insurance agencies, files that contained employer reports of who was working and their quarterly earnings. From these, we would produce estimates of impacts on what we considered the four primary outcomes: employment, earnings, welfare receipt, and welfare payments.[12] The expected cost savings from using existing records allowed us to expand the sample (reducing the size of effects that could be detected and producing reliable estimates for more subgroups of people), placed less burden on study participants, and reduced the survey problems of sample attrition or recall (that is, when sample members could not be located or could not accurately remember their past behavior). But there were limitations—fewer outcomes and some systematic exclusions (for example, neither the welfare nor unemployment insurance earnings records tracked recipients after they left the state, and the earnings records did not cover all types of work).

LESSONS FROM LOUISVILLE WIN LAB

Louisville's two tests of job-search assistance deserve special mention because they had an unanticipated impact on policy, research, and MDRC. Intuitively, job-search programs have strong appeal. Given the high cost, and at that time unproven value, of traditional employment and training services, this strategy presumes that, for many welfare recipients, the main obstacle to finding work is not the absence of specific skills or prior employment but inexperience in and ignorance about how to look for a job. The idea behind a job-search program is that, with instruction in how to do a job search and some structure within which to do it, many will, through their own efforts, find work and begin to support themselves.

The Program and Research

Irrespective of any theoretical potential the job-search idea might have, MDRC and federal staff were skeptical that Louisville's first WIN Lab project (operated from November 1978 through June 1979) would produce much in the way of results for two reasons. First, the proposed form of job-search assistance was minimal: female welfare applicants and recipients with children of any age would be offered up to six weeks of individual job search (sometimes preceded by a few days of instruction), during which they were expected, on their own, to follow up and report back on job leads provided by WIN workers. Second, Louisville already had a similar activity as part of its regular WIN program. The only innovation seemed minor: People would be given an opportunity to participate immediately on referral to WIN, rather than with the usual delay of two to ten weeks while their welfare application was processed, and would be offered accelerated reimbursement for child care, transportation, and other costs. The site reasoned that, because these services would reach women sooner—when they were more motivated to seek work—they would increase the number who got jobs. But the new program would be voluntary. Even with added resources to provide job-search and support services, would more people actually participate? Compared with other WIN Labs, this seemed like a small idea; yet ironically, of the four initial tests Louisville was the only one that increased employment.

To find out whether the job-search plan would work, most women registering for WIN were randomly assigned to an experimental group (offered the new, voluntary program and, after six weeks, the regular WIN program) or to a control group (offered conventional WIN services including individual job search, subject to normal procedural delays).[13] The random assignment process, which MDRC controlled, proceeded smoothly, and a total of 1,619 women were assigned and followed for twenty-seven months using unemployment insurance records and for thirty-three months using AFDC records. In an unusual sign of its commitment to the study, the Louisville office also agreed to randomly assign staff to units that worked with either of the two groups, eliminating the possibility for any bias that might be introduced if, for example, the best counselors were selected to serve the experimental group.

The result was a program that, although operated in only one office, was realistic in intent and implementation. It was run by normal WIN staff within the regular office. There were added funds to serve more people but not for frills.

Historically, most Louisville welfare recipients received no WIN services and, as expected, only 5 percent of the controls got job-search assistance, and few entered any other WIN activity. To reverse this, Louisville planners set an ambitious and arbitrary target to get 70 percent of experimentals to participate in job search. The result was that, although the program was technically voluntary and people could not be sanctioned (that is, have their grants cut) for refusing to take part, staff strongly encouraged participation, and so some welfare recipients might have thought the program was mandatory. Because, as a result, the experiment included people with different skills and needs— from those whom staff considered were ready to look for work to others who seemed more like supported workers—the research could address a policy issue that took center stage in later welfare reform debates: What share of the WIN population would participate in and benefit from an activity such as job search?

As the second WIN Lab project, Louisville tested a more intensive group job-search program, modeled on the approach pioneered by Nathan Azrin but without the mandatory component. In the job clubs—operated from October 1980 through May 1981, but with shorter follow-up (six months for earnings and twelve months for AFDC)—participants were offered one week of classroom instruction in job-search skills followed by up to five weeks in which they were required to make at least fifty calls a day to prospective employers from a telephone room at the WIN office.

The Findings

Many of the findings on Louisville's individual job-search program were surprising. First, despite its extremely low net cost (less than $140 per person in 1985 dollars), the program generated impacts that were positive and relatively stable for the almost three years over which the sample was tracked.[14] Women who were offered the opportunity to participate found jobs sooner, and women in the control group never caught up. For example, during a three-month period a little more than two years after random assignment, the employment rate for experimentals was 5 percentage points higher than for controls (36 percent versus 31 percent), earnings were 18 percent higher ($513 versus $436, averaged over people who did and did not work), and

AFDC receipt was 6 percentage points lower (63 percent of experimentals were still on the rolls versus 69 percent for controls).[15]

Second, and as a result, the program was highly cost effective. A streamlined cost study showed that, within a short period, job search more than paid for itself in public funds, with savings in AFDC payments alone substantially exceeding program cost. Although a direct comparison with Supported Work was not made at the time and certainly would not have been appropriate (since Louisville served a wide range of women on welfare and Supported Work only the most disadvantaged), the implication was startling. For a small fraction of the expense, Louisville produced impacts of a similar order of magnitude, which meant that it generated much larger earnings gains per dollar invested.

Third, again there were clear limitations. More experimentals than controls were working, but they did not obtain more-permanent or higher-paying jobs. Three years after job search, more than half the experimentals were still on welfare. Fourth, as in Supported Work (but nonetheless surprising for this low-cost program) high outcomes did not always translate into high impacts. People who were more job ready were more likely to end up with jobs, but the program made a greater difference for people who were less job ready.

Louisville also produced important insights on participation. Under pressure to raise rates—and with some modest additional funding—Louisville staff got more than half the experimentals to become active in job search. In the process, the study also confirmed that many women on welfare want to work. Large numbers of people volunteered, which in the second Louisville test meant that they engaged in the arduous process of making fifty telephone calls a day to prospective employers.

Finally, the two Louisville studies revealed the fallibility of staff judgments on who could work. Initially staff were sure that they could tell who was job ready (and would therefore benefit from job search) and argued that other people should be excused. We countered that they might be right, but we wanted all eligible people to be randomly assigned and asked staff, before serving them, to rate people on their job readiness. The counselors agreed and based their ratings on their perceptions of people's motivation and skills. The study found that the ratings were not good predictors of women's subsequent attendance in the job club or success in finding a job, both of which were heavily affected by unpredictable situational factors (for example, children's health or transportation or housing problems). This supported what came to be the belief of many job-search proponents: that the labor market, not counselors, should determine who is employable, and thus most people applying for welfare should be enrolled, irrespective of judgments about their employability.

Although the DOL-MDRC team considered these findings highly relevant to the WIN system, Leiman also cautioned against overgeneralizing from one site. "While the Laboratory concept is well designed to foster the incubation and testing of new ideas, these ideas should then be replicated elsewhere under similarly controlled conditions if they are to be accepted as truth. Next steps may logically require the controlled testing of the Louisville program in additional sites" (Goldman 1980, viii).

LESSONS FROM WIN LABS MORE GENERALLY

The WIN Labs project both built on the lessons from Supported Work and broke new ground. Although at the time we thought the innovations tested were disappointing, they and the collaborative style Hans advocated were to have an outsized influence on future studies.

Research Methods

The WIN Labs project—with Louisville as its most ambitious example—produced three breakthroughs in research methods. The first was to demonstrate that random assignment could be conducted in operating WIN offices without overly disrupting program intake or burdening staff. This vastly expanded the terrain of the feasible. I had come to the project, fresh from Supported Work, thinking that a tied sale—random assignment as a condition of site participation—with a hefty financial incentive and somewhat rarified context were critical to success. I left seeing that, at least at the scale tried in the WIN Labs, another strategy—combining joint ownership with modest funds and careful attention to minimizing the burden on staff and insinuating this process into normal intake procedures—could also clinch the deal. The importance of this was twofold: it meant that researchers could conduct such studies in a new arena and that, under the right incentive structure, states and localities could be valuable partners.

The second breakthrough was the extensive use of administrative records to measure the impacts of an experiment. Although an earlier experiment had used AFDC records to assess an administrative reform in one state, WIN Labs used records from several agencies in several states to measure the effect of a programmatic change and used WIN staff to gather basic background data. This may not sound like a big deal, but combined with the first breakthrough it set the stage for an order-of-magnitude expansion in welfare studies, from single-digit thousands of people before 1980 to double-digit thousands in the following decades. Not only were future studies larger, but it became feasible to track people for many more years—a key to addressing questions about the relative effectiveness of different welfare reform approaches. The result was an alternative research model that stressed the value of answering a few questions well and using smaller subsamples or future studies to pursue more refined questions.[16]

A third finding was the importance of using multiple methods to address complex questions. Although the impact and cost findings got a lot of attention, those on participation and staff behavior also contributed lasting lessons, since mandates and participation rates quickly became salient political issues.

Evolution of Experiments

In contrast to later experiments, the negative-income-tax, Supported Work, and WIN Labs projects shared several features. They were specially funded pilots in which participation was voluntary; and researchers and funders fully or partly controlled the design of both the program and the study. The negative-income-tax studies were centrally controlled, laboratory-like projects. Designed and run by researchers and fully funded from Washington, they were extraordinarily ambitious in their use of complex experimental designs intended not simply to determine whether one particular program approach was successful but to refine estimates of behavioral responses to precisely defined incentives. Supported Work was relatively similar in scale and also centrally designed by the funders and their agent (in this case, MDRC). Supported Work differed from the negative-income-tax projects, however, in that it was implemented by small (sometimes new) community organizations, had supplementary funds to cover all of the research and much of the program operations, and used a simple experimental design intended to assess one particular new program. The WIN Lab experimental designs were simple, as were those in Supported Work. But they moved social experiments even further out of the relatively contained conditions of researcher-operated or specially created programs—into mainstream WIN offices. The WIN Labs sites were partnerships, with a substantial measure of state and local control.

Impact on Policy, Practice, and Research

In 1981 the Reagan administration decided to close down the WIN Labs project. However, even before the new appointees took over, the Labs had been running out of steam. Both Hans and Rosen had retired (the former in February 1980, the latter in January 1981), the three active sites were having difficulty generating new ideas, MDRC had concluded that the management demands exceeded the research yield, and DOL's interest was waning as the Carter administration shifted its focus to welfare reform, making WIN and the WIN Labs seem irrelevant. Leiman pointed to another reason that the sites lost interest: It took a very long time to enroll a large enough sample and get results in a study conducted in only one, relatively small office. Nonetheless, this small project had a large effect on welfare research and policy during the Reagan era and beyond.

The first effect came from the vindication of Hans's idea that rigorous testing of innovations is more likely when state and local staff and researchers work together. In a prescient comment, the MDRC 1981 annual report concluded that

> in the last analysis, the greatest value of the WIN Labs may prove to be not so much their specific findings as the way in which those findings were developed. Enlisting the cooperation and commitment of WIN office staff, the demonstration was able to produce quality research on a small scale. With the center of gravity for employability programs shifting from the federal government to the states, the WIN labs experience appears to be a useful model for research—one that allows both for variation in local policy development and, through its creation of a network of local research efforts, for national dissemination of new information.

The WIN Labs also delivered on another aspect of Hans's vision. They showed that if rigorous research could be done within the system—involving typical civil servants who faced the normal pressures and uncertainties of such work—the programs tested and the results were more likely to be replicable, relevant, and used. Our experience suggested yet a further insight: it was not the WIN Lab idea per se that made cooperation possible but rather the relationship built with states and localities.

The second effect came from the validation of a specific approach: job-search assistance. As Berlin recalls, the Louisville experiments were not the first tests of job-search assistance, but at that time they were the most independent and robust. As a result of those studies—and the ones that followed, in part shaped by them—all the states picked up on this strategy, making it a central pillar of subsequent welfare reform efforts.

The third effect was the flip side of the first. From the beginning, DOL and MDRC staff were worried that the WIN Labs strategy might encourage studies of incremental reforms that did not address important national concerns, in contrast to the more ambitious changes of either the Supported Work or the negative-income-tax variety. Whether this was a weakness in the strategy or failure of either of the national partners to come up with significant ideas and adequate funds, the result was modest innovation and modest findings. As this model became the template for research in the 1980s and beyond, it limited what was tested and thus known. However, as succeeding chapters show, the partnership strategy did not necessarily mean limited ambition.

A final effect was on MDRC's skill set and style of work. As Barbara Blum, MDRC's next president, later wrote, the WIN Labs showed MDRC that "states are willing to try new ideas and to subject their programs to rigorous analysis" and prepared MDRC well for a future of working more directly with states (Leiman with Seessel 1982, vii–viii).

YOUTH INCENTIVE ENTITLEMENT PILOT PROJECTS

In July 1977, the same month Congress passed the Youth Employment and Demonstration Projects Act, the Department of Labor—reflecting the urgency to get started quickly and the mammoth challenge of the knowledge development effort called for by the law—("its scale and complexity dwarfed any research and development effort undertaken by the Department of Labor before or since" [Elmore 1985, 283]) asked for a special meeting of MDRC's board. At the meeting—attended by Rosen, his boss William Hewitt, Robert Taggart (the newly appointed head of the Office of Youth Programs), Kramer, and others from DOL—the department appealed to MDRC to oversee YIEPP, the most innovative and demanding of the four new programs in the act. The scale of the enterprise, as noted at the beginning of the chapter, was vast: a $240 million demonstration of a job guarantee that eventually employed 76,000 youth in seventeen communities, including entire cities and multicounty regions. The guarantee extended to all low-income youth on condition that they remain in or return to high school (or its equivalent) and meet academic and job performance standards.

Despite the highly visible and political nature of the project, and despite other board members' concern that MDRC was taking on too much too soon, Ginzberg urged a positive reply, according to the minutes of the July 19 meeting: "Since DOL had been partially responsible for the creation of MDRC, their strong request at this time should be responded to positively, if at all possible." He also noted that this would be a good test of "the MDRC instrument" for managing federal demonstrations. The board acquiesced, and MDRC immediately shifted gears, staffing up to run the vast effort. Five months after the legislation was signed, sites had been funded; by March 1978, the first youths were assigned to jobs; and by the end of 1978, 42,000 youth had enrolled.

Although YIEPP did not use random assignment, it had substantive, methodological, and institutional links to the 1980s programs discussed in later chapters. The substantive link came from the job guarantee. The project was not a "program" that offered opportunities to a fixed number of youths but one that gave open access to a job guarantee for as long as youths remained eligible. Reflecting this, the authorizing legislation asked for information on the feasibility and cost of creating enough jobs and specified that the jobs had to be real and productive, not "make-work." Getting reliable answers to questions of management and feasibility meant operating the program at a real-world scale and widely publicizing the job guarantee. Thus managing YIEPP was closer to running a means-tested, work-conditioned welfare entitlement than to operating a traditional employment and training program. Although YIEPP offered paid jobs, the challenges it faced were not unlike the ones that would surface five years later around unpaid workfare, conceived as a saturation work-for-your-benefits program for AFDC recipients.

The methodological link followed from that. In studying YIEPP implementation, we examined three issues that proved central in later studies of welfare-to-work and workfare programs: the factors affecting participation in potentially universal programs;[17] the likelihood that the programs provided either real or make-work jobs; and the feasibility of enforcing performance standards that involved both employment and education systems and both public and private sector employers. In developing a design to estimate impacts, we concluded that the entitlement or saturation nature of the job guarantee ruled out random assignment; instead, we opted for a comparison city design. The positive and negative lessons from the impact study (conducted by Abt Associates) affected our thinking about evaluating later large-scale, and potentially saturation, welfare reform demonstrations. Furthermore, a 1985 National Academy of Sciences report (Betsey, Hollister, and Papageorgiou 1985) assessing the Youth Employment and Demonstration Projects Act research stated that random assignment findings are far less biased than other methods. This conclusion was to play a possibly decisive role in the fight for random assignment in welfare reform. (The same report also concluded that the YIEPP design produced convincing estimates of the dramatic increase in employment when the program was operating—a doubling of the employment rate for African American youth, effectively reversing a dramatic twenty-five-year deterioration—but not of whether there were or were not postprogram impacts.)[18]

Finally, the institutional link flowed from the good and bad impacts the YIEPP evaluation had on MDRC itself. The evaluation propelled us out of the laboratory-like environment of relatively small-scale experiments into the real world of full-scale programs run by public agencies, although in this case the subjects were the workforce and educational systems rather than welfare agencies. It led to a dramatic expansion in our staff size (from around sixty in mid-1977 to one hundred in 1979) and capacity to monitor large and complex local programs, design and operate a massive management information system, and conduct a rigorous study of implementation and participation. However, it also greatly increased our dependence on funding from a single federal agency, DOL. Thus, inadvertently, it helped set us up for potential disaster when Ronald Reagan was elected in 1980 and WIN Labs, YIEPP, and other projects (including tests of Supported Work with new populations and plans for its institutionalization) were abruptly terminated by a DOL that had become hostile to research and demonstrations.

CONCLUSION

Making smart policy depends on knowing what works and what does not. The most definitive way to find out is to use a social experiment. But in 1970, people wondered: Was a social experiment for welfare and employment policy feasible? Could it be used to answer important questions? The series of pioneering negative-income-tax experiments had shown that under two conditions—in a controlled, laboratory-like situation and looking for evidence of the work incentive effects of cash payments—the answer to both questions was yes. But what about operating employment and service programs, where issues of politics, people, and context loomed large? Were experiments feasible and useful in that context? This and the previous chapter tell how two major projects showed that, in conditions that move several steps into the real world, the answer was, again, yes. The story of how this was done illuminates the decisive roles played by people—social entrepreneurs, civil servants, researchers, and managers—in foundations, the government, and the private sector.

In the process, the two initiatives described so far—Supported Work and the Louisville WIN Labs—provided convincing evidence that some social programs could increase work effort and be cost effective. They produced early insights into enduring issues, such as who benefits most, how success should be judged, the importance of control group behavior, and why high outcomes may not reflect high impacts. They showed the limits to change. Both experiments produced improvements but not solutions, modest advances but not blockbuster drugs. They also revealed that progress in determining whether social programs worked was not accompanied by comparable evidence on why they worked.

There was good news also for people searching for ways to bring rigorous evidence to policy debates often dominated by anecdotes or untested claims. Once it was clear that the experiments had been meticulously implemented, there was widespread acceptance of the validity of the findings. The transparency of the method and the simplicity with which the results could be explained made random assignment a powerful communications tool. Complex mathematical models may be fascinating to statisticians, but discussions among experts about what their implications mean for real-world action can cause glassy-eyed stupefaction, and disbelief, among the many who must be convinced if real-world policy improvements are to be made. In these two cases, people differed, as they always do, on the implications for policy and raised questions about whether the results could be replicated in other places or on a larger scale. But at the conclusion of these experiments, there was not the familiar back-and-forth among experts that followed studies using more complex, and ultimately less interpretable, methods.[19]

The result, for the key funders (the Ford Foundation and DOL) as well as the institution set up to manage the projects (MDRC) and its key research partners, was a conviction that random assignment was an essential tool for estimating program effectiveness and an increased awareness of the shortcomings of alternative approaches. This also led to greater confidence in the value of the try-small-before-you-buy-big model of policy making. At the micro level, the parties involved drew lessons on the circumstances that made random assignment feasible and useful: the need to balance research goals against on-the-ground realities to get the most knowledge without overloading operating programs; the importance of large samples and attention to data quality; and the reasons no legal or ethical challenges had been encountered along the way. In the process, the WIN Labs, Supported Work, and YIEPP set a high standard for evaluating programs and provided major lessons on the art of implementing program evaluations.

NEXT STEPS

At the end, we were left with an even bigger question, particularly since YIEPP's nonexperimental evaluation design precluded shedding light on several important issues. Experiments are hard work and expensive. Are they worth it? Robert Solow's (1980, 10) comment about Supported Work well expresses MDRC's conclusion about experiments more generally: "That is expensive knowledge, but I am convinced the price is worth paying. Governments must be made to realize that even such large sums pale into triviality next to the much larger amounts that get poured down rat-holes in the belief that it is more important, or at least better politics, to respond hastily and visibly to social needs on the basis of no tested knowledge at all."

Solow did not know then that the federal government was poised to slam the door on funding for such studies. Would social experiments end or be reincarnated? Fortunately for us at MDRC, Merwin Hans's vision—that if states and localities believe a project can answer their questions and if they have a relationship with the researchers, they are more likely to stay the course, help the study, and value the answers—provided us with an insight we were able to build on as we worked to help transform social experiments in the 1980s. As Blum put it, "The WIN Labs have provided MDRC with an unusual opportunity to understand and begin to prepare for a new and difficult era" (Leiman with Seessel 1982, viii). Since MDRC was a major research actor in the 1980s, this expertise helped define the next phase of welfare research.

CHAPTER 4

Inventing a New Paradigm:
The States as Laboratories*

[Should MDRC be] putting ourselves out of organizational
existence?

—William J. Grinker[1]

Who let those closet socialists evaluate our program?

—Reagan administration official[2]

Political transitions can sound portentous but may bring little change. For our
story, however, Ronald Reagan's election in 1980 was a true revolution, mark-
ing a dramatic turning point in welfare policy, the role of the states, and the
nature and origin of welfare research. Support for a welfare entitlement and
for voluntary programs such as Supported Work yielded to the harsher language of mandates and obligations. Policy initiative shifted from Washington
to the more varied and less predictable terrain of the states. Funds for demonstrations evaporated, and social science researchers came to be viewed with
suspicion, as advocates for the liberal policies they typically assessed.

The prospects for continued, large-scale, government-supported random
assignment research looked bleak. Each of the conditions that had nurtured
such studies—enthusiastic federal commitment, generous funding for test
programs, and centralized clout—disappeared, in some cases permanently. Yet

*Chapter 4 authored by Judith M. Gueron.

in these seemingly hostile conditions, this type of research not only flowered but, within the decade, produced results of greater policy relevance and impact than the negative-income-tax or Supported Work experiments. The emerging new style of research prompted no less a sage than Senator Daniel Patrick Moynihan to proclaim that research had played a central role in shaping and facilitating the passage of federal welfare reform legislation in 1988.

This chapter begins to tell the story of that transformation, the most far-reaching and unlikely of MDRC's forty-year history, and corrects the myth that random assignment studies of state initiatives were the result of federal insistence on this approach. As this and subsequent chapters recount, the original impetus came from outside government, to be embraced only years later as a central tool of federal waiver policy.

THE REAGAN REVOLUTION

Reagan came into office at a time of shifting attitudes toward women, work, and welfare. These changes fed anger at a welfare system that many felt encouraged dependency, undermined family structure, and unfairly supported people who could work but did not while others struggled at low-wage jobs. As a result, public debate shifted permanently from whether welfare mothers should work to who should work and how to make that happen. Reformers sought to balance four goals: reduce dependency, increase work, reduce poverty, and save money—all without harming children.

Workfare, Mandates, and Devolution

Reagan brought to Washington a conviction that government could not solve the problems of poverty, in fact made things worse when it tried, and should basically get out of the way and let the market do its job. To implement this, the new administration promoted two elements of the strategy Reagan had attempted as governor of California: changes in the calculation of welfare benefits and workfare, in which welfare mothers with school-age children would be required to work for their benefits.[3]

One attraction of workfare was that it appeared to offer something for nothing. In place of a Work Incentive (WIN) program, in which most people escaped the intended mandate, workfare sounded simple: require people to earn their benefits by working (for the number of hours determined by dividing the grant by the minimum wage), with no compensation beyond limited reimbursement for work expenses. Defenders of this approach argued that it would bring welfare into line with prevailing values, provide work experience for the poor and useful services to the public, encourage people (including those with off-the-books jobs) to leave the welfare rolls, provide the dignity of work, and ultimately increase public support for Aid to Families with Dependent Children (AFDC). Opponents characterized it as "slavefare" that threatened mothers and children; they also estimated that it would cost, rather than save, money.

Concerned about the likely outcome from workfare, as a March 7, 1986, *Washington Post* editorial later put it, "an uneasy Congress deflected the issue to the states, allowing them to set up work programs if they chose." The relevant legislation, passed in August 1981, was the Omnibus Budget Reconciliation Act of 1981 (OBRA). The legislation included a long list of provisions defining how states should calculate benefits and eligibility (several of which substantially reduced work incentives) but also gave the states new flexibility in designing programs to promote employment. In particular, for the first time, they could routinely require AFDC recipients to work in public or nonprofit agencies in return for their benefits, a provision formally titled the Community Work Experience Program (CWEP).[4] They could also use welfare grants to fund on-the-job training in the private sector. In addition, under the WIN demonstration provisions, state welfare agencies could opt to run the WIN program without the participation of the state's labor department.

Thus in place of Reagan's workfare vision Congress reaffirmed the more nuanced concept of a reciprocal obligation, which throughout this book we call a welfare-to-work program. Under this set of provisions, welfare recipients who were subject to WIN mandates (mostly single mothers with no child under the age of six) could be required to accept a job, search for work, or participate in work-directed activities, including workfare (in states that chose to adopt it), or face the loss of some or all of their benefits. Public agencies, in return, would have to provide services and supports that would help people get jobs and participate in activities. Thus rather than create a new federal program, Congress left each state to seek its own balance between opportunity and obligation, between reducing poverty and reducing dependency—thereby starting a shift in policy initiative that continued for the next fifteen years.

But wasn't this just a restatement of WIN with a new option (workfare), with no change in who could be required to participate or in the amount their grants could be cut if they refused, and no new money? Not quite. There was a sleeper in OBRA, one introduced by Congress, not by the administration—the handing over of WIN to the state welfare agencies. The WIN structure in each state at the time involved two agencies with different missions: the Labor agency responsible for assigning people to activities, and the Welfare agency responsible for enforcing sanctions and providing support services. As a result, welfare commissioners, the people who administered the AFDC program and were under the gun to reduce the rolls, felt no ownership of WIN. If a state took up the WIN demonstration option under OBRA, in contrast, the state welfare agency would become responsible for the whole program, with new flexibility to design a welfare-to-work program on its own. Amazingly, this change (which at first blush sounded like a minor administrative wrinkle) breathed new life into WIN, transforming it from a highly prescriptive federal program to a state initiative.[5] Governors grabbed the opportunity to put their mark on welfare reform. It is clear, in retrospect, that what had changed was not so much the set of rules as the willingness of states to enforce them.

Questions on Feasibility and Effectiveness

There was reason to expect that flexibility would unleash change—interest in workfare was not sparked by OBRA but preceded it. Gordon Berlin recalls that, from his post in the WIN office, he had seen a steady stream of state requests for demonstrations of workfare and related mandates. However, the results (including from Governor Reagan's demonstration in California) had not been encouraging: only a small proportion of AFDC recipients technically required to do so actually participated. "Basically . . . the key question of operational feasibility remains unanswered. . . . Since the AFDC workfare model had not been implemented effectively, there are little reliable data on operating costs, deterrent effects, welfare savings, or long-term impacts on earnings and employment" (Gueron and Nathan 1985, 424, 426).

IMPACT OF THE REAGAN CHANGES ON MDRC

Very quickly, the Reagan administration's actions threatened to engulf MDRC. How could MDRC, an organization that received almost all its funds from the federal government and defined itself as a vehicle intended to rigorously test positive ways to improve the well-being of low-income people, survive? This chapter explains how we responded and presents the new partnership paradigm that evolved.

On the Cusp of the Reagan Revolution

From the time MDRC decided it was open to a life beyond Supported Work, we faced the challenge of generating new projects. Before 1980 we did this by responding to the entrepreneurship of our funders, primarily DOL and the Ford Foundation, both of which viewed the learning strategy embodied in Supported Work as a valuable new tool to advance their own missions and sought to sustain MDRC as a management vehicle to make that happen.

During these years, MDRC built its reputation on transforming relatively undeveloped ideas into productive demonstrations through quality implementation and research. We had become superb at realizing the dreams of others but not at implementing our own. Notably for what follows, we had stayed aloof from the typical competitive procurement process by which the federal government funded research contractors.

For that strategy to succeed, the obvious prerequisite was that people in control of money at Ford and DOL be interested in MDRC's skills and type of work and willing to sole source large amounts of funds. This approach worked for five years. As I observed in a December 1983 memo to MDRC's president, Barbara Blum, "This was the best—and in some ways the easiest—of worlds, except that it did leave a continued anxiety about 'what next' and about whether the corporation was too 'reactive,' and whether that would limit its scope. However, as long as there was enough of quality to react to, and friends such as Howard Rosen and Mike Sviridoff, there was a sense that MDRC would continue and a confidence that Grinker would figure out how."

The outcome was rapid growth, from a $5.5 million budget in 1975 to $23.9 million in 1980, but about 90 percent of the latter came from the federal government. In 1981, alarmingly, virtually the entire MDRC budget came from DOL, which that year provided fully 95 percent of our funding and was the major or exclusive funder of all five of our active projects. To make matters worse, philanthropic support was similarly concentrated; MDRC was viewed as the Ford Foundation's baby, even though during that year the foundation covered less than 3 percent of our budget.

With the exception of the WIN Laboratory project, our activities focused on disadvantaged youth and teen mothers. However, we did have a project in the pipeline—developed with Ford and the National Governors' Association and dubbed the Human Reinvestment Project—to test the usefulness of ear-marking some career jobs in state or local governments for AFDC recipients. The project had features of both Supported Work and WIN Labs but had a greater focus on state government. As of January 1981, sixteen states were involved, and we anticipated commitments from the foundation and DOL within the next few months to support a five-year, $13 million budget.

Threat of Extinction

This was not to be. In a February 1981 memo to the board, William Grinker reported that the change in administration "has brought us to a state of day to day funding crises, since all of our ongoing projects were awaiting either previously committed grant modifications and/or extension when the new administration took office. . . . Like Pauline, we continue to be rescued by sympathetic bureaucrats at the last moment and we continue to function on the basis that commitments will somehow be honored." But this did not last.[6] By March, it was clear that the new leadership in DOL was focused on cutting costs, did not feel bound by past commitments, and was leaving the business of research and large-scale innovative projects. Although he assured the board that staff were not panicking, Grinker presented alternative scenarios for closing down MDRC activities "depending on the severity of federal budget cutting." The description of the transition from Jimmy Carter to Reagan included in a National Academy of Sciences report captures the mood: "The posture of Reagan appointees in the Department of Labor toward these unfinished projects, by most accounts, ranged from indifference to outright hostility. 'When the new administration arrived,' one insider recalled, 'an immediate freeze was put on all extensions and refundings of the ongoing research efforts. They wouldn't even let the entitlement [YIEPP] research be completed until an editorial appeared in the *Washington Post* that created a Congressional uproar'" (Elmore 1985, 330).

The Department of Labor cuts threatened every aspect of our work, but most relevant for the welfare story was the impact on the Human Reinvestment Project. Not only did it quickly become clear that the administration would not support the project, but the very idea behind it—reserving state jobs for welfare recipients—seemed increasingly unrealistic as states anticipated federal cuts that would force them to lay off staff and phase down the public-service jobs program.[7] The emphasis on voluntary participation and paid work also seemed out of touch with Washington's message of workfare and mandates. Scrambling to salvage something from the development work, we shifted gears to accommodate the administration's interest in job search assistance and to include some locations, such as San Diego, with close ties to the Reagan people.

By May 1981, the ax had fallen. In a traumatic series of actions, Grinker reduced the staff by 45 percent and informed the board in a May 28 memo that in the fall, when he would have a clearer picture of feasible alternatives, he would provide options "for continuing MDRC as it is, changing its nature, or phasing it out." Thinking back on those years, Robert Solow recalls: "We all thought it was going to be extremely difficult. . . . These people, they know the answer before they asked the question, so what do they need us for, or people like us. And, we also . . . felt that MDRC's kind of problem, going after disadvantaged populations, was not going to be popular with the Reagan administration. Perhaps not popular with American society at the time of the Reagan administration and might not attract foundations, so I might have given at best a 50-50 chance of [MDRC's] surviving."

What Next?

While we were thus occupied, staff at the Office of Family Assistance (OFA), the HHS agency responsible for the AFDC program at the federal level, were well aware of the discouraging story of earlier workfare attempts. Before passage of OBRA, but anticipating some form of workfare legislation, they sought to arm themselves and the states with information on best practices with the hope that this would prevent a replay. As part of this, in June 1981 they launched a competition for a contractor that would design CWEP approaches appropriate for varied conditions, help the states implement these models, and assess, in the words of the *Federal Register*'s June 11, 1981, announcement, "the legal, regulatory, organizational, administrative, and socioeconomic issues and other problems encountered in attempting to implement CWEP" and determine what models worked best in which types of settings. Notably absent from the long list was any attempt to measure the impact of workfare on welfare receipt and employment.[8]

MDRC hesitated to respond. On the political side, we were concerned that, once under federal contract, we would be called on to help make workfare work or be constrained on how honestly we could report our findings. On the substantive side, we worried that a study limited to assessing feasibility and best practices would not tackle the key question of whether workfare actually helped people get unsubsidized work and become self-sufficient. On balance, seeing no prospect of alternative major federal demonstrations and convinced of the importance of learning about feasibility, we broke with our past and submitted a proposal. Based on our work with the states and our WIN Labs and YIEPP experience, we thought we had a good shot. However, for reasons that are still obscure, and despite rumors that selection was imminent between the top contenders—of which we heard we were one—the competition was abruptly canceled in October.

Our board met the same month in an atmosphere of crisis, anticipating further federal cuts and the resignations of both its founding chairman and president. In a September 22, 1981, memo to the board, Grinker—who had planned to leave a year earlier but stayed on to help reposition the organization—had posed the existential questions: "Where do we go from here? . . . [Should we be] putting ourselves out of organizational existence?"[9] Encouraged by the Ford Foundation's indication that it would provide $1 million in general support to develop new work over the next two years, the board reached two critical decisions: to attempt to keep the organization alive and to stick to its focus on the disadvantaged. To guide us in charting a new course, the board elected as its chairman Richard Nathan, a professor at Princeton's Woodrow Wilson School of Public and International Affairs and a Republican with a strong interest in state government. It also began the search for a new president. In the interim (March to July 1982), I served as acting president.

Back when we had all been wondering whether we could sustain MDRC without Grinker, I received a note from Solow (written on October 5, 1981) that reflected the commitment of the board and reminded me why the effort would be worth whatever it would take: "I want to tell you in particular that I intend to stay active on the Board and you can count on me to keep supporting the integrity of the research effort. It's not going to be easy to survive at all, but if we do survive, it better be on terms we can be proud of."

FILLING THE VACUUM

The Omnibus Budget Reconciliation Act —combined with early evidence that states were likely to respond with controversial programs, a chance to bring reliable analysis to bear on a debate colored by emotion and ideology, and no plan for federal evaluation (plus a suspicion that, were one to be resurrected, it might not be objective)—created a void that we immediately saw

Table 4.1   Timeline of the Work/Welfare Demonstration and Related Events

Date	Event
November 1980	Ronald Reagan elected president
May 1981	MDRC lays off 45 percent of staff
August 1981	Congress passes Omnibus Budget Reconciliation Act (OBRA)
October 1981	HHS cancels planned federal study of OBRA changes
October and November 1981	Grinker announces resignation; Nathan replaces Ginzberg as MDRC board chair
May 1982	MDRC submits proposal to Ford Foundation for challenge grant to fund Work/Welfare demonstration
July 1982	Blum becomes president of MDRC
1982–1984	Eight states sign on
1984–1988	MDRC publishes interim and final state reports
August 1986	Gueron becomes president of MDRC
1986–1987	MDRC and Ford publish synthesis monographs
October 1988	Reagan signs Family Support Act

Source: Author's compilation.

as the opening for an independent, Ford-sponsored initiative. The resulting Demonstration of State Work/Welfare Initiatives (the Work/Welfare demonstration) has been called "a watershed in social experimentation" (Greenberg, Linksz, and Mandell 2003, 214). Unprecedented in scale and structure, the project ultimately included tens of thousands of welfare families in eight separate experiments in multiple offices in a representative group of states (see timeline in table 4.1). Each state tested its own distinct variation on the welfare-to-work theme, but all were subject to the same research design and, in some form, had to come up with evaluation money.

Summing up the effect of HHS's decision not to evaluate OBRA, Michael Wiseman (1991, 658–59) notes that the result was the opposite of what was intended. Instead of stifling inquiry, it stimulated research that had a larger impact because it was

not tainted by federal government sponsorship. . . . The administration of then-Governor Reagan never encouraged a significant evaluation of the California welfare reforms of 1971, and the actions of the administration at the beginning of the 1980s hardly reveal fervor for serious investigation of the effects of OBRA. But by forcing MDRC to obtain funds outside of government, and to seek as clients the states themselves instead of HHS, the administration set into motion the process that would produce many of the virtues . . . in the package of results MDRC had to offer in 1986. Every gardener knows that pruning does not necessarily make plants flower less: if the administration thought in 1981 that reducing federal funding of research would necessarily diminish the strength of the competition it faced in pursuing its welfare agenda, it was wrong.

MAKING THE WORK/WELFARE DEMONSTRATION HAPPEN

Although MDRC initiated the process—thereby breaking from its earlier reactive mode—its ability to deliver required the simultaneous alignment of six moving parts. The first three were the forces that would shape the initial vision: an entrepreneur to develop the concept and drive the design and implementation, a demonstration structure that responded to political and funding realities, and a feasible and compelling research strategy. Actions on these three fronts would determine whether the project could attract and hold the other three players essential to success: a major, long-term funder; committed state partners launching programs of interest; and federal officials who would cooperate with or at least tolerate the endeavor.

For MDRC, the fall of 1981 and the ensuing years were a struggle for survival. Crisis prompted the project and necessity inspired the brinkmanship and passion that helped make it a reality. The threat of extinction mobilized the board and staff to stake the organization on our ability to succeed. We were well aware of the risk and had no back-up plan. The resulting intensity and determination unleashed unusual creativity and effort. The project might not have happened in calmer times, but MDRC's effort would have been for naught without the partnership and support of the Ford Foundation, the positive response from state administrators, and the quiet backing of HHS officials. Thus although what follows addresses the six ingredients sequentially, they were in fact in simultaneous play, with decisions on goals, ambition, design, scale, cost, funding, and ultimate feasibility the result of iterating actions and reactions from the key actors.

The Entrepreneur: Staying Alive

To us, the opportunity and likely saliency of a major research initiative was clear. In his last important act as president, Grinker grabbed at the opening—seeing this as our only lifeline to staying in business in a form true to our mission—and, always a master at envisioning funding collaborations, pitched it to Ford's vice president for U.S. and international affairs, Susan Berresford, as a project that would enable MDRC to remake itself and position the foundation and us to assess the cutting edge of the Reagan revolution. As he and Berlin both recall, Grinker told Berlin at the time that he was determined to leave MDRC with a major new project that would give it a shot at survival, even if he was not the diplomat needed to court the states and make this vision a reality.

Although this was basically a leap into the unknown, we brought much to the challenge. In the aborted Human Reinvestment Project, we had built links to a number of states and found widespread interest in OBRA's flexibility and a new resolve to make WIN participation requirements more meaningful. Our work on HHS's CWEP proposal not only provided a partial blueprint but prompted us to distill what we knew about work programs, the behavior of AFDC recipients, the variety within WIN, the potential of voluntary job search and work experience, and the hazy line between voluntary and mandatory programs. Furthermore, Supported Work and WIN Labs had given us a model of rigorous evaluation and some early insight into the likely magnitude of impacts and thus the required sample sizes for reliable findings. The Labs also revealed the potential of a partnership approach and a way to conduct research on the cheap. In addition, we were just completing the YIEPP evaluation. Although YIEPP (voluntary paid work for youth) and workfare (mandatory unpaid work for welfare recipients) clearly differed, many of the research challenges—measuring participation, determining feasibility, and assessing real work versus make-work in a saturation context—convinced us that guaranteed paid jobs and work-for-benefits positions were points along a continuum rather than totally distinct.

Although MDRC staff strengths were obvious, what may be less apparent was the important role played by our board. At no time since its creation to implement the Supported Work demonstration—and at no subsequent time—was board guidance on political and policy issues, hand holding, and active fund-raising as essential as during these years, when the organization tottered on a precipice. Of particular note was the unconditional commit-ment and confidence of Richard Nathan, our new chairman. Nathan's recol-lection thirty years later as to whether he ever doubted our survival is em-phatic: "We had . . . lots of smart people, a wonderful mission, and the Ford Foundation. . . . We just had to be strong. I didn't have doubts."

BEING OBJECTIVE ABOUT WORKFARE   Before we could take up this challenge, MDRC's board and staff had to address two internal constraints. The first was ideological. In early mission statements, captured in its 1978 and 1979 annual reports, MDRC described itself as designing, managing, and evaluat-ing social programs "to help disadvantaged members of society improve their positions and prospects for the future." Although we had flourished under both Republican and Democratic administrations and prided ourselves on being hard-nosed about seeking truth and communicating failure as well as success, we had always tested approaches that we considered positive: that is, the programs were voluntary and were directed primarily at increasing work and self-sufficiency, not at reducing dependency. Should we, could we, now assess an avowedly conservative approach such as mandatory workfare? Since a major question with workfare was feasibility, was there a risk that we would slip into our familiar technical assistance mode and help states make workfare work, thereby affecting the conclusion on a highly controversial approach?

The minutes from our November 2, 1981, board meeting reveal the early debate. Solow asked how we would handle the situation if we found that workfare was a success. Staff responded that we would have to be committed to a level of detachment that would enable us to report the findings as they were. Then Carl Holman, whose words carried special weight given his posi-tion as not only our board's vice chairman but also president of the National Urban Coalition, made a comment that we often repeated in staff discussions: workfare should be assessed, and MDRC was the most capable organization to carry out that assessment because we would be evenhanded and objective.[10]

By April, the internal debate had become more nuanced, because staff concluded that the very word "workfare" was polarizing and almost useless. As an April 1982 memo to the board put it, "We do not employ it [the term] . . . because workfare itself does not represent the key dimension in evaluating a work/welfare program determined to establish a quid pro quo for welfare receipt; that key dimension is the stringency and certainty of the participation condition, be it established by workfare, job search, supported work, or train-ing." Putting this concern clearly behind us, the same memo reported to the board, "We are not willing to concede that workfare is an inherently repressive idea, with no potential for fair and productive administration. . . . Given the emotion and chaos surrounding the work/welfare issue, staff feels that this is the optimal position for us to stake out at this time: to provide dominant ideas with their best shot at working, and report on their strengths, weaknesses, impacts, feasibility, and replicability." In the step-by-step process of resolving this issue, MDRC had transformed itself from an organization that saw its mission as testing generally progressive ideas to an explicitly nonpartisan in-stitution that believed in subjecting conservative as well as liberal approaches to the same rigorous evaluation standard and telling an evenhanded story on what it learned.

Although internal, this debate had obvious external implications. Federal funding had been essential to all our projects. As early as October 1981, Grinker had told the board that "political support or at least not having a 'liberal reputation' counts for a great deal in Washington these days." Though we were prepared to conduct an evaluation of Reagan-inspired reforms with no federal support—or even with active federal opposition—we sought to disabuse potential critics of the fear that our research would be prejudiced by an underlying leftist agenda. Through evaluation design, products, and dis-semination, we sought to demonstrate that the organization could be trusted to present the unbiased truth of what it learned.[11]

BUILDING RESEARCH CAPACITY   The second reinvention challenge centered on our skill set and our way of doing business. At this stage, we saw ourselves primarily as a vehicle to manage the testing of new approaches. As such, we sought to address three of the challenges in any demonstration: ensuring that the new idea got a fair test, balancing research ambition against operational feasibility, and ensuring a high-quality evaluation. To achieve the first, we had hired staff we hoped could help the local operators (the people who ran the programs we assessed) accelerate up the learning curve, so the study could measure somewhat mature programs, rather than programs in a shaky start-up period, and do so before the audience's patience evaporated. To achieve the other two goals, we hired a few senior researchers. But the balance, in the 1970s, was toward operations. We subcontracted all survey, impact, and ben-efit-cost work (with the exception of the Louisville studies described in chapter 3) and focused on helping local programs implement the intended models, actively directing subcontractors, and assessing the how, what, and why questions we viewed as closely linked to what we learned from working with the sites.

Early in 1981, a number of factors prompted us to conclude that survival required a change in both style and staffing. First, in the absence of special operating funds and central control, new projects were more likely to resemble evaluations of state initiatives than demonstrations of centrally designed and funded new models. This shift would require relatively less MDRC operational assistance to communities seeking to implement the models.

Second, the nature of the emerging Work/Welfare demonstration and the more cost-conscious research environment suggested an expansion of in-house responsibility for impact research. The record of WIN and workfare implementation problems, and the varied treatments states were proposing in response to OBRA, suggested the value of a close linkage between the study of participation and operations and the analysis of program impacts. For example, it would be essential to establish whether a finding of no impact (were that the outcome) meant that implementation had been weak or that services and mandates had been available and enforced but did not affect behavior. As I put it in a December 13, 1982, internal memo, "It will be important to go beyond the 'black box' vision of the program inherent in most impact studies if we are to understand the implications of the process and participation story for the generalizability of the impact results." To ensure that this integration occurred and to minimize coordination costs, we wanted to lodge most impact, process, and benefit-cost work in-house.

Third, financial and strategic considerations also suggested an increase in research capacity. We had always known that our aloofness from the regular process of competitively bid requests for proposals (RFPs) carried risks. At the November 2, 1981, meeting of the board, with opportunities for sole-source funds evaporating, Nathan summed up the board's sentiment that MDRC "should be wary of getting heavily involved with RFP bidding, but should do so on a selective basis." We also expected the environment to get much more competitive. We were concerned that without a stronger in-house analytic capacity we would have trouble bidding alone on any rare future federal research procurements, and we worried about our leverage in bidding with other firms. Finally, we anticipated great difficulty in raising the $7.2 million projected for the study and saw little logic to giving a substantial share of it to sustain organizations that we increasingly viewed as competitors. As a result, at a time of great uncertainty, we hired Daniel Friedlander and David Long to head up the impact and benefit-cost studies, respectively.

Having resolved our internal constraints, we still had to address the remaining five moving parts: How should we structure the demonstration? What was the research agenda? Would states be interested in participating and if so, under what terms? Who would pay for the study? Would the federal government seek to block or cooperate with the project?

The Demonstration Model: Learning What Works in the Real World

Before the 1980s, experiments were centrally funded tests of voluntary programs or policies of substantial national interest. Policy makers and researchers designed the model that would be tested and called most of the shots on the research agenda. The federal government not only was the primary research funder but also put up the money to pay for all or a large part of the special programs that were the subject of study and directly or through intermediaries created or contracted with local agencies selected because of their expressed interest in uniform replication of the planned design. Although Supported Work and WIN Labs moved a few steps out of a laboratory-like atmosphere into the real world, they were not evaluations of regular programs run by public agencies.

The upside of those controlled conditions was clout and stability plus the opportunity to test new and sometimes expensive ideas unlikely to emerge from normal operations. An important downside was the risk that key local actors would be indifferent to or ignorant of the endeavor or that they would perceive it as impractical, made by elite social engineers, and not affordable, feasible, replicable, or owned by the delivery systems or political actors that would be responsible for running any ongoing program. These factors probably hindered the expansion of Supported Work and were certainly the rationale for Merwin Hans's partnership vision of the WIN Labs project.

The Work/Welfare demonstration differed in almost every dimension. Most of the programs were mandatory. They emerged from the regular political process and reflected the varied ways states chose to respond to the new federalism environment of OBRA. There was no special federal or other money to provide leverage over the sites.[12] Relative to the study's ambition, research funds were also limited. These factors prompted a new model in which random assignment and the other attributes of a high-quality study were integrated into normal welfare operations; people were required to participate in the research, and informed consent played a more limited role; and study samples were large, prompting heavy reliance on state administrative data rather than on specially collected surveys.

TESTING SYSTEMS CHANGE States sought to reconcile ambitious rhetoric with the reality of shrinking funds by testing their proposed demonstrations in a subset of counties or for part of the caseload. Thus though the tests were realistic in intent and operation, they were not full-scale or permanent statewide programs. Furthermore, most of the reforms were tests not of a single component (such as job search, supported work, or workfare) but rather of a new multidimensional system of components, messages, mandates, and services. As a result, this study would use randomized trials as one of its central innovations to evaluate a moderate- to large-scale system change implemented and funded by the mainstream service providers.[13]

In its effort to launch this project, MDRC visited more than thirty states, seeking at least eight that would include several large urban areas, cover the major program models emerging in response to OBRA, meet the research and funding requirements, be able to plan and administer the program effectively, and be broadly representative of variation across the country in economic conditions, welfare benefit levels, and administrative structure. By late 1982, we concluded that states were focused on one of two basic models: either conditioning welfare receipt on active participation in work-related activities (which would mean that states would need to create a sufficient number of such activities) or using innovative techniques to increase the transition to unsubsidized employment. Although the programs varied in complexity and cost, the primary mechanism for the former group was variations in job search and unpaid work experience, and for the latter group grant diversion–funded on-the-job training.[14]

The combination of devolution and the funding structure meant that, in contrast to earlier randomized trials and demonstrations, the major mechanism for shaping what we could test would be the programs states chose to implement and the process of site selection and negotiations—rather than the more direct mechanism of writing guidelines and providing and controlling operational funds. Rudolph Penner, a member of the MDRC board, observed at the July 14, 1982, board meeting that this structure might provide the same type of invaluable information on the mechanics of implementation that emerged from the administrative agencies part of the earlier Housing Allowance experiment (sponsored by the Department of Housing and Urban Development), noting that "the fact that we can't control the states is an opportunity and not just a problem."

Lack of MDRC control over operating funds had obvious implications for leverage over the design, stability, and evolution of the state projects themselves. In addition, these evaluations were undertaken at a time when states were swamped by Reagan-era changes in the AFDC rules, WIN cutbacks, and the restructuring of the employment and training system under the Job Training Partnership Act (adopted in 1982).

DIVERSE RESEARCH FUNDING   A second funding difference between the Work/Welfare demonstration and earlier major studies was in resources for and control of the evaluation. To compensate for the absence of direct federal involvement, MDRC sought 50 percent of the research and related funds from a Ford Foundation challenge grant and anticipated that the rest would have to come from diverse state and local philanthropic or public sources. Although the state dollars usually proved to be mainly or sometimes totally a pass-through of federal funds (see further discussion below), the price of access to the state programs was that MDRC agreed not to operate as the typical independent research firm but, instead, to be under separate contract to welfare agencies in each state, giving them some leverage over the research in a structure that was presented as a new type of partnership.

This plurality of relationships meant that the evaluation would have to produce products and services that would satisfy both its state and national clients. States would want reliable answers to their questions about the success of their new programs and some technical assistance on program design and implementation. A single analysis using data pooled across all the states—as in the Supported Work project—would not meet this need. Instead, there would have to be comprehensive, free-standing reports on each state project, and project samples would have to be large enough to support reliable estimates. MDRC and the Ford Foundation, in contrast, were also interested in addressing issues relevant to national policy. To meet both demands, the study was structured as a series of parallel tests. The state evaluations would be somewhat responsive to local concerns but would have to address a common core of questions and produce findings using identical measures and reporting structures, all designed to facilitate subsequent comparison and combined analysis. (Throughout this discussion, I refer to the evaluation clients as states, but in county-administered welfare systems, such as those in California, the counties were separate and sometimes equally demanding consumers.)

Initially, we feared our lack of leverage would result in a study that could fall apart as states dropped out or refused to cooperate. But as early as 1982, the flip side of the cutback in federal funds suggested tantalizing potential benefits, as I said in a presentation at the time:

> Despite an elegant design and clear-cut results for the AFDC group, the supported work model has yet to be funded and implemented on a large scale. . . . In this demonstration, the participating states have a direct interest in the program they are testing and the lessons from the evaluation. . . . Individual states view it more as an evaluation of their program initiative that will help them in the formulation of state policy. Thus, while the initiation and implementation of the project is difficult, the road from research lessons to program implementation may be shorter. (Gueron 1982, 13–14)

Several years into the project, we concluded that the structure had indeed delivered, initially in building state ownership and allegiance and ultimately in impacting policy.

Barbara Blum—who was a welfare commissioner before she became president of MDRC in mid-1982—analyzed, in a retrospective article, how the outside-the-system nature of the Supported Work and negative-income-tax experiments partly explains why senior state officials ignored the results, in contrast to the direct link they felt toward the Work/Welfare demonstration. With state ownership came the challenge of shared control but also the gift of commitment. "In the past, MDRC had, through its national financial backers, exercised a great deal of authority to ensure that local programs adhered to its research agenda. Now it was the states . . . holding the purse strings, and it was thus public officials who were in a position to set the terms for the studies" (Blum 1990, 7–8). That the project was viewed as having the state welfare commissioners' blessing influenced staff to do more and governors to pay attention and overall "contributed to the success of a difficult undertaking" (Blum with Blank 1990, 10).

The Research Plan: Answering Key Questions Well

In developing a research design for this new type of study, we knew that a final plan would be shaped by many factors, including the following: the programs that states would implement; who would fund the study and at what level, overall and by state; the key questions in Washington and the participating states and how much it would cost to answer them; and whether random assignment proved possible. We dealt with all this uncertainty by developing a four-part preliminary design that drew on our past work and on initial reconnaissance visits and anticipated a dynamic and interactive process, in which knowledge gained would be used to generate hypotheses for testing and revisions in the plan—a high-level version of the sequential design described in chapter 2.[15]

FOUR-PART DESIGN The first component in our design focused on participation, particularly the feasibility of imposing a participation requirement. That Congress had passed OBRA did not guarantee that much would actually happen, especially since there was no new money. Because earlier WIN and workfare programs had been unable to establish meaningful obligations, those programs became a series of components and services for some but not a change in the basic rules of the game for welfare receipt. A major issue after OBRA was whether the existing or restructured bureaucracies—in some cases invigorated by becoming a WIN demonstration or by the increased public support for mandates—would be more successful. Questions abounded. Would states be willing or able to operate tough programs and substantially increase participation? Would workfare emerge as a large part of the action or a small component? Would public employee unions object? How would states differentiate recipients who could not work, or should be excused, from those who should be penalized for noncompliance?[16]

Given past failures, we saw as the core of the evaluation a quantitative and qualitative process study to address these issues, and we cautioned against extensive up-front expenditure on a sophisticated impact analysis until it became clear that there were programs that justified it. And getting accurate participation data proved more costly than anticipated, eating into resources for other parts of the analysis. The process study also expanded because the seemingly straightforward concept of participation turned out to be anything but straightforward. We found ourselves asking, what is really meant by participation? Are we asking whether people participate at all? Or whether they participate continuously while on welfare? What should be counted in the participation rates? Showing up for any activity? Or for only certain ones? Should the concept of participation be expanded to include sanctions, welfare exits, and regular paid work while on welfare—a concept MDRC staff called "coverage" and viewed as better capturing the effective reach of the program's mandate? Even more fundamental, what constituted successful implementation of a saturation or universal mandate: a participation rate (however defined) of 25 percent, 50 percent, or 100 percent?

Second, we designed a work site study to explore what workfare programs might look like in practice. Much of the debate about workfare hinged on the nature of the work-site experience: Would the positions be judged as punitive, demeaning "make-work" or as activities that produced useful goods and services and provided dignity? Would they help people develop skills (as required by OBRA) or serve as a dead end? Would welfare recipients view workfare as fair? We proposed to address such questions by surveying a random sample of work-site supervisors and participants.

Third, we would perform an impact study to determine how welfare-to-work programs affected behavior. The OBRA changes were controversial, with great uncertainty about the likely nature, size, and even direction of impacts. Advocates of welfare-to-work mandates felt the changes would increase work and reduce dependency, either because they would make welfare more burdensome and less attractive or because they would provide people with assistance and skills in locating jobs. Others questioned the assumption that people would move off the rolls to avoid the mandate and saw no need to create a work ethic that they maintained was already there. They felt that people stayed on welfare because there were too few jobs and because existing programs were not doing enough to increase skills. They also pointed to the risk of unintended consequences of mandates, especially for children in welfare families. (The impact of mandates on children was not addressed until ten years later in the Job Opportunities and Basic Skills Training evaluation, as described in chapter 9.)

A key early design decision was to focus the impact research on answering a few questions well rather than exploring more questions less reliably. Several factors drove this choice: the likelihood that state programs would have low costs and limited participation, the extremely tight research budget, and a judgment that there were indeed clear, first-order questions that should take priority. The expectations on cost and participation meant that we would need large samples scattered across multiple offices in each state. This would be necessary if we were to detect with reasonable precision impacts that, though small on average, could be of sufficient magnitude to determine whether a program generated savings that exceeded or fell short of its costs. The only affordable strategy to track so many people in eight or more states for at least twelve months was to rely on administrative data rather than the richer data possible with (much more expensive) surveys.

Building on what we had done in WIN Labs, we felt the study would be worthwhile if it could produce valid estimates of impacts on the four outcomes that could be tracked in administrative records—employment rates, earnings, welfare receipt, and welfare benefits—for clearly identified subgroups of the welfare population. These were not only the most relevant to the debate but were also highly transparent and understandable and could easily be compared with costs. Other outcomes—including hourly wages, attitudes, child welfare, health, and comprehensive measures of family income and poverty—would have to either come from the one or more states with resources to conduct small surveys or await a future study.

Large samples, good data, and adequate follow-up were necessary but not sufficient for getting reliable estimates of impacts. The other critical factor was the design, which for us meant determining whether we could use random assignment.

Finally, we would perform a benefit-cost analysis to assess whether welfare-to-work programs cost or saved money. When OBRA was enacted, there was enormous uncertainty about the net cost of state programs. I recall discussions with staff at the Congressional Budget Office about the football-field-wide range of uncertainty around their projections, particularly for CWEP. Cost data were not only scarce but also typically inaccurate, since previous studies usually failed to account for costs to agencies other than the one running the program, did not subtract the cost that would have been incurred anyway (as measured by a control group), and drew on unreliable local records. Furthermore, some assumed there would be large offsetting savings as people were deterred from applying for welfare, left the rolls to avoid the hassle or because of the programs' assistance, or were sanctioned when they did not show up for required activities. Others pointed out that it would initially cost substantially more (for administration, supervision, and services, including child care) to operate the programs than to pay benefits, and they doubted that compensating savings would be enough to offset the operating costs.

Benefit-cost analysis, as noted in earlier chapters, offers a potentially powerful tool to settle such issues. It can judge whether a program increases economic efficiency (that is, produces positive net social benefits, defined as an increase in society's overall resources). It can also address how these net benefits or losses are distributed among different groups (that is, who pays the costs and who reaps the benefits). These are questions of primary interest to economists. Policy makers as a rule are much more interested in a third question: Would the programs pay for themselves in direct budget savings? An example of the importance of the budget impact is a comment from a California legislator about the San Diego program we studied, captured in an internal MDRC memo of March 25, 1983: "Senator Garamendi, the sponsor of the State legislation establishing and providing funds for the Employment Preparation Program, has publicly proclaimed that the program saves $3 in welfare benefits for every $1 in program costs. . . . Many people have 'promised' net benefits for [the program]—there is an expectation (or hope) that MDRC's evaluation will support these promises." For the Work/Welfare demonstration we decided to focus on the budgetary impact (whether the program would produce net budget savings over five years—a much shorter period than was chosen for Supported Work) and whether welfare recipients would be better or worse off financially.

SELECTING REPRESENTATIVE STATES   Early in the project, we opted to study not a random group of states but a group selected judgmentally. From an operational perspective this was a no-brainer, since MDRC had no power to require states or counties to be in the study. We also thought that an estimate of the average or typical response to OBRA (strict external validity) would not be useful, since our goal was to determine whether a diverse group of states that seriously intended change could in fact impose a real participation requirement, not to document that many states planned and accomplished little.

We were careful in our selection, however, because we needed to deflect two possible criticisms: that we missed the important policy initiatives and that our specific selection of sites was largely responsible for the results. To counter the former, we sought sites that would fairly reflect the spectrum of state actions. To counter the latter, we sought a group of sites that, in addition to being demographically and geographically diverse, would reflect the national environment in terms of the incentives faced by welfare recipients, the strength of the local labor market, and some measures of administrative capacity. To achieve this, we ranked all states in a multidimensional matrix, showing the characteristics of the existing AFDC program (benefit level, error rate, employment rate), economic conditions (urban or rural, unemployment rate, growth of employment, percentage in manufacturing), the performance of their existing WIN program (as measured by the percentage of people unassigned to any activity and the percentage placed in jobs), and our judgment on the likely participation rate in the new program.

DECIDING ON RANDOM ASSIGNMENT From its inception, MDRC was committed to rigor. This did not, however, automatically translate into random assignment. Among our first five large-scale projects, for example, only Supported Work and WIN Labs were experiments. But our experience—including selling and watching the reception to our findings—convinced us that we should try to use random assignment in every major project and turn down work where this, or an alternative convincing approach, was not possible. Given the controversy surrounding workfare, we particularly wanted to avoid a debate about methodology when the time came to present the results. Also, our comparative advantage was in random assignment studies. We knew how to do these well and, at the time, had never done a nonexperimental impact study in-house.

Despite this, because we thought the Work/Welfare demonstration was important even if the impact design was less than ideal, we made two separate decisions: first, to push to study impacts; second, to look for an opening to do random assignment. However, from the behavior of people in the control groups in our prior work, WIN operating data, and early studies of welfare turnover conducted by RAND researchers, we knew that many welfare recipients move off the rolls quickly, and we doubted our ability to predict turnover and thus to construct a reasonable counterfactual. As I saw it during those years, "To detect the impact of [the new state programs] against the background 'noise' of normal caseload behavior promised to be difficult. Moreover, since the 'treatments' were relatively low cost and not intensive, it would be important to be able to measure accurately small changes in participants' behavior" (Gueron 1985, 6).

As of the end of May 1982, we had concluded that random assignment would be neither feasible nor appropriate, and we favored comparison sites within the same state. One month later this changed, however, and we anticipated using random assignment in at least four of the five states that were leading candidates for inclusion in the project, compared with only one (West Virginia) that relied exclusively on comparison counties. By late 1983, we were close to agreement on the final eight states, with random assignment as the key design in every one, including the study of single parents in West Virginia. How did we end up with random assignment at a scale never attempted before, ultimately covering 28,500 people in the study samples and another 12,500 under an early design in Chicago?

In terms of the technical reasons, we knew that the research design should follow reality on the ground. (The political reasons states accepted random assignment are discussed later in this chapter.) We had viewed random assignment as inappropriate when we thought states sought to change the rules of AFDC for all targeted eligibles in the demonstration areas. A research design that artificially exempted some people (through random assignment to a control group not subject to the mandate) risked producing misleading results, since it might make implementation easier than in a regular program (because there would be fewer people to serve), or affect the behavior of people in the control group (who might hear about the requirements and think they were subject to the new program), or reduce welfare impacts (if it led to dilution of the mandatory message).

As the months passed, however, the combination of federal funding cutbacks, limited availability of support services, and evidence that operating a universal program would cost money up front (with the hope of offsetting savings only in the future) led states to propose initiatives that were not universal. Rather than risk replaying the WIN experience of large numbers of untreated people, states would recognize capacity limits and impose a mandate on only part of the targeted group in specified geographic areas. This opened up the possibility for a control group. The new reform would be publicized but at a lower volume and only to those subject to the mandate.[17]

Because we were looking for an opportunity to shift the design to random assignment, we jumped on this change. The question quickly became not whether to do random assignment but how to implement it, including what to tell people, how to protect controls from the message, what the control treatment (AFDC only or WIN?) should be in order to answer the question the state cared about, and where to locate random assignment to measure the full impact for those to whom the mandate was applied. Usually, this meant that, at welfare application or recertification, one randomly determined group of people (the treatment group) would first be told that the rules had changed and then be subjected to the new program mandate, and another (the control group) would be excused from the mandate and, in half the states, also from the WIN program.[18] The result was stronger and more uniform designs in each state, which promised greater confidence in our ability to detect impacts and compare results.

The evolution in three states (Arkansas, West Virginia, and California) illustrates how this played out. The original design in Arkansas assumed saturation and relied on a comparison between counties. When limits on support services (primarily child care and transportation) prompted the program to serve only the most employable 30 to 45 percent of the caseload and place others in an inactive "backlog" pool, we and the state agreed to switch to a random assignment design.

The original West Virginia program required men in two-parent welfare households to work for their benefits as long as they received AFDC. Our evaluation compared results in nine counties that had supplemental foundation funds to provide workfare to all men on the caseload with results in eight matched counties funded to serve 40 percent of the caseload. Based on the operational success of this program and the popularity of workfare, the legislature subsequently extended the program to single mothers but had resources to involve only a limited number of people, prompting an agreement to evaluate it using random assignment.

The route was more direct in California, where the state's RFP for a research contractor declared random assignment the preferred methodology.[19] In San Diego, we made a further innovation, reflecting the interest of both the state and the county in evaluating two distinct programs (job search followed by workfare and job search alone) and in isolating the incremental effect of the workfare component. To do this, we randomly assigned people to three groups: a control group eligible for the regular WIN program, a group eligible for the full program sequence, and a group eligible for job search only.

The Ford Foundation: Funding Innovation

Without money, good ideas often remain a dream. The Work/Welfare demonstration simply would not have happened without the Ford Foundation. The power of the foundation's actions flowed from both the amount and style of its support. Ford made a large, multiyear commitment, a particularly gutsy act given the unprecedented nature of the project. The funds were explicitly flexible, to leverage the maximum knowledge gain and matching funds. Ford's good name shed an aura of power, prestige, and inevitability on the endeavor. Foundation staff related to MDRC as active partners and enablers.

For us, the knowledge that Ford shared and supported our vision and ambition inspired and liberated us to think big—and to commit ourselves fully to what we saw as a highly uncertain effort.

History and the foundation's style explain some of this, but so do individual actors. In a series of grants over the seven years leading up to Reagan's election, the foundation had made a $7 million investment in establishing MDRC as a new intermediary organization. This history exemplified the foundation's unusual style of seeding and sustaining organizations through core and project support and of taking pride in its offspring, seeing their success as an important part of its legacy. Although by 1982 Sviridoff, MDRC's creator, was no longer there, both Franklin Thomas, the president, and Susan Berresford, the newly elected vice president, knew the history and embodied this tradition.

This background and Berresford's awareness that MDRC's survival was at stake helps explain her commitment, reflected in the minutes of an October 2, 1981, meeting of our board, to provide general support and work with us in areas of mutual interest. By the time of our April 16, 1982, board meeting, staff morale had made a turnaround—from preoccupation with survival following the layoffs and Grinker's departure to optimism and a focus on the business at hand. I attributed this to the announcement that Blum would be joining MDRC as its new president, positive state response to the concept of the Work/Welfare demonstration, and the foundation's preliminary positive reaction to the project.

Our development work culminated in a May proposal laying out the broad outlines of a three-year, $7.2 million project and requesting Ford support of $3.6 million (50 percent of the total, on condition that this would be matched by other public or private funds). We estimated that states would spend tens of millions on the operation of the programs. Our proposal gave the following rationale for Ford action:

> The MDRC staff and board strongly believe that this effort is particularly important at this time when pressure is on state governments to devise cost-efficient programs to reduce welfare rolls and increase the transition of recipients to unsubsidized work, with substantially decreased federal resources. This demonstration would provide an important source of real knowledge to guide programmatic and policy direction in an area often dominated by emotion and ideology. . . . The work/welfare issue continues to play a central role in

public policy debate, and without some form of demonstration effort to examine the various initiatives being undertaken by the states, it is unlikely that the debate will be any more enlightened in the future than it is now.

The imperative for evidence fit with the importance President Thomas had always attached to combating policy by anecdote. As he remembers it,

> Good work by itself isn't enough. You need to be able to document it so that it is available to those who are interested in policy questions and social protection systems. And one of the vehicles through which you could get this kind of work done was MDRC. . . . We said that, when the time comes, when there is a change in attitude at the federal level and they are interested again in social protection systems, we need a body of experience out there that will buttress this shift in policy and form the basis for continued support for these efforts and respect for them.

TAKING THE RISK The guts of our proposal was a challenge grant. To draw down Ford funds for each state study, we had to have private or public commitments for an equal match. But the system was flexible, reflecting uncertainty on the number of states and recognition that they were likely to vary in availability and source of local funds, start-up date, and design. Thus though overall the states would have to come up with at least 50 percent of the funds, the ratio could vary by state.

The project held obvious promise, but there were also clear risks. Could we recruit and retain enough states, raise the matching funds, obtain the state administrative records that were the cornerstone of the study, build the needed in-house capacity to conduct the work, deliver a high-quality project within budget, and avoid political backlash and public controversy? Would the states launch and maintain reforms that warranted evaluation, and would they sustain their commitment to an initiative that imposed burdens on highly political programs, promised no money, and offered only knowledge and prestige? Would the federal government support or seek to undermine the initiative? Would the findings be compelling and have an impact?

In addressing these uncertainties, our proposal offered no guarantees and explicitly anticipated a high state casualty rate. To provide Ford some comfort, we proposed a three-phase process in each state: a short reconnaissance phase, a brief developmental phase, and a multiyear final phase to implement the demonstration and research. Before any state could move into the expensive third phase, we would provide an operational plan, including evidence of a firm commitment for the local share, and the recommendation from a specially created oversight committee composed of MDRC board members and outside experts. A positive Ford response would be needed to trigger the release of funds.

In short, the foundation was being asked to make a $3.6 million commitment toward a $7.2 million budget, knowing that there could be costly schedule slippage and that the budget was very tight given the ambition. Furthermore, Ford was being asked to gamble on its own. For the first time in any large-scale social experiment, no direct federal funding was anticipated and, thus, no partner with deep pockets to share the risk. The foundation would also be accepting another risk—greater responsibility for the survival of MDRC. With this new grant, Ford's share of MDRC costs would rise from less than 3 percent in 1981 to around one-third (albeit of a much smaller budget) in each year from 1983 through 1985. Twenty-five years later, Berresford recalls that "several people here—myself, Frank [Thomas], and others—just thought that MDRC was such an important institution and had done such incredible work already that the idea of it disappearing was unthinkable. . . . And the challenge MDRC was facing was not because it was ill conceived, or poorly run, or had a lousy board, or where you couldn't imagine it would have another generation. . . . So, it was not a complicated decision. . . . The question was how we were going to help it survive, not whether we should do anything."

Reflecting further, Berresford notes that Ford's response addressed a broader discussion within the foundation of three concerns raised by Reagan's election: how to protect certain organizations the foundation had created and supported; how to help states respond effectively to the shift in power from the federal level; and how to avoid sliding into policy by anecdote rather than evidence, in particular, in response to the administration's use of stories about welfare queens and cheats: "MDRC . . . was going to develop very solid knowledge of what worked and what didn't and counterbalance some of the anecdotal stuff that was going to be driving policy. And we wanted to preserve this institution. . . . This was a huge investment we had made and we just had this deep respect for the institution."

Another reason for the foundation's response may have been their perspective on the risks involved, which differed from MDRC's. In asking the key actors—Prudence Brown and Gordon Berlin (the program officers responsible for our grants during this period), Thomas, and Berresford—whether they had thought the grant was risky, I was surprised to find they do not share my memory of ulcer-producing anxiety. Brown recalls that MDRC's reputation convinced them that, even if we did not deliver on all aspects of the proposal, we would produce something of clear value. Berlin comments that his greatest concern was enlisting the states, but that even there he was not very worried, given his experience with WIN Labs. But he also notes, "I probably wasn't savvy enough to fully understand how crazy it was to think you could give the states the money and they would match it with the feds. . . . And while I knew you were bringing the research in house, frankly, from Ford's point of view, you had been supervising and managing it in the past and we didn't know the details of the different roles." Berresford recalls, "I don't remember it as a matter of risk. I remember it as an experiment and adaptation to a new landscape. . . . What I remember was that we were congratulated for trying to do things in new ways because you had to do that. And MDRC had such a strong record. We believed in the capacity of the institution to adapt, however that might work, and if it meant us providing funding in some novel ways, we got credit for that from Frank [Thomas], for being flexible, for being adaptive, and not worrying too much."

Thomas's recollection reveals the culture he created: "I think of the Ford Foundation as the research and development arm of the society. That by definition means you take risks. Without risk there's no progress. . . . So, both answers are accurate: No, we didn't think it was overly risky; yes, there were clear risks involved. And that was what the Ford Foundation was about."

THE POWER OF ENABLING PHILANTHROPY The power of the Ford grant flowed both from its magnitude and from how it was structured and managed. Not only did Ford make a large commitment, but it made it at one time and using an innovative approach that responded to devolution. There were trigger points, but the structure allowed us to craft and publicize the full project and launch a strategy to deliver on it. Instead of sitting around waiting for poorly designed RFPs, staff could aggressively identify important initiatives, help states structure them to facilitate learning, push the schedule forward, and creatively leverage the resources for an adequate assessment. Berresford describes how this approach fit with her funding philosophy:

The money should be the least of your worries at a time of crisis. I have always differed from some of my Ford colleagues and colleagues in other foundations who say: "In a time of crisis, give people a little bit and see if they can begin to work their way out, then take the next step with them and, kind of step-wise, work it. . . ." I think if you trust people, give them a nice block of money that makes sense and take that burden of uncertainty off them and then let them be tremendously creative, with confidence. . . . If you measure everything in little . . . segments, you not only miniaturize ambition, which I am very concerned about with philanthropy, but you also miniaturize the courage and experimentation that a grantee can have.

In terms of management style, the Ford program officers, Brown and, later Berlin, consistently acted as partners seeking ways to help the initiative succeed. Berlin attributes this to the message from the top: "Frank [Thomas] believed profoundly that it was the grantees that mattered. . . . He was determined to change the culture of the organization. It was to be driven by grantee needs, not some kid or older guy sitting in the foundation saying 'do this, do that.'"

An ongoing expression of the "What can we do to help?" and "We are willing to take risks to make this succeed" spirit was Brown's extraordinary flexibility in the use of Ford funds in the context of a rolling enlistment of states, where the number of states and timing of claims on the challenge grant did not become clear for several years. Although Brown now dismisses their efforts—"in the scheme of things, these were just bureaucratic issues; that was our job"—it was obvious to us that this flexibility substantially increased the foundation's risks and workload and our momentum and resources.[20]

Finally, the foundation's aura of power helped us successfully solicit the challenge funding we needed and solidify the commitment of the states, with the unexpected result that no state dropped out of the study. I recall vividly the atmosphere in the foundation's boardroom in November 1985, when Ford hosted the participating welfare commissioners, who were gathered to hear and discuss our early findings. The majesty of the setting amplified the commissioners' pride in being part of the select group that would ultimately contribute the definitive findings on welfare reform during that period.

Looking back more than two decades later, both Berlin and Berresford point to that meeting as evidence of the project's success. Berlin recalls "a real feeling that you'd pulled it off. Look, these administrators are around the table; they are getting the research side; they care about it; they are experiencing real learning. It felt really powerful. . . . And at the [Welfare Studies] Advisory Committee meetings, you had prominent academics reviewing this stuff. The feeling was that we were really advancing understanding at a crucial time." From Berresford's perspective, "It was serious participation, and that impressed us enormously because that was exactly what we were looking for—serious consideration at the state level of the kind of results that you all were pulling together. So, I think maybe the grandeur of the room worked for the state officials and the behavior of the state officials worked for the foundation."

In addition, Ford's sponsorship helped MDRC escape the limitations of being a typical state contractor. It gave us freedom to define the research agenda, not only to satisfy each state's interests but also to address larger lessons in a highly visible and politically charged area of national policy. It let us insist on data confidentiality procedures, which in some cases led us to refuse state requests to provide identifiable data on people participating in the research. It made it possible for us to negotiate publication rights that gave states an opportunity to review and comment on our reports but not to suppress or rewrite them. And it was Ford (particularly through its general support grants) that funded MDRC's dissemination to audiences outside the participating states, without which the project would not have had its unusual impact on policy and practice.

The States Sign On: Administrators Become Heroes

So far the key players in our tale had shown creativity and taken risks, but they were motivated by their own missions and in our case by the drive to survive. Webster's dictionary defines *heroism* as "extreme self-sacrificing courage especially in fulfilling a high purpose or attaining a noble end." Many of the welfare commissioners and the senior staff running the state and local programs that joined the project qualify. At a time when they were launching controversial reforms that put staff under great strain, these people accepted the added work and potentially explosive risk of inserting a lottery into the stressful welfare intake process and participating in a demanding and independent study that could as easily show failure as success. In the history of welfare experiments, they were the lead actors at the pivotal moment. In contrast to Supported Work, where programs received millions of dollars to create jobs, or later studies that followed a track record of successful experiments, the Work/Welfare demonstration states were in uncharted territory. The rewards for joining and staying were not obvious. How did we sell the project? And why did the states opt in?

CONDITIONS AND SALES PITCH   To pull off the Work/Welfare demonstration, we needed to enlist eight or more states that could simultaneously satisfy five conditions: They planned a significant initiative at a scale that would produce a reliable impact estimate and agreed to keep the program operating during the evaluation period. They agreed to cooperate with research demands, including random assignment and the monitoring and restriction of services received by a large share of the caseload. They maintained and were willing to share administrative records of sufficient quality to track participation and to measure welfare and employment outcomes. They provided, directly or indirectly, 50 percent of the funds for the evaluation. And, as a group, they were broadly representative of both the national response to OBRA and the variety of local conditions.

MDRC used a number of arguments to sell the project as a win-win opportunity, in a process that had elements of an elaborate courtship ritual. Our first highlighted the value of getting answers on impacts and costs. The Omnibus Budget Reconciliation Act had put state welfare commissioners in an uncomfortable position. The AFDC program was unpopular; the commissioners had new flexibility and authority to take charge; and they were often under intense pressure—from the state legislature and the governor—to get tough and cut the rolls. Yet commissioners understood better than the typical legislator the cost and difficulty of reform, the diverse characteristics of the people on welfare, and the need to balance multiple goals. Although they had almost no reliable evidence on the likely results of specific policies, at least some of them suspected that the performance data they normally produced would not provide the correct answers. They might not use the phrase "welfare dynamics," but they knew that people left welfare on their own, and they were not sure whether welfare-to-work programs would speed this transition.[21]

Thus commissioners were primed for our three-part message: you do not know whether these programs will work, typical outcome measures will not answer that question, and you need to find out the program's impacts. To hammer these points home, we came to each meeting armed with a reputation for quality research and gold-plated data: the evidence from Supported Work and the Louisville WIN Labs. In state after state, we used those data to explain how impressive performance measures (showing, for example, the number of people in the experimental group who leave welfare for a job) might represent success or failure, depending on how many participants would have found jobs on their own, as shown by the control group. We argued that, without us, they would only know about outcomes; but if they participated in a rigorous impact study—which by mid-1982 we had redefined as a random assignment evaluation—they had the opportunity to measure the actual accomplishments of their program, to answer other questions they cared about, and to get results that would be simple, credible, and defensible.

Two factors further strengthened our hand. The first was the federal policy that there had to be some type of independent assessment of the section 1115 waivers that most of the states we were meeting with needed to operate, and in some cases partially to fund, their demonstration programs.[22] The second was our offer of 50 percent Ford funding for a study that could meet that requirement, plus a commitment to help states raise the rest. The promise of a heavily or even fully subsidized evaluation proved essential, as it soon became apparent that the project would not get off the ground if it had to depend on states' putting up substantial funds for research.

A third selling point, which resonated powerfully with most administrators, was the promise of ongoing access to our staff, who—through their experience operating similar programs, their knowledge of what was going on across the country and of past research, and their expertise in developing data systems—could offer real-time insight and advice on how to design and strengthen state programs. In addition, we promised periodic conferences designed to share early findings and exchange lessons in an atmosphere that also built camaraderie and a network of peers.

Fourth, we were able to address diverse political concerns. Some administrators responded to the opportunity to gain visibility and cachet by being selected for a high-profile Ford Foundation initiative. Others sought to defend themselves against further changes imposed by state legislators or Congress. In particular, for administrators facing legislators gung-ho for workfare but harboring their own doubts and aware of funding cutbacks, a demonstration could simultaneously appear prudent and serve as a holding action to fend off expansion.

Finally, an essential tool in selling the study was the evidence that we had already successfully inserted random assignment into the intake process in several WIN offices in the WIN Labs project. However, this new project upped the ante. Its scale was greater than that of any previous project. Furthermore, both the programs and the random assignment intake process would be mandatory. And in most states, random assignment would be conducted in the regular welfare (not the WIN) office and thus would be integrated into the high-stakes eligibility review process. Administrators understandably feared some combination of bad press, objections from client advocates, lawsuits, negative impacts on operational performance, and additional burdens on hard-pressed staff. Overcoming these concerns took intense effort, tough negotiations, and our commitment to work with the state staff and local community to develop procedures that seemed fair, ethical, and relatively unobtrusive.[23] As in Supported Work, we concluded that "MDRC's arguments were probably particularly persuasive because they were not made primarily by researchers, but by staff who had themselves operated projects and clearly respected the need to balance research priorities and programmatic needs. Ultimately this worked because the state staff had a degree of confidence that MDRC understood their interests and concerns, would be reasonably flexible and responsive to operational demands, and would produce results that would not be overly academic or arcane but speak to pragmatic concerns" (Gueron 1985, 9).

Together, these arguments proved effective, and we moved from the can-it-be-done phase in April 1982 to a conclusion by mid-July, when we were on our way to signing up several states, that it would be difficult but feasible. From that date forward, our ability to get access to the state welfare commissioners and our sensitivity in pitching the project were greatly aided by the fact that one of their own, former New York State commissioner Barbara Blum (who, while chair of the American Public Welfare Association's Council of State Administrators, had forged close relationships with other commissioners) took over as head of MDRC and became a key salesperson for the project. Several years later (in 1985) Blum also became head of the association. The marriage of Blum's insight into what made administrators tick with our staff's operational and research savvy proved a potent combination.

CHALLENGES AND DELAYS Despite all this, recruiting states proved unexpectedly difficult. Instead of the anticipated year of developmental work, it took two years and repeated visits to more than thirty states to lock up the final eight full-study states (plus three others in a process study of welfare grant diversion). Finding interested states was not the challenge. From the beginning, interest was high among both liberal and conservative administrators. But it turned out to be hard to pin down what a state planned to do, including the project's likely nature, scale, stability, and competence. It also took time to determine data quality and availability.

The toughest hurdle of all was obtaining matching funds, which delayed start-up and added to the roller-coaster ride of enlisting states. The West Virginia courtship illustrates the challenges, despite an auspicious beginning. Berresford made the initial contact and in December 1981 invited us to join a meeting with Paul Jenkins, the executive vice president of the Pittsburgh-based Claude Worthington Benedum Foundation (a family foundation that concentrated its giving in West Virginia and southwestern Pennsylvania) and Leon Ginsberg, West Virginia's welfare commissioner. At the meeting, Berresford signaled that Ford would partner with Benedum if Benedum funded West Virginia's participation in the MDRC initiative, and everyone expressed interest: Jenkins in leveraging Ford funds for West Virginia, Ginsberg in an evaluation of their planned program for welfare fathers, and MDRC for including this serious workfare effort in the national study.

Nonetheless, it took almost a year to reach final agreement. In the process, it became clear, not surprisingly, that Benedum sought mainly to fund activities that would have a direct impact on citizens of West Virginia, rather than an out-of-state evaluation, and that the foundation was worried about political stability, the depth of the state's commitment, and the longevity in office of the commissioner. At one point Benedum staff asked Ginsberg directly whether this was his preferred way to spend their money and whether the project was really useful to the state. The discussions ended happily only because Ginsberg repeatedly affirmed his interest in seeing the demonstration happen. Time and again, when the easy course would have been to move on, he urged Benedum to support the evaluation. The result was ultimately positive, with Benedum making an exceptional three-year commitment for the full 50 percent matching funds: $670,000, 60 percent of which would go to the state (for local office staff and workfare participants' allowances). Given the importance of West Virginia's participation to building early momentum and creating a sense of reality in a project that until then was only a vision, I put Ginsberg high on my list of heroes.

Benedum proved the exception, however. Despite similar efforts elsewhere, we were successful in getting only one other local foundation involved, the Winthrop Rockefeller Foundation in Arkansas, but for a much smaller amount ($90,000 over three years). By mid-1982, in a July 7 memo, I reluctantly informed our board that foundations were not a likely source of matching funds and that it was also proving extremely difficult to get direct state dollars, because "subsidized evaluation is attractive, but only up to a point."[24] Fortunately, we were by now discovering a number of promising ways to tap federal funds.

These difficulties, combined with the urgency to show that the project was viable by quickly enlisting a minimum number of reasonably diverse states, meant that staff efforts to recruit sites were not initially based on rigorous guidelines. Only after October 1982, when the project passed the reality threshold, did we explicitly seek to fill some of the remaining empty cells in the multidimensional matrix we had set up for site selection. By the end, we concluded that we had succeeded well enough: the states were representative of the diversity of responses to OBRA, met the other criteria in our matrix, and did not appear exemplary (in the sense of being too good to be representative) in past or likely future performance. Blum (with Blank 1990, 8) describes the frustrations of the recruitment process: "We encountered administrators who would entertain the idea of a program study only if they could be certain that it would be quick and positive—or at least not negative. In other cases, state officials were interested in an objective study; but subsequently we discovered that it was unlikely their programs would generate the number of participants needed for an adequate sample size. Or we discovered that all of the prerequisites for a study were there except the willingness of state legislators to support it."

EIGHT STATES SIGN ON   Of the eight demonstrations (see table 4.2), six were mandatory, in that they required people to participate in activities as a condition of receiving welfare. The remaining two were smaller voluntary programs that emphasized grant diversion–funded on-the-job training.

For four of the six mandatory demonstrations, the requirements were relatively modest, low cost, and short term—job search of some form followed by about three months of unpaid work experience. This use of workfare as a transitional activity (not an ongoing requirement) reflected the general national response to OBRA. Only West Virginia (where program planners, facing the nation's highest unemployment rate, saw workfare as a way to keep up

Table 4.2   Key Characteristics of Projects in the Work/Welfare Demonstration

Location and program	Model	Study area	Target group	Sample size
Arkansas WORK program	Mandatory. Job search workshop followed by individual job search and twelve weeks of unpaid work experience	Two of seventy-five counties (includes Little Rock)	AFDC applicants and recipients with children aged three or older	1,153
Baltimore Options program	Mandatory. Choice of individual or group job search, thirteen weeks of unpaid work experience, education, job skills training, on-the-job training	Ten of eighteen welfare offices	AFDC applicants and recipients with children aged six or older	2,823
			AFDC-UP applicants and recipients with children of any age	349
Cook County WIN demonstration	Mandatory. Two programs: individual job search, and individual job search followed by thirteen weeks of unpaid work experience	Countywide (includes Chicago)	AFDC applicants and recipients with children aged six or older	11,912

Program	Description	Coverage	Target population	Sample
San Diego Job Search and Work Experience demonstration	Mandatory. Two programs: job search workshop and job search workshop followed by thirteen weeks of unpaid work experience	Countywide	AFDC applicants with children aged six or older	3,591
			AFDC-UP applicants with children of any age	3,406
Virginia Employment Services program	Mandatory. Individual or group job search followed by thirteen weeks of unpaid work experience	Eleven of 124 local welfare agencies representing the statewide program	AFDC applicants and recipients with children aged six or older	3,149
West Virginia Community Work Experience Program	Mandatory. Unpaid work experience of unlimited duration	Nine of twenty-seven administrative areas	AFDC applicants and recipients with children aged six or older	3,695
Maine Training Opportunities in the Private Sector program	Voluntary. Employability training, twelve weeks of unpaid work experience, and on-the-job training funded by grant diversion	Statewide	AFDC recipients on welfare for at least six months with children of any age	456
New Jersey Grant Diversion program	Voluntary. On-the-job training funded by grant diversion	Nine of twenty-one counties	AFDC recipients over the age of eighteen with children of any age	1,943

Source: Author's adaptation, based on Gueron 1987, Table 1, and Gueron and Pauly 1991, Table 3.1.

skills and morale, not as a route to regular jobs) required workfare for as long as people were on welfare.

The studies varied in scale, from a sample of fewer than 500 in Maine to almost 12,000 in Illinois (Cook County, including Chicago). Most operated in only part of the state and were targeted to mothers with school-age children—the group traditionally required to register with WIN—who represented about one-third of the adult AFDC heads of household. Some worked with subsets of this group (for example, only applicants in San Diego). None covered the full AFDC caseload.

The states also emphasized different goals. Seven operated under the WIN demonstration authority; but as the program names suggest, the message of state ownership resonated. Programs were not called WIN but rather Arkansas WORK or Baltimore Options, reflecting local values and conditions. Some focused on helping people obtain better jobs and long-term self-sufficiency and others on immediate placement and welfare savings. They also differed in the extent to which they emphasized and enforced participation. Although most planned to increase participation above the levels they had achieved in WIN, few articulated a goal of full or universal participation.

DELIVERING ON COMMITMENTS   Our strategy for working with the states had evolved from working with sites in earlier demonstrations and from Blum's personal experience and style. Her message to staff was to be honest about demands, answer states' questions, and deliver on commitments.

As a result, in our early visits we made it clear that, though the study offered real benefits, it also brought burdens. We communicated that, though we sought to satisfy our ambitious national research agenda, we were open to adding questions or supplemental studies (many of which would not require random assignment) in cities or regions key to that state. This helped, although commissioners still complained about the many demands on staff time, the abstruse nature of the research, and the unfamiliarity of the impact measures we reported. They repeatedly urged us to simplify and summarize, present fewer statistics, use layman's language, and talk more about implications.

Because we suspected cooperation would be higher if state staff understood the point of their efforts and how it fit with their mission, training at all levels included a clear explanation of the importance of the evaluation, what would be learned, and the planned procedures. Over the years, it became increasingly apparent that state staff cared about making a difference, understood the details and benefits of random assignment, and bought into the value of getting more reliable answers to their basic questions. As reflected in a memo I wrote at the time, Frederick Pond, our point person in Virginia, noted in November 1985, "It's nice to know the truth rather than the fishy numbers of the past. Those numbers never fooled the workers. They knew the gross savings weren't real. Realistic numbers help with the workers. They can deliver this."

Ownership, collaboration, and partnership are often empty slogans masking business as usual. But in 1982 it was clear that our powerlessness vis-à-vis the states required a genuinely new style, in which leverage was based not on funding and control but on the quality of the working relationships, the usefulness of technical assistance, and the creation of a strong mutual interest in and commitment to obtaining credible findings. Robert Ivry, MDRC's vice president for operations in 1983, remembers it this way:

> The evaluations became a sort of insurance policy that could withstand political transitions. To my knowledge, none of our studies was cancelled with the election of a new governor, even if the political party changed. This is really astonishing since new governors usually discontinue the policies and programs of their predecessors. This sustainability of the evaluations, which also helped sustain the programs, was probably due to a combination of the movement toward a middle ground in welfare reform (mandates in return for services), the growing receptivity to the value of good research, and the key support of the bureaucrats who survive political transitions. It is also a tribute to our relationship building with states and the luster and visibility of the overall project: states were part of something larger than their particular evaluation, they were part of a privileged group.

Through multiple visits to the field and eight conferences for commissioners and other senior administrators, MDRC staff built genuine friendships and a peer network, with the result that local staff often came to value and enjoy the experience, to trust MDRC staff enough to be forthright about problems they were confronting, and ultimately to look back with pride on what we had accomplished together. The greatest evidence of this is that some of the county and state staff volunteered for subsequent random assignment studies.[25]

MEETING POLITICAL CHALLENGES   Working with states proved to be the antithesis of the "stealth" Supported Work study and gave new meaning to the phrase high-profile research. During these years, governors won or lost elections—and in the cases of Bill Clinton and Michael Dukakis, ran for the presidency—based in part on their claims to be successful welfare reformers. Knowing this, their welfare commissioners and the staff accountable to them hammered at the political repercussions of MDRC's actions and findings. The surprise was which issues proved electric and which did not.

One dog that did not bark was random assignment. We went into the project fearing active resistance from line staff or hostile press coverage. This did not happen, although it did in subsequent studies. In part, this can be explained by our efforts to tailor random assignment to each site's intake procedures and to streamline paperwork so that the total process took less than fifteen minutes per person. In part it may have resulted from the procedures used to inform people in the control group about the process and satisfy legal and ethical concerns. But the biggest factor was the unflinching support at the top that our win-win appeal had generated.

That line staff did not undercut the study did not mean they favored it. As James Healy, a longtime MDRC senior field representative, remembers about Arkansas, "The only enthusiasm for random assignment at the county level came after staff finally realized that it was reducing their caseloads and they had fewer individuals to contact regularly."

One potential risk political appointees took by participating in a study by an independent evaluator was that state officials would lose control over their own story. This issue of independence also turned out not to be contentious, at least up front. Most state administrators had never participated in such a high-profile study and did not anticipate the power that would follow from the transparency of the findings and the active dissemination strategy MDRC would develop. They also had no reason to predict the nature or magnitude of the impacts or to expect that MDRC would insist on releasing them, whether positive or negative. Although issues of independence surfaced in some states later in the project, this was limited, in part because we worked closely with each state on the interpretation and release of the results.

The dog that did bark was the use of a new metric (impacts) to measure program success. The use of impacts meant that the state's program would be assessed by a standard that was unfamiliar and was almost certain to produce numerical results that would be much smaller than the familiar outcomes— the measures embedded in the federal WIN allocation formula and touted by governors in states with programs that were not subject to comparably rigorous evaluation. For example, at the same time we were conducting the Work/ Welfare demonstration, Massachusetts governor Michael Dukakis was garnering headlines about the success of the state's Employment and Training Choices program. As Commissioner Charles Atkins (1986, 20–21) reported, "Since October 1983, more than 20,000 welfare recipients in Massachusetts have obtained full- or part-time jobs through the state's employment and training choices program. That is 20,000 families who chose a paycheck over a welfare check—and in the process saved taxpayers $60 million in welfare benefits. . . . The long-term goal of the program is to place 50,000 people in jobs over a five-year period for a total savings of $150 million."

A state in the Work/Welfare demonstration might also place 20,000 people in jobs (that is, that many would have left welfare for work). But MDRC's evaluation would report that something like 90 percent or more of them would have gotten jobs anyway (as shown by the control group)—and that the program, therefore, actually produced only a 5 to 10 percentage point increase in the employment rate, with correspondingly lower welfare savings.

State welfare staff repeatedly pleaded with us to give them some cover and reduce the liability of being in the study—as reported in a series of internal MDRC memos, written at the time, quoting what was said at our November 1985 conference for state staff. For example, Rowena Bopp, the special assistant for operations in New Jersey's Department of Human Services, recounted that her governor, after reading a press clipping that cited outcomes in praising Dukakis's achievements, sent the New Jersey commissioner a handwritten note saying, "Get me the same kind of results." Bopp asked, "How could our study help, or compete?" Others echoed her appeal: "We are paying for the Massachusetts publicity by the heightened expectations"; "The Illinois legislature wants drama"; "You need to distinguish 'realistic' use and 'political' use. You can't sell the program on the impacts"; "It is important for MDRC to help state staff understand that impacts are enough." Although some stated that "Massachusetts places a burden on us to present accurate numbers," Bopp ultimately concluded at the meeting that she would have to revert to using outcomes.[26]

My own summary of the conference, included in a January 14, 1986, memo to our board, shows how this type of reaction worried MDRC. "One issue—the Massachusetts oversell—really haunted the conference. . . . That is, with Massachusetts claiming that all placements represent *increases* in employment, can another state survive with *net* impacts of 5–10 percentage points? State Commissioners and staff lamented the endless notes they get from their governors pushing for similar press and claims. The challenge to MDRC is quite acute: is the truth sufficiently saleable, particularly if someone else is effective selling another message?"

The problem was not only external. Ivry worried that MDRC staff would themselves become demoralized when other states pushed to outdo Massachusetts by launching glitzy initiatives that were not based on the research findings.

We responded to the challenge by relentlessly seeking to educate the press, advocacy groups, senior state and federal policy makers, congressional staff, and others about the distinction between outcomes and impacts, the erroneous use of outcome data, what could be learned through a control group and random assignment, and the encouraging results from the states in the study. We made it clear that the Massachusetts program and others reporting only outcomes might have actually been successful (as measured by impacts) but that quoting only outcomes fostered unrealistic expectations and contributed to a climate in which real success appeared puny in comparison.[27] States in the study were helped by the visibility of and attention paid to our findings and became much more sophisticated in their understanding of program data and claims of effectiveness as time went on. As Commissioner Coler later stated, "The demonstration helped me to understand that welfare caseload trends are complex economic indicators. Some of the people who participate in a welfare-to-work program would have found jobs if there had been no program" (Blum with Blank 1990, 9).

In the public relations war between outcomes and impacts, our staff sometimes felt hopeful that good data were driving out bad. This seemed to be the case by the late 1980s. Congressional staff and Congressional Budget Office analysts distrusted the outcome claims and relied on the random assignment studies in drafting and estimating the costs of the 1988 Family Support Act. Some editorial writers and key reporters also recognized this distinction. As the longtime MDRC board member Isabel Sawhill stated at a board meeting on October 10, 1986, "Massachusetts in the case of [the Employment and Training Choices Program] . . . showed a fear at getting reliable evidence. As a result, they won the battle (in the short run) but lost the war." However, at other times, we were sobered by the realization that this message needed to be repeated over and over and over again, to each new set of actors and reporters, requiring time and resources beyond the scope of the project.

That the commissioners joined and stuck with the study despite the beating they took on this issue is one reason we came to view them as heroes. Barbara Blum (with Blank 1990, 9) captures this spirit in her reflections on administrators' actions:

> By no means did [welfare administrators] view the demonstration solely as a disinterested search for the truth. . . . Still, just by having taken the step of entering the demonstrations, the administrators had to have a threshold level of respect for research. . . . All those who accepted the offer to have their programs evaluated by MDRC indicated they understood there were no guarantees that research would produce favorable program results. At the outset, recalls Ray Scott, former administrator in Arkansas, "We opted to 'low-key' the demonstration. . . . We kind of put it together in the middle of the night." One of the reasons for this was that "we didn't know whether it would work or not." While hardly conforming to traditional images of the way in which scientific truth-seekers behave, Scott's strategizing in fact reveals the very same willingness to tolerate uncertainty about outcomes that we praise in pure researchers.

Our efforts to accurately measure participation was another area where it was hard to set realistic expectations. As Ray Koenig, who comanaged the San Diego project, put it at MDRC's November 1985 conference with state staff, "It is hard to explain that, despite the 50 percent rate, San Diego did have high participation relative to the past. To the uninformed it may seem low." At the same meeting, welfare commissioners suggested we count all positive activity—including working and getting off welfare—as "good nonparticipation."

The Federal Role: Building a Stealth Partnership with Washington

MDRC launched the Work/Welfare demonstration with three big unknowns: Could we get the money? Could we get the states? Would the federal government cooperate with or seek to block the study? The answer to the third question, which surprised us, turned out to be closely linked to success on the first.[28]

As described earlier, we had seized on HHS's decision not to evaluate the

Community Work Experience Program to explore the feasibility of an independent study. Originally, we anticipated relying solely on state and private funds, with no federal role beyond that which HHS would play vis-à-vis the states in reviewing their OBRA plans and demonstration requests. In late 1981 and early 1982, we met a number of times with staff in the two relevant federal offices in HHS (the Office of the Assistant Secretary for Planning and Evaluation and OFA) to tell them about our plans and find out what they were doing, to assure ourselves that we were not duplicating efforts. By March we were convinced the road was clear, with no other significant evaluation on the horizon. During the same period, our visits to the states had confirmed that federal section 1115 waivers and demonstration grants would be important both programmatically and as a possible source of evaluation funds to match the Ford grant.

But in early April, when we were moving ahead full steam recruiting states and preparing our proposal to the Ford Foundation, we heard confidentially that HHS had begun to discuss a possible demonstration that sounded quite similar to our effort but had more federal funding for states (including both planning and demonstration grants) and a large, multiyear research contract. Concerned that such a project would entice states to jump ship and thus undercut or supplant our work—and also result in a more politically motivated study—Richard Nathan and I immediately set up a meeting with high-level HHS staff, which took place on April 12, 1982.[29]

Our pitch was direct: we have the Ford money, we have deep knowledge, we know what is going on across the country, we have strong state interest based on our ability to provide technical assistance and get them recognition, we have a comprehensive and powerful research plan, we will be objective and independent, we hope to work closely with HHS on this project as we have in past MDRC demonstrations, and we anticipate having six states start in 1982 and up to six more a year later. Although all of this was accurate, it was also a high-stakes bluff. We hoped the deep pockets of the Ford Foundation and the power of the project's design and progress would convince HHS that our project had unstoppable momentum and would deliver what they were seeking from their competing effort.

We left the meeting thinking it had been a positive exchange that might even result in a joint or coordinated project. I was thus startled by a confidential call two days later from one participant, who reported that, though the vocal federal officials appeared to favor a public-private partnership, another more silent group had been outraged by what they saw as a stealthy and inappropriate invasion of their territory by "Carter people" whom they feared were out to discredit workfare. And it was they who posed the question about "closet socialists" quoted at the opening of this chapter.

This attitude horrified us. But it also solidified our determination both to make the study happen and to ensure that it was nonpartisan and objective. We had grappled internally with the very issue that concerned the Reagan administration officials: our ability to honestly assess conservative policies. We had emerged committed to imposing a research design strong enough to withstand attack or manipulation and to reporting whatever results it produced. But at the time HHS staff had no reason to know or believe this.

Although the April meeting stirred up a hornets' nest, it left a positive legacy. First, the bluff worked. In my notes of June 29, 1982, I recorded being told that HHS had decided not to move ahead with a separate project, since "MDRC had preempted us on this, as you had more dollars and a better project. . . . Any [Office of the Assistant Secretary for Planning and Evaluation] effort would only be duplicative." This may be a rare example of the Ford Foundation's pockets appearing to be deeper than the federal government's. The same caller who reported this also said, however, that "cooperative funding . . . was unlikely in the current political environment" and that "there seemed to be little interest from the political types in an objective study in this area." Second, the initial determination to stop or undermine the study quickly ended—possibly because, as Blum observed when I consulted with her, HHS would find it difficult to convince the states not to participate at the same time that the Reagan administration was trying to encourage local initiative and public-private partnerships. Third, the animosity and suspicion of some in HHS were gradually replaced by trust; the public-private partnership did emerge, even if it was more a silent than a direct one.

Several factors probably explain this evolution. On our side, we repeatedly stated that we would not prejudge the results but intended to conduct an impartial study. We explained that the design of the process and work-site studies would provide early answers on controversial issues and that the use of random assignment—if well executed and honestly reported—protected the states and HHS against researcher bias. Later on, I took to saying that reports from random assignment studies "wrote themselves," in that the analysis was so straightforward that the researcher could not obscure the findings behind abstruse statistical manipulations. Possibly HHS also came to believe we were indeed committed to building a science of evaluation rather than advocating for a political agenda. It probably also helped that Blum soon took over as head of MDRC, since she had working relationships with the HHS secretary and others leading the agency and was known as no ideologue. Finally, our reports (the first one on San Diego's program came out in February 1984) were widely viewed as evenhanded and fair.

Whatever the cause, the result was growing cooperation. On our side, time only increased our incentive. Over the first half of 1982 we had grown more aware of the challenge we faced in raising the $3.6 million to match the Ford grant. We met with local foundations in all the states, as noted, but only two provided funding. Furthermore, most states put up little or none of their own money. With research such a hard sell in the tight state budget climate, we shifted our focus to Washington. Although we did not anticipate receiving any direct federal funds (and thus would have no constraint on our independence), we were learning more about the ways that states could indirectly access federal money—in particular, via special section 1115 evaluation or operating grants or the regular, open-ended 50 percent federal match to state administrative costs (since evaluation was judged a legitimate administrative activity). Using these approaches, states could in fact come up with 50 to 100 percent of their 50 percent match by passing through federal funds.

We reached out to include HHS in our planning and over the next year built a spirit of partnership, with federal staff attending site conferences and becoming increasingly interested in the findings and data. Examples of HHS's cooperation included their suggesting critical research questions and identifying ways for states to draw down federal matching funds. On MDRC's side, examples included providing special briefings and offering advice on ways to strengthen HHS's own demonstrations. (It was at one such briefing in July 1982 that Howard and I first met.) This joint activity provided the playing field for a new generation of HHS staff, who had not been part of the earlier DOL-run WIN experiments, to learn the benefits and challenges of random assignment and to understand, with almost an insider perspective, the emerging findings and open research questions.

Probably the most striking symbol of the transformed relationship was how we worked in tandem to find a way to fund Maryland's participation in our project. Starting in January 1982, we had been meeting with state staff in an effort to develop a study of the state's WIN demonstration. Enthusiasm was mutual—on the state's part to obtain MDRC technical assistance and get

Ford Foundation support for the required WIN demonstration evaluation and on our part to include a large eastern city with a program that contrasted sharply with San Diego's. But one small problem persisted: money. Under the AFDC regulations, the federal government could match funds donated to a state provided there were minimal strings attached, including that the donor had not designated the recipient of funds. After initial optimism, George Merrill, the savvy coordinator of Maryland's welfare employment initiatives, concluded (in a September 20, 1982, letter to Robert Ivry) that state funds were unavailable, but he identified the donated funds policy as a way to tap federal dollars. As he put it, in a bland statement of what we ultimately came to call matching the unmatchable, "It is our understanding that funds made available to MDRC by the Ford Foundation will make up the 50% State share of the evaluation's cost; the remaining 50% will be paid from the Federal share."

Unfortunately, the Ford funds had already been awarded, and they designated MDRC as the recipient, precluding federal matching. The Office of Family Assistance agreed to an unusual interpretation of the section 1115 waiver authority to allow matching in the case of Maryland but made it clear that it would not repeat this exception (once, but never again was the message). Prudence Brown, our program officer at the foundation, was originally leery of this arrangement, fearing that HHS could back out at any time. However, when HHS approved the plan, Brown correctly read this as encouraging evidence that the department had turned a corner by not (as she put it in a November 29, 1982, memo to Berresford) taking "this fairly easy opportunity to block the MDRC project."

Ultimately, the states' ability to tap federal funds proved absolutely critical to the Work/Welfare study. By October 1982, MDRC was projecting that, in the first five states, 53 percent of its funding would come from the Ford Foundation, 12 percent from local foundations, 7 percent from state funds, and 27 percent from state-directed use of federal funds. This conversion of HHS from a feared obstacle to a trusted partner was one of the surprises and more enduring legacies of the Work/Welfare initiative.

PAYING FOR QUALITY: THE MANAGEMENT CHALLENGE

With the six moving parts aligned, we still had to complete the project. The fit between the ambitious vision and the actual budget contained in our proposal to the Ford Foundation was a best guess, but we knew the ultimate cost was uncertain.

Relatively quickly, budget pressure hit. Almost every task took longer and required more effort than anticipated. Furthermore, not only did each state request at least two reports, but as findings began to emerge in early 1984 pressure mounted for summary monographs, testimony, and presentations. The stomach-churning anxiety of those years returned full force when, in reading through materials for this book, I opened a musty 1985 file and came across a budget report with my handwritten note, "Will overrun in January," attached to a memo asking the project director to end discretionary work, reassess priorities, and consider dropping data sources or cutting the scope of the final report.

To some extent, the memo reflected the normal challenge of managing research, particularly in a nonendowed, nonacademic institution in which there are minimal or no funds to subsidize projects. In that environment, every study has to cover its cost, including the salaries of staff working on it (and collectively the projects must cover the organization's expenses). Because most multiyear studies face uncertainties, their contracts usually have aspects of a cost-plus arrangement, in which the scope of work and the budget are set but contingent on certain conditions (including the major factors that drive costs) being met. If those conditions change, both funder and contractor understand that the budget or work plan will be reconsidered. An alternative type of contract—in which the product and budget are truly fixed—is usually avoided; unless the budget has slack, a firm will not want to run the risk of getting to the end and either not being able to produce satisfactory work or losing money.

What made the Work/Welfare demonstration a special case was the intensity of the pressure and its de facto fixed-cost structure. This was a transitional project, falling between the more generously funded 1970s and the later studies—when we, other researchers, and the federal government (which by then had become the major sponsor) knew more about what such work cost. In this project, both the ratio of ambition to resources and the uncertainties were higher than in any project I have been involved in before or since. Also, there was no clear funder to go back to when state delays led to cost increases. Ford had made a large and generous grant, and we felt heavy pressure to meet our part of the deal without asking for more. On the state side, we had already struggled to raise the match reflected in the contracts and now were obliged to deliver.

The result was a five-year challenge of trying to complete the initiative for the available resources. After cutting anything that looked remotely peripheral, we were down to balancing what we could afford against what made the project shine. The choices felt stark: Should we hang in there, spending money in the hope of raising more in the future? Or have we committed ourselves to unaffordable quality, in which case should we jettison some major aspect of the study? These choices were revisited over and over again as mounting costs for data collection and required early reports squeezed the budget for other areas.

It might seem obvious that customers define what they are willing to pay for and contractors deliver it. But our problems were aspirational, not contractual. From the start, we knew our ambition and style of work exceeded states' expectations, but states' expectations felt largely irrelevant. Our goal was not to be a contract research firm but to learn what works and through that process to improve the well-being of low-income people. We also sought to reach an audience that extended beyond the states and included federal and local policy makers and practitioners, the public, the media, and fellow researchers. In the process, we sought to build our reputation and fulfill the vision we had presented to the Ford Foundation.

But how were we to manage for excellence when we knew that we lacked the resources to meet that standard? At some level it came down to figuring out how to do more for less by asking the staff to work harder and more efficiently. To recruit, retain, and inspire excellent people to make a special effort we needed to enlist their passion, their pride, and their sense that the project was worth the personal sacrifice. We had to offer something they really valued, such as an opportunity to be part of a path-breaking project, to do work that met the highest standards and to see they were making a difference in something they cared about. For MDRC—and I saw similar behavior in other fine research firms—this came from our joint belief in the organization's mission and our ability to align our ambitions with that mission. When staff met about budget crises, no one suggested cutting quality or dropping a key study area. To varying degrees, we all wanted to advance knowledge, prove random assignment feasible, change social science research, and make government more effective. As a result, without saying it explicitly, everyone volunteered to work harder. The challenge for management was to deliver worthwhile opportunities, to balance the pressure to perform against our desire not to exploit staff or ultimately erode morale, to keep pushing for more money, and to search for a more cost-effective style that would not affect quality.

Seen this way, we were our own worst enemy. Every few months I would write to the board about staff overwork. Yet despite efforts to the contrary, I and others running the organization were encouraging this behavior. We were urging the people responsible for data not to compromise on accuracy; field staff to go the extra yard to build relationships and spread the word; researchers to do what it took to deliver high-quality, credible evidence; and a report review style that consumed resources in our drive for quality, clarity, and policy relevance. We knew that maintaining our standards in an environment of scarce resources was the critical issue facing the organization. But identifying a problem does not solve it; and while staff got more efficient over the years, I and others running the organization failed miserably in finding a solution.

MDRC's board struggled with these issues when it discussed how to respond to the continuing budget crises and position the organization to have a future. In meetings in early 1984, some members argued that the past was gone and the staff had to readjust and go where the money was: If what we do does not sell, we change the price. If there is no market for social science experimentation, we change what we do: explore new fields and consider less expensive activities, such as technical assistance. Nathan, our chairman, counseled against despair, pointing to our progress in devising more economical ways to design demonstrations, in getting states interested in our work, in tapping new foundations, and in linking process and impact analysis. Carl Holman, the vice chair, joined others in advising that we not abandon a focus on the disadvantaged, urging that in the current climate such work was more important than ever. Paul O'Neill, the board's treasurer, reinforced the view to stay the course, arguing that the focus on the disadvantaged and the integrity of the research in identifying what works and what does not were the very factors that held the organization together. He advised against following the money, going so far as to say that the organization was actually strengthened by its work with states and by having fewer resources. Gilbert Steiner, who often reflected the soul of the board, noted the déjà vu quality of this survival discussion and, in a prescient comment, urged the staff to involve the Ford Foundation in the debate, given the critical role it played for MDRC.

In the end, through much scrambling and Ford, state, and federal support, we got through with both the study and MDRC intact and experienced little staff turnover. Nonetheless, in June 1985 we eventually did go back to the Ford Foundation to fund supplemental activities. The basic Ford grant and matching funds had been allocated to the state studies, culminating in a marathon sprint to complete the final state reports. Although these were well received and generated extensive press coverage, they were perforce long and relatively technical.

Given the high policy interest in welfare reform, there was a large audience for publications that would synthesize the lessons in a more accessible format. Our staff hungered for an opportunity to be more reflective and to produce such documents, but we lacked the resources to fund time to work on them. So we turned again to the Ford Foundation, identifying three audiences: program administrators and government officials, congressional staff, and academic researchers. In addition to written products, we sought funds to disseminate the findings beyond what we could do with general support funds. We argued that, given the intense interest, this strategy would maximize the yield and leave a lasting record from Ford's substantial investment.

In the same musty 1985 file mentioned earlier, I found my write-up of a meeting with Berresford, Brown, and Berlin, describing their response to this request. In their typical style, all three agreed on the importance of getting resources to spread the word, made it clear that there was basically no question about the need for this effort, and moved on to discuss options to fund it. Reading this more than twenty years later, I again felt a sense of almost physical support from the fellowship they conveyed.

A year later, the foundation delivered the supplemental funds that, in combination with general support funds, allowed us to produce the monographs, articles, and dissemination effort described in chapter 6. At the same time, HHS provided funds to extend the follow-up in several states; and we were able to raise foundation and public funds for complementary studies that indirectly relieved some of the budget pressure.

NEXT STEPS

This chapter describes how the Work/Welfare demonstration pioneered a new vision of social experiments, in which MDRC, by building real partnerships with welfare administrators, was able to convert state initiatives into random assignment studies. At the time, we had a hunch that the very structure of the studies—the combination of rigor and real-world tests—would make the findings particularly relevant. I return in chapter 6 to whether the project delivered on its potential. But first, in the next chapter Howard, from his vantage point as a senior career civil servant at the time, recounts how the Reagan revolution affected his professional life at HHS and paradoxically fostered the re-entry of HHS into the policy research and evaluation arena during the early 1980s

CHAPTER 5

The Reagan Revolution and Research Capacity Within the Department of Health and Human Services: From Near Destruction to New Growth*

> When I was introduced to the idea [of random assignment] with the [Seattle-Denver Income Maintenance Experiment] hearing, it made a lot of sense to me. Then I learned a lot more about the intricacies of research designs when I was at OFA and [later] ACF and how comparison designs don't necessarily work, so during that time I became a true believer in the power that getting that kind of information can have.
>
> —Jo Anne Barnhart[1]

When Ronald Reagan won the presidency in 1980, the Department of Health and Human Services (HHS) had already played a substantial role in what was then the relatively brief history of social experiments. Although the first such experiments were initiated by the Office of Economic Opportunity, through the 1970s HHS had initiated and supervised the operation of several negative-income-tax experiments, participated in the Supported Work demonstration, and been responsible for what is arguably the most policy-influential single social experiment ever conducted—the RAND Health Insurance Experiment.[2] The HHS expertise that developed from this experience was housed in

*Chapter 5 authored by Howard Rolston.

Table 5.1   Institutional Home of Howard Rolston Within HHS, 1978 to 2004

Date	Event
1978–1980	Welfare Reform Planning Group, Social Security Administration
1980–1986	Office of Family Assistance, Social Security Administration
	—State Data and Program Characteristics Branch, 1980–1981
	—Division of Research, Evaluation, and Statistics, 1981–1985
	—Office of Policy and Evaluation, 1985–1986
1986–1991	Office of Policy and Evaluation, Family Support Administration
1991–1995	Office of Policy and Evaluation, Administration for Children and Families
1995–2004	Office of Planning, Research, and Evaluation, Administration for Children and Families

Source: Author's compilation.

the Office of the Assistant Secretary for Planning and Evaluation (ASPE). When the Reagan administration took over, the new negative attitude toward policy research led fairly quickly to the radical reduction (through layoffs and resignations) of much of the staff (in the Department of Labor as well as ASPE) who had fostered and learned from these experiments.

In this chapter, I relate how the events described in chapter 4 appeared from inside the Reagan administration. I write from the vantage point of a career civil servant who was relatively insulated from the firestorm Judy describes and was lucky enough to play a growing role as part of a cadre of both career and political appointees who worked together over many years to make random assignment the standard for policy and program evaluation. Table 5.1 sketches the chronology of my major moves within HHS over my two and a half decades there.

By 1980 I was already at HHS, tucked away in a small corner of the Social Security Administration (SSA), the Office of Family Assistance (OFA), whose main responsibility was operating the Aid to Families with Dependent Children (AFDC) program at the federal level. Although these earlier experiments were known in OFA, and to me, certainly no expertise existed there in the design or management of social experiments.

By the end of the 1980s, however, much would be changed. My office (by

Table 5.2   Timeline of the Rebuilding of HHS Research Capacity and Related Events

Date	Event
June 1981	First CWEP request for proposals issued
August 1981	OBRA becomes law
October 1981	First CWEP request for proposals canceled
May 1982	Second CWEP request for proposals issued
July 1982	MDRC briefs OFA on Work/Welfare demonstration
Fall 1982	All-day briefing at MDRC on Work/Welfare demonstration
December 1982	Research authorities and budgets transferred to OFA
Spring 1983	Jo Anne Barnhart becomes associate commissioner for family assistance
May 1983	Grant diversion request for proposals issued
June 1984	Saturation Work request for proposals issued
April 1986	Family Support Administration is created, with Wayne Stanton as its assistant secretary
May 1986	Teen Parent demonstration request for proposals issued

Source: Author's compilation.

that time I was in the Office of Policy and Evaluation in the Family Support Administration, since a reorganization had taken place in HHS) would include a staff with substantial experience designing, initiating, managing, and partnering with other organizations on large-scale social experiments. By the end of the 1990s my office—now in the Office of Planning, Research, and Evaluation in the Administration for Children and Families (ACF), through yet another reorganization at HHS—would be the leading force for social experiments in the federal government, having designed, initiated, funded, and overseen dozens of experiments, primarily in welfare policy.

This chapter relates the early part of this story. It describes how my office and I became involved with experiments and how our capacity grew. We made significant mistakes in the process, but we also learned how to do things more effectively and take on bigger and more important projects. It is paradoxical that this new policy research capacity should have begun to grow during the very period when the Reagan administration was radically reducing the strong capacity that had been built in the 1970s in ASPE, another part of the same federal department (see table 5.2 for the timeline of rebuilding HHS research capacity).

BACKGROUND AND CONTEXT

I begin my account of this development at the transition from the Carter to the Reagan administrations for three reasons. First, although the broader federal role in social experiments began much earlier, in the late 1960s, the transition was a critical turn in how the experimental method would be applied in welfare (and ultimately in other fields). Actions taken in 1981 by the Reagan administration not only were the impetus for MDRC to undertake the Work/Welfare demonstration but also laid the groundwork, in several subtler ways, for later federal government initiatives that promoted the use of random assignment.[3]

The second reason for starting with the change in administrations is that both career civil servants and political appointees (who change when the administration changes) played critical roles in these initiatives. My office, and more broadly the federal government under the Reagan administration, came to support and initiate experiments in welfare because of actions by the two distinct groups, in their separate roles as well as in how they worked together. The actions of individuals and the organizational and social relationships in which they typically operate underpin what happens in government, and transitions between administrations are especially illuminating of these relationships. The third reason I begin at this point is that, although I had worked on welfare issues somewhat earlier and would not become involved in experiments until somewhat later, it was that transition—and the issues I confronted in it—that led me to become an advocate for experimental designs.

Such transitions are stressful times for civil servants, but they are also opportunities. The stresses require little explanation, as they reflect the difficulties we all have in dealing with workplace changes: Who will be my new boss? Will I have the opportunity to show what I can do? How will I adapt to operating within the framework of a different set of policies? These questions are particularly pressing when career staff know that a deep shift in policy will occur, as was the case in January 1981. The outgoing president had unsuccessfully attempted to federalize welfare, and although expectations for the incoming administration were not clear, federalization was surely no longer on the table.

The opportunities of a transition are closely related to the stresses, as a change provides the circumstances in which to display the skills that define an effective civil servant—the ability to further the policy agenda of the appointee (or appointees) of the elected president to whom he or she reports, and the ability to apply objective, professional judgment to the set of problems at hand. In addition to exercising these two skills, balancing them is important. Will appropriate deference to the policy choices of the senior policy officials veer into suppressing one's professional judgment in order to get ahead? Will the overly zealous exercise of professional judgment substitute one's own personal views for the policy choices of those who occupy their positions as a result of an election?

HOW I CAME TO BE INVOLVED IN WELFARE AND THE LEGISLATIVE PROCESS

I started my involvement with welfare research and policy almost by accident. My academic training was in philosophy, and after an undistinguished four and a half years as an assistant professor, I went to work as a junior analyst in HHS—specifically, in the agency within SSA that was responsible primarily for hearing appeals of denied disability claims. Several years later, in 1978, my boss, Deborah Chassman, went on to head the policy unit of the Welfare Reform Planning Group, an organization within SSA tasked with managing the transition to federal operation of welfare that would be necessary if President Carter's initial welfare reform proposal, the Program for Better Jobs and Income, became law. In this proposal, the administration advanced a major reform initiative that included federalizing AFDC, creating a national minimum benefit, extending eligibility to two-parent families in all states, and providing public service jobs for those expected to work. Because I thought very highly of Chassman and I had little interest in disability hearings, I asked her for, and was successful in getting, a job that I began in August 1978.

In my new job, I split my time between doing legislative policy work and designing and implementing a system to automate and use federal AFDC administrative data. I had little knowledge of welfare but was soon engrossed in the work, as welfare issues seemed to me to get at fundamental social concerns. Carter's first welfare reform proposal was already pretty much dead, and the administration had proposed incremental reform in its place, under which states would continue to operate AFDC but be subject to additional federal requirements, primarily entailing more generous eligibility and benefit levels. Although a modified version of this proposal passed the House, it went nowhere in the Senate, and by 1980 SSA disbanded our group and moved staff

into other positions. Because of my work on automating AFDC administrative data, I was moved to a semi-moribund branch of SSA's Office of Family
Assistance that had responsibility for data analysis, still working for Chassman, who had become the director of the broader OFA Division of Research,
Evaluation, and Statistics. Thus at the time the Reagan administration was
forming in early 1981, my job consisted primarily of working with the AFDC
administrative data that states reported to the federal government.

It was not long before Chassman, being a capable and respected bureaucrat,
got herself and her staff involved in the Reagan administration's new proposals
for AFDC. I had not played a role in developing these proposals, but I was
soon involved in "the numbers." When an administration advances a legislative proposal, it provides estimates of additional federal costs or savings expected should that proposal become law. These estimates normally become
part of an overall budget submitted to Congress, but because the time is too
short after the inauguration, incoming administrations typically do not submit a full budget in their first year. In the case of the many programs with fixed
authorizations, such estimates are not an issue. But open-ended entitlements
such as AFDC require an estimation of how passage of proposed legislation
would affect the number of individuals who participate in the program and
their level of benefits. Since changes in these program rules can cause changes
in behavior, behavioral change must be included in the estimation process. For
example, the Reagan administration's proposals to treat earnings less generously in determining AFDC benefits and eligibility required the estimation,
for an average month over a five-year period, of how many people would be
working and what their earnings would be, which also required an estimation
of how much more or less they would work as a result of the change.

The administrative branch is not the only authority that produces and dis-
seminates numbers, however. Since its creation in the mid-1970s, the nonpartisan Congressional Budget Office (CBO) has produced the official numbers
that will be used for budgeting in the congressional process of considering the
legislation. CBO's estimate of whether a proposal will cost or save money, and
if so how much, can be critical in determining whether a proposed change
actually becomes law. As a result, an administration must be able to defend its
numbers effectively to CBO. Although the administration's numbers may
have some rhetorical power in debate over the legislation, they will ultimately
be irrelevant if CBO's estimates are materially different. This powerful CBO
role would contribute to more rigorous program evaluation.

Since the Reagan administration had developed its AFDC proposals and budget estimates in great haste, it had provided only a very limited rationale for them; my task was to develop the strongest case for the estimates for a subset of the proposals.[4] Typically, administrations change estimates only at specific points in the process, and thus the estimates I was given to work with were set in cement. My task was not to reestimate them but rather to find the strongest evidentiary basis to support them as they stood.[5] With more than twenty proposals covering a great deal of ground, the task was highly educational, forcing me to review a large number of research results and reports.

The negative lesson I learned during this arduous review process proved to be of particular importance in areas related to work effort, especially the Reagan administration's proposal to mandate that all states operate a community work experience program (CWEP). The numbers I had to defend estimated that the requirement would save hundreds of millions per year. But neither of the two main studies that had evaluated CWEP-like programs had a credible approach to estimating what would have happened in the absence of the program, making it impossible to determine what employment or welfare changes, if any, had occurred in response to the program. A third evaluation of a work experience program, limited to men on AFDC in Massachusetts, was based on an experimental design, but I could not use its findings to justify estimates that predicted reduced costs, as the findings showed no significant impact on employment or welfare benefits. My frustration during this initial estimation experience was substantial, because I could not use existing evidence to produce a rationale for the administration's estimates that even I found convincing—not to mention the difficulty of convincing others, including CBO, that were not already sold on the proposal. I would pursue the issue of employment program impacts for the rest of my career and still find it compelling thirty years later.

My work on the CWEP estimates was also important in less directly substantive ways. I became the numbers guy regarding legislative estimates and direct support staff to the new politically appointed associate commissioner of OFA, Linda McMahon. Although young and not long on experience, McMahon was both substantively knowledgeable and a good manager. Having been on the Senate Finance Committee staff, she was also smart in the ways of Congress. As any civil servant understands, there is no greater opportunity to prove both one's capacity and one's loyalty to an incoming political official than through frequent interaction on a high-priority initiative. As a result of my numbers reputation, when a reorganization of OFA resulted in Chass-man's promotion to director of the newly formed Office of Policy and Evalu-ation, I took over as acting director of the Division of Research, Evaluation, and Statistics in the summer of 1981, despite the fact that I had no direct background in evaluation.

How I came to be involved in the policy and program questions that are the substance of the evaluations described in this book illustrates important features regarding how government operates. These are the features surround-ing the decision process that enabled random assignment to become the dom-inant method for evaluating welfare-to-work reforms. When the federal gov-ernment promoted random assignment designs, career civil servants typically served as initiators. Although, for the most part, political officials were not initiators, with important exceptions they were strong supporters and served as powerful advocates and protectors of experimental initiatives. Had either career bureaucrats or appointees not played these roles and done so in concert, it seems impossible that what did happen could have happened.

This close working relationship between political appointees and career civil servants sounds like a gloss on what is really a less seamless, more con-flicted interaction between career and politically appointed staff. I can hon-estly say that I experienced very little of this. With only one exception, the appointees I worked directly for cared every bit as much as I did about good research and good policy. Although I saw little conflict between career and the political staff I was fortunate enough to work with, however, I did see a lot of fighting among the political staff, plausibly motivated by the relatively short time appointees typically have to get their favorite ideas implemented. In these latter struggles, the career staff line up overwhelmingly with their im-mediate political boss. To do otherwise would break an important bond of trust without which there can be no honest exchange of ideas and strategy—in which the professional judgments of career officials are expected, even if they conflict with those of their immediate supervisors. On a more basic level, career civil servants who make a habit of acting against their political boss will almost surely find themselves relegated to mundane duties.[6]

HOW FEDERAL POLICY AND EVALUATION ARE ORGANIZED

It is common for policy (sometimes called planning) and evaluation (some-times called research) to be colocated organizationally. And there are several reasons for putting them in the same office. One broad reason is to facilitate the application of research findings to policy development. For those who have an interest in seeing that policy is informed by evidence, this is a good reason. And in the agencies in which I worked, this was the dominant way in which research related to policy. However, it is not uncommon for policy makers to have decided on what policies to put forward based on their own understanding of the evidence or—even more commonly—on value perspectives that may be quite independent of the weight of the evidence. In such cases, it is particularly useful for the work of policy and evaluation staff to be closely aligned, as evaluation staff who understand the full body of evidence are in the best position to help formulate the best defense that can be made of a policy to which a political official is committed and to attack the quality or relevance of evidence put forward by the defenders of opposing policies. The task I was given—making the best defense of cost estimates already made public and not up for change—falls into this category.

Such a process does not sound like such a good thing; but it is at the heart of policy debates in this country, and probably to some extent in any democracy. And it can be viewed from a more positive perspective. It allows advocates for a policy position to advance the best case for that position, somewhat analogous to lawyers making the best case for their clients. The use of research findings to support a position already determined is a skill that senior policy officials probably value universally, even when they also value the use of research findings to develop policy. Much of everyday policy development in fact has both elements, although the increasingly partisan approach now characterizing the policy debate on many vital questions appears to favor givens that are adopted without much attention to evidence.

Another reason for organizing policy and evaluation together is to facilitate control of the latter by the former. Although this sounds entirely bad (and some of it can be), it also has a positive perspective. It is not unusual, for example, for totally independent research and evaluation units to use limited budgets on projects that are irrelevant in the policy context of the time. Such projects can occasionally be forward looking with respect to where the policy context is moving, or even help create a new context; but they can also waste scarce research dollars by reflecting researchers' personal interests that do little to help programs improve or to inform current policy debates. By facilitating the coordination of policy and evaluation, the research is likely to be more relevant. The choice of what questions to address with limited federal research resources will always reflect some policy perspective, of course. But relevance to a viewpoint that is rooted in the democratic election of a president is certainly a meaningful standard. Although some notions of control are abhorrent, including outright cooking of the results and suppressing the publication of findings, during my government career I observed no tampering with evidence and only a few examples of suppression of results.

This accounting of reasons, along with my assessment of good and bad, is relevant to our story because it provides the setting in which political appointees and career staff make choices about research, as well as the central basis on which they develop relationships with and expectations of one another. From my experience, political appointees overwhelmingly enter government to pursue the implementation of policies to which they are strongly attached. The policies may or may not be rooted in strong evidence; and most often appointees have not formulated many of the details that govern how those policies would be implemented. With the exception of those who head agencies with a narrow scientific focus, few appointees enter government for the purpose of overseeing the conduct of research, even appointees with distinguished careers evaluating the policies and programs they join the government to manage. Assistant secretaries come to change the world, not to learn about it. Mary Jo Bane, certainly the most accomplished and influential researcher I have worked for, recalls her motivation for becoming assistant secretary of the Administration for Children and Families this way: "Actually I wasn't thinking very much about the production of research. . . . I was thinking mostly about the delivery of programs and about the changing of policy. That's just the honest answer. You know I figured that I had the opportunity of having a varied career. Research was a part of my life in the university, but it certainly wasn't something that I came to [government] thinking would be a focus."

Furthermore, once political appointees with limited direct operational responsibilities, unlike those who head agencies such as SSA or the Internal Revenue Service, are in their positions, their long hours are taken up primarily with two activities—developing and implementing policy and putting out fires (such as the Head Start program whose building is shut down by a hurricane or the public misbehavior of the head of a grantee agency)—when they are not managing a large organization and attending to the needs of their political superiors.

This is not to say that senior political leadership is uninterested in research or fails to contribute to it. Almost universally the assistant secretaries for whom I worked cared deeply about both the application of reliable evidence to improve programs and the funding of projects with high standards of rigor to produce that evidence. As Olivia Golden, former assistant secretary of ACF recalls, "I'd always thought about the ways you could combine . . . a research perspective and reflection with actually finding ways for that information to be important and useful."

Additionally, they frequently made important contributions to strengthening their agency's capacity to conduct high-quality research. Golden, in her earlier tenure as the commissioner of the Administration on Children, Youth, and Families,[7] hired staff who subsequently had important leadership roles in ACF. This is how she describes the high priority she placed on research in her early days as commissioner: "Once I came [to the Administration on Children, Youth, and Families], a very early area of focus was trying to understand what [research] capacity we had. . . . I had to deal with the people aspect as well as the content aspect."

The upshot of all this is that, although political appointees often make important substantive contributions to the direction of federal research programs, they typically lack the time to focus their energies on the research function. Instead, the overall creation, management, and day-to-day operations of research programs typically fall to senior civil servants.[8] Who are the career bureaucrats who end up exercising these authorities? Overwhelmingly, they are individuals viewed by the political appointees with whom they interact as capable and loyal, both to the particular appointee and to his or her interpretation of the policy goals of the current administration. More concretely, senior civil servants with research responsibilities typically need to prove their loyalty and competence in three major policy-related ways: using research findings in the development of policy, using them in defending policy, and creating a research agenda that furthers the administration's policy agenda. Of course, being competent and creative in developing and managing the research agenda is important. But the ability to perform the three policy-related activities effectively is almost always viewed by senior political staff as part and parcel of the narrower research and management skills required of the job.

Although we were naïve at the beginning, before long we learned that random assignment can be controversial and lead to both internal and external disagreements. And these struggles can easily get swept up into broader policy and political fights. A successful program of random assignment studies—or any other prolonged, complex, and accretive research strategy—requires that a political appointee trust a career manager to exercise good judgment on substantive matters and act to minimize the risk of blow-ups. Conversely, career staff can feel free to be more ambitious and entrepreneurial if they know their political boss will back them up if difficulties do nonetheless arise. Jo Anne Barnhart, HHS associate commissioner from 1983 to 1986, puts it well: "In one way or another, every research project involves uncharted waters. Sometimes, just embarking on the research is risky. A strong relationship between career and political staff is absolutely essential. If I hadn't had complete faith and trust in the expertise, intellectual integrity, and loyalty of the career staff, I wouldn't have had the knowledge or confidence necessary to resist political pressures and to insist on research criteria and designs that would yield the most meaningful—not necessarily the most 'popular'—results." When such mutual trust is missing, the chances that any sustained policy research program will be successful are much diminished.

THE NEW ADMINISTRATION BEGINS ITS WORK

The Reagan administration pursued a two-track strategy for promoting state adoption of community work experience programs. First, as part of a broader set of changes to the statute, it proposed to Congress that the law require all states to operate the program. Second, through demonstration authority it sought to incentivize states to adopt it even in the absence of the passage of legislation.

The Administration Advances Legislative Proposals

Shortly after the inauguration, the administration put forward a list of more than twenty proposed changes to AFDC, the main thrust of which was limiting the eligibility of families with access to other income and resources. These proposals were advanced under the rubric of preserving the AFDC safety net by targeting resources on those with limited income and resources—the "truly needy." Although the proposed changes covered a number of policy dimensions, only two are of direct significance to our story: reducing eligibility for families with earnings and requiring all states to operate workfare or CWEP programs.

With respect to eligibility, a set of five interlinked proposals had the effect of counting a larger proportion of earnings in determining a family's AFDC eligibility and benefits. Back in the 1960s, with the goal of increasing the incentives for welfare parents to work, Congress had replaced the policy of reducing benefits by a full dollar for every dollar earned with an earnings disregard (the thirty-and-one-third rule) that reduced benefits by about 67 cents for every dollar earned—leaving the AFDC recipient with about 33 cents of additional income for every dollar earned. One of the Reagan admin-istration's most significant proposals was to limit the application of this disre-gard to four months. If enacted, this set of provisions would render ineligible almost all families of AFDC parents who were working full time.

Under the workfare proposal, as Judy describes in chapter 4, states would be required to operate some type of workfare program and could require AFDC recipients to perform work that served a public purpose, up to the number of hours that resulted from dividing their AFDC grant by the higher of the state or federal minimum wage. As in the 1960s and 1970s, requiring welfare recipients to work as a condition of receiving benefits was contentious. Conservatives generally favored it, regarding workfare as an appropriate form of reciprocity for society's provision of benefits to individuals; liberals gener-ally opposed it, using words like "slavefare," since it was mandatory work.[9] Although values were the basis for much of this disagreement, competing empirical views regarding the extent to which requiring participation in CWEP would actually increase recipients' employment and earnings also played a role.[10]

The community work experience program would have been a sweeping change to AFDC had states required a significant number of recipients to participate. But the Reagan administration was silent on just how many indi-viduals a state would need to include and provided no penalties for states that failed to comply. Thus it was certainly imaginable that under the proposal states would be operating CWEP with few participants.

With Its Legislative Proposals Before Congress, the Administration Decides to Launch a CWEP Demonstration

Consistent with the role of a career research manager in supporting an ad-ministration's policy agenda, shortly after Ronald Reagan's election Chass-man, my boss, began working with staff to develop a proposed research agenda. Given that the incoming president had been a strong supporter of workfare as California's governor, Chassman assumed this would be a high-priority area for the new administration. Current regulations at the time barred federal matching for benefits made in the form of payments for work performed (*Code of Federal Regulations,* title 45, sec. 233.140), thus prohibiting states from requiring AFDC recipients to work in exchange for their benefits. However, section 1115(a) waiver authority could overcome this prohibition in the context of a demonstration, which is how HHS had allowed California, under Governor Reagan, to do so between 1973 and 1975.

It would be hard to characterize California's experience operating a workfare program as anything other than unsuccessful. The research design for the demonstration was to implement the program in thirty-five counties and then compare those counties' AFDC caseloads, applications, case closings owing to earnings, and expenditures with those of the remaining California counties—a very weak counterfactual. In fact, because of a combination of rules about whom the counties could require to participate and substantial local opposition in many of them (especially the more populous ones), few individuals were required to work in exchange for their benefits. The report the state developed on the demonstration (State of California 1976), which was produced by a Democratic administration after Governor Reagan had left office, concluded that because the level of implementation was so low the program could not have had a significant effect on the target outcomes, even if the counterfactual had been stronger.

Based primarily on this negative experience, the research branch of Chassman's staff developed a potential project with two separate but linked elements. The first would advertise to interested states the availability of section 1115(a) waivers and provide federal matching funds "to initiate CWEP at the earliest possible time and to assess various approaches for CWEP." A separate competition, funded under a different research authority (section 1110 of the Social Security Act), was to provide a grant to a nonstate organization to develop models of CWEP that could be implemented in four to six states, develop data on the projects, and analyze the data with an ultimate goal of providing "states information on the best arrangements for CWEP." The basic thrust of the overall project was to allow states to implement CWEP, to help them do so well, and to capture information so that other states could replicate their efforts. However, no effort to measure the impacts of implementing CWEP on caseload dynamics or subsequent employment was contemplated.

In March shortly after McMahon arrived to head OFA, Chassman presented her with the idea for the project, and McMahon agreed to move ahead. Staff developed draft language for a *Federal Register* announcement, which designated an OFA analyst as the contact for the two, linked projects. The influence of policy on research priorities is well illustrated in a memorandum from McMahon to her counterpart in SSA, Larry Thompson, a career civil servant who was associate commissioner for policy. The April 28, 1981, memorandum asserts that "priorities need to be revised to reflect OFA's current priorities" and that research sponsored by the agency should replace projects dealing with the Medicaid notch and benefit levels (certainly not Reagan administration priorities) with the two CWEP projects.[11] The memorandum then makes it clear that McMahon did not see this as a matter for negotiation between her and Thompson: "Jack Svahn [commissioner of SSA] and I see these Community Work Experience projects as central to the administration's changes in the AFDC program." Finally, she asks for "expedited support" of Thompson's staff in issuing the announcements and directs him to meet with her: "You and I need to meet with our principal staff support for this important effort early next week. . . . I will telephone your office to make specific arrangements."[12] The announcement appeared in the *Federal Register* on June 11, 1981, and generally conformed to the approach described in attachments to the McMahon memorandum.

The guidelines for the two competitions spelled out issues of interest to HHS, including criteria for selection of participants; assessment and work-slot development strategies; the relative emphasis on training, job search, and work; provision of day care and other supportive services; the kinds of CWEP positions (sector, level of supervision, and duration, in hours per week and months); procedures to handle client rights and ensure health and safety; the sanctioning process for noncooperating clients; the administrative structure and relationship to the Work Incentive program (WIN), the Comprehensive Employment and Training Act, General Assistance programs, the Food Stamp program, and any workfare projects; and how all this would vary for clients with different characteristics. Notably absent was any attempt to measure how workfare would actually affect welfare receipt and employment.

Shortly after the competition was announced—at a June 24, 1981, conference for a group of states organized by the National Governors Association and the Ford Foundation to discuss coordination of federal and foundation-sponsored research—Chassman stated that the organization that won the grant competition would assist the states with implementation and trouble-shooting with respect to administrative and implementation issues, since these had undermined past projects. According to Judy's contemporaneous notes about the meeting, Chassman also added that there was currently funding available only for technical assistance and the beginning of data collection; she also commented that the topic was "not ready for impact analysis" and that states might favor strong work requirements even if implementing them increased program costs.

The initial timetable for both competitions was ambitious, with proposals due at the end of July 1981, selection in early September, and state projects up and running shortly thereafter and to last for three years.[13] The offer of section 1115(a) waivers became moot (at least theoretically) before the end of the summer. With the president's signing of the Omnibus Budget Resolution Act of 1981 (OBRA) in August, states had the option of operating CWEP, so waivers were no longer a federal requirement. However, the second element of the project—model building, provision of technical assistance, and documentation—was equally relevant regardless of whether a state implemented CWEP under waivers or under the newly passed statute.

HOW THE ADMINISTRATION APPROACHED THE POTENTIAL OPPORTUNITY TO LEARN ABOUT OBRA'S EFFECTS

Passage of OBRA created major opportunities for learning how large program changes affected low-income families. Yet with few exceptions, the Reagan administration ignored this potential. Although this lack of interest in learning is evident in several areas, it is most clearly displayed by examining the administration's waiver policy in the early 1980s.

Welfare Waivers and Their Relevance to Program Evaluation

Section 1115(a), commonly referred to as waiver authority, became law in 1962 as part of a larger set of changes to the Social Security Act. It contains three authorities, the first two of which are relevant to this discussion: the authority to waive state plan provisions, section 1115(a)(1); and the authority to provide federal matching payments for benefits and services not otherwise allowable, section 1115(a)(2).[14] Although section 1115 applies to a broader set of programs in the act, except where otherwise noted (particularly with regard to Medicaid) I describe section 1115 in the context of the AFDC program.[15]

The actual waiver authority, section 1115(a)(1), provides that in the context of an "experimental, pilot, or demonstration project" the secretary of

HHS "may waive compliance" with any AFDC state plan requirement. Ultimately, this consisted of more than forty requirements covering a broad range of subjects, including the treatment of income and assets in determining eligibility and benefit levels, the requirement to include specific individuals in the household in the AFDC family unit, which individuals were subject to work requirements, and the individual entitlement to AFDC. Sections of the statute that were not on the list of state plan requirements were subject to waiver by reference. For example, after the Family Support Act of 1988 was signed into law, one plan provision required states to operate a program in conformity with the Job Opportunities and Basic Skills Training program section of the statute; a waiver of this plan requirement by implication could waive all or part of the program.[16] Thus the waiver authority provided enormous flexibility for the secretary to rewrite most of the AFDC and JOBS programs in the context of a state experimental, pilot, or demonstration program.

The second authority—dubbed "matching the unmatchable"—provided (also in the context of a section 1115 demonstration approved by the HHS secretary) that "costs which would not otherwise be included as expenditures . . . shall, to the extent and for the period prescribed by the Secretary, be regarded as expenditures under the state plan." Like the waiver authority, the authority of the secretary to provide federal matching for activities not normally covered in the statute is very broad. For example, before the JOBS program was created, under the Family Support Act of 1988, welfare agencies could obtain federal AFDC matching for only three specific work program activities added in the early 1980s—job search, work supplementation (a form of grant diversion), and community work experience. Section 1115(a)(2) authority allowed the secretary to permit expenditures for a broader range of activities to receive federal matching.

The extreme flexibility these two authorities provide for the secretary to override statutory provisions and regulations promulgated to interpret them is not narrowed by section 1115's description of the criterion by which they can be invoked—namely, where "in the judgment of the Secretary, [the project] is likely to assist in promoting the objectives of" AFDC. One of these was "encouraging the care of dependent children in their own homes, or the homes of relatives by enabling each State to furnish financial assistance and rehabilitation and other services . . . to needy dependent children and the parent or relatives with whom they are living to help maintain and strengthen family life and to help such parents or relatives to attain or retain capability for the maximum self-support and personal independence consistent with the maintenance of continuing parental care and protection" (Social Security Act, sec. 401).

Furthermore, the secretary may provide waivers "to the extent and for the period he finds necessary to enable such State or States to carry out such project." Three things are notable here. First, the stated objectives of AFDC are very broad. Second, the sole standard set forth is the secretary's judgment that a project will further these objectives. Third, the Secretary's finding of the necessity for a waiver for a specific extent and period is again simply left to his or her judgment. It is breathtaking that Congress, which detailed so many specific provisions regarding how a state must operate a program, at the same time authorized the executive branch to cast aside all these rules in a demonstration, solely on the basis of one individual's determination that another set of rules would produce some subset of a broad list of better outcomes.

Even so, the flexibility is not limitless. Most significantly, the secretary must use the waiver and matching authorities to enable the conduct of projects. This has several important implications. First, the waivers are not simply programmatic relief from legal requirements, even where providing them for this purpose might further the objectives of the act. Conduct of a project is not the same as operation of a program. As the HHS general counsel's March 1964 draft memo states, "A project is limited in time" and "suggests something specific and special"—which, for example, would rule out simply increasing federal matching for activities that were normally a part of AFDC but might be subject to funding limitations.[17]

Another key limitation is embodied in the concept of experimental, pilot, or demonstration, which HHS has consistently taken to imply that section 1115 projects must include an evaluation component. Although it is stated in the context of distinguishing section 1115 projects from research, the same March 1964 memo lays the foundation for this position: "An experimental, pilot or demonstration project would ordinarily involve some recording of information, evaluation, and reporting." (Subsequent, more formal, HHS legal interpretations would remove the word *ordinarily.*) This requirement would play a central role in how section 1115 became a key vehicle for the use of randomized experiments in welfare evaluations. Again, however, reflecting the broad discretion granted to the secretary, the nature and extent of the required evaluation is not specified. This discretion would also play a central role in providing administrations broad flexibility in waiver policy regarding evaluation requirements imposed on states as a condition for operating section 1115 projects.

A final point for our story is that the section 1115(a)(2) authority provides the possibility of new federal funding for activities in the framework of the normal matching processes of the program. With respect to AFDC, there were two primary matching rates.[18] The largest expenditures in AFDC were for benefits to families; the federal government matched these dollars at 50 to 80 percent, depending on the median income of the state, with higher rates for poorer states. The second matching rate was for the administrative costs of running the program; these were matched at a uniform 50 percent.

Thus HHS had vast legal discretion in the use of section 1115(a) with respect to the AFDC program. It also had enormous substantive flexibility in what it could waive. Furthermore, the circumstances regarding when to use that flexibility were almost entirely at the secretary's discretion. Given this flexibility in circumstances, although a project had to include evaluation, its nature and the other conditions HHS might attach to the receipt of waivers were equally broad. As a consequence, the vast majority of decisions about whether to approve a waiver request from a state and what conditions to attach to it were matters of policy, not law. Nonetheless, all waiver approvals required review and clearance by HHS general counsel, although usually, but not always, the legality of the waivers themselves was straightforward.

RESTRICTING EARNINGS DISREGARDS   After passage of OBRA in August 1981, the Reagan administration quickly promulgated regulations, and already by the fall and winter of that year states were applying those new rules to their caseloads. Not all states preferred the new (less generous) earnings disregards, however; and two of them, Wisconsin and Utah, expressed interest in section 1115 demonstrations to revert to prior AFDC law. The administration's response was clear. The requests were denied in letters to the states citing evidence that more generous disregards tended to prolong welfare use and that approval would decrease a parent's capability for self-support and, as a result, would not promote the objectives of the Social Security Act.

Although the Reagan administration had considerable nonexperimental evidence on its side that the indefinite thirty-and-one-third disregard was not effective in promoting work (Levy 1978; Barr and Hall 1981), limiting its application was also highly controversial at the national level, and liberals, by and large, argued that the four-month limitation would indeed reduce work effort. The requests by states not to operate under the new disregards opened the possibility that a rigorous experimental test could be conducted to determine whether this was true. The Department of Health and Human Services could have given the states waivers to use the old disregards while also requiring them to conduct an experimental evaluation by randomly assigning a portion of their caseload to the new, more limited disregards. Nobody envisioned this possibility at the time. And even if someone had raised it, HHS would have been unlikely to make the offer, given the administration's desire to enforce the national policy it had advanced successfully in the legislative process. From the administration's perspective, approving a waiver demonstration for even two states would have been forgoing precisely the policy it advocated.

The administration did allow an evaluation of OBRA changes through another avenue, however. Shortly after passage of OBRA, my office contracted with Research Triangle Institute for an evaluation of the OBRA changes that drew nationally representative samples of working and nonworking AFDC recipients both before and after the OBRA changes, in a before-after cohort comparison design. Research Triangle Institute (1983) found that working recipients did not quit their jobs and there was no decline in the uptake of work for nonworking recipients. The length of follow-up was only twelve months, however; the sample of nonworkers was not very large, given that uptake of work was quite slow for a cross-section of nonworking AFDC recipients; and the lack of a randomly assigned control group left open the possibility that non-OBRA factors may have accounted for the lack of observed change. The issue of more or less generous disregards would not be subject to further, more rigorous evaluation until much later in the decade.

WIN DEMONSTRATIONS A second important category of waiver requests in the early 1980s was the extension of work requirements to broader segments of the welfare population for states operating WIN demonstration. A key provision of that legislation established that the WIN demonstration participation requirements were to be those in force in the state at the time it began its demonstration. The participation requirement in the regular WIN program was set forth as universal but with exemptions, the largest adult category of which was single parents (primarily mothers) with a child under the age of six. This exemption removed about half of all AFDC adults from WIN participation requirements. Because the participation requirements were described in a state plan provision, they fell under the authority of section 1115(a)(1), enabling them to be waived in the context of a demonstration if the secretary determined that doing so would further the objectives of the Social Security Act.

At that time, about a half-dozen states were interested in reducing the age of the youngest child that triggered the exemption. Most of these wanted to lower the age from six to three, but some wanted to remove the exemption altogether and make age-of-child exemptions on a case-by-case basis or lower it to one year. These states submitted section 1115 applications to HHS, but for the new rules to apply to their WIN demonstrations they needed approval before the time the rules were to be implemented.

The Reagan administration had not taken a position on reducing the age-of-child exemption for mandatory WIN participation. But it was interested in increasing the employment focus of AFDC; and exempting a large proportion of the caseload, some for many years, limited the extent to which this could be accomplished. Consequently, HHS approved all state requests for age-of-child waiver demonstrations, even though some applications were very brief and provided few evaluation details, on the basis that they would promote the self-support goals of the statute.

As with the disregard waiver requests, the approved WIN demonstration waiver requests provided an opportunity to learn that, again, the administration was not interested in pursuing. Typically, the states proposed to evaluate their waivers by comparing employment rates for parents with children under six with those with children six and over, and HHS found this approach acceptable. This is not uninteresting information, but it fails to assess whether requiring participation in the work activities provided under WIN improved employment and earnings outcomes or affected the children of either group of parents. Rather than regarding waivers as an important learning opportunity, the administration focused on using the waiver authority to allow states to implement a policy that appealed to them ideologically. Except for the case of Arkansas—where MDRC would take the initiative in experimentally addressing whether extending work requirements to parents of younger children improved their employment and earnings outcomes (see chapter 4)—HHS would not be proactive in addressing this question rigorously, or the question of potential effects of the policy on children, until nearly a decade later.

Similarly, HHS did not see the WIN demonstrations themselves as an opportunity for rigorous evaluation, although the statute required the department to conduct an evaluation of them. Instead, the evaluation requirement was met by HHS's requirement that WIN demonstration states provide a subset of the information that the Department of Labor required regular WIN states to report, primarily concerning such subjects as employment entry and retention. Ultimately, my office produced a report summarizing these data and comparing WIN demonstration states to regular WIN states. However, there was neither any analysis to determine whether this comparison was methodologically appropriate nor any effort to consider how the evaluation requirement could be used to determine which programmatic elements were effective in improving employment and earnings outcomes.

CWEP Demonstration

Although the June 1981 CWEP grant announcement did not suggest any examination of the impacts of state programs, it did focus on technical assistance and learning about implementation issues. But even this turned out to be irrelevant, because the whole thing was canceled the following October. The administration appeared to be entirely turning its back on learning about CWEP.

In May of 1982, however, a second grant announcement was issued, this one providing funds to the states for the purpose of piloting CWEP programs. This announcement, considerably more detailed than the earlier one, sought to provide funding of about $300,000 over two years to any state "to test innovative program designs, techniques, and procedures for implementing CWEP." Like the earlier announcement, it was aimed at improving "administrative effectiveness," describing as its "primary objective" the testing of "implementation processes and administrative procedures that constitute 'best practices' for operating CWEP." The announcement certainly did not call for an evaluation of the impact of CWEP on subsequent employment; but it did not rule it out, either. Thus the objective was qualified as "primary," administrative effectiveness was never defined, and it was not unreasonable to assume that best practices might be determined, at least in part, by success in improving employment and earnings of programs that implemented these practices.

Ultimately, states that were part of MDRC's Work/Welfare demonstration submitted a number of applications for grants, of which two were approved even though the grants indirectly funded MDRC's impact evaluation—in the sense that, to the extent that HHS funds covered part of the implementation evaluation, presumably other funds were freed up to cover the impact evaluation. That HHS was indirectly funding evaluations they would not initiate strongly suggests to me that, at least at McMahon's associate commissioner level, she was willing to ignore this implication. It further suggests that the problem was not so much the impact evaluations of CWEP as it was the tension the Reagan administration felt about initiating impact evaluations of CWEP at the very same time it was proposing to mandate it on all states.

Policy and Evaluation

In 1981 the policy of the Reagan administration regarding approval of section 1115 waiver demonstrations was straightforward. To the extent that requested waiver projects were consistent with overall administration policy with respect to AFDC, HHS determined them to further the objectives of the Social Security Act; to the extent that proposed projects were inconsistent with that policy, the department denied state applications to conduct them (in some cases even failing to continue projects that had been approved by the previous administration). Furthermore, the evaluation requirements attached to approved projects were minimal; the main goal was to allow the state to implement the policy, and no serious consideration was given to gaining knowledge of the policy's effects.

Many observers regarded the Reagan administration's actions in this area as based on a desire not to know the truth about the consequences of its proposed policies. Certainly, the administration placed a low value on obtaining rigorous evidence about these consequences and on research more generally. Furthermore, its use of the section 1115 waiver authority, though consistent with the letter of the law, was less in keeping with its spirit. But there is a simpler way to construe the administration's actions, which I find at least as plausible: initiating an impact evaluation can justifiably be taken as implying some agnosticism—some level of uncertainty about the effects of the tested policy. The Reagan administration had attempted to require all states to operate CWEP (and would continue to do so in its budget submissions over the next several years), and it had constrained disregard policies in all states. Clearly, Reagan appointees believed in the intrinsic value of CWEP, but the administration also had to estimate the consequences of adopting this policy as part of its proposed budget, claiming that large savings would accrue from these policies to both the federal and state governments. To initiate impact evaluations of these policies, either through federal research projects or federal approval of state waiver demonstrations, would be tacit acknowledgement that these estimates were in doubt.

Perhaps this contradiction would not have been such a problem had not so many states opposed the policies. But in this hostile environment, acknowledgement of cost uncertainty would have further undermined the possibility of successfully passing legislation requiring states to operate CWEP. In addition, it would open up the disregard limits that had already been successfully enacted. Thus, the problem with the administration's approach can be seen less as its failure to pursue evaluation of the policies it promoted than its insistence that the policies be put in place universally while lacking the empirical justification for so doing.[19] So although it could tolerate research by others, it could not initiate and remain consistent with the policies it advanced. The upshot was that by not pursuing any research strategy regarding the effects of CWEP, HHS created a vacuum that left the field open to MDRC.

HOW I BECAME COMMITTED TO THE EXPERIMENTAL METHOD

The period from August 1981 to December 1982 was a formative period for me. I developed a strong commitment to the value of the experimental method in program evaluation, and although the implications of that commitment were unknown to me at the time, they would play out over the rest of my government career (and beyond). A number of key experiences played a role in this development, but the setting I was in also contributed in important ways.

My Growing Involvement in HHS Evaluation Decisions

As mentioned earlier, the HHS/Office of Family Assistance office I had come to lead did not directly administer the AFDC research budget at that time. Because, except for the Research Triangle Institute evaluation of the OBRA benefit and eligibility changes mentioned earlier, my office had no direct responsibility for managing research grants and contracts, my staff was initially small. But whereas reductions in workforce were widespread in many human services programs in the early days of the Reagan administration, we were adding substantial new staff. Strengthening OFA's capacity for welfare initiatives and federal oversight of AFDC was clearly an administration priority. With passage of WIN demonstration authority as part of OBRA of 1981, my office became responsible for operating the demonstrations; and the responsibility for administering WIN research funds, but no research staff came from the Department of Labor to my office, so we had no access to the institutional knowledge of previous WIN research, including the studies described in chapter 3. The centralization of research authority was completed in December 1982, when my office became responsible for the entire research function and budget for AFDC. My office was slowly acquiring the elements for implementing a significant welfare research agenda, although for nearly a year and a half my day-to-day responsibilities for evaluation and research were pretty modest. This was valuable time for a newcomer to develop a perspective.

Another large advantage of my situation, and throughout my career, was that I was able to play both a research and a policy role. In the early 1980s my staff and I collectively remained the "numbers people," which forced me to see the need for research that could lead to more accurate and better-supported numbers for policy analysis. Most important, it was natural, while playing this kind of policy role, to think about research investments as delivering information to the policy process. The perspective I developed over this period on the research sponsored by the office previously responsible for AFDC-related research was based on this role. Overall, I came to believe that too much of the research budget had gone to projects that lacked any direct connection to improving AFDC. Stated simply, too little funding was devoted to program evaluation. In addition, it seemed to me that the funding had previously gone to too many small projects and that learning something credible and usable for policy required substantial resources. I became convinced that better prioritizing and funding fewer projects were essential if solid progress was to be made.

Given the Reagan administration's focus on work, I continued to search for reports regarding what was known about the effectiveness of different approaches to moving welfare recipients, or other low-income adults, into work. I read the emerging experimental literature on the effectiveness of job search that had been sponsored by the Department of Labor during the 1970s, including Nathan Azrin's work on job clubs and MDRC's Louisville WIN Laboratory Project. Equally important, I read about a sophisticated nonexperimental evaluation of the Comprehensive Employment and Training Act that was sponsored by the Department of Labor. Program data were collected on a sample of program participants, which the evaluation matched, along with subsamples from the Current Population Survey, to Social Security earnings records. The evaluation then compared the employment experience of these two groups. Several highly respected research organizations (including Westat, which was responsible for the evaluation) analyzed the data and, famously, came up with divergent assessments (Barnow 1987).[20]

Some time in 1982 I obtained and read two draft reports of those analyses. I recall few details, but I was particularly interested in what was known about the effectiveness of different work activities; and I do remember that I found the results confusing. This was especially true when researchers analyzed the effectiveness of various activities for different subgroups. At the time I had limited ability to assess the actual statistical techniques used. But reading subsequent reanalyses of those analyses makes it pretty clear that better training could not have helped me much; to this day there is no agreement among experts on which of the analyses yielded more reliable results. Barnow (1987, 189), for example, concludes, "It is clear from the wide range of approaches used by the studies reviewed in this paper that there is not agreement at this time on how earnings functions should be specified nor how the selection process should be modeled."

Learning about MDRC

I first met Judy Gueron in July 1982, when—with McMahon and my immediate boss, Michael deMaar—I attended an MDRC briefing on the project they were undertaking with the states. Three months later we briefed MDRC staff on the states to which we had provided grants for CWEP projects, two of which (California [San Diego] and Virginia) were also part of MDRC's Work/Welfare demonstration. Later that fall MDRC invited me to their offices in New York City to spend a day learning more about their demonstration. Lengthy give-and-take sessions gave me my first chance to delve into the project in some depth, learn details, and ask questions.

I remember walking from MDRC's offices at the end of the afternoon and thinking that experiments were an eminently practical way to learn about the extent to which different work programs and their components improve or fail to improve employment and earnings outcomes. I already had a strong appreciation for the value of random assignment, but I came away with an even stronger sense of how right it was for the particular questions at hand. I thought that such a design would make it possible to determine what difference CWEP and other activities really made for recipients and that, although the information was not currently available, the MDRC demonstration (and future projects) could make it available over the longer run. I was sold on random assignment experiments. I also saw how, given our research budget, we could initiate this kind of work ourselves, in a way that would complement MDRC's effort.

Grant Diversion

Launching an initial effort proved to be surprisingly simple. In contrast to the type of complex decision-making process that Judy describes in chapter 4, the decision to move forward on grant diversion involved just three people: deMaar, my immediate boss; Jo Anne Barnhart,[21] who had recently become head of OFA when McMahon became the state director of California social services; and me. I proposed the idea of a demonstration, the three of us discussed it, and Barnhart made the decision. She recalls it this way: "I don't remember the specific waiver you talked to me about the very first time, but I just remember that . . . I really started to understand the capabilities of the federal government to do that kind of experimentation."

About six months later, on May 11, 1983, OFA published its first annual set of research and demonstration priorities, transmitted to the states over Barnhart's signature. In addition to two projects on the improved identification and reduction of fraud and payment errors (one of which expressed a preference for projects that proposed using control or comparison groups), there were three work-related projects. Two were CWEP-related—one to develop best practices for training CWEP participants to provide day care for other AFDC recipients and the other to develop a "model CWEP management information system." Both were similar to the earlier CWEP demonstration efforts in focusing on improving the operations of CWEP but not attempting to assess its impacts. The third, however, represented OFA's first step to initiate projects that would use experimental methods to assess the effects of a work program; it offered funds to states for a demonstration of grant diversion.

Grant diversion is a concept that came into welfare and employment policy in the 1970s (see chapters 2 and 4). The idea is that funds that would otherwise provide welfare payments to AFDC recipients be used to provide wage subsidies to employers who would hire the recipients. To quote the announcement, "Grant diversion is a technique whereby the recipient's AFDC cash grant is diverted to a public or private employer that employs the recipient."

Although Supported Work had other elements—such as structured, increasingly demanding work experience—the underlying mechanism for partially funding the work experience positions for AFDC recipients under the program was grant diversion. The work supplementation program, passed as part of OBRA, was also a form of grant diversion.[22] Grant diversion differed from CWEP in that it created a wage-paying job that established an employer-employee relationship; CWEP, in contrast, required the AFDC recipient to provide work in exchange for his or her benefit without status as an employee.

Since grant diversion is aimed at creating job opportunities, not simply providing a windfall to employers who would have hired recipients anyway, the key policy question for grant diversion is whether it results in increased employment and earnings for participants during and after the period of the subsidy. These are the kinds of questions that lend themselves to an experimental design, because the control group will be a reliable representation of how much employment recipients would have been able to obtain without the subsidy. The OFA grant announcement required that a control or comparison group be used and gave preference to "projects utilizing an experimental design with random assignment."

The language of the announcement provides an important clue (and an interesting lesson) to why the Reagan administration was willing to initiate a project intended to determine the impact of grant diversion, in contrast to its resistance with respect to CWEP. Grant diversion is described as a technique. For the administration, use of this language implied an attitude of neutrality and agnosticism about whether the technique actually worked; and, in fact, grant diversion was a nonpartisan, politically neutral issue. Although a similar set of questions was also relevant to CWEP (that is, does it increase AFDC recipients' employment and earnings), the administration would never have referred to CWEP as a technique. In the same grant announcement, in fact, the CWEP day care project uses the term *technique*; but it does so not to describe CWEP itself but rather to describe approaches to using CWEP to meet the day care needs of other AFDC recipients. Similarly, in both earlier CWEP announcements the grantee was expected to demonstrate techniques for operating CWEP; but CWEP itself was not described as a technique.

Describing a program as a technique implies that its value is instrumental—it has no value unless it actually produces a desired end. The community work experience program, obviously, was viewed by administration policy officials not only as a means to the end of increased employment but also as a reflection of the moral value of expecting welfare recipients to work in exchange for their benefits and thereby produce something in return for the community (that is, an end in itself). Because high-level Reagan administration officials so strongly held to this value claim, and because they had staked themselves out on its effectiveness in reducing welfare caseloads, they could not yield any ground on the empirical claim about the effect of CWEP on increasing work outcomes. These considerations were not a constraint for them with grant diversion as it was merely a technique.

Although in retrospect the Grant Diversion demonstration was an important initial step and an equally important learning experience, as a demonstration it had limited success in addressing the utility of grant diversion in increasing employment and earnings. And even this limited success was primarily a product of MDRC's design and implementation rather than of OFA's original design. The six programs we funded yielded only two impact reports, one for the Maine Training Opportunities in the Private Sector program (Auspos, Cave, and Long 1988) and one for the New Jersey Grant Diversion program (Freedman, Bryant, and Cave 1988). In the Maine program, grant diversion was a relatively small component in which only individuals who had been unsuccessful in gaining regular employment from two earlier activities typically participated. New Jersey's history of operating reasonably large-scale on-the-job training programs enabled it to convert fairly quickly to being funded by grant diversion; so it implemented a program large enough for an impact evaluation. None of the other state projects was able to deliver a program of sufficient scale for an impact analysis. The six states together produced only about 15 percent of the roughly 8,000 job placements they had originally projected for the first two years. In addition to the two impact evaluations in New Jersey and Maine, MDRC's design also yielded a useful cross-state implementation study in the six states we funded, using funds it obtained from the Ford Foundation (Bangser, Healy, and Ivry 1985).

The Maine and New Jersey grant diversion evaluations illustrate the implicit partnership that was developing between OFA and MDRC, even in the absence of any explicit coordination. MDRC had been in dialogue with both states about participation in the Work/Welfare demonstration before OFA's grant diversion announcement, but lack of a local match prevented their inclusion in the project. According to Judy, without the OFA funding neither would have been in the demonstration. Equally, without MDRC's efforts and matching funds from their Ford Foundation challenge grant, our grant diversion evaluation initiative would have produced little of research value and no impact findings at all. Thus as was true of the CWEP grants, OFA's funds indirectly provided financing for MDRC's Work/Welfare demonstration, increasing the value of both Ford's and OFA's investments.

There were two major, interrelated problems with the project that stemmed from my and my staff's lack of experience, and that of OFA more generally, with both work programs and program evaluation. First, our assumptions were naïve in failing to recognize the operational difficulties involved in establishing grant diversion programs at significant scale. The rhetoric at the time emphasized that grant diversion was a win-win-win proposition—good for the individuals who got jobs, good for employers who received the wage subsidies for employees, and good for government and the public because welfare caseloads would be reduced. Although there was already considerable evidence that the share of employers receptive to hiring subsidized welfare recipients was small, we were simply unaware of it. As a result, we devoted far too little time and resources to overcoming this problem. Over time, OFA and its successor agencies would make progress on understanding how to be reasonably certain a program was operating in a manner that would make a successful evaluation plausible; but our progress would occur only in incremental steps as our experience increased.

Second, and consistent with this failure to appreciate operational problems, the project itself was severely underfunded. It provided each state with a total of only about $600,000 over three years. Both the sum and the duration were far too small to fund the development of a program and its evaluation. Even if the funding had been more generous, getting a program up to scale, accumulating sufficient sample size, and following that sample for a reasonable period of time was just not possible within three years unless a program was already operational. The one positive aspect of our grant diversion project was that the shortcomings, which became apparent pretty quickly, taught us much that we were able to use in other projects.

Thanks to MDRC, the findings from these studies were quite relevant to policy. The three components that together made up the Maine program had moderate earnings impacts, although its relatively high cost and failure to reduce AFDC use resulted in a negative benefit-cost ratio from the government perspective. The New Jersey program had similarly moderate earnings impacts. But these were noteworthy in that the control group received all the

WIN services the experimental group did, with the single exception of the on-the-job training funded by grant diversion. Furthermore, because its costs were much lower than those of the Maine program, and it did reduce welfare receipt, it was estimated to pay for itself over a two-and-one-half-year period.

Nonetheless, the predominant finding of both the Maine and the New Jersey impact reports, as well as the implementation report MDRC produced for all six states, was that subsidized employment was likely to remain a minor element of any welfare-to-work strategy. Although more time, resources, and effort would probably have resulted in larger programs, their scale would most likely still have been modest. Despite the attractiveness of the grant diversion funding mechanism in the abstract, subsidized employment may be inherently limited by a demand side constraint—few employers are typically interested in the subsidy.[23]

Saturation Work Programs

The Reagan administration's first set of legislative proposals would have required all states to operate a community work experience program; the law Congress actually passed made it a state option. However, even had the original Reagan proposal become law, it set no minimum standard for the scale of mandatory enrollment in the work program. Throughout the early to mid 1980s, the administration advocated a series of legislative proposals to establish participation standards and to extend the permissible set of work activities. In addition to proposing a requirement that all states operate CWEP, for example, it proposed to mandate that the principal wage earner in a two-parent family participate. The administration also proposed to give state welfare agencies the option to require applicants and recipients to look for work, for which it would provide federal matching funds. The optional activity—job search—passed, with some limitations, as part of the Tax Equity and Fiscal Responsibility Act of 1982, but the state mandates for CWEP did not. The administration continued to press for new state mandates over the next several years, but without success. For example, the Reagan administration proposed that states be required to involve increasing percentages of nonexempt welfare recipients in a limited set of work activities in any given month. It was in this context (setting monthly participation standards for mandated work activities) that OFA initiated the work saturation demonstrations.

On June 1, 1984, OFA published its second annual set of research priorities. The major project it proposed to fund was a demonstration of saturation work programs in an urban area. As background, it asserted that "there has been no large-scale attempt in a major urban center to involve *all* employable recipients in a comprehensive group of work activities, i.e., to 'saturate' the caseload." It proposed a project in a city of at least 400,000 inhabitants that would operate a program to include job search, work experience, and other work activities, with a goal of actively involving at least 75 percent of all eligible recipients in any given month. We funded the project much more generously than the grant diversion projects, potentially up to $2.1 million over three years. The effort was clearly intended to serve as a model for how the proposed legislation would operate.

This linkage to a legislative proposal (and its associated budget projection) had a significant effect on the nature of the evaluation. That the highest priority was an impact evaluation is reflected in the language of the announcement: "Emphasis will be on measuring levels of employment among participants, welfare grant reductions, [and] . . . deterrent effects . . . attributable to this demonstration. . . . An additional significant objective of the project will be the development of models." In a significant change in approach, the Reagan administration was now willing to propose a demonstration with an impact evaluation of a key legislative priority. Several factors were responsible for this major shift, including changes in senior political positions and the fact that this was a demonstration not of CWEP but of a broader, more comprehensive program.

Most important, however, was the administration's growing recognition that its legislative efforts to require states to operate more extensive and comprehensive work programs was being undermined by its own inaction in producing supportive evidence: the lack of evidence that these programs would result in substantial increases in employment and reductions in welfare dependency could be used to support opposition to the legislation. Anticipated impacts on welfare savings were particularly crucial, because the nonpartisan CBO was consistently crediting the Reagan administration's legislative proposals with AFDC savings that were much smaller than the administration's own estimates.[24] For example, in the president's budget for fiscal year 1984, the administration proposed to require states to operate mandatory job search and CWEP programs and estimated net savings in federal AFDC costs of $501 million for fiscal year 1985. By contrast, CBO estimated $40 million in savings for the proposal, with net savings for Job Search, based on the Azrin random assignment studies Judy describes in chapter 3, and net costs for CWEP, based in part on the negative Massachusetts experiment (Peskin 1983). By 1984, CBO's estimates were bolstered by MDRC's findings from its San Diego Work/Welfare site that following job search with workfare did little to increase its overall effects. In this way the congressional budget process—along with a group of bean-counting civil servants at CBO—came to have a significant influence on program evaluation. The Reagan administration, seeing that it could not ignore this process, began to take steps to build strong evidence in support of its legislation rather than simply continuing to rely on the existing weak evidence that was convincing only to those already convinced. As the Work/Welfare demonstration results became available, they played the central role in cost estimates for legislative proposals related to work. Janice Peskin, who was responsible for CBO estimates in this period, remembers estimating the effects of the work provisions of the Family Support Act: "I used MDRC's published results extensively and used all those available at the time that I had to complete the estimate. . . . I cannot imagine how these estimates would have been completed without the availability of the MDRC experiments."

The emphasis on impact evaluation for a project that embodied a high legislative priority was a step forward, in that the administration was now willing to invest in developing evidence for its policy proposals. But lack of a requirement for random assignment was a step backward from the grant diversion announcement, although this omission was more a feasibility and methods calculation than a policy or political concern. From the feasibility perspective, we considered it very important to initiate a saturation project but were unsure we could find a site both capable of operating a saturation program for even a subset of its welfare population and open to an experimental design. Even more important, we were interested in measuring the deterrent effects of a saturation program but were uncertain whether states would propose to saturate an entire geographical area, which would leave no unserved recipients to form a control group.[25] Because of these uncertainties an experimental design was not required, but it was also not precluded.

As it turned out, two promising projects emerged, both based on individual random assignment, one of them again thanks in good part to MDRC. MDRC took the initiative to create a strong proposal with the state of California and the county of San Diego that had, as noted, previously been a site in MDRC's Work/Welfare demonstration. The essence of the proposal was to add a component to the previous sequence of job search followed by CWEP, which would assess individuals who were unsuccessful in finding work after the first two components and move them into a broad set of work activities that would keep them continuously engaged. This, the Saturation Work Initiative Model (SWIM), was clearly our first choice among the applicants. The second proposal was from the state of Pennsylvania to conduct a saturation project in Philadelphia—the Pennsylvania Saturation Work Program. The Philadelphia design was a more open and less fixed sequence, but it also included a significant CWEP component. Because Philadelphia had much less experience in running work programs, and because the state itself proposed to conduct the evaluation, we understood that such a project was much riskier than San Diego's. Nonetheless, the opportunity to run two projects, one of which would be in a major city in the Northeast, led us to take on the risk; so we doubled the funding and awarded grants to both California and Pennsylvania.

The Pennsylvania demonstration was somewhat successful, but in the end it failed for the reasons that concerned us at the outset, plus some more. In addition to lack of programmatic experience, there was a struggle between the more conservative state and the more liberal city over whether to operate CWEP at all. State staff worked hard to carry out the evaluation and might have accomplished it had staffing cutbacks not made it impossible. Remaining state staff produced a preliminary report suggesting that random assignment had been successfully carried out and that the project had modest but positive impacts on earnings. However, refining the results required much more data cleaning and analytic effort than state staff could accomplish, despite their best efforts. The state higher-ups did not regard failure to produce a final report as a black mark, as a quality research organization would have. Once again we learned an expensive but valuable lesson; and we approved no more projects in which state staff were proposed as evaluators.

The Saturation Work Initiative Model, however, would lead to important implementation and impact results (Friedlander and Hamilton 1993), as Judy summarizes in chapter 6. For the heads of single-parent families, SWIM produced a combination of earnings increases and welfare reductions that, over five years, produced a return to government of $2.30 for every $1 invested in it. Even more significant for the national policy debate over participation rates were the implementation findings, which revealed more clearly than previous studies how welfare dynamics as well as other situational factors lead to much less than ongoing, universal participation. Despite working with all mandatory participants, SWIM reached an average monthly engagement rate of only about 50 percent. Because of the rigor of both design and implementation, the SWIM evaluation strongly suggested that maximum feasible monthly participation rates were much less than 100 percent.

Teen Parent Demonstration

The Teen Parent demonstration (TPD) would mark our most significant step forward in this period of building institutional capacity to design and fund experimental evaluations. Although further procedural improvements would be made as the agency and its successors funded subsequent evaluations, in this demonstration we addressed and overcame many of the weaknesses of previous efforts.

The main roots of TPD were a series of studies on welfare dynamics funded in the early 1980s by ASPE. The most famous product of that series was the first, a study of the distribution of lengths of AFDC spells noted by Judy in chapter 4 (Bane and Ellwood 1983). Among other things, it firmly established the reality of long-term dependency for part of the caseload and linked early childbearing to long-term recipiency. They found two broad categories of welfare recipients. The large majority of mothers who entered AFDC had relatively brief spells of welfare, and these mothers typically were older, relatively better educated, and divorced rather than never married. But a relatively small proportion of entrants stayed much longer, and their accumulation of time on AFDC meant that they made up the majority of current recipients at any point in time. They typically had children earlier in life, had not completed high school, and had never married the fathers of their children.

After funding a follow-up to the Bane-Ellwood (1983) study by June O'Neill and colleagues at the Urban Institute (O'Neill et al. 1984), ASPE funded Mathematica Policy Research, with a subcontract to David Ellwood (1986), to examine whether targeting self-sufficiency interventions to likely long-term recipients of AFDC would be an effective strategy. The resulting study suggested that early intervention could have a payoff in reducing long-term dependency.[26]

By 1985, when the analyses from the Ellwood (1986) study were becoming available to HHS, we in OFA had now become the primary advocate for mandatory work programs for AFDC recipients. To me it seemed a natural extension of this perspective to test mandatory participation of teen parents in self-sufficiency activities appropriate to their young age. Given the age of the mothers, political officials in the administration were likely to be open to a broader range of work activities for the young mothers, including education. Since teen parents were typically exempt from WIN because they had children under six, the project would be structured as a section 1115 project, and we would provide the necessary waivers to states operating the demonstrations. Barnhart approved the basic approach of the proposed project, and my office pressed ahead with planning for it.

REORGANIZATION AND A CHANGE IN LEADERSHIP Barnhart's initial approval of the project, however, was soon to prove insufficient for its implementation. In December 1985, the former governor of Indiana, Otis Bowen, became the secretary of HHS. By early April 1986, OFA had undergone a substantial reorganization—becoming, along with several other HHS components, a new operating division, the Family Support Administration.[27] When Wayne Stanton, a former head of Indiana's Department of Public Welfare, was named assistant secretary for this new agency on April 4, 1986, Barnhart resigned as head of OFA, and Harvey Veith, who had previously directed the Office of Community Services, replaced her.

The shift in political leadership left me in a precarious position. In November of 1985, when my immediate supervisor left government to become a consultant, I had been appointed acting director of OFA's Office of Policy and Evaluation. The acting directorship was a senior executive service position, which would be a major promotion for me. But the actual promotion would take time, and given the reorganization, it was not at all clear that the position would remain at the senior executive service level. By the end of the week in which Barnhart resigned, Stanton came to OFA and addressed the entire staff. He stated his view that the most important program in the new Family Support Administration would be Child Support Enforcement. His view was already widely known and no real surprise. But things got worse. He went on to describe OFA as a weak and ineffective agency, a "rubber-stamp" organization in his terms, and said that things would soon change under his leadership.

I was angry, wanted to leave, and put out feelers, particularly to contacts in SSA, asking about other job possibilities. But I soon cooled off (and nothing else immediately materialized), realizing that if I wanted to continue doing welfare policy and evaluation, and if I wanted a promotion, I would have to get the higher-level staff job, and this meant I would have to report directly to Stanton. (Senior executive service slots are tightly allocated, and clearly there would be no new ones in OFA.) To do so, I would have to establish a relationship of trust and competence with Veith, which proved easy to do, and much more important, and much harder, with Stanton.

Veith signed off on the Teen Parent demonstration, and we issued an announcement to states on May 1, 1986, advertising the availability of grants to run TPD programs. It took somewhat longer for me to establish a relationship with Stanton. My first step began with the submission of OFA's legislative budget. My staff and I put together a set of legislative proposals that were pretty much what the administration had submitted the previous year, and I made a special effort to meet with Stanton and have him approve our submittal. The meeting worked to my advantage, as I was able to showcase my understanding of the Reagan administration's welfare policy and, even more important, confirm my deference to his authority by clearing the proposals with him (which not all my peers in the other programs did). By the fall of 1986, I had been promoted in an acting capacity to a higher-level policy and evaluation job, the associate administrator for policy and evaluation for the recently created Family Support Administration. In this new position I was able to obtain Stanton's approval to continue the launch of the TPD project the following January.

Working directly with Stanton was neither easy nor pleasant. However, it did have large advantages quite apart from the promotion. Stanton cared little about welfare and even less about research. Since through my policy role he came to trust me, by and large he delegated these areas to me. With respect to research, which necessarily had much lower visibility, my staff and I were able pretty much to exercise our judgment on major projects. Since this was the only example of my having a less than forthright relationship with an assistant secretary for whom I worked, I count myself fortunate—although I continue to think the strategies I felt it necessary to use in that instance occur far less frequently in reality than conspiracy theorists may be tempted to believe.

NEW INSIGHTS INTO FUNDING AND MANAGING AN EVALUATION   By the time we began planning TPD, we had come to appreciate the operational difficulties of putting new interventions in place and to understand that insufficient funding contributed to these problems. We had also learned that our own limited travel funds gave us too little ability to monitor demonstration sites directly and to assist them in overcoming implementation problems. Furthermore, it had become clear that high-quality evaluation (quite apart from the cost of the demonstration itself) was more expensive than we had been assuming and that the overall funding structure had to be separate, so that the operational and evaluation concerns did not compete with each other. Finally, we had realized that giving money to states via grants to both provide the intervention and conduct the evaluation left us with insufficient control over not only the evaluation (the evaluator had a contract with the state, not the federal government) but also the intervention (we had no good agent to push for quality). Although giving money directly to states could produce successful results with an accomplished research firm involved, on average the yield of winners was too low.

Accordingly, TPD was structured differently. There were two separate funding processes: one offered grants to states to develop and operate the programs; a second procured a contract with a research firm to conduct the evaluation. To aid the local programs in designing and operating an intervention of sufficient quality and scale to be a fair test of the core idea, the evaluator was also tasked with providing technical assistance to the states and their local sites. Even in the grant announcement there was an entirely new level of detail. The substantive project descriptions of both the grant diversion and saturation work announcements were three paragraphs, the last of which was about funding level and mechanism. Although the TPD description itself was only six paragraphs, it was accompanied by a fifteen-page section on grant guidelines that, though it allowed for substantial flexibility, was also quite prescriptive. For example, the guidelines required that the intervention be mandatory, with sanctions for individuals who did not cooperate; be full time, minimum participation being thirty hours per week; include case management and a self-sufficiency plan; provide for necessary child care and transportation; require full participation and thus include all teen parents who were assigned to the program group; and provide for a balance of education and more directly work-oriented activities according to the age and education attainment of the teen parent. In addition, the requirements for paternity establishment and child support enforcement took up a page and a half of the guidelines. With respect to meeting evaluation needs, the announcement required the state to make 3,600 teen parents available for random assignment over a three-year period and to cooperate with the evaluator, which would be chosen by HHS. To support the operation of the demonstration, we provided each state with about $3.25 million over four years.

One consequence of moving from a grant to a contract vehicle was that in TPD and subsequent major procurements, I played no role in selecting the contractor. Once I had reviewed and approved the request for proposals and appointed a review panel, the actual selection of a contractor was out of my hands.

We decided to broach the idea of a partnership with ASPE, because we thought it would improve the odds for success. As noted, ASPE had funded the underlying research, suggesting that earlier intervention with teen parents on AFDC might improve their economic outcomes, and still had staff who were well versed in that research. It seemed to me that having more good heads working on issues could only improve the outcome. This was especially true given that TPD would make the federal government much more directly responsible for the result (the point of the new approach, after all) than had the earlier approach of providing grants to states. Sharing the responsibilities would also have the advantage of sharing the costs of this unusually expensive project.[28] Finally, although most of the ASPE staff experienced with random assignment studies had left, the agency had a strong history in that arena.

ASPE's response was positive. We quickly worked out an arrangement in which my office would fund the grants to the states and the technical assistance portion of the contract, and each of us would provide half the cost of the evaluation. We also agreed that ASPE would officially manage the contract (Reuben Snipper served as project officer), and we would officially manage the grants (Nancye Campbell was the project officer). Finally, we agreed that the two agencies would make all decisions on contracts and grants jointly and that, informally, Snipper and Campbell would comanage both parts of the project. This worked out well in practice and was a form of arrangement we would repeat in later projects. One great benefit of the partnership is that it supported a more general partnership in support of experimental design, which both my office and ASPE continued.

As expected, the increased resources directed to operational issues played an important role in improving implementation quality. Although TPD had only modest impacts on employment, that was not a result of implementation failure. In addition to the resources themselves, the greater responsibility for the evaluation that the contract mechanism entailed resulted in greater agency ownership and sense of commitment to ensuring project success.[29] This was most evident in connection with ensuring that the states and local sites adhered to the program model set forth in the request for proposals. To us, the mandatory nature of the intervention was central, which the grant guidelines made clear. For example, they described how individuals were to be sanctioned and stated that supervisory approvals were required for exemptions. Nonetheless, despite the agreement that the states (New Jersey and Illinois) had made, the local sites resisted sanctioning noncooperative recipients. Campbell and I made trips to both states and met with the human services commissioners and their staffs to reiterate that mandatory participation was not an option but a condition of their having accepted the grant. Even more important were Campbell's skills and her commitment to operational success. Having started her career as a food stamps supervisor in a local welfare office, she has one of the best "noses" for implementation quality of anyone I have ever met. She probed and pushed the local sites continuously and effectively. As Rebecca Maynard, the principal investigator for the project recalls, "Without Nancye Campbell, there wouldn't have been a TPD."

NEXT STEPS

The resulting skills of HHS staff and their dedication to overseeing high-quality evaluation, as well as their growing capacity to manage large-scale experiments, would become a critical building block for the more substantial and ambitious agenda of experimental studies that followed. Our new partnership with ASPE also proved crucial in pursuit of that agenda, as the two agencies continued to cofund and comanage subsequent random assignment studies.

Judy continues our story in chapter 6, with an extended discussion of the results of the Work/Welfare demonstration and the impacts of those results on policy and practice. In chapter 7, I describe the evolution of the waiver story, in which my office and ASPE proved to be key allies and partners in the internal challenges we would shortly confront, with crucial help from the Office of Management and Budget, as we sought to expand the role of random assignment in government-sponsored evaluations. In chapters 8, 9, and 10, Judy and I describe the major random assignment studies that moved our evaluation agenda forward and, together, built a body of knowledge that was much more comprehensive than the simple sum of its parts.

CHAPTER 6

The Work/Welfare Demonstration: Lessons About Programs, Research, and Dissemination*

Research at MDRC was the basis of our 1988 legislation.

—Senator Daniel Patrick Moynihan[1]

The state programs constitute almost a work-and-welfare laboratory, and the well-regarded Manpower Demonstration Research Corp. has carefully studied [many] of them. The results . . . suggest that work requirements may be neither as punitive nor as effective as past debate on the subject has made them out to be. The reports could help defuse this issue.

—*Washington Post*[2]

Training taught me the advantage of [random assignment], but when I came to Washington I realized that it wasn't just an advantage, it was an absolute necessity.

—Ron Haskins[3]

The Work/Welfare demonstration was the major turning point in our story. If Supported Work and the WIN Labs put a toe in the real world, this project was an immersion. At the start, we at MDRC fretted over all of the prerequisites to success: recruiting the states, getting the money, gaining federal coop-

*Chapter 6 authored by Judith M. Gueron.

eration, implementing random assignment, obtaining quality data, sustaining the project long enough to produce meaningful results, and completing the studies within budget. Once those challenges were overcome, we moved on to the payoff of distilling and sharing the lessons.

LESSONS ABOUT PROGRAM AND POLICY

The Work/Welfare demonstration ended up being a random assignment study of eight state programs. The six mandatory ones and the San Diego Saturation Work Initiative Model (SWIM) evaluation were successful in answering five fundamental program and policy questions.[4] Was it feasible to impose a participation obligation? Was workfare more than simply makework, and was it considered fair? Did the programs increase employment and reduce welfare? Did the programs save money for taxpayers? Were outcomes and before-after comparisons potentially misleading?

Imposing a Participation Obligation

The threshold question was whether states would really make people participate. Our conclusion was yes. Despite limited funds, states were serious about imposing obligations. However, the combination of welfare turnover and realistic administrative lags meant that the maximum participation rate was around 50 percent.[5]

We further found that, depending on the state, 75 to 97 percent of welfare recipients who had not participated in the program had either satisfied the mandate (if not through participation then by getting a job or leaving welfare) or been sanctioned (that is, had their welfare grant reduced). That meant that at most only 25 percent were left uncovered by the programs. This impressive accomplishment was balanced against the reality that the requirements were generally short term. Because job search came first in a sequence, the only activity most people engaged in was looking for a job for several weeks; far fewer were in some form of workfare (at most a fifth of those who were eligible) or (with the exception of Baltimore and SWIM) education or training. Nor were the programs statewide. Subsequent studies (the California Greater Avenues for Independence program and Florida's Project Independence evaluations, discussed in chapter 8) explored the potential for full-scale implementation.

Workfare, Makework, and Fairness

Much of the workfare debate hinged on the character of the work-site experience. Supervisors judged the work important and said that participants' productivity and attendance were similar to those of most entry-level workers. The majority of welfare recipients reported that they were satisfied with their assignment, believed they were making a useful contribution (even though they would have preferred a paid job), and thought the work requirement (usually limited to three months) was fair. As one of our field researchers observed, "These welfare programs did not create the work ethic, they found it."

Increase in Employment and Reduction in Welfare

The states sought, in varying degrees, to increase work, reduce welfare, and make families better off. Overall, we found modest improvements on the first and a mixed story on the second and third. In five of the seven programs, in most years following random assignment, more mothers in the experimental than in the control group held unsubsidized jobs—for example, between 4 and 8 percentage points more at the end of the first year. Although there were many possible explanations for failure to show improvements in the remaining two states, we concluded that the most likely reason in West Virginia (where program planners anticipated no impact) was the extremely high unemployment rate and in Cook County (a very low-cost program that mainly monitored people and sanctioned those who did not participate) the program design.[6]

Some of the programs also produced welfare savings. The largest cut in the rolls occurred in Arkansas and SWIM, where at the end of the third year there was a 7 percentage point reduction in the share of people on welfare. Average total income from these two sources generally increased, but not by much. Because we relied on administrative records, we could not measure the impact on official poverty rates, but the results suggest it was minimal.

Savings to Taxpayers

The programs were relatively inexpensive, with average net costs per enrollee between $120 and $950. In most cases, this up-front outlay was more than offset by savings within two to five years, showing that social programs could be investments with clear payoffs, rather than a waste of public funds. (The first San Diego program, for example, returned $2.50 for $1.00 of initial costs.) This result set a high bar for judging the success of future programs.

Together, these findings show that states responded to the challenge of the 1981 Omnibus Budget Reconciliation Act (OBRA) legislation with reforms that dispelled the notion that welfare-to-work programs do not work. However, the initiatives were more incremental than radical, and the resulting programs, though often highly cost effective, had modest impacts on welfare and work behavior.

Outcomes and Before-After Comparisons

Experiments, as we stress repeatedly, determine the success of programs in terms of impacts, as measured by the difference in outcomes between the program groups and the control groups. As discussed in chapter 2, because the background pattern of behavior differs for different groups and contexts, high program outcomes do not necessarily reflect high impacts, and there may be differences among subgroups.

The welfare-to-work studies reaffirmed this conclusion. What we learned revealed that the commonsense strategy of giving priority to the most job-ready welfare recipients would have been a mistake. Although more disadvantaged welfare mothers (for example, those without recent work experience) were less likely to work and get off welfare after being in the program, they nonetheless showed the greatest improvement compared with similar people in the control group. This is because people with a work history were more likely to succeed even without the program.

As can be seen in figure 6.1, before-after comparisons can also be misleading. A focus on outcomes for the experimentals (the only people managers normally observe) suggests that both the Baltimore and Arkansas programs reduced welfare receipt (the figure on the right). The trend lines indicate that more than 90 percent of experimentals in Baltimore were on welfare at the start of the study and fewer than 50 percent three years later, a reduction of around 45 points. That looks like a whopping achievement. Arkansas also did well, with more than 65 percent initially on the rolls (the number is lower because random assignment occurred at application and some people never got on welfare) and close to 30 percent at the end of the demonstration.

But to say that the Baltimore program cut welfare in half clearly overstates its accomplishments. To have an impact, as shown by the vertical distance between the experimental and control lines in the figure, the program had not only to reduce welfare receipt but to reduce it more than the rapidly declining counterfactual. Arkansas did this; Baltimore did not. This has profound implications for the usefulness of common performance standards in assessing welfare reform programs. The employment data on the left side of the figure tell a similar story. Employment rates for people in the Baltimore program went up more over time than for people in the Arkansas program; however,

Figure 6.1   Trends in Average Quarterly Employment Rates and AFDC Receipt, Arkansas and Baltimore

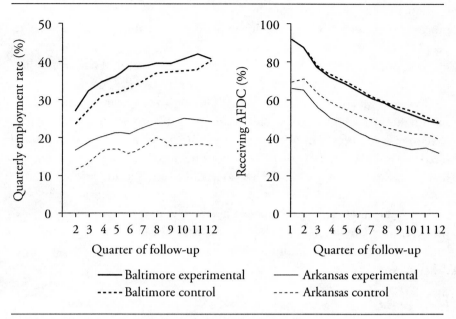

Source: Author's compilation based on Gueron and Pauly (1991, figures 4.4 and 4.6).

since the same is true for people in the control groups, Arkansas had the larger long-term impacts.

LESSONS ABOUT RESEARCH METHODS

David Greenberg, Donna Linksz, and Marvin Mandell (2003) conclude that the overall success of the Work/Welfare demonstration in producing superior information in a new and challenging context (state control, mandatory programs, regular offices) influenced the shape of subsequent social experiments. It also taught us a great deal about three specific methods issues.

Random Assignment in Welfare Offices

We had already conducted random assignment for AFDC (Aid to Families with Dependent Children) recipients in Work Incentive (WIN) offices (see chapter 3). The Work/Welfare demonstration broke new ground in conducting random assignment when people were applying for welfare.

To address the obvious fact that program staff generally dislike random assignment, we expanded on the strategies used in earlier projects. We sought to limit the burden by lodging the experiments in each site's unique intake process in a way that would minimize disruption, maintain the number of people served, and maximize intellectual yield. We also provided extensive training, aimed to persuade staff that the study's success could have real value for them and possibly also for welfare recipients.

However, we did not rely on trust; we sought to keep direct control over the intake process so that people could not get onto welfare or into the welfare-to-work program, initially or later, without passing through a monitored gateway. At first, bowing to local pressure in two sites, we made mistakes that let staff game the system.[7] We then regrouped and put in place a uniform process that involved phoning in to MDRC. This both determined who was subject to random assignment and designated people's experimental or control status. In later studies, as we gained confidence in our ability to ensure local cooperation, and as computer systems improved, we further streamlined the process.

Legal and Ethical Concerns

The second major change from our 1970s studies was in the handling of the legal and ethical issues raised in any random assignment study, as well as those specific to the new context, including the following:

- establishing procedures to inform people on welfare about the study and provide them with information about whether they could refuse to participate in the program or surveys or refuse access to their administrative records
- minimizing the extent to which the research exposed people to risks, including how to avoid an unacceptable or illegal denial of services or benefits
- establishing grievance procedures
- protecting data confidentiality and sharing data with other researchers

The Work/Welfare demonstration was the first to attempt random assignment in the 1980s reality of state control. We knew from the beginning that inadequate attention to ethical concerns could not only harm people in the study but also generate a backlash that could force delay or cancellation of the evaluation and poison the environment for future work. Both the risks and the stakes seemed especially high, since we were assessing highly political and controversial initiatives in studies that required the support of state commissioners and sometimes even governors.

LIMITING CHOICE AND INFORMED CONSENT   The mandatory nature of the programs, and our position as a state contractor, immediately put us in new territory. This surfaced during our initial 1982 meeting with the San Diego people (the first site to start random assignment). State and county officials preferred not to tell sample members about random assignment or seek informed consent, while we argued that, at a minimum, people should be told they were part of a special study and allowed to opt out of interviews.[8] Following from these different perspectives, MDRC and state staff wrestled with how the new issues posed by mandatory programs—when the mandate came not from the evaluator but from the state—should affect policies that in the past we had resolved by setting up special committees to deal with the protection of human subjects.[9]

At the states' insistence, we agreed that the research would not give people a choice of opting out of program requirements (because they were the law) or out of the basic study (which relied on a brief form completed as part of the intake process plus regular administrative records), since states had the right to use such records to assess their programs. The final design in all sites included the following elements: Random assignment would be used to create an experimental group subject to the new law and a control group excused from both the newly required services and the threatened financial penalties. People in both groups would be told they were in the study and subject to a lottery, informed of the grievance procedures, and given a choice about responding to any special surveys. Because people could not opt out of either random assignment or the records follow-up, the study would produce an unbiased answer to the basic question about the effect of the program on all people subject to the new requirements.[10]

The logic behind these decisions (which conformed to our reading of the federal regulations) was that the study did not impose risks beyond those that might flow from what the state planned to do anyway, since states routinely matched AFDC data with earnings information from unemployment insurance earnings records to check AFDC eligibility; people in the control group would continue to receive all entitlements and could volunteer for

other services in the community; and there would be no reduction in service levels.[11]

Welfare advocates did not object, in part because at this time they viewed
the new mandates as punitive and thought the controls were being favored
rather than denied a benefit—quite the opposite of their reaction to random
assignment in voluntary programs. Similarly, career staff (many of whom were
social workers) were less predisposed to mandates than the political leadership
and hence did not balk if some recipients were exempted.

Protecting Confidentiality and Sharing Data   Although states viewed the
evaluation as an integral part of their administration of welfare and informed
consent as neither required nor appropriate, they were extremely concerned
about protecting the privacy of their records. Thus our contracts required
that we keep any personally identifiable data confidential and use administrative records exclusively for the purpose of evaluating each state's program.

We strongly supported this emphasis on confidentiality but ran into problems when we considered the state as an outside party. From the state perspective, even though the money came mainly from the Ford Foundation and
federal funds funneled through the state, MDRC was the state's contractor.
State contract shops drew up agreements that usually contained language
more appropriate for purchasing a truck than an evaluation, prompting
lengthy negotiations as we sought minimally acceptable terms.

We successfully resisted one state's demand for access to our surveys with
workfare supervisors and participants so they could investigate practices that
concerned them. But issues about the appropriate handling of administrative
records were less easily resolved—a burgeoning problem, since by 1985 outside researchers began requesting access to the data.

In responding, we sought to balance staff morale, legal, business, and political issues. MDRC's staff—after spending years frenetically assembling the
data and churning out reports for each state—wanted the first crack at doing
less contract-driven analysis. Those of us running the organization wanted to
provide them this opportunity, when they finally had some free time and resources to act on it. Also, provisions in some of the state contracts and the
AFDC statute complicated the release of data to researchers who were not
associated with MDRC, and possibly even to those at MDRC, for analyses
that went beyond the agreed-on work. Furthermore, we had to ensure that the
release of data did not compromise confidentiality; yet we had no funding to

create public-use files, or to document the files so that others could access them, or to make staff available to respond to requests for assistance. Finally, we faced a conflict between viewing the data as a valuable corporate asset and being true to our general commitment to academic freedom, particularly since the project had been funded with foundation and public funds.

As a result, we made decisions that were subsequently criticized. In particular, we did not press to quickly resolve the access issue, contributing to a not undeserved view that we were being unduly proprietary about sharing data. However, by late 1985, we began negotiating with the states to resolve the legal issues and get agreement to three changes: permission to use the data to conduct additional analyses not funded under state contract, provision of administrative data for several additional years (beyond the twelve to twenty-four months in the final reports) so we could study longer-term impacts, and permission to share the data with other researchers. Reflecting the delicate nature of these negotiations, one state responded by asking us to return all their records data and refusing to provide data to extend the follow-up. Three others eventually provided the records and agreed to our and others' further analysis, and MDRC made the files available to outside researchers on request.

I now think the objections had a strong basis and that I should have pushed earlier and harder to make the data available to others. But hindsight is easy, and time dulls memory of the pressures.

Feasibility of Reliance on Administrative Records

The third major change from prior studies, as noted, was reliance on state and county administrative records, both to measure participation and to track the experimental and control groups' behavior at a scale that was vastly greater than the WIN Laboratory Project effort described in chapter 3. On balance, the strategy proved successful for measuring impacts. With persistence and the support of state commissioners, we were eventually able to obtain AFDC and unemployment insurance earnings records in all the states, and these were judged to be sufficiently accurate to produce unbiased estimates.[12]

It proved much more difficult to get good data on participation in activities provided by the test program or other community agencies. Since we did not have the funds or leverage to impose new tracking systems, we had hoped to rely on typically existing, but sometimes new, state and local WIN tracking systems—although we were concerned about quality, since the data were usually neither used by program operators nor tied to a high-stakes state function such as paying accurate AFDC benefits. Extensive quality control reviews confirmed our fears. At best, the data tended to show only whether someone was assigned to or scheduled for an activity, not whether he or she actually showed up, let alone for how many hours or days. In one state, there was no tracking system at all. As a result, we had to retreat from our plan to track everyone in the sample; for some states we even had to use costly case-file searches, manual logs, or sampling from community college and other records. Barbara Goldman, who headed the data collection effort, recalls that "there were huge problems. The WIN data were garbage . . . especially in education and training. We ended up using some of it, but always had to say that it measured assignments, not actual participation. . . . To this day, there is not one project we are part of that we haven't had to quality control and caveat the administrative records on participation. . . . Because of this, in later studies, we began using surveys as our primary way to measure participation."

As Carl Holman, a longtime member of the board, remarked at its May 15, 1986, meeting, the poor data reflected a deeper problem: "If they can't give you the data, they can't make the program work." This also meant that federal participation standards rested on the same weak foundation.

Although the success of our work encouraged researchers to rely on records data in most subsequent large-scale welfare evaluations, the experience also revealed that these data were much more difficult and costly to obtain and use than initially anticipated and were a key reason for the project's delays and budget problems. Quality varied, we had to improvise back-up strategies, and states were frequently implementing new systems at the very time we were negotiating access, suggesting that success depended on a combination of determination, flexibility, high-level intervention, and art.

THE STUDY'S EFFECT ON POLICY AND PRACTICE

We began the Work/Welfare demonstration with the goals of learning what works and informing others about the findings in the hope that better evidence would promote more effective policy. We consciously sought to avoid the Supported Work experience of a beautiful study that largely died on the bookshelf. In recounting how others saw our work, I use direct quotes liberally to minimize any bias I might have.

A wide variety of people—headed by New York's senator Daniel Patrick Moynihan—concluded that the research did have an unusual direct effect. They point to how it shifted thinking about welfare and welfare recipients, affected the design of state and local programs, and helped forge the consensus that led to new federal legislation. The result was a bill, the 1988 Family Support Act (FSA), that in its central provision replaced WIN with the Job Opportunities and Basic Skills Training program that increased funding for welfare-to-work programs, recast them in part in response to the findings, and even required a subsequent random assignment study. As a result, two studies of the welfare experiments conclude that FSA "is arguably the high mark of the political influence of evaluation *results*" (Rogers-Dillon 2004, 46, emphasis in original); "possibly more than any other social experiments, the welfare-to-work experiments have played an important role in policymaking" (Greenberg, Linksz, and Mandell 2003, 238).

Unprecedented Impact

Not all the provisions of the Job Opportunities and Basic Skills Training program built on expanding the programs to which MDRC's findings applied. A number of key ones were based on faith. Examples include the call for a greater investment in basic and remedial education (requiring that it be offered to people who lacked a high school diploma or had low basic skills); targeting intensive services on more disadvantaged recipients (most of whom remained on welfare after participating in job search or workfare programs); requiring high rates of participation; and extending the mandate to single mothers with children three to five years old. However, there was pretty universal agreement that MDRC's findings, and their dissemination, were more than usually influential, given that politics and values are all more influential than evidence and even in this case often proved "relatively impervious to facts" (Haskins 1991, 630).

The most telling comments came from some of the key actors. Senator Moynihan, who in January 1987 became chair of the subcommittee of the Senate Finance Committee responsible for drafting the Senate version of welfare reform, was a vocal supporter. A special symposium on passage of FSA, which featured contributions by both welfare researchers and welfare reform participants and observers, included the views of two people who played important roles as Democratic and Republican staff, respectively, for the relevant Senate and House committees—Erica Baum, recruited by Senator Moynihan in 1986 to draft the Senate's version of welfare legislation, and Ron Haskins, Republican staff member for the House Ways and Means Committee.[13]

From the beginning, according to Baum (1991, 603, 606), she and Senator Moynihan wanted the bill to reflect the best knowledge available: "the education, training, and work requirements in the legislation were substantially influenced by the evaluations of welfare-to-work programs conducted by the Manpower Demonstration Research Corporation, and the conduct of MDRC in the dissemination of these results contributed significantly to the effort's political success. . . . [MDRC's evaluations would] revolutionize the conduct of welfare-to-work program evaluations, help pave the way for FSA, and revitalize the link between social science research and policymaking."

Haskins (1991, 618, 622), tracing how research was used at all stages in the legislative process, notes that two studies were particularly influential:

> The Family Support Act offers a model of how research can help initiate a policy debate, how it can play a role in shaping the terms of the debate, and how members of Congress can become convinced that a given policy action should be taken because it will produce good outcomes in the long term. . . . The hearings record shows not simply that research is part of the routine process of congressional debate, but even more remarkably that MDRC . . . and the Bane and Ellwood studies . . . were virtually common knowledge among witnesses and members. . . . The studies seemed to create a common seedbed of reference carrying two messages: Lots of welfare mothers stay on the rolls a long time; and states know how to get more welfare mothers to work and save a little money in the process.

Michael Wiseman (1991, 658), the symposium editor, states that "MDRC built its contribution from the ground up as specifically an evaluation of programs intended to affect the duration of welfare spells and the extent of welfare dependence; the result was a triumph of entrepreneurship, analysis, and communication that will hereafter serve as a counterexample to those who deny the feasibility of positively affecting policy through social experimentation."

Peter Szanton (1991, 591, 597), also in the symposium, concludes that MDRC's studies had a "near-unprecedented impact" and "were pivotal to the passage of FSA." Here is his summary of what he learned from interviews with

House and Senate staffers, lobbyists, reporters, and others in the months following passage of the bill:

> I found a surprising consensus. The central players in the bargaining that pro-
> duced the legislation believe that without the findings of a timely set of analy-
> ses, the bill could not have retained its most significant elements—its employ-
> ment and training provisions. . . . The effect of [MDRC's findings] was
> profound. The staffer who drafted the Senate bill recalls: "That early pamphlet
> on 'Reforming Welfare with Work' was absolutely crucial. It was central to our
> argument for increased funding. It proved that some things worked." As a key
> lobbyist put it, "The MDRC studies . . . gave credibility to the governors' cen-
> tral position: that the states were doing things that worked." . . . According to
> [a National Governors Association] official, "For the first time, we could char-
> acterize reform as an investment." And a veteran Senate staffer remarked, "It
> was unique. In all the years I worked on welfare reform, we never had a body
> of data that showed what worked. Now we had it. And those findings were
> never contested at any level."

Lawrence Mead (1997, 50–51) writes later about how the 1980s studies
changed the debate.

> The disappointing results of voluntary education and training programs con-
> tributed to the sense in the 1970s and early 1980s that . . . the effect of any
> antipoverty program when evaluated was likely to be zero. . . . The verdict that
> nothing works was reversed mainly by the mandatory work programs that de-
> veloped in the 1980s. . . . When the early San Diego results became known in
> the mid-1980s, they deeply impressed Congress and the research community.
> Along with the political appeal of social contract, they do much to explain why
> the Family Support Act aimed to expand welfare employment programs
> around the country.

According to Szanton (1991, 597), the effect was felt on both sides of the
aisle: "The opinion of a key House Republican staff member is that 'MDRC's
big effect was on the Republicans. The Democrats wanted to spend the money
anyway. MDRC gave respectability to the idea that training programs had
some promise. After [the Comprehensive Employment and Training Act],

that was pretty remarkable. Without MDRC we either would have had no bill, or simply a benefit increase bill—and then probably a veto.'" Jonah Edelman (1995, 104) concurs: "The MDRC results affected Democrats as well. By showing that work for benefits . . . wasn't necessarily viewed as punitive, and that welfare recipients didn't especially mind working, MDRC's findings made many liberals, advocates in particular, accept that mandatory welfare-to-work programs weren't necessarily bad."

The view that research helped forge a new consensus was echoed by the press. Subsequent to the *Washington Post* editorial quoted at the beginning of the chapter, a *New York Times* editorial on August 24, 1987, said that MDRC "created the data base that convinced Republicans and Democrats that welfare recipients are willing and capable of working" and, in a March 9, 1993, article, quoted Senator Moynihan as crediting the MDRC studies with "providing the grounds for a Congressional consensus on overhauling the welfare system."

All these comments describe the effect on federal legislation and the research community. But to alter practice, the Work/Welfare demonstration had to change the behavior of state and local actors. The studies were designed to reach this audience, of course, since states and sometimes counties were the direct partners in the study and were customers for the results. And there is good evidence that the partnership strategy proved successful. By 1986, Arkansas had expanded its work program statewide, and ten counties in Maryland had adopted versions of the Baltimore model. Most impressive were developments in California, where the San Diego results helped propel the 1985 legislation in creating the statewide Greater Avenues for Independence program, which in its ambition was one of the forerunners of FSA.

Reasons for the Impact

Analysts of the 1980s generally point to five factors that explain the studies' unusual impact: their credibility, the findings themselves, their timeliness, the aggressive marketing of results by an organization regarded as impartial, and the policy environment. The credibility came from the combination of random assignment, replication, and relevance.

CREDIBILITY Research design, though regarded as arcane by many players in the policy arena, was front and center. A key Senate Democratic staffer told Szanton (1991, 598) why MDRC's conclusions were so readily accepted.

"'Experimental design, experimental design, experimental design! That was what mattered to me. For the first time we had random assignment, and controls, and replication across lots of states!' . . . A key Republican staffer concurs: 'You couldn't question the results. It was just much better than anything else we had. In the end, everybody was quoting MDRC. The only other authoritative source was [the Congressional Budget Office], and [it] was relying on MDRC's stuff.'"

Reinforcing the view that when experts argue, the research is ignored, Baum (1991, 609) notes that Congress reacted to the 1980s results because they were unambiguous and never challenged on methodological grounds:

> We took particular note of MDRC's findings and did not rely much on the claims of success being made on behalf of Governor Dukakis's much discussed Employment and Training (ET) program. ET supporters declared that their program was responsible for moving huge numbers of welfare recipients into the workforce and saving the state of Massachusetts millions of dollars. But Massachusetts was also enjoying an economic boom and an unemployment rate of about 3 percent. Without the same sort of rigorous research design employed by MDRC, it was impossible to say how many Massachusetts welfare recipients would have left the AFDC rolls for jobs anyway, even if ET had not existed.

As a sign of how this viewpoint had spread, a January 19, 1988, editorial in the *Washington Post* noted, "It is difficult to study such programs because many people are leaving welfare all the time. A governor can claim his work program moved some impressive percentage of mothers off welfare, and it turns out most of them would have moved off anyway. To guard against this, MDRC used control groups." Baum (1991, 609) also observes that MDRC found positive results across nearly all the states studied, despite the variation in design, conditions, cost, population, attitudes, and administrative capacity; and that the programs were delivered by regular staff in regular offices: "This is no minor matter. In the past, elaborate programs pilot-tested by sophisticated social scientists or a small number of program experts produced worthwhile findings. But when the programs were transplanted to real-world social agencies . . . the positive results disappeared. Since MDRC found that diverse state and local administrators could succeed on their own . . . we could be relatively confident that . . . other cities, counties, and states could do likewise."

The advantage of our having tested programs in communities with a range of experience and resources was felt at least as strongly at the state and local levels. On July 11, 1985, I went to Arkansas with Daniel Friedlander to brief Ray Scott, the director of the Department of Human Services, on the latest findings. Scott noted the importance of Arkansas's inclusion in the study, pointing out that its achievements were relevant to more parts of the country than were the stronger results from the far more costly program in San Diego. From his perspective, the Arkansas findings also indicated that any new federal law should allow substantial state flexibility rather than aim to set some dogmatic nationally uniform standard.

These reactions suggest that policy makers valued what researchers call external validity, though not in any formal statistical sense. Our three-part strategy—selecting states that were representative along the dimensions politically savvy folks viewed as most likely to affect success; collecting good descriptive data; and having samples large enough to produce valid estimates for each location—proved convincing. Staff at MDRC concluded that the structured but judgmental sampling process gave more face validity than would probably have come from a random selection of a smaller number of locations. In many situations, this is still likely to be the case.

Ron Haskins (1991, 619–20) shares Baum's view of the importance of random assignment, noting, "Of all MDRC's remarkable achievements, getting states to agree to random assignment—the sine qua non of social science—is its most important." Wiseman (1991, 662) states that the unusual impact on policy makers flowed not just from random assignment but also from the particular attention MDRC paid to keeping the methodology simple and presenting results in a consistent format: "Comparison of means between experimental and control groups given random assignment is as simple as methodology can get, and in the OBRA [Work/Welfare] demonstrations MDRC adhered slavishly to a common format for reports that emphasized straightforward presentation of regression-adjusted control and treatment group means for key variables and the difference between the two." David Greenberg and Marvin Mandell (1991, 643–45) add to this list the fact that the findings were interpreted by a single organization and spokesperson, fit a consistent pattern, and were viewed as positive and noncontroversial.

NATURE OF THE FINDINGS Thus methodology was clearly important, but so were the findings themselves and that they were accurately understood. As

Jason DeParle (2004, 99) writes, "Critics had called mandatory programs ineffective and punitive, arguing that the money would be better spent on volunteers. But participants told MDRC they considered the work rules fair. Plus the programs saved money—while some up-front costs were involved, the investment more than paid for itself, usually within five years. . . . Soon blue-ribbon panels were hailing a 'New Consensus.' Conservatives would agree to 'invest' more in welfare-to-work programs; liberals would agree to require some people to join. Spend more, demand more—it was a compelling idea."

These comments suggest that the research responded to the front-and-center issues facing welfare policy makers. The impact research was important, but so were the benefit-cost study and, in particular, our decision to estimate the effect on federal and state budgets. This evidence that a social program could be an investment that more than paid for itself in the not-so-long term was both unexpected and almost irresistible. But the work-site and process findings also proved critical to the politics of reform. The former helped convince liberals that mandates were not necessarily punitive. The latter provided support for advocates of devolution by showing that the states could be trusted to run programs that at some level both imposed demands and were successful.

TIMELINESS   Analysts of this period agree that the timeliness of publication helps explain the impact of the findings, but they differ on how much this was attributable to luck, our actions, or some of both. From her unusual perch in Moynihan's office, for example, Baum (1991, 608) argues the importance of luck: "What we didn't know, until MDRC's paper [Gueron 1987] appeared, was whether the OBRA demonstration programs produced any effects, good or bad. . . . Having the data on time to help shape and promote our legislative efforts was nothing short of amazing, and it was sheer dumb luck that MDRC's research reports reached us, as they did, just one step ahead of each critical juncture in the legislative process." Szanton (1991, 601) agrees with Baum that timing was "the most crucial aspect of the story," but in his opinion, "it was entrepreneurship, a nose for the key question, a supportive foundation, and organizational persistence, not dumb luck, that produced MDRC's findings when they were needed."

Greenberg and Mandel (1991, 643–45) point to another way in which timing augmented the studies' impact. Because we communicated results to

Congress almost as soon as they were produced, there was no time for others to gain sufficient familiarity with the findings to challenge the interpretation or methodology, which contributed to the impression that the findings were unambiguous.

On the "sheer dumb luck" front, it was also helpful that Bill Clinton was both governor of Arkansas during MDRC's study and the chairman of the National Governors Association during congressional debates around FSA. Our memos from this period provide a window on the future in describing the staff's awe at Clinton's mastery of the research and his political skill in the briefings and press conferences around the Arkansas interim and final reports. As the governors' spokesperson on welfare—for a bill that Senator Moynihan repeatedly labeled the "Governors' bill"—Clinton knew not only the issues but also the reality of participating in and interpreting a social experiment.

AGGRESSIVE MARKETING   Analysts of this period also uniformly conclude that credibility, timing, and the findings themselves were necessary but not sufficient to explain the unusual impact of the Work/Welfare demonstration findings. For that, they credit several aspects of the communication strategy and style. Here is Szanton's (1991, 598) description: "MDRC reported its results in a flood of technical reports, pamphlets, press releases, summaries of findings, seminars, and briefings. More than a hundred presentations—briefings, lectures, testimony—were made on some aspects of its work and welfare studies during 1986 and 1987."

Haskins (1991, 620, 629) discusses the process and its impact thus: "MDRC included a diverse set of groups in its briefings, all of which were playing an important role in welfare reform. . . . MDRC showed that timely distribution of reports, testimony before congressional committees, and perhaps most important, meetings with key congressional and administration staffers, can produce knowledge about and acceptance of research findings."

Baum (1991, 609–10) emphasizes the importance of the widespread perception of impartiality and lack of hype. "As a private, nonprofit research organization, MDRC had no axe to grind, political or otherwise. . . . No one got special treatment. The federal government had not hired MDRC to do the 1982 studies and had no control over the studies' design, the substance of the findings, or the timing of the release of those findings. Individual states had been required to contribute part of the research costs, but MDRC told their participating states the unvarnished truth—including those instances when their programs failed to produce favorable results."

Szanton (1991, 598) notes that one important result of our marketing strategy was press coverage, and that this in turn had an effect on Congress. "Asked what difference it would have made to welfare reform had MDRC not existed, a House Republican staffer . . . began by saying, 'Well, there wouldn't have been any media coverage—not on the WIN demo programs. No reporter would have known what they proved.' . . . But as it was, MDRC's work produced a stream of stories whose import was quite clear."

Although obviously taken with MDRC's style and impact, Szanton concludes that the studies and marketing would not have mattered had policy makers resisted change. Henry Aaron (1990, 278) reaches a similar conclusion: "The lesson of this experience seems to be that social science can facilitate policy when it finds that measures congenial to the values of elected officials are at least modestly beneficial."

POLITICAL CLIMATE How does one explain the fact that, during this period of fiscal austerity, moderately positive results were viewed as sufficiently encouraging to be offered as support for making expanded welfare-to-work programs the centerpiece of reform? From a longer-range vantage point, why was a strategy that was hailed as a success in 1988 recast as inadequate in 1996?

As the foregoing makes clear, one reason the findings resonated is that they appeared at a time when attitudes toward work, welfare, the poor, and federalism made action possible. Another is that, although key people responsible for FSA were well aware from MDRC's results that welfare-to-work programs were no panacea, they may nonetheless have thought this the most promising strategy or hoped the new provisions would boost effectiveness.

But was there yet another reason why the rhetoric of modest change was effective in 1988? After a speech I gave in 2006, a questioner asked, "How important was the role of Senator Moynihan?" Obviously, I cannot know the answer. But I can offer some insight as one who found herself in an unusual position from which to view the senator as a consumer of research.

Before the events leading up to passage of FSA, I knew the senator only through his writings and reputation and one experience of his unique style, when I testified before the Senate in February 1987. But that changed in July

1987, when I got my first phone call from him. Researchers do not expect senators to call them to inquire about data, ask whether the evidence supports a draft bill, or seek insight on how to deal with opposition. But Moynihan reached out to me repeatedly on all these issues. I anticipated his deep knowledge of the history and politics of earlier reform efforts. But I was stunned that he personally read research monographs and sought to understand the nuances of interpreting the data. I was also impressed by his unwavering integrity in using the findings. Even at moments that Senator Moynihan characterized to me as "live or die events" in the struggle for legislation he obviously cared deeply about, he did not overstate the results but consistently argued that, given the complexity of the problem, incremental improvements were to be expected.

A selection of the senator's comments before and after passage of FSA demonstrate his style. In hearings before the Senate Committee on Finance, October 14 and 28, 1987, "The message that MDRC has brought to us is that there is not a great deal that can be done suddenly; but there are important things that can be done steadily, and particularly now that we have the demography going for us." As quoted in the *Congressional Record* of July 31, 1992, "Since year one, we have always made clear that a program of this kind takes time to work out problems, gain understanding, and to change the bureaucratic behavior of people who for 50 years, have been coming into the welfare office, signing up and getting their checks and going away." And speaking before the Senate on August 7, 1995, "Spectacular results? No. We did not tell anybody to expect anything spectacular in the face of this demographic change. But real? Yes. . . . Remember, we did not promise a rose garden. We did not say it would be easy."

My conclusion is that having a remarkably sophisticated consumer of social science research in the Senate made a substantial difference. Here was someone who could fit new findings into a twenty-year debate about welfare reform, distinguish quality evidence from hype, and leverage research results for maximum impact. Would welfare legislation have passed if Moynihan had not been in the Senate? Possibly. Would it have been as much informed by research? Probably not.

However, if Moynihan had been alone, the research would not have resonated as it did. What also struck me during those years was the quality of the staff in the House and Senate and the extent to which they recognized, welcomed, and used reliable evidence.

MDRC'S STRATEGY FOR INFORMING
POLICY MAKERS

I have thus far concentrated on what others said about whether, how, and why the Work/Welfare studies affected policy. Here I describe what MDRC did. Although our initial vision was crude, communication was central to our thinking from the beginning, since the whole project was based on faith that reliable evidence on important issues, shared with the right people, could make a difference in the policy process. The leap from this hypothesis to a tactical strategy evolved opportunistically from the interaction of ambition, funding, and learning through doing, filtered through the externally focused lens that Blum, as president, brought to MDRC. In the end, we concluded that our impact was the result of many of the same factors others identified.

As was his wont, Michael Bangser, our general counsel and a senior reviewer for the project, started the internal debate on our public posture in a memo to Blum on October 15, 1982, shortly after she took over, posing a number of questions: Should we actively disseminate our findings? If so, how should we address subjective and judgmental issues about what approaches seem most promising? What should be our process for fielding press calls? How do we respond if states issue public relations pieces touting their programs and using participation in the MDRC-Ford project as evidence of legitimacy and significance? How do we avoid being identified with a particular state program, especially if we offer design assistance? Would providing such assistance affect the actual or perceived objectivity of our research? When do we share information with the states? What will we do if we discover abusive, unfair, discriminatory, or just plain stupid things going on? Do we defer comment until the final report?

Preconditions for Having an Impact on Policy

In addressing these and other questions, we started by putting the key building blocks in place. We then responded to three interacting factors: determining what we wanted to say, deciding on our audience and how to reach it, and obtaining some flexible funding.

ADDRESSING IMPORTANT ISSUES   The most important action was the starting point. We consciously designed the state studies to meet what we saw as the precondition for impacting policy: having something to say at the end, no matter how the research came out, about an issue that would be central to future national and state policy. Although our first cut at the research agenda emerged from our past experience, it did not stop there. The state–Ford Foundation–MDRC partnership forced us to test-market the research questions up front, through the process of selling the states and other funders on joining the study and then again on release of each of the twenty or so major reports. Thus it was no accident that the resulting narrative was relevant.

PRODUCING DEFENDABLE FINDINGS   The push for rigor, in contrast, came from within MDRC. Our brief institutional history had convinced us that we should not start a study unless we believed we would be able to defend it at the end. As a result, in setting the research agenda, we sought not only to identify the salient questions but also to understand which of them could be most definitively addressed. This led us to push for random assignment. But rigor was not limited to impacts. We firmly believed that, to reach the right conclusions, we needed a good understanding of implementation.

ENSURING VISIBILITY, INDEPENDENCE, AND REPETITION   Three other aspects of the project aided but were not all essential to success in impacting policy. First, these were not stealth initiatives. At the state level, they were often high-profile reforms, sporting the governor's name. At the national level, the states and cities selected gave relevance and weight to any findings. This suggested that our problem might not be how to generate interest—we were able to create impatience at the beginning merely by describing the study—but how to manage it responsibly. Second, though we expected and got political pressure on how to release findings, we were not subject to real control. In part thanks to the Ford umbrella, we had been successful in negotiating contracts that gave the states an opportunity to review and comment on our reports but not to embargo or rewrite them. Moreover, the federal government had no direct control over what we said and published. Third, the design of the project—state contracts requiring multiple reports and the two-year rolling state enrollment in the study—meant that once the reports started, we were producing a new one every three months for almost five years. This helped us create a media crescendo, where each topic would be discussed first from results in one state and then, again and again, from results in others.

Although ex post these points may seem obvious, many have overlooked their importance or gotten it backwards. Even research of the highest quality cannot address policy questions or yield lessons if it has not been structured to do so from the start. For research to be policy relevant at the end, one has to do the heavy lifting up front.

Six Operating Principles of Message and Style

We knew we would be releasing findings into a climate of shifting and sharply ideological disagreement. In this environment, we saw our role as educating people on what we learned and on some of the nuances—methodological, practical, and in terms of policy trade-offs—so that they could interpret and use our and others' findings in pursuit of their goals. In presenting the evidence, we also were affected by the strengths and limitations of the data: for example, we could produce highly reliable estimates of impacts on earnings and welfare, less reliable measures on income, and no direct evidence on children. In preparing reports and presentations, we debated how much to say and what to emphasize. We knew we had to be careful, since we might not have a second chance to get it right. This led us to rely on six operating principles—with some trial and error and without articulating them clearly at the time.

USE A SIMPLE AND UNIFORM STYLE IN ALL REPORTS   Our audience, our goal of cross-state comparison, and budget pressure all prompted a strategy of transparency and standardization. Since our most direct audience was state and county officials and legislators, people who typically were not familiar with the refinements of program evaluation, our first challenge was to make the results simple. In a meeting of the board on January 24, 1987, longtime member Carl Holman urged us to avoid complexity and jargon: "You got to put the fodder down where the stock can reach it." For openers, this meant we had to explain what the control group represented and what was meant by program impact, since as one state official put it, researchers and welfare officials "don't even speak the same language" (Greenberg, Linksz, and Mandell 2003, 291).

Our task was to make sure that our presentation did not obscure the great advantage of random assignment—that the analysis is straightforward and the results relatively easy to understand. We made an early decision to use the simplest possible graphs and tables, always showing in three columns the outcome for experimentals, the outcome for controls, and the difference between the two. Later we added a column for the percentage increase or decrease over the control group. We used easily understood measures, such as quarterly earnings or the percentage of people receiving welfare. The reports were free of equations, the tables not cluttered with statistics. The text walked the reader through each column and definition. Even so, we found that our public—after years of hearing effectiveness measured with before-after comparisons of outcomes—had great difficulty absorbing this unfamiliar vocabulary.

The push for standardization was in part related to the audience. Once people understood one set of outcome measures and how to read one set of tables, the last thing we wanted was to switch styles. In addition, we want our readers to be able to flip across reports and compare state results. To accomplish this, we reordered and restructured the administrative data into identical measures and presented them the same way every time.[14]

The other reason to standardize was to meet the demands of relentless budget pressure. We sought to contain staff time and gain economies of scale by making the reports follow a similar format. Nonetheless, the state reports were not identical in that they reflected the varying budgets, data, issues, and wishes raised by each state. The variation also reflected the evolution of the analysis over the three-year span of final reports, with later documents building on what was learned and tackling new questions. Thus over time Friedlander and his colleagues got increasingly sophisticated in subgroup analysis and in integrating what we knew about welfare turnover into the assessment of participation and impacts.

Share Positive and Negative Findings on Multiple Goals   Because good news for some could be considered neutral or bad news for others, our strategy was to release all state results to the public, not to privilege one outcome or goal over others, and to make a balanced presentation of the evidence and the trade-offs. Our challenge was to communicate several messages without confusing our audience and undermining our goal of simplicity.

Think Hard About How to Characterize the Results   Beginning with the first report on San Diego, we had endless discussions about how to characterize the impacts. Were they small, moderate, or important? The option to present the numbers and let the audience judge success or failure was tempting, but we knew that our first-level audience, those same state officials, had no context of other rigorous studies to judge our results and were thus likely to compare them with the more familiar operational or outcome data that were not tempered by a control group.

Our internal discussions went beyond how to characterize the impacts to deciding on the most appropriate number to use: the experimental-control difference or the percentage increase or decrease over the control group, which yielded a bigger absolute number and was probably what people thought we were saying anyway. Over the years, we came to believe that many people did not understand the difference and worried that, by stressing the former, we were understating results. We finally resolved to cast the findings as modest but important and eventually to show the findings both ways.

But though we sought to communicate the limited magnitude of change, we were also increasingly impressed by our findings—well aware of how hard it was to beat the null hypothesis of zero impact, given the tough standard of random assignment. As statistically significant and relatively consistent effects appeared—and we learned that the programs more than paid for themselves— we worked hard to combat the reaction that modest change was not worth the bother.

BE QUICK, PROTECT THE BRAND, AND SPEAK IN ONE VOICE   There is an inherent tension in research between getting the story out quickly and getting it right. In each state, we operated under contracts that usually specified a first report fifteen months after the program started (California called for one every year). In one sense this was helpful: we simply had to produce. But we also sought not to repeat the negative-income-tax story, where people struggled with limited success to retract findings that were released prematurely (Coyle and Wildavsky 1986, 179). And push as we might, there were some immutable realities. It takes time before an adequate number of people have been in the program and can be followed for long enough to judge impacts, it takes time to obtain and organize the data, and it takes time to conduct and write up the analysis. In addition, since almost all prior MDRC impact and benefit-cost work was produced by subcontractors, getting this work done meant hiring new staff and putting them on a data collection, analysis, and report-writing treadmill. Finally, we were determined that, though this project was really eight separate social experiments, it should remain one study, with a common intellectual agenda and an integration of the lessons.

To accomplish this, we made three structural decisions. First, we adopted a divide-and-conquer approach: identifying some meaty issues that could be answered early rather than waiting to have all the answers or rushing out results we were unsure of. Thus to the extent that we could get away with it, we limited the first reports to findings on implementation, participation, and workfare rather than impacts. Second, we set up a matrix management structure, with some people responsible for key study areas (process, work sites, impact, benefit-cost) and others assigned to coordinate the story in each state. Third, we set up a centralized review process to ensure a uniform quality brand for all MDRC reports and a clear and cumulating message. This last step worked, but it meant that the same small group of executive staff and, in most cases, our outside research advisory committee were involved, potentially creating a bottleneck.[15]

One part of protecting the brand was our concern with the tendency to rush to judgment. As I told our board in a January 10, 1985, memo, when we were preparing to release our first reliable impact and benefit-cost results thirty months after the start of random assignment, "Developing a plan to communicate this story will be important. We will need to both explain the complexity and not oversell the conclusiveness or generalizability of results from San Diego [the first such report], since we may find very different outcomes in other states."

Ten months later, in a November 30, 1985, memo to the board, Blum emphasized a corollary to the widespread press attention—the "continuing challenge to convince the press and legislators that we *really* are still analyzing data from the Work/Welfare Demonstration sites, and that our findings are still to come. . . . There is little understanding that solid information takes time to develop—or perhaps there is just no willingness to wait." As we worked to combat this, we continually sought to balance statements on rigor with cautions that results might change and that open questions remained.

EDUCATE PEOPLE ON METHODOLOGY AND INTERPRETATION　If we wanted our varied audiences to give special credence to our results and interpret them correctly, we had to help them in three areas: assessing the quality of other evidence purporting to address the same questions, explaining what lay behind the numbers, and being clear on what we were not saying.

In the first area, as is clear from comments quoted earlier in this chapter, we focused particularly on the unique strength of random assignment and the difference between outcomes and impacts, and we made headway on both issues, though from our perspective it felt like an unending task: we had to start from scratch with every new audience, a process that took scarce time and money.

In the second area—explaining what lay behind the numbers—we were much less successful. Several examples give a taste of the problem. One perennial issue was helping people interpret average impacts, given that people in the study did not experience the "average." We might report that experimentals earned an average of $2,000 a year, for example, or $400 more than controls. This would prompt a reaction: "How can people earn so little? What's the value of $400?" We knew that the $2,000 average included large numbers of people with no earnings and that the impacts were quite likely a combination of little or no change for people who would have worked anyway and big changes for others. Our difficulty was that, though we could state the problem, we could not easily solve it within the random assignment context.[16]

We were even less successful in explaining the distinctive nature of the 1980s studies. Previous random assignment evaluations of welfare or employment programs assessed an activity that was one component of the WIN or employment systems (for example, the Supported Work and the Louisville job search programs). Since the people studied were volunteers selected by the programs, I dubbed these selective-voluntary programs. Such programs are expected to affect only the high percentage of people in the study who actually participate in program services. In contrast, the Work/Welfare demonstration estimated the impact of changing an entire service delivery system, which included mandatory administrative practices and multiple activities. Because the systems studied were intended to reach a wide range of people eligible for regular AFDC or WIN—typically including both welfare applicants (some of whom never even completed the application process) and recipients—I called them broad-coverage programs. Such programs were expected to change the behavior of people who actually participated in the mandated job search, workfare, or other activities as well as those who did not participate but were subject to the monitoring, the message, and the threat or reality of financial sanctions for failing to meet program requirements. To capture both types of effects, we placed random assignment as early as feasible (often at welfare application), so the measured average impact of broad-coverage programs showed the effect of a system (not just the direct services) on diverse people subject to its requirements, only a minority of whom typically received employment services (Gueron and Pauly 1991, 70–78).[17]

Another way we explained the numbers was helping people interpret the path of program impacts over time. Impacts that were hoped to last for years often decayed or even vanished because either experimentals left or lost their jobs or people in the control group eventually got jobs and caught up. Did this mean the program was a failure? This might be a reasonable conclusion for a skills training program for people not on welfare—where the raison d'être for the up-front outlay was increasing long-term earnings. But welfare reformers have diverse goals, prominent among which is saving money. A program that gets people jobs sooner produces real savings: the state and federal governments avoid welfare outlays. Even if the impacts do not continue, the savings do not go away. The savings are banked. Thus from the budget perspective, short- and long-term results both matter. Control catch-up does not wipe out past gains.

In the final area of explaining what we were not saying, we sought to make a distinction essential to evidence-based policy, between not knowing whether something works and knowing it does not work. The need to do this increased with MDRC's reputation. As we emerged in 1987 as the authoritative source on welfare employment issues, both our results and our statements about open issues were used by various groups to defend assorted and often contradictory positions, as a kind of Good Housekeeping seal of approval. However hard we tried to be clear up front and refute misstatements, conscious and political misuse by some was inherent in the territory.

DRAW THE LESSONS, BUT STOP SHORT OF ADVOCACY   There is a continuum in communicating research—from sharing only the numbers in which one has the utmost confidence, to sharing a broader range of findings and insights, to providing a context for interpreting the findings, to suggesting the implications for policy and practice, to offering technical assistance, to advocating for a particular policy. In determining our comfort zone along this spectrum, we balanced internal and external pressures against our desire to protect our reputation for nonpartisan research.

The internal pressure came from our mission. MDRC was not created to be another excellent research center but to learn what works and to communicate what we learned in ways that would enhance the effectiveness of public programs. As we evolved in the late 1980s from primarily a learning organization (with only a few projects under our belt) to also a teaching organization (with unique expertise on welfare-to-work programs), the board and staff debated how far to push the teaching function. We had qualitative and quantitative research findings and a reservoir of insights gained by our operations staff during their years of observing and working with local programs. Every time staff spoke about our findings, they were asked for their views on issues that included but usually went way beyond the ones directly addressed in our formal research. Should we respond cautiously and share only what we were reasonably sure of, or should we be broad enough to be helpful to our impatient audiences in Congress and the states, which had to make decisions now and were convinced that we often knew a lot more than we were willing to say?

Robert Ivry, who led our operations staff during these years, pushed for a more active role in his December 27, 1983, memo to Blum: "It is time to do a better job both communicating what we know through available forums and capitalizing on our expertise in future technical assistance work. There should, however, be some ground rules for technical assistance. It should be limited to activities related to our demonstrations and confined to the lessons we have learned. We should not attempt to become another management consultant agency. . . . We should not be ashamed of this or need to apologize that this compromises our integrity. 'Technology transfer' as [the Office of Family Assistance] calls it should be an essential part of demonstrations."

At MDRC, we viewed providing technical assistance as a form of dissemination, but with a clear difference. In this work, we were usually applying what we knew in a context set by a paying client whose ultimate decisions we did not control. As we revisited the issue many times over the years, our overall conclusion was always that technical assistance should be part of our education toolkit, that we had a responsibility to share our knowledge if it could help others, that this type of activity would have positive feedback on MDRC (as professional development for staff and by making us more aware of the real issues on the ground), and that there was a style of such assistance that could go far in protecting us from being seen as the designers and advocates of the programs our clients ultimately adopted (programs that might bear no resemblance to our advice).

Nonetheless, although we conducted eleven technical assistance projects between 1984 and 1987, two factors kept it a small part of our portfolio: it often did not pay for itself, and it demanded time from senior staff who were already heavily committed to managing the larger projects. In later years, when we were able to get more foundations to provide support for some technical assistance projects, we used it to produce some of our most widely read publications. But overall we failed to institutionalize and efficiently deliver this type of knowledge.

The external pressure on us to provide technical assistance came from a number of directions. One was the Ford Foundation. As Gordon Berlin (then at the foundation) put it in an internal April 1986 memo, "Unless attention is paid to implementation of research findings in state and local programs, the transferability of those findings to real life settings may be lost. Because program design assistance can contribute immensely to the quality of services disadvantaged people receive, it is an important part of MDRC's future activity plan."

Pressure also came from client advocates. In 1987 MDRC staff concluded that, though our work was well known to state and federal administrators, it was less known and understood by people in advocacy groups. This led us to invite 100 national and local organizations to a forum at which we would share our findings and explain what we did, and they would share their views on the research and the priority open questions. The seriousness with which advocates took this opportunity underscored their view of the power of research in the congressional debate.

At the forum, no one seemed to question the integrity of our work, but many questioned our political neutrality and whether we addressed the right questions. Some blamed MDRC for the draft legislation's focus on work programs; others said we were too neutral in our presentations and urged us to advocate actively for certain interpretations and policies. With passions heating up and people pushing us to produce a one-page statement defending voluntary programs, Robert Greenstein, the highly respected head of the Center on Budget and Policy Priorities, one of the seven cosponsors of the event, stood up and said, "MDRC is not a lobbying organization. It is our job to produce such a statement." Although the discussion was at times testy, it was clear where the pressure was coming from, especially since some of the attendees were candid in telling us that a statement issued on MDRC's letterhead would be much more effective than an identical statement issued under their auspices. In the end, both the advocates and we went away convinced of the value of ongoing exchanges. We began to seek advocates' early and regular input in our future work with states, which led to their crucial support when opposition to random assignment exploded a few years later in Florida.

Other groups—the press, congressional staff, and state or federal officials—also pushed us to become more active participants in the debate. We were asked not only for comments and input on legislation but also for support on specific proposals, for a statement of our position on an issue, whether we would settle for certain language, and whether we would change the timing and content of our testimony.

Our response was to draw a sharp distinction between informing policy and lobbying for any particular result. In our state reports, we stuck closely to the findings. In cross-state monographs and testimony, we pushed to identify broader lessons and open issues, both still very much tied to the research. In state and local technical assistance, we went a step further, providing our best judgment based on research and broader operations knowledge while working to distinguish the evidence base for the two. In technical assistance, rather than advocating for any one solution we also adopted a style that related goals and means: for example, if the goal is increasing employment, this is what is known about how to do that; if the goal is reducing poverty, this is what is known, and so on.

Our application of these six principles created both political advantages and risks for the states. Although they had signed on for an independent evaluation, they clearly had not reckoned with the visibility the results would garner. When coverage was positive, they basked in the glow; when less than that, they sought relief or an acceptable way to move forward. States could not veto our reports, but they could pull the plug on the study by failing to supply the data or canceling our contract. We wanted to be honest, but we also wanted the opportunity to finish the work.[18] Overall, we found that the states could accept a straight story. But we also knew we were fortunate in having some positive results. We were well aware that, had we found negative or no impacts, or even no employment gains, we might have been out of business.

Spreading the Message

Although MDRC had gotten impressive press coverage for the Supported Work findings, at that time we were hardly a communications powerhouse. By the summer of 1982, Blum had begun a four-year transformation. She took an expansive view of our audience—including people in government (politicians and administrators) at the state and county as well as federal levels, the key interest groups, policy analysts and scholars, foundations, and the press and public. She knew the terrain and actors and sought to get our work on the agenda of what she considered all the key meetings—initially to introduce the study and then to share the findings. Although she was clearly operating strategically, her view was that communications was not a science, that you could not know in advance which presentation would bear fruit, and that as a result we should go after as many audiences as we could afford with face-to-face presentations, diverse written products, and outreach to the press. By the time I took over as president in mid-1986, Ivry, I, and others had absorbed her proactive strategy and continued to spread the word with the hope of contributing to a common base of accepted wisdom.

TARGET MULTIPLE AUDIENCES   Our communications strategy differed depending on our audience. At the state and county levels, we followed a retail strategy for states that participated in the demonstration, hosting conferences, testifying at legislative hearings, and conducting numerous briefings. The result was that welfare administrators often became effective communicators of the evaluation results and able to apply them as policy evolved in their state. In contrast, we adopted a primarily wholesale strategy in reaching other states and practitioners. At the federal level, in addition to keeping key people routinely informed on the progress of the project, we scheduled formal briefings around major new findings.

Over time, this strategy created a community of congressional staff and people within a wide range of Washington agencies who learned the findings together in real time. Since many of them stayed in their departmental or related jobs for years, key people working inside and outside government heard the emerging story, complete with cautions and limits; learned (with us) that random assignment could be done in this context and how other approaches fell short; had an opportunity to ask questions (some of which we could address in future reports); and, through this, came to own the methodology and the findings enough to apply them in their own work.[19]

Our outreach to the research community was less structured. In addition to delivering speeches, teaching occasional classes, and publishing articles, in 1984 we created the advisory committee, which had an unintended benefit that we did not realize until later: the review process brought prominent welfare researchers—in addition to those already on our board—into our learning circle and thus helped create advocates for the methods and spokespeople for the findings.

DEVELOP DIFFERENT PRODUCTS   Our desire to reach multiple audiences also affected the nature of our products and our policy of distributing them free to many audiences. We sought to go beyond lengthy research reports and occasional academic articles to separately published executive summaries, articles in journals likely to be read by welfare administrators, monographs, and short brochures. We struggled with mixed success to find a balance between pressures to produce detailed reports and more-analytic and shorter papers.

Another visible product was testimony, which we used to highlight both the basic findings and several overarching themes:

- Set realistic goals, since funding is limited and impacts modest.
- Give states flexibility, since resources vary and research has not identified a single most-effective model.
- Be cautious about outcome-based performance standards, since they might prompt states to target the most job-ready recipients, who benefit least from low- to moderate-cost activities.
- Set realistic participation standards, since findings suggest that the maximum feasible monthly activity rate, even in exceptional circumstances and with unlimited funds, is 50 percent.

REACH OUT TO THE PRESS   In earlier years, our media outreach was limited largely to periodic announcements and follow-up on major reports, plus occasional responses to requests for information. As our reputation grew in the mid-1980s, we began to be contacted regularly and widely cited. Many people contributed to this, but Sheila Mandel, our director of public affairs from 1978 until her death at the end of 1987, was the linchpin.

Although we were always gunning for coverage, in crafting and marketing press materials, our primary goal was accuracy. As a result, even more than in reports, we labored over press releases in an effort to make the findings important enough to spark interest, simple enough to generate an accurate sound bite, and nuanced enough not to overstate the findings or hide their complexity.

From the beginning, we adopted a few guidelines to help us deal with state officials who saw risks and opportunities in the substantial local and national coverage. We gave them draft press materials in advance and responded to suggestions; but, as with all our work, we did not let the states censor our releases and did not include quotes from state officials.

The combination of the study's nature, our press strategy, and the unusual times hit a high point in 1987, with three editorials in the *New York Times* mentioning MDRC in seven weeks. Even more gratifying was the thoughtful quality of much of the coverage, as illustrated by the response to our February 1986 release (which prompted articles and editorials in the *New York Times,* the *Wall Street Journal,* and the *Washington Post*; was picked up by all the major wire services; generated hundreds of articles across the country; and was covered by ABC, CBS, and CNN news). The headline in the February 24, 1986, *Chicago Tribune* read, "Workfare Findings: A Help but Not a Cure."

Seeking Funding for Communications

Presentations, products, and press outreach all take time and money. From the beginning of the Work/Welfare demonstration, the participating states made it clear that none of their funds could be used for activities beyond their specific study. In many cases, state staff—including commissioners—could not even use state funds to pay for travel to meetings or out-of-state conferences related to the project. Ford Foundation staff, in contrast, made equally clear both the high value they placed on ensuring that research spoke to policy makers and practitioners and their understanding that making this connection cost money. We had originally anticipated that Ford's Work/Welfare challenge grant could support our initially modest vision of dissemination and cross-state reports, but the budget pressures left us scrambling to stretch these funds to complete the core state studies, leaving that much less for communications activities.

How could we possibly pay for an expanded communications strategy? Credit for getting us through it goes to the Ford Foundation, which complemented its project support with generous general support, and to a number of other foundations. Many people have written about the key role such funding plays for nonprofit organizations, and the difficulty in obtaining it. MDRC was no different. For most of the organization's history, general support funds were almost our only flexible resources, resources we treasured and dedicated to two life-blood activities: developing new work and disseminating what we learned from all our projects. If our communications strategy was indeed a key explanation for the Work/Welfare studies' unusual impact on policy and practice, general support funding was the agent that made it happen. At the end, as noted in chapter 4, Ford supplemented this even further.

NEXT STEPS

MDRC emerged from the Work/Welfare demonstration with a strengthened commitment to random assignment. We realized that, despite innovation in many other states, the legacy of the early 1980s would come from the small number of such studies. We saw the power of impact and benefit-cost findings that were so credible they kept the witch doctors at bay, combined with other types of research that addressed attitudes, feasibility, implementation, and replicability.

We also saw that we were not alone in reaching these conclusions. Many of the relevant actors—among congressional staff and in federal and congressional agencies, public interest groups, and the states—and a small group of researchers had also come to value this type of evidence, providing a core community of supporters. Furthermore, participating states saw the experience as the entry ticket to a privileged learning community and the national limelight. This fed an enthusiasm to apply random assignment to further questions. If modest change produced modest results, would a greater investment in education and training make a greater difference, particularly for very disadvantaged welfare recipients, most of whom remained unemployed and on the rolls? Could success be replicated at larger scale? Would other approaches not only increase employment but also reduce poverty? As one sign of interest in questions such as these, in the Family Support Act of 1988 Congress required that the Department of Health and Human Services use random assignment in evaluating the act's centerpiece. "By funding this new evaluation, the federal government, in effect, paid homage to the usefulness of the information previously provided by the welfare-to-work experiments" (Greenberg, Linksz, and Mandell 2003, 244).

On the government side, the seeds had been planted for a new strategy to emerge. In chapter 7, Howard describes how the Department of Health and Human Services and the Office of Management and Budget would increasingly over time use their waiver leverage to compel states to conduct such studies.

On our side, we had gained a storehouse of knowledge, more diversified funding, and the skills to conduct large projects that required a blend of operational know-how and research expertise. But the future remained uncertain. The spark for our success in this new context had been a challenge grant from the Ford Foundation. Could we replicate that? Could we compete for and win large federal contracts? Could we get enough foundation funds for projects that fit our mission and thereby avoid becoming captive to the federal or state request-for-proposals process? Would states continue to be willing partners? In chapter 8, I continue MDRC's story.

CHAPTER 7

Waiver Evaluations: How Random Assignment Evaluation Came to Be the Standard for Approval*

> To accomplish these things we had to go to Washington and kiss someone's ring to say, "Please give us a chance to try something that might work."
>
> —Governor Tommy Thompson[1]

> Paraphrasing Senator Daniel Patrick Moynihan, political officials are entitled to their own policies, but not their own science.
>
> —Richard Bavier[2]

Throughout the first Reagan administration, the Department of Health and Human Services (HHS) applied the approval standard described in chapter 5 to section 1115 waiver applications: it approved waiver requests from states whose policy proposals were consistent with administration policy and denied those from states that wished to try anything different. Evaluation requirements were minimal, which was plainly permissible as a legal matter, given the simplicity of the standard and the broad secretarial discretion accompanying it. In this chapter I recount how that approval standard became increasingly untenable, as the federal stance on welfare reform shifted to the more federalist approach of encouraging states to test their alternative options for reform.

*Chapter 7 authored by Howard Rolston.

Table 7.1   Timeline of the Welfare Waiver Story and Related Events

Date	Event
July 1985	HHS offers North Carolina waivers for random assignment
February 1987	Reagan administration budget proposes waiver authority for a number of low-income programs
February 1987	Wisconsin governor Tommy Thompson meets with HHS secretary Otis Bowen to describe upcoming waiver request
July 1987	President Reagan creates ILIOAB
August 1987	OMB proposes randomly assigned cost control group
September 1987	HHS approves New Jersey demonstration without random assignment
November 1987	ILIOAB adopts guidelines with random assignment as the preferred design
April 1989	President George H. W. Bush creates the LIOB and directs it to provide substantial deference to state requests for nonrandom assignment designs
February 1992	Bush administration budget announces states as laboratories initiative
April 1992	Wisconsin governor Tommy Thompson agrees to random assignment for Bridefare
February 1993	President Bill Clinton tells governors of his support for waiver flexibility
August 1996	Temporary Assistance for Needy Families (TANF) becomes law, rendering waivers irrelevant

Source: Author's compilation.

In the process, federal officials gradually changed the waiver approval standard to one that focused primarily on holding the federal cost of state-initiated reform initiatives no higher than a ceiling—which they eventually decided to enforce by requiring inclusion of random assignment evaluations, using the control group experience to establish the cost cap (see table 7.1 for the major events in the welfare waiver story).

THE FIRST SKIRMISH

On April 19, 1985, less than three months into the second Reagan administration, the governor of North Carolina, James G. Martin, sent a letter to HHS secretary Margaret Heckler requesting a waiver of the state Aid to Families with Dependent Children (AFDC) plan to permit an increase in child care for welfare mothers. The requested approach was as follows: Child Care Resources, Inc., which administered public day care funds in Mecklenburg County, North Carolina, had received a $300,000 matching grant from the county, with which it had successfully raised an additional $300,000 from a number of private and public funders to establish a Child Care Recycling Fund. The purpose of the fund was to increase the availability of subsidized child care for AFDC-eligible parents who wanted to go to work by "recycling" the federal, state, and county AFDC (and food stamp) funds that would be "saved" because of reduced benefits to the AFDC parents who would go to work.

To us at HHS, this was an all too familiar claim—that spending more money to provide new benefits to welfare parents would increase employment and reduce welfare expenditures sufficiently to offset the cost of the new benefit. It was clear that every AFDC case that left the rolls and received subsidized child care to support employment would generate transfers to the fund, whether or not that mother would have found employment without the subsidized child care. In the vocabulary of program evaluation, the proposed recycling fund would rely on an overstatement of savings to AFDC because gross outcomes, not net impacts, would be the basis for the calculation. A further mark against approval, in the eyes of the administration, was that the child care benefit was simply continuing dependency, albeit in another form. Thus it would have been straightforward to deny the waiver request on the same ground used to deny the expanded income-disregard waivers—the project would not further the objectives of the act—except for one important fact. The executive director of Child Care Resources, Inc. was the niece of Jesse Helms, the conservative senator from North Carolina, and his office was supporting the North Carolina request.

After a delegation from Child Care Resources met with the HHS secretary (rather than receiving the standard denial), I was sent to North Carolina to meet with state and local officials as a follow-up. Secretary Heckler wrote Governor Martin on July 19 that the proposed project was potentially fundable under section 1115. The letter went on to assert that "a critical element of all experimental or demonstration projects is the evaluation component." It then described a list of eight specific issues that should be addressed in an application, which included the following: "To measure the effects of the project accurately, an experimental design will be needed." Unable to deny the request politically, we had elected to require a rigorous test of a policy we opposed. The thinking was that either the state and county would turn down the offer, or if they approved it, the evaluation would shed clear light on the policy—including not only an unbiased estimate of its impact and whether it did save the government money but also confirmation that some of the control group would obtain employment. The state elected not to accept the offer in that form. The Department of Health and Human Services, however, provided a grant to the state to plan for a similar project down the road. Two years later, after major changes in the administration's policies regarding the use of section 1115, North Carolina submitted a waiver application that HHS would approve, under essentially the same conditions as those stipulated in the earlier offer the state had rejected.

SHIFTS IN WAIVER POLICY

Throughout the first half of the 1980s the states expanded their use of the work option alternatives made available in the Omnibus Budget Reconciliation Act of 1981 and subsequent legislation. Although it was supportive of states' taking up these options, the Reagan administration continued its effort to require them to operate community work experience programs (CWEP)—that is, compulsory work for welfare recipients in return for their benefits. This made no headway in Congress because of both opposition from the states and lack of credible evidence to support the administration's claims for CWEP's effectiveness. The administration also introduced the notion of participation standards, which would require states to involve increasing numbers of recipients in a limited number of work activities. This policy push was equally unsuccessful. Most important, despite the growing welfare-to-work options, federal funding for these options was still very small; $264 million was available under the Work Incentive (WIN) program and the WIN demonstration for fiscal year 1985 but was declining every year, and states probably claimed another roughly $50 million per year under the title IV-A options in the AFDC program.

All this was to change dramatically in the second Reagan administration, however, owing in large part to the efforts of Charles "Chuck" Hobbs, who from 1985 to 1989 was director of the Office of Policy Development (OPD), an office within the White House. Hobbs believed that the vast majority of means-tested federal funds supported a "welfare industry" designed to support dependency and that the public funds spent on this industry would be better directed to empower individuals—a perspective that focused on the whole panoply of means-tested programs and the total amount spent on them rather than on specific proposals for changes to individual programs (Hobbs 1978). The consequence of this shift to a broader view of the welfare system as a whole was evident in President Reagan's February 4, 1986, State of the Union address, which directed "the White House Domestic [Policy] Council to present me by December 1, 1986, an evaluation of programs and a strategy for immediate action to meet the financial, educational, social, and safety concerns of poor families. I am talking about real and lasting emancipation, because the success of welfare should be judged by how many of its recipients become independent of welfare."

Following that State of the Union, Hobbs initiated a broad study of means-tested programs that culminated in *Up from Dependency: A New National Public Assistance Strategy* (Domestic Policy Council Low Income Opportunity Working Group 1986), a report that largely followed his view that enormous sums of money were spent to combat poverty in an ineffective manner. President Reagan used one of its statistics in his January 21, 1987, State of the Union address: "We've created a welfare monster that is a shocking indictment of our sense of priorities. Our national welfare system consists of some 59 major programs and over 6,000 pages of federal laws and regulations on which more than $132 billion was spent in 1985." He went on to say, "I will propose a new national welfare strategy—a program of welfare reform through state-sponsored, community-based demonstration projects." And he did. In February of 1987, as part of the president's fiscal year 1988 budget, the administration proposed that Congress allow states to apply to a statutorily created interagency board to operate demonstrations that could potentially involve waivers of federal law for any federally funded antipoverty program. Senator Robert Dole and Representative John Duncan sponsored the Low Income Opportunity Improvement Act, introducing it on February 27, 1987. The condition of this state flexibility would be a requirement that any state effort under the waiver authority result in no extra cost to the federal government. Nothing was said about how any "extra cost" would be identified and measured. To exercise this demonstration authority, the legislation would also create an executive branch board in the White House.

This multiprogram waiver proposal was viewed within the administration with varying degrees of enthusiasm. Outside the White House OPD, and even to an extent within it, there was skepticism that Congress would remove the many rules it had put in place for low-income programs. First, such an effort would face a daunting array of committees of jurisdiction. Second, and equally important, the proposal implicitly dismissed the incremental progress that had been made in the development of state welfare-to-work programs and the body of welfare-to-work findings, suggesting that even relatively modest state programs had demonstrated effects on increasing employment and decreasing welfare use. Among those in the administration, particularly in the Office of Management and Budget (OMB) and HHS, who continued to favor proposals to strengthen AFDC work requirements by establishing participation standards for states, there were concerns (supported by MDRC's emerging research) that previous legislative efforts had failed, at least in part, because they were too restrictive with respect to the work activities states would have had to require.

The Department of Health and Human Services, at the encouragement of OMB, developed a legislative proposal that would require states to increase participation in work activities over a five-year period; it would also reduce exemptions but allow much greater latitude than the administration had previously proposed regarding what activities states could count as meeting the standard. This proposal, titled Greater Opportunities Through Work, became part of the president's fiscal year 1988 budget, along with Hobbs's multiprogram waiver proposal. Although the administration's coupling of a waiver proposal and a work proposal defused the policy disagreement between Hobbs and OMB momentarily, the underlying tension between the OPD (which favored a welfare reform strategy based on federalism) and OMB and HHS (which favored one based on federal work mandates) would play out over the remainder of President Reagan's second term.

TESTING THE WATERS

On February 24, 1987, Tommy Thompson, the new governor of Wisconsin—an important part of whose agenda was to reform welfare in his state—met with HHS secretary Otis Bowen, himself a former governor (of Indiana). The purpose was to describe a package of welfare reforms requiring waivers of federal AFDC and Medicaid policy that Wisconsin intended to submit to HHS. The broad goal of the proposal was to reduce welfare dependency, with planned actions under waivers that would

1.   expand AFDC work requirements to parents with children under the age of six
2.   expand earnings disregards so that AFDC phased out with increased earnings more gradually than the four months that the thirty-and-one-third rule provided[3]
3.   extend the length of time former recipients who had left AFDC for work could receive Medicaid
4.   require teen parents and thirteen- to eighteen-year-old dependent children to attend school as a condition of AFDC eligibility (dubbed Learnfare)
5.   pay a lower benefit level to new arrivals to Wisconsin (dubbed Two-Tier)

Governor Thompson presented these proposals in the context of the White House task force's recommendation that states have flexibility to design their own welfare programs. He also proposed to reduce AFDC benefits by 6 percent (actually a 5 percent reduction, plus withholding of a scheduled 1 percent increase) that did not require federal approval. By this reduction he hoped to fund the expansion of Wisconsin's work programs and to claim additional federal matching from the federal savings that would accrue from the benefit reduction. Finally, the governor said that his preferred approach would be a block grant to the state so it could retain the full state and federal savings from any reduction in caseload and payments, although he acknowledged that this would require passage of the president's multiprogram waiver proposal.

Although it affirmed that much in Thompson's approach was consistent with the administration's waiver proposal, HHS's internal review focused on how the Wisconsin plan compared with administration's AFDC policy—that is, according to the then-current (Reagan's first term) standards for assessing section 1115 applications. For example, internal analyses dated February 20, 1987, prepared before the meeting between Secretary Bowen and Governor Thompson, noted that the state's narrowing of exemptions from mandatory work requirements was broadly consistent with the Greater Opportunities Through Work proposal. One such analysis also noted with respect to the expansion of earnings disregards that "the net outcome of such policies has been increased rather than decreased dependence on welfare." The department's initial perspective was to apply the "approve what we like, disapprove what we don't like" standard to Wisconsin's proposed demonstration, at the same time that another memo also preceding the meeting acknowledged that from a legal perspective, "much of what the State wants to do could be done under existing waiver authority. The limitation to this approach is that the waivers may result in additional Federal expenditures," unlike the administration's multiprogram waiver proposal, which "limits Federal monies to what would have been spent in the absence of the demonstration."

The response the secretary is reported to have made to the governor in the meeting also reflected the standards of the first Reagan administration. A memo by the Wisconsin Nutrition Project, based on a conversation with a state staff person in attendance at the meeting and dated the following day, described HHS as open to a proposal to lower the age of the youngest child that exempted a parent from work requirements and favorable to a requirement of school participation by teen parents and sixteen- to eighteen-year-old youth. It further noted that HHS had raised doubt about the authority to alter the disregards but also offered to "put staff on it and work with Wisconsin to figure out a possible project."[4] In addition, HHS was quoted as saying it lacked the legal authority to allow the state to continue to provide Medicaid to some lower-income non-AFDC recipients if it reduced benefits, as it had proposed.

Having a newly elected governor of the president's party meet with the secretary on an issue of high priority to both of them was certainly enough to capture our attention at HHS. In a follow-up to that meeting, Nancye Campbell and I visited Madison, Wisconsin, on March 19 and 20 to discuss options the state might pursue. Obviously, since the state was proposing waivers HHS would previously have denied out of hand, we were being sent not to negotiate but rather to explore the policy space for potentially viable middle ground that might prove acceptable to both parties and to provide technical assistance on the mechanics of developing an application.

As an example of this exploration, in discussing how the state might provide an earnings disregard that would more consistently leave working recipients better off than if they did not work, we discussed the possibility of a disregard less generous than the current thirty-and-one-third but one that would last longer (specifically a thirty-and-one-sixth disregard that would apply for twelve rather than four months). This was not something HHS would necessarily approve, just something we could analyze to determine whether it might receive favorable consideration. The discussion was based on the idea that such a policy change might be roughly neutral with respect to its effects on dependency and costs, since it would narrow eligibility for some, broaden it for others, and still be consistent with the state's objectives. The implication was that, although HHS might ultimately deny the waiver request on policy grounds (as it previously had), cost neutrality had also entered the negotiations as a consideration.[5] We were working under the assumption that, before any action could be taken, HHS would estimate the waiver's cost neutrality. There was still no sense that we would actually monitor the waiver's effects.

When Campbell and I arrived in Madison, we were surprised to see that the schedule for our meeting included a time slot for me to participate in a press conference with Governor Thompson.[6] The Madison press were present and, although the governor did most of the talking, I did have to answer a few questions, most of which related to the innovativeness of the governor's proposal. The surprise press conference gave me my first glimmer that when governors make welfare reform a major issue, visibility—and therefore stakes—can escalate dramatically.

Wisconsin submitted a formal section 1115 demonstration application on May 1. Not much movement occurred on the application until a June 25 meeting in Hobbs's office, called to discuss the Wisconsin proposal. I put forward the position that HHS should approve the overall project but deny the expansive provisions—the Medicaid extension and thirty-and-one-sixth—because they did not further the objectives of the act. The Office of Management and Budget supported my view, and the meeting reached agreement on this approach. Hobbs asked HHS to draft a letter to the state detailing the agreed-on position, for review by OMB and OPD.

At about the same time we began discussions with New Jersey, another state with a Republican governor—Thomas Kean, who would later chair the 9/11 Commission. On June 18 Drew Altman, the commissioner of the New Jersey Department of Human Services, wrote Hobbs requesting his support for a welfare reform project named Realizing Economic Achievement (REACH). On the same day, he submitted a section 1115 waiver application. The main feature of REACH was the removal of many of the existing exemptions to work requirements—including lowering the age of the youngest child that exempted a parent from six years to two years, achieving much higher participation rates, and extending Medicaid for up to a year when individuals left welfare owing to increased income from work. Altman's application estimated that these changes would result in $290 million in federal savings over five years. It also expressed concern with the fragmented waiver process and reminded Hobbs that Governor Kean was a supporter of President Reagan's legislative proposal to give states greater flexibility.

By the spring of 1987 it had became clear that the administration's bill proposing the use of block grants to allow states to demonstrate alternatives to a wide range of federal means-tested programs was unlikely to pass. At that time, Richard Bavier, a career civil servant at OFA (and later OMB policy analyst) who had supervised the AFDC waiver process and been detailed to OPD to work on *Up from Dependency*, wrote a memo to Hobbs explaining that the Food Stamp program, like AFDC and Medicaid, had statutory authority to provide states with waivers for research purposes and that rental assistance programs also undertook demonstration research using regulatory authority. Although some of these authorities were more limited than that for section 1115, Bavier suggested using them to waive provisions of low-income programs, pending (unlikely) passage of the president's legislative recommendations for a broader waiver authority. This led to a wider discussion that resulted in a July 17 memorandum to President Reagan recommending that he establish an Interagency Low Income Opportunity Advisory Board (ILIOAB). The board's role would be to coordinate the administration's low-income strategy and "to encourage and facilitate state [welfare] reform experiments." The board would also provide governors with "one-stop shopping." Exercise of waiver authority would remain with individual department secretaries, as the statutes governing the relevant programs required, but the ILIOAB would serve "as a forum to discuss system-wide implications of waiver requests, particularly those requests which cover more than one program." On July 21, the White House announced creation of the board. The press release was not explicit about the ILIOAB's role in waiver requests, but it did state that the board would review "policy alternatives . . . especially multi-program reform concepts or proposals of the States." In neither the recommendation nor the press release were criteria articulated on which the board would base its recommendations. The board chairman was identified: Charles Hobbs.

As the administration was forming the ILIOAB, Hobbs withdrew his support for the agreement reached in his office the previous month to place limits on the Wisconsin proposal and attempted to move the process to a more favorable decision for Wisconsin. For this purpose, he held two meetings in his office on the same day that formation of the ILIOAB was publicly announced. My political supervisor at that time, Wayne Stanton, was normally the person to approve or disapprove AFDC waiver requests. As such, he—along with William Roper (the head of the Health Care Financing Administration, the agency that administered Medicaid), who had waiver authority for that program, and Robert Helms, the assistant secretary for planning and evaluation—were the three HHS members of the ILIOAB. However, since Stanton's primary interest was child support enforcement, he by and large delegated his role on the board to me. As Hobbs had requested earlier, I brought to one of the July 21 meetings the letter Hobbs had ordered to be drafted, which approved the overall Wisconsin project but disapproved the proposed changes to the earnings disregards and the extension in Medicaid coverage.[7] This was, of course, the HHS preferred position and fully consistent with the agreement reached at the earlier meeting with Hobbs. But since Hobbs's desire to provide more flexibility to the state was not an issue HHS political leadership wanted to fight over, I was told to resist somewhat but ultimately go along with approving Wisconsin's current application unchanged.

The Department of Health and Human Services, however, was not the only party that needed to be convinced, nor the most powerful bureaucratically. The Office of Management and Budget, which also had formal membership on the board, had long held concerns about HHS's previous use of the section 1115 waiver authority to approve Medicaid expansions that ultimately proved costly. Several years earlier it had used its bureaucratic leverage in apportioning appropriated funds to HHS to successfully require the department to submit to OMB for prior review any section 1115 demonstration approvals that could result in additional costs of more than $1 million or affected more than 300 individuals.[8] The Office of Management and Budget now saw Hobbs's move to provide greater flexibility to governors as having the potential to open the flood gates on three open-ended entitlements—AFDC, Medicaid, and food stamps (which had a similar authority to section 1115 but, because of statutory restrictions prohibiting benefit reductions, was even more vulnerable to additional costs). The risk was particularly pronounced for Wisconsin and New Jersey, which were representing eligibility expansions as investments they claimed would actually save money because of incentive effects that would induce more welfare recipients to go to work. No career civil servant in either HHS or OMB believed that existing research supported these claims.[9] Indeed, contrary to what the states were asserting, most of us believed these elements of the state's proposals would almost certainly represent additional costs to the federal government.

At the July 21 meetings in Hobbs's office, HHS agreed to approve the Wisconsin waivers, but OMB strongly opposed doing so and continued to argue that the earnings disregard and Medicaid extension waivers should be denied. Representatives of OMB argued that the overall project would not clearly be cost neutral to the federal government, even if the state were allowed to count the benefit reduction as savings, despite the fact it did not require waivers. Most important, OMB laid down two key principles. First, we should not just estimate cost neutrality in advance but we should also monitor it during the project. Second, since section 1115 was a research authority (with which HHS, of course, agreed), an appropriate evaluation design should be part of any project approval. Underlying the second principle was the idea, similar to our thinking in the North Carolina case, that if HHS were going to approve state policies that the administration would have vigorously opposed at the national level, it should certainly want a rigorous evaluation of their actual effects.

Given the large political importance governors were beginning to place on welfare reform, at both HHS and OMB we were greatly concerned that, in the absence of a rigorous evaluation design, the incentive to proclaim success would trump the desire to produce objective evidence. There was still no discussion of any specific details regarding how to either monitor cost neutrality or design the evaluations. However, OMB did go so far as to urge that there be publicly articulated rules for how the administration would review section 1115 proposals (that is, that it should not be done simply on a case-by-case basis).

The OMB position was the first full articulation of federal cost neutrality as a principle for approving section 1115 waiver demonstrations, although all the agencies participating in the internal debate were known to agree on it (any differences were about how to measure and enforce it).[10] I believe this unstated policy consensus grew primarily out of the multiprogram waiver legislation, which required that there be no increased cost to the federal government—a consensus that was probably reinforced by everyone's realization that the Medicaid waivers granted earlier in the decade had indeed increased costs. Even Hobbs supported the principle of federal cost neutrality in theory; but given his later emerging views about measuring effects on costs, in practice he certainly was concerned more about providing flexibility to governors than about protecting the federal budget.

The meeting ended with agreement that staff from the participating agencies would work together to develop cost estimates, which was done over the next month, August 1987. Since all were used to developing cost estimates for legislative proposals, applying this experience to a proposed demonstration was familiar territory. We agreed to credit Wisconsin with savings from the benefit reduction, although it did not require waivers, and on the broad approach to costing out the proposal. Nonetheless, because of small differences in assumptions, all HHS's estimates showed the overall project saving money, whereas OMB presented a range of estimates including some that showed net cost increases. This kind of difference was not unexpected, since a large number of assumptions, most of which had only limited empirical basis, drove these estimates (which is still the case). The OMB estimates gave the agency further ammunition against approval (which an uncharitable observer might suspect could have influenced the assumptions they chose to use in the first place).

AN INSPIRATIONAL IDEA

Toward the end of August a new idea emerged that would, over a number of years, introduce a level of rigor into the evaluation of section 1115 projects that was unimaginable at the time. David Kleinberg, a senior career executive at OMB, suggested that we measure cost neutrality by a randomly assigned group of recipients who would continue to receive benefits under the old rules, and that this group—a cost control group—be the basis for estimating a cost-neutrality baseline. In other words, an extrapolation from the level of expenditures on the control group would constitute a cap on federal AFDC and Medicaid payments to the state during the demonstration period. According to Bavier's recollection, another senior career executive, Barbara Selfridge, who would carry much of the weight of OMB's battle with the White House OPD, described Kleinberg's proposal as an inspiration, and it certainly was.

As Kleinberg recalls, however, arriving at the idea of a cost control group was a group process, not his individual insight: "We kicked around ideas for a long time, a lot of different ideas. I don't remember them all. In fact, I don't remember very many of them. . . . There were probably five or ten internal meetings. . . . It was not some insight that I personally had." Using experimental methods to evaluate individual waiver demonstration policies was not a new idea. Knowledge of its feasibility and credibility was also widespread in the Washington welfare policy community as a result of MDRC's widely disseminated findings and OFA's sponsorship (one in partnership with the Office of the Assistant Secretary for Planning and Evaluation) of three significant experimental projects. What was new about Kleinberg's proposal was the suggestion to apply the experiment to the entire set of demonstration policies, thereby creating a systematic counterfactual. The benefits of using this randomly assigned cost control group were several. First, it removed the need to rely on estimates, about which there would always be competing but unverifiable assumptions and, hence, disagreement. In looking back, Kleinberg describes this as the central goal: "The objective was to have a reference point, that people would say, 'Yes, that works.' . . . How do you do something that is the least contentious way of doing it?"

In an interview in 2012, Keith Fontenot, who at the time was in Kleinberg's shop and participated in the internal discussions, affirmed Kleinberg's account of the group process from which the idea of a cost control group emerged. In addition, he added another interesting dimension—efficiency in handling the expected waiver workload.

> We arrived at the idea of a cost control group as the confluence of two considerations. The first was that we wanted to have solid, indisputable information for both policy making and cost control. The second was, given what we saw as an impending deluge of requests, we needed a template, a technique, that would enable us to manage the workload and not require the negotiation of an entirely unique evaluation and cost-neutrality arrangement for each state. We were a small shop with a big workload and needed to be able to say without a lot of complex analysis and negotiation, "If you adhere to these standards, it will be much easier to approve a demonstration."

The reference point Kleinberg and Fontenot describe would allow the administration to apply uniform rules to all states regardless of assumptions about their projects' likely costs. For example, both HHS and OMB thought the Wisconsin plan would probably be cost neutral (despite OMB's most pessimistic estimates) but that the New Jersey plan would most likely increase federal costs. However, if both states would agree in writing (as a condition of receiving waiver approval) to claim no more funding than a baseline established by expenditures for the control group, HHS could approve both waiver requests and allow both to continue without risk. Even if they proved to be not cost neutral overall, they would be cost neutral to the federal government by agreed-on design. Furthermore, by selecting a control group from the case-load that existed at the start of the demonstration and incrementing it with newly approved cases, the control group would remain representative over time. Finally, the evaluation would rely on the same control group used for budget neutrality as the basis for deriving unbiased impact estimates.

Using a randomly assigned control group that would receive the old program was a brilliant administrative solution to a cluster of problems, and it became the key lever that drove the policy. It was the gateway to allowing states flexibility to implement policies the administration would otherwise oppose, because, if enforced, it would ensure federal budget neutrality and provide for an objective evaluation of those policies. Not all parties embraced the idea, however, despite its brilliance. The important opponent was Hobbs, who knew random assignment would antagonize states and result in fewer approved waivers—undermining his primary goal of devolving welfare to state and local government.[11] The two states in question had also already expressed strong resistance. Wisconsin had strenuously objected to exempting individuals from Learnfare, although it had already agreed (in a July 24, 1987, letter) to use random assignment to evaluate the Medicaid extension (the program element of most policy and cost concern to the administration). New Jersey claimed (in an August 19 letter) that because the program would be "mandatory for most AFDC recipients, it precluded the full use of random assignment." My personal assessment at the time was that, although OMB had put forward a great idea, Hobbs's opposition made it unlikely that the proposal would resolve the current problem.

New Jersey's opposition to using random assignment to evaluate its REACH initiative is an interesting illustration of the political risks that motivated governors to resist it. The state had a long history of random assignment evaluations in welfare going back to the original negative-income-tax demonstration. Later in the 1970s it had two Supported Work sites, and in the 1980s it participated in three important HHS experimental evaluations—Grant Diversion, the Health Care Financing Administration's AFDC Homemaker-Home Health Aide, and OFA's Teen Parent demonstrations. But in this case it wanted no part of random assignment. Michael Laracy, at the time a senior career civil servant in the state, recalls the situation: "[The governor] really envisioned this not as a demonstration, but as reform. . . . This was not an experiment; he was changing the system like Dukakis had. . . . There was also concern that we might get some findings that wouldn't be laudatory, and he didn't want this to be looked at too closely." That is to say, the political agenda would not be well-served by an independent, rigorous evaluation. So even where there was no opposition to random assignment per se, a rigorous evaluation of what was billed as welfare reform was still viewed as a threat.

On September 2, the ILIOAB recommended that HHS approve the Wisconsin application; the next day Secretary Bowen called Governor Thompson to tell him that he had conditionally approved the project. What that meant was not clear, since there was no agreement on the conditions of approval, about which OMB and OPD were still in deep disagreement. New Jersey also began to press its case by claiming that for budgetary reasons it needed to have an approval before October 1. Since we had made even less progress with New Jersey, this seemed a particularly daunting task.

In the last week of August, New Jersey representatives had come to Hobbs's office to discuss their application and urge its approval by October 1. They strongly resisted using random assignment, and Hobbs asked staff to work with the state to determine whether there were viable alternatives. From OMB's perspective, Hobbs had indicated more flexibility than they would have liked: OMB associate director Jay Plager followed up with a September 25 memo to Hobbs and to HHS expressing concern that a "misunderstanding arose from the meeting" and strongly reiterating what OMB had taken to be agreement to take a harder line.[12] The memo asserted that alternatives to a randomly assigned control group should be the basis for paying states only if the latter were "wholly impractical," not simply because the alternative was the "state's preference." It also insisted that the burden was on the state to demonstrate that the alternative would protect the federal government and that such an alternative be "developed prior to granting a waiver."

Bavier, who served as the board's secretary, and I responded to Hobb's request to develop alternatives. Bavier's idea for cost neutrality was to use a caseload-model estimation technique to establish a baseline for program expenditures. In this approach, to the extent the state's caseload was less than an agreed-on lower bound of that estimate, savings would be granted to the state to match the unmatchable for section 1115(a)(2) costs related to approved activities (such as the Medicaid extension). If the caseload exceeded an agreed-on upper bound, HHS could cancel the project. I suggested a design based on a prior experience sample, such as had been used by Research Triangle Institute (1983) to evaluate the amendments to the 1981 Omnibus Budget Reconciliation Act. Under this design a historical cohort of recipients would be tracked longitudinally before implementation of REACH and compared with a similar post-REACH cohort. Both these alternatives were clearly much weaker than a random assignment design.

The Roosevelt Room in the West Wing of the White House was usually the location of ILIOAB meetings and where states were typically invited to present their proposed demonstrations.[13] As a bureaucrat used to more humble surroundings, I always found it a pleasure to enter the darkened room, with oils of the two Roosevelt presidents on the walls and comfortable leather chairs. We usually conducted negotiations with states in the Eisenhower Old Executive Office Building, however, across a driveway from the White House. Hobbs had his office there, a nice space with a fireplace that had many years before been the office of the secretary of the Navy.

As New Jersey continued to press for approval by October 1, a negotiation was scheduled for the afternoon of September 30 not in Hobbs's office but in a National Security Agency conference room in the same building, notable for the clash between its restored mid-nineteenth-century painted walls and ceiling and its raised floor, suspected by many to have been built three feet above the normal level to accommodate electronic equipment. The commissioner, Drew Altman, led the New Jersey delegation, which also included his deputy Dennis Beatrice, career staff Michael Laracy and Ray Castro, and an attorney. Hobbs and Plager, along with Robert Helms from HHS, were the administration negotiators. About 5:00 p.m. the meeting moved to another conference room, down the hall from Hobbs's office, where Jim Miller, the OMB director, joined the group and established himself at the head of the table. After a period of no movement by either side, New Jersey's lawyer launched into a tirade about the administration's intransigence. Miller said OMB directors expected to be treated with greater respect and stormed out, not to be seen again that evening.

As negotiations continued past midnight, HHS lawyers who attended throughout the meeting drafted two and a half pages of agreed-on terms and conditions for the project's approval.[14] The core of the agreement was along the lines Bavier and I had developed (including my weaker evaluation terms and Bavier's weaker approach to cost neutrality). Sometime in the early hours of the morning, the New Jersey team drove back to their state and the rest of us went home. Over the next few days, we wrote more detailed terms and conditions regarding the evaluation they were to perform, and Secretary

Bowen sent a formal letter of approval (backdated to October 1 as the state wanted) to Commissioner Altman.

The Office of Management and Budget never told the rest of us why it eventually backed down; most of us assumed the political stakes were just too high that night for it to stick to its guns. Perhaps Hobbs and OMB made an agreement that New Jersey, and (given what happened later) Wisconsin, would be exceptions and that states would be subject to more rigorous and uniform standards in the future, a view OMB later took explicitly in arguing that New Jersey and Wisconsin did not constitute precedents. It might have been possible, if we had had Hobbs's support, to convince both states to follow the OMB approach; it was inconceivable without it. How did Hobbs pull it off? He was not the kind of effective bureaucrat who built and relied on alliances with others—someone later said of him that the only person in the executive branch he could deliver was the president. And nobody, even in a position like Hobbs's, can make that happen often. Maybe that night was such a time.

Undoubtedly unhappy that, though he applied first, Governor Kean had beaten him to the punch, Governor Thompson wasted little time in pressing Wisconsin's case. On October 20, Stanton approved the Learnfare waivers, and on October 28, Wisconsin state officials came to Washington to negotiate the remainder of the approvals. Their revised proposal offered to use a 10 percent randomly assigned control group to monitor and evaluate the Medicaid extension and the thirty-and-one-sixth rule for benefit reductions, but continued to resist using an overall cost control group. Once again OMB acceded to an accounting arrangement that was less than the model it advocated. It was better than the terms New Jersey had negotiated, however, particularly since Wisconsin had agreed to use control groups for what were the most worrying (to the administration) and potentially most costly components. The next day Secretary Bowen formally issued an approval to the Wisconsin secretary of health and social services.

RANDOM ASSIGNMENT AS THE PRESUMPTIVE EVALUATION DESIGN

The Office of Budget and Management lost these two battles. But the fight had been on difficult terrain. First, the internal struggle began and OMB's proposed cost control group solution emerged only well after the start of discussions with the two states. Second, Republican governors who had publicly staked out claims to reforming welfare led both states, and both had strongly resisted using a randomly assigned cost control group. Having shown flexibility, however, OMB was now well positioned to win the next stage of the war. It had strengthened its position to push for standards, and it did. An ILIOAB meeting on the day that the final Wisconsin negotiation took place discussed draft procedures (circulated by Bavier, as the board secretary, and dated October 21) that included the assertion that "to determine what federal spending would have been in the absence of the demonstration, a preferred method is a control group." That meeting also discussed material on the extent of waiver authority in low-income programs. After considerable internal negotiation, similar language describing randomly assigned control groups as preferred was contained in the final version of the guidelines issued by the White House on November 30, 1987, although with a little more room for exceptions. The new procedures would be particularly important, because it had become quite clear that the administration's block-grant legislation was going nowhere in Congress. The administration would henceforth be urging states to submit waiver proposals as an alternative way to foster devolution.

With substantial outreach throughout 1988 led by Hobbs's office and the departments, including regional meetings with states, twenty-six states submitted section 1115 applications, of which sixteen were approved by the Reagan and Bush administrations. State responses to the preference for random assignment of individuals were by and large negative, and in only five states was the presumptive design of individual random assignment achieved. In four others, the approved design involved matched and randomly assigned offices. Washington state's Family Independence Plan and Alabama's Avenues to Self-Sufficiency Through Employment and Training Services program, for example, used such an approach. In Washington the design divided all but one office in the state into four geographic strata and then paired them within strata based on nine matching variables related to both the economic and demographic conditions of the counties. Five of those pairs were selected randomly. The selection probability was proportionate to size, and of each selected pair one member was randomly assigned to treatment, the other to control. In Alabama, where more systemic reforms involved integrating AFDC and food stamps into a single program, we matched three pairs of offices based on historical similarities and randomly selected one of each pair as the treatment office.[15]

In Ohio and New York, the state leadership did favor random assignment of individuals, both for unusual reasons. Ohio's deputy commissioner Paul

Offner, who would later become an aide to Senator Moynihan, had learned about federal waivers as a state senator in Wisconsin and saw the opportunity to introduce innovations through flexibility while remaining committed to serious research. Although Ohio initially proposed the use of nonexperimental designs, the state quickly agreed to individual random assignment for two of their initiatives and matched, randomly assigned counties for a third.[16] In New York, professor Mary Jo Bane, on leave from Harvard, was commissioner—and a member of MDRC's board of directors—and the state supported the requirement for random assignment in the special Family Support Act (FSA) language that authorized the demonstration. A few other states reluctantly accepted the random assignment of individuals. North Carolina was one of these, essentially agreeing to an approach that it had not taken up three years earlier.

The OMB leadership in promoting high-quality evaluation is an illustration of how the impetus for rigor can come from unexpected places. It also illustrates how a range of motivations can lead to the same conclusion. The agency was concerned with the cost of the demonstrations themselves and that, in the name of decreasing federal cost, welfare programs operating at the state level would actually increase federal expenditures. But its primary motivation, I believe, was policy more generally—the fear that weak and manipulable evaluation results, combined with governors' interests in claiming success in expansive welfare policies, would enable open-ended entitlements to be expanded legislatively in the name of decreasing costs when their actual effect was the opposite. The use of random assignment removed this risk.

The struggle also illustrates the key role played by civil servants. Throughout the months of struggle, Selfridge was the primary representative of OMB, and it was Kleinberg and his staff, who came up with idea of using random assignment to establish a cost-neutrality baseline and for evaluation. However, at all times OMB was able to get random assignment accepted as the preferred design only because the political appointees within it, including Plager and his successor Arlene Holen, had bought into the approach and were willing to battle over it.

A BUMP IN THE ROAD?

With the passage and signing of FSA in October 1988, state interest in waivers decreased significantly but did not entirely disappear, especially for states that had applications still in the pipeline. Consideration of these applications continued into the first year of the George H. W. Bush administration.

One of President Bush's early staffing acts after being sworn in on January 20, 1989, was to appoint John H. Sununu, then governor of New Hampshire, as his chief of staff. New Hampshire had had significant dealings with HHS and the ILIOAB the previous year, and Governor Sununu had been personally involved, even hosting one of several regional meetings the ILIOAB conducted to encourage state waiver requests. The appointment of Governor Sununu raised significant issues for the ILIOAB's waiver policies and particularly its preference for experimental designs.

New Hampshire had developed a concept paper for a demonstration in November 1987 and submitted a request to the Health Care Financing Administration for a one-year Medicaid extension. An AFDC waiver request submitted by the state the following February included a number of changes (generally expanding eligibility) that would have simplified eligibility determinations, coordinated them with food stamps eligibility, and reduced the age (from six to three) of a youngest child that would exempt a single parent from work requirements. Since the state proposed to implement the demonstration statewide at a single point in time, it asserted that "construction of valid comparison groups through random assignment or other techniques cannot be achieved" and proposed instead comparison of outcomes before and after implementation of the changes. After extensive negotiations we reached apparent agreement, based largely on an approach proposed by the state in a June 2 letter to Hobbs, that the state would phase in the programs in three waves over two years in matched, randomly selected offices and complement this design with a series of prior experience samples similar to what had been agreed to with New Jersey. (The Medicaid extension would be evaluated only with a prior experience sample, because New Hampshire had already implemented it statewide with state-only funds.) The Department of Health and Human Services submitted draft terms and conditions to the state on June 29, 1988, but the state did not act on them. In early December, Sununu, still the New Hampshire governor, wrote to Hobbs saying that the state was reviewing its demonstration plans in light of FSA passage, which had rendered many, but not all, of its waivers unnecessary.

The transition of political appointees from the Reagan to the Bush administration was a gradual one. Although President Bush named Louis Sullivan as secretary designate of HHS in January, most of the Reagan administration assistant secretaries remained in place into the spring of 1989. So did Hobbs. At the end of January he tried to force decisions on the ten state waiver proposals that remained before the ILIOAB. On January 31, he wrote Secretary-designate Sullivan that he had scheduled negotiations with Iowa and South Carolina as well as a series of board meetings. He also asked the new secretary to designate someone who could represent HHS in the negotiations and said that he, Hobbs, needed to make a recommendation to the new president by March 1 as to whether the board should be continued.

Hobbs also made unsuccessful efforts to weaken the board's preference for random assignment. On January 31, for example, he issued a memorandum to members of the board asserting that "many states" found it "impractical to exclude some recipients from full participation in their demonstrations" and complaining that "federal agency staff feels obliged to attempt to fit the experimental design to every proposal." Of course, it was not surprising that staff did "attempt to fit" these designs to every proposal, because it was the presumptive design, and there were no methodological or serious practical impediments to doing so. Hobbs instructed the federal lead agency to provide a detailed assessment of the method in cases where the agency or OMB did not find proposed state alternatives to random assignment sufficiently rigorous. In essence, this would have changed the presumptive design from random assignment to whatever the state's alternative might be.

Hobbs made little progress on his efforts to move state proposals by attempting to weaken evaluation and cost-neutrality standards, however, thwarted in large part by two Reagan holdovers who represented the most affected departments—Robert Helms (HHS) and John Bode (Department of Agriculture)—and John Cogan, acting as OMB deputy director. On February 23, Terry Branstad, the governor of Iowa, wrote to Sununu complaining about HHS's unwillingness to grant waivers for several components of Iowa's demonstration, including waivers to allow federal funding for one-year post-AFDC extensions of Medicaid and child care benefits. FSA provided that individuals who left AFDC because of increased earnings were entitled to twelve months of Medicaid and child care, similar to what many states had proposed. However, to reduce their cost in the short run, these provisions would not be effective until April 1, 1990. As was the case with New Hampshire's Medicaid extension, Iowa had already implemented these provisions with state funds and wanted to get federal matching for them before the April 1990 FSA implementation date. In his letter to Sununu, Governor Branstad stated that Hobbs had encouraged submission of the waivers and "the certainty of his remarks caused us to devote a considerable amount of time and resources in pursuit of a waiver, only to have our request delayed and finally denied."[17]

The Department of Health and Human Services had in fact had extensive negotiations with Iowa and been unable to reach agreement on a cost-neutrality mechanism. The state had pressed for using a caseload model, but based on the use of such a model in New Jersey, we were not amenable to approving it again. The caseload model in that case estimated that the REACH program reduced New Jersey caseloads by 7 percent—highly implausible, given that REACH had been implemented in only a few counties and the caseload reduction in those counties was no more than in the rest of the state. More generally, in the transition between administrations HHS was acquiring a stiffer spine, partly because we appreciated the value of random assignment but also no doubt because Hobbs was approaching the end of his White House tenure. As the most senior Reagan holdover, Helms, also a lame duck, was the key political official.[18] On December 5, 1988, Hobbs had written HHS requesting that draft terms and conditions be prepared that included the disputed provisions with a nonexperimental design. Because of its concerns with the weak design, the department resisted doing so and sought OMB's backing for its position. With the Iowa application still open, on March 2 Sununu replied to Branstad's letter, expressing his sympathy and reassuring the governor that "no formal decision" had been reached. On the same day Hobbs presided over his last meeting as the ILIOAB's chairman.

Although Hobbs was not able to make any direct headway in weakening the board's standards, Sununu, who was in a much stronger position, took steps to do so. Just eight days after Hobbs's last board meeting, Sununu signed a March 10 memorandum to the president in which he recommended that the president "reestablish the ILIOAB as 'The Low Income Opportunity Board'" with William Roper, a physician who specialized in health policy, as chair. Roper, who had previously served on the ILIOAB as the Health Care Financing Administration's representative responsible for Medicaid waivers, had now taken Hobbs's place as head of the White House OPD. In the memorandum, Sununu recommended that "as a condition of its reestablishment, [the new board] adopt within 30 days a range of acceptable evaluation and budget neutrality assurance arrangements, including methods other than those relying on control groups, from which the States can choose. It should be further directed to give substantial deference to states in the use of other than control group methods if the proposing State finds control group methods unacceptable because of cost, potential legal challenges, or projected adverse impact on people in need of public assistance."

On March 30, Sununu informed the affected agency heads that the president had reestablished the board (now the Low Income Opportunity Board [LIOB]), with Roper as chairman, and asked them to designate representatives for its initial meeting on April 7. The memorandum also stated that the president had directed implementation of Sununu's recommendation.

At the April 7 meeting, Sununu and his deputy, Andrew Card, addressed the LIOB. Sununu urged it to be constructive. Card, who had headed the White House intergovernmental relations unit at the end of the Reagan administration and interacted with the ILIOAB in his role as liaison with the governors, encouraged the LIOB to be creative in finding ways to recommend approval of state demonstration proposals. Roper described the president's charge to develop options for assessing cost neutrality other than random assignment and assigned LIOB staff member Peter Germanis to develop such a list for board discussion.

At the next board meeting on April 19, the sole topic on the agenda was "evaluation and budget neutrality assurance methods."[19] Before the meeting, Roper had distributed a paper by Germanis describing past practices of the ILIOAB and its preference for experimental designs, along with a general discussion of various alternative methods. In both the paper and his presentation, Germanis was clear that other methods of controlling for external circumstances and selection bias were weaker than random assignment.[20] In the discussion that followed, many of the standard concerns for and against random assignment were raised, with both OMB and HHS on the side of experimental methods. Roper noted that many state demonstrations included provisions for Medicaid and child care extensions similar to those contained in FSA and asked whether these could not simply be implemented earlier. The two agencies pointed out that there was no programmatic authority to do so, and that section 1115 research authority was HHS's only mechanism. Another LIOB staffer, Dee Martin, provided a status report on pending state applications, including the fact that two, Kansas and Utah, had withdrawn because of their concern with the rigorous evaluation requirements. Roper closed the meeting by urging the agencies to work with Germanis to propose more specific nonexperimental methodologies and the circumstances for their use.

Germanis convened another meeting of LIOB and agency staff on April 25. Among those present were Bavier, who had moved from the board to OMB, Mike Fishman from the Office of the Assistant Secretary for Planning and Evaluation, Steven Cole from the Department of Agriculture, and me.

Most of us held to our view, along with Germanis, that allowing the use of nonexperimental methods for cost neutrality and evaluation with no established standards was a recipe for unreliable evaluation and runaway claims of success. Between the last board meeting and this one, Bavier had advanced the idea of allowing nonexperimental methods where they could be subjected to an empirical, out-of-sample test before the onset of the demonstration, and this was also discussed at the meeting. Germanis reflected the consensus of the meeting in a memorandum to Roper the following day: random assignment should remain the board's preferred method. Where a state was unwilling or unable to use an experimental design, there should be a test of the alternative approach proposed by a state to see how well it would have predicted past out-of-sample outcomes. The group recommended that the LIOB reserve the right to require random assignment when policies of high concern were part of the demonstration. In addition, both caseload models and approaches that simply followed demonstration participants over time with no external comparison group were deemed inherently unreliable. The basic consensus was to move very little from the current presumption of random assignment.

Roper distributed Germanis's memorandum to LIOB members before the next meeting on April 28, along with a cover note saying, in part, "I personally find the proposed alternative unsatisfactory in meeting the Board's charge to develop a range of acceptable . . . methods." He also suggested that the board "seek the counsel of experts from outside the government to help us resolve these issues." Although the announcement for the following meeting lists minutes for the April 28 meeting as an attachment, the copies I have seen do not include them. Thus the description that follows is based on my recollection, as well as those of several others who were present. Most members were from agencies that lacked waiver authority and were not directly involved in state proposals (for example, the Departments of Labor, Justice, Education), and some had little technical knowledge of evaluation. By and large, these members were silent. Generally, HHS and OMB staff argued that the consensus staff approach described in Germanis's memorandum—that is, to retain the presumption for random assignment but in some circumstances allow exceptions for a validated nonexperimental approach—was a feasible way to increase options for states while not abandoning objective standards for cost neutrality and evaluation. The meeting did not result in a resolution, and Roper did not yet have what he regarded as a satisfactory way to implement the chief of staff's approved recommendation to the president.

Since the LIOB had responsibilities beyond coordinating state waiver requests, including coordinating the administration's public assistance policy, beginning with the next meeting on May 19, 1989, it began to consider options for development of a Bush administration antipoverty agenda. Views within the board were widely divergent, with HUD secretary Jack Kemp favoring an ambitious program and OMB and HHS favoring caution. This subject more and more dominated LIOB meetings and continued for more than a year, into the summer of 1990. As these broader policy concerns came to the fore, issues regarding waivers moved gradually into the background. State interest turned to implementing FSA, and either the federal departments approved the remaining waivers through a series of compromises or states abandoned them. Occasionally the issue of greater flexibility arose, for example, when, in a July 31 address to the National Governors Association, President Bush stated that he had asked the LIOB "to make flexibility the guiding principle, so that states will have greater freedom to experiment with welfare reform." Although the proceedings of its September 23 meeting show that the LIOB did consult with outside experts on the subject of low-income assistance policy, I can find no record, nor can others I have asked, of consultations with such experts on the use of nonexperimental methods. The president's directive was never implemented, and the LIOB's preference for random assignment remained in effect, although its implementation was largely dormant. Its dormancy, including lack of pressure from the states, allowed Germanis (a mid-level political appointee) and a group of civil servants to defeat the approved recommendations of the president's chief of staff, saving an important principle for use at a later time.[21]

Was this a case of the bureaucratic intransigence so frequently alluded to by politicians? Certainly, it was not insubordination.[22] We operated in a totally open way, and nothing prevented board members, all of whom were political appointees, from carrying out the president's directive. Nor did we drag our feet. From our perspective we were simply unwilling to call approaches reliable when we did not think they were. Germanis recalls the motivation for his actions this way: "At that time I must've been convinced along with everyone else that there was no credible . . . alternative. . . . I've always thought that my job was to give the best advice possible."

Fishman, the senior ASPE career staffer on LIOB issues, describes it this way: "I cared because I thought it was right. . . . Frankly, to me, while the cost control side made a good argument, and gave us more power than we would have [had] without it, that wasn't the driving issue. We had the ability to do this in a way that we could learn something useful from these waivers, and I didn't think we should be giving states the opportunity to just do whatever they wanted without learning something from it. And this was the best way to learn something we could have confidence in."

NEXT STAGE IN THE WAIVER STORY

By the summer of 1989, action on state waiver applications had pretty much wound down, and states submitted few new applications until 1992, the year running up to the election of Bill Clinton as president. From 1989 to 1991, developments further strengthened the case for random assignment, which were important in the second round of waiver applications at the end of the Bush administration and the torrent after Clinton took office.

One of these developments was yet another waiver request from Wisconsin, one of the exceptions to the general hiatus in waiver applications as states turned their attention to implementing FSA. Wisconsin governor Tommy Thompson was moving to expand his state's efforts to require AFDC parents to have their children attend school regularly. On July 21, 1989, he met with HHS secretary Sullivan to seek support for a proposal to expand Learnfare requirements to families with children aged six to twelve. At the meeting, Secretary Sullivan indicated his support for the planned expansion, and on September 12, Governor Thompson submitted a preliminary waiver application. On November 7, HHS's support for the proposal was reiterated in an interim letter to the governor.

The original Learnfare program had been extremely controversial, and extending it to younger children was no less so. The independent evaluation had not yet produced information on the program's effectiveness. But that did not stop Governor Thompson, who used his own internal analysis to claim that the program was successful in increasing school attendance and that these benefits should not be denied to younger children. This kind of claim was, of course, one of the primary reasons for requiring rigorous, independent evaluation. Although such claims are not preventable, over time rigorous evaluations can contradict or confirm them.[23] Critics had never liked Learnfare because of its reliance on penalties and its lack of support services to help families ensure their children's attendance. Supporters viewed the program as simply reinforcing existing parental responsibility and truancy laws. The proposed Learnfare extension produced an outpouring of correspondence to HHS—

from members of Congress, the Wisconsin state legislature, and a number of nongovernmental organizations—most of which opposed the extension.

Within HHS there were senior political appointees who were opposed to approving the application on policy grounds. However, since the secretary had twice indicated his support, and since a denial would prompt a call from Governor Thompson to the president's chief of staff, and we would certainly be told to reverse ourselves, an approval seemed all but given. In the end, after some steps to disapprove the application, we at HHS settled on conditions that required Wisconsin to spend some of its demonstration savings for services to families subject to Learnfare requirements (to respond to a frequent complaint of its critics) and to use an experimental design for evaluating the Learnfare expansion. On June 6, 1990, Jo Anne Barnhart, who had been confirmed as assistant secretary the previous month, notified the state that the project had been approved.[24]

Early in the same general period, the Minnesota Family Investment Plan had been authorized by Congress on December 19, 1989, as part of an omnibus reconciliation bill (Public Law 101-239). This project was unique in several important respects.[25] Minnesota did not oppose using an experimental design, and indeed had supported its inclusion in the federal legislation after not including it in the draft it provided to congressional staff. In addition, the state worked closely with MDRC in both the design of its program and its evaluation. The Minnesota plan was a critical part of the way that MDRC used the states' interest in welfare reform not simply to evaluate individual state reform efforts but to craft an agenda to answer important, more general, research questions.

The Minnesota Family Investment Plan also illustrates the important role played by key congressional staff in supporting random assignment designs. If staff on the two key committees with jurisdiction over AFDC (House Ways and Means and Senate Finance) had supported state efforts to resist experimental designs, it would have been much more difficult to impose such a requirement. In the case of the Minnesota plan, for example, House Ways and Means staff convened a meeting on June 29, 1989, which included both Minnesota and executive branch staff and advocates, to discuss legislative language. The original draft provided only a loose requirement for the state to evaluate the plan. Representing HHS, I offered alternative language that would require a random assignment design. On July 5, Minnesota submitted a new draft of the authority, which included random assignment and reflected agreements reached at the meeting. This quick change reflected the state's readiness to conduct an experiment, but it also reflected the fact that congressional staff supported the administration's emphasis on rigorous methods.

To my recollection, Ways and Means and Senate Finance staff in every case supported random assignment. In some cases this support was a result of their previous training and experience. For example Ron Haskins, who was on the staff of the Ways and Means Committee, is a developmental psychologist who earlier in his professional life had personally participated in an important experiment.[26] The strong support for random assignment among less scientifically trained staff surely resulted in part from the frequent MDRC briefings on findings from its Work/Welfare demonstration.

Unlike most states, Minnesota was not pressing for immediate statewide implementation. Instead, it had begun several years earlier to plan and design a pilot program that was also programmatically unique. Its primary goal was to reduce poverty, not dependency. Many difficult issues needed to be worked through with Minnesota, but the careful planning, thoughtfulness, and integrity of the state's staff made the entire process a pleasure. Our experience was a model of how program development can be advanced and evaluated by rigorous research.

Perhaps the most important development in this period was the emergence of significant problems in some state demonstrations where cost neutrality was not based on individual random assignment. The New Jersey REACH program was a leading example. The caseload model implied that the state had saved the federal government more than $20 million. However, the caseload decline was no steeper in the three counties where REACH had been implemented earliest than in the remaining counties in the state. Furthermore, the early evaluation results from the prior experience design implied that the program had not had a significant effect on caseloads and that the implementation of the program had been very weak (Decker 1991). With two other demonstrations, Alabama's Avenues to Self-Sufficiency through Employment and Training Services program and Washington's Family Independence Plan, cost neutrality arrangements implied that the states owed the federal government amounts on the order of what the federal government owed New Jersey. These problems would provide valuable ammunition in the subsequent struggle to establish random assignment of individuals as the normative standard for waiver demonstrations.

RANDOM ASSIGNMENT BECOMES THE DE FACTO STANDARD

After the AFDC caseload reductions that accompanied the Omnibus Budget Reconciliation Act of 1981 (which were fully in place by the spring of 1982), most of the 1980s was a period of relative stability with a trend of slowly rising caseloads. However, in 1989 the caseload began to rise sharply and continued to do so until the spring of 1994. Although it is not clear that this rising caseload directly affected it, by the end of 1991 governors' interest in welfare waivers began to emerge again, and the George H. W. Bush administration was aware of numerous states that had specific changes they wanted to implement.[27] Based on this interest, and possibly also the fact that the president was running against candidate Bill Clinton, who promised to "end welfare as we know it," OMB included an initiative in the 1993 president's budget to encourage the use of research waivers in welfare programs to further the states' roles as laboratories.[28] In his State of the Union message in February 1992, President Bush said, regarding the renewed state interest, "We are going to help this movement. Often state reform requires waiving certain federal regulations. I will act to make this process easier and quicker for every state that asks for our help."

Following that State of the Union address, internal discussions began regarding how the administration would implement President Bush's initiative. In September 1990, the LIOB had been replaced by the Empowerment Task Force, chaired by Jack Kemp, the secretary of housing and urban development. This task force provided a venue for the discussion of various antipoverty strategies but did not assume the ILIOAB and LIOB role of coordinating state requests for welfare demonstrations. That there was no coordinating body in the White House meant not only that the preference for random assignment was no longer formally in place but also that President Bush's directive for the LIOB to establish alternative evaluation and cost-neutrality methods for states was likewise irrelevant. It was now clear that there were just four key organizations involved in establishing section 1115 demonstration policy—the Administration for Children and Families, the Office of the Assistant Secretary for Planning and Evaluation, OMB, and the White House OPD.[29]

Career staff in the first three of these organizations strongly supported the establishment of strong "waivers for an experimental evaluation *quid pro quo*," which would be deviated from minimally and primarily where an experiment was inappropriate on methodological grounds. Furthermore, we were well positioned to build higher-level support from the political leadership. Barnhart, my supervisor at the time, had been a strong advocate for experimental designs ever since her role as head of the AFDC program in the mid-1980s. Martin Gerry, the assistant secretary for planning and evaluation, was primarily focused on other priorities and by and large deferred to Barnhart on welfare reform demonstrations. He delegated most decisions in this area to Fishman, who was also a strong supporter of experimental methods. Finally, at OMB, which had originally formulated the experimental standard, Bavier was the key player. From the outset, the three of us, along with other HHS staff, saw the task as implementing an approach that would make experimental evaluation, and cost neutrality, the truly preferred approach of the administration.

The first step was to convince the key leadership in the fourth agency, the White House OPD, in this case Gail Wilensky, a deputy assistant to the president for domestic policy whose primary areas were health and welfare policy. Clearly, her office would field high-level complaints from governors to the White House, so it was critical that she be on board. Wilensky was a health policy specialist who, before moving to the White House, had headed the Health Care Financing Administration (now the Centers for Medicare and Medicaid Services). Although years earlier she had been substantially involved in welfare issues and knew the negative-income-tax experiments, she had much less recent experience in welfare policy. She was well versed in research methods, and her doctorate was in economics. But in this case her background could have proved a double-edged sword. Although she was perfectly capable of understanding the arguments for and against random assignment, the research with which she dealt on a regular basis seldom relied on experimental methods. The latter aspect initially led her to be skeptical of the position that Bavier, Fishman, and I advocated. At one point she even politely suggested that it was almost anti-intellectual to limit welfare demonstration evaluation methods to experimental designs. As she had a fundamentally empirical attitude about such issues, however, she was more than willing to listen and discuss.

To argue our case, in early April Bavier drafted and circulated for comment among our group a memorandum to Wilensky articulating the case for random assignment in state welfare demonstrations. The final April 6, 1992, version cited and provided copies of critical methodological work in the area (including Stromsdorfer 1987; LaLonde 1986; Fraker and Maynard 1987; and Ashenfelter and Card 1985). In addition, Bavier described the history of the Comprehensive Employment and Training Act (CETA) evaluation as "pivotal" and explained that it had led an advisory panel and the Department of Labor to halt a CETA-style evaluation of the Job Training Partnership Act in favor of an experimental design.[30] The memorandum also laid out the problems with the evaluations that were not based on individual random assignment and had been approved under the ILIOAB and the LIOB. It also noted that high-quality nonexperimental evaluations were just as hard and expensive as experiments. The memo closed by setting out what we all believed to be a key concern: that although in a particular case a nonexperimental design could not be ruled out a priori, once the administration approved a poor design, other states would "expect the same kind of deal." Bavier's memorandum, along with a meeting in Wilensky's office, did the trick. She was convinced that in this setting experimental designs were the right approach, and she was prepared to play the critical backstop role in the White House.

Never one to hold back a waiver request, Wisconsin governor Tommy Thompson applied for a new demonstration in March. He proposed to conduct a five-county demonstration to require and provide education and employment services to teenaged two-parent families. A combination of carrots and sticks, the project would loosen requirements for eligibility for two-parent family benefits and increase their earnings disregards, but it would also reduce the incremental benefit the family would receive if it had additional children while on welfare. The state proposed that the program be evaluated using a nonexperimental design. Although its official name was the Parental and Family Responsibility Initiative, it soon became known as Bridefare.

Wisconsin's rapid submittal of an application was an important opportunity for us. If the state's proposed project was to be the first in a series of state submittals, it would be important to establish a precedent that the federal expectation for evaluation and cost neutrality would be individual random assignment. Since Wisconsin had not historically favored experimental designs and only reluctantly accepted them on some occasions, Governor Thompson's agreement to such a design would send an important signal. Furthermore, I believed that Wisconsin state officials had always been irked that New Jersey had been approved before them in 1987, and that the governor would place a high value on being first in whatever round of waivers might follow. It also seemed to me that we could sweeten the pot for the state even more if I planted the idea that being first this time could result in a White House event with President Bush. I would tell them truthfully that I had no ability to directly influence whether such an event occurred (and in fact I never tried). But I felt confident that once the idea was in his mind, Governor Thompson would place the right calls to make it happen.

After running my plan past Barnhart, who liked the idea and told me to give it a try, I called my counterpart in the state and laid out the deal. If Wisconsin would agree to random assignment, I was confident that HHS would quickly approve its project. I also reminded her that Wisconsin had been burned in the nonexperimental evaluation of Learnfare, which found no effect of the program on school attendance. (A subsequent experimental evaluation found the same, but that result was not known at the time.) I also speculated that since the president had announced the initiative to help states with rapid waiver approvals, and since it was a presidential election year, it seemed plausible to me that the White House would like to make some positive publicity by having the president announce a fast approval with the nation's leading governor on welfare reform.

This turned out to be the rare case where everything worked exactly as planned. Wisconsin leapt at the idea, and we worked quickly together to agree on terms and conditions. On April 10, three weeks and a day after the state had formally submitted its application and only about two months after 1989 State of the Union address, HHS approved the application, and Governor Thompson appeared with President Bush in the White House as the approval was announced.

Over the next four months applications were submitted by Oregon, Maryland, New Jersey, Michigan, California, Virginia, and again by Wisconsin. The trick now for staff was to take the precedent established with Wisconsin and use the now strong internal agreement to establish a standard. This meant a combination of persistent cajoling and quiet insistence that states agree to random assignment on a one-by-one basis. The art was to convince states that unreliable evaluations were not in their interest and to show, in a detailed manner, that the nonexperimental evaluations they were proposing would produce unreliable evidence.

The next several months were critical. Meetings were held with several states interested in pursuing waiver demonstrations, typically even before they submitted applications. One of the first of these meetings was with New Jersey. A key state legislator introduced legislation that would cap family benefits so that children who were conceived while their families were on welfare would not trigger an increase in the family's benefits and would include stronger financial incentives for such families to work. The state was developing a section 1115 demonstration to implement the legislation and, as with REACH in 1987, was arguing that no families should be left out of the treatment. This was also the view of the key legislator. In support of its position, New Jersey had developed a nonexperimental design.

From HHS's perspective, we believed we needed to argue convincingly to the state that the design they proposed would very likely fail to produce credible results and that failure placed both the federal government and the state at risk. Staff in HHS and OMB spent much time dissecting the state's proposed design and exposing its weaknesses. On April 24, New Jersey's human services commissioner William Waldman came to HHS to present the state's proposal. He and Barnhart kicked off the meeting and then left staff to argue out the design. The New Jersey staff came prepared to argue strongly for their position. But since they were also well trained and came in knowing the weakness of their position, they had difficulty deflecting criticisms of their design. When Commissioner Waldman and Assistant Secretary Barnhart returned at the end of the day, the New Jersey staff acknowledged the problems that HHS and OMB had pointed out and agreed that an experimental design would be much stronger and more reliable than the design they had proposed. This meeting put us on a path toward random assignment for New Jersey's demonstration.

That meeting illustrates what seemed to us to be frequently the case: our state counterparts appeared to agree with us that the only credible design was random assignment, but they argued, at least for awhile, for their political leaderships' positions. Michael Laracy, at the time a senior career official in New Jersey, describes his handling of the situation thus: "Both [Wayne Bryant, the state legislator sponsoring the reform] and the new governor, Florio, were very committed to pronouncing this a success as soon as they could. . . . So I just pushed as hard as I could to try to get it right, and . . . you guys were pretty strong on it, so I just portrayed it as I thought we had to give in to you guys, all the while being happy to do so."

In the next two months meetings were held with several other states, including Maryland, California, and Michigan, and the consistent federal message was that experimental designs would best protect both the state and the federal government. Like New Jersey, none of these states initially supported experimental designs to evaluate their demonstrations, but all came around. Word of federal expectations spread, creating a new atmosphere about what would be negotiated and what would not. On May 21, the head of the California Human Services agency, Russell Gould, met with Barnhart. He told her that, although he did not prefer random assignment, he would not fight it if that was what other states were going to have to accept. Later, in a critical meeting on June 8 with Gerald Miller, who headed the Michigan Department of Social Services, Wilensky and Barnhart set forth the same expectation. It is notable that in other contexts both Gould and Miller were not opposed to random assignment, and perhaps that made them less intransigent. The Greater Avenues for Independence program (GAIN)evaluation was still under way in California, Michigan was currently host to two sites in the Job Opportunities and Basic Skills Training (JOBS) program evaluation, and David Butler of MDRC and I had personally met with Miller to recruit Michigan into the latter evaluation. But clearly, without the support of senior political appointees the random assignment policy could not have held for the waiver demonstrations.[31]

By the close of the Bush administration, HHS had approved ten state projects, all but two of which included evaluation and cost neutrality based on random assignment. Oregon, which we knew would resist random assignment, had proposed to tighten several work requirements and had no expansive waivers, so a strategic decision was made not to push them very hard. The Wisconsin Two-Tier demonstration, which paid a lower level of benefits to recipients who recently entered the state, did not lend itself to an experimental design.[32] In some cases, flexibility was shown regarding the unit that would be individually randomly assigned. For example, because Michigan had a system of assigning cases to workers that would have been damaging to disrupt, its evaluation randomly assigned workers rather than recipients.

So finally, by the end of 1992, the standard that had been first enunciated in 1987 became a full-fledged reality. Looking over the longer term, the enormous progress of a decade is clear. In chapter 4, Judy describes how, through May 1982, MDRC did not consider random assignment feasible or appropriate as it began to develop the Work/Welfare demonstration. That view changed over the next several months, and the resulting demonstration would become a critical lever in altering views of the feasibility and desirability of using random assignment to evaluate welfare reform efforts. In addition, the findings would be applied directly in the policy-making process. For example, an April 1987 publication from the Congressional Budget Office (1987), titled "Work-Related Programs for Welfare Recipients," drew heavily on MDRC's research. And in the mid-1980s, the work cited earlier as influencing our discussions with Gail Wilensky, which used the Supported Work findings to cast doubt on the reliability of nonexperimental methods for evaluating work programs, began to emerge. This was further bolstered by reports from National Academy of Sciences and Department of Labor expert panels that were critical of comparison group designs. Thus as the second Reagan administration debated internally about how to assess cost neutrality, and more generally to estimate the effects of state waiver demonstrations, the feasibility and desirability of random assignment designs were becoming well established.

The next five years would further establish the utility of random assignment. The findings on GAIN and similar demonstrations, the launch of the JOBS evaluation, and the emergence of other important experiments only served to strengthen the case made over the previous five years. The consistent failure of nonexperimental evaluations of state welfare waiver demonstrations added further support. Thus it took almost ten years for random assignment to become the de facto standard for welfare waiver demonstrations. It is ironic that the use of random assignment to enforce rigorous program evaluations at the state level—thereby enabling the federal government to enormously increase state flexibility—would be undercut again in 1996, when Congress and President Clinton replaced AFDC as an individual entitlement with a system of block grants to the states but with no evaluation strings attached. In the meantime, the waiver story continued.

A NEW ADMINISTRATION TAKES OVER

Bill Clinton was elected to the presidency in November 1992, an event for which I had been hoping. Although I began working on welfare issues under the Democratic administration of Jimmy Carter, I had spent most of my career—twelve years—in Republican administrations. Professionally I had grown somewhat tired of working for the same political party and wanted to demonstrate my capabilities as a career civil servant, not just a contributor to Republican administrations. In addition, although my personal views had been strongly influenced by conservatives' strong emphasis on work, the incoming president was one of the few national Democrats who also articulated that emphasis. Furthermore, whereas the George H. W. Bush administration spent a good deal of time debating whether to have an explicit welfare reform and antipoverty program—with the debate finally spilling over into the press in July 6, 1990, when the *New York Times* published a story on how the president's Domestic Policy Council rejected any "bold" options—President Clinton was elected having famously made the pledge "to end welfare as we know it." Thus I was sure there would be interesting work to do, interesting new appointees with whom to do it, a high presidential priority associated with the work, and the possibility of actually accomplishing positive changes in the welfare system.

By the end of February 1993, the Clinton administration's new faces began to appear. At HHS the key political appointments related to welfare reform were the two professors from Harvard's Kennedy School of Government who had collaborated on some of the most influential research on welfare dynamics—Mary Jo Bane, nominated as assistant secretary for the Administration for Children and Families and David Ellwood, as assistant secretary for planning and evaluation. Their seminal 1983 scholarly work on welfare dynamics was not their only credential for their new jobs. In addition to her research contributions, Bane also had extensive experience in government service, having been both deputy commissioner and commissioner of social services for the state of New York. Ellwood (1988) had published *Poor Support*, which had proposed time limits on AFDC receipt and had clearly influenced the incoming president's campaign positions on welfare. At OMB, the key person with responsibility for welfare budget and policy was Isabel Sawhill, another noted welfare researcher. Coincidentally, all three had affiliations with MDRC, with Bane and Sawhill having served on its board of directors (as they do today) and Ellwood on its Welfare Studies Committee.[33] I was delighted to see the caliber of the incoming appointees and confident that exciting things would be happening.

A Torrent of Waiver Requests

Given the priority the incoming president had given to welfare reform in his campaign, the most immediate focus of his appointees was how to organize a process for developing the administration's legislative proposal. However, it did not take long for the issue of section 1115 waiver requests to rear its head. The state of Vermont had submitted a request the month before the election that included a time limit after which recipients would be required to work. Although by December we at the staff level had already worked out approvable terms and conditions with the state, the outgoing Bush administration decided not to act on the application but to leave it for the incoming administration. Vermont's Democratic governor, Dr. Howard Dean (of later fame as a presidential candidate himself), soon pressed the new administration for approval.

The tension between their central responsibility to design a nationally reformed AFDC program that would end welfare as we knew it and continuing to grant section 1115 waiver demonstrations was, of course, obvious to both Ellwood and Bane. The national focus would entail additional federal requirements on state AFDC programs that would reduce flexibility; the waiver process, at least as implemented by the Bush administration, provided states virtually total flexibility.[34] Early on, however, President Clinton had made it clear that he was prepared to live with this tension: on February 2, 1993, he addressed the National Governors Association on welfare reform, stating explicitly that his administration would move forward with national reform and also with approving state waiver demonstration requests, even those with which he disagreed. Thus on April 12, 1993, the incoming HHS secretary Donna Shalala approved the Vermont application, the first of a great many welfare reform demonstrations she would ultimately approve.

The opposition between advancing national policies for welfare reform and providing state flexibility through section 1115 would continue right up to enactment of welfare reform legislation, the Personal Responsibility and Work Opportunity Reconciliation Act (PRWORA) in August 1996. There was a huge amount of internal discussion and external negotiation with states about sensitive policies and their details, especially family caps and time limits and protections afforded to recipients under the agreed-on waiver provisions. What was conspicuously not discussed in the internal debates was random assignment, not surprising given the views of the senior political officials and the fact that the quid pro quo policy was already in place. There was some initial resistance from governors, including personal appearances (as by Iowa governor Terry Branstad, who pleaded his case to leave no Iowan out of his welfare reform, which he asserted would be a big success). But this resistance faded as the expectation of a randomized trial became firmly established as Clinton administration policy.

With the growing interest in state welfare reform and no national legislation on the short-term horizon, state section 1115 demonstrations grew by leaps and bounds. The masses of state waiver applications had major consequences for the work of my office. Almost 90 percent of states would ultimately submit at least one demonstration request, and many submitted multiple requests or modifications of previously approved projects. At any one time, twenty to forty applications could be pending. The great bulk of staff time was taken up processing waiver demonstration requests, and staff who did not normally work on welfare issues were recruited to help. We met weekly with Bane to update her on every application, discuss how to set priorities, and strategize about the details of negotiations with each state. In addition, we would periodically review our internal processes to streamline our production of approvals.

By the summer of 1996, HHS had approved such demonstrations in forty-five states, almost all of which included a random assignment evaluation.[35] Waiver approvals continued right up to enactment of PRWORA, even in the period between the bill's passage by Congress and its being signed into law by the president, for two reasons. First, since President Clinton had already vetoed two versions of welfare reform passed by Congress, it was unclear until late in the game whether any such legislation would be enacted. Second, there was the possibility that a provision inserted late in the drafting of the legislation—which would allow states to continue the policies embodied in approved section 1115 waivers, even where those policies conflicted with the law itself—might actually become law. This provision was in fact included in PRWORA, becoming section 415 of the Social Security Act.

PRWORA Changes the World of Welfare

The legislation Clinton signed into law on August 22, 1996, though more stringent than some senior officials in his administration would have preferred, did indeed fulfill his campaign promise to change the world of welfare. The replacement of AFDC by Temporary Assistance for Needy Families was the most dramatic change, but the new law also had profound implications for the implementation of section 1115 waivers, which remained applicable to title IV-A (the title of the Social Security Act that authorized both welfare programs), as well as other titles in the Social Security Act. Because the new program provided states with greatly enhanced policy flexibility, much of what states sought under section 1115 was now available to them without relying on federal approval—particularly to states that had waiver demonstrations in place. Section 415 was henceforth simply a state option regarding policies rather than a demonstration authority. There was no longer any implication that the policies it permitted required evaluation or, given the block-grant structure, that cost neutrality had to be observed.[36]

LESSONS FROM THE HISTORY OF WAIVERS

Several factors stand out as crucial in the overall history of waivers: the high political stakes of the period, the universality of the waiver requirement (no state was off the hook) along with examples of its feasibility, the capacity of a cadre of major research organizations to conduct high-quality evaluations, the availability of public funding, and the role of federal staff involved in the waiver approval process. Some of these unambiguously helped the cause of rigorous evaluation; others both helped and hurt in different ways.

The High Political Stakes of Welfare Reform

The high political stakes surrounding welfare reform had two major effects on the effort to make waiver approval contingent on a random assignment evaluation of the proposed demonstration. First, it is hard to imagine the intensity of the senior-level federal advocacy of experimental designs that I describe (in both HHS and OMB) in the absence of the following sequence of events. Two high-profile governors who shared political affiliation with the White House made welfare reform an important political issue in their states. In addition, another governor, Michael Dukakis, was touting outcome measures as proof that his reform (Massachusetts's Employment and Training Choices program) was reaping major budget savings.[37] Such claims raised two concerns among senior federal officials: that the actual costs of the demonstrations themselves would turn out to far exceed estimates and, more important, that the states' waiver initiatives might prove to be the camel's nose under the tent of federal welfare budgets, should the touted reforms become national policy.

The second effect of the high political stakes was fear that the governors, who, but for a handful, were resistant to the imposition of random assignment for their waiver projects, would take their complaints directly to the White House, along with the usual dramatic stories of bureaucratic quibbles standing in the way of progress. Ongoing concern that governors would successfully override the waiver approval process and make deals at the highest levels required constant vigilance on the part of the senior bureaucrats involved to avoid the damage of escalating waiver disputes. We learned how to present random assignment as a fair test, the only way of ensuring states that their interests would be as well protected as federal ones. We also became adept at the negotiating skills required to cajole and convince staff that, although rigorous evaluation would be more difficult, it would avoid the kinds of unknown and incalculable uncertainty to which state initiatives would otherwise be exposed (of which we were able to give several unsettling examples). Our strategies were not dissimilar to the ones MDRC used when seeking the cooperation of state and local partners for their experimental evaluations.

The objectivity of the test was also important in the broader policy community. High political stakes in welfare, as in many other fields, means high controversy. In this case, what conservatives thought of as reform was viewed by liberals as retrogression, and vice versa. Liberal elected representatives in both Congress and state legislatures, along with welfare advocates, saw federal requirements as a bulwark against conservative policies and state flexibility as a threat. Thus they were often opposed to HHS's granting particular waivers, and as state policies grew more conservative, they became increasingly concerned with the flexibility that HHS was providing. Although it did not provide much solace, that random assignment would result in an objective evaluation at least meant that governors who were trumpeting success would ultimately have to face the reality of hard evaluation findings.

The Universality of the Waiver Requirement

Universality helped the effort to impose random assignment in three major ways. First, it gave state human services staff leverage with their legislatures and with budget staff (who might otherwise have preferred a cheaper evaluation route). "We're not the only ones who the feds are making do this; all the other states have to do it too" was often a useful tool for state staff. Second, universality made experimental designs more routine as their feasibility became better established. The argument that an experiment was impossible in waiver demonstrations became progressively weaker as there were ever more examples that it was being done. The growing recognition that experimental evaluations of welfare reform options were indeed feasible solidified the examples of MDRC's Work/Welfare demonstration, the GAIN evaluation, HHS-initiated experiments, and others. This was a major accomplishment that carried well beyond the period of waivers and was central to random assignment's becoming part of the normative structure of the welfare community. Finally, that state staff actually had to procure and manage the independent evaluations did much to expand their research capacity well beyond that of MDRC's studies.

In another respect, however, universality had mixed consequences. The large numbers of projects that tended to have similar elements made it more likely that patterns of findings could be reliably generalized beyond each individual state. But the flip side of this virtue was that the binding requirement for all states became the lowest common denominator of random assignment designs. Even where there might be good reasons for a more complex design in a particular demonstration, that other states had not been asked to do more than the minimum could be used as an effective counterargument. In the summer of 1992, for example, our office looked carefully at a proposed demonstration design that would have required five different treatment groups to isolate the separate effects of different policies within the demonstration package. In the end, its complexity made us decide it was a politically impossible fight to win. Making it even more impractical was the fact that the strongest bureaucratic force for random assignment was cost neutrality, which required nothing more than comparing the full set of reforms in a given demonstration with the whole hodgepodge of policies that made up unreformed AFDC. From an evaluation viewpoint, evaluating a black box of different incentives adds less to the knowledge base than estimating the separate effects of an incremental change in a clearly defined program component or comparing two alternatives in a head-to-head test.[38]

Research Expertise in Conducting High-Quality Evaluations

The achievement of random assignment as the waiver approval standard was helped immensely by the existence of a select group of research organizations with the capacity and expertise to conduct large, high-quality experimental evaluations—mainly MDRC, Abt Associates, and Mathematica Policy Research. Of these, MDRC was by far the most crucial at the time. First, although other research organizations produced strong evaluations of individual demonstrations, MDRC was the one that established the feasibility of pursuing random assignment in regular welfare offices (see chapter 4) and also the only one that pursued a structured strategy of deciding which policies would be the most important to learn about before selecting state programs for evaluation based on their ability to illuminate those chosen policies (see chapter 8). Second, OMB's familiarity with MDRC's experience in eight states in the early to middle 1980s certainly must have played a key role in advancing the idea of random assignment as a way to establish cost neutrality.

The Availability of Public Funding

High-quality evaluations are not cheap. Although they vary greatly in cost, depending on the number of sites and the amount of survey work (a substantial contributor to the overall cost), a waiver evaluation of a major reform would most likely range from $1 million to $5 million. In the case of the waiver demonstrations, the evaluation funds were split equally between the states and the federal government. Because federal AFDC policy allowed the cost of evaluation to count as an administrative cost of the program, it provided federal matching of state dollars one for one. The states were willing to come up with their half in exchange for the flexibility they sought through waivers. The federal government was willing to match those costs to get the evaluations it sought. The federal funding was also particularly easy bureaucratically. Since it came from the open-ended entitlement for AFDC administration, there was no opportunity cost of tapping into it. Without the happy circumstance of open-ended federal funding, the whole approach might have foundered. Federal research budgets were clearly too small to support the large number of projects that emerged, and there would have been direct trade-offs with other important evaluation projects.[39] And if states had been required to foot the whole evaluation bill, they would almost certainly have fought even harder against random assignment.

The Role of Federal Staff

The firm commitment of HHS senior staff to random assignment evaluation designs was also crucial to the story. Initially, although we believed strongly that experimental methods were the best approach for evaluating welfare reform, there was great skepticism that such methods could be imported into the waiver process. However, once their feasibility became apparent, staff commitment to establishing and maintaining random assignment as the presumptive approach never faltered, extending, when necessary, to proactive strategizing with staff at OMB and the Department of Agriculture. Furthermore, as waiver applications started to come in at a much faster pace in the last year of the Bush administration and in the Clinton administration, the commitment spread to many additional staff. The workload was enormous, for several years eclipsing most other research projects for which the Administration for Children and Families staff were responsible, and it really wore people down. Nonetheless, staff believed that completion of the waiver evaluations would create an enormous body of evidence. As a result, the work never seemed pointless from an evaluation perspective. Had the evaluation designs been suspect, some staff would almost certainly have begrudged the necessity of forgoing work that could build real knowledge in favor of work that was masquerading as a way to find reliable evidence. Karl Koerper, a senior analyst and ultimately director of the division responsible for waiver applications, provides this assessment of the likely consequences of losing random assignment: "I think morale would've suffered a lot. It goes to what our purpose was. We had already learned to a certain degree we weren't learning anything from studies that weren't random assignment. . . . Are we just there to facilitate states' changing their policy or are we there to do research? . . . Some staff that had the skills, especially the better staff, would have looked elsewhere for work." This is consistent with my experience that random assignment has a way of supporting commitment to hard work and high standards.

Externally, random assignment was a struggle throughout, although over time it became less so. Internally, the struggle continued for almost five years before it became a settled issue in the last year of the Bush administration and throughout the Clinton administration. Fishman describes the years before internal agreement was reached: "I remember getting pushback on this issue continuously from the political level. When we had new people coming in with Bush . . . we had to continually to push for this. . . . I remember us really working to figure out how do we make the case in terms that would be persuasive to them, which was always a struggle. Because at the end of the day, they had the predisposition to really just let states do what they wanted to do. They didn't care about this one way or the other."

That there was substantial continuity in the views and roles of a group of civil servants who crossed administrations was an immense asset in the struggle. Again, in Fishman's words, "I don't think we could have succeeded in what we did had there not been this collective of senior career people who felt the same way. . . . I felt that was pretty critical. If we had broken ranks, if there had been someone in that group . . . if any of the three of those key legs of the stool [the Administration for Children and Families, the Office of the Assistant Secretary for Planning and Evaluation, and OMB] had fallen out, it would've been a lot harder. . . . We reinforced each other."

Not all the experiments that flowed from the waivers yielded worthwhile results. Quite a few never began, most were not completed, and some that were completed were badly done. Furthermore, given the large number of changes that welfare reform involved, the knowledge gained was much less than it might have been had more complex designs been the rule. Certainly if one had been able to design a process to maximize learning about welfare reform, it would not have been as inefficient as the waiver process, and it quite likely would have been more effective. Overriding all these limitations, however, was the indisputable fact that the large numbers of evaluations contributed to changing the evaluation norms in the welfare policy community in a way that smaller numbers would not have. Furthermore, the random assignment requirement (even though it came down to the simplest lowest-common-denominator designs) was the only way this could have been achieved.

NEXT STEPS

The body of waiver experiments spread knowledge of the value and feasibility of experiments in a way that took welfare evaluation to a stage beyond what the previous Work/Welfare and HHS-initiated studies had done. It is also important to emphasize that, among the large body of dross, several jewels shone out in the waiver period, some of which are included in the next four chapters.

Judy's chapter 8 describes two important MDRC evaluations designed to assess the effectiveness of education and training approaches in increasing the likelihood of welfare recipients' getting jobs. The first is the California GAIN evaluation, which began in 1986 and concluded its final impact and cost-benefit studies in 1994. The second is Florida's Project Independence, for which the planning began in 1989 and the final report was issued in 1995. Both GAIN and Project Independence later became their states' JOBS programs.

My chapter 9 discusses the environment in which the JOBS evaluation was developed and implemented and the lessons learned. The evaluation contract for JOBS was awarded to MDRC in 1989. The evaluation itself continued beyond passage of the PRWORA in 1996 and, along with the GAIN evaluation, transformed the welfare landscape.

Chapter 10 continues the story with Judy describing MDRC's plans for, and execution of, a policy research agenda that included evaluating demonstrations (building on the knowledge gained from evaluating programs to help people find work) to make work pay enough to reduce poverty. Two of these, in Wisconsin and Minnesota, operated under waiver authority.

CHAPTER 8

Expanding the Agenda: The Role of Basic Education*

> Under the guise of research to determine how well the program is working, roughly 15–20 percent of the applicants . . . will be shunted into a control group that will receive no job counseling or support services. . . . This is shameful and inhumane, and shouldn't be allowed to happen.
>
> —*St. Petersburg (Fla.) Times*[1]

> If we're going to put thousands of people through something, we ought to be willing to find out whether or not it works.
>
> —Don Winstead[2]

We have seen that real-world experiments proved feasible and credible; that most welfare-to-work programs were successful; that politicians and public officials listened and acted; that states could be willing partners; that a major foundation sparked these changes; and that several government agencies endorsed experiments as uniquely reliable. If welfare research had gone no further, it would already be unusual in its influence and in the use of multiple, large-scale experiments to determine the potential of a reform strategy.

But the story did not end there. What makes the saga exceptional is that the momentum was sustained and resulted in a comprehensive and coherent body of reliable evidence about a range of policy alternatives. In the process,

*Chapter 8 authored by Judith M. Gueron.

welfare researchers demonstrated the potential of using random assignment in increasingly demanding environments and of learning more from such studies. In the ten years from 1986 to 1996, these distinctive new contributions began to emerge. There was a flowering of experiments, a sort of golden age—complete with fresh victories and intensified battles—that generally followed the new paradigm laid out in the early 1980s but with four key differences that interacted to create the larger whole: the entrepreneurs, who were the sources of innovation; the policies tested; the questions asked; and the scale of the programs and the experiments.

During these years, three parties took the lead in shaping the knowledge-building agenda: the federal government, MDRC, and the states. At the federal level, the Department of Health and Human Services (HHS) funded many of the major studies and brought researchers at several organizations, particularly Mathematica Policy Research and Abt Associates, into the field. At the state level, although governors sought to change welfare, not to conduct research, they sometimes ended up in random assignment studies because they needed federal waivers and encountered staff at HHS and OMB, who made budget neutrality, as measured by an experiment, the price for flexibility. In other cases, exceptional state officials who learned about the growing success of such studies decided that this approach held enough promise to be worth the political risk, in the process becoming determined converts and occasionally even writing random assignment into law. As a result, for the first time, some of the champions of random assignment—the people who bore the brunt of the fight—were state staff.

These three parties knew about the modest but positive effects of the first generation of welfare-to-work programs and asked whether something else might work better. For some, doing better meant producing larger impacts and reaching the more disadvantaged by increasing the focus on education and training. For others, it meant helping single mothers not only obtain work but move out of poverty by supplementing their earnings, getting them higher-paying jobs, or increasing child support payments. For still others, it meant extending services and obligations to a wider range of people, including mothers with younger children, teen parents, and fathers who were not living with their children on welfare. For yet others, it meant tougher mandates and limits on how long someone could receive welfare.

Whereas early 1980s studies addressed the first-order queries about welfare-to-work programs—Do they increase work and reduce welfare? At what cost?—people now sought answers to more refined questions: What works best for whom, under what conditions, and why? Were there trade-offs, with different policies producing different benefits at different costs for different people? What metrics should be used to judge success: more work, greater participation, higher wages, reduced poverty, reduced dependency, lower costs, or better outcomes for children? How much did different factors—design, implementation, context, who participates—explain why some programs are more effective than others?

Earlier experiments assessed special demonstrations of programs designed by researchers or funders (such as Supported Work or the negative-income-tax experiments) or state-run initiatives that, though large compared with the prior studies, were still pilot projects targeted to selected groups in a few locations. Although both these types of experiments continued, for the first time random assignment was used to evaluate full-scale, ongoing programs.

These four factors prompted an array of studies that pushed the frontier on complexity, size, conditions, and the use and integration of different research methods within the random assignment context. What led these three disparate actors to produce what ex post resembles a coherent knowledge development strategy? Why did this, on occasion, ignite strident opposition?

This chapter first describes how MDRC developed an agenda that we hoped to promote through a combination of challenge grants from foundations and selective responses to federal, state, and other initiatives. The rest of the chapter provides examples of some of the projects and shows why, despite past victories, the fight for random assignment in real-world conditions was far from won.

Why the military language? From the current vantage point, the value and feasibility of random assignment may seem so obvious as to be uncontroversial. My point throughout is to remind readers that gaining this reputation took relentless determination over a long time. There was continuous resistance from administrators, politicians, advocates, and most academic researchers, who argued that such studies were some combination of unnecessary, undoable, unethical, illegal, overly burdensome, unreasonably expensive, or uninformative. Surprisingly, given the relatively smooth sailing of the ten prior years, the changing nature and increased ambition of what was tested after 1986—plus some blunders—raised issues and prompted occasional explosions that, in at least one case, endangered the whole endeavor. Insults were hurled and lawsuits threatened, prompting public officials to confront the appropriateness and limits of this new tool and evaluators to adjust their plans. Were it not for the rare academics who supported this work and the stalwart converts among congressional and state staff and in advocacy groups, the fight (or at least particular battles) could easily have been lost.

DECIDING HOW TO PROCEED

By August 1986, when I replaced Barbara Blum as MDRC president and the Work/Welfare demonstration was winding down, we had emerged as the premier research organization working with the states. From our virtual monopoly on rigorous welfare-to-work evaluations, we had unparalleled knowledge about the potential and limits of such programs, the technique of inserting experiments into real-world settings, and the issues governors and their commissioners cared about. One result was that states increasingly sought MDRC assistance in research and program design, particularly after passage of the Family Support Act (FSA) in 1988.

Some things, however, had not changed. We still lived on soft money and in most years were under the gun to close large budget gaps. We still had no heritage of strategic planning and certainly no grand scheme to build a research field. But we also had been weaned from a reactive style and were determined to take charge of our future.

Leading from Strength

MDRC, as an organization, had a twofold vision of its mission: learning what works to improve the well-being of low-income people and using our research and the active communication of our findings to enhance the effectiveness of social policies and programs. We started from this definition and those factors we thought explained our past success: picking the right issues, having staff with strong research skills and operational know-how working in teams, insisting on rigorous and multidisciplinary research, producing accessible and timely products, and implementing an aggressive communications strategy that stopped short of advocacy.

We sought to maintain two types of work we believed contributed to our distinctive brand: demonstrations that tested new ideas at small scale, as a possible prelude to an expanded program; and evaluations of new or existing programs. In concept these two are distinct. In demonstrations, our multifaceted role would include some or all of the following: initiating or managing the test, raising funds, providing technical assistance to local programs that usually operated outside the mainstream service delivery system, and overseeing or conducting the study. In evaluations we would apply the research tools honed in the demonstration environment to assess regular operating programs designed by others. After 1981, however, when funding limits generally ruled out Supported Work–style demonstrations, the distinction became blurred. Demonstration programs had only token funds for operations and were therefore grafted onto existing funding streams and delivery systems. We called these unfunded demonstrations. Our evaluations of state programs were hybrids, in which we evaluated and sometimes modestly helped shape state-sponsored reforms that were often large but not full scale.

Nonetheless, there was still a difference, and we remained committed to conducting demonstrations. However, mounting demonstrations took substantial up-front time and money (in some cases from a dozen or more foundations). This could not be our only activity. In contrast, evaluations were often funded through federal or state procurements, involved little or no foundation fund-raising, and could be started relatively quickly. Their downside was that they did not draw as much on our operational skills and were likely to be funded via contracts, giving us less independence and possibly less control of the scope and quality of the research.

Conflicting Pressures

In considering how to move forward, we sought to balance several pressures. The first was the need to raise money. The easiest way to do this would be to cash in on our reputation and respond positively to state requests, even if this meant conducting studies that did not answer new questions. The second was a desire to prevent the staff from growing stale, and to keep the organization dynamic and not overly specialized, by doing projects that advanced knowledge and methodology. A third pressure came from our growing recognition that one study—even a large experiment—was unlikely to put an issue to rest. We had heard again and again that it was the replication of findings in diverse conditions that inspired confidence. As a result, we sought to avoid a scattershot approach and, instead, build clusters of our and others' studies, so that we could speak with greater conviction about the comparative value and trade-offs of different strategies.

An obvious way to reconcile these pressures would have been to grow enough to do it all. But the memory of large layoffs was still fresh enough to make us fear that a short-term bubble in demand for our services could lead to unsustainable expansion. Also, much of what we treasured about MDRC—its management style, the nature of our products, the collective work and approach to quality control—would change if we got much bigger.

Weighing all these factors in 1987, we decided to limit new welfare research to projects that addressed priority unanswered questions, thereby explicitly ceding some of the market to potential competitors. This strategy resonated with our view of MDRC's raison d'être, even though it meant a more uncertain short-term future and the draining hustle to fund new demonstrations. Ironically, our success in implementing this strategy led us to grow anyway—from 69 staff in 1986 to 97 by 1989 (back to our size in 1979) and to 159 by 1996—creating the very pressures to raise more money and change how we did business that we had sought to avoid.

Priority Questions

We next turned to the crystal ball of issues likely to be most salient over the next five to ten years. We asked ourselves and others, What are the major policies affecting low-income people that would be most valuable to assess in the coming years? The resulting list, which evolved over the next five years in response to the changing context, outreach to the policy community, and what we learned from each successive study, contained six priority questions.

1. Do welfare-to-work programs emphasizing education or training have larger payoffs (particularly for more disadvantaged people) than the lower-cost programs operated in the early 1980s?
2. Is it feasible or effective to implement universal welfare-to-work mandates (the scaling-up question) or to include mothers with young children?[3]
3. Do programs for teen mothers reduce long-term dependency and improve outcomes for young mothers and their children? [4]
4. Would efforts to increase work and reduce poverty be more successful if there were greater financial work incentives?
5. Would extending services or mandates to noncustodial fathers of children on welfare increase child support payments or improve outcomes for them or their children?
6. What would happen if there were a limit on the length of time that families could receive welfare?

Thinking back, Robert Ivry, our most politically shrewd insider and the senior person at the time responsible for recruiting sites in our projects, marvels at the combination of serendipity and agency that fueled the agenda-building strategy.

> You know, we always talk about incremental knowledge-building at MDRC, where you do one study, you answer a set of questions, this generates hypotheses and unanswered questions that you use as a foundation for the next project. . . . There's this continuous, circular feedback loop. . . . I think it's truly astonishing . . . how we were agile enough to adapt our welfare studies to policy changes and zero in on exactly the right questions at the right time. And even though people complained that by the time the results came out the issues would have moved on, the timing was always almost perfect anyway because these issues don't go away in a year.

Necessary but Not Sufficient

By the fall of 1986, MDRC staff had come a long way from our stance in 1982, when we were not sure random assignment was feasible in regular public agencies and were thus open to alternatives. We now felt that we could design an ethical experiment that would answer important questions and that we should be ready to walk away rather than build a large project on a weaker foundation. However, we needed to be sure our board was behind us, particularly because at that time we were in the very early stage of two next-generation experiments that raised multiple red flags: the California Greater Avenues for Independence and Job Training Partnership Act evaluations described later in this chapter. To find out, we held a far-ranging discussion of random assignment, including the recent reports from expert panels at the National Academy of Sciences and the Department of Labor, chaired by Robinson Hollister and Ernst Stromsdorfer, respectively, on both of which I served.[5] Each panel separately concluded they did not believe the results of most comparison-group studies—including our multimillion-dollar study of the $250 million Youth Incentive Entitlement project (see chapter 3) and the Department of Labor's $50 million or so outlay on the Comprehensive Employment and Training Act evaluation—and saw no alternative to random assignment, given existing statistical techniques, if one wanted to produce credible data on program effectiveness.

Board members supported the staff, some unequivocally, others because they thought the environment put a premium on evidence; still others urged us not to lose sight of the limitations to the technique. Staff resonated to the cautions. We took to heart Eli Ginzberg's warning that MDRC should not become an organization that had only the hammer of random assignment and as a result took on only small nails, rather than going after the major open issues with a more varied toolkit; and Richard Nathan's urging that we strengthen our effort to understand why programs did or did not work—that is, nonimpact research focusing on implementation, management, institutional change, and program context.

Support for a wider agenda came also from our foundation funders and the participating states and sites. During these years, we were eager to diversify and expand foundation funding, seeing it as vital to our stability, independence, flexibility, and ability to control our agenda and conduct demonstrations. Even if the federal government was getting back into the business of funding experiments (as Howard describes in chapters 5 and 7), we were wary of becoming overly dependent on contract research, fearing it could disappear at any time, be overly narrow, or impose a political agenda. We had seen the brutal shift from the Rosen-Hans epoch to the highly political early Reagan years and wanted to limit our exposure.

This meant aligning our work with foundation priorities. These varied greatly, of course, but across the years we found that most foundation staff wanted to see a direct connection between their resources and benefits to people. Thus they were more interested in supporting service programs or the application of knowledge—dissemination and technical assistance and research focused on how to improve programs—than impact studies. Although they responded to our mantra about the risk of promoting policies on a hunch and discrediting them on an anecdote, there was rarely deep enthusiasm for funding the creation of evidence at the level of rigor we sought. After all, large-scale evaluations are expensive. Foundations had limited funds and tended, quite reasonably, to see this activity as a federal responsibility. There was also a tendency to disparage the gold standard as excessive and to think one could learn the same thing, or other things just as valuable, with lower-cost methods.

These concerns partly explain why MDRC never wanted to trumpet an experiment simply as a scientific triumph but instead sought to show that the effort was worth it—in that we gained important insights that would not have emerged from weaker methods, that this was a way to identify approaches the government might not promote, that the quality of evidence was appreciated by some influential audiences, that the findings helped build stronger programs, and that the studies informed (and sometimes affected) legislation that foundations cared about. This also explains why we sought to combat perceptions that we were purists who valued only quantitative analysis, were weak on replication, or cared only about the national audience and not about sharing operational lessons. In various ways we tried to communicate that our mission was not to validate methodology per se but rather to learn what works as a route to improving the well-being of low-income people. As part of this, we emphasized dissemination and produced many publications targeted at practitioners.

I remember making an admittedly self-serving argument to foundation leaders about the value of iconic studies that build the durable evidence to support whole fields. My theme was leverage and legacy: You are the nation's risk capital; you have limited funds but ambitious goals; one route to get there is to fund evaluations that can distinguish what works from what does not; failure does not mean learning that something does not work but not learning whether something works; through research, you not only support programs individually but redirect larger public resources toward potentially more effective uses in areas you care about. Slowly, as it became clear that social experiments were indeed judged uniquely credible in policy debates, we found more champions who made sustained commitments.[6]

Lack of Academic Support

Although MDRC was committed to random assignment, we knew we would have to continue converting or rebutting the naysayers and (even as we tried to obscure this reality from the states and some funders) that there was little vocal support for this work in the academic community. Reflecting that reality, twenty years later, Thomas Cook, a renowned scholar of research methods, asked me, "Why, as an economist, did you persist and advocate for random assignment experiments . . . in that place and time when you were in such a minority and the glitterati in the field were against it and favored selection modeling and instrumental variables?"

My answer is that throughout these years colleagues at MDRC and I were not focused on the academic elite. As a result, and in retrospect fortunately, I was not aware of the depth of vitriol or of the personal disdain some academics felt toward what they called "contract shops."[7] Of course, we had to deal with particular harsh blasts, the most formidable from James Heckman, who asserted (1992a and 1992b) that experiments produce results that are likely to be biased (because random assignment alters the programs being analyzed) and are of dubious scientific value (because they yield no basic or cumulative knowledge). In doing so, we felt (rightly or wrongly) that when the sparks flew only a handful of scholars (most notably, Hollister and Gary Burtless) could be called on to defend the value and ethics of experiments and give them a legitimacy that we, the obviously self-interested practitioners, could not.[8] For this reason, I emphasized the just-in-time endorsements of experiments by the prestigious National Academy of Sciences and Department of Labor panels noted above in our fight to implement such studies in California and Florida.

Although stung by the attacks and the drag of swimming upstream, we plowed on and really did not understand why the opposition appeared so unrelenting. After all, random assignment was invented by statisticians, and the first social experiments were launched by academics. Yet when it moved beyond the lab into the real world, and others were devising the tools and gaining the savvy, most academics were not in the front lines or even in sight but seemed to enjoy throwing darts at the shortcomings (which they often accurately identified) without acknowledging the strengths. It seemed to me there were two groups of dart throwers: the economists who said they could get the same or better answers at less cost by using statistical modeling that would solve the selection bias problem, and the qualitative and institutional researchers who said we were addressing narrow and relatively unimportant questions.[9]

I had a hunch this fight was playing out on several levels. On one level, it appeared to be an interdisciplinary and intradisciplinary and organizational competition for money, influence, and legitimacy. On another, it felt like an argument about what econometric methods could do, the importance of theory, the audience and goals of research, and different views of truth, knowledge, and science. As part of this, I felt that, from the perspective of some academics, what we were doing in experiments was simple to the point of trivial, revealed our lack of methodological expertise or imagination,[10] and that the work would not be worthy of a Ph.D., let alone tenure.[11]

Finally, we were clearly living in worlds with different cultures and senses of what was at stake. My insistence that all reports include estimates of the same basic impacts, identically defined and presented, and only then go on to new analysis, is one example.[12] I saw our job as making it as easy as possible for busy, nontechnical readers to find and understand the results, not to showcase how smart we were. Thus I was delighted but not surprised to hear from Howard (a key audience) that when he got an MDRC report he went straight to a specific table to compare findings from the new study with prior ones. Some academics recast this deliberate simplicity as an indictment.[13] Henry Aaron (1990, 279) contrasts the two value systems well:

> The values of the academy, in which most social scientists are trained and many are employed, may be inconsistent with the value of the policy world. The former praises technical virtuosity and elegance and rewards analytical innovation. The latter insists on simplicity and transparency and is indifferent to analytical innovation. The paper that wins tenure is not likely to influence the decision makers. The paper that influences a member of Congress is likely to be dismissed as recreational, not professional, activity by one's academic colleagues. But that situation is a commentary on the values of the academy, not of the standards for good policy analysis.

To many in the academic community this type of debate is riskless and engaged in with enthusiasm—a familiar jousting where the heated back-and-forth and identification of weaknesses are the best way to arrive at scientific truth. For MDRC, where random assignment felt central to delivering on our mission and even to our institutional survival, the risks were enormous. Too much dispute could not only kill particular studies but also undermine the singular strength of experiments—their ability to rise above the cacophony of methodological debates that Aaron (1978, 158–59) recognizes can lead to policy paralysis.

Reflecting on the lack of academic enthusiasm for randomized experiments during these years, Robert Solow, in a personal communication with the author in late 2012, observes that "much of this tension is just like the traditional tension between scientists and engineers or even between theorists and experimentalists within a science. The reputational payoff in economics is mainly for originality and generality, and has always favored theory over empirical work unless the latter is especially ingenious. . . . Recently the fashion within economics . . . has shifted toward data-driven empirical studies . . . and the intellectual payoff now goes to finding clever 'natural experiments.'"[14]

IMPLEMENTING OUR AGENDA

Choosing the questions and committing to random assignment were critical first steps; the hard work was finding the answers. We had not developed the questions based primarily on what we thought was most fundable. But our choice of questions had been influenced by several pragmatic factors: our reading of the market, our conviction that we could influence that market, and the strong interest many welfare commissioners were expressing in being part of a new MDRC project (what board member Bernard Anderson called the Tiffany effect).

We did not start with a well-developed game plan. But we did have a strategy. First, we viewed MDRC as only one actor in the knowledge-building enterprise. The Department of Health and Human Services and the Department of Labor were funding major demonstrations and evaluations that involved other research firms. Our aim (not always successful) was to be the ones responsible for the more innovative projects. Second, we envisioned an iterative and interactive process in which we would simultaneously test-market the questions, promote their importance, and be ready to pounce on opportunities to address them. As part of this, we listened closely to the interests of potential partners to identify possible projects and funding coalitions and to refine the research design. In particular, we talked with Howard and his colleagues to learn which issues they wanted to address through federally sponsored evaluations.

Third, for institutional reasons, we hoped to end up with a combination of one or two demonstrations and some evaluations or hybrids. For the evaluations, we planned to respond selectively to federal and state competitions and requests. For the demonstrations, we had in mind creating public-private partnerships. For the hybrid studies, we planned to seek another Ford Foundation challenge grant so we could replicate the strategy of the early 1980s and transform state reforms into high-quality studies. We thought FSA would prompt state initiatives (as the Omnibus Budget Reconciliation Act had in 1982) and wanted to ensure again that at least some of the thousand flowers that might bloom would leave a reliable trail.

Fourth, there was another, more intellectual dimension to this interactive process. We were always pushing to integrate what all the research told us and make sure new studies raised the bar substantively or methodologically (or both). While we were doing this, so were Howard and his colleagues.[15] This dance, in which we were consciously circling around each other and inviting the states and foundations in as partners, in part explains how knowledge cumulated and how later studies systematically addressed questions or refined methods raised by earlier ones, so that at the end it made a cohesive whole.

Over the next ten years, MDRC conducted more than a dozen major experiments that addressed all six questions on our agenda (see table 8.1). Both our actions and unexpected events shaped this: invitations from some states and the Canadian government to take on intriguing experiments, two more multimillion-dollar challenge grants from the Ford Foundation, HHS's insistence on random assignment as the price of waivers, our ability to build large coalitions to fund demonstrations, and an explosion of increasingly radical state proposals to reshape and then end Aid to Families with Dependent Children (AFDC).

The result was a collection of studies that shared many firsts, including use of random assignment to evaluate full-scale programs, its expansion to new populations and venues, and its integration with multiple research methods. The expanding track record of success and recognition of the unique strength of experiments generated new converts and contributed to the conviction that, if you wanted to learn about the success of welfare reform, no other style of research would be taken as seriously.

As anticipated, the homegrown demonstrations proved the hardest to launch, starting with the need to assemble as many as two dozen funders and build a network of local programs. Pulling this off took an unusual combination of optimism, drive, salesmanship, resilience, and faith. MDRC's undisputed master of this—part rainmaker, part visionary, part ambassador—was and is Robert Ivry. I particularly treasured Ivry's work because he took on and excelled at what I hated most—begging for support—and showed a remarkable talent for transforming funding appeals into an exchange of ideas and ultimately a mutually valued relationship.

The rest of this chapter focuses on two of these experiments—California's Greater Avenues for Independence (GAIN) and Florida's Project Independence (PI) programs. Together with Canada's Self-Sufficiency Project (SSP), Milwaukee's New Hope demonstration, and the Minnesota Family Investment Program (MFIP),[16] these five studies illustrate several characteristics of this phase of our story. First, senior state officials became advocates for random assignment. Moreover, corny as it sounds, they did this not primarily

Table 8.1   MDRC Welfare Experiments, by Priority Question, 1986 to 2000

| Welfare-to-Work Programs | | | | |
Emphasizing Basic Education	Universal or Including Mothers of Small Children	Learnfare, Teen Mothers	Financial Work Incentives	Noncustodial Fathers	Time Limits on Welfare
California GAIN[2] Florida PI[2] HHS JOBS evaluation[2] Los Angeles Jobs-First GAIN		Ohio LEAP, New Chance[1]	MFIP[2] New Hope[2] Canada SSP[2]	Parents' Fair Share[1]	Vermont Welfare Restructuring Project Florida Family Restructuring Program Connecticut Jobs First Program

Source: Author's compilation.
[1]Homegrown demonstrations in multiple sites.
[2]Focus of chapters 8, 9, or 10.

because they needed federal waivers but because they thought it was the right thing to do and the only means of getting defensible answers to their questions. (MDRC, as their contractor, became part instigator, part partner, and part catalyst in realizing and embellishing their vision.)

Second, states put up some of their own money for evaluation and more foundations participated. These changes did not reduce the importance of the Ford Foundation's challenge grants, which again allowed us to aggressively identify initiatives, structure them to maximize learning, leverage other resources for an adequate evaluation, and insist on our right to publish findings and use data after completion of a contract.

However, support at the top did not mean the fight for random assignment was won, because we and the states kept increasing the demands on the method. As far as I know, California's GAIN study was the first such evaluation of a new, highly visible and political, full-scale statewide program. Florida's Project Independence was all these and was also an ongoing program. Both examples showed the importance of building and mobilizing a community of supporters. This was particularly true of the firestorm that started in Florida, spread to a major federal study, and was ultimately extinguished by a coalition of unexpected allies.

Many people concluded that the studies had an impact on policy, practice, and research. They also agreed that the nature of the lessons would most likely not have been revealed or believed had we used anything other than random assignment. Together, the results suggested that policy makers faced a trade-off, with different reform strategies proving more or less successful in reaching different goals. This echoed through and was substantially reinforced by the study of the federal Job Opportunities and Basic Skills Training (JOBS) program that Howard discusses in chapter 9.

CALIFORNIA'S GAIN PROGRAM

In 1984 California's Republican governor, George Deukmejian, and Democratically controlled legislature came under pressure to reverse the state's escalating welfare rolls. With exceptionally high grants, the state had only 11 percent of the U.S. population but 15 percent of the nation's AFDC caseload and accounted for 21 percent of total AFDC outlays. By September 1985, the state had enacted the most ambitious welfare-to-work initiative to date: the GAIN program.

Forged by a bipartisan committee led by the conservative Republican secretary of California's Health and Welfare Agency, David Swoap, and the liberal Democratic state assemblyman from San Francisco, Arthur Agnos, GAIN combined elements of San Diego's earlier mandatory job search–workfare program and Massachusetts's voluntary Employment and Training Choices program.[17] The result was a program that allowed each side to claim victory and, for different reasons, expect better outcomes—particularly for long-term welfare recipients, the group of greatest concern—than the modest but positive results MDRC had found for San Diego. For the political right, GAIN imposed a stronger obligation: throughout the state all applicants and recipients with school-age children (200,000 mostly single mothers, or slightly more than one-third of the adults on welfare), unless specifically exempted, would be required to participate in work-related activities, including workfare, for as long as they remained on the rolls; those who failed to meet the requirement would face sanctions. For the left, it offered greater opportunity: People would be provided with child care and a range of services, including remedial or basic education (but not higher education) and skills training, intended to help them obtain work, get a better and longer-lasting job, and move out of poverty. To satisfy both sides, the legislation was targeted and proscriptive, with high-cost activities reserved for those deemed to need them. Thus the emphasis was education first for those with limited academic skills and getting a job quickly for the rest, backed up by other activities and involving choices and contracts.[18]

However, since this was California—where counties ran welfare and work programs under state supervision—the state agency could translate the law into policy, but each of the fifty-eight counties would transform that policy into a locally controlled and delivered program that reflected their diverse conditions, attitudes, welfare populations, and views of the appropriate balance between opportunity and obligation.[19] Thus from the beginning, policy makers anticipated many variants on the GAIN theme.

The GAIN concept represented a major departure from business as usual for the welfare system. Its goal was to ensure that people would always have to do something in exchange for their cash grants. Given the spotty history of the Work Incentive (WIN) program and the limited intensity, scale, and duration of the early 1980s efforts to change it, pulling off this second-generation program would be a major management challenge and serve as an important precursor to the JOBS program of FSA. Impressively, California recognized that, at least initially, GAIN would cost more than just paying cash welfare.

Thus the program had a projected budget of $335 million a year when fully operational, almost as much as the whole country had spent on the Work Incentive program at its peak.

Origin of the Evaluation

Unlike the state studies in the Work/Welfare demonstration, MDRC did not use the sweetener of a Ford challenge grant to entice the state into a rigorous study. Nor did a request for federal waivers play a role.[20] The GAIN legislation required the welfare agency to undertake an evaluation of "program cost, caseload movement, and program outcomes" and specified that it could contract with a qualified organization to do it.

James Riccio (1997, 244), who directed MDRC's GAIN evaluation, says that the program's origin "helped to sow the seeds for an evaluation. . . . All in all, it was quite a complex model. But, was it feasible? Would it work? How much would it cost? Would it be worth the price?" The program's reliance on basic education came from evidence that many welfare recipients had poor skills and correlation data showing that people with low skills had low income. But it was by no means clear that mandatory education would pay off. During the legislative debate, both sides had cited MDRC's earlier San Diego study and connected GAIN's passage and design to its lessons.[21] As a result, according to Riccio (1997, 244), "a few important legislative staff . . . and some key lawmakers apparently came to appreciate that reliable evaluation research could be a valuable tool. . . . They wanted to insure that in the future the legislature would be in a position to decide whether GAIN was worth continuing, or how it could be strengthened, on the basis of facts and not have to rely just on ideology and anecdotes."[22]

Two people played particularly central roles in the negotiations on GAIN and were also key to its evaluation: Carl Williams, the point person for Swoap, who became deputy director in the State Department of Social Services (SDSS) responsible for GAIN, and Julia Lopez, the main aide to Agnos, who became the chief consultant to the legislature's joint oversight committee.[23] Both agreed that, given its enormous budget, GAIN had to be rigorously evaluated and that this meant random assignment. Lopez ties her conviction to the San Diego evaluation: "It was unimpeachable. . . . It no longer became ideological. This was the power of it. . . . I knew this was the gold standard."[24] In addition, she links her commitment to Agnos: "[GAIN] was his baby. . . . He was so convinced that this would work, he wanted to prove it beyond a reasonable doubt."

Table 8.2   Timeline of California GAIN Evaluation and Related Events

Date	Event
1982–1988	MDRC's Work/Welfare demonstration, includes first San Diego random assignment study
1984–1988	MDRC shares results from San Diego and other sites
1985–1989	San Diego SWIM experiment
September 1985	California passes GAIN legislation
January 1986	MDRC begins GAIN evaluation
1987–1991	MDRC publishes GAIN implementation and participation findings
March 1988	Random assignment starts in first GAIN county
October 1988	President Reagan signs Family Support Act establishing JOBS program
1989	GAIN becomes largest state JOBS program
1992–1994	MDRC publishes GAIN impact and benefit-cost findings
July 1996	MDRC publishes working paper on five-year GAIN impacts
August 1996	President Clinton signs PRWORA, replacing AFDC entitlement with TANF block grants to states, tougher work requirements, and a lifetime five-year limit on federal assistance

Source: Author's compilation.

Williams attributes his conviction both to his training in experimental psychology and to having seen Senator Moynihan change his opinion on a guaranteed annual income when confronted with findings from the Seattle-Denver income maintenance experiment. Another factor was Williams's earlier work in Massachusetts, where he had witnessed firsthand the contradictory nonexperimental evaluations of Employment and Training Choices, something he wanted to avoid in the GAIN evaluation. History may have also played another role. For those legislative staff who had followed the two San Diego experiments (see timeline in table 8.2), the problem-free implementation of random assignment had defanged the dragon by making the method almost familiar.

Williams took the next step and suggested that the state engage MDRC. His logic was straightforward. He wanted a broad-ranging and scientific evaluation. He had read the San Diego reports, thought they did not look preprogrammed to come out a certain way, and considered MDRC the premier research firm in the area. As he puts it in retrospect,

I was trained in the scientific method, so to me, one of the reasons I liked MDRC so much was because I saw really good science being done. You know, there is a lot of schlocky social science. . . . [Researchers] give the answers that people want and all that kind of stuff. But the one thing about MDRC was, it looked to me that you guys were doing really honest, straight up, good social science. . . . You're not a political organization; you're not being emotionally driven into your answers; you are not biased; you're coming at it with a scientific approach, and that was very impressive to me.

Reflecting his desire to get the program up and running quickly, in October he approached us, asking us posthaste to submit information that might justify a sole-source contract.

We thus found ourselves in an unprecedented situation where the entrepreneur pushing for an evaluation and for random assignment—and willing to pay for it with state funds—was the lead state official.[25] Here was an ideal opportunity to get some answers to the first two of our six priority questions. Not only did GAIN promise to be a much more intensive program than those of the early 1980s, but it would be operating at full scale and in a state that would give the findings obvious political and policy significance. But we did have a concern. Until then we had used the leverage of partial Ford Foundation funding to head off pressure to weaken the research design or reports, to protect data confidentiality, and to give us some flexible money. Although we decided to proceed, we drafted protective contract language and moved quickly to set up an office in California headed by the politically astute former director of employment and training programs for San Mateo county, John Wallace, who would have many occasions to use his skills to sustain the study over the next eight years.[26]

To lock it up, we and SDSS faced three interrelated challenges: Could we win over state legislators who had objected to an out-of-state firm conducting the evaluation under a sole-source contract? Could we use random assignment? Could we devise a research plan that would satisfy the counties, the state welfare agency, and the state legislature? MDRC could not have overcome these hurdles alone. They were too political and too local. I tell the story in some detail because it speaks to the importance of allies.

In addressing these challenges, we drew on our two exceptional advocates: Williams and Lopez. Both were smart, knowledgeable, strategic, and politically savvy; both understood research and were determined to get an objective study that was done right.[27] They were also very direct. Williams said he was not willing to supervise a program of this size and complexity unless it had a really sound evaluation. Lopez warned us that senior legislators had a strong interest in serious research and feared a cozy relationship between MDRC and SDSS. Her message was sharp: This is not like the San Diego study; keep in touch, listen, relate to us and not just to SDSS. In turn, she quickly demonstrated her ability and willingness to advise us on how to negotiate Sacramento's treacherous political terrain.

The out-of-state challenge soon boiled down to whether we could win over state senator Bill Greene, a Democrat from Watts, the powerful and intimidating leader of two key committees: the Industrial Relations Committee and the finance subcommittee that oversaw health, human services, and employment. As Lopez recalls,

> Greene had a visceral belief in the human capital model and during the negotiations around GAIN insisted that there had to be remedial education before job search: He said, "You're not going to send someone out there who can't read and write and unless you do that, I'm not on." That was nonnegotiable. He also hated welfare so much he really believed in GAIN being an alternative. . . . He used to say that . . . this is the end of welfare as we know it; from now on it is about a path toward a job and independence. . . . And Bill Greene really believed in that. So, I think for Bill it was really the universality of the program that ultimately got him to question the random assignment decision.[28]

We got the answer quickly. Williams and I walked over to the capital, in mid-February 1986, thinking we would meet with Greene's assistant, Alan Davenport, to discuss the senator's concern about random assignment. But we ended up in a two-hour exchange with Davenport, Ben Munger (the senator's long-term economics guru, whom Lopez calls "the unsung hero" of the evaluation), and the senator himself. It started with a dressing down by Greene about how no out-of-state firm could understand what was going on and that there were good firms in California to do the job and that he supported GAIN because it offered "something real," education. Despite the hostile start, we ended positively and moved forward. This proved to be the first of a number of meetings MDRC had with Senator Greene in an effort to convince him that we were not part of a Deukmejian administration effort to kill his GAIN program; nonetheless, he remained uneasy about random assignment and two years later launched an almost fatal challenge.

The Fight for Random Assignment

The second challenge (using random assignment) came to a head quickly and interacted with the third (reaching agreement on the research plan). From the start, Williams had anticipated legal and political opposition, and in November 1985 he reported that he had gotten a preliminary reading that the GAIN statute would not permit random assignment. Undaunted, he requested a statement spelling out how alternative designs would weaken the study, and I shot back a memo fortified with quotes from the fortuitously timely National Academy of Sciences and Department of Labor expert panels (both released that month) that concluded with a plea:

> The GAIN program is a major state initiative with a clear legislative mandate to determine program impacts. . . . What these two panels concluded was that, given what we know now, alternative strategies yield results that simply are not believable. In determining program impacts we thus face a choice: either use a proven and defensible random assignment design or do not try to determine program impacts. The alternative to random assignment is to launch into a major impact study, spend substantial sums, end up with uncertain results and face the assault from critics. The GAIN evaluation is too important to burden with this risk.

Rereading the file drawers full of memos from those years, I was struck by how much effort, patience, art, and trust were involved in managing the GAIN evaluation; and how uncertain was the outcome. The image that struck me was a bubbling cauldron. For more than two years, issues would float to the top, be "resolved," and then sink from view, only to get propelled back to the surface (often agitated by state-county friction) in the same or slightly altered form and repeat the process.

Four main factors explain why random assignment provoked repeated legal and ethical objections that had not come up, or been more muted, in the first generation Work/Welfare demonstration state studies.

1. Scale: GAIN was intended to be universal for all who met the mandatory criteria.

2. Permanence: GAIN was implemented not on a trial basis but as a new, ongoing, statewide initiative.
3. More opportunity: GAIN's emphasis on education, even though mandatory, made the denial of services to controls more controversial.
4. County variation: Finally, counties, as noted, had substantial control of their programs.

Several other aspects of the GAIN law and California context affected the process as well. The state could not force counties to participate in the research, and we did not want them to try, fearing that unless counties volunteered they would find a way to undermine the study.[29] Counties were given two years to plan their programs and five to phase in the full caseload, providing ample time for protests to gather steam. In addition, different people had strong opinions on what they wanted to learn and what was feasible and appropriate; because of the program's prominence and state funding of the research, these counted much more than in our prior studies.

Michael Bangser, MDRC's general counsel, reviewed the legal and ethical issues for the board in a September 30, 1986, memorandum. His bottom line was that, although no court had specifically addressed these issues for programs such as GAIN, California's SDSS had been right to push for a clarifying amendment before we started random assignment. In this SDSS had been successful; in June 1986 the state legislature had amended the law to provide that random assignment "shall be utilized . . . [to] ensure a valid evaluation of the GAIN program's effectiveness."

This, however, did not end the debate. The first three issues—scale, opportunity, and permanence—interacted to raise more ethical red flags. To get a clean answer to SDSS's and the legislature's central question—Is GAIN effective?—required that the control group get no GAIN services.[30] But GAIN was an ongoing program, not a demonstration. Also, GAIN offered both education opportunities and tough mandates, with the result that some people thought controls were denied benefits while others thought they escaped obligations and penalties. And, most important in those early days, when no one knew what GAIN would cost, people assumed that funding would be adequate to support a universal program, raising the risk that the experiment itself would reduce the number of people served. Did these conditions rule out random assignment, as we had thought saturation would in 1982? Were we inadvertently crossing a line and denying people a quasi or real entitlement? We knew that, in their normal operations, states routinely experiment with programs, modify rules, and deny people services. Certainly Lopez thought the state had not only the right but the obligation to find out whether GAIN worked. She remembers how she felt: "We were spending a boatload of money. . . . We had to do this. It never crossed my mind not to do it." Williams had a similar reaction. Nonetheless, the message of universal coverage was out there. Was the amendment that required a control group sufficient? How would counties respond if controls wanted GAIN services?[31]

With the universality issue front and center, we worked intensely in Sacramento and each county to resolve whether, how, and where to use random assignment.[32] The greatest challenge remained before us: convincing enough counties—and not just any ones but a representative group of them that had to include Los Angeles—that the benefits of being in the study exceeded what many perceived as the political liabilities. Things began badly. San Diego, which because of its prior experience in two MDRC random assignment studies carried a lot of weight with the other counties,[33] initially voiced the strongest objections that the research would dictate the program (the analogy was to how a photographer controls a wedding) and thus interfere with county autonomy; make the program look bad (by starting random assignment too soon and ending the follow-up before it had captured benefits that could ultimately offset the up-front investment); and focus on impacts and neglect important institutional and attitudinal changes. Other counties piled on.

The campaign seesawed back and forth, with SDSS and legislative staff deflecting lawsuits and other efforts to make random assignment illegal. One of my worst memories from these forty years is the time the Santa Clara welfare director called Goldman, MDRC's director of GAIN research during the initial years, a Nazi to her face. As the counties delayed starting their GAIN programs and decisions stretched out, time itself became our enemy: until random assignment actually began, people could not be called unreasonable for doubting whether it could work.

Why was the experiment ultimately embraced by many counties and supported strongly over its eight years, an eternity in state politics? The first factor was that Williams and Lopez were unyielding in their determination to see it through. From the beginning it was clear that MDRC was not out there alone. There was a united front, a shared passion. As Williams puts it, "We were going to get random assignment one way or another."[34] Their successors held the same line. In this sense there was drama but never despair.

The second was the open, inclusive, bipartisan, and collaborative process Williams and Lopez put in place to resolve design issues and adjust to changing circumstances.[35] Repeatedly, MDRC would prepare option papers and go over them with SDSS and a core group of county and legislative staff, with all focused on getting maximum knowledge from what was viewed as a capped research budget.[36] At the same time, we and SDSS sought input from service providers and welfare rights and child advocacy organizations. As Riccio (1997, 245) puts it, "They were all stakeholders in the GAIN program, and we wanted them to become stakeholders in the evaluation as well."

This process not only ensured that decisions would be widely accepted and would hold up over time but also created a level of trust and a community of allies who understood how particular actions and conditions would affect the study or the questions it could answer and came to believe in its value. As a result, even when Williams and Lopez left around the time random assignment began (March 1988), there was deep support for the next phase—most notably, from Dennis Boyle, Kathy Lewis, and Bruce Wagstaff (at SDSS) and among legislative staff, particularly Paul Warren, who replaced Lopez.[37] On our side, Wallace, Goldman, and Riccio had the right strengths to support this process and market the results: they were plain talkers, good listeners, patient, tenacious, and creative.

The third factor that got us through was self-interest. SDSS made it clear to the counties early on that random assignment came directly from the legislature. Lopez left no doubt: "GAIN is not a block grant to solve county fiscal problems. We have certain expectations and interests." The threat was explicit: High hopes are pinned on GAIN, but the program was as yet unproven. GAIN's generous resources would dry up without convincing evidence that it worked.

The fourth was MDRC's style of working with the state and counties, in which (as always) we sought to build a relationship of mutual respect that made them part of a learning community, created a sense of privilege and collegiality, gave them broad national visibility, and assured them that the evaluation addressed their concerns. We limited the impact component of the evaluation to six diverse counties. But these counties together represented 50 percent of the state's AFDC caseload, and we made sure the design would include enough people (33,000) to provide reliable estimates of effects and net costs for each of those counties and for key subgroups. Furthermore, the design was simple enough—random assignment to GAIN or a control group—so that it would not constrain how counties chose to operate GAIN, initially or over time. Counties would also be reimbursed by the state for research-related costs. To give the six counties a chance to work out the kinks, random assignment would start about ten months after the program began, and the sample would be followed for three (eventually extended to five) years. People in the control group would receive no GAIN services but could participate in the extensive other programs available in the community.[38]

We also committed ourselves to addressing an issue of major importance to all parties. GAIN was a multidimensional program. Everyone wanted to understand the extent to which different components, strategies, or local conditions affected participation patterns and ultimate success for key subgroups. For legal and political reasons, we had to rule out randomly assigning welfare recipients to diverse aspects of GAIN. Instead we fell back on an approach we all recognized as second best: collecting more detailed information than had been done in the past on a range of dimensions—how the programs were managed and implemented, changes in welfare and related institutions, the attitudes of staff and recipients, local conditions, the use of child care—and testing hypotheses about their relationship to county-specific impacts.

The fifth factor that drew fans to the evaluation was that, starting in 1987, we issued reports on program implementation that proved useful to the managers and also showed we could be flexible and respond to the state's concerns. Thus shortly after Lewis took over as the hands-on manager of the GAIN program, she faced a barrage of questions about the use of child care funds, which was much lower than expected. Was this because people did not understand their new entitlement to child care, were not offered the required choice of providers, or could not find care that suited their needs and preferences? At her request, we produced a report showing that underuse resulted from a combination of people's preferences, legitimate nonparticipation in GAIN, and the normal movement of people off welfare. That report, and one published a month earlier, revealed the power of a simple visual tool developed by Gayle Hamilton, MDRC's expert on measuring participation: a flow chart of the paths followed by a typical 100 people registered for GAIN, indicating how many reached key mileposts and why they fell out of the expected sequence.[39] Ivry notes that Hamilton's funnel diagram was pivotal for research and an eye-opening technical assistance tool for managers. Riccio recalls that Lewis's positive experience with these reports motivated her to take an active role in shaping the research agenda and advocating for a high-quality study.

The final factor—the one that at last made opponents such as Senator Greene feel comfortable with random assignment—was the state's budget crisis. In February 1988, only a month before we were slated to begin random assignment, we learned that Senator Greene was determined to block it and to urge Los Angeles to pull out (a lethal threat, since the county had more than a third of the state's welfare caseload). At just that time, new projections showed GAIN's costs running substantially higher than original estimates because more people than anticipated were judged to need remedial education. The state's decision to hold the budget line effectively ended the concept of a GAIN entitlement for all and required the counties to come up with some way to deny eligible people access to services.[40] This had an immediate impact on the senator. Instead of denouncing the study when we met a few days later, he told us that, since the budget crisis meant an excess demand for slots, a lottery would be a fair way to give everyone an equal chance.

What followed was anticlimactic, given the scale and complexity of the intake process. A number of controls wanted to be in GAIN, and others rejoiced at having dodged the obligations and penalties. But basically random assignment went off without a hitch, so smoothly, in fact, that Riverside and Los Angeles counties opted to participate in subsequent experiments, and one county decided to continue the lottery after the study ended (as an objective means to limit staff caseloads).[41]

Not all stories have a deeply moving ending, but this one did. In 1992 Senator Greene, then retired and ill, called to thank Wallace for our new report, the first to show GAIN's impacts: "You've answered my dreams; you've contributed more to the people, and me, than you know. . . . The beauty is in the honesty of the research; it is the most honest I've read. . . . You've made a dream of being a public official a reality."

Lessons About Program and Policy

The GAIN program had been based on the hope that emphasizing basic education for those with limited academic skills and helping the rest get a job quickly would produce better results (particularly for long-term welfare recipients) than the shorter-term, primarily job search approach common in the early 1980s—and that the higher cost would be worth it. The study was destined to be important because it was California but also because Congress had made a similar bet in making JOBS the centerpiece of national reform.

The findings were mixed. When the results for all six counties were lumped together, GAIN's mixed-service model outperformed the job search–based programs on some measures, generating larger, longer-lasting impacts (still robust five years later) and having greater success with more disadvantaged recipients.[42] Nonetheless, the big picture remained in the range of modest but positive: over five years, in the average three months, 28 percent of single mothers assigned to the program worked, compared with 24 percent of controls; by the last three months, 39 percent received some AFDC benefits, compared with 42 percent of controls. Cumulatively, over the five years, people in GAIN earned an average of $2,853 (23 percent) more than those in the control group and received $1,496 (7 percent) less in welfare payments. But in contrast to most of the earlier state studies, GAIN did not pay for itself, returning seventy-six cents in budget savings for every public dollar spent to run it. On the other hand, GAIN did better in raising participants' incomes, leading to a small (3 percentage point) reduction in the share of families in poverty, and also showed that positive impacts could be replicated at full scale, until then a major unknown.

The findings for one particular site, however, were considerably more impressive. Riverside, a large county located east of Los Angeles, stood out for the breadth, magnitude, and consistency of its positive effects and for its lower costs. Over five years, 33 percent of those in GAIN worked in the average three months compared with 24 percent of controls, and people in GAIN earned a total of 42 percent more than those in the control group and received 15 percent less in welfare payments (see table 8.3). Moreover, the good news occurred for many different categories of people, including very-long-term recipients and those with poor academic skills. As a result, the program was highly cost effective, returning to taxpayers almost three dollars for every dollar invested. Here was something to cheer about: for the first time, solid evidence that a welfare-to-work program produced results that broke out of the modest range. Even the well-known and vocal skeptic Charles Murray (1994, 28) calls the early Riverside results "dramatic."

REASONS FOR GAIN'S SUCCESS IN RIVERSIDE   The research team wrestled with what to make of Riverside. Was it a fluke that was not replicable, or did the study offer convincing insights on what drove these results? Fortunately, since

Table 8.3 GAIN's Impact on Average Earnings of Single Mothers

Country and subgroup	GAIN group ($)	Control group ($)	Difference ($)	Percentage change
Riverside	16,974	11,936	5,038***	42
Do not need education	24,046	18,121	5,924***	33
Need education	12,307	7,797	4,510***	58
San Diego	18,193	15,318	2,875***	19
All six counties	15,067	12,215	2,853***	23

Source: Author's compilation based on Freedman et al. (1996, tables 1, 2, and 3).
Note: Data are average total earnings of single mothers in the five years following random assignment. Averages include zero values for women who were not employed.
***Statistically significant at the 1 percent level.

SDSS had anticipated that counties would take different approaches, we had collected extensive quantitative and qualitative data describing how the program was implemented and managed, which Riccio and his colleagues used to systematically test different theories about what approaches worked best. Through this, they identified a range of practices not found in other counties that they concluded may have contributed to Riverside's broad success: a strong and pervasive message that encouraged all participants (even those deemed to be in need of basic education and even those in education or training programs) to get a job quickly; heavy reliance on job clubs but also substantial use of basic education (what came to be called a work-focused, mixed-services strategy); special staff to help people find jobs; adequate resources and a commitment to enforce the participation requirement for all people required to be in GAIN; and a cost-conscious and outcome-focused management style.[43]

What we learned about Riverside surprised us. As Riccio (1997, 249) has noted, "Like many people following the welfare reform debates, we didn't think the Riverside approach, which gave less emphasis to education and training, would be the one that performed better. But, that's what we found, and it changed opinions."[44] The experience reminded us of what we had discovered long before in Supported Work: programs that feel and look the best do not necessarily do the best.

We knew that the Riverside story—with its counterintuitive findings along a key liberal-conservative fault line—would be a big deal. We were confident of our estimates for each county, because these were based on random assignment and large samples, but we were less confident about why effects varied across counties, since we had not randomly assigned the same people to different GAIN approaches. In communicating the results, although we tried to distinguish what we knew with more or less confidence, we sometimes found ourselves criticized for overselling the findings and not making it clear enough that Riverside's program included some education.

Riverside's results did not sit well with the other counties. Lawrence Townsend, the county's tough-talking, astute, and opinionated welfare director, had a very particular view. He did not buy the idea that people who failed a math or reading test necessarily needed more education to get a job or that GAIN should seek to place everyone in the ultimate job for them. His motto—Any job is a good job and a potential stepping stone to a better job— rubbed many the wrong way (including, initially, some people on his staff).[45] Other counties disagreed, a few vehemently. When presented with the one-year findings, their reaction was: Just wait; once people complete education and move into the labor market, they will get better jobs, and we will overtake and then surpass Riverside. To many people, it just seemed axiomatic that the greater investment in education would pay off, particularly for people without skills or a high school degree. But the two-year, three-year, and then five-year results confirmed a different story: Although impacts in the other counties did grow over time, Riverside stayed in the lead and, crucially, proved to be the most successful with more disadvantaged recipients.[46]

Even though Riverside produced the largest impacts found thus far in a welfare-to-work experiment, it did not transform participants' earnings potential. More people got jobs than would have without the program, and got them sooner, but these were usually not "better" jobs. Total income was only slightly increased (since welfare benefits continued to be cut, often dollar for dollar, when people went to work), and reductions in poverty were small. Thus five years after enrolling in Riverside GAIN, 31 percent of welfare recipients were still receiving benefits, although some were receiving reduced grants because they were working.

LOWER OUTCOMES BUT HIGHER IMPACTS   As in Supported Work and the Work/Welfare demonstration, GAIN outcomes sometimes sent a false signal on which groups benefited most. The first three rows of table 8.3 present one outcome measure (the average amount single mothers earned during the five years after random assignment, lumping together those who did and did not work) for three groups in Riverside county: all people in the sample, people the GAIN skills test and other criteria found not to need basic education (the more advantaged people), and those determined to need basic education (the more disadvantaged recipients). Column 1 shows that for women randomly assigned to the GAIN program, average five-year earnings were almost twice as high for those found not to need education as for those found to need it ($24,046 versus $12,307).[47] But column 2 (the control group) shows something more: the more advantaged group also did much better on its own, without access to GAIN. As a result, GAIN's impact on that group (column 3) is only a third higher. Similarly, column 1 shows that, after assignment to GAIN, people in San Diego earned slightly more than those in Riverside ($18,193 versus $16,974). But column 3 tells us that this difference in outcomes is misleading: GAIN raised average earnings by $5,038 in Riverside compared with only $2,875 in San Diego.

Without random assignment the findings would have been suspect. As Wallace puts it, "If there hadn't been a GAIN evaluation with a control group, Larry Townsend in Riverside would have been an ideologue out in the desert saying 'any job is a good job.' Our staff didn't like it; his staff didn't like it. But the experiment showed it worked." In the process, Townsend became a celebrity and Riverside a go-to place for presidents (Jimmy Carter and Ronald Reagan) and governors (Pete Wilson and George W. Bush).

Lessons About Research Methods

The GAIN evaluation advanced research methods in two areas. First, it showed that it was feasible to operate and conduct a random assignment test of a full-scale, complex welfare-to-work program and that scale did not seem to alter effectiveness. Scaling up is a big issue in evaluation. Most random assignment studies are of small interventions. In welfare-to-work programs we have a rare three-stage example of going from a test in one office, the Louisville jobs search program, to a demonstration for part of the welfare caseload in San Diego and elsewhere, to the California statewide GAIN experiment.[48]

The second innovation, Riccio (1997, 243) notes, was "to go further than any preceding welfare-to-work study in integrating implementation and impact research and in trying to 'get inside the black box' to learn how different program strategies might influence program impacts." This involved several steps. First, we had larger samples and used multiple methods—observing the program, in-depth interviews, formal surveys of staff and participants, and data from case files and an expanded set of administrative records—to help us understand why some worked better than others. Moreover, MDRC went on to collect identical measures of management attitudes and practices, individual characteristics, services, and economic conditions in later random assignment studies, thereby facilitating a subsequent pathbreaking synthesis that pooled data for 69,000 people in fifty-nine local offices (Bloom, Hill, and Riccio 2005). Second, we used surveys to collect the same participation data on people in GAIN and the control group, so we could reliably report the extent to which the program increased activity over what we found to be the substantial service use (mostly of training and postsecondary education) by controls. Third, we ranked the six impact counties along a variety of measures and examined whether these were consistent or inconsistent with specific hypotheses about how county practices influenced participation and impacts.[49] Finally, we used the survey to collect data on a wider range of outcomes than in past work-welfare analyses, including the quality of jobs, employment dynamics, income sources, and education.

The final methods lesson concerns the value of cumulative evidence. We had found that Riverside's employment-focused mixed strategy was more effective than earlier job-search-first programs or GAIN programs that pushed basic education. But we concluded that this finding was too influential—and too counterintuitive—to be supported by a cross-county comparison in one state. Fortunately, HHS structured the evaluation of JOBS called for in FSA to include both the assessment of other mixed-service programs and the random assignment of welfare recipients to a control group or to one of two different programs operated in the same community.

Impact on Policy and Practice

For reasons similar to those cited in chapter 6 for the influence of the Work/Welfare demonstration findings—credibility, transparency, repetition, timeliness, and active dissemination—the GAIN findings seemed to impact policy and practice. The first two flowed from the experiment and its scale and the strategy of telling a simple story, using no fancy statistics. Wallace recounts that everyone could understand the numbers in a table such as table 8.3: "The fact that you have an E[xperimental] column, and a C[ontrol] column, and the difference, it does away with so much ideology and preconception. It's right there. . . . And we spent a lot of time doing that in the briefings, whether they were in L.A. County or in the [California Department of Social

Services] conference room with legislative staff, going through here's what it means in the E column and here is the C column. Here is the difference. . . . So, it was an easy sell from that perspective because the methodology lends itself to an easy sell."

In the same vein, Haskins, the Republican staff director of the Human Resources Subcommittee of the House Ways and Means Committee between 1995 and 2000 and one of the principal architects of the Personal Responsibility and Work Opportunity Reconciliation Act (PRWORA), recalls the visual impact of the paired bar charts for the GAIN group and controls showing the number working, on welfare, and the costs: "In all three cases the experimental group was different from the control group. . . . These were not huge differences but you could detect it visually. . . . That's a big deal, because who knows about the p-level." He also credits the cumulation and consistency of studies.

> It was not so much any particular study that made the difference. There were a lot of studies over a period of time. . . . This is important in that it showed what could be done with research and that you really could, over a period of years, learn a lot and develop almost a sequence of learning. . . . I think it was a triumph. People really came to appreciate the importance of scientific research, governors included. . . . I think it got to be a real winner for them politically. In the past most studies showed nothing worked, or not very much, and then all of a sudden you get these and they show you really can have an impact and people work more and all the stuff we want.[50]

The result was that no one questioned the findings or debated methodology; discussion shifted to the implications and how to interpret the county comparisons.[51]

The fourth reason was timeliness. This was a challenge, since we did not want to jump the gun and have to retract results. Our solution, as in the earlier studies, was to divide up the research, producing some meaty results annually between 1987 and 1994. In rapid succession during these years, states had to redesign their work programs in response to FSA; state governors launched ambitious reforms; the Clinton administration and Congress debated how to "end welfare as we know it"; and states then had to remake welfare to meet the options and requirements of the 1996 law. Given the later start of the federal JOBS evaluation, for many years the GAIN study provided the only available evidence on the effectiveness of a large-scale JOBS program. The environment was also changing in California, with a breakdown in the bipartisan coalition that had originally supported GAIN. The result was that policy makers absorbed the GAIN results as rapidly as we could churn them out.

The fifth reason was the aggressive marketing of findings by an organization broadly viewed as having no ax to grind (Weaver 2000, 144). Taking off from the dissemination practices described in chapter 6, we added an even greater role for state, county, and legislative staff. The partnership style used to resolve design decisions had fostered a reservoir of trust. Looking back, Wallace and Riccio use similar terms in describing the GAIN evaluation, saying that it took on "mythic" or "iconic" stature for the parties involved. This resulted not only from the contract and funding structure but, more important, from the high stakes within the state. Because GAIN was a major and costly initiative, this was never a closet study. Reflecting this, we regularly got requests—from the state or the staff of senior legislators—for the latest findings to inform budget decisions.

When the information became available was nearly as important to the state as what the information was. As one senior official put it to Wallace, "The main advantage of getting information earlier was that it could affect people's positions *before* they become frozen and could thereby prevent unnecessary and wasteful fights and bloodletting."[52] At one point in 1991, Wallace reported a call from a staffer to the president of the state Senate: "Don't you have any data available to help us make these decisions? Not even a single county. . . ? You can't tell me you don't know. . . . We've got to make decisions now. . . . We have to have your findings before then." Although the words certainly increased the pressure to push schedules forward as much as the data flow would allow, the caller ended by saying he had tried his best and understood our position. In other words, in both SDSS and the legislature, people had a stake in protecting the integrity of the study and their investment in it; no one wanted to compromise its aura of objectivity and quality.

As a result, we developed a multipart strategy. First, key state and county welfare administrators and legislative staff reviewed draft copies of our reports.[53] This was no pro forma exercise. We got line-by-line and sometimes word-by-word comments in a process that increased the accuracy of the reports but did not (despite what we had feared) involve heavy-handed pressure to change the bottom-line message. Second, we adopted a two-pronged approach to spreading the word, one for California and one for the rest of the country, but in both cases we included audiences whose own communications would have a multiplier effect. Within the state we conducted extensive briefings for state and local officials, people from advocacy groups, and of course the legislature. Nationally, relying primarily on grants from Ford, for general support, but from other foundations as well, we arranged briefings in Washington for White House staff, Senate and House staff, congressional agencies, and people at major liberal and conservative organizations. We made presentations at numerous conferences and testified multiple times to Congress. Finally, we issued formal press releases, and our communications director, Judith Greissman, reached out to California and national reporters, with stunning results. The outcome, Haskins recalls, was that people in Congress came to know and believe the results.

The study's impact within the state was clear.[54] At the county level, administrators became convinced that Riverside's achievements were real and relevant. The most moving response came from Los Angeles, where the leadership not only did not reject the finding that their program came up short but adopted their neighbor's employment-focused strategy and, in an act Lopez recalls as "unheard of," commissioned MDRC to conduct a second random assignment study to see whether their performance improved (it did, in both higher earnings gains and reduced cost). If replication "is the ultimate test of truth in science," this is an example of social science research heading in the right direction.[55]

At the state level, good news was embraced as vindication and bad news as a bombshell that sometimes left SDSS fighting off threatened budget cuts. As an example of how seriously state officials took the study, Riccio (1997, 245) says that, when the economy went into recession and drastic cuts were made across the state budget, the study's findings saved the program: "Understandably, there were also calls to cut GAIN program funds dramatically and to make major changes in the program model. However, early impact findings had recently been made available and showed promising effects. Some legislators used these early results to argue successfully that big changes in the program should be put off until the final evaluation results were in. Others agreed, and the program survived largely intact."

Later, when the Riverside findings came out, policy makers revised program regulations to focus more on rapid employment, a legacy that endures in the work program California operates under the 1996 welfare reform legislation. Lopez credits the benefit-cost budget estimates as particularly influential, providing rare, convincing evidence that a social program can save money.

Looking back at these years, when he was covering welfare and poverty issues for the *New York Times*, Jason DeParle (2004, 111–13, 209) describes the effect of the GAIN Riverside findings on Congress and other states:

> In the spring of 1993 . . . MDRC published the most influential study of the end-welfare age. . . . "Get a job, any job," was the Riverside mantra. After two years, Riverside had raised its participants' earnings by more than 50 percent, making the program about three times as effective as its rivals. Most states were still pushing education and training in their JOBS programs, so the study had the effect of turning the conventional wisdom—train first, then work—on its head. The idea of forsaking education in favor of "dead-end" jobs may sound cruel, and the thought can be taken too far (Riverside did have some education and training). But it's often what recipients want, at least initially. . . . The Riverside philosophy quickly became the philosophy nationwide: work first. . . . "Work first" was rising beyond program design to the realm of secular religion. . . . [By 1997] virtually every state regarded an entry-level job as preferable to the education and training efforts they had run in the past.[56]

The welfare-to-work studies clearly had an impact on how states structured their programs. But did they influence or even inform the most far-reaching welfare legislation since 1935, the 1996 bill that ended the AFDC program? At the time, I argued that PRWORA was a leap into the unknown—based on hope rather than knowledge—and evidence that politics trumps research when the stakes are high enough.[57] I saw the overall lesson from the experiments as encouraging: If Riverside's results could be replicated (admittedly, a big if), we would finally have found a welfare-to-work approach that could make more than a modest difference. It seemed to me that the 1996 law ignored this, opting for an untested and risky strategy. I was therefore mystified when Haskins repeatedly said the bill was driven by research. As he recalls it,

> Work really is the central issue of welfare reform, and the idea of work took on even more significance as an important, achievable goal because of the experiments. They took that potentially contentious issue off the table by showing that states could actually do things to get more people to work and save money.

As a result of the experiments, by something like osmosis everybody in Congress came to understand this, it became the new conventional wisdom, and this had a dramatic effect on the welfare debate. . . . It is the best story I know of how research influenced policy.

But the bill also set a strict time limit on federal assistance (rather than providing a subsidized job after the cutoff, as originally envisioned by Clinton), called for an unprecedented engagement in work-related activities before the time limit, and ended the AFDC entitlement. Nothing in the experiments per se supported a view that most people could find and keep a job and survive without welfare or that states could meet the participation requirements. Instead, the push for drop-dead time limits bubbled up from the states in their escalating competition (via waiver requests) to show who could be the toughest on work.

With some distance I now think the research did have an impact in positive and negative, direct and indirect ways. Experiments provide reliable evidence, they do not set policy goals or resolve trade-offs. Although modest impacts and findings of cost-effectiveness had been considered sufficiently encouraging to foster expanded funding for welfare-to-work programs under FSA in 1988, they were recast as inadequate five years later, after the welfare rolls had increased sharply (despite the new JOBS program), support for an AFDC entitlement had eroded further, and the debate had become more stridently partisan. Thus as R. Kent Weaver (2000) documents, conservatives concluded that more was needed, a kind of shock therapy.[58] In that sense, the work-welfare research—combined with the facts on the ground and views about the negative effects of welfare—was used to support radical and untested ideas, such as time limits, that promised not just improvements but solutions to the welfare problem. Indeed Haskins (2006) himself, in his insider account of the making of PRWORA, makes clear the unsurprising extent to which values, philosophy, politics, circumstances, and personalities drove decisions.

At the same time, as both Haskins and Weaver note, people drafting the bill drew positive lessons from the research. First, they interpreted the body of work-welfare and waiver studies as showing that states could run effective programs, which encouraged Congress to give them even more authority under block grants (and convinced key Republican governors that increased discretion could have financial and political rewards) (Weaver 2000, 374; Haskins 2006, 328). Second, specific provisions of the law (promoting work, setting tough participation standards, and limiting participation in education and training) were influenced by (or at least defended with) evidence on the success of mandatory programs that emphasized getting a job quickly, including findings from GAIN and the JOBS evaluation discussed in chapter 9 (Haskins 2006, 179, 317).[59] Furthermore, the MDRC experiments were also used to estimate the cost of PRWORA and to define the numerator and denominator of the participation rate in ways that would make attainment somewhat more feasible (Greenberg, Linksz, and Mandell 2003, 249–50).[60]

Jo Anne Barnhart—who during these years held senior welfare positions in the Reagan and first Bush administrations and as a Senate staffer—takes issue with this cautious conclusion. After reading a prepublication manuscript, she observed that, by focusing on whether the specifics of the bill reflect policies tested in the studies, Howard and I understate the overall effect of the experiments. In Barnhart's words,

> The debate over how to reform welfare could aptly be described as contentious, emotional, and partisan. When President Reagan brought his ideas about Community Work Experience (CWEP) to Washington, a stark line was drawn in the sand. Hence the divided view on human capital vs. labor-force attachment. . . . Without the incremental insights provided by the random assignment experiments, it is difficult to imagine the two conflicting sides coming together. Thanks to the authors' work, fact-based information gleaned from the research provided a "neutral" common language for the divided political rhetoric. Thus, although PRWORA did not exactly mirror the research findings, it would never have been possible without them. . . . The shift in thinking with respect to welfare reform was the reward [for] the research effort.

INCENDIARY PRESS IN FLORIDA

The challenge of selling random assignment in California proved a tepid warm-up for what happened next in Florida, where the toxic combination of gubernatorial politics, a concerned state legislator, and an ill-considered decision in a separate study fed an explosion of inflammatory press that almost led the state legislature to ban control groups and in the process both jeopardize a major federal research project and potentially poison the well for future studies. I relate this fight, the worst that I encountered, because it shows both the magnitude of defense needed and the way earlier work (including the GAIN study) created a community of allies who, in a crisis, went to bat for a

Table 8.4   Timeline of Florida Project Independence Evaluation and Related Events

Date	Event
June 1987	Florida legislature creates Project Independence
May 1988	Ford Foundation awards MDRC second welfare challenge grant
October 1988	President Reagan signs Family Support Act, creating JOBS program
September 1989	HHS selects MDRC to evaluate the JOBS program
October 1989	MDRC starts Project Independence evaluation
January 24, 1990	Florida assemblyman proposes ban on control group research
February 11, 1990	Texas newspaper condemns HHS random assignment study
February 12, 1990	HHS secretary halts Texas study
March 7, 1990	Florida legislature lets random assignment study proceed
April 1995	MDRC publishes final Project Independence impact and benefit-cost report

Source: Author's compilation.

research method they believed in. It also reveals how, even in the pre-Internet era, a flare-up from a state could ricochet, pointing to the need for constant vigilance about the ethics and politics of research. Finally, it is an opportunity to pay tribute to officials who, in the face of criticism that could wither the strongest spirit, persevered in supporting random assignment.

Between 1984 and 1988, MDRC had conducted the outreach, described in chapter 6, that introduced a wide array of policy makers and advocates to the credibility of random assignment studies. These then became a reference point in congressional debate about welfare reform. In May 1988 the Ford Foundation awarded us a second challenge grant to address some of the major unanswered questions on welfare reform and provide technical assistance to states (see table 8.4). Later that year, Congress passed FSA, which created the JOBS program that expanded and restructured welfare-to-work programs to emphasize education and training and required parents with preschool-age children to participate. To accommodate this, and because mandates for mothers with younger children were controversial, FSA directed states to provide child care to participants and extended transitional child care and Medicaid coverage to those leaving welfare for employment.[61] In September 1989, HHS selected MDRC to conduct the random assignment evaluation of JOBS called for by the legislation. In October MDRC, funded in part by the new challenge grant, signed a contract with Florida for a five-year study of Project Independence, its ongoing JOBS program.

Staff in Florida's welfare agency, the Department of Health and Rehabilitative Services (HRS), date the origin of the study and the decision on random assignment to a 1986 retreat for a handful of legislators, agency staff, and representatives of public interest groups convened to explore ways to improve the state's welfare-to-work initiative. At that meeting, MDRC's Bangser had stressed the importance of defining success in terms of net effects rather than job placements and described the advantage of having a control group. The bill that emerged in 1987 created a statewide program (which in 1989 became the state's JOBS program) that required participation for AFDC mothers with children aged three and older and specified up-front job search for those assessed as job ready and education and training for others. It also called for an evaluation, using language lifted from the GAIN bill with the addition of the specification that it "shall . . . utilize control groups."

In mid-1988, we were prospecting for states to include in the new Ford challenge grant and thought Florida's Project Independence offered an opportunity to study the potential of mandatory services for women with young children. At the same time, several factors raised the state's interest. First and most important, Gregory Coler, the secretary of HRS, wanted to participate in a second round of Ford-sponsored MDRC random assignment studies. This was particularly impressive, since he had been the commissioner in Illinois during the earlier Work/Welfare demonstration, when we used this approach to declare his program ineffective. Second, according to Don Winstead, the assistant secretary for economic services in HRS, his department had launched three unsuccessful attempts to respond to a legislative requirement for a report on Project Independence's progress. At first, HRS estimated cost savings by assuming that every person who left welfare would have remained on the rolls without the program, thereby producing what Winstead calls "big numbers . . . that had no validity." Next, they engaged someone from a local university, who, Winstead says, "came up with some methodology that I never fully understood and . . . with a report that wasn't viewed as particularly credible. And then the auditor general . . . came up with an estimate and it wasn't very credible either, but it was different from what the department had come up with. It then got to be kind of controversial, with these dueling estimates, none of which was particularly credible."

At that point, Coler suggested that Winstead ask my opinion on the diverse methodologies. I declined the request, referring him to Hollister and suggesting that Winstead read the National Academy of Sciences report by the panel Hollister had chaired (Betsey, Hollister, and Papageorgiou 1985), thereby launching what Winstead dubs Lesson 1 in his education on random assignment and impact studies.[62] According to Winstead, Hollister "wrote a [letter] that basically said this is bunk and, oh, by the way, what the department had done previously was bunk also and here's why and here's how you do these things and that's not what you've done." Next, Winstead recalls, "I got hauled in front of a legislative committee in the [state] Senate that was interested in all of this and I gave them a copy of Hollister's letter and said, 'Look, we tried to do it and it doesn't hold up. The auditors tried to do it and it doesn't hold up. What we really need to do here is drop back and get somebody that really knows this business to do it the right way as Professor Hollister is suggesting.' That was then the trigger to actually doing the Project Independence evaluation."

Winstead says that this experience, his reading of MDRC reports on GAIN and other programs, and his review of the legislative history of FSA (including Senator Moynihan's statements about the role played by MDRC's research) persuaded him that "the only way to get out of the pickle of these dueling unprovable things was to get an evaluation of unquestioned quality and go forward." When asked why he offered MDRC a sole-source contract for a random assignment study, he notes, "I thought the only way to salvage the credibility of the program was to make sure that the best people of unquestioned ability did it, and based on the prior work. . . . I felt that you all were the only firm in the country that could do this."[63] On random assignment, Winstead says the key was having the secretary's support, not any HHS pressure related to waivers. He remembers that Coler was committed to finding the truth and had declared unequivocally, "We're in favor of control groups. . . . Go ahead, do it."

As we began planning the study, HRS, since they placed priority on estimating statewide impacts, suggested that we choose the counties through a random process.[64] Because, in contrast to the California case, the Florida department directly administered programs throughout the state, staff in Tallahassee were confident that they could require local offices to participate in the experiment. Two ripples in the relatively routine start-up gave a hint of the tidal wave to follow. In August 1989 the state shared MDRC's initial proposal with the district offices (without the prior face-to-face briefings we had used in past studies) and heard strong opposition to denial of services to controls and concern about adverse publicity, lawsuits, and increased workload that could negatively affect their ability to achieve state-imposed performance goals. In October, someone forwarded these objections to Florida assembly-man Ben Graber, who chaired a legislative subcommittee that had responsibil-ity for some HRS programs, including Project Independence. On January 23, 1990, Graber dropped his bombshell, writing to Coler, "Please be advised that I intend to file legislation which . . . would include an amendment to . . . delete the reference to utilization of control groups. I consider the arbitrary denial of benefits to a random sample of eligible citizens to be an unacceptable practice. I believe the state of Florida should not participate in this form of social experimentation."

His press conference the next day prompted a string of inflammatory ar-ticles over the following two weeks in the *Miami Herald* and other Florida papers, attacking HRS and quoting Graber to the effect that the agency was treating welfare recipients like "guinea pigs." "I think even one client who suffers from it is too many. . . . To use a research project to hurt someone is wrong (*Sun-Sentinel* [Broward and Palm Beach counties], January 25, 1990). The *Miami Herald* (January 25, 1990), "We don't need to spend millions of dollars or even one dollar to see what happens to people if they don't get social services. . . . We can see those results every day in our streets."

The *Miami Herald* followed its first article with one the next day saying, "Several sociologists said Florida's plan reminded them of the infamous Tuske-gee Study of the 1930s when the federal government sponsored a public health study of male syphilis."[65] On January 29 the *Miami Herald* continued, with an editorial calling the plan "misguided, wasteful, cold-hearted, and just plain dumb"; a cartoon in the *Sun-Sentinel* characterized HRS staff as unethi-cal scientists pulling the legs off spiders just to see what would happen; and on February 4 an editorial in the *St. Petersburg Times* titled "Project Inhu-mane" called the study a "cruel joke": "That's right, millions will be spent to deny 5,500 needy people, mostly mothers with small children, the chance for self-respect and survival. Millions will be spent to keep them from learning critical skills necessary to land a job with decent wages."[66]

Here was our worst nightmare. The state agency was blasted, our work was equated with the poster child of abuse against human subjects (the Tuskegee study), random assignment studies were condemned as immoral, advocates were indignant, and the Ford Foundation was swept into the mix by implication. In addition to the immediate danger to the Florida study, we feared the contagion would spread (already reporters were phoning California officials to discuss the GAIN evaluation) if the story were picked up by the national press, threatening our simultaneous recruitment of states for the JOBS and other evaluations.

Worse was soon to come, and from an unexpected quarter. On Sunday, February 11, two weeks after the Florida story broke, the *Dallas Morning News* ran a front-page article on a completely separate HHS-sponsored random assignment study of transitional Medicaid and child care benefits in Texas. This study had started out as a test of enriched benefits for experimentals, with controls continuing under existing law. Then Congress passed FSA, which required that, as of April 1990, the enriched treatment would become an entitlement for all. However, to preserve a study they thought had value, HHS had decided to hold the two groups in place for two more years, in effect denying some controls access to the new transitional benefit entitlement. Several articles lumped together the Texas study (approved under the waiver process described in chapter 7), random assignment in general, and the recently launched federal JOBS evaluation and concluded self-righteously that, after the current outrage, Texas had correctly refused the invitation to participate in the JOBS study. All but the most informed readers would have been utterly unable to distinguish between what was going on in Texas and what was proposed for the JOBS evaluation. These articles were picked up by the Associated Press and soon hit California papers and even the *New York Times*.

The coverage, particularly the repeated comparison with the Tuskegee study, frightened everyone involved, including HHS secretary Dr. Louis W. Sullivan, who the next day issued a press statement that "no person receiving welfare in the state of Texas has been denied or will be denied benefits to which they are entitled" and instructed HHS staff to revise the study accordingly, leading to a February 14 headline in the *Washington Times*, "Public Protest Precipitates End of Welfare Experiment."

We at MDRC and staff in HHS knew we had to act quickly. In an atmosphere of crisis, we met a few days later with the new assistant secretary for policy and evaluation, Martin Gerry, and others at HHS. Our basic goal was to draw a red line between studies of an open-ended entitlement program (such as the new transitional benefits in, for example, the Texas case) that is explicitly funded to serve all eligible applicants and programs such as JOBS

(Project Independence in Florida and GAIN in California) that may have the rhetoric of universality but lack the funds to support it (the distinction we had been wrestling with since the 1980s and revisited in GAIN). When denial of services to some is an inevitable part of implementing the program, it does not come from the research. As Mary Jo Bane—a former welfare administrator, longtime Harvard professor, and member of MDRC's board—put it in a March 1, 1990, letter supporting the Florida study, "The alternative to random assignment is not service availability for everyone, but instead an alternative rationing procedure," be it on the basis of first come, first served or on an attempted assessment of need.

Simultaneous with the HHS meetings, a few of us at MDRC—including Ivry and Goldman, who was initially responsible for the Project Independence study—began a campaign to understand the Florida situation, line up support, and seek a way to address the issues. From the beginning, we saw the possible ban on control group studies in Florida or any similar legal precedent as not simply a contract issue but a fundamental challenge to our work (and survival) and to social policy research more generally. So we threw resources and time into educating people in the state (including scores of in-person meetings) and the broader community.

As was the case in California, we could never have navigated this maze alone. Our guides were Winstead and his colleague Sheffield Kenyon, HRS assistant deputy secretary for programs. As best we could determine, events in Florida were driven by the unusual combination of a hotly contested gubernatorial election,[67] an advocacy community that distrusted the welfare agency, a welfare commissioner who was a lightning rod for attacks on the governor and the agency, a study mandated by the legislature, the allure of the national spotlight, general suspicion about random assignment, and a welfare department that, though solidly behind the study, was making things worse by claiming that Project Independence (a large-scale, ongoing program) served everyone.

Our first challenge was to get HRS to reverse this long-standing line, which they reluctantly did, recognizing that it was essential to refute Representative Graber's claim (similar to what had troubled Bill Greene vis-à-vis GAIN) that the control group research, rather than a funding shortfall, was responsible for service denial. Our second challenge was to understand and, without undercutting the research, address the concerns of advocates, public interest groups, and legislators, including Graber. We quickly got rid of the fear that our no-bid contract meant we had some kind of sweetheart deal and would be writing a puff piece for the state: people checked us out with colleagues in other states and national advocates and became convinced we would be independent and do quality work. It probably helped that we consistently took the high ground, stating our willingness to walk away from the study rather than either waste resources on an evaluation that would show inconclusive findings or see MDRC sucked into endless litigation.[68]

Although advocates raised many objections, the key one was that controls who enrolled on their own in education and training should have the same access to child care as would members of the experimental group engaged in similar project-funded activities.[69] Resolving this issue was complicated by what was described at various times as the poisonous, adversarial, confrontational relationship between key advocates and HRS, since an important ingredient in moving forward would be whether either party trusted that the other would stick with any agreed-on compromise. A key figure was Mark Greenberg, a senior staff attorney at the Center for Law and Social Policy in Washington who had previously been a legal aid lawyer in Jacksonville and knew the Florida players. Greenberg, a member of an informal advisory group Ivry regularly consulted on MDRC's evaluations, had become an avid consumer of research.[70] As soon as the story broke in the press, local advocates called Greenberg to check on MDRC and the legal issues, including his thoughts on child care. Greenberg's view that, under FSA, members of the control and experimental groups should be treated the same way in their access to in-program child care carried great weight.

By mid-February, we were unsure whether the Project Independence study could be salvaged but thought the outcome would depend largely on our ability to work out a compromise with the advocacy community.[71] The situation was complicated by our and HHS's recognition that how we resolved the child care issue in Florida would set a precedent for the national JOBS evaluation. Although some at HRS and HHS initially resisted (arguing that in-program child care was part of JOBS and not an entitlement and that providing it to controls would reduce the JOBS program's estimated impact), by late February all agreed that we could not tough this out in the current climate, especially given Secretary Sullivan's statement.[72] Once HRS agreed to give controls equal access to child care, to fund a separate child care utilization study, to create a statewide advisory group that included advocates, and to clarify that Project Independence did not serve everyone anyway, most advocates withdrew their opposition and with it their support for Graber's amendment.

Simultaneously we worked to address legislators' concerns before the March 7 hearing on the amendment. As one step, we went to Washington to alert Senator Moynihan and numerous congressional staff, federal agencies, and public interest and advocacy groups, whom we hoped would be voices of reason with the press and Florida legislators. During the same period, Winstead orchestrated a marathon round of one-on-one meetings with several dozen Florida legislators. In general, their response was positive, with a typical caveat: We're with you, unless there is a smoking gun.

The hearing itself was anticlimactic. We submitted letters of support from advocates, state officials, and researchers.[73] Winstead and I testified. Graber's amendment banning control groups was withdrawn. The state agreed to set up a panel to review future projects. And, with the TV cameras rolling, the legislature endorsed random assignment and decided to continue the study.

I concluded my testimony with a word on the press coverage, particularly the comparisons to the Tuskegee study:

> For a researcher these are fighting words. In the Tuskegee study, poor black men in Alabama were not told they had syphilis or that a new treatment, penicillin, existed. If we had a readily available wonder drug to help people be self-sufficient and off of welfare, I am sure there isn't a person in this room who would not use it. If Project Independence is that, I assume you would put more money into it. Since we don't know that and the funds are not there, you would be wise to get the answers first. . . . I am convinced the study will deliver information of value to you and others and in the process treat welfare recipients with respect and dignity.

In my view, several factors account for this outcome. First, the leaders in HRS did not walk away from the study but persevered and gave enormous time to keep it alive. Seeing an agency fight to get its program independently scrutinized while taking a shellacking from the press is stunning. Especially devastating was the ABC national nightly news on the day of the hearing, which dedicated fully one minute and forty-five seconds to this complex issue and called for an end to "intentional deception by the government in an apparent effort to determine how social programs work." Throughout this experience, the highlight for me was watching Winstead in action. Why did he persist? Two decades later he says,

> I remember at one point when you were down there you said to me, "Now look, you understand whatever we come up with it's not going to be nearly as good as what your press releases say." And I had read enough stuff by then, I knew that. I think, it sounds sort of naïve, but I became convinced that it was the right thing to do and that we ought to do it and if we're going to put thousands of people through something, we ought to be willing to find out whether or not it works. And that was pretty much it.

What would he have done if we found that Project Independence didn't work? He says: "Do something else. It's not like the impact results were all that astonishing to us."

A second factor was the work of numerous advocates in Florida who came to believe in the value of our research. Once we resolved the child care issue, they pitched in to review the details of the evaluation, resulting in a study that retained its rigor and had broad-based support. Several prominent Washington-based advocates, particularly Greenberg at the Center for Law and Social Policy and Robert Greenstein at the Center on Budget and Policy Priorities (both of whom used high-quality evaluations in their own efforts to improve social programs), provided the backbone of support that gave their Florida counterparts the confidence to move forward.

A third was the willingness of state legislators to take a fresh look. Graber had raised important questions about the legitimacy, equity, and even constitutionality of control group studies; the press had pounced; and in the cauldron of electoral politics it would have been easy to get on that bandwagon. Instead, we found that most legislators listened, and many changed their positions. In part this reflected one of the unintended consequences of new federalism: the strengthening of state legislative staff who consistently worked behind the scenes to support the study. Winstead draws a simpler conclusion: "We prevailed because we were right, and ultimately most of the members understood this."

A fourth factor was the widespread support for random assignment and MDRC that we found among congressional staff working for both Republicans and Democrats, people in states where we had conducted evaluations, and a small number of academics. We asked many who had used our work to speak up about it, and we were moved to see how they responded and the sincerity of their belief in its importance.

Although we had won this round and avoided both a ban on experiments and a law suit on random assignment, we were still losing in the press and knew that the coverage would make the implementation of the JOBS evaluation much harder. The Department of Health and Human Services seemed settled in for the fight (which Howard describes in chapter 9), but we had seen firsthand that the glare of TV was a terrible environment in which to debate this kind of issue, and we buckled down to the potential for similar fights.

Although this fracas had delayed the study, it also created a strong coalition committed to its successful implementation. This proved useful, because we soon encountered severe problems getting local staff to do random assignment rigorously and provide quality baseline data. In contrast to GAIN, where we conducted the lottery in the tranquil work program offices, in Florida we implemented it in the more chaotic welfare offices, where staff were also determining benefits and resolving crises. The problems were particularly acute in Miami-Dade, where we trained (and often retrained) up to 450 harried staff working in difficult conditions. We eventually turned much of this around by stationing adjunct staff in the offices and then went on to the challenging task of collecting administrative records while the state changed its computer system.

The final report in 1995 pointed to the strengths and limitations of Project Independence, which, under the pressure of rapidly increasing welfare caseloads and worsening economic conditions, evolved into a relatively low-cost program focused on getting people off welfare and into jobs quickly. The program modestly increased employment and earnings and reduced reliance on welfare, and it accomplished this at no overall net cost to taxpayers. The impact on earnings was greater in the early years, when the program was implemented as intended, and sharply reduced (particularly for women with young children) when caseloads rose and child care and other resources became more limited. Winstead recalls concluding that child care was critical to success and, as a result, to persuading the legislature to guarantee real access to child care when, several years later, it set a time limit on welfare receipt.

The difference in effectiveness for early and later enrollees in the study provided a timely warning about the risks of stretching a program's services below the threshold level at which they can be effective. In addition, the reason there was no net cost to taxpayers was that the project was very cost effective for women with school-age children, saving taxpayers (over five years) more than a dollar and a half for every dollar spent on the program. In sharp contrast, for women with younger children (for whom child care outlays were higher and the program's achievements smaller), taxpayers lost money, and welfare families had less income. These benefit-cost results challenged administrators to confront the difficult task of reducing dependency among women with very young children, since FSA for the first time required all states to serve this group—pointing to the importance in the JOBS evaluation of determining whether other strategies would be more effective.[74]

Winstead also remembers feeling that it took a long time to get impact results and that, until then, he was "kind of flying blind." As a result, when MDRC conducted a study of Florida's time-limited welfare program, Winstead built his own admittedly incomplete and nonlongitudinal database to track experimental-control differences on an ongoing basis.[75] He recalls that the positive Project Independence experience made him comfortable participating in this later random assignment study.[76]

NEXT STEPS

The GAIN and Project Independence studies, as noted, were state-sponsored evaluations of JOBS programs mandated in the 1988 FSA. In chapter 9, Howard puts them into the context of the even more ambitious federal JOBS evaluation, its design, implementation, and lessons to be drawn. Although MDRC had only once before bid on a major federal contract, we jumped at the opportunity to conduct that study, which we saw as a means to answer intriguing questions raised in the GAIN evaluation, and we were fortunate to be awarded the contract.

Following Howard's discussion of JOBS, I return to the next stage of MDRC's institutional journey. We were still very much involved in the JOBS, GAIN, and Project Independence evaluations well into the 1990s. At the same time, however, we were aware of the emerging general view that past reforms (including the yet to be fully implemented JOBS program) would not deliver transformational change. The spark for this discontent was the dramatic growth in AFDC caseloads between 1989 and 1994, which, after ten years of relative stability, suddenly increased by more than a third, to 5 million families. The resulting budget pressure returned welfare to center stage but this time under a harsher spotlight. As I discuss in chapter 10, at MDRC we debated how to convert this context into an opportunity to refine still unanswered questions and to devise evaluation projects that would enable us to address them. Chapter 10 focuses on one area—what came to be termed "making work pay," the general hypothesis being that if work pays enough to support a family, people are more likely to take a job and less likely to return to welfare—because it exemplifies the growing support for random assignment and the changing nature of the studies.

CHAPTER 9

The JOBS Evaluation: Cumulative Evidence on Basic Education Versus Work First*

> The evolution of the [JOBS evaluation] design . . . was really quite a phenomenal experience. . . . To me it was a terrific experience of folks just working together—ACF, ASPE, MDRC—to try to coax a design out . . . that would yield the most knowledge we could possibly get.
>
> —Mike Fishman[1]

Along with the Greater Avenues for Independence program (GAIN) evaluation (later, California's JOBS program), the Job Opportunities and Basic Skills Training (JOBS) evaluation would profoundly alter the views of policy makers, program operators, and researchers about the effectiveness of alternative strategies to move welfare parents into the workforce.[2] Within a decade, the perspective underlying the JOBS program would be substantially undermined, and welfare-to-work programs would be very different from their predecessors under JOBS. Work programs under Aid to Families with Dependent Children (AFDC) and, later, Temporary Assistance for Needy Families (TANF) would be focused much less on basic education and much more on job search, rapid job entry, and other short-term work-focused activities (a not very precise set of activities often referred to as work first).[3] Although many factors played a role in this transformation, the findings from the GAIN and

---

*Chapter 9 authored by Howard Rolston.

Table 9.1   Timeline of JOBS Evaluation Design Planning and Related Events

Date	Event
October 1988	Family Support Act signed
March 1989	Decision memorandum recommends initiating the JOBS evaluation
June 1989	Request for proposals issued
September 1989	Contract awarded to MDRC
Fall 1989 through the end of 1990	Postaward redesign period
November 9–10, 1989	National Academy of Sciences meeting
March 1990	Contract modified to include JOBS Child Impact study
June 1995	First impact report on three labor force–human capital sites issued
December 2001	Final report issued

Source: Author's compilation.

JOBS evaluations were particularly important. The JOBS evaluation marked major steps forward both in experimental evaluation of employment programs for low-income parents and in how the Department of Health and Human Services (HHS) conducted these evaluations. These steps included not only the substance of what was evaluated but also the research design for the evaluation and advances in measurement.

In this chapter I describe the origins of the JOBS evaluation, how it came to have its central design features, as well as how these features represented advances over previous research on welfare policy. The JOBS evaluation originated in a series of events that played out over a period of roughly a year and a half and involved typical choices that need to be carefully addressed to conduct rigorous and policy-useful evaluation. (See table 9.1 for the timeline of major events.) Recruiting the sites and implementing the study design were not without problems, but the main story here is of the hard but exciting work of building a strong study design.

THE REQUIRED STUDY THAT WAS NOT REQUIRED

Section 203(c)(2) of the Family Support Act (FSA) directed the secretary of the Department of Health and Human Services (HHS) to conduct a study of the relative effectiveness of different approaches to operating the JOBS program in reducing long-term dependency. The study was to be an evaluation based on demonstrations in five states, using experimental designs with random assignment to experimental and control groups. A total of $10 million was authorized, to be appropriated over fiscal years 1990 and 1991. Outcome measures were to include education status, employment and earnings, AFDC receipt, and, to the extent possible, poverty status.

The text of FSA would certainly suggest that to be in compliance with the law HHS was required to conduct the study. But in fact the study was never conducted as such, and no law was broken. Two critical facts led to this outcome. First, the language of the bill, "authorized to be appropriated," in itself made no funds available. As usual with an authorization, further action by Congress as part of its annual appropriations process would be necessary to actually fund the study.[4] Second, section 203(c)(2) of the act was a freestanding authority. If Congress had amended the Social Security Act, HHS would have been compelled to conduct the study, even if Congress did not appropriate specific funds. It is not uncommon for Congress to create special authorities that the executive branch is required to carry out, but only to the extent that Congress actually appropriates money under the authority, and FSA included many such authorities. In the case of 203(c)(2), funds were never appropriated, leaving HHS under no legal obligation to conduct the study. The existence of the effectiveness study authority would, nevertheless, play an important role in the JOBS evaluation that eventually took place.

A key impetus for HHS to move ahead with an evaluation of JOBS was section 203(b), which did amend the Social Security Act by adding a section 487, titled "Performance Standards." This latter section required the secretary of HHS to develop "recommendations for performance standards . . . with respect to specific measurements of outcomes and be based on the degree of success which may reasonably be expected of States in helping individuals to increase earnings, achieve self-sufficiency, and reduce welfare dependency, and shall not be measured solely by levels of activity or participation." Section 203(b) also required that these recommendations be "based, in part, on the results of studies conducted under section 203(c)" and that they be reported to Congress no later than October 1993.

Although five years to develop a report to Congress may seem like a long time, that the recommendations depended on the effectiveness study actually made it, for all practical purposes, impossibly short. For example, on the assumption that it would take a year to accumulate and randomly assign a sufficiently sized sample and that the sample would be followed for three years, this would leave only a year for both planning and analysis—that is, to identify sites, establish a way to fund the evaluation, design the evaluation, collect the data (earnings records typically lag by about six months), analyze the results and their relevance to performance standards, develop the recommendations, and, finally, write and clear a report to Congress. Although we knew it would be impossible to meet the deadline, we thought it important to present a plan to senior political officials that would make a good faith effort and come as close as possible to meeting the specified schedule.

The situation was further complicated by the fact that President Reagan had signed FSA only the month before George H. W. Bush was elected president, and it was not immediately apparent how the transition to the new administration would occur. By February 1989 it was clear that many of the Reagan political appointees still in their jobs would not be staying long. But it was also clear that waiting for the new appointees to arrive would effectively rule out a procurement in the current fiscal year, since the key decision makers required Senate confirmation and following that probably a lengthy process of education. So Carl Dahlman, still the deputy assistant secretary of income security policy in the Office of the Assistant Secretary for Planning and Evaluation (ASPE), and I decided to push forward with the existing cast of characters: Robert Helms, still head of ASPE, and Catherine Bertini (who would soon replace John Bode as the assistant secretary for food and nutrition) who, as acting head of the Family Support Administration, was my boss. Dahlman and I developed a joint decision memo to Helms and Bertini seeking their sign-off to move ahead and forwarded it to them on March 31, 1989.

This partnership between Dahlman, a political appointee, and me provides an excellent illustration of how relationships between career and political staff forged in policy development can provide the foundation for teamwork on research. We and our staffs had worked closely together on state waiver requests and on the administration's analysis of legislative proposals that were part of the congressional process that led up to passage of FSA. Helms, a more senior appointee whose primary focus was health policy, was also deeply involved in these issues. The long days and occasionally nights we spent struggling internally to develop policy positions and effective strategies for presentation externally created strong bonds of loyalty and trust.

Bertini, also a political appointee, had been director of the Office of Family Assistance, which administered AFDC, and over several years she and I had established a strong relationship. Unlike Helms, she had little research background; her focus was policy. FSA required rapid development of regulations for JOBS, and before she was elevated to acting assistant secretary, Bertini had already approached me with the challenge that we work together to meet the stringent statutory deadlines, which then became the highest priority for my office.[5] As a result, when Dahlman and I were preparing the JOBS evaluation memorandum, I was also managing a team of career staff that was just completing the proposed JOBS regulations. Given Bertini's limited background in research, this certainly created a set of circumstances in which she readily deferred to me on moving ahead with the procurement.

I strongly believed, as I am confident Dahlman did too, in the value of further randomized trials, not only for developing performance standards but also to determine what approaches would work best in JOBS. However, since the only statutory urgency we could claim applied to the development of timely performance standards based on reliable impact data, this was our memo's central argument for evaluating JOBS. Despite my own skepticism (and that of many of my HHS colleagues) that we could actually achieve performance standards sufficiently rooted in impact findings, the recommendation report requirement was our best argument for moving ahead quickly with an experimental evaluation.[6]

Although the request for proposals (RFP) provided for the possibility of site-level random assignment "if appropriate or necessary," the primary approach was random assignment of individuals, and there was no provision for a nonexperimental design. We never discussed any impact design other than random assignment, reflecting the conviction we had come to during development of the waiver evaluation standard (chapter 7). We had already spent a year and a half trying to persuade states to use random assignment to evaluate their demonstrations. And during the very same month we were developing the RFP for JOBS (April 1989) we were fighting in the Low Income Opportunity Board to thwart implementation of President Bush's executive order to dilute the waiver standard. It was simply inconceivable at this point that either career or political staff at HHS would have considered a design other than random assignment.

Our memorandum presented both the program improvement and the performance standard benefits of conducting an experimental evaluation of JOBS, including a lengthy discussion of the potential trade-offs between the two. Emphasizing performance standards would argue for selecting sites that reflected the broadest range of programs' economic- and benefit-level settings.

It would place little weight on the specifics of program design, since the main purpose of the information garnered would be to adjust outcome standards for different program circumstances, not to "constrain the choice of approach." Emphasizing program effectiveness, in contrast, would argue for systematic variation in that regard, to find out which program designs were more effective in improving outcomes. We presented these two options as different approaches for program selection into the evaluation. Both would select programs purposively to fill the cells of a matrix. But the dimensions of the matrix would vary depending on the primary objective of the evaluation. Our memorandum advocated doing both, thereby doubling both the number of sites and evaluation funds required.

Although we described the JOBS evaluation as "mandated in the Family Support Act," we understood, of course, that without the appropriation of funds it was no more mandatory than the several other mandated but unfunded FSA studies. We chose to push our related study and ignore most of the others, based on our view that the knowledge gained from evaluating JOBS using an experimental design would be potentially valuable in furthering the success of the program, whether by setting performance standards or by establishing which program designs were most effective. Our presentation of the study as required was meant not to mislead Helms and Bertini, both of whom we informed of the real circumstances, but rather to highlight its endorsement by Congress and its urgency.

Because we were not bound by the statutory language, we also felt free to pick what we liked in it and reject what we did not. Thus we seized on the random assignment language but ignored the suggestion that we give the funds to states that presumably would contract with research organizations. We could ignore the funding language, because there were no funds under that authority, and our funds were from a different source. We preferred the route of our contracting directly with a research firm, because it gave us greater control and offered an opportunity for us to hold a competition and choose the strongest bidder. The intentional ambiguity in the way we publicly described the mandatory status of the JOBS evaluation did cause some confusion, however.[7]

As in all cases of rigorous field research, except where funds are appropriated for a study by Congress (not the case with the JOBS effectiveness study), financing the evaluation was a critical issue. Fortunately, the history of collegiality between our office and ASPE facilitated the pooling of research funds, without which the scale of the study would have been impossible.[8] As our experience with joining forces for the Teen Parent demonstration had been positive, both organizations found it easy to agree to a joint undertaking.

A CRITICAL TWO-STAGE DESIGN PHASE

As with all evaluations, the JOBS design phase, both before the RFP had been issued and after the contract was awarded, was critical to the quality of the eventual evaluation design. Because we placed such high importance on the study, we were eager to get external reactions to our ideas early. ASPE, which had a multiyear grant to the Institute for Research on Poverty at the University of Wisconsin, requested that the institute convene a group of experts, which included Judy, to comment on all aspects of the proposed evaluation. We provided a discussion draft for the meeting participants, extracting the substance of our memorandum to Helms and Bertini and appending eleven discussion issues. The meeting, which took place on April 14, 1989, would significantly change the focus of our design in two important respects.

Shift in Site Selection Criteria

The most critical change was in how to select sites for the evaluation. Overwhelmingly, participants counseled that trying to obtain a semi-representative group of sites was neither desirable nor feasible. First, the state JOBS programs were likely to be at various stages of implementation, depending on localities' implementation of the previous AFDC work options and the Work Incentive demonstration program. Second, they would be in a state of flux for some time, since some state work programs would have to be modified substantially to meet federal JOBS requirements. Third, even if we were able to obtain a representative set of sites initially, by the time we had results the programs would have changed.

Consistent with this, participants urged us to avoid evaluation of programs that were just being implemented—selecting, instead, "mature programs," to avoid "evaluating start-up," which would not provide a fair test of what program models could produce. We were strongly encouraged to develop good information on the effectiveness of different programmatic approaches to help states in designing their JOBS programs and to de-emphasize selection based on formulating performance standards. Judy advanced the view (in line with MRDC's development of a research agenda as described in chapter 8) that we should first assess past and ongoing evaluations for what was, and would be, known about program effectiveness and then see what key questions had still to be addressed. The information sources we could, in her words, "cobble together" to help inform state JOBS program choices included MDRC's Work/Welfare demonstration programs, the section 1115 waiver demonstrations under way, and the GAIN and Teen Parents demonstration evaluations. That we should not think of what the JOBS evaluation would deliver in isolation, but rather see it as part of a broader agenda of studies, would prove to be the right prescription.[9]

Although we had some concerns about moving away from a more representative selection of sites, the approach the experts almost universally recommended made a lot of sense to us. Beginning with grant diversion, our history with employment experiments had been to try to figure out what works; and we had a much weaker commitment to performance standards, about which we remained skeptical. Adopting a more strategic and piecemeal approach would mean that we would not be able to say anything about the effects of the average JOBS program. But since we could not compel state or local programs to participate in the evaluation, we knew we could not guarantee a representative sample of states in any case—a realization strengthened by the Department of Labor's recent failure to enroll a randomly selected group of sites in its experimental evaluation of Job Training Partnership Act of 1982 (which had to revert to purposive selection because so many sites refused to participate).

With substantial support from the group, Judy also advanced the idea that in some sites we should test two alternative programs against each other and a control group. This would provide much stronger evidence of the differential effectiveness of alternative approaches than simply comparing each approach with a control group in each site, by removing any potentially confounding effect of independent site-level differences. I expressed the concern that it would be difficult to recruit sites into the evaluation if they were expected to run dual programs. But Paul Offner, who at the time was deputy director for the Ohio Department of Human Services, which was currently involved in two state waiver evaluations that used random assignment (the Ohio Transitions to Independence demonstration and the Learning, Earning, and Parenting program), argued that we could find willing states.[10] He not only proved to be correct but ultimately put his own state on the line when Columbus, Ohio, become a JOBS evaluation site that tested, head-to-head, two alternative approaches to JOBS case management.

The Request for Proposals and the Procurement

The RFP was issued on June 23, 1989. Its content clearly reflected important elements of the April 14 meeting discussion. The largest change was abandonment of the site matrix; the RFP included the March 31 discussion draft as appendix IV, but with a strong qualifier at the top of the first page: "Since this paper was written, the Government's thinking has changed. . . . The RFP does not require that sites be selected on the basis of any specific stratification variables. . . . There is far less emphasis now on using study results as a basis for developing performance standards."[11]

The request for proposals also reflected the heightened priority we held to learn about the effectiveness of a range of JOBS program designs. The RFP's list of the ten "key policy issues to be addressed by the evaluation" began with two questions: "What strategies—such as program components and sequencing strategies—work best in helping welfare recipients to increase employment and reduce welfare dependency? Do they prove cost effective?" The list had only a single question on performance standards, which came at the very end: "How should JOBS performance standards be designed?" The restructuring of priorities proved a critical decision. In designing an impact evaluation, a fundamental question is whether its primary goal is to estimate the impact of an average program or the impact of well-implemented models within an overall program.[12] In theory one could do both, but in practice the high cost of doing so usually forces a choice. In the case of JOBS, we could not in fact answer the average impact question well because we could not compel programs to participate, which ruled out any effort to achieve a representative group of sites.[13]

This was not a binding constraint for us, however, because we also judged it more important to focus substantively on discriminating among strategies. This decision to focus on a range of program models proved more crucial to the value of the evaluation findings than any of us realized at the time, given the demise of the JOBS program in 1996, when changing social attitudes and the unambiguous success of work programs had made them an inherent part of the welfare debate. By the time the JOBS evaluation findings were available, the crucial question on everyone's mind was not whether welfare-to-work programs were effective (they were), or what the average JOBS program had produced, but rather which type of welfare-to-work program worked best.

A further change in the RFP was an explicit emphasis on the intended focus on differential impacts: "In some sites, there may be more than one treatment group to which participants could be randomly assigned." The RFP gave no guidance regarding the substance of those programs, which would be determined over the next year. Although not yet specified in content, the head-to-head tests would prove central to the enduring value of the evaluation.

Another change, which would be momentous in its consequences, occurred between the memorandum and the RFP: a decision to explore the feasibility of measuring the impact of JOBS programs on children. Although Richard Nathan had first raised this issue, particularly with respect to FSA's child care benefits, in the April 14 meeting two career ASPE staffers, Ann Segal and William Prosser, would become the drivers for what would become the JOBS Child Impact study. Segal and Prosser had somewhat limited experience with welfare policy, having come from the area of ASPE that dealt primarily with issues of child development and programs such as Head Start and child care. Both of them saw the JOBS evaluation as a means of gaining information on what had long been a contentious issue in that area: Did requiring welfare mothers to go to work negatively affect their children? Looking back, Segal says, "There was still a lingering debate about whether forcing moms to go to work was going to harm young children. Both Bill and I had a null hypothesis on that. . . . We thought that in a lot of these cases, kids would end up in the same kind of child care as they were in their homes; they would not experience a whole big difference."

But, as would turn out to be even more important, they also saw the study as an opportunity to draw attention to the fact that there had been little focus on children's outcomes, despite AFDC's stated purpose of aiding children. Segal puts it this way: "The focus was here we're going to have this massive study on what happened to the adults, but it gave us the opportunity to look at the kids." Thus apart from the impact questions that could be addressed in the study simply by adding measures of child outcomes, Segal and Prosser viewed the study as a way to get descriptive information—what Segal calls "a deeper dive"—about how children on welfare were faring in a varied group of locations that would become a subset of the JOBS evaluation sites. And as part of this deeper dive, they thought the study could be a vehicle for creating validated measures for low-income children.

The upshot was inclusion of an RFP task related to measuring the impacts of JOBS on children. Because of considerable internal disagreement about this, it was added as an additional task to assess its feasibility, with an option to include a further task of measuring such impacts based on the results of the feasibility study. The main feasibility question—whether interviewers trained to conduct surveys would be able to conduct child assessments originally developed for administration by psychologists—had already been answered affirmatively by inclusion of similar measures in the 1986 fielding of the National Longitudinal Survey of Youth. The feasibility option simply reflected a bureaucratic way to move the RFP forward while deferring resolution of our internal disagreement.

An important advance for HHS was how the RFP dealt with site selection. This did not reflect the substance of JOBS directly but rather was the continuation of our learning how best to enroll productive sites in an evaluation. The RFP provided substantial flexibility for sites to enter the study, including both a process by which states could apply for grants to participate and a process by which the winning evaluation contractors could recruit promising sites even if they had not applied for a grant. The RFP provided for funds for the winning evaluator to conduct site visits and to develop a technical memorandum that would include site selection criteria and recommendations for which sites to select, with a site-by-site justification for each selection. Including the evaluator so deeply in site selection was an important step forward from the model developed for the Teen Parent demonstration, for which HHS had already selected the sites on the basis of a paper grant-application process but no direct contact with sites and awarded the evaluation contract and site grants simultaneously. The JOBS evaluation decision was a result of several factors, by far the most important of which was to achieve a much more informed selection process by spending more time gathering firsthand information about how potential sites were operating.[14] Its manifest superiority over the earlier separate and simultaneous processes of identifying an evaluator and sites made it the model HHS would use in future large-scale experiments.[15]

At the end of a hotly contested competition, the department awarded the contract to MDRC on September 30, 1989, the last day of the federal fiscal year, reflecting the typical statutory requirement that federal funds be obligated in the fiscal year for which they were appropriated or be lost to the agency (by automatically reverting back to the U.S. Treasury).[16]

Post-Award Redesign

As is typical of major evaluations, one of the initial stages of the JOBS evaluation was to redesign the project, as called for in the third task of the request for proposals. This stage is always necessary because the formal federal procurement process requires the program office funding the evaluation to remain at arm's length from the bidders. Although there is some back-and-forth between the two, it is mostly in writing and limited to determining the strongest bid, and always mediated through a contract officer. The central parties can have direct in-depth discussions only after the contract is awarded. These discussions can even lead to important changes, although all revisions must occur within the framework of the contract specified in the RFP that governed the procurement.

A central goal of the redesign stage is to review the contractor's proposed approach in greater detail and begin to flesh out how the project will be carried out. The resource constraints facing any major evaluation involve inevitable trade-offs regarding what the findings will teach. The nature of these emerges ever more clearly as implementation details are added, and the agency's priorities in launching the project are continuously revisited and rebalanced to determine how the actual implementation can best accomplish the evaluation's goals. Although the prioritizing of resources continues through the end of the contract, the choices the agency makes at the outset are the most fundamental and have the largest resource implications. For the JOBS evaluation, a series of exciting and vital meetings—in which my office, ASPE, and MDRC analyzed, debated, and ultimately shaped the evaluation—began in the fall of 1989 and continued throughout 1990. Mike Fishman, who was director of the ASPE Income Security Policy Division at the time, recalls the rigor and energy of the meetings: "We would create an agenda to discuss particular topics and then MDRC would come down for a face-to-face meeting. We would spend the better part of a day in a conference room working through the issues. MDRC would bring well fleshed out options with the implications of each. The discussions were very spirited—with new ideas raised and discussed. It was a very interactive, iterative process."

LABOR FORCE ATTACHMENT VERSUS HUMAN CAPITAL DEVELOPMENT MDRC's proposal recommended including both sites in which a JOBS program would be tested against a no-JOBS services control group and sites in which two treatment groups would be tested against each other along with a no-JOBS services control group. For these powerful head-to-head tests, one treatment, which seemed most in consonance with the thrust of JOBS, would be what they called the Basic Education Mandate. Under this approach, a program would require mandatory JOBS recipients who lacked a high school diploma or tested below a minimal reading or mathematics level (with limited exceptions) to participate initially in an education activity. MDRC also described a second treatment, termed Client Assessment/Choice. This would allow for a more flexible, individualized treatment under which the program would screen mandatory JOBS recipients with a more comprehensive assessment tool, and the caseworker and recipient would jointly determine the initial activity in JOBS. However, MDRC proposed to implement this test only if the government elected an option to include five additional sites. Their concern was that the early development of the states' JOBS programs might make the alternative approaches virtually indistinguishable, thus undermining the value of the multiple-stream tests.

Instead, MDRC proposed an alternative for the second treatment, dubbed Job Search Sequence, that would, with limited exceptions, require all mandatory JOBS recipients to look first for work. It might then assess those unsuccessful in finding significant employment and place them in other kinds of activities "but at limited and sharply lower participation rates." MDRC judged that the Job Search Sequence stream was probably not feasible under JOBS because of the latter's emphasis on education. However, given that this proposed stream was much like the programs MDRC had evaluated in the early and middle 1980s, they felt it would provide a test of whether the "education or assessment models are more effective than an up-front job search sequence." Since JOBS represented a much more generous federal funding stream than the previous welfare-to-work authorities, the Job Search Sequence stream would represent the earlier state of affairs, and JOBS evaluation sites would have to agree to limit access to JOBS activities for this stream to much lower levels than permissible under the JOBS program.

Thus under MDRC's original proposal, the strongest method for determining the relative effectiveness of two programmatic approaches—random assignment to one of two different treatment streams—would not be used in the JOBS evaluation to determine the differential impact of two different kinds of JOBS programs but rather to assess the incremental impact of JOBS models and funding levels compared with pre-JOBS approaches and funding. Since the highest priority of the evaluation was to identify the most effective approaches for operating JOBS programs, this struck me as a misalignment of resources in not using the most powerful method to address the highest-priority question.

My approach to addressing this priority question was further, and strongly, influenced by the policy role I had played in the legislative process leading to passage of FSA, which was the high-water mark of my involvement in legislative policy. My staff and I had played an extensive role in analyzing various congressional bills, as well as the offers and counteroffers advanced in negotiations between the House and Senate. I had also served on a small group of mostly political staff working with the HHS undersecretary on devising a departmental legislative strategy and was one of four members of the administration's negotiating team led by Joseph Wright, the deputy director of the Office of Management and Budget. In all these capacities what struck me most about the developing legislation on JOBS was the House's insistence on requiring that states provide substantial segments of AFDC recipients with basic education services, despite the almost total lack of evidence that such services were effective in increasing employment. Although research established a correlation between low education levels and longer-term welfare recipiency, MDRC's strong impact evidence on the effectiveness of pre-JOBS interventions related entirely to programs based primarily on job search and work experience and with minimal basic education. Since the original House bill would have virtually entitled individuals with low basic reading and mathematics skills to training in basic education skills, states would have had no choice but to provide low-skilled individuals with these services, were they mandated to participate in JOBS.

Over time, the Reagan administration had moved from the narrow position of mandating that states require recipients to be in community work experience program (mandated work in return for benefits) to the more flexible position of emphasizing participation in some activity determined by a state to promote higher employment. Although the Senate was not eager to advance participation standards (it ultimately included much lower participation rates to secure the administration's support), it was generally in support of state flexibility regarding the content of work activities. In meetings with Senate Finance Committee staff, I stressed that the House bill would preclude states from running programs that had been proved successful in MDRC's rigorous evaluation—and that, although it would make sense to move beyond those relatively narrow programs, it would not be good policy to bet on basic education doing better than more work-focused activities and rule out the latter. Senate staff was sympathetic to my argument, but because they were also aware of their need to deal with the House, they chose a strategy that would keep the House's general framework but build in qualifications to provide greater state flexibility. From a legal perspective, this strategy proved effective. An initial assessment was required, but the JOBS program as finally legislated did not mandate that it occur before any participation in a JOBS activity. Furthermore, although the legislation required states to include education as an activity for those over the age of twenty who lacked a high school diploma or equivalent, substantial exceptions were allowed based on the state's employment plan for the individual. Finally, although development of that employment plan had to include consultation with the recipient, the state was the final arbiter of its contents. The upshot of my participation in developing the legislative language to which both the House and Senate ultimately agreed was that I understood its qualifiers, and how all the parts worked together, in a way that was not apparent to readers of the legislation who had not been privy to those discussions.

From my perspective, the JOBS debate and negotiations reflected two opposing ideological positions, neither of which was independent of empirical claims or totally lacking in factual support. The liberal perspective held that poor basic skills kept the majority of welfare recipients from employment and that the education deficit would need to be remedied for these recipients to get and succeed at work. Certainly, the low average skills of many welfare recipients were well documented, with about half of current recipients not having completed high school. But there was no experimental or other credible evidence that an intervention designed to improve basic skills would improve either employment or education outcomes.

Conservatives were skeptical of any intervention short of work. They believed the welfare system had undermined incentives to work, that most AFDC recipients could work, and that doing so would give them experience and improve their economic situation. But the conservatives' most favored work activity was the community work experience program, the evidence for which was weak. Conservatives also liked job search, since it had the potential to connect individuals to jobs in the regular economy. Furthermore, MDRC's Work/Welfare demonstration and San Diego's Saturation Work Initiative Model showed that interventions that included well-structured job search did have positive employment and earnings effects, albeit modest ones.

These two ideological perspectives also underlay the core design choice for JOBS program operators. They could either follow the overt education path or take advantage of the covert flexibility to implement a more work-focused approach. A JOBS evaluation that included multitreatment-stream sites would, therefore, be ideal for shining a rigorous research spotlight on the empirical claims embedded in the two competing approaches.

For this purpose, MDRC's proposal was close to what was needed but was not quite there. Their Basic Education Mandate seemed exactly on target and right in line with the basic theme of JOBS—remediation of basic skills to improve employment. But their Client Assessment/Choice model did not seem fully compatible with the JOBS emphasis on education. Nor did it seem consistent with where states were heading in designing their JOBS programs. Most important, because MDRC staff could not have an insider's understanding of the JOBS statute, they did not appreciate that, with the right modifications, the job search approach could be consistent with the law. The law did allow for all JOBS assignees to be required to search for work initially, but it also required that those who were unsuccessful be evaluated and provided further services. Limiting these services in the way MDRC had proposed was not consistent with JOBS and failed to capture the idea that JOBS programs should incorporate the success of pre-JOBS welfare-to-work programs but also build a more intensive set of services on them. The key change needed was to include post-job-search services for unsuccessful job seekers that were consistent with a focus on rapid employment (for the most part short-term skills development) and to remove arbitrary restrictions on service levels or cost. If this job-search-plus approach turned out to be less expensive than the Basic Education Mandate, this would then be an important empirical finding—not a preimposed design limit.

For the first redesign meeting, I drew up a hand-written chart that described the two streams I proposed be tested head-to-head within sites. One I dubbed Human Capital Development (in this chapter hereafter referred to as the Human Capital approach), the other Attachment to the Work Force (later renamed Labor Force Attachment and hereafter referred to as the Labor Force approach). Some concern was expressed that the Labor Force approach would not be consistent with the statute and might require waivers. To me it was critical that the evaluation be designed not to require waivers, since I was also interested in demonstrating the flexibility inherent (though not necessarily highlighted) in JOBS. My goal was to be consistent with the letter of the law but not necessarily its broader theme. (In fact, few states initially picked up on this flexibility, and it was only well into the 1990s that states began to shift their JOBS programs away from being predominantly basic education services, influenced in part by the emerging early findings from the GAIN and

JOBS evaluations.) After some debate, most staff in ASPE and MDRC liked my approach, assuming that it could pass legal muster, and this was the direction we decided to pursue.

As we refined the initial conception of the models, we worked to ensure that each was stylized to create a sharp difference between them with as little overlap as possible. MDRC then moved quickly to identify potential three-stream sites for the Labor Force versus Human Capital test, and within a year we chose three: Atlanta, Georgia; Grand Rapids, Michigan; and Riverside, California.[17] Although the JOBS evaluation would provide a wealth of policy and program information across all sites, these three would be its core strength, confirming Judy's advocacy for such an approach and its broad support in the previous spring's seminal meeting of experts convened by the Institute for Research on Poverty.

STRENGTHENING THE BASELINE   Evaluations based on nonexperimental designs almost always require collection of information on individuals before entry into the program or policy undergoing evaluation to derive any impact estimates, even if biased.[18] Since random assignment designs require only comparison of outcomes after random assignment, baseline data are not necessary to produce unbiased estimates, as long as random assignment has been successfully implemented and the groups do not differ systematically. Baseline information is of great value, however, for confirming that random assignment was indeed random. Baseline information contributes greatly to the value of an experiment in additional ways as well, by

- providing a quantitative description of those who were randomly assigned,
- increasing the statistical precision of the impact estimates,
- helping to assess and adjust for response bias in follow-up surveys, and
- identifying any subpopulations that may have been differentially affected by the treatment.

Sufficient data are almost always already available to assess the success of random assignment and to serve all the additional purposes except the last on the list, which is the reason typically invoked for moving beyond already collected data to a special baseline survey.

The theoretical potential of subgroup analysis is that any subpopulation within the experimental group, as defined by pre–random assignment characteristics, constitutes a mini-experiment of its own, yielding estimates for that subpopulation that are unbiased (that is, internally valid). Take as an example the random assignment of both men and women to participate in an employment program. Estimates for the total population, for men, and for women, will all be internally valid. Since the latter two populations will be smaller than the total, such estimates will be less precise, and impacts of a given size will be less likely to be detected if they exist.[19] But the estimates will still be unbiased. This feature of experiments has led many to posit that one of their primary values is not just to determine whether a program or policy is effective but also, as commonly phrased, "what works for whom." Understanding that some subgroups are helped by a program and others are not, for example, could potentially lead to better targeting of resources by excluding, or modifying the program for, those who are not.

Before the JOBS evaluation, MDRC's welfare-to-work experiments had relied for baseline data primarily on a one-page client information sheet, which was expanded for the JOBS evaluation. More significantly, in the JOBS evaluation planning, sentiment was strong to try a deeper, more theoretical approach that would capture welfare recipients' motivation and internal and external circumstances, to see whether those would provide stronger measures of what might differentiate program effects. This led to development of a brief, self-administered baseline survey, the Private Opinion Survey, that would be succeeded by the follow-up surveys in the three core sites testing the Human Capital and Labor Force treatments head-to head and in Portland, Oregon, a site that tested a more flexible work-first program.[20] Considerable disagreement about what exactly should be in the survey led to several changes in its specific contents. In the end, questions covered attitudes toward balancing work and parenting, risk of depression, locus of control, problems arranging child care or transportation, and health and family problems. Because of topic sensitivity, the survey was administered separately within the intake process through procedures established to ensure confidentiality of the responses from staff operating the program. Baseline data for the JOBS evaluation consisted of the Private Opinion Survey augmented by the usual administrative records on earnings and welfare receipt and standard demographic information captured in the intake process.[21]

DUAL RANDOM ASSIGNMENT   Important choices often have to be made in social experiments about the point of random assignment. First, the point where a social intervention begins is typically not well defined. Second, only some points in the program entry process are suitable for carrying out the allocation of individuals to groups. Selecting among the range of possible random assignment points has important consequences not only for what will be learned but also for the relative cost of that knowledge.

For the JOBS evaluation, the important random assignment choice was whether it should occur at the welfare office (where initial and ongoing eligibility and benefit levels were determined) or the JOBS office. In most AFDC programs the two functions were performed by different staff in different locations. This was important to the JOBS evaluation, because the determination as to whether someone was JOBS mandatory was typically part of the income maintenance function (that is, before the person ever appeared at the JOBS office).[22] This determination could be made either when persons were present (in which case they were also given the time and location of a required appointment at the JOBS office) or in their absence (in which case they were informed by a letter that also included the JOBS office appointment time and place).

In some evaluations this choice might have been unimportant. For JOBS (as had been the case in the Work/Welfare demonstration and the GAIN and Project Independence studies), however, the point of random assignment had important implications for what would be learned, because the mandatory JOBS requirement meant that the program might plausibly affect individuals' employment outcomes in at least two ways. First, the services might increase employment by improving individuals' skills and therefore employability. But second, the mandatory aspect of JOBS might itself have positive effects on measured employment, independent of the services received. For example, some of the individuals who were told they would be required to participate in JOBS might decide not to bother with the services and just find employment on their own. Others, who might be working but not informing the welfare office of their employment, might have to choose between keeping either their job or their welfare benefits (to the extent that their work commitments were incompatible with their JOBS participation). This phenomenon, commonly referred to as "smoke out" because it reveals off-the-books employment, could have a real effect on employment—positive if individuals decided to work more to make up for the loss of benefits, or negative if they quit their job or reduced their hours to comply with the work requirement. Even if they did not in fact change their hours of work, the mandatory nature of the program could still have had a real effect in reducing their welfare benefit amount.

This dual potential effect of JOBS mandatory programs was important for an additional reason: the often significant drop-off in the number of individuals told to report and the number who actually turned up at the JOBS office. Although part of this would be an effect of the dynamic nature of welfare receipt noted in earlier chapters, with many individuals' circumstances changing quickly, some of it would potentially be an effect of the known requirement to participate as a condition for continuing to receive AFDC benefits.

In the end we decided on a dual approach wherever it was feasible, because of the downsides to each approach taken separately. The downside of randomly assigning at the JOBS office was that any effects of the mandate that occurred before a person actually showed up there would be missed, thus understating the true program impact. The downsides of random assignment at the earlier welfare office stage were several. First, once individuals were randomly assigned, they had to be included in all data collection and all analysis, to maintain the required analytic equivalence between experimental and control groups. This would almost certainly increase the costs of the evaluation by requiring the tracking of increased numbers of individuals who did not then participate in JOBS at all. Second, it would potentially dilute the sample for analysis if in fact the initial mandate did not affect behavior (thus making it harder to find any effects of JOBS itself). Finally, in some cases collecting baseline information in the welfare office was difficult, sometimes impossible, for AFDC program staff, not only because of enormous workloads but also because not all applicants were seen in person at the point they became mandatory.

MDRC, having presented all these issues in their proposal, recommended designs that randomly assigned at the JOBS office. However, MDRC also advanced an approach that would do a "double random assignment." The first would take place at the welfare office and would create a small control group and a large JOBS mandatory group. To hold down evaluation costs, the basis for comparing outcomes would be limited to administrative data. A further random assignment of those assigned to the JOBS mandatory group at the welfare office would then take place at the JOBS office, thus creating a second control group that would not be subject to any further requirements. Since the states showed evidence of taking the JOBS mandate more seriously than ever before, we were reluctant to give up on measuring these effects and decided to investigate the extent to which random assignment at both the welfare office and JOBS office was possible. As discussions with potential state and local partners were continuing, it became increasingly clear that random assignment in both welfare and JOBS offices was simply not feasible at all the sites. We did, however, identify two sites, Riverside and Grand Rapids, where it was feasible, so we were ultimately able for the first time in a welfare-to-work study to pursue the dual random assignment strategy.

ENTREPRENEURIAL MANEUVERING ON THE JOBS CHILD IMPACT STUDY[23] OPTION

Segal's and Prosser's original motivation in advancing the inclusion of an in-depth study of the impact of JOBS participation on children was threefold:

1. To find out whether requiring women with young children to work would negatively affect their children (the do-no-harm perspective). This had become particularly relevant since JOBS had lowered the youngest age of children whose mothers could be required to participate from six years to three (and to one at state option), ages at which children were not yet uniformly in school.
2. To develop validated outcome measures for low-income children.
3. To develop in-depth descriptive information on how children on AFDC were faring.

Although a feasibility assessment of such a study had been approved for inclusion in the RFP, to paper over internal disagreement on whether to conduct the study at all, the disagreement continued, with several competing views both for and against conducting it entering the discussion.

The MDRC contract proposal presented the initial complication. MDRC had proposed to subcontract primary responsibility for the feasibility study to Child Trends, a research organization with a substantial history in measuring the well-being of children. Nicholas Zill, its president, and Kristin Moore, who would succeed him, were lead authors of the relevant proposal section. The best evidence, according to their write-up, suggested that maternal employment was not harmful to children's development; but they acknowledged that this finding was based on primarily middle-class mothers who had chosen to take up work outside the home (although perhaps pressed by financial need). This view was consistent with where we at HHS had started (the do-no-harm criterion), but the proposal developed the motivation for the study along two complicating dimensions.

The first was the large number of factors they described as potentially affecting child outcomes (either positively or negatively), including the quality of child care, potential demographic changes (such as lower fertility or changes in household composition), loss of Medicaid, job satisfaction, or job stress.[24] They also emphasized that any or all of these could vary greatly among individuals depending, for example, on psychological variables (such as a mother's attitude toward working outside the home versus being a full-time homemaker). All these potentially moderating and mediating factors led the proposal writers to hypothesize that potential effects on children were likely to differ by subgroups, even if there were no clear hypotheses about the direction, or existence, of an overall effect—implying, in turn, that power calculations would need to take into consideration not just the overall sample size but also the likely size of potentially policy-relevant subgroups.

The second complicating dimension in the proposal was an emphasis on the strong presumption in JOBS of remedial education and consequent hypothesized linkages between parental education and positive child development: that any improvement to the mothers' education that came from JOBS might lead to improved child well-being. The hypothesis that the education element of JOBS could be viewed as a positive force for child development represented a major shift from the initial perspective that child outcomes should be assessed against the negative hypothesis implied by the do-no-harm criterion: that requiring mothers with young children to participate in JOBS might lead to worse child outcomes.

The combination of the positive impact hypothesis and the many-pathway perspective implied an enormously broad measurement strategy, including measuring children's cognitive development. This is not to say that hypotheses of how JOBS might affect children in many domains, including cognitively, could not be derived from the do-no-harm perspective. But emphasizing the potentially positive aspects of JOBS education services was certainly more congenial to such a hypothesis. As a consequence, the MDRC proposal suggested that the child impact study be concentrated in sites that emphasized the education component.

A third perspective complicated the child impact issue even further, this one coming primarily from outside HHS and outside MDRC's proposal. This viewpoint emphasized that JOBS was an opportunity to improve child well-being, especially to the extent that it focused resources on high-quality child care and used a mother's participation in JOBS as an opening to bring additional services that would promote children's positive development to bear directly. In other words, JOBS program operators should not focus simply on mothers' employment but rather should develop two-generational programs that would also directly aid their children. Although this programmatic perspective was not strictly focused on evaluation, it was certainly consistent with the broader measurement view that stressed assessing child well-being across multiple domains. It would take well into the 1990s to resolve the debate over the purpose for, and manner of, assessing the effect of JOBS on children. But that debate began in earnest within two months of signing the JOBS evaluation contract.

On November 9 and 10, 1989, the National Academy of Sciences held a long-planned meeting to discuss assessing the effects of the Family Support Act on children and a more general focus on two-generation approaches. The primary funder of the meeting was the Foundation for Child Development, whose president was Barbara Blum, the previous president of MDRC. Her intention was to use the meeting to draw lessons from past research to influence implementation of FSA so that it would be beneficial rather than harmful to children and to encourage research on the new act to learn more about poor children. A large number of individuals involved in research and policy related to low-income children and families attended, and the meeting was structured around a series of solicited papers. Its location was the crowded Lecture Room in the main building of the National Academy of Sciences on Constitution Avenue, in Washington, D.C. The secretary of HHS, Louis Sullivan, was the invited speaker at a dinner held in the academy's Great Hall in the evening of the first meeting day.

The initial paper was written by two faculty members of the John F. Kennedy School of Government at Harvard—David Ellwood and Julia Wilson. Ellwood, of course, had been the coauthor, with Mary Jo Bane, of seminal work showing that, although most who entered welfare received benefits relatively briefly, a subset of AFDC recipients were long-term welfare stayers. The paper he and Wilson gave at this meeting took the position that JOBS was unlikely to have much effect on child well-being. Their primary argument was that any effects on children were likely to come from increased maternal employment, on which pre-JOBS programs had only modest effects. They argued further that, although JOBS might have larger effects than its precursors, these were unlikely to be substantially larger. Since the literature suggested that employment at best weakly affected child outcomes, it was highly unlikely that the expected modest maternal employment changes would lead to detectable effects on child well-being. My own view, essentially the same as theirs, was that a major investment in examining the effects of JOBS on children seemed highly questionable, although I was open to a modest investment to address the do-no-harm concern.

The view that JOBS should implement two-generational programs with the goal of improving both adult and child outcomes, which was championed by many outside government, troubled me on two separate grounds. First, although I liked the idea in principle, it seemed to me that urging such approaches on program operators would run the risk of both diluting their mission and greatly complicating the difficulties most state and local welfare agencies would surely face in implementing an employment program. Changing welfare agencies across the country into employment-focused organizations would itself be an extremely difficult task; transforming them further and, at the same time, into the locus of improved child development seemed impossible. Two-generation programs were best developed and evaluated in the context of well-funded demonstrations, I argued, not the initiation of JOBS programs. Second, adding improved child development as a JOBS goal seemed like setting states up for failure—even if they were successful in improving employment outcomes, they would be labeled as failures unless they also managed to improve child well-being.

As happens more often than not in Washington, the public debate was intense and interesting, but the real action took place behind the scenes. The role the National Academy of Sciences meeting played in designing the Child Impact study resulted from what occurred in the HHS Humphrey Building offices across and up the Mall.

Several days before the meeting, ASPE staff suggested that we exercise the JOBS Child Impact study option and that the upcoming meeting would be an ideal venue for the secretary to announce HHS's commitment to learning about the effects of JOBS on children. On its surface, this suggestion was certainly premature; the contract was not two months old, the project was barely under way, and the purpose of the feasibility study was described as gathering evidence to inform a considered decision on whether to proceed. In fact, however, although many important technical hurdles still had to be overcome, the raw feasibility of the study was never really in doubt, just its substantive value. Staff in ASPE saw the National Academy of Sciences meeting as a valuable opportunity for resolving the design issue in favor of conducting the type of study they had conceived and advanced.

Although my staff and I raised the concern that acting when the feasibility work was just getting under way was no way to proceed, it was clear that ASPE held the high cards. The secretary and his chief of staff, Michael Calhoun, were both acutely conscious of the ambiguity of the secretary's public persona. From the beginning of his tenure, conservatives were suspicious that he was insufficiently pro-life, while many liberals regarded him as a minority face in a conservative administration. Studying the impact of JOBS participation on children looked like an excellent way to demonstrate his concern with child well-being to the latter group without offending the principles of the former. One did not have be an expert on decision making in government to see that an announcement at the National Academy of Sciences would appeal to the secretary's closest advisers and that the head of ASPE, Martin Gerry, would also be pleased with the idea of the study and the locus of the announcement.

My staff and I, in contrast, owing in part to the conservatives' rejection of the first of Secretary Sullivan's candidates for assistant secretary for family support, had no Senate-confirmed supervisor to carry the water for caution. In addition, since ASPE had committed itself to covering the bulk of the extra cost projected for the child study, my biggest concern—that my office, which was responsible for 80 percent of what was already a $9 million and growing tab for the main study, would become responsible for 80 percent of another $2.7 million to answer a question that would only confirm the null hypothesis—was removed.[25] So I made no effort to press the issue within HHS and simply accepted the likely outcome of the process.

Segal, however, was not so passive. The previous summer the HHS senior leadership had held a retreat to establish the policy priorities the new administration should pursue. ASPE had suggested then that the department's adoption of a more two-generational perspective in programs for low-income families could produce better outcomes for both parents and children, a view that had been warmly received. So, when the secretary's speechwriter came to ask Segal's help on giving the secretary something to say about the department's two-generational efforts, Segal, as she herself says, acted as "an opportunist. . . . We didn't have a lot of examples of two-generational studies. . . . I saw that as a way for the secretary to announce this big new two-generation study and indeed wrote a couple of paragraphs for the speechwriter. . . . It was a career decision [of mine]. . . . I don't think it went up to the political level."

Segal did not elevate the decision up the chain of command. She felt confident that the language passing through the various levels of department clearance would constitute its acceptance. Furthermore, it was a safe bet that the secretary would read it exactly as was, since he seldom, if ever, deviated from the text of speeches written for him.

The night of the speech containing the announcement, Segal and I sat together at the dinner. I remember turning to her and saying, "Well, I guess we're going to do it." Within a few months, on February 21, 1990, Fishman and Patrick Fagan sent forward a decision memorandum to Gerry recommending exercise of the JOBS Child Impact study option, saying, in part, that "Secretary Sullivan has publicly announced his support for the study of families and children." Approval of the recommendation followed, and on March 30, 1990, the contract was formally modified. As a fellow bureaucrat, I could not help admiring the deftness with which Segal had sized up the opportunity and seized the moment to realize a goal that represented what she viewed as not only an important policy issue but also a priority of her agency.

Of course, even a capable civil servant like Segal needed support from key political appointees. According to Fishman, Gerry was a strong supporter of the JOBS Child Impact study and played a key role in helping to manage ongoing dealings with the HHS contracts office and ensuring that there were sufficient funds to sustain the study at a high level.

INTEGRATING THE JOBS CHILD IMPACT STUDY EFFICIENTLY INTO THE OVERALL EVALUATION   Although the key decision to undertake the JOBS Child Impact study occurred early, analyzing alternative ways to carry out the study as efficiently as possible within the broader JOBS evaluation took a great deal longer. It took intensive work to arrive at a set of survey measures that was substantively optimal without being too lengthy for easy administration but even more to arrive at an efficient subsampling design for its implementation. The original plan had been for the Child Impacts study survey to be administered to a separate subsample from the main study survey (which itself was to be administered only in certain sites). Despite the substantive reasons for separating what could be thought of as two different populations, the efficiency arguments for integrating the two surveys in the end proved overwhelming.

Even when that decision had been made, there still remained the question of which subsample should be administered the integrated survey. The first plan had been to administer the integrated survey at two and five years after baseline in the three sites where the Human Capital and Labor Force approaches were being tested head-to-head—but only to the Human Capital stream and the control group. The reasons for this decision were that the Human Capital approach represented what was then thought to be the typical JOBS program, with its emphasis on basic education skills; that provision of education services to parents might improve education outcomes for children; and that the financial resources in the contract at the time were not sufficient to survey all participants in both streams. Once again, an outside advisory panel produced compelling reasons to change the design—strongly urging that we assess child impacts for the Labor Force stream as well.[26] Panel members were concerned that the do-no-harm criterion was not being given sufficient weight. This resulted in our funding the survey for the Labor Force stream also.

In addition, the Department of Education provided a multimillion-dollar contribution to expand the evaluation to study the education aspect of JOBS in more depth. This funding enabled the study to analyze the education effects of JOBS on both parents and children by testing the educational achievement of both groups, gathering teacher evaluations of how children were doing in school, and tracking the children's school performance via administrative records.

FINAL DESIGN, KEY DESIGN ELEMENTS, AND MAJOR FINDINGS

The design that emerged from the long and crucial process just described led directly to the strength of the key findings. The utility of the results to policy makers depended on each key design choice.

Final Layout of Sites, Treatments, and Data Collection

The JOBS evaluation was implemented in seven sites, each of which also included a no-JOBS control group, and tested a total of eleven different JOBS program models:

- Atlanta, Georgia; Grand Rapids, Michigan; and Riverside, California: Labor Force versus Basic Education head-to-head tests

- Columbus, Ohio: Basic Education with traditional case management (with separate caseworkers for benefit eligibility and JOBS services) versus Basic Education with an integrated model (with a single worker combining both).
- Detroit, Michigan, and Oklahoma City, Oklahoma: Basic Education.
- Portland, Oregon: Mixed, with elements of both Labor Force and Basic Education.

About 57,000 individuals were randomly assigned across the seven sites, with data collected as follows:

- Administrative records data, including unemployment insurance wage records and welfare benefits, were collected for all individuals.
- Baseline data on personal characteristics (such as demographics and welfare and education history) were also collected for all individuals.
- The Private Opinion Survey and reading and math tests were administered in the three Labor Force versus Basic Education sites and in Portland.
- A client survey was administered to a subsample in the same four sites at five years and to a subsample in all sites at two years.
- The special child-impact data collection was administered in the three Labor Force versus Basic Education sites at two and five years (to a sample of individuals who had a focal child aged three to five years at the time of random assignment).

Design Elements That Contributed Most to the Policy Value of the Findings

Four features of the JOBS evaluation stand out as critical to the definitiveness of its findings and their policy value: the systematic, unified nature of what the JOBS evaluation tested; the head-to-head tests; improved measurement strategies; and two-stage random assignment. Each made an important contribution to our knowledge of welfare policies and programs.

THE UNIFIED HYPOTHESIS UNDERLYING THE JOBS PROGRAM   The primary hypothesis of the JOBS program, which underlay the design of the JOBS evaluation, was that providing basic education to adult welfare recipients with low basic skills would improve their employment and earnings.[27] The evaluation systematically tested this hypothesis by requiring that all seven of the sites implement at least one experimentally tested treatment requiring welfare recipients with low basic skills to participate in remediation services. Second, in the three Labor Force versus Human Capital sites, the evaluation also tested a contrasting treatment, consistent with federal JOBS program requirements, that was built on a different model—that, with help, welfare recipients with low basic skills could find employment without first undergoing remediation.

The authorities to get welfare recipients to work in the early 1980s were a more scattered set of options, allowing state welfare agencies variously to operate the Work Incentive program with greater federal flexibility; require welfare recipients to work in exchange for their benefits; require welfare recipients to look for work; and provide subsidized employment for welfare recipients using welfare benefits as the subsidy. If these can be said to constitute a hypothesis, it is a weak one, going something like this: If we try several plausible approaches, they may increase welfare recipients' transition to work.

In contrast to the actual separate authorities enacted in the early 1980s, the basic design of MDRC's Work/Welfare demonstration had a relatively unified underlying theme: in four of the eight sites, the model for the program was initial job search followed by workfare for those who had been unsuccessful in finding jobs.[28] Although the other four sites certainly added important information for policy and practice, the four sites that shared a more common program model built a more coherent story, even if not as unified as that for JOBS.

HEAD-TO-HEAD TESTING Even with the more unified approach of the JOBS program, systematic assessment required that the Human Capital stream be tested in multiple sites, not only against the control experience but also in contrast to the Labor Force stream.[29] The power of this contrast in three different sites—along with the single treatment designs in three other sites and the two separate Human Capital streams with different case management models tested in the Columbus site—added substantial weight to the JOBS findings.

MEASUREMENT IMPROVEMENTS Two major improvements in measurement were also important to the value of the JOBS evaluation. First, the JOBS evaluation used a more comprehensive measurement of baseline characteristics, allowing a more systematic analysis than previously of whether program effects differed by the characteristics of the individuals assigned to them.[30] Second, and even more important, was the more systematic measurement of outcomes for young children, allowing the first rigorous assessment ever of whether work requirements for welfare parents had positive or negative effects on children. Added value was the quick extension of the same measures to numerous other studies (experimental and nonexperimental), fulfilling Segal's and Prosser's original vision (see discussion in chapters 10 and 11). As Segal says, "I think the biggest [value to us] was that we got validated instruments for the first time, and these . . . influenced the field; people picked them up."

TWO-STAGE RANDOM ASSIGNMENT   Without the two-stage random assignment in two sites, the evaluation could not have begun to disentangle how much of the effect of JOBS treatments derived from the actual job services and how much from the simple fact that service receipt was mandated and the participants knew this up front.

Key Findings
The central findings of the JOBS evaluation are clear:

- Both the Labor Force and Human Capital approaches represented fair tests of their respective hypotheses. Each, as implemented, was clearly distinct from the other, and each was consistent with its underlying model.
- Both approaches had positive effects on employment, earnings, and welfare receipt. But the positive impacts of the Labor Force approach were larger than those of the Human Capital approach in all three of the head-to-head test sites. The time trend of the impacts differed between the two streams, however. At the three-year follow-up, the impacts of the two streams were about equal. At the five-year follow-up, neither had significant impacts on the main outcomes. However, when measured over the entire five-year period, the Labor Force programs' impacts were larger, because its impacts were larger over the first two years.
- The Labor Force approach was less expensive to operate, with costs running about 60 percent of the costs of the Human Capital approach.

- The Human Capital approach had no significant effects on education achievement.
- The earnings and welfare receipt findings for the sites testing only the Human Capital approach were generally similar to the findings for the Human Capital stream in the head-to-head sites. Portland was an exception, with larger and more persistent effects on earnings and welfare receipt than any other site, including the Labor Force approach in the head-to-head sites. This finding is further discussed later in this chapter.
- In the Columbus site, integrated case management proved more effective in improving employment outcomes than separate case managers for income maintenance and for employment.
- The mandate, even with no subsequent services, had significant positive effects on increasing employment and reducing welfare use.
- With respect to the JOBS Child Impact study, no consistent pattern of effects, either positive or negative, was found, confirming the null hypothesis of no impact. There was a slight pattern (inconsistent across sites) of small negative effects on adolescents' school performance, but the limited data collection on older children and the unclear pattern among sites limits confidence in this finding.[31]

How the JOBS and GAIN Findings Influenced Policy and Practice

The Greater Avenues for Independence program, in California, was built on the same underlying general hypothesis as JOBS: that low-skilled welfare recipients could best advance in the workforce by placement first in adult basic education.[32] In addition, since GAIN was begun earlier, its evaluation results became available earlier. The one-year GAIN impact results, published in 1992, showed stronger impacts for Riverside than for the other counties, all of which placed a greater emphasis on basic education. Although many were skeptical that Riverside would remain at the top of the heap, the two-year impacts published the next year and the three-year impacts published in 1994 dispelled much skepticism, and the findings began to have a significant effect on policy and practice.

In the following year, the first JOBS evaluation findings from the head-to-head tests provided powerful confirmation of the much stronger GAIN impacts found in Riverside County, which stressed rapid job entry and constrained the use of education, than in the other GAIN evaluation sites. The finding of the success of work first itself now having been repeated in two separate random assignment tests—and most powerfully in the JOBS head-to-head tests, where confounding site and treatment was not an issue—ruled out the possibility that the Riverside findings resulted from some site-specific idiosyncrasy.[33]

The primary effect of the two studies on policy and practice was to undermine the basic education hypothesis of the JOBS program. In so doing, it strongly supported the conservative perspective that work programs, even without remedial education, could improve welfare recipients' employment outcomes, even those with low basic skills. Ron Haskins, the key staffer in developing the welfare provisions of the 1996 welfare reform, puts it this way:

> I'm really confident in saying that the most important effect was that this knowledge developed . . . [that] if you had job search programs, more people would go to work, and . . . you could save money. Those were the two biggest messages, and I think it had a dramatic effect on the welfare debate. It took what could have been the central issue right off the table. There just wasn't discussion of whether these programs would work. . . . Democrats didn't want to do what we were trying to do, and they would've loved to say these programs don't work. . . . [But] you'd be antiscience, you'd be against Judy Gueron, plus you probably couldn't get away with it.

It is worth noting that—as familiar as Haskins was with the research, and as well-trained a researcher as he is—he now describes the findings and their role in policy in terms of messages, not evidence. Furthermore, although he is answering a question posed specifically in the context of the JOBS evaluation, he neither identifies the particular study nor associates specific findings with it or any study.

The progressively stronger evidence that work first was more effective than basic education first, and at lower cost, is highly consistent with the direction policy and practice in fact took, although this direction was based on a very general view of the findings and went considerably further than the evidence underlying them. For example, although the findings did strongly undermine the JOBS program view that basic education was central to improving employment outcomes, the findings did not address questions about the effectiveness of other forms of human capital development such as occupational skills training (as opposed to basic education).

A second important effect of the findings came from the lack of effects, positive or negative, on young children. Had the Human Capital approach documented positive effects on children, it might have continued to have advocates despite its smaller (relative to the Labor Force model) effects on parental employment, particularly since it would have been possible to argue that there were generational trade-offs for the Human Capital approach. If negative effects on children had been detected, these would also have been likely to have affected policy. Haskins says in that regard that "had Democrats been able to present credible evidence from state welfare reform demonstrations or other reliable sources that showed strong work requirements were associated with bad outcomes for kids, the bill would have been in serious jeopardy. Even if Republicans had passed the bill in the House and the Senate, President Clinton would probably have vetoed it."[34]

Since the findings for Portland have played a prominent role in the welfare debate—used, interestingly, by both liberals and conservatives—it is worth discussing them somewhat further. Although the JOBS evaluation was highly unified, there were inevitably differences among sites. The difference between the Portland program and those in the other Human Capital sites was particularly significant for the hypothesis being tested because, although Portland was more flexible than the strict Labor Force sites in allowing basic education and skills training at the outset, it nevertheless strongly emphasized early job search (in this respect it was similar to Riverside GAIN, the outlier site in the GAIN evaluation). In analyzing the Portland findings, MDRC described that program as mixed (as they had described Riverside GAIN), signaling that it had elements of both the Human Capital and the Labor Force models, although less rigid than elsewhere in the selection of who entered each and in what sequence individuals received them.

Despite large and sustained effects, Portland's findings have not led practitioners to take up the model.[35] I think this is the result of two very different factors that affect the use of research results. The first is that evidence from a single site is unlikely to convince policy makers or researchers without some degree of replication. For example, although MDRC suggested that the unique success of both Portland JOBS and Riverside GAIN in producing large and sustained impacts may have been attributable to their mixed models[36]—a description that MDRC developed after the GAIN findings became known rather than as part of the theory underlying the design of the evaluation—other analyses show that attempts to determine the cause of a program's success in this manner cannot reliably do so (Greenberg et al. 2001). One cannot get inside the black box of any particular program in a single site, unless alternative treatments are tested either head-on or in a multisite design with a large numbers of sites. This need for more complex designs is probably most influential with researchers.

The second factor, which is related more to influencing policy and practice than to research acceptability, is timing. This can be observed in the very different reception given to the Riverside GAIN and Portland JOBS findings. The evaluation results from the former program had a very large influence on policy and practice, even though they were confined to a single site, but not by direct replication. Given the frustration of rising caseloads and a social turn in a more conservative direction, the Riverside GAIN results provided not so much a model for replication as a different vision for welfare-to-work services and requirements. Outside Los Angeles County, other program operators did not implement the Riverside version of the GAIN model; rather, they turned to it thematically and shifted from a focus on basic education to one on job search. The salience of timing and consistency with broader social directions, rather than narrow research findings, is well illustrated by both Riverside's and Portland's own reactions to their findings. Even though the Riverside GAIN model performed better than the Riverside JOBS model (this was not, of course, a head-to-head test), the county operated a program more like the latter than the former. And by the time the Portland results emerged, the program had in fact become much more like the typical Labor Force model; even after the final results emerged, its programming did not revert to the model tested in the JOBS evaluation. Thus, as reflected in the Haskins quote, it was the message that came through, not the literal findings, and the message resonated with the times.

Why is it that findings are not applied more directly both in policy and program operation decisions? How is it that specific impact estimates morph into general messages? It is notable that even in study reports we describe findings and interpret them in a natural language and not just equations and that we could only expect our policy and operational discourse to be even less precise. It seems clear that some simplification is inevitable and even desirable (what would it be like for members of Congress to be speaking as scientists?). Policy makers typically need to make quite general decisions, and most often the estimates we produce even in the strongest evaluation do not directly generalize to all populations or even all subpopulations within the research population, leading to overgeneralization. Studies with stronger external validity could help to reduce this form of oversimplification.

However, simplification often involves an even greater degree of distortion, for example, when the size or importance of impacts is exaggerated or when the description of the program is different from what was actually implemented and evaluated. It is likely, I believe, that at least some of this distortion occurs because both empirical information and values undergird policy and practice. This certainly was the case in welfare. And strongly held values can sometimes color our interpretation of evidence. Policy and program discourse is a complex of empirical and value claims that are not easily sorted out in a clear logical chain of argument.

That value positions often distort empirical findings might lead some to pessimism about the possibility of achieving the goal of evidence-based policy, but this does not follow. Evidence is most useful when we share a common end, for example, increasing work among adult welfare recipients, and strong evidence is built with regard to how best to achieve this. But often we attach values to means and are not simply interested in the most efficient way to produce the largest effect on a given outcome. How we balance the weight given to empirical considerations and that given to values is itself a value judgment. But our values themselves are subject to reconsideration based on what we learn. Better studies can change how we weigh evidence versus values but can also change those values themselves, and the findings described in this chapter have done just that. Twenty years ago, many liberals opposed job search before remediation as unfair, forcing unprepared individuals into the workforce. Now many (not all) of the same people, although they still support government help for low-income parents' efforts to improve their skills, no longer oppose what they earlier viewed as unfair. That is, knowing that a practice improves outcomes can change our mind about its fairness. Even when people disagree about ends, new empirical findings sometimes can reduce these differences. I may initially rank one outcome higher than another, but if strong evidence suggests that the latter can be improved readily with few or no downsides, and the former is intractable despite multiple attempts to change it, my ranking may well change. Thus the continued building of a body of strong evidence can affect our judgment not only about how we can more effectively bring about a given end but also about a practice more generally. Although we should not expect, nor would it be possible or appropriate for, findings to mechanically dictate our actions, we should expect that as evidence becomes stronger, it will have greater potential to influence program and policy choices through our altered appreciation of both facts and values.

THE REPORT TO CONGRESS ON JOBS PERFORMANCE STANDARDS

The language of the Family Support Act made clear that the performance standards HHS was to recommend to Congress were to be about outcomes, not processes, and that they were to measure success in achieving impacts on individuals: "recommendations shall be made with respect to specific measurements of outcomes and be based on the degree of success which might reasonably be expected of States in helping individuals to increase earnings, achieve self-sufficiency, and reduce welfare dependency, and shall not be measured solely by levels of activity or participation" (Social Security Act, sec. 487(a)(2)). Although most of us at HHS believed the current state of the art would not support department recommendations on JOBS performance standards that would actually promote positive impacts, we did have a statutory obligation to submit a report to Congress. To assist us in this effort, we had included a task under the JOBS evaluation contract for the contractor to conduct analyses, draft sections, and convene meetings. The program's performance standards were a topic of the second meeting of the JOBS Evaluation Advisory Panel held in December 1991; we also held external meetings on JOBS performance measurement in July 1992 and November 1993. After back-and-forth on several drafts that MDRC produced, we received a draft in October 1993 that we believed was ready to be circulated within the department.

The general tenor of the draft was skepticism about our ability to recommend JOBS performance standards that would benefit the program. The report raised, and illustrated with examples, four general concerns: inconsistent and unclear relationship between outcomes and impacts; difficulty establishing a level playing field across states and over time; difficulty determining who should be in the denominator, thereby avoiding creaming and gaming; and recognition that state programs had different objectives. The draft report did not advance any recommended measures or standards and did not promise to do so in the near future. Rather, it suggested three options that were a combination of further research and allowing states to explore implementation of performance standards.

Mary Jo Bane and the other senior political officials found the approach too negative. The Clinton administration was strongly advocating the collection and use of information on program outcomes, and this was a central element of Vice President Gore's Reinventing Government initiative. Furthermore, Bane promoted outcome measurement, even though I am confident she understood full well the technical problems in aligning outcomes with the added value that impacts represent. The only plausible argument I ever heard that advancing outcome measurement would improve programs was that it would focus them on the outcome rather than simply putting people through programs. As far as I was concerned, nobody ever satisfactorily explained why they believed that a system of outcome-based performance standards would actually recognize and reward high performance.

The report to Congress, submitted in 1994, was much more positive. The report included much of the analysis in the earlier draft regarding the four challenges to developing outcome-based JOBS performance standards without offering any concrete solutions to them, beyond future analysis of data (including what would become available from the JOBS evaluation). Nonetheless, it committed the department to a process that would result in final publication of outcome-based performance measures by October of 1996 and performance standards two years later. What the department would have proposed and how that might have worked will never be known. Passage of the Personal Responsibility and Work Opportunity Reconciliation Act and the elimination of the JOBS program prevented any of that from coming to pass.

As both drafts of the report indicated, and as Judy describes in chapter 12, a necessary condition for outcomes to measure real performance is that they be proxies for impacts. I believe we are nowhere close to being able to identify such outcomes for any area of social policy; thus outcome-based performance standards are science fiction, not science. Nonetheless, under the Clinton, George W. Bush, and Obama administrations, ever increasing requirements have been imposed on state and local programs funded with federal dollars to report on outcomes to the federal government. This reporting costs untold millions of dollars to produce data that are uninterpretable and bear no relationship to performance (as measured by impacts). If we want to know what programs are producing, we need to evaluate them. There are no shortcuts.[37]

BUILDING A STRONG SYNTHESIS OF EVIDENCE

From the perspective of building substantive knowledge, rather than sending policy messages, the most vital element is no single study in itself but the broader agenda of research in which it is embedded. The only rigorous way to get at this broader evidence building is through research syntheses—that is, a variety of methods for analyzing impact estimates across studies to construct more systematic, generalizable findings, the formal "cobbling together" Judy referenced at the Institute for Research on Poverty design meeting more than a decade earlier. Three important syntheses provide valuable illustrations of the contribution large numbers of diverse studies can make if analyzed together.[38]

The first—carried out as a special study in the JOBS evaluation (Michalopoulos and Schwartz 2001)—includes data from evaluations of JOBS, GAIN, the Florida Family Transition Program, San Diego's Saturation Work Initiative Model, and the Minnesota Family Investment Program, all of which were conducted by MDRC.[39] The synthesis that the authors analyzed pooled, individual-level data for more than 70,000 individuals for the main analyses and data on 17,000 to 20,000 individuals based on the JOBS evaluation's Private Opinion Survey.

The second important synthesis (Greenberg and Cebulla 2005) is an aggregate-level meta-analysis of a database with impact estimates of thirty-six experimental evaluations of mandatory and voluntary welfare-to-work programs in which the midpoint of random assignment was, except for one case, between 1983 and 1996.[40] Twenty-nine of the thirty-six were implemented by three large research firms with substantial experimental and analytic experience: MDRC conducted just over half (nineteen), Abt Associates seven, and Mathematica Policy Research three. Because some of the studies provide multiple estimates for a given outcome (for example, the JOBS evaluation produced separate estimates of earnings impacts for eleven programs), the number of observations is substantially larger than the number of evaluations, approaching eighty impact estimates for some outcome variables. More complicating methodological issues arise than in the special study in the JOBS evaluation (Michalopoulos and Schwartz 2001) because the analysis is not conducted at the program-participant level. Its great strength lies in the vast number of studies included.

The third synthesis in the group (Bloom, Hill, and Riccio 2003, 2005) is a groundbreaking example of the strength of evidence that can be developed using a methodologically sophisticated approach to a well-coordinated body of experiments.[41] The core analysis was a multilevel model based on 69,000 individual-level observations in fifty-nine local offices that were part of three MDRC studies: the GAIN, Project Independence, and JOBS evaluations.[42] In addition to unemployment insurance earnings records for each individual, in all three studies MDRC collected the same information in several key domains (including how frontline workers and their supervisors described their programs), as well as information from treatment and control group members about their participation in various activities (such as basic education and job search). The focus was on estimates of earnings impacts over a two-year period for each office (because of the large number of individuals in the study, these estimates were precise enough to produce very reliable estimates at the office level). The explanatory variables included individual-level characteristics, program characteristics in each office based on the staff surveys, the office-level impact on program activities, and a measure of local economic conditions. Thus the model used in the synthesis estimated the relationship between the size of the earnings impacts and six implementation features, three program differentials, a variable measuring the local economic environment of the programs tested, and a group of characteristics of the program population.

The three syntheses address important questions regarding welfare-to-work programs. The findings that emerge are striking.

Almost all subgroups of welfare recipients experienced increased earnings from welfare-to-work programs, with surprisingly little variation in earnings impact. In this case the story was in the subgroups, primarily because subgroups turn out to matter less than we expected. This finding comes most directly from Charles Michalopoulos and Christine Schwartz (2001), who examine effects by subgroup. In their synthesis, annual earnings impacts over the first three years after random assignment were about $500. Earnings impacts were largest for the moderately disadvantaged ($599), and similar for the least ($404) and the most ($421) disadvantaged; because of the very large sample sizes, these differences were statistically significant.[43] Viewed abstractly, these differences could be considered large, in that impacts for the moderately disadvantaged group were roughly 50 percent larger than for the other two. But from a programmatic perspective, they do not suggest that the three groups should be treated differently or that any group should be excluded from participation. Remarkably, characteristics (such as attitudes toward work and child rearing) and the presence of barriers to employment (such as perceived lack of child care or transportation) made no difference in impacts. The study concluded that "if the objective of welfare-to-work programs is to increase earnings, this set of programs worked well for almost every subgroup" (Michalopoulos and Schwartz 2001, ES-5).[44]

Before this study was conducted, evidence on the differential effects of welfare-to-work programs was mixed, with the strongest being Daniel Friedlander's (1988), a much smaller study that suggested an inverted U, with larger earnings effects for the middle group (which the Michalopoulos and Schwartz [2001] synthesis confirms), as well as some evidence for larger effects for the most disadvantaged in other studies such as Supported Work. Either side could be, and was, argued on a theoretical basis: that effects would be larger for the more disadvantaged, because those who were better off could find work without help; or that effects would be smaller for the more disadvantaged, because they could not find jobs without more help than the programs were providing. Michalopoulos and Schwartz (2001) show that neither was relevant in a policy sense and that, given the kinds of welfare-to-work programs that were widespread, there was no reason to target particular groups of welfare recipients or exclude others. This finding for a main outcome is a considerably more important finding for policy makers than most fields of social policy have the evidence to address.

The other two syntheses yield largely consistent findings. Howard Bloom, Carolyn Hill, and James Riccio (2003) find that the individual characteristics of an office's population of welfare recipients account for only about one-fifth of the explained variation in earnings impacts. Furthermore, although a few characteristics are weakly associated with higher earnings impacts, most are not, and no particular pattern emerges among the scattered few that are. As the authors state, "First, it appears that welfare-to-work programs can be effective for many types of clients, not just for those with a few particular characteristics. Second, it appears that targeting clients according to how hard or easy they are to serve will not necessarily influence program effectiveness" (Bloom, Hill, and Riccio 2005, 66).

David Greenberg and Andreas Cebulla (2005, 54) conclude from the findings for their primary model that "it is not clear whether the welfare-to-work interventions tend to be more or less effective in serving relatively more disadvantaged caseloads than more advantaged caseloads." In separate subgroup-focused analyses, they do find some evidence that impacts are larger for more disadvantaged groups, especially long-term welfare recipients. But overall, they agree strongly that whatever differences exist are too small to justify targeting any category of individuals for inclusion in, or exclusion from, program participation.[45]

Staff emphasis on rapid job entry is associated with larger earnings impacts; measured increases in participation in basic education are associated with smaller ones. Surveys in the three evaluations reported by Bloom, Hill, and Riccio (2003, 2005) asked staff a number of questions on the extent to which the program emphasized rapid job entry and how much it provided individualized attention. In the multilevel analysis, programs that had a stronger emphasis on quick movement into the workforce had much larger earnings impacts than those with a weaker emphasis.[46] Based on participant surveys, percentage point impacts on participation in basic education and job search were also available and used in the analysis. Larger increases in basic education participation were found to be negatively correlated with earnings impacts, and the intensity of job search had no association with earnings impacts. The latter finding is somewhat surprising, given quite consistently positive earnings impacts of experiments in which the treatment was job search, either by itself or as a significant component. In addition, Greenberg and Cebulla (2005) find that a greater increase in job search is associated with higher earnings impacts. One possible explanation for the disparity is that the staff survey information on degrees of emphasis on rapid job entry was collected only in the three MDRC studies on which the Bloom, Hill, and Riccio (2005) study is based, not the whole set of studies included in the Greenberg and Cebulla (2005) meta-analysis. Bloom, Hill, and Riccio (2003, 568) discuss the issue in the following terms: "This finding does not necessarily mean that job search is unimportant for program success, or that some programs could operate just as effectively without it. Instead it might be the case that the particular kinds of messages and assistance that get conveyed to clients within job search activities may determine whether these activities are effective."

Higher local unemployment is associated with smaller earnings impacts. A bad economic environment clearly decreases employment outcomes and the chance of getting a job. It is less clear, at least a priori, whether a poor economy is associated with decreased employment impacts. Some have speculated that in a poor economy, impacts would be lower since it would be harder to get a job and thus welfare-to-work interventions would be less effective.[47] Others have argued, in contrast, that impacts would be lower in a good economy, when anybody can get a job (leaving little room for programs to increase outcomes). The Bloom, Hill, and Riccio (2005) and Greenberg and Cebulla (2005) syntheses examine this question, and they agree that a weaker economy is, in fact, associated with smaller earnings impacts. For example, the former find that a 1 percentage point increase in the unemployment rate is associated with a $94 decrease in two-year earnings impact, from a mean impact of almost $880. Experiments further confirm that job search programs have some positive impact in all but the worst economies.

As important as these studies are in shedding light on the relationship between various program and environmental features and the size of impacts, they are not without limitations. Both Bloom, Hill, and Riccio (2003, 2005) and Greenberg and Cebulla (2005) are correlational studies; thus we must be cautious about inferring causality from the statistical relationships they establish. For example, it is possible that other, unobserved factors are responsible both for a program emphasizing rapid job entry and for its higher earnings gains, for example, the character of the programs' leadership. We need to randomly assign treatments with these different characteristics to sites if we are to establish strong evidence of causality. Similarly, although the results for subgroups that Michalopoulos and Schwartz (2001) focus on are experimental, and thus we can safely infer that they represent unbiased estimates of impacts, any inference that the subgroup characteristic is what causes the impact estimate would not be experimental, as an underlying unobserved characteristic could be responsible.

NEXT STEPS

As always, even in instances such as GAIN and JOBS, important questions remain unanswered. And sometimes policy speeds ahead in ways that may guide the questions policy researchers examine but are implemented before crucial policy-relevant issues are resolved. The next two chapters are cases in point.

In chapter 10, Judy discusses the next stage in MDRC's research agenda—how to make work pay—which was guided by the policy decisions to make people work combined with the evaluation findings that the positive effects of welfare-to-work programs on earnings did not carry with them corresponding decreases in the numbers in poverty. The argument is that, if indeed people are expected to work rather than draw welfare, this will only actually reduce poverty if the mandated work also increases income enough to move them out of poverty.

As I note in this chapter, GAIN and JOBS did not address whether skills training (as opposed to basic education) helps employability. In chapter 11, I describe subsequent work designed to address systematically the effectiveness of approaches to moving beyond job finding to job retention and advancement.

CHAPTER 10

Expanding the Agenda II: Three Experiments to Make Work Pay[*]

People who work hard and play by the rules shouldn't be poor.

—Robert Kuttner[1]

With the welfare debate shifting rapidly toward the right in the early 1990s, work-for-your-grant (workfare) and related policies that had been denigrated as slavefare ten years earlier looked benign next to calls to end support. The tipping point came when the Democratic presidential candidate, Bill Clinton, made "ending welfare as we know it" and "making work pay" central parts of his platform, and the shift culminated in the 1996 law ending Aid for Families with Dependent Children (AFDC).

During these years, as state governors proposed various combinations of carrots and sticks to influence a host of behaviors,[2] we at MDRC debated what was likely to emerge as the most salient reform options: the ones worth major experiments. We were still heavily involved in the Job Opportunities and Basic Skills Training (JOBS) and Greater Avenues for Independence (GAIN) studies to determine the most effective design of welfare-to-work programs (work first, education first, or mixed strategies) and had become intrigued by Irwin Garfinkel's proposal that the government ensure a minimum level of child support (see Garfinkel 1988), which David Ellwood

*Chapter 10 authored by Judith M. Gueron.

(1988) had popularized (along with a broader focus on making work pay) in his influential book, *Poor Support*. Our focus evolved into an interest in addressing the underlying tensions between two goals: how to increase family income without discouraging work; and how to enforce work requirements, cut dependency, and save money without harming children. Not surprisingly, since we all swam in the same policy waters, the approaches we wanted to test were also the main ones pursued by states and the new Clinton administration.

Two strategies—putting a limit on how long people could receive welfare and changing the financial incentives so that people would not be worse off working than staying on welfare—emerged as the main new tools to foster what some called a work-based safety net. Those who thought the major cause of poverty was poor people's behavior (out-of-wedlock births, single-parent households, low rates of employment) emphasized setting a time limit on welfare, on the theory that the best way to change that behavior and encourage people to make it on their own was to make welfare even less attractive and ultimately to end it. Those who thought the cause was the decline in earnings of low-skilled workers combined with perverse incentives that discouraged work proposed strategies to make work pay and to encourage both mothers and fathers to jointly support their children.[3] Proposals included reducing tax rates within the welfare system, providing earnings supplements outside the welfare system (including a large expansion of the earned income tax credit (EITC) for low-income working families), and increasing child support payments from noncustodial parents (backed up by a guaranteed minimum benefit from the government).[4]

As we surveyed the landscape for promising projects, our board pushed staff to be creative. Eli Ginzberg, Isabel Sawhill, and Gilbert Steiner urged us to avoid small ideas and "tireless tinkering": Try things that have the promise of producing big effects. Look for the bolder, most radical but still relevant state proposals. If these are not forthcoming, go out and create public-private partnerships to launch more far-reaching demonstrations. Be both entrepreneurial and opportunistic. Rebecca Blank warned against calling these new areas—particularly supports for working poor families—"welfare," with its pejorative connotation. Her message: The problem for most people (this was said in 1995) is not job availability but low wages. These new reforms do not envision welfare as an alternative to jobs but provide services, supports, and supplements that will turn bad jobs into better ones.

Using the approach outlined at the beginning of chapter 8 (and armed with a new Ford Foundation challenge grant), we sought to assemble clusters of creative tests of the two main state strategies. Because what we could study depended heavily on what states wanted to do—and states were putting together components they saw as mutually reinforcing but were sometimes, in fact, pushing in different directions—we found ourselves often assessing what Robert Ivry dubbed "policy stews," which included various combinations of time limits, financial incentives, JOBS programs, and other approaches. To determine the separate contribution of the various components, or to address other unanswered questions, we used increasingly complex designs with multiple experimental groups. The result was that sites had to enforce challenging rules on what they could and could not offer different people and to run, out of the same office, multiple programs with varied sequences, activities, and messages. By consciously pushing the envelope on experimental design, we tested feasibility anew. Finally, to address issues not covered in state evaluations, we promoted or jumped to take on demonstrations.

THE PROGRAMS AND DECISIONS ON RANDOM ASSIGNMENT

Although each of the experiments had its champions and challenges, I focus here on three that illustrate the improved climate for random assignment and how it was used to answer new questions. (The timeline of events is presented in table 10.1.) Each study sought to determine whether, if jobs reliably paid more than welfare, more people would work and, as a result, there would be less poverty and better outcomes for families.[5] At the time—based on nonexperimental estimates of prior changes in AFDC tax rates and the 1970s income maintenance experiments—the conventional wisdom among researchers was that financial incentives alone did not have much overall effect on work effort and might reduce it. Yet program administrators who witnessed the welfare trap firsthand saw it differently, and by 1995 more than thirty states had proposed more generous incentives. At the same time, the federal government was greatly increasing the EITC (one version of such an incentive). We wondered what would happen if incentives were tied to some kind of work requirement. What if, instead of giving people welfare when they did not work, you paid them only when they did? Would the results be different? And, even if they were, would the cost of reducing poverty be prohibitive? Would benefits to children in some way offset that cost?

Table 10.1   Timeline of Earnings Supplement Experiments and Related Events

Date	Event
June 1991	Canadian government invites MDRC to help set up and test the Self-Sufficiency Project (SSP)
December 1991	Social Research and Demonstration Corporation (SRDC) created
September 1992	Ford Foundation approves third welfare challenge grant
November 1992	Bill Clinton elected president
November 1992	SSP operations begin
1993	Minnesota (MFIP) and New Hope studies begin
1993	Congress substantially increases EITC
1995–2003	SRDC publishes results on SSP
1995–2005	MDRC publishes results on MFIP and New Hope
August 1996	President Clinton signs Personal Responsibility and Work Opportunity Reconciliation Act (PRWORA)
1999	MDRC launches the Next Generation collaboration to synthesize child and family impacts
2001–2002	MDRC publishes reports and briefs from Next Generation collaboration

Source: Author's compilation.

The Canadian Self-Sufficiency Project

Our first opportunity to get answers came from an unexpected source. In June 1991 the Canadian government—in the form of Human Resources Development Canada (HRDC), at the time Canada's counterpart to the U.S. Departments of Labor and Health and Human Services combined—approached us with an invitation to help design and conduct a large demonstration of a work-based alternative to welfare: an extremely generous, temporary earnings supplement for long-term welfare recipients that HRDC hoped would reduce poverty and promote self-sufficiency, called the Self-Sufficiency Project (SSP). From the outset, they made it clear that they wanted to use random assignment and had the money (their initial estimate was C$50 million for eight years) to pay for a 1970s-style demonstration, including the full freight for operations, research, and subsidy payments. They also said that they came to us only because they lacked the in-country expertise and saw MDRC as the sole firm that could handle this assignment, but that turning to a U.S. firm was politically dicey and their explicit goal was to use the project to end their dependence on U.S. talent. Thus part of the deal was that we would establish and work side by side with a Canadian firm to teach Canadians the tricks of the trade about social experiments.

In the glow of hindsight, this offer might seem a no-brainer. The policy was of great interest and had never been tested experimentally; we saw no remotely comparable opportunity on the U.S. horizon; it offered an opportunity to export our message on social experiments and gain a useful international perspective; and it was fully funded, a luxury we had almost forgotten how to imagine. After ten years, here was a chance to get out of testing programs constrained by what states could afford and use our full array of intermediary skills.

Yet we hesitated. First, this was Canada, and our focus was poverty in the United States. Was the welfare population or benefit system too different or the proposed subsidy too large or oddly structured for the results to be relevant? Second, the Canadians were on a fast track and asking us to take responsibility for the whole show—that is, all development, design, implementation, research, and operational aspects (including setting up a system to process and pay the subsidies)—broader responsibility than we had ever had in a project. Could we agree on a schedule that would not compromise our other projects? Third, basic budget logic suggested that it would be hard to fund an entitlement under a fixed budget. Would we be at financial or ethical risk if the experimentals' take-up rate for the subsidy was unexpectedly high, or would there be someone with deep pockets standing behind us?[26] Fourth, the Canadians wanted us to create a new company, transfer expertise and (in short order) leadership, and work under a yet-to-be-specified contract structure. Could we do this and ensure that, given the high opportunity cost and potential exchange-rate risk, we gained enough from the experience? Finally, could we get the same long-term commitment and assurances of independence that we had achieved in all our U.S. work?

Within a month—reflecting the flexibility, determination, and decision-making ability of the people in charge at HRDC (Barry Carin, the assistant deputy minister; Louise Bourgault, the director general of the Innovations Branch; and John Greenwood, the director of research for the Innovations Program) and the overdrive of the MDRC team led by Gordon Berlin—we had satisfactory answers to all these questions and decided to go forward pending resolution of two final issues: the design of the incentive program and agreement with the two preselected provinces (British Columbia and New

Brunswick) on the conditions required for a successful random assignment study.

The design issue came down to devising a subsidy structure that met HRDC's vision, had a shot at having big effects, was supported by economic theory and research, was an implementable test of clear policy value, and met ethical norms.[7] We also sought to ensure that the study was of a structure and had a large enough sample to answer the key questions. As Greenwood recalls, the context for SSP was the dual pressure on the Canadian government to reverse rapidly escalating welfare costs and substitute "active" labor-market policies for "passive" income support that "gave people money to do nothing." HRDC's idea that the participation in SSP should be conditioned on work came from the income maintenance experiments. Canada had attempted to do a negative-income-tax (NIT) experiment, the Manitoba Guaranteed Minimum Income experiment, in the 1970s but canceled it midstream when it ran way over budget and people in the government were no longer willing to continue it. Barry Carin knew that one factor that had killed the NIT concept was the small negative labor supply effect and thought that SSP, if conditioned on full-time work, could avoid repeating that failure and hopefully deliver on its multiple goals of increasing income, increasing work, and getting people off welfare.

Working with Canadian and U.S. advisers—including Philip Robins and David Greenberg (who had played lead roles in the Seattle/Denver Income Maintenance Experiment), Jon Kesselman, Craig Riddel, Gary Burtless, Robert Moffitt, Henry Aaron, Charles Michalopoulos, Robert Lerman, and John Bishop—in an exceptionally comprehensive design effort, we specified the major alternatives and commissioned a team to simulate their likely effects and costs.[8] In the process, we identified one risk that Aaron and others agreed could be lethal and thus had to be carefully quantified: the possibility that the subsidy might have the perverse effect of inducing people to go on (or stay longer on) welfare to become eligible for its benefits, a phenomenon termed "entry effect."[9]

Pulling all this together, we reached agreement on the following design: SSP would offer monthly cash payments for up to three years to a cross-section of single parents, in Vancouver, British Columbia, and parts of New Brunswick, who had been on welfare for at least a year and then left to work full-time in a low-wage job. An individual's decision to participate in SSP and work would be voluntary, and supplements would be paid as long as the person worked at least thirty hours a week and remained off welfare. The subsidy would vary with each month's earnings and was set so that people were typically C$3,000 to C$5,000 a year better off in SSP than if they had worked the same amount and remained on welfare.[10] The goal was that, at the end of three years, wages and income would have gone up enough to reduce the incentive to return to welfare.

The initial design vision was for a single experiment, comparing long-term recipients offered SSP with people in the existing welfare system. Subsequently, two others were added: one that tested the program's effect on welfare applicants (a creative way to determine whether the supplement's lure would keep people on welfare longer, one form of entry effect) and another, called SSP Plus, that tested the effect of adding pre-employment and postemployment services (job search, job coaching, job development, and case management) to the supplement. In total, more than 9,000 single parents were randomly assigned and followed for up to six years.

Our second challenge was to determine the depth of support for random assignment in Ottawa and the two provinces. We were quickly reassured on the former. Greenwood traces HRDC's commitment to Carin's concern about not repeating the polarized Canadian 1970s debate on the negative income tax. Carin was convinced that SSP would be controversial. He knew the program would be costly and could be justified only if there were significant benefits; he wanted to find out whether people would opt for earnings supplements rather than traditional welfare; and he wanted a rigorous test in real-world operating conditions so the results would reliably reflect what could be expected if the program were later replicated on a large scale.[11] In short, he wanted reliable evidence and feared that, if HRDC did not proceed carefully and use "unassailable methodology," a similar dispute would ensue, and they would again end up arguing about methods rather than results.

As one step in determining what was the most rigorous methodology, Greenwood set out on a cross-country U.S. tour. At all his stops—MDRC, Robert Spiegelman at the Upjohn Institute, the Institute for Research on Poverty at the University of Wisconsin–Madison, and the Battelle Memorial Institute (a nonprofit research and development organization)—people urged him to use random assignment.[12] He also pored through the literature and recalls being struck by the increasing tendency in the United States to use experiments to evaluate welfare reform and by the assertion (in the 1985 National Academy of Sciences report [Betsey, Hollister, and Papageorgiou 1985], which carried sway in GAIN and Project Independence) that, without randomized experiments, they could not believe any of the findings. As Greenwood fed what he was learning up the line, he says, Carin became convinced that an experiment would produce the most unimpeachable evidence. He notes further that Carin "wanted to say: Nobody has ever successfully done a large-scale randomized trial [in Canada], and I want to do it."

But wanting to do it was not the same thing as knowing how to do it. As Greenwood recalls, at the beginning a lot of people thought the undertaking was simply not feasible. "We had no experience in it. . . . The one experience we had (Manitoba) ended badly. And we weren't exactly sure how to go about it. . . . But we were given a lot of confidence by having talked to people in the U.S." After exploring options and finding no single Canadian organization that was either able or willing to take on a project like SSP, as Greenwood remembers it, HRDC turned to MDRC because it was pioneering such studies, was a nonprofit organization, and had both operational and research capacity.[13] As a result, we were asked to set up a Canadian analogue, the nonprofit Social Research and Demonstration Corporation (SRDC), and take on the explicit mission of technology transfer.

We next sought to gauge provincial support, the critical unknown since HRDC had chosen the provinces before outlining the research requirements, could not force them to cooperate, and wanted to start operations as soon as possible. We were warned that the challenge would be aggravated by two other objections: that SSP was a national office, "Ottawa" project and that the award of what was a big contract had gone to an American company (considered especially bad given the recession, anger about the free trade agreement, and an upcoming election). Thus we were cautioned to lay out all the requirements up front to ensure that the provinces would stay involved over the long haul.

Within the provincial welfare bureaucracies the reaction was split. People at the top, who had served on the project's advisory board long before we came into the picture, were very supportive. (This was key, because Canadian federalism gave more power to the provinces, particularly on welfare policy, than the U.S. system gave to states.) For them, the program was a pure win: HRDC paid for the subsidies and local operating programs and the provinces got to keep (with no strings attached) their 50 percent share of savings from people who left welfare to participate in SSP. Furthermore, because this was both a research demonstration and an employment program, Ottawa was not seen to be interfering in welfare, an area of provincial jurisdiction. However, we still had to win over the political people (an effort that included a one-on-

one meeting between Berlin and the provincial prime minister in New Brunswick), line staff, and the advocates.

The reaction of local office managers was mixed. There was the expected complaint that we were a U.S. firm; however, because the Canadian and U.S. systems turned out to be quite similar, our knowledge of the real world of welfare and the details of how to integrate an experiment into operations countered that effectively. We also heard occasional concerns about experimenting with human subjects, protecting confidentiality, and not imposing new workload burdens, as well as a fear that welfare staff might be caught in the middle between local advocates and the central government. But the main objection was that they would lose control over their clients. Echoing views we had heard in offices throughout our own country, starting with the Louisville Work Incentive staff in the 1970s (see chapter 3), they said, "We know who is going to benefit from this; you should let us (not some random process) decide who will and won't get the supplement." Support from the leadership (both in HRDC and the key provincial staff) helped us overcome this, combined with the enormously important fact that Statistics Canada (the highly respected Canadian equivalent of the U.S. Census Bureau) would be our partner in selecting and assigning the sample, collecting and assembling the data, and developing the informed consent and confidentiality procedures.[14]

Our meetings with numerous local advocacy groups also went well. Their objections focused less on random assignment than on whether SSP addressed the real needs of recipients or would lure them to work and thereby to neglect their children.[15] As anticipated, they too questioned the use of an American firm; but we were able to convert many by explaining that most of the funds for the project would stay in Canada, that participants could benefit substantially from a program rewarding rather than penalizing work, and that random assignment was a fair way to allocate the subsidies. But their warning about unintended negative effects on children did not go unheeded. Partly for defensive reasons, but also out of an interest in looking at potential positive effects, HRDC added a study of child impacts to the evaluation.

The fight for random assignment turned out to be more courtship than conflict. As Berlin, who orchestrated the process, told MDRC's board in an October 1, 1993, memo,

> When we began the project, we expected to have difficulty in two areas: the
> ethics of random assignment . . . and the involvement of Americans in testing

new Canadian social policies. For example, citing an entitlement mentality, provincial officials warned us that random assignment would not be feasible because elected officials would intervene to get people in their . . . district who are selected into the control group moved into the program group. . . . Similarly, Statistics Canada staff expected those selected into the control group to withdraw from the study in large numbers. They also expected high [interview] refusal rates among those selected to be part of the study. Finally, there was concern that the provincial Income Assistance staff would subvert the project because the supplements would make some of their clients better off than the staff. After nearly a year of operation, and after more than a year and a half of briefings with advocates, politicians, academics, and local Income Assistance casework staff, we have experienced none of these difficulties.

Having made the decision to go forward, we worked with HRDC to assemble the consortium of institutions required to implement it, starting with the creation of SRDC in December 1991.[16] To ensure a rapid start-up and to facilitate technology transfer, MDRC executives Berlin and Robert Granger initially served, respectively, as SRDC's executive director and chief financial officer, and MDRC board member Rudolph Penner served as its chairman.[17] Berlin quickly hired Canadian staff to take the lead in implementing the study and to work with MDRC staff on all aspects of the research and later, after casting a broad net, selected David Card, the distinguished Canadian and U.S. economist, to serve as co–principal investigator. SRDC succession planning was in the works from the beginning, and after a formal search, Greenwood became deputy director in 1995 and executive director in 1998.

Two Complementary Models

Although SSP promised to the a major, multi-site experiment, in 1992 we were intent on building a cluster of studies, having seen in the preceding ten years the power of replicating results in different contexts. As we scanned the United States for the best complements to the Canadian study, two options stood out as ambitious, innovative, carefully planned, and having both strong local support and a leadership committed to random assignment.

NEW HOPE   The first was New Hope, an antipoverty initiative in Milwaukee, Wisconsin, that had been shaped over ten years by an unusual coalition of community activists, which included labor organizer Julie Kerksick; David

Riemer, a policy expert whose book (1988) became the blueprint for New Hope; and later a businessman, Tom Schrader. Starting from four principles—that people who are willing and able to work full-time should have the opportunity to do so; that people who work full-time should not be poor; that people who work more hours should take home more pay; and that full-time work should make people better off financially than they would be on welfare—they proposed a voluntary program for people willing to work at least thirty hours per week. It included a package of incentives and case management that participants could receive for up to three years: help in obtaining a job (including short-term, minimum-wage community service jobs for people who did not find full-time work), an earnings supplement to bring income above the poverty level, subsidized health insurance, and subsidized child care. The program would operate independently of Wisconsin's welfare system and would be open to all low-income adults living in two target areas, whether or not they had children or were on welfare.

Although New Hope was always viewed as a pilot program with a learning agenda, the business leaders pushed to spell out a strong evaluation component. This prompted the project's board in 1991 to turn to Robert Haveman at the University of Wisconsin–Madison, who convened a panel to recommend how the program should be assessed and later to oversee the study. Panel members—notably including Robinson Hollister—strongly endorsed the project but only if it was structured as a social experiment, which they termed essential for it to "stand up to the scrutiny of the research community."[18] In August 1992, when the New Hope project team issued a request for proposals for the evaluation, they stated that they were committed to giving the concept as full and fair a test as possible: to learn what works, what does not, and why; and to use a random assignment design. At the bidders' conference, the team made the depth of their support for the evaluation even clearer, saying that, though they hoped the program worked, if it helped only the people it served it would be a failure. Their goal was to influence national policy, and they saw a credible evaluation as the route to achieving this. As Kerksick, who later became New Hope's executive director, said, "We haven't spent all of these years of hard work just to deliver a program to seven hundred people. However proud we are of the program, we wanted to change policies for all low-income working families" (quoted in Duncan, Huston, and Weisner 2007, 10).

THE MINNESOTA FAMILY INVESTMENT PROGRAM   The second promising U.S. option was the Minnesota Family Investment Program (MFIP). When Minnesota officials set out to reform welfare in the late 1980s, they sought to reduce poverty, reduce dependence on public assistance, and increase work. Their deliberations were unusual in that they placed as much emphasis on poverty reduction as on employment increases; recognized that, in the short run, the rolls would increase and reform would cost more, not less, than the then-existing welfare system; and proposed to operate MFIP as a seven-county pilot before deciding on a statewide program. MFIP's designers also held a particular view of welfare dependency. In their terms, people who worked and received a supplement (that is, a reduced welfare grant) should not be considered dependent in the same way as those who relied totally on welfare (that is, did not work at all). Reflecting this, officials characterized the program as an investment. The MFIP final report described it this way: "The hope was that, to the extent that MFIP led to higher costs than the AFDC system in the short run, the up-front investment would be 'purchasing' important improvements to child and family well-being in the longer run" (Miller et al. 2000, 3–4).

The resulting program, launched in 1994, differed from both SSP and New Hope—both of which operated as alternatives to welfare and provided supplements only for full-time work—in that it changed welfare itself and rewarded both full- and part-time work. MFIP modified the AFDC system in two key ways. First, it increased financial incentives by allowing people to keep more of their benefits when they worked and thus to more easily mix work and welfare.[19] Second, it required long-term recipients to work full time (defined as at least thirty hours per week) or participate in services designed to move them quickly into jobs. (Long-term recipients thus received the full MFIP' program, whereas applicants and new recipients received the MFIP incentives but had no full-time requirement.) MFIP also folded AFDC, general assistance, and food stamps into a single cash grant.

John Petraborg, the deputy commissioner in the Minnesota Department of Human Services, explains the decision to have a rigorous evaluation in terms similar to those used by Carin in Canada: "We were aware . . . that this was a pretty big change and that we were taking a chance by staking out a position that was out of the current mainstream—the antipoverty goal was pretty unique during the Reagan era. . . . Bringing the credibility of an outside evaluation to that process and not inconsequentially the credibility of an organization like MDRC was important to us."

Several factors drove the leap from there to a social experiment. David Butler, our lead liaison with the state, says that the first was Joel Kvamme, MFIP's designer and first director, who cared deeply about research and championed random assignment. "This was his baby. . . . I think it would not have happened if not for Kvamme. . . . He was the heart and soul." The second was that an earlier MFIP research design (prepared by the Upjohn Institute) had proposed an experiment, and multiple visits by our staff (to disseminate results from prior studies and explore opportunities for future work) had reinforced the value and feasibility of this approach. Third, Petraborg recalls that the state was well aware of MDRC's track record on evaluations and wanted to claim the authority and visibility that went with it. "That was an avenue for national recognition for us and we had a neighbor to the East [Wisconsin] with a governor [Tommy] Thompson, who was playing the political communication card and I think we really wanted to be able to get some attention based on the substance of what we were doing. So there was a little bit of . . . competition between the two states." Although Minnesota did need waivers from HHS and the Department of Agriculture to run the program, that requirement did not drive the random assignment decision.[20]

The final result was an ambitious design. To disentangle the effects of MFIP's two major components (financial incentives and mandatory employment and training services), families were randomly assigned to three groups: full MFIP, MFIP incentives only, and regular AFDC.

We hesitated before closing the deal on either study. A central purpose of our 1992 Ford challenge grant was to assemble a coherent group of studies that would leave a legacy on work incentives comparable to the one we had created on welfare-to-work programs. On the positive side, these were both impressive studies, they both called for random assignment, and, though less generous, they shared several principles with SSP. On the negative side, unlike the fully funded SSP, we were convinced that the New Hope and MFIP evaluations were underfunded and would together require more than $1 million in Ford funds. Was this the best use of that grant? Would we be passing up more valuable opportunities if we went ahead with these two projects?

Both evaluations also raised substantive concerns. On New Hope, we worried that the sample (eventually increased to close to 1,400) might simply be too small to detect an impact, even if one existed, given the need to examine the diverse groups separately. On MFIP, we also thought the initial sample was too small, given the multigroup design, the interest in determining impacts for several subgroups, and the modest nature of the incentive.[21] In addition, we worried about whether MFIP (with its expectation of increased welfare rolls and costs) was too liberal an outlier in the increasingly harsh political climate. Finally, we were concerned about generalizability and would have preferred to have at least one larger and more diverse state rather than three projects straddling the U.S.–Canadian border. However, on balance, and doing our best to read the tea leaves, we took the plunge and began work on both projects in early 1993.

Implementing Random Assignment

The principle of random assignment generated remarkably little opposition in the make-work-pay experiments, for which I can think of five major reasons. First, all three projects were pilots, explicitly set up to determine how potentially expensive earnings supplements affected behavior and income. As such, it was clear from the beginning that budgets and slots were limited and that getting defensible evidence on benefits and costs would be essential to selling any future expansion. Second, once they were on board, people in the sponsoring agencies themselves pushed for random assignment, under the conviction that only this method would produce the evidence they needed. Third, in SSP and the New Hope project, participation in the research and thus the program was voluntary. Fourth, the projects brought opportunities and new money to the people and communities involved. Since funding limits meant slots had to be rationed somehow, it was not hard to argue that a lottery was fairer than a more discretionary form of selection. In short, this was more akin to the try-before-you-buy world of voluntary Supported Work (with entrance via informed consent) than mandated GAIN, Project Independence, and JOBS. Finally, recent experiences had made us better at explaining random assignment—from preemptive outreach to advocates in Canada, to describing the incentives to participants and training intake workers, to answering critics and the press—and we were able to transfer this expertise to Canada's SRDC.

Although there was little opposition to the principle or practice of random assignment, its actual implementation was by no means easy to pull off. Recruitment was a major problem for New Hope, for example, and random assignment doubled the challenge. As Kerksick recalls, random assignment put serious strains on staff: since this was a community initiative, many of the program staff lived in the target neighborhoods and knew the people coming in, making the need to reject persons assigned to the control group personally difficult. Even so, as Tom Brock (who led MDRC's study of the program's implementation) recalls, New Hope never considered dropping out because they believed they needed high-quality evidence to influence national policy, and key funders insisted on a control trial, particularly Julia Lopez, who had moved from California to the Rockefeller Foundation.[22]

In Minnesota, the major difficulty turned out to come not from random assignment per se but from the arduous task of implementing the three-group design and convincing the state to keep both the program and control groups in place long enough to complete the study. On the first, the three-group design translated into asking program staff to run a complex switching station—directing people to, and operating side by side, programs with different activities and messages. Remarkably (as with the head-to-head tests in the JOBS evaluation discussed in chapter 9), it worked, and the system did not overload. Butler and Virginia Knox (who led the evaluation) attribute this to the depth of staff support for MFIP's antipoverty goals, the talent of the central state team that oversaw and worked with our staff to train the counties, the quality of the training, and the designation of one group of state staff to work with the two MFIP groups and another to work with the control group still on AFDC. The challenge to keeping the programs and control groups in place long enough was political. Minnesota was implementing MFIP at a time when Governor Thompson in neighboring Wisconsin was getting unparalleled national visibility for tough reforms focused on work and personal responsibility. Ivry links Minnesota's ability to keep the program and research in place to MFIP's combining a mandate with the supplement—which state staff used, Butler noted at the time, in a "disguise the sheep in wolves clothing strategy" (that is, focusing implicitly on poverty reduction but hiding the fundamental goal in a tough-sounding welfare reform package).

A NEW FOCUS ON CHILDREN

After 1988 several factors converged to increase interest in studying the effects of welfare reform on children. Until then, welfare-to-work studies had focused on economic outcomes, even though helping children had been the rationale for creating AFDC in the first place. However, the Family Support

Act's extension of mandates to single mothers with preschool children (as young as age one year, at state option) prompted concern about whether requiring mothers to work would hurt young children—leading ASPE's Ann Segal and William Prosser to push the federal JOBS evaluation to address the issue.[23] At MDRC, a number of us involved in that study had initial doubts whether, given the anticipated modest changes in parents' employment, we stood a chance of detecting positive or negative impacts on children, even if there were some. Fortunately, HHS forged ahead, and the ultimate importance of the study owed a great deal to strenuous efforts to make the design strong enough to yield reliable findings.

Shortly thereafter, following up on the advocates' concern that SSP might harm children, the Canadian government added a study of child impacts. Since the goal of SSP's generous earnings supplement was reducing poverty and helping families, MDRC staff thought there was a good chance of creating a design that would capture such effects, if there were any. Our actions on that study contributed to the momentum for exploring child impacts in other evaluations, including five by MDRC: the New Hope and MFIP evaluations and the studies of time-limited welfare programs in Connecticut, Florida, and Vermont.

The entrepreneurs were Robert Granger at MDRC, staff in Minnesota, and Howard at the U.S. Administration for Children and Families, working with Segal, Martha Morehouse, and colleagues in ASPE. Granger had directed our evaluation of New Chance (a demonstration testing comprehensive services for low-income young welfare mothers and their children that included a study of child impacts) and was overseeing our New Hope evaluation and other work on children. As Knox recalls, Granger pushed to assess not only the possible harm to children from harsh time limits but also the potential benefits to children from New Hope's supports. (Granger was more skeptical about finding any effects by adding such a study to MFIP, with its less generous subsidy.)

Granger served on a research network, sponsored by the John D. and Catherine T. MacArthur Foundation, that was charged to improve the understanding of how poverty affected children and families. Although a lot of nonexperimental research suggested that poverty did affect children adversely, it could not establish definitive cause-effect relationships. In late 1994, Granger approached the network with several options to study causation in the children and family area by enhancing ongoing MDRC experiments. They "leaped at the chance" to build on the evaluation of New Hope, with its enriched health care, child care, and subsidy payments specifically intended to help families (Duncan, Huston, and Weisner 2007, 46). Although most of the network members who eventually worked on the New Hope Child and Family Study had no experience with large-scale field trials, the opportunity to leverage the MDRC infrastructure and staff know-how offered a ready-made solution. At the same time, it helped MDRC build expertise by providing mentors (particularly Greg Duncan and Aletha Huston) for our newly hired child development researchers.

With funding from the MacArthur, William T. Grant, Annie E. Casey, and several other foundations and the National Institute of Child Health and Human Development and other public agencies, the groundwork laid by Granger led to a multidisciplinary and multiorganizational partnership among scholars in the MacArthur Network, MDRC, and elsewhere, plus staff at the New Hope project, to estimate new outcomes and explore the processes by which the program might affect them. This work included collecting information from parents, children, and teachers and in-depth ethnographic interviews with a smaller number of families to determine the program's effect on children's psychological well-being, school performance, and social behavior, as well as family dynamics, parents' health, and parent-child relationships. The excitement among network scholars is reflected in the reaction of Althea Huston, the lead child development expert, who had firsthand experience with experiments.[24] As she recalls it,

> In 1987, I spent a year studying public policy analysis as part of an internal sabbatical program at the University of Kansas. . . . When I discovered the income maintenance experiments and the early welfare reform experiments, I had two reactions: first, excitement that true random assignment experiments were being used to test policy, and second, frustration that the outcomes sampled were almost all adult economic variables. . . . Hence, when Bob Granger suggested to the MacArthur Network that we might add assessments of children and families to some of the MDRC studies, I did think I had died and gone to heaven.

In contrast to the New Hope situation, the addition of a child study in MFIP came not from MDRC or HHS but from Charles Johnson, who had replaced Kvamme as project director. From the beginning, MFIP design papers had included vague references to studying children and, as Knox recalls, "Chuck Johnson never forgot it. He always had in his mind that if he could raise the extra money he would like to add that." Seeing an opening, he turned to the Northwest Area and McKnight Foundations to make this a reality.

With funding in place—from these efforts and the HHS study described in chapter 11—to analyze the impacts on children in the JOBS evaluation, the three make-work-pay studies described in this chapter, our three evaluations of programs that combined time limits with other requirements and incentives, and several other state projects—both Howard and his colleagues in the Administration for Children and Families and ASPE, and Granger and others at MDRC turned to their larger agendas of creating a coordinated body of work on child impacts.

Staff at HHS worked with ChildTrends to define parallel measures for use across the studies and conduct further analysis. At the same time, starting in 1999, Granger assembled a consortium of funders (the David and Lucile Packard, Grant, and MacArthur Foundations) and an interdisciplinary team of researchers at MDRC and eight other institutions under the rubric of the Next Generation project to pool and reanalyze more than 30,000 child observations from seven experiments (Morris, Gennetian, and Duncan 2005) and from an even larger number of studies for adults (Bloom and Michalopoulos 2001). Although results from the individual programs were already generating substantial interest, Granger argued that looking systematically across the studies would amplify their power by clarifying how different welfare reform choices affected families and children. Building on the work of the project teams and the virtually identical data that MDRC had collected in each of the experiments—and focusing analysis on the high-priority questions identified by people in the policy and practice community—the result was a series of research syntheses that provide an example of the point Howard makes in chapter 9: that a set of studies, if analyzed collectively, can have a payoff much larger than the sum of its parts.

LESSONS ABOUT PROGRAM AND POLICY

Since the 1960s, reformers had sought to change welfare in order to increase work, reduce dependency, save money, and reduce poverty. Most mandatory welfare-to-work experiments had produced positive, if generally modest, success on the first three, little or no effect on poverty, and (until the JOBS evaluation) no evidence on children.[25] The make-work-pay tests were set up to add to the knowledge base by asking whether supplements tied to work reduce poverty by increasing both income and work effort, and, if so, would they benefit children?

The answer to both questions was yes. All three studies during the period when the programs operated showed positive effects on income, work, and elementary school–age children's school achievement. Although each study had drawbacks on its own, that they produced similar results across a range of approaches and contexts (and used the same measures as our simultaneous evaluations of other reforms, thereby facilitating comparisons) added heft to the conclusion that making work pay was a strategy that worked and need not cost much.[26]

Charles Michalopoulos, Pamela Morris, and others summarize the findings for the five to seven years after random assignment for SSP, New Hope, and MFIP as follows:[27]

- The programs increased employment, earnings, and income. People offered earnings supplements were more likely to work, earned more, and had more income, in some cases substantially more, than control group members.[28] However, some people (particularly in MFIP, which rewarded part-time work) reduced how much they worked.
- Effects on welfare receipt varied with the structure of the earnings supplement. For example, families in SSP had to leave welfare to receive the supplement, and SSP reduced welfare use below what it would have been. Families in MFIP had to remain on welfare to receive its supplement, and MFIP increased welfare use.[29]
- The effects diminished over time, in part because the programs ended and in part because the early employment effects did not lead to lasting wage gains. The designers of SSP and New Hope hoped that people who were encouraged to work would gain skills that would permanently lift them to higher-paying jobs. That did not happen. At the end of follow-up, impacts were close to zero. The pattern of impacts suggests that offering the supplements for a longer period would have resulted in long-term effects on income and welfare receipt but not on employment.
- Effects on employment and earnings were larger and somewhat more persistent for very disadvantaged families. The effects were sometimes

substantially larger for long-term welfare recipients who had not worked recently and had not graduated from high school.[30]

- Combining earnings supplements with employment services produced larger effects than supplements alone. Some of the programs required participants to look for work or provided services to help them find and keep jobs. Adding such requirements or services produced larger and longer-lasting effects on employment and earnings, although the programs' effects on income stemmed primarily from their earnings supplements.

- Earnings supplements typically cost the government money. Costs (over and above what was spent for the control group) ranged from $100 to about $2,000 a year per family.[31] All three studies showed that costs could be reduced by paying supplements only to people working full time and to those least likely to work on their own, such as long-term welfare recipients and the long-term unemployed.

- Young children in families who were offered supplements did better in school than their counterparts in the traditional welfare system. During the years that the programs operated, earnings supplements produced small improvements in the school achievement of children aged two to five when their parents entered the program; in later years, benefits declined somewhat, in parallel with the reduced effect on family income. This contrasts with the findings discussed in chapter 9 that mandatory welfare-to-work (JOBS) programs typically increased employment but not income and had few if any effects (positive or negative, short- or long-term) on young children.[32]

The value of random assignment—especially the multigroup designs used to get inside the program black box in MFIP and SSP—speaks for itself, as does the building of a cluster of comparable studies. Knox sums up the advantage of the MFIP design in retrospect:

The three-group design helped disentangle the effects of work mandates from the effects of the carrot of extra make-work-pay money. . . . That the benefits for children all came from the income gain and that parents going to work per se did not have positive or negative effects was very clear from the way the random assignment results fell out. We could not have stated that with the same degree of confidence without a design that made all of the comparisons in the same site and conditions, rather than by comparing across studies. . . . This study helped to confirm what you saw in [the decades of nonexperimental research], but in a way that was more definitive because of random assignment.

In developing the research designs and analysis plans (and developing a model of the mechanisms through which the programs might affect their objectives), all three studies involved interdisciplinary teams. As part of this, they also included extensive implementation research that pointed, for example, to the importance of program operators clearly explaining and marketing the incentives. Berlin (2000, 41) highlights this: "For a program to have positive work effects, those targeted must know about and understand the likely effect incentives will have on their total income. If there is little or no marketing, then only people who would in any case have gone to work and left welfare would receive incentive payments—driving income transfer costs higher without any change in work behavior. Thus marketing, outreach, and careful explanation are essential."

IMPACT ON POLICY, PRACTICE, AND RESEARCH

Our starting point in communicating results from the make-work-pay research was similar to that in the GAIN activities described in chapter 8: separate press releases and dissemination around findings from each study. However, we were rapidly accumulating comparable data from a score of different reform programs. We knew that, just as a single study cries out for replication, so a large group of studies (multiple treatments, sites, and populations) produces too much information for most people to absorb. We saw one of our roles as pulling it together in an accessible format, using nontechnical language and simple graphics. Fortunately, a group of funders backed us (the Annie E. Casey, Charles Stewart Mott, David and Lucile Packard, Ford, George Gund, and James Irvine Foundations), and staff produced a series of cross-cutting monographs focused on the trade-offs and choices states faced under the historic 1996 Personal Responsibility and Work Opportunity Reconciliation Act (PRWORA).

We further ramped up syntheses and communications under the Next Generation project, which we had explicitly sold as an opportunity to leverage ten years of work and reach new audiences. To do this, we added short, glossy policy briefs (with a memorable histogram showing child impacts with and without earnings supplements), expanded the use of our website, and mobilized the multi-institutional team to reach out to diverse audiences.[33] With a powerful story to tell—providing financial support for low-income workers increases work, reduces poverty, and helps young children but costs money; work requirements without supplements increase self-sufficiency, can save money, and do not harm young children (as some opponents had feared) but do not help them, either—we issued press releases that generated hundreds of articles around the country and tens of thousands of visits to our website, and over two years we conducted more than 100 briefings and presentations in Washington and the states and at professional meetings. We explicitly targeted people across the political spectrum, so that the key actors in the upcoming 2002 debate about the reauthorization of Temporary Assistance for Needy Families (TANF) would know the results.

In disseminating the child impact findings we faced a new challenge. As described in chapters 6 and 8, MDRC's consistent strategy in earlier studies had been to keep it simple and focus on measures that are readily understood, uniform, and capture what policy makers ultimately care about, such as how many people are on or off welfare, the amount (in dollars) of changes in earnings, transfer payments, and income, and whether a program costs or saves money. At times we differed on how to categorize impacts—that is, whether they were small, modest, or large—but the units in which we measured them had a transparency that allowed policy makers to reach their own conclusions on whether the magnitude had policy significance.

This changed when we turned to measuring children's cognitive or achievement outcomes, social behavior, and health. To compare effects measured on different scales (most of which had no inherent meaning) or for quite varied samples, the researchers expressed impacts as effect sizes, calculated as the difference between the average program outcomes and control group outcomes divided by the standard deviation of the control group members. For the layperson, these standardized measures were neither meaningful in themselves nor easily interpretable. To compound the challenge, the children's young age meant that the outcomes were intermediate or proximate measures (for example, gain in school achievement at the age of six) for the long-term goal (high school graduation or ultimate labor force success). Since the concept of effect size meant nothing to policy people, we were constantly pushing for translations, falling back on definitions such as "the short-term effect of earnings supplements is analogous to increasing young children's scores on an achievement test from the 25th to the 30th percentile" or "the effects on children are about one-half to one-third as large as those on adult economic outcomes."[34]

Did the research and dissemination affect public policy? The answer is not obvious, given the many factors at play. At the time, I was told the results helped frame the discussion and were widely cited. In particular, they empowered advocates, who issued press releases and included them in testimony to buttress their argument not to cut block grants to states despite the sharp decline in welfare caseloads.

However, the findings came out during a rapidly changing policy environment. In a few years, many of the underlying concepts—supporting people when they worked rather than just giving them money, making work pay more than welfare and enough to move families out of poverty—had moved from radical ideas to the mainstream of the Clinton administration and national policy. As a result, it is not clear whether the studies themselves moved the debate (and prompted nearly all states to include make-work-pay incentives in their new TANF programs) or primarily ratified trends already under way. My guess is a little of both. Once welfare became time limited and most families were expected to work, policy focus shifted to how to put some kind of safety net under working families. By showing widespread benefits—including, most influentially, benefits to children, which practically speaking ended when the subsidies did—the three studies provided strong support for those seeking to assist low-wage workers, to protect welfare supplements during an economic downturn, and to make benefits ongoing, as in the various child credits and state EITCs.[35]

Thinking back to their experiences, the officials responsible for the projects drew a number of lessons. Petraborg points to three from the Minnesota Family Investment Program. First, the timing, quality, and national visibility of the results had enabled them to take the project statewide as the centerpiece of the state's program under PRWORA.[36] Second, the nature of the cooperative partnership with MDRC had been important in sustaining state officials through the ups and downs of a project that took ten years and spanned the tenure of five welfare commissioners and multiple governors. Third (echoing Lopez, Carl Williams, and Don Winstead in California and Florida), good government is possible, and a bipartisan approach, combined with an emphasis on data, enabled policy makers to get beyond an ideological debate so that people of good will could actually look at the evidence. (Butler is more downbeat, noting his disappointment when the state sharply reduced the financial incentive while continuing to call the program MFIP and to tout the positive findings.)

Kerksick concludes that Milwaukee's New Hope had a mixed effect on the design of Wisconsin's welfare reform, called W-2. It failed in getting W-2 to adopt an antipoverty goal and to pay wages rather than require people to work for their benefits, but it did contribute to Wisconsin's atypical commitment to affordable health insurance and child care. In terms of the research design, recalling that she ran New Hope as an experiment only because "I certainly didn't see that I had any choice," she remains confident that the decision was a wise one: "New Hope would not have gotten the attention it has without random assignment." However, she also greatly values the qualitative research, stating that the impact study showed them whether the program as a whole worked but not why participants reacted to the New Hope offer as they did. To learn that, she notes, "the broad brush of the impacts was aided by the finer bristles of ethnography."

Greenwood thinks Canada's SSP had multiple repercussions. First, it showed the feasibility of doing large-scale social experiments in Canada. Second, it had an indirect effect on how the debate was framed. Although SSP itself was not replicated, it prompted a more broadly based program through the tax system and was a "major input into the decision to implement the Working Income Tax Credit [modeled partly on the U.S. EITC] in Canada." Third, it generated widespread interest in using demonstrations to test new approaches before making a decision on the details of a full-scale program. But Greenwood also blames Carin's insistence on doing SSP as a grand "Cadillac version" (too much time and money) as setting back the cause of random assignment as an evaluation tool in Canada and regrets the lack of an incentive comparable to the U.S. section 1115 waiver evaluation requirement.

The make-work-pay experiments had other effects as well. Ivry thinks they raised interest in determining whether different forms of financial incentives and conditional cash transfers would affect diverse types of behavior. Subsequent MDRC examples include random assignment tests of rent incentives in public housing, retention incentives for training programs, performance-based scholarships in community colleges, and payments to poor families in New York City intended to improve health, education, and employment outcomes.

Huston notes that the studies also contributed to methodology and highlights the value of the interdisciplinary research teams:

> Throughout my work . . . I have been aware not only of the value of random assignment, but also of its limitations. . . . One of the major weaknesses is the "black box" problem—little enlightenment about the processes responsible for effects. Correlational studies can help to illuminate process, but investigators can also build these questions into a random assignment design. One of the ways New Hope differed from many of the other welfare reform experiments was our extensive measurement of potential mediators or process variables. We worked from an elaborate conceptual framework. . . . A major contribution of Next Generation was methodological—building ways of testing mediators using the experimental designs to remove possible selection and other forms of bias.

REFLECTIONS ON CONTROL GROUPS AND MODEST IMPACTS

The experiments described in this and earlier chapters tell a surprisingly upbeat story. A range of reforms produced consistently positive effects: work went up, welfare went down, and there was no collateral harm. Some strategies also benefited young children and even substantially reduced poverty. Given the skepticism about social programs prevalent in the 1970s, the findings of favorable impacts—plus the unexpected discovery that some programs really were investments that more than paid for themselves in tangible dollar savings within a few years—were encouraging.

But the results also sent another message. Success was generally modest. A major reason impacts were modest is that participants in a control group do not stand still. In all the evaluations discussed in this book, many controls got jobs or left welfare—either on their own or with the assistance of or with incentives provided by the existing employment, training, welfare, education, child care, tax, and other systems. This normal behavior—the counterfactual—sets a hurdle that all reform programs have to overcome to have an impact (that is, value added).

Experiments answer the question, Does the reform achieve more than the services and incentives already available? They do not answer a second question, Are the services, incentives, and rules embodied in the reform effective in changing people's behavior?

Whether a reform makes sense thus depends on the net gain and cost of introducing the new regime on top of the existing system. But the reality of control services can cause confusion because, although people often agree up front that the first question is the right one, they subsequently interpret the findings as though they had answered the second question. And in the political arena there are often obvious rewards for such an interpretation, which is why it is so crucially important to measure the control group experience with extreme care and continually work to educate the political world that the counterfactual is ignored at the cost of jeopardizing the formulation of wise policy.

And if the control group catches up, can this be interpreted to mean that there is no need for the program? "Just let the world be the control group. Everyone will get to the same point in the end"? In the field of cash assistance, the answer may be an easy no. When welfare benefits are replaced by earnings, the government spends less. Depending on how much the program costs, the result may be real savings that can be used to meet other needs—even if the saving does not continue indefinitely. Moreover, even when net costs exceed net savings, other benefits (such as positive effects on children) may be judged worth the cost.

In a 1990 review of several books about the prior twenty-five years of policy research, Edward Gramlich (1990, 284–85) warns that social problems are complex, program funding limited, institutions hard to change, and reforms cautious, making it "next to impossible for interventions to make large changes." He worries that even MDRC's positive welfare reform findings—those that passed the economists' test (that is, the winners won more than the losers lost)—"can almost never provide results that satisfy political expectations. The best results that can be expected from any real world test of the policy usually are not good enough to raise the odds that the policy will pass, and may well lower these odds."

There are many influences on people's lives that compete in determining their futures. The search to disentangle those influences will continue, and random assignment experiments can be a powerful tool in identifying improvements. But policy advances depend, as well, on the continuing struggle to educate policy makers that few reforms (incremental or radical) are likely to produce big impacts. The problems are too tough and the other influences on people's lives too strong.

WAIVER EXPERIMENTS FAIL TO PREDICT THE AFTERMATH OF PRWORA

A competing explanation for modest impacts is often advanced—that the very fact of requiring a control group prevents any experimental evaluation from capturing the full effects of a policy change. Supported Work, the Canadian SSP, and GAIN all tested innovations that were ambitious in their scope and cost. Nonetheless, none of these tested universal changes that filled the airwaves with a radical reform message or fundamentally changed either side of the labor market. This left open the question of whether a community-wide saturation combined with a universal message of change would have produced bigger impacts or could have been tested in an experiment.

The experience following passage of PRWORA—replacing the AFDC program with temporary assistance under TANF—shines a spotlight on this issue. Before 1996, MDRC and others had begun random assignment evaluations of a number of state time-limited waiver demonstrations, all of which found modest impacts.[37] Then, after TANF's implementation, most of us were stunned to see caseloads cut in half and an unprecedented increase in the number of welfare recipients going to work. Did this mean the experiments failed to estimate the real effects, or that the post-1996 reforms were different and more powerful, or that simultaneous changes in economic condition or other policies drove down the rolls?

The explanation is probably some combination of all those reasons. The waiver experiments were of specific versions of time limits, most of which had many exceptions—what might be characterized as time-limits "lite"—and multiple components (including expanded work requirements and services and increased financial work incentives). Although the studies were generally well implemented, they usually did not isolate the effects of time limits and most likely did not capture the programs' full impacts, since they were not designed to measure any effect on welfare applications and were conducted at a time when "many recipients and staff were skeptical about whether the time limit would really be imposed" (Farrell et al. 2008, 75), and "some control group members mistakenly believed that they were subject to some form of time limit" (Bloom and Michalopoulos 2001, 39). As Dan Bloom, who led MDRC's time-limited waiver evaluations, recalls, "Although caseworkers generally didn't tell the controls that they were subject to time limits, they couldn't shield them from the strong message 'out there' that it was not acceptable to stay on welfare anymore."

According to Mary Farrell et al. (2008), state policies under TANF block grants are much tougher, but only part of this is because of time limits: only half of welfare families headed by adults live in states that usually terminate benefits when people hit time limits; however, most states enforce tough sanctions (including closing the case) when recipients fail to meet work or other requirements, and half the states have diversion programs that provide lump-sum payments to people who agree not to reapply for assistance for some fixed period of time.

Finally, states implemented TANF in highly unusual times, with an exceptionally strong labor market, a simultaneous major expansion in the EITC and child care subsidies, and an increase in the minimum wage.[38] Blank summarizes the many studies that sought to determine how much of the dramatic caseload decline and employment increase during the five years following PRWORA was attributable to the exceptionally robust economy and how much to policy changes (including time limits). Although the numbers vary, all studies concluded that both played an important role and that neither explained the magnitude of behavioral change, leading Blank (2006, 59–60, 64–65) to offer two hypotheses: an incredible synergy between economy and policy and a behavioral shift among low-skilled women in response to the strong antiwelfare message. Reflecting on those years, Gordon Berlin reaches a similar conclusion: "There were three main reasons the waiver [experiments] failed to predict what happened after PRWORA: (1) the treatment that produced the impact on the caseload was overwhelmingly the strong economy, and we did not have a prior test of that; (2) the next most important thing was the 'message' of time limits (one type of community effect), and arguably the waiver studies did not provide a real test of that either; and (3) the synergy argument—we did not have a test of time limits plus making work pay plus a strong economy."[39]

In terms of the general usefulness of the experimental method, in my view the push for random assignment did not limit what was evaluated. If states, before 1996, had piloted tough time limits and administrative practices, these could have been assessed using random assignment of individuals, or better yet (to capture entry effects) locations (offices or counties), with the important caveat that would likely have made the estimates conservative; although a strong message could have been transmitted to people in the experimental group, the message could not have saturated the airwaves, as that would most likely have altered the behavior of controls. Whether the targeted message would have substantially reduced the impact is not obvious. However, this does not change the reality that laws creating or eliminating nationwide entitlements or enacting universal changes, once adopted, do not lend themselves to random assignment evaluation.[40]

REFLECTIONS ON MDRC'S 1986–2000 EXPERIENCE

Prior to 1986, random assignment experiments were rare tests of special demonstrations. Over the next 15 years, they became the preferred approach for evaluating a wide range of ambitious and sometimes full-scale welfare reform strategies. MDRC's experience during these years suggests a number of lessons.

Building Support

The successful implementation of the increasingly ambitious welfare experiments resulted from multiple factors. In 1982, when we first asked state commissioners to convert their reforms into tests with random assignment, we encountered incredulity about its feasibility and doubt about its value. We overcame this by delivering real benefits: answers to their questions, a subsidized evaluation, a spot in the limelight, membership in a privileged group, and evidence that it could be done. Success made this new paradigm the model for subsequent studies.

EACH SUCCESS MADE MORE AMBITIOUS EXPERIMENTS POSSIBLE   By 1986, state and national policy makers who were aware of the earlier experiments had crossed the feasibility and value thresholds. They had seen that such studies need not be toxic and could both produce useful lessons and bring unanticipated credibility, visibility, and prestige. Then the GAIN and Project Independence studies—which sought to use random assignment to evaluate full-blown reforms—encountered opposition not faced in the earlier smaller-scale tests. We and HHS mobilized to overcome the objections, and our efforts worked. The momentum continued; increasingly complex designs were implemented; and within a few years it became clear to more people that, if they wanted to have a national impact or be able to defend an evaluation, they should use random assignment.

THE COMMITMENT OF SENIOR ADMINISTRATORS PROVED CRUCIAL Successfully conducting a large-scale random assignment experiment requires a marriage of technical skills, operational wisdom, political savvy, and (at times) courage. We had the first two, but none of the studies highlighted in chapters 8 and 10 would have gotten off the ground without local champions who brought savvy and courage. In each case, busy administrators—sometimes teamed with senior legislative staff—opted for random assignment not primarily to obtain federal waivers but for the loftier goal of getting to the truth and, in some cases, gaining validation and a place in the national spotlight.[41] Although officials in California and Florida may not have anticipated the attacks, they did not retreat under pressure. We at MDRC found their unshakable determination to battle it out because "it was the right thing to do"—a response not unique to those states—an inspiration.

The three make-work-pay studies did not encounter the same opposition at the state and local levels, but supporters at those levels still played a vital role. Every independent evaluation requires leaders to take risks. Not only must they open their program to scrutiny—and thus lose control of the story and at some level admit a priori that they do not know whether the program will work. They must also make a multiyear pledge to follow protocols and provide data. Strikingly, despite gubernatorial and state staff turnover during periods of up to a decade, not a single study was canceled or even compromised.

A SMALL COMMUNITY OF EXPERTS, ADVOCATES, AND PUBLIC OFFICIALS LENT CREDIBILITY In 1986 few academics visibly endorsed large-scale field experiments, yet decision makers wanted some stamp of approval of this methodology, that it was sound and ethical. When called on to provide such reassurance, we sought to create an aura of scholarly blessing by directing them to the same band of supporters. The extreme example of how one person made a difference was Hollister, who had been a key figure in the income maintenance and Supported Work experiments, chaired the National Academy of Sciences panel that endorsed random assignment, served as the consultant who prompted the Florida Project Independence experiment, and was a strong voice on the panel that convinced the New Hope board that only this approach would give them national credibility.

Four other groups were major defenders of random assignment: state officials who had lived through experiments and attested to the limited burden and large rewards; advocates who had used the findings to reassure colleagues that the technique could be moral, objective, and useful; state and federal budget officials and congressional and state legislative staff who vouched for the credibility of the findings, particularly when they used them to cost out legislation and wrote random assignment into law; and the small cadre of senior civil servants at HHS and OMB who made it the quid pro quo for waivers, thus endorsing its unique legitimacy.

Why did they do this? It seems to me that, since the early 1980s, we all participated in a mutually reinforcing learning experience. Probably few of us started as random assignment zealots, but our experience convinced us that there was a gold standard, that it was attainable, that what it provided really could help build and defend better policy, and that the alternative was a methodological quagmire. In particular, that prominent liberals and conservatives believed that experiments produced a truth that was above politics made converts. As a result, government officials and people in the advocacy community valued the method and were there when we reached out for allies. In my view, this community did not arise out of thin air but was nurtured at least in part by a conscious effort to shape studies so that they addressed issues of importance to these diverse actors, whom we viewed as stakeholders and partners. Although it is likely that no group alone could have held the line against an attack such as that in Florida, collectively they contributed to the illusion of a consensus and, by promoting success, helped solidify it. Yet there were still ten long years to go before the mirage of widespread academic support became reality.

Producing Important Findings

The two reform strategies highlighted in chapters 8 and 10 emphasized different goals and, as summarized in table 10.2, produced different results. Mandatory welfare-to-work programs did better in reducing welfare dependency and government spending; earnings supplements did better in reducing poverty and benefiting young children.[42] In general, impacts were modest, and no single policy maximized all goals.

Table 10.2   Trade-Off in Benefits from Two Reform Strategies

Goal	Earnings supplement	Welfare-to-work mandate
Reduces poverty	Yes	Usually no; at best, small
Benefits young children	Yes	No
Increases work	Usually yes	Yes
Saves money	No	Often yes, but depends on design
Reduces welfare	Depends on design	Yes

Source: Author's compilation.

Affecting Policy

The link between research and policy is complex and murky at best. None-theless, our experience suggests actions that can increase the probability that experiments will be successful in informing policymakers.

THE EXPERIMENTS HAD DIRECT AND INDIRECT EFFECTS ON POLICY   Many people stated that the welfare-to-work experiments changed conventional wisdom and actual policy. In particular, the findings that states could design and run effective programs that could save money and (from GAIN and the JOBS evaluation) that work-focused, mixed-service programs that included job search could have larger and more pervasive impacts than other alternatives, including programs that emphasized basic education, directly influenced the language of PRWORA and the design of state welfare-to-work programs. In contrast, the evidence that well-designed earnings supplements could boost income and help young children without cutting work effort seemed to have a more indirect effect—by contributing to a view that, once welfare ended, the new work-based safety net should not only require but also reward work and to a broader interest in using financial incentives to affect other types of behavior.

METHODOLOGY, PRESENTATION, AND MARKETING MATTERED   The experiments of-fered scientific evidence replicated across multiple and diverse settings that reform could make a difference. But Supported Work had convinced us that evidence alone would not carry the day. If we wanted to change accepted wisdom, we needed important findings, simple and straightforward presentation, and the money and strategy to spread the word. Throughout the 1980s and 1990s, the Ford Foundation remained the major angel behind our ability to do this. Others joined later, and we fashioned a robust communications plan that pushed the findings, implications, and trade-offs but (we hoped) did not cross the line to advocating for a particular policy. As a side effect, by giving visibility to the programs' architects, these activities also contributed to the perception that experiments benefited participating states and sites, which helped generate candidates for later studies.

RANDOM ASSIGNMENT IS NECESSARY BUT NOT SUFFICIENT   Random assignment does not guarantee that a study will be valuable. It is the gateway to an opportunity. Making the most of it requires not only the clarity of the method (plus its quality implementation) but also the money and ambition to address additional issues vital to policy makers and practitioners: How and why did the program work or fall short? Can the program be replicated or made more effective? How do benefits compare with costs? In the cases explored in chapters 8 and 10, the responsible parties had opted for random assignment, but in my judgment (except in the Canadian case), the availability of unlimited federal matching funds in some cases (which effectively provided a 50 percent discount for welfare research) and of foundation resources in others paid for expanded samples, the collection of quantitative and qualitative data about the programs, and other enrichments that transformed these studies from likely to have disappointed into successes. Under the PRWORA system of block grants (where money for research trades off against money to serve people), states are unlikely to muster the political will to fund high-quality, multimethod evaluations. This is why the end of the AFDC program (and thus the end of matching federal dollars as an evaluation funding source) put at risk future research of this type. People interested in replicating the welfare story in other fields, or sustaining it in this one, need to focus on creating a comparable source of funds.

THERE WAS A CLEAR PAYOFF TO HAVING A RESEARCH AGENDA   Although we did not start with a fifteen-year plan—it emerged from an iterative process informed by many actors and by the findings themselves—the up-front process of identifying issues that were likely to be important three to five years out, and the rejection of work that did not advance methods or build knowledge, helped forge a coherent strategy that informed policy more effectively than a collection of uncoordinated studies, however high their quality, would have.

NEXT STEPS

This and earlier chapters recount the origin and growth of experiments. Although many actors and institutions played key roles, a subtext is the importance of the incentive structure embedded in the AFDC program: the benefit entitlement, which, by threatening an open-ended call on public funds, contributed to state and federal interest in finding out whether reforms would save money; the federal matching of state outlays for evaluation; and the waiver authority that HHS and MDRC leveraged to promote experiments.

As we had feared, after the demise of AFDC in 1996, there were no new state-initiated or state-funded welfare random assignment evaluations. In the next chapter, Howard describes how HHS used other tools and built different relationships to nurture experiments. MDRC responded to some of those opportunities and also conducted a nonexperimental study of the impact of devolution on families and neighborhoods. But more significantly, we shifted gears. Supported by multiple foundations and different federal agencies, we focused on promoting experiments in other fields and targeting diverse groups, including preschool through high school education, place-based initiatives, and programs for community college students, at-risk youth, and former prisoners.[43] We also expanded our explicit focus on methodology, exploring the randomization of intact groups or clusters (schools, classrooms, public housing developments) and other issues that applied the power of social experiments in new areas and increased what we would learn from such studies.[44]

CHAPTER 11

The End of Our Story: Welfare Reform Recedes from the Spotlight of Random Assignment Program Evaluation*

There are lots of disappointing evaluations, for example, of employment retention and advancement with respect to TANF. Do we say, "Let's give up on trying to help people retain jobs and advance in the workforce?" No. It challenges us to find different models.

—Wade Horn[1]

Both Judy and I have heard people say, even experts very familiar with the welfare evaluation field, that the rigor of the large body of welfare experiments was a result of the federal government's use of its 1115 waiver demonstration authority to require an experimental evaluation in exchange for programmatic flexibility (the quid pro quo). This explanation is appealing in its simplicity, but it is not how the random assignment or the waiver story actually developed. Since the waiver authority was never used to enforce the quid pro quo until 1987, and not used systematically for that purpose until 1992, as I described in chapter 7, it could not have stimulated the early-1980s' movement of social experiments from the arena of national demonstrations to evaluations of state work programs.[2] New welfare experiments were also initiated

*Chapter 11 authored by Howard Rolston.

independent of the waiver process during the 1987–1996 period, when random assignment was the standard for waiver experiments.

Even after PRWORA removed the incentive for states to request section 1115 authority for programmatic flexibility, federal-state-local partnerships using random assignment to evaluate welfare-to-work and broader welfare reform strategies continued.[3] The new policies that emerged in state waiver demonstrations and were embodied in TANF, especially tougher work requirements and time limits on benefit receipt, and the outcomes of those policies led such evaluation partnerships to new programmatic foci:

- How to help people who had successfully left welfare for work to stay off the rolls
- How to help people advance in the workforce, and
- How to help recipients with multiple significant problems be successful in work

In addition, these new policies heightened interest in their effects on children—potentially negative impacts from their parents leaving welfare without a job, and potentially positive effects from program impacts on their parents' skills and ability to become self-sufficient. The new content reflected three major factors: what had been learned about welfare dynamics from previous experiments and emerging nonexperimental research, a broadening programmatic focus in the states, and new evaluation methods and measures that had been developed in the process of implementing the earlier experiments.

In this chapter I review the experiments mounted in the 1990s and beyond to focus on strategies used to address these new questions. In the process, I show how we worked to build a research agenda systematically, by explicitly basing new evaluation efforts on the lessons of prior demonstrations (drawn from both failure and success) to maximize the additional contribution of a new effort to forge a cumulative body of knowledge.[4] (Table 11.1 presents a timeline of major events.)

A SUBSTANTIVE SHIFT IN DEMONSTRATION FOCUS: THE POST-EMPLOYMENT SERVICES DEMONSTRATION

Earlier we describe the important role the Mary Jo Bane and David Ellwood (1983) analysis of welfare played in formulating the hypotheses about reduc-

Table 11.1   Timeline of the Post-TANF Story and Related Events

Date	Event
April 1993	Decision to initiate the Post-Employment Services demonstration
June 1996	Initiation of Project to Evaluate Child Impacts of State Waiver Policies
August 1996	TANF replaces AFDC
November 1996	ACF Announces Funding to Continue State Waiver Evaluations
November 1996	First meeting of states and evaluators to design Child Impact study measures
September 1997	Five states awarded funds to measure child impacts in random assignment waiver evaluations
November 1998	First meeting with states to plan Employment Retention and Advancement project
September 1999	Contract awarded to MDRC for Employment Retention and Advancement demonstration
September 2001	Contract awarded to MDRC for Enhanced Services for the Hard-to-Employ demonstration
March 2004	Final Five-State Child Impact study report issued
April 2010	Final Employment Retention and Advancement demonstration report issued
March 2012	Final Hard-to-Employ demonstration report issued

Source: Author's compilation.

ing welfare dependency that led to the Teen Parent demonstration. That study was based on the Panel Study of Income Dynamics, a longitudinal survey that began collecting extensive data on a representative set of families in 1968 regarding their total annual income and its sources, including income from AFDC. The study had one major limitation for studying welfare dynamics, however: it collected only annual income measures.[5] Since AFDC eligibility was determined monthly, this constraint prevented the Bane-Ellwood analysis from capturing either very brief spells or exits and reentries that may have occurred within a given year.

By the early 1990s, the National Longitudinal Survey of Youth (NLSY) had collected about a decade of income data on a monthly basis. Since the original study design was a representative sample of youth aged 14 to 22 in 1979, later NLSY waves were not nationally representative of all adults. But since the NLSY database was large enough to reliably capture the behavior of younger individuals and their experience as recipients of Aid to Families with Dependent Children (AFDC) over time, its monthly income data made possible a more finely grained analysis of welfare dynamics. A dramatically new picture emerged. Many more exits turned out to result from employment than from marriage (the primary cause suggested by the annual data). In addition, the two archetypes of "short stayers" and "long stayers" emerging from Bane-Ellwood were joined by a third, the "cyclers." This group was characterized by multiple short-lived exits, primarily for employment, followed by re-entry to AFDC. For this substantial group of recipients, getting a job seemed less of a problem than staying employed.

In March 1993, my staff and I were working on a spending plan for the coming year's research budget. The bulk of funds, as always, would be committed to continuing multiyear projects; but decisions about new spending had to be made, and made sufficiently early in the fiscal year for funds to be committed to particular projects no later than its end (September 30), after which uncommitted funds would be lost to the agency. Fortunately, Mary Jo Bane, who would not be confirmed as Department of Health and Human Services (HHS) assistant secretary for children and families until the fall, had arrived by March as a part-time consultant, giving us substantial time for the research-planning process.

The welfare cyclers were high on our list. At the previous November's Association for Public Policy and Management conference, Nancye Campbell, the same career civil servant who had served so well as co–project officer on the Teen Parent demonstration, had heard a presentation by LaDonna Pavetti (finishing up a doctorate with Bane and Ellwood at Harvard's Kennedy School of Government and soon to be a consultant with the Office of the Assistant Secretary for Planning and Evaluation [ASPE], who described findings from her thesis on that very issue. Pavetti had used NLSY data to study a group of welfare mothers who cycled between work and dependence on welfare, and identified problems that appeared related to their difficulties in sustaining employment. When Bane arrived, she provided us with information on a Chicago program run by Toby Herr, Project Match, which had won an *Innovations in Government* award managed by the Kennedy School. (Herr would also soon be an ASPE consultant.) Through intensive and regular contact with welfare recipients, Project Match's goal was to move recipients into employment through a series of monitored activities. In the process, it had developed considerable longitudinal data on the participants, some of which yielded findings consistent with Pavetti's and other analyses based on the NLSY (see Herr and Halpern 1991).

As we brainstormed about research ideas to present to the incoming Assistant Secretary, Campbell suggested focusing on employment retention. She recalls her thinking this way: "It was a combination of now we're in a world with time limits[6] [and] our data suggest that people get jobs but don't keep them . . . leave welfare but come back, so that the getting the job part, which was a lot of what welfare reform was about until that time, suggested we had that part down. . . . The new policy context of using up your months and years because you can't stick in a job . . . seemed like the next place we should focus."

Campbell then created the first step in a new generation of research by translating the operational idea of Project Match, namely individual case management to help individuals solve employment problems, into the goal of assisting individuals who obtained employment to stay employed. The proposed Post Employment Services Demonstration (PESD) would assign a case manager (somebody in the welfare system but with a specialized role of only working with newly employed recipients) when a parent became employed. That case manager would offer whatever services were considered necessary to assist the parent to remain employed: helping to deal with an employer or re-arranging child care, for example, or resolving other problems undermining steady work. In the event that an individual lost her job, the program would also be responsible for providing services, such as job search, to enable her rapid re-employment. An experimental design would be the basis for evaluating the programs, and sites would be required to randomly assign at least 1,000 mothers who obtained jobs over an 18- to 24-month period.

Campbell also came up with an innovative funding suggestion for the project. In addition to the waiver and matching the unmatchable demonstration authorities, section 1115 provided $4 million annually for use as the state share of demonstration programs. By long-standing agreement, my office and its predecessors had $1.8 million for welfare and the Health Care Financing Administration had $2.2 million for Medicaid. Since these funds could be used as the state share, they were effectively doubled when added to the open-ended 50/50 federal match for AFDC administrative costs. The total amount of funds was even greater when they were claimed under the Jobs Opportunities and Basic Skills Training (JOBS) program matching rate of 60/40. Although these funds were typically used for state program operation costs that were part of a federal demonstration, as would be the case in the proposed PESD, Campbell suggested using the funds also to pay for a centralized evaluator for the overall project. This would be done by having one of the states selected to operate a PESD project compete a contract for the overall evaluation, but in close coordination with my office and under specifications we would determine.

On April 23, 1993, we presented the idea to Bane, who was enthusiastic and gave us the go ahead at once. Soon after, we issued a grant announcement and the following September awarded grants to four states: California (Riverside), Illinois (Chicago), Oregon (Portland), and Texas (San Antonio). Illinois was selected as the lead evaluation agency, and it awarded an evaluation contract to Mathematica Policy Research on April 1, 1994.

EFFECTS OF STRICTER WORK REQUIREMENTS AND TIME LIMITS ON CHILDREN: BUILDING ON TOOLS FROM THE JOBS CHILD IMPACT STUDY

As state waiver requests continued to grow in the 1992–1996 period, their content focused increasingly on stricter work requirements and time limits. There now seemed to be something of a bidding war, with both Republican and Democratic governors claiming they were "tougher on work." States were proposing more immediate and larger financial sanctions for failure to meet work requirements ("hair trigger sanctions"), as well as shorter and shorter time limits, including what were termed "drop dead" limits, which cut off parents or whole families after a set number of benefit months, independent not only of any efforts they had made to find work but also of whether jobs were available for them. Although the Clinton administration would only approve time limits that had some exception for individuals who cooperated with program requirements and had made good faith efforts to find employment, the requirements proposed by states (and approved) were often extremely stringent, making the dividing line between conditional time limits and absolute drop dead limits very thin. Other policy areas, such as requirements for teen parents to attend school and live with an adult (if they were minors) and family caps that did not increase benefits to a family when a child was conceived on welfare, also became common.

Given the wide range of human and social capital embodied in parents on welfare, it seemed to me that the overall thrust of where state policy choices were headed was likely to create not only winners but also losers under the new regimes.[7] Those who functioned well under a stricter AFDC program and found employment would likely have greater family income (especially when the recently increased earned-income tax credit was taken into account), but those who did not would likely see substantial decreases in family income. Children in the former situation might do better, but children in the latter could very well do worse. So, although I had been skeptical that the JOBS program would have a significant effect on children, I found it plausible that the new, more stringent welfare rules would change that, at least for certain subsets of the population.

With the growing number of waiver demonstration applications, the negotiation of terms and conditions had become more standardized, invariably beginning with a template that included a list of questions the evaluation should address. One of the questions on this list addressed effects on child well-being. This passage, from the December 1994 terms and conditions for an Indiana waiver, was typical: "Does the demonstration affect the well-being of children, including their long-term prospects for self-sufficiency? Outcome measures related to this question include, at a minimum: measures of child well-being such as reported child abuse and neglect; health and insurance status as in extant data available from local records and medical records; and incidence of school truancy."

The data gathering required under this provision was clearly minimal compared to the measures hammered out for the JOBS evaluation (see chapter 9). The reason was simple: cost. Since the federal requirements for an experimental evaluation implied state cost sharing, more detailed data requirements would have entailed costs far beyond what most states were willing to spend, potentially stimulating much greater state resistance to high-quality evaluation. I appreciated this constraint, of course. But at the same time it seemed to me that the measurement tools developed in the JOBS evaluation could, and should, be brought into a subset of the state waiver evaluations. How could this be done?

We—by now the Office of Planning, Research, and Evaluation (OPRE), the policy function having been split off into a new office—needed both state partners and money. Since testing the winner/loser hypothesis involved identifying subgroup effects (which might even cancel out and disappear in any overall effects), we needed state demonstration designs that involved good baseline (that is, pre-random-assignment) data on recipient characteristics and large enough experimental and control groups to allow for meaningful comparisons among subgroups. We also needed states that would voluntarily modify their evaluations in a way that would put them at additional political risk. They would have to be willing to undergo a rigorous, public test of whether their welfare reforms were helping or hurting children.

Money was the first requirement; no additional money would leave us with no partners. But as I began to formulate these ideas in late 1995, money was not readily available to HHS's Administration for Families and Children. Since annual appropriations for the research budget I managed for many years had been highly stable, I devoted little attention to protecting that budget other than writing a strong justification for a funding level each year as part of the budget process. I had done little to establish and maintain good relationships with the staffs of appropriations committees, although I was careful to do so with their counterparts on the authorizing committees. In the summer of 1995 my neglect came back to haunt us. The Republican majority elected the previous November had interpreted the many different research budgets in HHS as reflecting duplication. The budget managed by OPRE was deemed duplicative and was "zeroed out" in the fiscal year 1996 budget. Since we had forward funded the JOBS evaluation by several years, our major project was not at risk. But we had absolutely no funds for new initiatives.

On March 22, 1996, as I walked alone to a retirement luncheon for a colleague, I found myself thinking about the lost opportunity to augment the waiver demonstrations. Suddenly, the answer hit me—we could use section 1115 demonstration authority funds (the same source used for PESD) to persuade states to augment their evaluations. Since these were mandatory funds, they were not subject to annual appropriation. Just as quickly, it struck me that we would need a central mechanism to coordinate the state efforts into testing a common set of measures.

By the next day, I had a reasonably good idea about how to fund a coordinator for the state efforts: form a partnership with ASPE. Given its longstanding interest in measuring child well-being, I was confident that proposing a joint effort in this case would be well received. We met within a week and worked out a plan. ASPE would fund Child Trends, the organization with primary responsibility for the JOBS Child Impact study, by augmenting a grant Child Trends already had from the National Institute for Child Health and Human Development. My office, in turn, would provide funds for planning grants to enable states to work together, under the leadership of Child Trends, in developing a set of child well-being measures that all participating states agreed would fairly assess whether and how their reforms affected children. Child Trends would organize meetings and create documents to facilitate this joint planning process and would summarize the results.

We announced the availability of grants to states on June 7, 1996. Twelve states applied, and all were awarded planning grants on September 25. Between those two dates, the world of welfare and waivers changed forever. Congress passed, and on August 22 President Clinton signed, the Personal Responsibility and Work Opportunity Reconciliation Act (PRWORA), replacing AFDC with time-limited welfare and eliminating the waiver quid pro quo.

ARTICULATING A VISION OF WELFARE REFORM EVALUATION IN THE NEW SOCIAL POLICY WORLD

As many have observed, PRWORA was a major turning point in the history of U.S. social policy. It replaced the sixty-year-old AFDC program with Temporary Assistance for Needy Families (TANF). (Table 11.2 shows the major differences between the two programs.) It also had very significant effects on child support enforcement, Supplemental Security Income for children and adults, and immigrants' eligibility for means-tested assistance.

How we implemented section 413 of PRWORA, which provided $15 million in research funds to ACF, was central to how we moved ahead with the evaluation of welfare reform. There was a three-week gap between the House and Senate passage of the PRWORA conference bill and the president's signing the bill into law. Because of section 415, which allowed states to continue waiver policies, and the relief it would bring to states from federal requirements and potential penalties for not meeting them, a flurry of activity ensued—to complete pending state applications as well as a few new amendments to bring existing projects under the purview of the section. Although we could see light at the end of the tunnel of negotiating section 1115 applications, we had a few more weeks of intensive work before we could celebrate.

Our relief at having the end of this work overload in sight was mixed with considerable concern that the vast majority of the evaluations for which we had worked so hard would be abandoned. To ensure that not all would be lost, we were determined to exploit any assets we still had.

Table 11.2   Six Major Features of AFDC and TANF

Substantive area	AFDC	TANF
Definition of family unit and how income and resources affect eligibility and benefits	Highly prescriptive federal rules	State determined, except for requirement that family include a minor child
Individual receipt of benefits	Indefinite individual entitlement to benefits	No individual entitlement; federal benefits limited to five years (with 20 percent exception for state)
Federal and state funding	State entitlement with federal funds matching state dollars on an open-ended basis	State entitlement to a fixed block grant and requirement for state maintenance of effort
Work requirements on states	Modest participation rate standards with flexible activities	Higher participation rate standards with narrower list of countable activities
Existing waiver demonstrations	States required to comply with terms and conditions, including evaluation (usually random assignment)	State able to temporarily continue policies even where inconsistent with TANF with no evaluation requirement (section 415)
Research funding	State evaluation costs matched 50-50 with federal dollars	Federal research funding of $15 million annually (section 413)

Source: Author's compilation.

The main asset we had was section 413 and the $15 million it provided annually for research. Welfare reform research and evaluation had strong supporters on the staff of the two key authorizing committees, Ron Haskins at House Ways and Means and Margaret Malone at Senate Finance. Both believed it was vital that the new reforms be evaluated; they were also aware that the appropriations committees had eliminated my office's funding source for welfare evaluation initiatives. Committee staff often seek technical assistance from staff in the executive branch and from outside experts, and Judy and I were able to provide such input into the language that the authorizing committees developed for section 413. Senator Moynihan, who expressed disdain for the administration's and the Republican's legislation, did support the research funds involved. So did Sheila Burke, the chief of staff who famously spoke for Senator Dole.[8]

Our strategy for using the funds was based on establishing clear priorities. The top priority was to create a new overall relationship for working with states that could replace the waiver-for-research quid pro quo without threatening evaluation rigor. The second was to protect as much as possible of what was high value from among the waiver evaluations. The third was to extend and initiate new work with states that would be not only valuable but widely recognized as such.

Creating this new relationship required us to project a compelling vision. In many ways it was an old vision: federal and state governments working as partners to produce strong evidence of effectiveness. But something was truly new: the extent of state flexibility. The key element of our new vision had to be transforming that flexibility into a positive force for better research, rather than the chance for states to snub those of us who had for so long told them what to do. Many expressed concern that the era of high-quality welfare experiments might be over, but fortunately that danger turned out to be avoidable.

The central idea we had to sell was threefold: (1) that the many federal statutory rules of AFDC had limited state choices and therefore narrowed their need for information; (2) that the new choices created for the states by TANF had brought with them an intensified need for high-quality information to better understand the consequences of those choices; and (3) that, since experimental methods are often the strongest way to understand the consequences of program and policy choices, there was great potential for a continuing agenda for welfare reform evaluation rooted in experimental methods. This meant engaging states as partners throughout the evaluation process, including them in planning the objects of study so that our research agenda was responsive to what states believed they most needed to know. Our assumption that this logic would appeal to a significant number of states was the basis for our strategy and led to important decisions regarding how we engaged with states.

I had the opportunity to present our vision to a December 9–10, 1996, meeting of states in Phoenix, Arizona. I emphasized that HHS did not begrudge them their new-found freedom and had no desire to find ways to hold onto federal power. I made it clear that I still firmly believed requiring experimental designs as a condition of waiver approvals had been the correct decision, but I also recognized that important negative consequences had come with the necessarily universal nature of the requirement. The waiver process was over, and, though good had emerged from it, it was now time to say goodbye. "The old king is dead. Long live the new king." Most of all, I stressed how important it was that states have reliable information for policy making and program design, that experiments could be powerful in building that knowledge, and that my office was prepared to act in partnership with states to answer the questions most important to them. The questions and comments after my opening remarks were positive, and I left feeling that state-federal partnerships would emerge and could be successful.

PRESERVING THE BEST, AND SOME OF THE REST, OF THE WAIVER DEMONSTRATIONS

Four research areas were specifically authorized for funding in section 413, including resources "to operate and evaluate demonstration projects, relating to this part, that are in effect or approved under section 1115 as of August 22, 1996, and are continued after such date (section 413(h)(1)(D))." Our ability to cover 100 percent of the costs for the continuation of waiver evaluations was a critical asset, since the AFDC provision for the states and the federal government to split the cost of evaluation on a 50-50 basis was no longer in effect for those evaluations. A critical new limitation was that the post-PRWORA funding was a fixed annual amount, $15 million, whereas the federal 50-50 funding was open ended, meaning that the new funding would not adequately cover as many evaluations as were currently under way. At the same time, universality had led to far more evaluations being undertaken than could be supported by organizations able to accomplish them well. Thus abandonment of many of the waiver evaluations was, on balance, probably a good thing, since it allowed us to preserve a number of higher-quality evaluations without continuing those that had less chance of delivering strong evidence.

Having funding to support continuing research, we now needed states that had ongoing high-quality evaluations and were willing to continue those evaluations, including maintaining both treatment and control groups for a substantial period. Fortunately, it was clear that some states had a genuine interest in rigorous evaluation and in knowing how their reformed welfare programs compared with AFDC. This motivation was furthered by the fact that, although the issue of random assignment was contentious, we had established person-to-person relationships with evaluation staff in virtually all states. And many of them also found it satisfying to support work that was more rigorous and credible than the types of evaluations they were usually able to undertake. Finally, the research organizations conducting the evaluations did not want them to end prematurely. Both their self-interest in not losing business and their more altruistic commitment to seeing their work result in increased knowledge often made them key salespersons in urging states to seek funding. With these assets, as soon as President Clinton signed the bill we began strategizing about how to make funds available to states quickly, since we were concerned that they might precipitously drop their control groups before we had a chance to build an evaluation partnership with them.

The formal process for using a portion of section 413 funds to continue waiver demonstrations was initiated in a grant announcement to states on November 4, 1996, soliciting what we called Track One and Track Two applications. Track One referred to random assignment impact evaluations. Noting that the Administration for Children and Families had "approved 79 demonstration applications from 43 states" and that "these demonstrations can be expected to form the foundation of State program designs for the Temporary Assistance for Needy Families Program," the announcement said that funding the continuation of experiments "will provide early impacts on various specific welfare reform initiatives." With the majority of states invested heavily in the design and implementation of comprehensive reforms using waivers, and given TANF's vast flexibility (including that provided under section 415), many of the waiver programs would also effectively be TANF programs. Since the existing control groups would continue receiving welfare under the old, nonwaiver AFDC rules, this was a genuinely unique opportunity to measure experimentally how TANF, at least initially, compared with AFDC. It was also the last chance to make such a comparison. And since many of the evaluations were already under way, the findings could be available relatively soon. The announcement stressed the importance to states of high-quality information and asserted that TANF had not eliminated the need for experimental studies (although clearly in one sense it had) but rather had heightened the "importance of impact analyses which utilize random assignment."

Track Two, in contrast, was for planning grants to states that did not want to continue an impact and implementation study with an AFDC control group but wanted to modify their evaluations to learn other important things. The small planning grants would enable them to develop some aspect of their evaluation into either an implementation study, or a nonexperimental impact study, or possibly an experimental study of alternative approaches to a particular policy area under TANF (such as more strict versus less strict sanction rules for individuals who fail to comply with work requirements). We added Track Two to our plans for two strategic reasons. First, we wanted to have a wide range of states engaged in evaluating their programs and taking ownership of evaluation as an important state activity. In addition, we wanted to show states that we were not so committed to experimental methods that we recognized no other form of impact evaluation—as certainly must have seemed the case in our negotiations regarding evaluation designs of proposed waiver demonstrations before PRWORA.

By January 15, 1997, the due date for applications, we had received nineteen applications under Track One and twenty-four under Track Two, involving a total of thirty states. That more than a third of the states were applying for funding to support an evaluation based on an AFDC control group was extremely encouraging. During that spring, we approved nine of the nineteen applications for Track One projects (in Arizona, Connecticut, Florida, Indiana, Iowa, Minnesota, Texas, Vermont, and Wisconsin). The three major research organizations with the most experience in welfare experimentation—Abt Associates, Mathematica Policy Research, and MDRC—were conducting seven of the nine, giving us confidence in the commitment of those states to quality evaluation and the high likelihood that those evaluations would produce reliable findings. All twenty-four of the Track Two applications were awarded planning grants to develop new applications for grants to actually conduct evaluations. Eleven Track Two applications for grants to implement modified evaluations were approved in September of the same year, with another three added the following fiscal year, when we had a new infusion of $15 million. Most of these were in-depth implementation studies. A number were nonexperimental impact evaluations; we approved these, even with no real expectation that they would produce credible evidence, to demonstrate a good-faith effort to give states the opportunity to carry out nonexperimental impact evaluations. We approved two applications (from Nebraska and Virginia) to conduct within-TANF experiments—not enough to provide the body of knowledge required to learn much definitive about the effects of state policy choices under TANF, but a start. The only proposed projects we did not fund were ones we believed had absolutely no chance of success.

NEXT STEPS ON THE FIVE-STATE[9] CHILD IMPACTS STUDY

Continuing the best of the waiver experiments was important, not just in itself but also because it was a must if we were to augment a subset of state evaluations with more systematic, in-depth, and common measures of child well-being. Successfully accomplishing this had become even more urgent with TANF's passage. Debate about the effects on children of both TANF as a whole and particular TANF policies had been so vigorous, even vitriolic, that it would surely continue. Credible findings to inform this debate were vital. But the options for so doing were extremely limited. Given the lack of pre-PRWORA data on in-depth child outcome measures, even sophisticated nonexperimental statistical methods were unavailable. The only hope was to augment the experiments we had already approved to assess how the new state policies under TANF affected children.

We now engaged in the planning process with the states to which we had issued planning grants at the end of September. For the first meeting in that process, held on November 7, 1996, Child Trends had prepared materials to guide states through a systematic exploration of various domains of child development and potential measures within each. State representatives were enthusiastic as they discussed whether their reform demonstrations were likely to affect these measures. The back-and-forth was considerable, but before long a strong consensus emerged among the states to incorporate all the measures the researchers would have included except the cognitive assessments (which were universally considered by the participating states as extremely unlikely to be affected by their programs). This state consensus was adopted as the foundation of the common core of measures the federal government would fund in the project. The whole discussion made it crystal clear to us that states brought important insights into the analytics of what outcomes should be measured and that a federally imposed set of measures, just as we had feared, would indeed have undermined their sense of ownership and the federal-state partnership.

The successful initial convening of these state grantees and their evaluators was quickly followed by a second meeting on February 27–28, 1997. Its primary purpose was to present Child Trends' formal distillation of the first meeting and to provide guidance for the second round of competition for grants from section 413 funds that would support a subset of these grantees to include the child well-being measures in their evaluation surveys. The participants again were enthusiastic, and in late spring eleven of the twelve applied.

The decision on which states to fund turned out not to be difficult. Among the nine Track One states we had approved, six were also among the twelve child impact planning grant states, demonstrating both that their underlying welfare reform evaluations were among the best and also that their evaluations would be adequately funded. Several states also applied to assess child well-being in the context of less comprehensive programs (for example, only for teen parents). None of these were approved, given that we could fund only a limited number of states and we regarded states that represented comprehensive reforms based on varying the central policy choices (time limits, enhanced earnings disregards, and work requirements) as most critical to our research agenda.

On September 30, 1997, we awarded child impact implementation grants to five Track One states: Connecticut, Florida, Indiana, Iowa, and Minnesota. All the states had work requirements that were stricter than typical AFDC programs. Three had time limits (Connecticut, Florida, and Indiana), which for the former two were quite strict and for the latter less so. Iowa had an unusual form of time limit, a limited benefit plan under which applicants who refused to develop a self-sufficiency plan were limited to six months of benefits, after which they could reapply only after a set number of months had passed. Minnesota had no time limit. Connecticut and Minnesota had earnings disregards that were much more generous than the other three, although all five were more generous than AFDC. All five states had a strong evaluator: Abt Associates for Indiana; MDRC for Connecticut, Florida, and Minnesota; and Mathematica Policy Research for Iowa.[10] The McKnight, Northwest Area, and Annie E. Casey Foundations had already made a major investment in measuring child impacts in the Minnesota Family Investment Program evaluation. Annie E. Casey also made another that allowed Indiana to field a much-increased sample, greatly strengthening the likelihood that the evaluation would find any substantively significant findings.

The implementation phase for this Five-State Child Impact substudy functioned as well as the planning phase. Child Trends continued to coordinate the effort, and the three evaluation organizations, although they had their own ways of conducting surveys and measuring child well-being, worked smoothly together to develop a common core of measures. We were pleased to see that all the organizations involved seemed to relish working together to achieve a product greater than each could achieve alone. When the data collection was completed, the four research organizations, with the support of the states, my office, and ASPE, worked together to produce an initial interpretation of the findings and a common public-use data file (Tout et al. 2004).

Assessing the Returns on Our Investment: Track One, Track Two, and Child Impacts

The cost of the Track One evaluations was $17.2 million over five years, of the Track Twos $12.1 million over six years, and of the Five-State Child Impact study (all Track One add-ons) $5.9 million over five years. What was the payoff from the total of $35.2 million spent in this way?

The value of the Track Two studies is relatively easy to assess. At the national level, they quickly disappeared from sight or were never seen at all. The nonexperimental impact studies had difficulties throughout, sometimes in data gathering, other times in analysis. Even though we enlisted the aid of academics with both strong methodological insight and practical experience evaluating policies to provide technical assistance at the state level, not one of these studies produced findings that passed even the lowest standard of credibility. Karl Koerper, who at the time managed the division that initiated and oversaw all three sets of studies, describes the situation: "All the [nonexperimental impact] reports seemed to be flawed in one way or another, and none provided an adequate . . . counterfactual for estimating impacts."

The Track Twos also included a range of descriptive studies. Some of these involved looking at particular populations, such as Native Americans or individuals leaving welfare. Others examined how states implemented certain policies. Only some of the studies of welfare leavers, which were augmented by a much larger group that ASPE funded, supported with congressionally designated funds, were significant at the national level, although they may have played some role in helping develop policy at the state level. Of the two small experiments, neither was truly successful—an incoming governor canceled one, and the other compared two approaches that were not different enough to yield interesting findings.

One of the main motivations for the Track Twos was to strengthen relations with states for future evaluation partnerships that would use more rigorous methods. Whether we accomplished this is unclear. On the one hand, it is notable that several of the states that did conduct nonexperimental impact studies were strongly opposed to random assignment at the time and continued to be so after their projects were complete. And most of the states we partnered with in subsequent evaluations had previously been our evaluation partners outside the waiver demonstrations. On the other hand, our willingness to fund the Track Two projects may have helped to improve our relationships with states more generally. Adding all these considerations together, I think it highly unlikely that the Track Two investments returned the $12 million investment spent on them, either in research or state-relationship value.

The findings and research value of the Track One investments must be assessed along two distinct dimensions. With regard to the central provisions of TANF, their value needs to be considered in combination with other welfare reform experiments focusing on the specific issues involved. For example, what has been learned about financial incentives is a result of findings from not only these five but other experiments as well, such the Canadian Self-Sufficiency Program and New Hope, and even the original income maintenance experiments.

But testing TANF-related provisions was not the only focus of the Track One demonstrations. Perhaps their greatest value was to enable the Five-State Child Impact study. And the positive value of the investment in these studies seems clear. In 1999 MDRC began what has become known as the Next Generation project, which synthesized the child impact findings from ten experiments it conducted plus the two additional experiments in the Five-State study that were conducted by the two other firms. Not only did adding detailed child outcome measures enrich the studies of individual states; together they have produced substantial secondary analyses to determine and quantify broader conclusions.

The two sets of overlapping studies, Five-State and Next Generation, taken together, produced a strong body of evidence, despite the limitations of individual studies, that provides consistent knowledge about the impacts of welfare reform on children. Increasing both earnings and income by providing wage subsidies produces modest, positive impacts for young school-age children. Adolescents, in contrast, typically suffer modest, negative school-related effects across a broad range of welfare reforms, even in cases where family income increases. Outside these experimental studies, there is little strong evidence regarding the effects of welfare reform on children. Jeffrey Grogger and Lynn Karoly's (2005, 222) synthesis of the research on the effects of welfare reform concludes that the reason there are "so few observational studies of the impact of welfare reform on child outcomes" is that the data to support them do not exist.[11] The authors go on to describe the one methodologically sound study they were able to identify but then proceed to note its many shortcomings, primarily owing to a lack of necessary data Thus, experiments have been critical to our understanding of the impacts of welfare reform policies on children, including the Five-State study, which would have been impossible without the Track One investment.

Building on the PESD Findings to Study Employment Retention and Advancement Initiatives

In the fall of 1997, Mathematica Policy Research shared the initial impact findings from the four PESD evaluation sites, based on surveys of the initial 40 percent of the random assignment sample across all the sites. Even given their preliminary nature, the findings were discouraging. Not only were there no statistically significant impacts on employment or earnings (which might have been expected with the reduced samples); there were few suggestions of positive patterns. Of the thirty-two quarterly impacts estimates available across the four sites, ten were negative (none significantly so), and only a handful of the twenty-two that were positive were close to being significant even at the relatively weak .10 level. On the basis of this evidence, we could not plausibly expect large impacts in the final results, to be available in another year.[12]

When an evaluation with adequate statistical power fails to produce evidence that a program has had any impact on its intended outcomes, there are two broad hypotheses as to why this might be. One is that the program was not implemented as designed, in which case the program model did not get a fair test. In the case of PESD, the initial (and subsequent) evidence was that the program was implemented as designed, implying that the program model did get a fair test. The other hypothesis is that the theory of the program is wrong, that is, the causal mechanisms assumed to bring about positive change do not, in fact, lead to those outcomes, and that the initial assumptions need to be reexamined.

From this perspective, the timing of PESD—initiated in 1993, about six months before AFDC caseloads would reach their national peak and when the accelerated movement of welfare recipients into work was just beginning—proved prescient. By 1997, welfare caseloads had already shrunk substantially and the increase in work among single mothers was dramatic. With the greater focus by state and local programs on moving welfare recipients into work, program operators began to observe much more directly the retention problems of the many newly employed mothers who turned back frequently to assistance for financial support. In addition, the establishment of state and federal time limits under TANF made state and local staff much more conscious of the need not only to move recipients into jobs but also to establish them in the workforce less transiently. As a result, states increasingly began looking to stabilize welfare recipients' employment, many beginning to view their mission as helping recipients not just to get jobs but to keep them; and many states saw gaining information on how to do this as a high-priority need.

It was particularly disappointing that, despite the excellent timing in having initiated the right demonstration four years earlier, we had nothing positive to provide states by way of advice, just as they began to look for the information PESD was intended to provide. So we decided to initiate another major experimental research effort, beginning with a planning stage that would provide the groundwork for the Employment, Retention, and Advancement (ERA) demonstration. Although retention was the focus of PESD, we thought it was important to broaden the scope of the new research to include employment advancement as well. A large body of descriptive research established that job loss among newly hired former welfare recipients was substantial and also that job advancement was typically slow to nonexistent. Overwhelmingly, the welfare policy community had come to accept the proposition that society should expect parents to work to support their children, even if that meant requiring them to accept low-wage jobs, often with erratic hours. To many, including myself, it seemed that this obligation of self-support entailed some reciprocal responsibility for government to aid in providing the opportunity for these mothers to advance and, at least over time, establish themselves more in the mainstream labor market. Actual advancement for every low-wage mother was not likely, but providing the opportunity to do so seemed an appropriate governmental responsibility.

Consistent with our strategy to engage states early in the development of projects, in the spring of 1998 we announced the availability of grants to states to fund time for state staff to design programs and travel to meetings in

Washington, where they would discuss their proposed approaches both with other states and with experts on employment issues and interventions. Our vision was of a federal convening role that would help states work with one another, along with getting advice from outsiders in a systematic manner. The funds would also enable states to develop applications to compete for participation in a national random assignment evaluation of promising programs. Thirteen states applied for the grants, and we provided funds to all thirteen the following summer.

The need for planning grants reflected two key circumstances. First, unlike in 1981 when states were seizing new opportunities to implement work programs, in 1998 their interest was in improving retention and advancement, but few programs with these aims actually existed at any scale. Thus it was necessary to move from an evaluation strategy that assessed the impact of existing programs to a demonstration program that encouraged the development of new programs we could then evaluate. Second, we lacked the funds to pay for the implementation of demonstrations. Under AFDC, we had paid for demonstration programs using section 1115. But with TANF we had no federal dollars with which to match, let alone provide, the state share. States that wanted to participate in the project would now need to use their block grant funds to pay for the operation of the programs. Because of the large decrease in the cash assistance caseload such funds existed, but it was not clear whether states would use them for that purpose. MDRC staff would subsequently aptly describe the ERA as an "unfunded" demonstration.

Also in the summer of 1998, OPRE awarded a contract to the Lewin Group to coordinate the federal part of the ERA effort. The project director was Mike Fishman, who had previously played a key role in promoting high-quality research at both ASPE and the Food and Nutrition Service in the Department of Agriculture. Fishman and his staff quickly organized the first of what would be a series of meetings with state grantees, held on November 12–13. The project team and other attendees introduced state staff to a number of research findings, including the preliminary PESD results and a new analysis, funded by my office, of the employment dynamics of welfare mothers based on an analysis of the NLSY (Rangarajan, Schochet, and Chu 1998). This indicated that the reasons for job losses were multiple and not dominated by a small number of problems that could be readily targeted. As states worked to develop their programs, use of the PESD results was vital. At every stage, Lewin and federal staff raised the same question, which became a constant refrain: "What would this program provide that moves it beyond the PESD programs and would lead one to think this new program would be more successful?"

We initiated a procurement for the ERA evaluation stage in spring 1999 and awarded a contract to MDRC the following September.[13] The project enrolled states into the evaluation through a competitive process. The Lewin Group and MDRC continued to provide technical assistance through both site visits and meetings of the states until the evaluation stage was fully under way. Eventually, sixteen different program approaches were tested in eight states. Because retention and advancement were new areas of program development, and because each approach was distinctly homegrown, there were no strong similarities across the sixteen. The relative uniqueness of each program would, as it turned out, strongly influence the evidence ERA produced.

For the final ERA project report (Hendra et al. 2010), MDRC categorized twelve of the sixteen programs into four categories based on the characteristics of the populations served: three served unemployed TANF recipients, four employed TANF recipients, and five non-TANF employed individuals.[14] Most strikingly, and in sharp contrast to most of the earlier major studies, only three of the twelve programs, one in each group, showed a general pattern of positive findings on earnings. Given the variety of programs, there was no clear similarity among those that were successful and no clear contrast with those that were not. The single program that was successful for unemployed TANF recipients, the Texas Employment Retention and Advancement project, included the kinds of financial incentives and requirements that previous research described in chapter 10 suggests are effective in increasing employment. But the successful program for former recipients that most closely resembled the PESD programs that were unsuccessful was the Riverside Post-Assistance Self-Sufficiency program, making it somewhat inconsistent with earlier research.[15] Perhaps the clearest story was the difficulty program operators universally had in increasing the rate of participation in activities aimed at improving retention and advancement over the levels that control group individuals achieved on their own.

Since the ERA experience provides potentially valuable lessons for the design of future experimental studies, contrasting ERA with earlier studies with respect to design and findings is helpful. Particularly strong results come from studies where a single model is tested in multiple sites and where there are differential impact tests within sites aimed at contrasting the model with other contenders.[16] The JOBS evaluation represents this kind of case, and the Greater Avenues for Independence (GAIN) evaluation, though it lacked differential impact tests, did have a single underlying model with what proved to be important local variation. That the impacts were generally positive in these studies is important information. But studies without positive impacts can also produce strong evidence, for example, PESD—in which a reasonably uniform model failed to produce positive findings in any of four sites. For ERA, after the failure of PESD, we had no compelling model to test in multiple sites, nor did we have competing models in the field. We had little choice but to evaluate whatever programs the states developed.

Contrasting ERA with the Work/Welfare demonstration of the early 1980s is also useful. The goal of both was to capture state innovation at times of "letting a hundred flowers bloom." But the flowers were already blooming in 1981, whereas in 1998 seeds were just germinating. Neither examined programs based on a common underlying hypothesis. But in the earlier demonstration, four of the programs had some form of job search and work experience, in part because these were the two most significant AFDC work programs that Congress authorized welfare agencies to operate. Although not as focused as JOBS or GAIN, this core provided an important thread for the Work/Welfare demonstration, not only across the individual sites but also linking them to the earlier Azrin and Louisville Laboratory studies and the later JOBS and GAIN studies.

In addition to this thread in Work/Welfare, an important difference between it and ERA was that most of the former programs produced positive impacts, whereas most of the latter did not. The knowledge gains of Work/Welfare emerged in part from the fact that the programs' success implied that the choices of states generally led to improved employment outcomes for individuals and overall savings for governments. Thus AFDC work programs were proved a worthwhile investment, a conclusion that led directly to a large increase in funding in the Family Support Act. Although we cannot, of course, know in advance whether the programs will be successful in making such a choice, we should be aware that we are unlikely to learn much if there is no clear pattern of success or failure across sites. The success of evaluation is not whether the programs work but, rather, the utility of what we learn. A smattering of success in a sea of programmatic failure in a project where each site is unique is not very useful for informing program choices or for next steps in evaluation. In this sense, ERA produced little on which program operators could rely or to build a new study, having produced a clear pattern of neither success nor failure.

Enhanced Services for the Hard to Employ

How to improve employment outcomes for hard-to-employ welfare recipients was another priority need that states identified. A common view among states at that time was that, as the caseload decreased (by fiscal year 2000 the number of adult recipients had declined from 4.6 million in 1994 to less than 1.7 million) and the employment of single mothers rose, the proportion of the remaining caseload included increasing proportions of the hard to employ. There was the further perception that the strong emphasis on job search, which was successful with more readily employable recipients, was less suited for the harder to employ.

According to a number of studies examining the question of whether the caseload became more disadvantaged as it declined, little evidence has been found of major change toward greater disadvantage. Sheila Zedlewski and Donald Alderson (2001), for example, find no evidence of significantly greater disadvantage; Richard Bavier (2003) finds that this is so for several markers of disadvantage, but he also reports an increase in adults reporting a work-limiting health condition. Several plausible explanations have been advanced for this seemingly counterintuitive result. It may be that more-able parents did indeed leave to take a job but that less-able parents also left the rolls because they were unable, or unwilling, to meet the stricter worker requirements. It must also be kept in mind, as always, that the caseload under both AFDC and TANF was very dynamic, with families moving on and off the roles for reasons independent of any program. Thus state-level perceptions of a more disadvantaged caseload could have one of two causes. Since fewer individuals were either formally or informally exempt from work requirements than before, frontline workers were more often faced with the need to help them find jobs. The fact that no one is categorically exempt from the federal five-year lifetime limit has increased the pressure on welfare agencies to be successful with all recipients, irrespective of those perceived to be job ready.

With respect to the success of welfare-to-work programs for more disadvantaged parents (as well as other groups), research suggests—as we have discussed in previous chapters—that outcomes are unreliable indicators of impact, and the major syntheses discussed at the end of chapter 9 find that impacts for more-disadvantaged parents are comparable to those for less-disadvantaged ones. Thus there is good reason to engage hard-to-employ individuals in these activities. However, the same studies show that the outcomes for the more disadvantaged are lower. Thus if the hard-to-employ are only required to participate in common welfare-to-work activities, even though their outcomes are improved as much as those of the more advantaged, more of them will remain jobless. State perceptions were correct in seeing a problem regarding more-disadvantaged parents and that they needed additional tools to improve those employment outcomes.

Although launching a random assignment project to complement the ERA evaluation would clearly be a significant step in developing effectiveness information to assist states in their investment of federal and state funds, it would be several years before the needed funds became available. In fiscal years 2000 and 2001, my office would be spending a little over $4 million on the evaluations continued from section 1115 projects and the Five-State Child Impact study, down from almost $11 million in 1997. By fiscal year 2002, funding for these projects would be under $1 million. Although we had acquired some large new commitments, such as ERA, we had substantial room within the $15 million annual amount to fund a major initiative on hard-to-employ parents while still leaving many millions for the initiatives of an incoming administration. So in the summer of 2000 we began to scope out a project.

Although my office had launched ERA without a major funding partner, an evaluation of services for the hard-to-employ seemed to me a natural fit for another ASPE partnership. Approaching interventions for parents that could potentially improve child outcomes too would certainly appeal to ASPE staff, which continued to have a strong interest in such strategies. In fact, ASPE staff turned out to be a very easy sell. They were enthusiastic about the project and quickly added their own perspective—that some of the programs have an explicit two-generation approach with both elements aimed to improve adult outcomes and elements designed directly to improve child outcomes. We arranged a partnership team that would work on developing the project and a funding arrangement under which my office would fund two-thirds and ASPE one-third of the evaluation cost.

Timing was a problem, however, with the 2000 presidential election approaching. Beginning a procurement at the end of an administration that can be awarded only in a new administration is fraught with the risk that it will never actually get off the ground. Nonetheless, given the apparent broad consensus on the importance of the subject, and because the issue was high on the state information priority list, we proceeded to develop the project into the fall and winter of 2000–2001, knowing that the president and the party in power would be changing.

I made sure to inform the incoming transition team that the project was on the short list of priority decisions for OPRE that required a decision before the end of the fiscal year. As had happened on previous occasions when a new administration had arrived, the Senate confirmation process left me without a political supervisor until well into the summer of 2001. In addition, I had received no feedback on the project from either the transition team or other incoming political staff. Nonetheless, to prevent making the awarding of a contract within the fiscal year impossible, on May 4 we announced the procurement in the *Commerce Business Daily*, officially beginning the public procurement process.

On February 28 the president had announced his intention to nominate Wade Horn, the president of the National Fatherhood Initiative, to the post of assistant secretary for children and families. Since Horn would not be confirmed until July 25, and I would get no explicit direction from him until at least that time, I looked for clues about where he might stand on the project.

I was not entirely in the dark, since Horn had served in the George H. W. Bush administration as commissioner for children, youth, and families—the part of Administration for Children and Families that oversaw Head Start, foster care, and other related programs—and I knew from that experience that he was a strong believer in reliable evidence based on random assignment. A child psychologist by training with a strong background in experimental methods and statistics, he had launched a number of high-quality research projects as commissioner. He was also, and continues to be, enthusiastic about using experiments to provide credible evidence on the effectiveness of programs and policies. In June, he gave the keynote speech on welfare reform to an audience of state TANF directors, which added to my feeling that he might be favorably disposed. He spoke quite a bit about healthy marriage, his highest policy priority, but he also addressed the employment side of welfare reform. Most relevant to my concerns, he described the importance of effectively serving the hard-to-employ.

By mid-July, I began to think the unthinkable—awarding the contract for the Hard-to-Employ evaluation without further notification, including to

Horn after he was confirmed. I had started the process with the clear understanding that I was protecting a research opportunity, but I would never previously have completed a procurement without getting the explicit go-ahead
from whoever would become my supervisor (although the authority to go
ahead was delegated to me). Now I was beginning to question that approach.
Being an effective civil servant means being a loyal one, both institutionally
and to the person who is one's political superior; it means respecting the fact
that political officials are the decision makers who derive their authority from
the president whom the country had elected. By habit, I had already developed a sense of loyalty to Horn and had taken steps to protect his options,
including at least once to the potential detriment of my personal role in the
incoming administration. At the same time, I was becoming acutely aware
that effectively learning what works can only occur if the process is not subject
to every change in presidents or assistant secretaries. I began to think that
building knowledge requires loyalty too, and that this loyalty had to have a
place within loyalty to the democratic structure of our government.

These lofty abstractions on loyalty were, of course, accompanied by a long
list of more concrete interests. Most important, learning what were effective
services for the hard-to-employ was an important issue to a number of parties:
to parents who fell into that category, along with their children; to the welfare
reform agenda that required making work possible for as many parents as
possible; and to the states that were the engine of reform. Horn himself had
spoken eloquently about the subject. In addition, my office had invested a lot
in the procurement, as had the bidders. At a more mundane, personal level,
since I hated losing a good deal it would have annoyed me greatly if my office
had backed out after ASPE agreed to pay a third of the project costs, when I
knew ample funds would be available to build a research agenda for Horn that
he would like and that would further his goals. Finally, I believed I had done
my duty—I had used the transition process to alert the incoming administration to the impending procurement, and they had chosen either not to read
it or not to provide me any feedback. Thus I decided neither to stop the process nor to provide a final alert. On September 28, 2001, the department
signed a contract with the winning firm, MDRC.[17]

When Horn did find out we had awarded the contract, he was angry and
told me so. I defended myself, but I did feel uneasy about what I had done.
Being loyal had been helpful in achieving my career goals. My reputation for
loyalty had inspired a trust that had enabled me to do things that otherwise

would have been done by political staff and thereby to realize ambitions of my own. By this time I also knew my staff and I had valuable skills from which Horn would benefit, in effect making what I hoped would be ample reparations for my failure to be fully above board.[18] Furthermore, I knew that I was eligible to retire and planned to do so within a few years. To what extent was my previous loyalty based on principle and to what extent was it rooted in expediency? I shall never know the answer to that question and I am still uneasy about it, even though I do not regret the decision I made.

The Hard-to-Employ evaluation included four sites and five programs:

- In New York City, the evaluation design randomly assigned a sample of recently released offenders either to a subsidized employment program or to a control group.
- In Philadelphia, the evaluation design randomly assigned a sample of TANF recipients who had been on the rolls for more than twenty-four months to one of three groups: a treatment group assigned to a subsidized employment program (run by one provider); a second treatment group assigned to an intensive case management program (run by a different provider); or a control group.
- In Rhode Island, the evaluation design randomly assigned a group of parents on Medicaid who had previously undiagnosed depression either to a program that provided mental health services along with access to employment services or to a control group.
- In Kansas and Missouri, the evaluation design randomly assigned children whose parents were applying to a cluster of Early Head Start programs either to a two-generation program that supplemented its child development services to children with enhanced employment services to their parents or to a control group.

As in ERA, the programs were diverse; two programs do at least provide a similar service—transitional subsidized employment—although to different populations.

The final Hard-to-Employ report included analysis of these five programs as well as three from ERA (Butler et al. 2012).[19] There were no employment or earnings effects for the last three Hard-to-Employ programs. In the first two, the subsidized employment programs had initially positive impacts on employment and earnings, primarily as a result of the subsidized jobs, but these effects disappeared quickly after these jobs ended. Only one of the three ERA programs that targeted hard-to-employ individuals had significant employment impacts. The New York City Personal Roads to Individual Development and Employment program produced modest, sustained employment effects for its population of welfare recipients who had physical or mental health issues that prevented them from participating in regular welfare-to-work activities but were able to participate in modified alternatives. Some of the other programs affected other outcomes or had positive employment effects for a subgroup, but overall the results were discouraging from a programmatic perspective. Are they also discouraging from a knowledge-building objective?

In some respects, the problem is similar to that in ERA—a variety of different interventions, few of which were able to demonstrate employment and earnings gains. However, as with the positive impacts in ERA for the program that included financial incentives, the findings from the two subsidized employment programs in the Hard-to-Employ evaluation gain evidentiary value, because a number of other experiments have tested similar interventions. Beginning with the Supported Work demonstration and continuing through the 1980s, a series of evaluations generally found subsidized employment to be effective for women and less so, or not at all, for men (see, for example, Hollister [1984] on Supported Work; Barnow and Smith [2004] on the Job Training Partnership Act; and Bell, Burstein, and Orr [1987] on the AFDC Homemaker–Home Health Aide demonstration).

For the former-offender population, for example, the very weak, short-term earnings effects for released prisoners in the Hard-to-Employ evaluation are consistent with the findings in Supported Work for a similar population. Furthermore, findings from a project funded by the Joyce Foundation that examined four subsidized employment prisoner reentry programs also failed to find sustained earnings effects (Redcross et al. 2010). Thus the Hard-to-Employ findings add further weight to the concern that subsidized employment approaches may not be an effective employment strategy for the former-prisoner population.

For women, interpreting the lack of positive effects of subsidized employment in the Hard-to-Employ evaluation is more complicated, since previous tests of subsidized employment found positive effects for them. There are, however, substantial programmatic differences between the Hard-to-Employ and the earlier programs. One hypothesis for why this program was unsuccessful is that the time spent in a subsidized job in the Hard-to-Employ program was much shorter than in the earlier ones. The underlying theory of transitional subsidized employment is that it can overcome a lack of previous work experience and thus lead to greater future work. But although an individual could remain in a subsidized job up to six months, the average treatment group member in the Philadelphia program worked fifteen days in a subsidized job compared to nine and one-half months for the average welfare mother in Supported Work (Jacobs and Bloom 2011; MDRC Board of Directors 1980).[20] Furthermore, this modest amount of additional work in the Hard-to-Employ program was an increment to a much more substantial work history than AFDC mothers in Supported Work had going into that program. The earlier program included only mothers who had worked less than six months in the previous six years, while 55 percent of those in the more recent program had more than six months of work experience in just the past three years, with an average of ten months for the entire treatment group.[21] Thus in Supported Work the additional work experience was approximately one and one-half times the maximum amount a treatment group member had worked in the past six years, whereas in the Philadelphia program it was a small fraction of what the average treatment group member worked in the past three years alone. Based on this comparison, it is not surprising that the results in Philadelphia were different from Supported Work as the two were significantly different interventions applied to significantly different populations. In addition, given the theory of subsidized employment, the nature of these differences suggests that the later program would have weaker effects on employment than the earlier one. It is also possible that other different circumstances, such as the quality of the work experience, explain the lack of impact on this group. We cannot know the answer without further experiments with other programs—for example, those that include longer time in subsidized jobs.[22] All this, of course, further reinforces the notion that evidentiary strength is built not just on a single experiment or project but through a coherent agenda that accumulates findings from high-quality, rigorous studies over time and space.

Considering the ERA and Hard-to-Employ Findings Together

Given the variety of programs tested, it is not surprising that there is no clear answer to why only four of the twenty programs evaluated in ERA and Hard-to-Employ had significant persistent earnings impacts. Richard Hendra et al.

(2010) conclude that the programs that were unsuccessful were unable to create more than a small treatment differential beyond the control group. In some cases, especially where individuals in the control group were on TANF at some point, this was attributable to participation levels in standard welfare-to-work activities that the treatment group was unable to improve on. In other cases, particularly in more voluntary settings outside TANF, participation rates were low for both treatment and controls. The small treatment-control differentials were also true of the unsuccessful ERA programs that David Butler et al. (2012) analyze. The Rhode Island mental health program as well as the Kansas-Missouri Early Head Start program also were unable to create an employment service differential, although in these two cases both failed operationally to integrate a significant self-sufficiency component. Finally, I have suggested that a possible explanation of the two subsidized employment programs' lack of persistent employment or earnings impacts was their limited duration.

Does this provide the basis for answers to why the findings of the later studies are so much more disappointing than the earlier ones? I think they at least suggest some reasonable conjectures. The findings make it plausible that the very success of the kinds of programs in the earlier studies that have now been widely implemented has in part made later success more difficult. The high rate of mandatory control services suggests that some of the later interventions needed to jump a higher hurdle created by the earlier ones. In addition, except for a few of the Hard-to-Employ programs, the ever-employed rate over the follow-up period was in the 75 to 90 percent range, not including the programs targeted on employed individuals, where it frequently approached 100 percent.

However, other of the studies' findings suggests that this is not the whole story. Despite the high rates just described, except for a few programs that targeted those already employed, average quarterly employment was much lower, typically in the 40 to 50 percent range. This lower ongoing employment rate contributed to the control groups' annual unemployment insurance earnings (again with a few exceptions) that were typically below $10,000, and often only about half that amount. This suggests that the situation Nancye Campbell described at the initiation of PESD still persists—the welfare system has learned how to get many individuals to go to work, but it has not figured out how to help them stay employed or advance. It may be that the lack of success of the great majority of the ERA and Hard-to-Employ programs derives from two circumstances: the inclusion of control group work activities raised the bar, and the later programs were attempting to deal with deeper problems of human capital. Persisting in work as well as finding jobs with higher pay and more hours most likely requires stronger soft and hard skills than many low-income parents possess; the tested programs were simply insufficient in intensity and duration to address these lacks. The substantial success achieved earlier came from two decades of implementation that changed the incentives for being on welfare by imposing mandatory work requirements and taught relatively simple skills, such as how to look for work effectively, and this was what led to their achieving modest, relatively sustained positive effects on employment and earnings. They were also able to do it at relatively modest cost. It may be that demonstrating success at the next level will simply be more difficult and possibly require a greater investment in both time and dollars.[23] The studies briefly described in the next section will begin to provide evidence that goes beyond such conjecture.

I retired from OPRE and the federal government in January 2004, after we had made the choice of study sites but before findings were available for either ERA or Hard-to-Employ.

After ERA and Hard-to-Employ: The Next Cohort of Studies

ERA and Hard-to-Employ are not the end of the line, and a number of successor studies are under way. One of the larger studies, and one in which I am very involved—Innovative Strategies for Increasing Self-Sufficiency (ISIS)—is being conducted by Abt Associates for OPRE.[24] The study is intended to build on one of the goals of ERA, using a random assignment evaluation to gain further knowledge about how to help low-income adults advance in the workforce. Many of the lessons we describe in previous chapters influenced the design of ISIS. For example, following the JOBS evaluation model—learning a few things well—rather than the more diffuse ERA and Hard-to-Employ projects, ISIS is focused on evaluating programs with a common underlying conceptual framework. In addition, the project will be systematically involved with the field of policy and practice throughout, as was so much of the work described in this book. As we go to press, ISIS sites are early in random assignment, making it too soon to tell how well we will apply these lessons and what the consequences will be.

Substantively, the "few things" ISIS aims to learn about well are the effects of career pathways programs, a cluster of innovations that have developed over the past two decades. Career pathways interventions are human capital development strategies whose goal is to raise individuals' earnings through skills and credentials imparted in a series of manageable steps in high-demand occupations. The skills tested in these programs typically include occupational-specific skills with strong links to employers; employment-related soft skills, such as developing effective relationships with supervisors and co-workers; and life skills, such as managing time and money. Unlike the Human Capital stream of the JOBS evaluation, which focused on improving basic skills, career pathways programs (while often including remediation of these skills) universally include occupation-specific training. Although career pathways programs grew out of a context broader than that of the welfare-to-work programs, considering them in the programmatic context of the JOBS program helps illuminate these new programs along with how ISIS represents a next cohort of study.

The basic causal hypothesis underlying JOBS was that at least half the adults on welfare without high school credentials were prevented from establishing themselves in the workforce because of shortcomings in their basic mathematical and reading skills. Thus remediating these skills deficits was a necessary step to improving earnings outcomes. Of course, it was also notable that welfare parents typically lacked occupation-specific skills as well. Why wasn't that absence more of a consideration in JOBS? I think the primary reason was the perspective that improving basic skills for adults was a separate, isolated first step and a prerequisite for acquiring occupational skills. Programs that aimed at providing occupational skill training had eligibility cutoffs for basic skills that precluded the vast majority of welfare adults from qualifying for them. Although human capital development is certainly much broader than the basic education remediation programs studied in the JOBS evaluation, these remedial programs captured much of what the vast majority of welfare recipients could access at the time.[25]

The career pathways approach is rooted in three facts: for most low-income workers, advancing in the workforce requires gaining occupational skills; many of these individuals voluntarily undertake training and education to improve their employment prospects; but very few actually complete enough of it to improve their economic outlook.[26] Particularly in community colleges, which have increasingly taken on the role of providing workforce development training and education services for adult and other nontraditional students, raising completion rates has become an important goal. Career pathways innovations tackle this goal through changes in instruction, such as integrating the teaching of basic and occupational skills, contextualizing basic skills training, and accelerating training, as well as other approaches to accommodate adult learners who often have to earn enough to support a family while attending school. In addition to innovations in the delivery of education and training, career pathways programs are linked closely to economic development, focusing their occupational training in growth areas with skill shortages. Finally, comprehensive career pathways programs provide strong systems of support—ranging from intensive career counseling to financial assistance, including help with tuition and other training costs, child care, and even in some cases, stipends.[27]

The ISIS evaluation is not the only such study in the field. A large number of other random assignment evaluations are focusing on programs aimed at increasing employment and earnings for disadvantaged youth and adults. The Department of Labor is currently funding five randomized trials of such programs, for example.[28] OPRE is funding random assignment evaluations, or designs for them, in five employment-related areas in addition to ISIS.[29] Abt Associates, Mathematica Policy Research, and MDRC have continued to be major evaluators in this area, conducting not only most of the Department of Labor and HHS projects but also foundation-funded efforts. MDRC has been particularly active in initiating and implementing projects in community colleges that have many elements in common with career pathways programs.

Convergence and Divergence from Experimental Welfare Reform Evaluation

In addition to the goal of increasing employment and earnings, all but one of these HHS and Department of Labor studies share another strong commonality—few of their target populations are exclusively welfare populations.[30] The shift of experimental research away from welfare is a consequence of the huge decline in the number of low-income parents receiving assistance. This has had two important, related consequences. First, much of the effort to discover what was effective in increasing welfare recipients' employment outcomes was motivated by an interest in decreasing welfare dependency; that end has, for the most part, been accomplished. Second, whereas AFDC was an effective gateway program for providing employment services to low-income parents, TANF is much less so. Reaching a broad swath of low-income parents to help them stabilize and advance in the world of work requires efforts outside the cash assistance system.

NEXT STEPS

The story told in this book began in the mid-1970s with the National Supported Work demonstration. Although HHS was involved with the demonstration, particularly as it related to welfare recipients, the Department of Labor was the primary actor. This continued with the WIN (Work Incentive) Laboratory project. The Work/Welfare demonstration followed, with MDRC, state welfare agencies, and then HHS becoming prime actors over the next decade and a half. Sometimes this involved waivers, but often it did not. With 1996 welfare reform and the subsequent sharp declines in welfare caseloads, the wheel has turned again. Welfare populations are no longer the main disadvantaged population in need of employment help, and efforts to understand experimentally how best to help low-income youth and adults have turned their focus to this broader population. Three federal departments are in the lead: OPRE has expanded its population of interest to low-income parents more generally; Department of Labor support for random assignment studies has reemerged; and OMB has strongly supported both. This completes our story in a certain sense, since experimental research on welfare reform is again not the leading force for learning about effective employment programs for low-income parents. The wheel can turn again, of course, but nothing is in sight to make that likely in the foreseeable future.

In chapter 12 Judy and I conclude the main book with the major overall lessons from our story that may prove useful to those working to extend the use of random assignment evaluations to help improve social policy in non-welfare areas. Judy's coda then pursues the reasons why much of the ivory tower was reluctant to embrace random assignment experimentation as an evaluation tool for most of our story, and how that reluctance has been changing over the past two decades.

CHAPTER 12

Conclusion and Lessons*

In the preceding chapters, we tell of our long struggle to show that a relatively untried technique—large-scale, random assignment experiments (the social policy analogue to clinical trials in medicine)—could be used to answer important questions about complex social programs. We also show that the results were considered singularly credible and, in part because of that, were judged by some to have an outsized impact on policy and practice.

Our story is about one policy area—welfare reform—as viewed through the lens of two institutions that worked independently and in interaction with others to promote this method and to build a coherent and useful body of evidence. During the telling, we discuss lessons we learned along the way about the strategies that fostered success—lessons we hope will prove useful in other fields and other contexts. The recent explosion of interest in the general approach by public officials and researchers in the United States and elsewhere, as discussed in Judy's coda to our book, makes us optimistic in this regard.

WHAT WAS LEARNED

The forty-five years of experiments produced insights about programs, policies, research methods, research management, and effective strategies to build support and disseminate results. Three of our findings shape the lessons.

*Chapter 12 authored by Judith M. Gueron and Howard Rolston.

Large-Scale Field Experiments Are Feasible

Random assignment proved to be feasible in a range of contexts and forms: from relatively small researcher-controlled pilot projects, to larger-scale real-world demonstrations operated in partnership with states and communities, to full-scale statewide initiatives; from simple designs that allocate people to a test program or control group to more complex ones with multiple groups and levels of randomization.

This may now seem obvious. But proving it, as we recount, met with sustained resistance from adversaries at the state and county levels, among federal officials, and between governors and Washington. The fight involved, at different times, program operators, politicians, advocates, and academic researchers—arguing that such studies were some combination of unnecessary, uninformative, undoable, unethical or illegal, too burdensome, or too expensive. Had it not been for the courage of state welfare officials, the money from foundations and government that paid for the studies and (in the case of foundations) for their dissemination, the few academics who actively supported this work from the start, and the converts among congressional and state legislative staff and in advocacy groups who gave their commitment and their time, particular battles (or perhaps the fight) could have been lost.

And then, beginning in the late 1980s, three changes shifted the momentum in favor of random assignment: the visibility and prestige of the completed experiments and, as a result, the participating states; the successful five-year (1987–1992) struggle by the Department of Health and Human Services (HHS) and the Office of Management and Budget (OMB) to make random assignment the quid pro quo for obtaining federal approval of waivers in exchange for giving states the flexibility to launch state-based reforms; and a slowly gathering momentum among academics in support of randomized trials, which picked up speed in the early 2000s.

Experiments Answered Important Questions

Experiments tested most of the major welfare reform proposals advanced during these years and the theories and hypotheses that underpinned them. The findings were often unpredictable, sometimes counterintuitive—findings that would not have been credible without the control group experience. There are several reasons why.

For one thing, confounding the fears of some scholars and many skeptics that random assignment would always result in findings of no effect,[1] the majority of the welfare area studies found program-induced changes that passed the tests of statistical significance and, in some cases, policy significance. For single mothers (the largest group on welfare), almost all the reforms increased employment and most also reduced welfare receipt. But the reforms did not work miracles. Because of low wages and the formula that cut welfare benefits when people went to work, few strategies substantially increased income or reduced poverty. Chapter 10 reflects on the reasons why impacts were generally modest.

In addition, most reforms proved effective for a broad range of welfare recipients (from the least to the most employable); others made the most difference for the more disadvantaged but still left more of them on welfare and not employed. The clearest pattern was that impacts were greater for women than for men, who generally were more successful in getting jobs on their own. Related to this, programs and groups of people with higher outcomes (for example, those who got a job) often had no higher or even lower impacts (those who got a job as a result of the test program). Thus, programs placed more men than women in jobs, for example, but, since men were also more likely to get jobs on their own, programs were more likely to help women. In such cases, outcomes-based performance measures would send a false signal and lead to wasted funds and less effective programs.

Furthermore, there was the unexpected discovery that the up-front outlay on some welfare reform programs (particularly the lower-cost or more work-focused ones) was more than offset by tangible dollar savings within a few years. This evidence that some reforms really were investments with a quick payoff (through reduced welfare and other benefits and increased taxes as people went to work) resonated with budgeters and politicians. It also meant that, even if controls eventually caught up with people in the program, the savings were already banked.

It was also the case that different approaches had differential success in reaching different goals. Mandatory welfare-to-work programs usually increased work, reduced dependency, and often saved money but had almost no effect on poverty and did not benefit (or harm) children. In contrast, programs designed to make work pay (for example, by supplementing the earnings of low-wage workers) increased income (sometimes substantially) and improved the school performance of young children, although they cost more. This and other trade-offs explain why, depending on their goals, people reached different conclusions on whether particular strategies succeeded or failed.

As described in chapters 8 and 9, the Greater Avenues for Independence (GAIN) and Job Opportunities and Basic Skills Training (JOBS) evaluations together, along with subsequent syntheses that relied heavily on those two studies, provided strong evidence that more work-focused programs, involving a mix of activities but with a substantial job search component, had larger effects than programs focused on remedial education. The combination of the head-to-head treatment tests, along with the large number of single treatment–control tests of programs emphasizing basic education or getting a job quickly, was central to the strength of this body of evidence. These findings were counterintuitive to many—especially, as in the JOBS evaluation, the work-focused programs cost only about 60 percent of the cost of programs stressing remedial education. Another important point was that many of the findings were replicated (not identically, but consistently) as reform approaches were adapted across diverse sites and for small, mid-sized, and full-scale, statewide programs. At least for welfare-to-work programs, scaling up did not seem to reduce effectiveness.

Finally, although the effectiveness and cost findings were the centerpiece, they were not the only type of evidence (or even the most important) that would matter to policy makers. We always viewed the random assignment design as the skeleton on which to build an evaluation that used multiple techniques to address a broader range of questions—including those raised by practitioners and managers, and by researchers who used different methods to diagnose the problems and understand why people behave as they do and how social programs work in practice. It was clear from the start that the funders and state and local partners would not have been satisfied if all they got was a yes or no answer. They cared about why program participants and managers behaved as they did, why programs were or were not successfully implemented, and what could be done to improve the results.

High-Quality Evidence Mattered

Advocates for experiments were not naïve about the likelihood either that these studies would determine policy or that they should. Given the highly charged atmosphere around welfare leading up to the elimination of Aid to Families with Dependent Children (AFDC) in 1996, we knew that research would be a minor element at best in a highly value-laden and political debate. Nonetheless, an important rationale for the investment was the belief that policy makers could distinguish—and might privilege—experimental findings and that more sensible and effective policies could be formulated if they had access to reliable evidence on whether particular approaches would advance sought-after goals, and at what cost. Without it, they would be largely groping in the dark, relying on opinions, prejudices, anecdotes, and weak data.

Surprisingly, as recounted in chapter 6, by 1988 a substantial number of people concluded that the welfare experiments had shifted thinking and contributed to at least a temporary consensus that led to that year's round of legislation. They generally attributed this to the following factors: the political climate that made action possible; the credibility, content, and timeliness of the findings; and the forceful, nontechnical, evenhanded, and media-savvy character of their dissemination.

The widespread visibility and acceptance of the results—and the discrediting of alternatives—prompted a variety of people to agree that the experiments had an unusual impact on federal and state policy, while acknowledging that politics and values continued to play a more decisive role. In part as a result, experiments went from being rare tests pushed by a small number of true believers to the preferred approach for evaluating small- and full-scale programs. (See chapters 6, 8, and 9 for an extended discussion of the role of the experiments in the 1988 and 1996 legislation.)

STRATEGIES THAT PROMOTE EXPERIMENTS AND INFORM POLICY

That there were some welfare experiments is not surprising. During the same years there were also important experiments in programs for unemployed workers, low-income youth, former offenders, people with health problems, and preschool children. What is surprising is the number, continuity (the longest uninterrupted history of large-scale experiments), and cohesion of the opus of work that emerged.

Overarching Lessons

In recent years, interest has increased in other countries and fields—notably in education and development economics—in using experiments to determine effectiveness. Because the welfare story is viewed as particularly promising, we are often asked what explains the scores of reliable experiments, the sustained funding, the state and local involvement, and the impact on policy and practice. Although the welfare experience provides no algorithm for success, it does reveal the contextual factors, incentives, strategies, and skills (on the front line and within the halls of government) that paved the way to success and sustained momentum.

CREATE A LEARNING COMMUNITY The central factor that sustained forty-five years of random assignment studies was creation of a community—of researchers, welfare administrators and other public officials, funders, advocates, and state and federal legislative staff—that recognized and valued the distinctive credibility of such studies. Large-scale evaluations and demonstrations do not happen without deliberate entrepreneurship. People at HHS, OMB, the Department of Labor, MDRC, and other research firms, in varying degrees and at different times, showed the initiative and had the resources and technical skills required to pull off experiments. To succeed, however, they needed allies to provide the venue, overcome the obstacles, defend the method, and support the endeavor.

In our view, the most important group—the main heroes in this book—were the state and local administrators who displayed the courage, determination, and political skill needed to put their programs on the line, and in some cases, win the battles that erupted when we sought to open up real-world programs to a new type of scrutiny. This support was unexpected and far from universal. Federal and foundation officials could fund research, but they were rarely in a position to ensure access to programs and their staff or to welfare recipients. The people responsible for such programs had to agree to participate: they had to perceive that the rewards exceeded the clear risks of cooperation.

During the years when welfare was most contentious, there was logic to being reticent. Randomization involved unknown political and public relations risks and burdens: it interfered with normal operations by substituting a lottery for the prerogative to choose whom to serve; it was an a priori admission that you did not know whether a reform would work; and it produced results that were usually so cut and dried they were hard to fight or fudge. A welfare commissioner involved in such a study could no longer sell his or her achievements using familiar outcome-based performance data (long used as a management tool) but instead risked hearing about the inevitably more modest—and possibly even negative—impacts. Finally, there was the threat of public attack and negative publicity from participating in "scientific" research involving human subjects.

Yet some busy and often much maligned state officials agreed to—and in a few cases even sought out—random assignment evaluations. Sometimes, as we discuss in earlier chapters, they did this because they thought it would help them obtain the federal waivers they needed to operate their proposed reforms. In many of the major studies, however, the more important reasons were that they wanted to learn the truth (and did not think results from other states would be enough), thought it was the right thing to do, hoped it would give their state and governor a place in the national spotlight and an opportunity to contribute to national policy, and had come to see that the burden on staff would be less than they originally feared.[2]

A second critical group was private funders. Large-scale experiments cost money, and the federal government had not only the deepest pockets but also the most logical role, since research is a poster child for what economists call public goods (in that people can benefit from the studies without paying for them). However, the welfare story had more than one angel. In the early 1980s, as we describe in chapters 4 and 5, Washington took time out from funding most social policy research, and experiments were kept alive and substantively advanced by the Ford Foundation. The foundation's role went beyond money. It not only had launched Supported Work but, in a rare demonstration of leverage and of the value of sticking with an issue and an organization, gave MDRC a total of $11.6 million in three challenge grants that, over fifteen years, became the catalyst to create seventeen major experiments and numerous related research and technical assistance projects that collectively produced $42 million in matching funds. These challenge grants provided MDRC with flexibility and independence: the ability to be proactive in identifying and shaping evaluations of state initiatives and launching multisite demonstrations of new approaches, an opportunity to study strategies and issues that did not match Washington's priorities, and some clout in negotiations over publication rights. In later years, many other foundations also supported this work and, because their staff usually wanted to see a connection between their funding and benefits to low-income people, encouraged a focus on understanding how to improve programs and on producing information useful to practitioners. Collectively, this foundation funding helped MDRC resist becoming a hired gun for the feds or the states.

Individuals in government and other types of institutions also played vital roles: the initially small circle of academics who actively endorsed the experimental method as superior and ethical; people in some national advocacy groups who convinced hostile local advocates that rigorous evaluations could be a powerful tool to identify and defend worthwhile social investments; federal and state executive and legislative branch officials and staff who fought for the method (including against the periodic threats to its legality), defended the findings, pushed for the resources that nurtured this field, and as the ultimate sign of support sometimes wrote random assignment into law; and at critical times Senator Daniel Patrick Moynihan, who valued impacts and understood the reasons for modest effects, going so far as to dub Judy, in an obviously two-sided compliment, "Our Lady of Modest but Positive Results" (*New York Times,* March 9, 1993).

Several forces helped build this constituency. One was evolution within the research community. Although few of the people involved in the first experiments started as true believers, over the course of multiple evaluations, conferences, articles, and debates about research methods, a core group (located in firms practicing this craft, a few federal agencies, and universities) emerged that shared an unwavering commitment to random assignment as the clearest way to find the truth and isolate research from political pressures. We became convinced that, given the set of research issues at hand, there was a gold standard, that it was attainable, that it really could help build and defend better policy, and that its rigor and transparency helped it rise above politics.[3] We also became convinced, by the high-profile panels and studies mentioned in earlier chapters,[4] that the alternative was a methodological morass. However, for the first few decades, we played an embattled game. With little vocal support among academics (who in the thirty-five years following the negative-income-tax experiments were never the entrepreneurs behind major welfare experiments), and seeking not to scare off state administrators, we tried to mask the lack of consensus. As discussed in the coda that follows this chapter, during the first decade of the twenty-first century, this changed dramatically.

A second factor fostering this community was the potentially high cost of ignorance. Until 1996, welfare was an open-ended entitlement. Any eligible single mother could apply for aid and get benefits that were set and partially paid for by the states. The lack of any cap on expenditures, combined with bursts of increasing costs, meant that smart federal and state budget officials kept a close eye on reform efforts. Because they would pay for mistakes, they had a direct stake in high-quality information on whether proposed changes would save or cost money.[5] Federal budget staff were particularly quick to respond to the emerging evidence that random assignment was feasible and that reliance on outcome data and nonexperimental estimates was potentially misleading. As a result, OMB staff pushed for experiments to measure the fiscal impact of state reforms, and staff at the Congressional Budget Office favored experimental estimates in costing out federal proposals.

Third, since welfare supports some of the nation's poorest families, welfare policy has always echoed values and attitudes about equity, social justice, responsibility, and the role of women, all viewed through the prism of class and race. People who cared about issues of poverty and child well-being—not only in government but also in foundations, advocacy groups, think tanks, and research centers—were interested in ways to restructure the system to better assist these families. Some of them saw building, using, and endorsing evidence of effectiveness as one means to defend or resist policy change.

A final factor was the conscious style adopted by MDRC and HHS to promote this community. After concluding that the stealth approach used during the Supported Work demonstration had failed to build a constituency for the results, MDRC sought to involve the diverse audiences for its work (including academics) as partners in all stages of projects, from initial design to ultimate dissemination. The Department of Health and Human Services reacted similarly. Whereas its early experiments tested demonstrations of new initiatives, where random assignment was less contentious, HHS became acutely aware of the need to build allies and promote community as it applied the section 1115 waiver quid pro quo.

Although some of these supportive elements may not exist in other fields, people advocating for experiments now have two advantages we did not have in the 1970s through 1990s: a clear track record of success (making it harder to argue that it cannot be done) and the increase in academic support.

BUILD A PROGRAM OF RANDOM ASSIGNMENT STUDIES What gave power to the welfare experiments was logic and relevance. Although people in Howard's parts of HHS and at MDRC did not start out with a plan to create a coherent body of evidence about a range of policy alternatives, by the late 1980s they had each begun to think strategically about building knowledge that would inform policy. For the next twenty years, although other research firms played central roles implementing experiments, these two organizations crafted the agenda and shared an ambition to make sure new studies were accretive, substantively and methodologically. Working separately (to avoid conflicts of interest), we more or less consciously circled around each other, reaching out to the same intellectual community to identify the issues and inviting states and foundations in as partners. The result was not just a large number of experiments but a logical sequence of evaluations and demonstrations—each taking off from what went before and collectively addressing the rapidly shifting context, in the process generating the momentum that supported further experiments.

This evolution was both broad and deep. Some experiments assessed single activities (for example, Supported Work) and others comprehensive system reform; some approaches (for example, job search assistance) were tested at small, middle, and full scale; others (for example, work-first programs focused on moving people into jobs quickly) were assessed first by comparing impacts in different counties (as in GAIN) and then more rigorously by randomly assigning people to this or an education-first approach run in the same offices; some were tested immediately at large scale; some (for example, financial incentives) were clusters of related models run in different locations.

One important element that enabled MDRC and HHS to lead the building of this program was that each had access to, and control of, money. Although control of resources is not sufficient for leadership, it is a necessity. Taking any federal research budget for granted is dangerous, but setting priorities and funding work consistent with those priorities is a common function of the national government. More uncommon was MDRC's actively and consistently seeking private resources to independently create elements of the research agenda that were of little or no interest to the federal government at the time. For the welfare research agenda, this proactive stance was particularly important in the evaluation of community work experience programs, which the Reagan administration consciously avoided initiating (chapters 4 and 5), and later in the decade, assessment of the effects of financial incentives, which certainly was not initially an HHS priority (chapter 10). Whereas for the most part the other major research firms primarily relied on successfully competing for work that was part of HHS's agenda, MDRC was able to set priorities for an independent, though strongly complementary, agenda.

A number of specific factors fostered this history and investment. The first was sustained leadership. The relatively small number of people in research firms and government who advocated for and implemented the studies stuck around for thirty-five years, in some cases in positions from which they had access to the emerging lessons, could identify the substantive and methodological gaps, and could to some extent drive the process. In doing this, they were supported by a succession of leaders (particularly at HHS, OMB, the Department of Labor, and the Ford Foundation) and by longtime staff in Congress and congressional agencies. In the federal government, the combination of continuity of civil servants and, for the most part, support of political leadership led to not only the large number of experimental studies but also their cohering into an advancing agenda.

The second factor was the open-ended AFDC funding structure in the pre-1996 years, which not only encouraged state reform and fostered an interest in evaluation but had another, more obscure benefit. Because investing in research was deemed a permissible administrative cost, there was an uncapped source of matching federal funds to help pay for state-sponsored evaluations.

The third factor was the success in producing important and, at least in some cases, encouraging findings, thereby creating momentum both for reform and for applying random assignment to the big questions left unanswered. In addition, aside from the early Reagan years, experiments were seldom viewed as a Republican or Democratic tool, but an objective yardstick that garnered cross-party support.

The fourth factor was continuous attention to ethics. Despite occasional horrendous explosions against their efforts, the people involved were committed enough to the endeavor, and convinced of the morality of the practices they had devised, to fight the name-calling and to prevail. We were fortunate that various groups in the learning community supported testing ways to make welfare more effective: for example, when early studies showed that simply requiring people to look for a job (job search) was not helping enough very disadvantaged recipients get jobs, some people pushed for strategies emphasizing basic education; when welfare-to-work programs got more people to work but not out of poverty, others argued for incentives to make work pay. Although the pressure was often for reform not research, many came to view experiments as one tool to gather the evidence needed to advance these policy goals.

Finally, our story unfolded in a context that created both opportunities and an audience for evaluation. Most notably, the gubernatorial competition for welfare reform leadership prompted a variety of state initiatives that could be seized on to address important options. MDRC's challenge grant structure capitalized on that dynamic.

MAKE IT A CONTINUOUS LEARNING PROCESS   The forty-five years of welfare evaluations produced clear generations that addressed new, emerging questions. But the welfare agenda is not just a story about a series of evaluations of novel ideas and programs. New questions are vital to a living research agenda, but the return of old ones in a new guise is also a sign of strength. The incentive issue is a prime example. The income maintenance experiments (during the late 1960s and 1970s) explored in depth the question of financial incentives—how the treatment of earnings in determining benefits affects employment behavior. After that, the incentive issue lay dormant for more than a decade. But in the early 1990s, MDRC and the state of Minnesota, Canada, and Milwaukee's New Hope program brought it back to life in a new form (incentives conditioned on work) and examined not only the labor supply response but also the effect on poverty and children. Similarly, the Department of Labor undertook experimental research on job search assistance in the 1970s, and MDRC and HHS extended this research into the 1980s and beyond. Numerous rigorous studies support the effectiveness of job search, and it is a now near universal ingredient of welfare-to-work and more general employment programs. But the question of the relative effectiveness of different job search assistance strategies has not been explored in thirty years. During that time, major changes in the working population and the economy have occurred, raising the question of whether the findings from those studies pertain to our current situation. In 2011, the Office of Planning, Research, and Evaluation (OPRE), in the HHS Administration for Children and Families (ACF) awarded a contract to design an experimental study of the relative effectiveness of different job search strategies.

A vibrant research agenda not only produces credible information for the use of program operators and policy makers; it also provides the opportunity to advance the efficiency and productivity of the studies themselves. Although one of the great virtues of experiments is their conceptual simplicity, designing and implementing high-quality random assignment studies to maximize their value is not simple. The welfare research agenda developed studies with increasing value by improving a number of their dimensions. Two important areas where significant improvements occurred were in measurement and in synthesizing findings across studies.

A key breakthrough in measurement was MDRC's adoption of estimating employment and earnings impacts using existing unemployment insurance wage records. Use of unemployment insurance records dramatically reduced the cost of measuring these main outcomes over surveys (although at the cost of losing detailed information available about particular jobs, such as hourly wages). In addition, because unemployment insurance records cover such a broad swath of employment and are thus semi-universal, their use reduced the potential for attrition bias.[6]

A second measurement advance was more refined assessment of the characteristics of programs, with respect to both treatment and control conditions. The best way to get "inside the black box" to understand what aspects of a treatment are efficacious is a design that tests treatment variants directly against one another (a multiarm design); in this regard, no subsequent welfare experiment has approached the original income maintenance experiments. However, short of random assignment to multiple treatments, understanding as well as possible what the treatment group was exposed to and how it contrasts with the experience of the control group (single-arm design) can provide insight into what may be causally active. Even with multiarm studies (for example, Labor Force Attachment Versus Human Capital Development in the JOBS evaluation, see chapter 9), we need to characterize the treatment and treatment-control contrast in detail in order to say what produced the impacts we estimate. Here a major breakthrough was in the GAIN evaluation, followed by including the same measures in the JOBS evaluation and Project Independence. Measuring the treatment well can also produce evidence that is not simply interpreting impact results but can inform other policy questions. For example, MDRC's analysis of rates of participation in the Saturation Work Initiative Model illuminated what level of participation standards the federal government can expect of states.

The JOBS evaluation was important in improving measurement in two additional areas—baseline characteristics and child outcomes. Although the overall search for what works for whom tended to support the perspective that the programs had quite similar impacts (but not outcomes) for almost all groups, this was a convincing answer in part because of the richness of the characteristics information that the Private Opinion Survey captured on the research group. The one group for which the programs did not have positive impacts, those at risk of psychological depression, was also identified from the survey. Measuring child outcomes in order to estimate effects not only on parents but also on their young children, the second breakthrough measurement tool of the JOBS evaluation, quickly spread to other studies and formed the basis for understanding the effects of welfare reforms on children.

Viewed narrowly, typically what we learn about rigorously in an experiment is the effect of the treatment-control differentials to which the specific subjects of random assignment were exposed. In the rare case in which we randomly selected a representative group of sites, we learn much more: namely, what the average effects would have been for the population of sites from which we drew our sample. To move beyond the specificity of the typical findings, we must resort either to a more informal narrative approach or to nonexperimental methods to augment experimental impact estimates. Although the best we can do in most cases is the former, in the welfare studies three important examples of the latter—Charles Michalopoulos and Christine Schwartz's (2001) multiprogram subgroup analysis, David Greenberg and Andreas Cebulla's (2005) meta-analysis, and Howard Bloom, Carolyn Hill, and James Riccio's (2003) multilevel model (all described in chapter 9)— stand out.

The third study is particularly striking, not only in terms of its findings, but in its imaginative use of data that were not collected with multilevel analysis in mind. The contrast between MDRC's original analysis of the GAIN data (Riccio, Friedlander, and Freedman 1994) and the later one is remarkable. The initial analysis is able only to examine patterns of impacts in relationship to site characteristics. It is appropriately cautious about the analysis, saying that the results should be regarded as "suggestive, not conclusive." At the time of the original analysis, multilevel modeling was just beginning to emerge from its infancy, and less than a decade later Bloom, Hill, and Riccio (2003) use the same data (along with comparable data collected in the JOBS evaluation and Project Independence) in a much more powerful way and draw much stronger conclusions.

In addition to these general lessons, each of us has drawn up our own list of more specific lessons. Judy originally published hers fifteen years ago (Gueron 1997); it is striking that a decade and a half later the list is still current. Although it reflects her experience at MDRC, much of the list equally reflects Howard's experience at HHS. The major exceptions are her communication lessons, which grew out of the unique role MDRC played in communicating findings to policy makers, practitioners, and the news media. Because we both strongly affirm the importance of the first fifteen lessons,

Howard focuses on additional lessons that are more narrowly relevant to his experience at HHS.

Lessons from MDRC: Structuring Research to Inform Policy*

Over the years, MDRC has been judged particularly successful in structuring and sharing research in ways that inform policy and practice. As earlier chapters show, this was fostered by the fruitful tension between its in-house operations and research staff and by the two parts of its mission: to learn what works to improve the well-being of low-income people and to actively communicate the findings so as to enhance effectiveness. As a result, we were not in the business of proving the potential of a methodology per se. We were interested in experiments as a means to an end: gaining important insights about significant policy options that would not be revealed by weaker methods and producing findings that would inform policy. MDRC's experience suggests a number of lessons on how to do this.

LESSON 1: FOCUS ON IMPORTANT ISSUES   The starting point for influencing policy is having something of value to communicate. Since the life cycle of a major experiment is often five or more years, this means making the right decisions up front, not scrambling to repackage findings at the end. To be successful, the study should assess a policy choice that is compelling, that will still be relevant when the results come out, and about which there are substantial unanswered questions.

LESSON 2: HAVE A REASONABLE TREATMENT   An experiment should test a policy that is supported by past research or theory and looks feasible operationally and politically—where, for example, it is likely that the relevant administrative systems will cooperate, people will participate long enough for the program to make a difference, the program differs from the services readily available to people in the control group, and the costs will not be so high as to rule out replication. This sounds straightforward; but AFDC was not a national program, nor is TANF, which replaced it. States and even counties adopt different strategies, reflecting local values, resources, conditions, and the priority given to advancing particular policy goals. As a result, the aim of

*This section authored by Judith M. Gueron.

most of the experiments we describe was not to find one model that fits all circumstances but to test alternatives that inform those choices.

LESSON 3: RUN A REAL-WORLD TEST IN MULTIPLE LOCATIONS   The program should be tested fairly (if possible, after the initial start-up period), at a scale and in an operating context that resemble potential subsequent expansion (ideally, that means delivered by regular staff in regular offices) and, if feasible, in diverse communities and contexts. Although the welfare studies gave priority to ensuring internal validity, they almost always also addressed external validity by including sites that, although rarely selected at random, were representative of the factors likely to affect impacts. It has proved uniquely powerful to be able to say that similar results emerged from reforms tested in mainstream offices in multiple and varied communities.

LESSON 4: ADDRESS THE QUESTIONS PEOPLE CARE ABOUT   The first-order questions are usually the ones that flow directly from the experiment: Does the approach work? For whom? Under what conditions? How do benefits compare with costs? Is there a trade-off in reaching different goals? But limiting a study to that list misses an opportunity to address the next level of issues that are critical to practitioners and policy makers who also want to improve practice on the ground. They want insights into how and why programs work or fall short, whether results can be replicated or strengthened, and what factors drive operational performance.

LESSON 5: FIGHT FOR RANDOM ASSIGNMENT, BUT ACKNOWLEDGE ITS LIMITATIONS   A high-quality experiment is almost always superior to other methods for providing a reliable estimate of whether a program or policy caused a change in behavior. Yet over the years, proponents of experiments have had to overcome strong opposition from politicians, welfare administrators, advocates, and academics. The easy response would have been to accept a weaker design, but experience has shown the hazards of that choice. A striking aspect of all the studies in this book is that they were spared the often irresolvable disagreements about results that followed studies using weaker methods. Such disputes have a high cost. Policy makers do not want to take a stand and then find the evidence evaporates in the course of a technical debate among experts.

   In my experience, the more unimpeachable the evidence, the greater the likelihood that an evaluation will be judged believable and not just pressure-group noise. In explaining why the welfare studies played such a visible role in legislative debates, multiple actors and observers listed first and foremost the credibility that came from random assignment. Over the years, we have found a deep and nonpartisan interest in finding truth and identifying methods that can rise above politics. There was almost no debate about methodology. This does not mean the research determined policy, of course. The political process ultimately balances many different interests to reach decisions. The hope of those laboring to produce reliable evidence is that it can inform, and thereby possibly improve, the political process.

Finally, some have argued that experiments too often show that programs do not work. Twenty-five years ago, the prominent sociologist Peter Rossi formulated this rule (among several other "laws" about evaluation research): "The better designed the impact assessment of a social program, the more likely is the resulting estimate of net impact to be zero" (Rossi 1987, 3). Rossi's warning was well placed, but those who respond to small or null experimental results by attacking the method turn the goal of research on its head. A failed study is not one that provides clear evidence that the test program does not work but one where you get to the end, after much money and effort, and have to say "I am not confident of the result" (see Gueron 2008).

However, in advocating for experiments, it is also important to acknowledge remaining limitations and challenges. These include situations—less numerous than opponents often claim—where, for ethical or practical reasons, random assignment cannot be used (for example, evaluating entitlements or in situations where isolation of controls from the message or services is unlikely).[7] In addition, experiments have rarely addressed whether the treatment affects people not directly targeted (for example, if a new benefit encourages people to apply for welfare or a new mandate deters them). (See the discussion of entry effects and time limits in chapter 10.) Furthermore, though there has been much recent progress in expanding what one can learn from experiments by combining different research methods (getting inside the "black box" to understand what features of the program or its implementation account for success or failure),[8] many questions remain.

LESSON 6: CREATE A WIN-WIN SITUATION   Experiments in operating programs rely on the sustained cooperation of state, county, and program staff, as well as study participants. Since MDRC is in the business for the long term, we have always sought to leave our partners open for an encore. To do this, we evolved an art, reflected in mantras repeated by MDRC's operations staff: "If someone is unreservedly enthusiastic about the study, he or she doesn't understand it." "Remember, you want them more than they want you." "Protect the core of the study, and figure out what you can give on." "Money can fix some problems, but not serious ethical concerns." "Build a relationship with people at the sites."[9] Implementing this philosophy required careful balancing of research ambition and operational needs.

LESSON 7: PROTECT THE BRAND OF RANDOM ASSIGNMENT Random assignment's reputation does not start and end with the flip of a properly balanced coin. The metal can be debased if the practitioners of this craft fail to pay meticulous attention to the details of design and implementation. The how-to list is long—and everything on it matters—but key items include an adequate sample and follow-up, high-quality data, a way to isolate the control group from the spillover effects of the treatment, and meeting high ethical and legal standards. The last issue is particularly critical, since randomly selecting who gets services inevitably raises sensitive issues of equity as well as humane treatment. Inadequate attention to these concerns risks not only blocking a study but even poisoning the environment for future work. Our experience suggests some threshold preconditions: experiments should not deny people access to services (or benefits) to which they are entitled or reduce service levels and should include adequate procedures to inform people about the study and ensure data confidentiality.

LESSON 8: NO SINGLE EXPERIMENT IS DEFINITIVE Back in the 1970s, we used to describe a multisite random assignment study as definitive. It is now clear that no single study answers all questions. Uncertainty shrinks with replication in different contexts and times, as each study generates new hypotheses. In social policy as in medicine, the real payoff is when there are enough high-quality, experimental results to allow for different types of synthesis—to identify the trade-offs and to refine the evidence on what works best for whom under what conditions.

LESSON 9: SET REALISTIC EXPECTATIONS The welfare story definitively refutes the view that social programs are investments with no clear payoff. But it was a constant challenge to get people to appreciate the value of small or negative findings. Even when the impacts were positive, their absolute magnitude was usually small to modest. These were improvements but obviously no panacea. This is not a caution about random assignment, but it is evidence of some combination of (1) how hard it is to change behavior, (2) inadequate theory or programs, (3) outcomes driven primarily by the economy and personal factors rather than the test programs, and (4) the policies assessed being not dramatically different from the robust, and often increasing, level of services available to and used by the control group.

Whether changes of this magnitude were declared evidence of failure or success depended more on the political context than on the findings themselves. In the late 1980s, the discovery that programs could be triple winners (increasing work, reducing dependency, and saving money) was considered a victory; a judgment of modest but positive was cited as progress and a rationale for expansion. By the mid-1990s these same improvements were recast by many as the reason to try something radically different. People working in other countries or fields where there is now a strong interest in random assignment should ask themselves whether the proposed changes are likely to produce larger impacts. If not, would modest success be viewed as a building block to progress or rejected as a failure?

LESSON 10: CONTEXTUALIZE THE RESULTS   To have an impact on policy, it is usually not enough to carry out a good study and report the lessons. Researchers need to help the audience assess the relative value of the approach tested versus others. To do this, they should lodge the results of the experiment in the broader context of what is known about what works and what does not.

LESSON 11: SIMPLIFY AND STANDARDIZE   In our experience, if an advanced degree is needed to understand the lessons from a study, they are less likely to reach policy makers. One great advantage of an experiment—the essence of why it is such a powerful communications tool—is that anyone can see what was done: All you have to do is calculate the average of the outcomes for people in the program group, do the same thing for the control group, and subtract. Nonresearchers can understand this—it is the epitome of transparency—since it more closely resembles test-marketing toothpaste than statistical modeling. It also means that different analysts looking at the same data are likely to produce the same numbers, even if they choose to emphasize different findings or reach different policy conclusions.

Over the years, MDRC reinforced this simplicity in multiple ways. One was to develop a standard format to present results and stick to it. This helped policy makers learn to read the tables and interpret the results. A second was to shun research jargon. A third was to avoid overly complex research designs, although complexity did increase over time. But we did not avoid telling people that the findings themselves were nuanced or involved trade-offs or needed to be understood in the context of other research. A fourth was to use a standard set of inputs and explanatory variables. Finally, we tracked a common set of outcome metrics—the percentage of people participating in different activities, working, on welfare, or in poverty; average earnings and welfare benefits; and the amount of money the government got back per dollar invested—that were not only relevant but were also readily comprehensible to our diverse audiences.

In our view, the sustainability and cumulative impact of these studies would have been far less if we had told the welfare commissioner (who was after all a political appointee), "Your program had an effect size of 0.15" and then added, in response to the resulting stare, "This is a small effect."[10] Instead, we made such statements as, "Your program increased earnings by 25 percent and reduced welfare payments by 8 percent. This cost $1,000 per person. Over five years, you saved both the state and the federal government money." Since realistically a state could not eliminate all welfare, and most states wanted to restructure it to increase work and reduce costs, this was a clear winner. It did not matter that we called the effects small or modest; for administrators focused on increasing work and saving money, the findings pointed to a better way to run the system.

Moreover, this combination of simplicity and standardization, including the comparison of results to costs, fostered an ability to compare the achievements and trade-offs from different policy responses and helped put on a level playing field states that opted for different ways to spend the same amount: spending more on fewer people or less on more people. It also fed subsequent syntheses.

This transparency may be hard to replicate in other fields, such as education, where the treatments last many years, the ultimate outcomes are further in the future, and the goals more diverse and not convertible to a dollar metric. As a result, studies must rely on intermediate or proximate measures that are an uncertain stand-in for the ultimate goals and are usually calibrated in units that are not as readily interpretable.

LESSON 12: COMMUNICATE ACTIVELY AND OFTEN Politicians and funders are impatient consumers. Our welfare studies were usually structured so that some findings (including important lessons on participation rates and program design) came out in a year or two and were aggressively shared with the multiple interested audiences, including the news media. At the same time, we made a conscious effort to resist pressure to produce results so early that subsequent analysis and data risked reversing the conclusions.

LESSON 13: DO NOT CONFUSE DISSEMINATION WITH ADVOCACY The key to long-term successful communication is trust. If you overstate your findings or shape them to fit an agenda, people will ultimately know it, view you as another interest group, and reject what you say. One reason the welfare studies were believed and used by people with divergent political views is that the results were marketed in an evenhanded style by an organization widely viewed as impartial. We saw our job as sharing a program's success and failure in advancing different goals, not in promoting one goal over another (for example, saving money versus reducing poverty). We sought to identify trade-offs, not to advocate for a solution. MDRC was not alone in projecting that style. The small number of researchers in the other institutions conducting the work shared the same attitude and training, a culture that federal and foundation funders generally supported.

LESSON 14: BE HONEST ABOUT FAILURE Although many studies produced positive findings, results were often mixed, and some were clearly negative. State officials, program administrators, and funders do not welcome hearing that progress depends on discarding approaches (particularly their favorite approaches) because they are found not to work. And though state officials may not have grasped at first that a failed program was not a failed study, we found they did learn and move on from disappointing findings, even to the point of volunteering for subsequent experiments.

LESSON 15: GET PARTNERS AND BUY-IN FROM THE BEGINNING Major stakeholders can make useful contributions in each phase of the work: identifying the problem and proposed solution, specifying research questions, reviewing progress and findings, and developing the communications plan. If you can create a real partnership and help key players see the value of what is being learned, they will have a stake in the project and its lessons and be more likely to work with you to improve the study and communicate the results and less likely to attack the method or the findings.

Although these lessons distill much of what we learned about designing and implementing experiments to inform policy, I have so far ignored a key factor: luck. It is nice to say that null findings are a key to progress. But uniformly negative results would quite likely have put us—and possibly social experiments—out of business. One can tout how much money can be saved when policy makers identify and shut down ineffective programs. But if that is all we had learned, foundations and Congress would just as likely have shut down the research. It is also true that the lack of null findings was not mere chance. We had made determined efforts to avoid, at least in the extreme, four of the risks that push toward this result: assessing programs too soon (that is, before they have had a chance to work out the bugs), swamping programs under research demands, following too few people for too short a time to detect impacts, or testing dumb ideas. We also paid close attention to all the details that affect whether an experiment is worth doing and will produce valid results. Yet there was still an element of luck: what we learned produced something for everyone. The left could stress the findings that social programs were investments with quantifiable payoffs; the right could point to the positive results from participation and work-directed mandates. The result was widespread use—and inevitably some misuse—of the research.

The welfare story is often cited as the model of how to build knowledge and inform policy. But this is not a time to rest on our laurels. In addition to the humbling, and continuing, challenge of understanding better why programs succeed or fail, there is a second challenge: how to make random assignment a more useful management tool.

Systematic and repeated experimentation is one view of how to raise performance: use rigorous evaluations to identify successful approaches; replicate those that work and discard those that do not, keep modifying and retesting programs, and use this trial-and-error culling as a means of continuous improvement. Although I endorse this vision, I understand well why critics object to its cost and lag time and also argue that it is too static and ex post to serve as a means to foster innovation. There is another approach to using evidence to improve social programs: the performance management movement, which sees the real-time tracking of outcomes and other metrics (such as the rate at which people participate or get a job) as a way to achieve multiple goals. These include monitoring program effectiveness, checking compliance with regulations, quantifying staff achievements, holding managers accountable, and inspiring and rewarding improvement. This is a bottoms-up approach that sets expectations and leaves managers and staff free to decide how best to use their time and resources to meet or beat the standards.

Ideally, since they share a common goal of promoting effectiveness by creating a positive feedback loop, these two movements would reinforce each other, with performance metrics serving as a short- or intermediate-term way to inspire higher outcomes that would, in turn, result in higher impacts and cost effectiveness (to be periodically confirmed by experiments). But for this to be true, outcome standards must be a good proxy for impacts. If they are, they will send signals that are likely to make programs more effective; if not, they will increase the risk of unintended, negative effects. Unfortunately, the welfare experiments show that outcomes are not good predictors of impacts. As a result—by making apparent winners out of actual losers—outcomes can potentially send false signals about whom to serve, what managers or practices are most effective, or whether programs are improving over time.[11]

This poses a serious dilemma. It cannot mean that outcomes are unimportant, since by definition higher outcomes, if nothing else changes, translate directly into higher impacts. It also cannot mean that workers and managers should not try out and track the results of new ideas unless they are verified by an experiment, since this would deny the obvious value of hands-on experience, high expectations, and incentives. It also cannot mean that setting stretch goals and encouraging people on the ground to figure out ways to achieve them is useless, since that is the way most successful businesses foster innovation and high performance. But it raises a bright red flag that emphasizing outcomes can prompt people to game the system in a multitude of counterproductive ways. (The press is filled with examples of this response to high-stakes testing in education.)

At present there is a stalemate, with the two camps existing in parallel and not converging. The strengths of one are the weaknesses of the other. Experiments get the right answer about effectiveness but are not useful as a quick turnaround management tool. Outcome standards provide timely lower-cost data, tap into the "you-get-what-you-measure" mantra, and may stimulate change, but since by definition they measure the wrong thing, the innovation may be unleashed in pursuit of a mistaken target. Over the decades described in this book, we have built evidence of this problem but have not made progress on the solution. Although periodic, credible evaluations represent enormous progress, the challenge remains to more successfully put this beautiful tool, social experimentation, at the service of managers. It seems to me that a solution may come from further work in two directions: increasing the understanding of how features of people, programs, and context affect impacts and integrating random assignment into administrative procedures so that managers (in their routine testing of alternatives or rationing of services) produce counterfactuals that can be used as a lower-cost and more dynamic tool to improve effectiveness.

Lessons from the Administration for Children and Families: Sustaining a Policy-Relevant Research Agenda*

All the lessons in this section, in one way or another, address the core question of continuity: how to sustain lengthy projects and a research agenda across changes in administrations. As such, they are relevant for civil servants, political appointees, and even private funders. Wade Horn, the former assistant secretary for children and families under President George W. Bush, aptly describes the fundamental problem: "In academia we would never say, every four years, let's just have a whole bunch of new faculty and . . . new ideas and do something completely different. Yet that's what we do in government every four or eight years. You . . . have a new bunch come in with new ideas and they throw out the old stuff. . . . There is a discontinuity."

LESSON 16: COMMITMENT BY SENIOR CIVIL SERVANTS IS VITAL Senior civil servants typically have substantial authority, particular in research and evaluation areas. They are a natural source of continuity because, as a rule, they maintain their positions across administrations. As Horn says, "It is helpful if you have career employees . . . that can span different political leadership. . . . What is required is someone who is committed to evaluation and research, who is high enough on the food chain, and strong enough in their viewpoint to be able to forcefully make the case to changes in political leadership for the need to continue ongoing studies as well as a field of studies."

Jean Grossman, the former chief evaluation officer at the Department of

*This section authored by Howard Rolston.

Labor, giving as an example Naomi Goldstein, the current career head of the OPRE, echoes Horn and adds another vital element—hiring and development of capable staff: "The reason ACF does so well is because of Naomi. Leadership has a huge effect. When you have somebody who is really good leading and a serious researcher, that person brings good ideas, can attract good senior people, mentors good young people, and can make the argument for good research to the politicals in order to secure the funds to do it."

Civil servants also typically establish long-term relationships with other agencies and often with congressional staff and the broader program and policy community. In addition, as Grossman says, they manage and train staff who must have the skills to initiate and oversee projects effectively. In the last decade, senior political officials have initiated programs of experimental research at the Social Security Administration and at the Institute of Education Sciences. Whether these programs are sustained over time, and if so how, will add important insight to the institutionalization of experimental research programs in the federal government.

LESSON 17: IT TAKES A SKILLED AND COMMITTED INTERNAL TEAM   Except in rare instances, government restrictions on hiring and travel force any random assignment research program to be extramural and operated by independent research organizations. Conceiving, initiating, and managing these external projects, however, requires a great deal of skill within the federal funding agency. Furthermore, carrying out these activities for even a modest-size project is not done effectively by an individual working in isolation; it takes a strong team. This need is particularly crucial in writing high-quality requests for proposals; as the HHS experience of the early 1980s described in chapter 5 illustrates, it is not enough to say "random assignment is required." Producing a request for proposals that will foster a strong competition among fully qualified bidders requires sophisticated research design skills, understanding what is necessary to ensure credible findings useful to the practice and policy community, and ensuring sufficient funds are budgeted for the effort. Assessing proposals that are responding to a request for proposals requires the same set of skills.

Another great advantage of having a team with strong analytical skills is that research staff are frequently called on by senior political officials to do policy analysis in addition to straight research. Their ability to do such tasks well buys a lot of credibility and good will. Fortunately, skilled people want to do interesting and challenging work that can make a positive contribution, and they like working with like-minded, talented staff—making an organized hiring effort by current staff almost always successful.

LESSON 18: BUILDING A STRONG TEAM IS EMINENTLY FEASIBLE Staff who develop and manage rigorous research, including random assignment studies, appreciate that something important and lasting is accomplished by their work. Reflecting on how the office has been able to hire, develop, and retain talented staff, Goldstein says, "I think that most people do find the work inherently rewarding. One of our staff said she came here from another federal agency because she kept going to meetings where she noticed the people who were doing the cool stuff were from OPRE."

Furthermore, with the increased support for random assignment from academics that Judy describes in the coda to this book, although many of my government colleagues and I were generalists who learned on the job (and there is still much about actually doing high-quality experiments that requires on-the-ground experience), most newer staff enter with a much higher understanding of the fundamental issues than we did. Goldstein compares the current situation to her experience:

> The fields of public policy and program evaluation are stronger and larger than when I was educated in the 1980s, so there are more people coming out of a range of academic programs who are very well trained to take on the kind of work we do. At the time, we spent relatively little time on random assignment and the message was, "Yea, it's the best but you'll never get to do it, so let's move on and talk about regression analysis." And that's changed. I also left with the impression that random assignment studies were simple and not intellectually challenging. That's certainly not true.

Goldstein goes on to describe how the interest in rigorous work and staff quality interact to create a virtuous circle: "At a certain point we got a critical mass of smart, talented, collegial people, making this a good place to work—and that is somewhat self-perpetuating. I think that our reputation is solid and that helps."

LESSON 19: POLICY DEVELOPMENT IS CONSISTENT WITH AN OBJECTIVE RESEARCH AGENDA Everybody who engages in the policy process has goals and ideas about the effectiveness of means that go beyond the evidence. As a result, having the same organization develop and manage research as well as support policy development involves risks, particularly the risk that research will be conducted in a way that biases what gets studied and can even distort findings. Some argue for a strict separation of the two, and some agencies rely on a strong firewall between them. Although the research staff in organizations that observe a strong firewall can and do produce valuable studies, I believe that this type of strict separation, as a general rule, risks more than it gains. First, it runs the very real danger of leading to studies that are fascinating to the research community but largely irrelevant to central policy debates. Second, undue emphasis on the risks of policy involvement to research objectivity can result in interpretations of findings that are too narrow to provide much help to the policy and practice community. The history we describe in this book strongly demonstrates that it is not only possible but valuable for research and policy expertise to be tightly aligned within a sponsoring agency, and that this alignment is consistent with the production of objective research that is useful to—and used by—the policy and practice communities.

LESSON 20: HAVE RESEARCH FUNDS AVAILABLE FOR INITIATIVES BY INCOMING ADMINISTRATIONS   All new political appointees arrive with a basketful of policy ideas and initiatives they want to undertake. They seldom have as many research ideas, but they usually know that research funds are an important area of discretion for them. Finding out that the previous administration's priorities are encumbering virtually all their agency's research budget will not make them receptive to project continuity.

LESSON 21: HAVE IDEAS FOR PROJECTS THAT ARE RELEVANT TO THE CURRENT (AND INCOMING) ADMINISTRATION'S POLICY GOALS   As the history of the Reagan administration's initial antipathy to impact evaluations of the community work experience program illustrates, senior political officials will not necessarily want an objective test of their favorite policy ideas. It is an even surer bet that they will not be interested in evaluations unrelated to their policy interests. But as that history also shows, those officials may be amenable to random assignment evaluations of related approaches. Developing a range of research initiatives that can be explored with incoming political appointees shows that career staff understand the newcomers' interests and are prepared to create a research agenda relevant to them.

LESSON 22: HAVE MONEY!   My staff and I learned the hard way not to take a research budget for granted. At times of fiscal retrenchment (certainly the situation for the indefinite future), one does not need to follow the news comprehensively to see that research budgets can be easy targets. A single project an elected official can describe in a way that suggests pointy-headed irrelevance can make an entire budget vulnerable. To manage a budget well, it is important that staff in one's own agency budget shop, OMB, and appropriations and authorizing committee staff on Capitol Hill all understand the nature of the research your budget supports. For the most part, these are the staff with a large say in identifying programs that will be well funded and those that will be cut. Strong relationships with those key staff can also be vital to recovering from cuts; in our case, relationships with authorizing committee staff enabled our office to achieve new funds only one year after being zeroed out.

LESSON 23: HUGE ANNUAL BUDGETS ARE NOT A REQUIREMENT   Sometimes opportunities arise that lend themselves to relatively inexpensive experiments (for example, when a lottery is already in place and administrative records can provide the main outcomes), but most large-scale, multisite experiments are relatively costly in time and budget. Because of these core costs, it is often worthwhile to add components to maximize what can be learned, which further drives up total costs. Bur since an experiment with reasonably long-term follow-up takes a long time, the high total cost can be spread over many years.

LESSON 24: BUILD SUPPORT IN THE LEGISLATURE   In addition to ensuring support for a research budget, congressional staff can create opportunities for projects, ward off threats, and educate legislators and the public about findings. The use of experiments in welfare research benefited from ongoing bipartisan support from staff of the key authorizing committees: House Ways and Means and Senate Finance. On more than one occasion they successfully introduced language into legislation to require random assignment. And with respect to welfare waiver demonstrations, they supported the executive branch's requirements for states to use experiments for evaluation and cost neutrality.[12]

LESSON 25: CROSS-AGENCY RELATIONSHIPS ARE VITAL The federal government side of our story makes it clear that no single agency could have achieved the successes we describe without strong allies working across agencies. The Administration for Children and Families, the Office of the Assistant Secretary for Planning and Evaluation, and OMB all played critical roles in sustaining both particular projects and the experimental effort overall. At different times, different agencies were in a position to seize the initiative to push random assignment forward. In addition, at critical junctures we were able to come together, and stick together, in the face of strong resistance that might well have prevailed had we been divided. Another important benefit of cross-agency collaboration is added funding and intellectual perspective, which can enrich a study—such as the Department of Education's contribution to the JOBS evaluation, which added a whole new dimension to the project.

LESSON 26: THE SUCCESS OF YOUR AGENCY ALSO DEPENDS ON THE SUCCESS OF EXTERNAL ORGANIZATIONS External research organizations, foundations, and academics all play a vital role in moving a research agenda forward. Willingness to partner with and support the ideas of external organizations financially and through other means, even where they do not directly align with agency priorities, is a worthwhile investment. Some activities, such as federal procurements, are rightly competitive, and arm's-length relationships are necessary to them. But agencies also have an interest in there being strong competitors for contracts and grants; and informal cooperative relationships outside the competitive process can further this. In addition, partnerships with and informal support for the efforts of foundations with interests related to agency goals can enrich not only individual projects but also the overall body of evidence.

LESSON 27: BE WILLING TO FIGHT FOR HIGH STANDARDS By their status as appointees of an elected president, political officials make policy and determine spending priorities where these are not determined by law. However, disagreements about what constitutes good science are not resolved by elections, giving the views of political appointees as appointees no privileged position in scientific disputes. Career civil servants can helpfully advise on these matters, but since their views are not determinative, they must be willing to fight for high standards. They may not prevail, but unwillingness to fight when standards are threatened guarantees failure.

LESSON 28: LOYALTY IS COMPLEX   Without strong, trusting relationships between civil servants and political appointees, it would not have been possible to create and sustain the research agenda we describe. These relationships depend on loyalty to roles and loyalty to superiors. Loyalty in the form of a commitment to the need for continuity and innovation in a research agenda, and, above all, to standards of evidence is equally vital. Balancing organizational loyalty with these additional dimensions of loyalty enabled individuals both to stand up for high standards and to seize opportunities to push the welfare research agenda forward.

LESSON 29: INTEGRITY OF DESIGN IS PROTECTIVE   Even in cases where an incoming administration has no problem with the research budget allocation per se (see lesson 20), it may still oppose continuing a project that is vulnerable to the charge of having a weak or biased research design. There are no guarantees; but a strong, unbiased design, such as one relying on random assignment, can be protective in the sense of promoting project continuity.

LESSON 30: GOOD LUCK HELPS, BUT BE OPPORTUNISTIC IN USING YOUR LUCK
Good luck played an important role in advancing the random assignment welfare agenda. The initial pattern of positive findings was certainly more conducive to further experiments than a pattern of null or negative findings would have been. The strong support and advocacy for random assignment by almost all the political leadership at ACF and organizational predecessors was also incredibly good fortune. None of these leaders was selected because of their advocacy for experimental methods, yet all played a vital role in their support for it. The continuity of the research agenda benefited, in addition, from an extended period of confluence and continuity of interests, across the political spectrum, in increasing work by welfare recipients.

Luck alone, though, could not have achieved a forty-five-year research agenda built on random assignment. For example, had the methods not been viewed as objective and unbiased, the ongoing policy interest, combined with deeply divided views about what would work best, could well have resulted in policy makers simply dismissing findings that disagreed with their positions. In addition, where luck presented opportunities, the actions of individuals in a range of organizations—OPRE, ASPE, MDRC, and OMB, in particular—were crucial in seizing them and turning them into realities.

LESSON 31: WHEN POSSIBLE, EXPLORE CONTENTIOUS ISSUES Welfare is notoriously an area of policy driven more by values and anecdotes than by hard evidence. Yet welfare is unique in having such a long, continuous history of large-scale social experiments. One might be tempted to think that this continuity could be better sustained across changes in political leadership by studying only narrow issues that are not at the heart of the more fundamental disagreements. Although some subjects (for example, grant diversion) had bipartisan support and were not deeply ideological, others (for example, Labor Force Attachment Versus Human Capital Development in the JOBS evaluation) were, and remain, strong values divides. Yet it was possible to sustain the JOBS evaluation across Republican and Democratic administrations and for the results to be credible, and acted on, by both sides of the policy debate. The point of impact research is to replace conjecture with evidence; limiting this to second-order issues is neither necessary nor desirable.

Although all the ACF lessons I have summarized are potentially useful, my first three (lessons 16 through 18) are the most important—encompassing leadership and building and maintaining a staff of talented, energetic people. Many factors both external and internal to government are expanding the use of random assignment. I asked a number of current and former career and political staff what steps might most help to institutionalize experimental evaluation within the federal government. Several made specific suggestions, such as that experimental evaluation be formalized in legislation, as is currently the case for the Institute of Education Sciences, or that OMB take further steps to promote the use of experiments by federal agencies. However, the overwhelming response was that success depends on leadership and staff capacity. The story of this book is a story of people taking leadership roles but always working in cooperation with others to find the truth. It appears likely that though progress has been made in some federal agencies, institutionalizing random assignment will continue to depend on the determination and skills of people.

The welfare story is part of a broader movement to show that random assignment can reveal how to improve social policy and use resources more effectively. Our tale reflects a triumph of the scientific method under often harsh conditions. And each of us points to important lessons learned from our different perspectives—on the strengths and limits of the method and on how experiments are best viewed as part of a continuous learning process. A diversity of innovators—in government, private organizations, and major foundations—and the many groups that became advocates for such studies explain the almost half century of uninterrupted experiments. They provided the momentum and the leadership. Over these years, we have seen zeal for the method build, recede, and reemerge even stronger. The coming years will show whether the current enthusiasm represents a swing in the pendulum, a steady state, or a step toward even wider acceptance of the value of social experiments.

CODA

Random Assignment Takes Center Stage*

This book describes the struggle to promote randomized experiments as a campaign waged over many years, mostly by people outside the normal academic reward system. In recent years, this has changed, both in the United States and internationally, prompting me to ask a number of people (see the appendix) close to the past conflict or current transformation: How would you characterize academic and government support for experiments forty years ago? Has this changed? If so, why? Although by no means a systematic description of this evolution, their responses provide insight on the context within which our story unfolded.

WHAT WAS IT LIKE BACK THEN?

Larry Orr, among the handful of people with a forty-year role leading and promoting experiments, describes the early years thus:

> In the mid- to late 70s, other than the relatively small group of government types and researchers in various firms who were directly involved in [the early experiments], there was little knowledge of, and almost no support for, experiments. Why? Inside the government I think the biggest barrier we faced was the cost of these things. I remember, when I was trying to get the Health Insurance Experiment funded, the strongest opposition came from the health establishment in [the Department of Health, Education, and Welfare]. They

*The Coda is authored by Judith M. Gueron.

saw this project eating up funds that would have supported 100 of their small-scale academic grants—and all for what? To answer "some crazy economists' question" about the demand for medical care! Fortunately, policy makers—from assistant secretaries like Bill Morrill to under secretaries like Cap Weinberger to Vice President Jerry Ford (who once overruled OMB [the Office of Management and Budget] to save the HIE [Health Insurance Experiment], on the advice of Paul O'Neill)—were used to bigger numbers and found the price tag less daunting. The same was true of congressional staff, who earmarked money for experiments at several points in the 70s and 80s.

Academic opposition to experiments didn't really get cranked up until the 80s, as I recall, with [James] Heckman leading the charge. . . . The whole issue of selection bias didn't really rear its head until the end of the 70s. Heckman's 1979 article, in which he promised "a simple consistent estimation method that eliminates the specification error" (that is, selection bias[1]), was the leading edge of academic attention to the problem. . . . [I]n the early [19]80s, with Heckman's "simple" method in hand, most academics felt that the problem had been licked by clever (and inexpensive!) econometrics. I remember attending a conference on the income maintenance experiments in 1984 or so, at which Orley Ashenfelter remarked that he had "come to see them shoot the last of the dinosaurs."[2]

Robinson Hollister concurs that it felt embattled, primarily because Heckman was such a powerful figure. He recalls in the mid-1980s "despairing that maybe there weren't going to be any more random assignment experiments." However, Judith Singer suggests that we may have overreacted to opposition from economists and failed to reach out to potential supporters in other fields.[3]

David Card relates the disenchantment with the negative-income-tax (NIT) experiments more directly to the experiments themselves. "Early on there was a lot of excitement about the NITs and many major economists . . . were involved in the analysis." He asks, "Why did the profession seem to walk away from social experiments in the late 1970s just as the final results from the series of NIT experiments were published?" and offers four possible reasons: "(1) unhappiness over the complex designs of the NITs; (2) some unease that the experimental results somehow failed to show 'big enough' incentive effects; (3) dissatisfaction with the 'big institutions' that ran the experiments

. . . and (4) the rise of new econometric methods, and confidence that these methods could be used to infer something from observational data."

According to Larry Hedges, the path was different in education research. After an impressive start that predated the NIT experiments, experimental research went out of favor. The "demise of experiments in education had more to do with the substantive theory associated with them than methodology, per se. . . . Psychology as a discipline was associated with experimentation, and psychology was increasingly seen not to have all the answers for understanding complex social processes like schooling." The result was a decades-long qualitative revolution he characterizes as a "disaster (at least scientifically)," in which "standards for training and even scientific thinking slipped" and which did not change until the creation of the Institute of Education Sciences (IES).

HAS SUPPORT INCREASED?

The explosion in interest is described by Joshua Angrist and Jorn-Steffen Pischke (2010, 4): "Empirical microeconomics has experienced a credibility revolution, with a consequent increase in policy relevance and scientific impact. . . . The primary engine driving improvement has been a focus on the quality of research designs. . . . The advantages of a good research design are perhaps most easily apparent in research using random assignment, which not coincidentally includes some of the most influential microeconometric studies to appear in recent years." It is further noted and explained by many of the persons I communicated with on this issue:

Howard Bloom: "There has been a dramatic change in the use of randomized experiments and in the demand for more rigorous evidence about effectiveness and causal effects. . . . This is not a lonely business anymore; this is a team sport. There are a lot of people out there who understand the issues and who believe and care deeply about getting really rigorous evidence and understand that a randomized trial is in most cases the best way to do it."

David Ellwood: "Support for randomized controlled evaluations has certainly grown enormously over twenty years, and I think the welfare related experiments played a crucial role. I do not think there was real hostility in the economics profession before. Economists have always preferred reliable systematic methods, and there were major prior experiments, notably the negative income tax and the health insurance experiments. Rather I would say that most economists were not much interested in social policy and the limited group who were was using survey data to answer slightly different questions about the nature of poverty, as opposed to examining what works to combat it. Today, many of the brightest stars in empirical economics focus primarily on designed or natural experiments, such as the work in the poverty action lab led by Esther Duflo and others."

Jon Baron, president of the Coalition for Evidence-Based Policy: "There's much greater acceptance now of random assignment as the strongest method for determining whether a program works or not, and that's recognized, for example, now in OMB policy, regulations, and guidance on budget scoring. The Congressional Budget Office has recently said they prioritize random assignment studies in the evidence that they look at. . . . It has appeared in appropriations language and in a lot of different areas in Congress over the past ten years with increasing frequency."

David Greenberg: "University faculty members, especially economists (but also sociologists), and especially faculty at the University of Wisconsin, were very active in the earliest random assignment studies. . . . However, many faculty members expressed skepticism concerning the usefulness of random assignment studies. And faculty interest faded. . . . Over the last decade or so, however, there has been a great revival of faculty interest. . . . The subject matter covered by experiments has become much more diverse."

To support this, the people I contacted point to the change in economics textbooks and methods courses, the expansion in publications focused on experiments,[4] the increasing number of experiments and share of them taking place outside the United States,[5] and the growth in articles about experiments in leading economic journals (Card, DellaVigna, and Malmendier 2011).

The extent of change is reflected in Heckman's response to my query: "No serious social scientist would oppose social experiments and I have become a big fan. I still think they have to be supplemented and they do not answer all of the questions, but they answer certain questions—mean difference questions in localized (partial equilibrium) settings—very well. Unless we experiment on entire economies and consider the full range of populations affected by a policy we cannot use experiments to estimate the system wide impact of an intervention. We all know about the problems of attrition, crossover, etc. But random assignment is here to stay."

WHAT FACTORS FOSTERED THE TRANSFORMATION?

Respondents agree that change was gradual—there was no single tipping point—and that many factors drove it, confirming Angrist and Pischke's (2010, 5) statement that "accounting for the origins of the credibility revolution in empirical economics is like trying to chart the birth of rock and roll. Early influences are many, and every fan has a story." People highlight five causes: studies showing the weakness of alternative methods, the successful implementation of numerous experiments, the roles of the IES and OMB, the actions of independent groups promoting experiments, and personal relationships and exposure to random assignment studies.

The first, and the one that probably had the most decisive impact on economists, was the repeated studies showing that alternative methods using carefully constructed comparison groups could not replicate experimental results. As Angrist and Pischke (2010, 5) put it,

> From the trenches of empirical labor economics, we see an important impetus . . . coming from studies questioning the reliability of econometric evaluations of subsidized training programs. A landmark here is [Robert] LaLonde (1986), who compared the results from an econometric evaluation of the National Supported Work Demonstration with those from a randomized trial. The econometric results typically differed quite a bit from those using random assignment. LaLonde argued that there is little reason to believe that statistical comparisons of alternative models (specification testing) would point a researcher in the right direction.[6]

Thomas Cook points to the importance of the first two factors. On the first, he describes the agenda of econometricians in the 1970s, 1980s, and early 1990s as

> to come up with a very, very general theory . . . so that you could easily model selection in any circumstance. [Arthur] Goldberger worked on that, the early Heckman worked on that. That was the sort of Holy Grail. . . . Now, as [younger people] went through this work in the 1980s and early 1990s, it became clear that you could not have a general model of selection without lots

and lots of assumptions that were not easily testable, and it began to look like a house of cards. . . .

These people despaired of a general selection model (people like Angrist and [Guido] Imbens and the like . . . and said we need something more modest and transparent, and random assignment was [that]. It only works under certain circumstances for certain causal questions, but when it works it is really clear. It was that abandonment of the more ambitious general selection model in favor of something more modest and transparent that led to the ability of young economists . . . to buy into the experimental agenda in the 1980s and 1990s.[7]

Cook also emphasizes the impact of the second factor:

Places like MDRC [showed that] for certain kinds of questions this was clearly an implementable, transparent strategy. . . . So the model was there of how to do it, not just theoretically but practically in the field. . . . This took away one of the main objections to random assignment studies, which had been that they were not feasible. . . . It was very empirical in that respect. [Before that] things like the NIT experiment had been around and labor economists and micro economists had used it as a template from the 1960s and 1970s. They were aware of it, it was just that in the 1970s they assigned it low value, as something not very interesting given that we could get a general theory of selection that could be used with all kinds of problems. But that failed, it failed miserably. It was a noble effort, but it didn't work. So this [random assignment] was the great fallback. It was available, it worked, it was transparent, the people in statistics blessed it. So why not?

Others agree on the influence of diverse experiments. Hollister remembers hearing MDRC's early 1980s description of cobbling together the Work/Welfare demonstration (chapter 4) as offering a possible lifeline to a sinking ship. Angrist and Pischke (2010, 4, 15) highlight the importance of random assignment tests of the Progresa program (offering conditional cash transfers in Mexico), the Moving to Opportunity program (offering housing vouchers in four U.S. cities), and Project STAR (testing class size in Tennessee). Greenberg distinguishes the impact by audience: "I'm not sure that 'evidence of feasibility from past random assignment studies, and in particular those testing welfare and employment programs' was especially important in changing the views of academics or others in the evaluation community. I think most such persons thought that experiments were feasible under certain circumstances, although they may have doubted their usefulness. I do think demonstrations of feasibility influenced policymakers and administrators at the federal and (especially) the state and local levels and also in other countries."

Baron's experience working in Washington supports Greenberg's second point:

> In terms of the factors that stimulated that transformation, the precedent from welfare was critical. . . . The fact that some models produced big increases on employment and earnings, reduced welfare dependency and food stamps, and actually saved the government money was tremendously important. When I first started the Coalition, I would give examples from medicine. . . . I stopped doing that because I think the initial reaction was "but can you really do that kind of thing in social policy?" So welfare provided the premier example for how random assignment [can have] an impact on national policy.

Kathryn Stack, a senior career official who spent most of her thirty years at OMB focused on education, recalls her reaction on first hearing about the welfare experiments in 2005.

> I remember thinking "God this is great." It was the stark contrast between the reality of what I lived with for a couple of decades in education—tons of money spent on layers of new programs but no data whatsoever—and then seeing MDRC, with a history of successful evaluation under its belt, so unlike a lot of the IES research, which was just starting. . . . At that point we were still joking about the What Doesn't Work Clearing House and the fact that Russ [Whitehurst] had set up a whole structure that had challenged the education research establishment around the country but had no product as yet. The welfare story gave me an alternative vision: "Okay, this is how it is supposed to look. These guys have done the studies. They come back with the data; there are disappointments, but they can also point to some positive impacts."

Still others point to the distance traveled from the 1970s, according to Angrist and Pischke (2010, 6), when journal articles disparaged the credibility of empirical work in economics yet concluded "useful experiments are an unattainable ideal."

Hedges: "I always believed that experiments were probably the only reliable way to estimate causal effects in complex settings. . . . I used to worry about feasibility, but I have come to see that experiments are much more feasible, in more situations, than I thought 20 years ago."

Bloom: "You don't hear anymore that you can't do randomization. It is done all the time, and it is done better than it used to be. I think one of the big innovations in randomized research in the last decade, perhaps the single biggest, is the randomization of intact groups, or cluster randomization, and an understanding of the statistics of that and an ability to analyze it properly. It was done occasionally in the past out of necessity—schools might have been randomized—and often times it was analyzed improperly and things looked far more significant than they really were."[8]

The third factor was two changes in Washington: the creation of the Institute of Education Sciences in 2002 with Grover (Russ) Whitehurst as its founding director and the priority placed on experiments by OMB.[9] On the former, respondents agree with Hedges that the "IES has had a tremendous influence."

Hollister: "I think that is the most amazing accomplishment in governmental innovation that I've seen in all the years that I've watched this stuff. I really respect Whitehurst. He built it pretty much on an NIH [National Institutes of Health] model . . . and it is the best government office since the 1970s, when we had all the academics in there working on these things. And it is the full structure of it that most people don't know about."

Bloom: "[Whitehurst and the IES have] had the single biggest effect on experiments in the last 10 years. . . . That was a sea change, right there."

Rebecca Maynard: "[The IES] sent a clear message to the education research community that well designed and implemented experimental evaluations generate more credible evidence of the effectiveness of interventions than do well-designed and implemented quasi-experiments."

People point to Whitehurst's public acknowledgment that decades of research had provided little reliable evidence on effectiveness and credit his multipronged strategy for the IES's immediate and potentially enduring impact: building an expert permanent staff; matching research methods to questions, with a strong preference for randomized trials in the downstream efficacy and scale-up stages and other approaches to develop new programs and identify promising practices; transformation of the regional laboratories; creation of the What Works Clearinghouse to serve as the "central and trusted source of scientific evidence on what works in education" (Whitehurst 2012, 116);[10] the funding of a new professional organization (the Society for Research on Educational Effectiveness) emphasizing experiments; and the funding of very high-quality predoctoral and other training programs in education schools. Bloom expands on this last element:

> Those doctoral programs are one of the most important things to have happened in education research. They have transformed the mindset and the ability of students to do really high-quality quantitative impact research in education, and they haven't just given them a set of tools but have really given them a way to think about impacts and effects. [In the past, people] would be trained . . . to do cross sectional analyses or longitudinal analyses from secondary data, they would have very, very little knowledge about what randomized trials were, or for that matter what the stakes were with respect to what randomized trials or a high-quality quasi-experiment like a regression discontinuity design [could do], how they could support causal inferences in ways that these other approaches can't. They didn't appreciate that difference; they weren't trained to understand that difference.
>
> [Methods courses] have changed remarkably, and it is not just about experiments for them, but it clearly is a real sensitivity to making causal inferences. . . . They get the math, but they also get the logic. It must be drilled into them. . . . The next generation is being taught differently and, because the money is there to do this kind of research, the next generation is actually getting to do it.

Singer points to the IES's funding of experiments as transforming the field.

> I came out of a Stat department—and did a chunk of my course work in the biostat department at Harvard, where medical [randomized controlled trials] were standard operating procedure—and I believed this was something that (a) one should do, and (b) one could do, but (c) that it required money. And the rubber hitting the road was that educational research was just not funded at the level that other fields were getting funded. . . . The confluence was: there wasn't money to fund the work; in certain fields of education there wasn't the

interest in doing the work; and the swing in many education schools was not evidence based. . . .

[The] IES has had a huge impact. . . . When IES was founded, Russ said "I am going to put my money" (and he had a lot of money) "into doing much more serious educational research." Money . . . all of a sudden was made available, if you were going to do it his way . . . and at the kind of scale that you need given that education research is multilevel and longitudinal. It is just that much more expensive.

Whitehurst's reply, when asked why he took such a strong stand in favor of random assignment and whether he was aware of or influenced by the forty-year experience in welfare and related areas, reflects the multiple routes to the spread of experiments and the distance across disciplinary and policy silos.

My doctoral training was as an experimental psychologist. My research and the research of most of my colleagues in child and clinical and cognitive psychology for the 30 years in which I was an academic prior to federal service focused on developing interventions and evaluating them using randomized experiments. I taught the graduate research methods course in a leading psychology department for over a decade, in which I addressed systematically the strengths and weaknesses of various research methods with respect to causal inference. Cook and Campbell was a core text for my course. In short, conducting experiments to draw conclusions about the impact of social and cognitive interventions was part of the air I breathed my whole professional career prior to federal service.[11] On the flip side, during the later period of my academic career my research came to focus on preschool education and as a result I was thrust into settings in which research was being carried out that was to me shockingly deficient in methodological rigor. Thus I came to the U.S. Department of Education with both a strong grounding in the methodologies that the canon of the empirical social sciences identifies as appropriate to questions about what works, and with an aversion to what was passing for rigorous research in the areas of education with which I had come to be familiar. It seemed obvious to me that education research was in bad shape, could not be any better than the empirical methods on which it was based, and badly needed a reboot to bring it into the mainstream.

I was peripherally aware of randomized trials in welfare reform and employment training but my touchstones were the early federally sponsored trial of

Project Follow-Through, the [randomized controlled trial] of the Abecedarian Project, the considerable body of [randomized controlled trials] in clinical psychology, and clinical research on pharmaceuticals and health interventions.

The second major change was at OMB and the White House. As Haskins and Baron (2011, 6–7) describe it, "A remarkable aspect of the Obama evidence-based initiatives is that the President intended from the beginning of his administration to fund only programs that had solid evidence of success. . . . As early as his inaugural address, the President made it clear that an important goal of his administration would be to expand programs that work and eliminate programs that don't. . . . No president or budget director . . . has ever been so intent on using evidence to shape decisions about the funding of social programs as President Obama, former Budget Director [Peter] Orszag, and other senior officials at OMB."[12]

Baron, describing his ten years working with OMB, makes it clear that the seeds of this began under President George W. Bush, when few people there, other than those involved in the earlier welfare work (see chapter 7), understood that random assignment was unique.

PART [the Program Assessment Rating Tool used in the Bush administration] . . . was not originally focused on rigorous evaluation. . . . There wasn't that much understanding of the importance of a valid counterfactual. But that began to change. Robert Shea, who eventually became Executive Associate Director of OMB, became a strong supporter and advocate for random assignment studies, as did Kathy [Stack]. I remember coming out of a meeting in 2006 [in which] OMB was pushing random assignment studies and thinking "Wow, things have really changed." But a very large turning point was when you had people at the helm of OMB at the start of the Obama Administration who had done random assignment studies. . . . There were a lot of initiatives that went forward, including OMB's rigorous impact evaluation initiative, the tiered-evidence initiatives that crossed the agencies which called for rigorous evaluation using random assignment where feasible. Those made a big difference.[13]

A fourth factor was groups outside government advocating for, doing, and supporting experiments. The most remarkable is the Abdul Latif Jameel Poverty Action Lab (J-PAL) at MIT, founded in 2003 by Abhijit Banerjee, Esther Duflo, and Sendhil Mullainathan "to reduce poverty by ensuring that policy is based on scientific evidence."[14] As their website states, J-PAL's worldwide network of professors is united by their use of randomized evaluations to test and improve the effectiveness of programs and policies aimed at reducing poverty. It is hard to overstate their role in raising the profile of experiments internationally, with hundreds of evaluations completed or in progress and an outpouring of awards and publicity.[15]

Although they acknowledge that experiments cannot always be used and offer no miracle cure—and that building evidence is a slow process requiring continuous feedback between findings and theory—Duflo and her colleagues are breathtaking in their ambition: "Just as randomized trials revolutionized medicine in the twentieth century, they have the potential to revolutionize social policy during the twenty-first" (Duflo and Kremer 2008, 117). From this unusual perspective, Duflo responded to my three questions: What set you on the path of pioneering the use of experiments in development economics, and in particular was the success of U.S. experiments a factor? How would you describe the forty-year evolution of support for randomized field experiments by academics and international organizations? and If support has changed, why? Her answers follow:

1.   We knew about the RAND Health Insurance experiment, the [negative-income-tax] experiments, and the MDRC experiments. This showed us that it was doable. Without the experiments that existed in the U.S., we wouldn't have known we could do it.

2.   I have a better perception of the last 10–15 years than before. . . . My impression is that among academics, support for [randomized controlled trials] was always big, but they did not think this is something they could easily do. What has then changed is that, especially with experiments in developing countries, which are much cheaper, it suddenly became a way to do business. So the interest has literally exploded over the last 10–15 years, with academics starting their own projects or starting to participate in large projects. In the last 3–4 years or so, there is something of a backlash, with a view in the profession that this has gone too far, experiments are not the only way to go, experiments are a bit "stupid" (they don't require you to be intelligent). But the number continues to grow . . . so I guess this is the normal.

      Among international organizations, as of 15 years ago, there was considerable skepticism. They really felt that this was not feasible, too expensive, not worth it, etc. This has changed dramatically, starting with the

World Bank (and now people at the Bank are really leading the charge), then other agencies, progressively (DFID [the UK's Department for International Development], USAID, etc.). . . .

3. I think just getting started. . . . Both academics and people in those organizations saw it could be done, the barriers were not so formidable, the results were worth it. And then excitement grew.

A second group promoting experiments—but focused on the executive branch and Congress—is the Coalition for Evidence-Based Policy. Set up by Baron in 2001 with the mission "to increase government effectiveness through the use of rigorous evidence about what works" and to advocate for the widespread adoption of programs proven to be effective, the coalition's website affirms that "evidence of effectiveness generally cannot be considered definitive without ultimate confirmation in well-conducted randomized control trials."[16] A recent assessment concludes that the group has been successful in educating policy makers on the value of random assignment in large part owing to its independence and the fact that it has no agenda other than promoting good public policy and thus no conflict of interest. The same review credits the coalition with a role in OMB's requirement that many discretionary programs be subjected to rigorous evaluation and in legislation containing similar provisions (Wallace 2011, 2).

Stack, from her seat on the receiving side of their message, credits Baron with an unusual ability to reach across audiences and use the welfare reform story as a motivator.

He would do this spiel about "Look at what happened in welfare reform because of these experiments." And because people in the education world didn't have any experience with using rigorous evaluation to actually improve the delivery of services or to inform policy decisions on how to structure programs, he could articulate the welfare reform example to show how they (1) figured out how to seize dollars that were going out the door anyway, and (2) used waivers, set up experiments, and learned from that experience in ways that could influence policy. Just the example itself was illuminating in that, okay, research *can* be relevant to how we run programs.

He used that example a lot, but it became especially relevant whenever you [didn't have] a lot of new money. . . and you had to get smarter about how you used existing money. And his welfare experience captured people's imagination—both at the end of Bush, when they were trying to think about how do you reform and tighten up the use of resources at the same time, and then in this administration. . . . The welfare model gives you hope that in a time of declining resources, maybe we can still learn through flexibility and waivers, and the experiments that are tied to them, so we don't all have to sit around and say that now budgets are tight we can't learn anything.

A third group, which Maynard credits with being a major force in promoting experimental research among academics, is the Campbell Collaboration, the social policy analogue of the Cochrane Collaboration in medicine.[17] She particularly notes the pioneering roles of Robert Boruch and Lawrence Sherman in building on the early experiments in the area of crime and justice.

Ivry, while acknowledging that many foundations continue to doubt the usefulness of experiments (too slow, too expensive, not needed) or see them as a federal responsibility, points to the evolution in philanthropy as another factor fostering experiments. "There is a small subset that are not only strong proponents of evidence but that will actually pay for evaluations to produce that evidence. That has been part of the evolution in a deepening understanding and acceptance of the value of strong evaluations and the distinctions between good and weaker ones. [The] Edna McConnell Clark [Foundation] is probably in a class by itself. Evidence is a precondition for their investments, both in terms of what evidence you have in the past and building toward stronger evidence in the future. . . . Even if you have done an experiment and then scale up, you still have to do a [randomized controlled trial] around the scaling up."[18]

A fifth factor was the role of personal contacts and chance encounters in spreading what Hollister calls the "virus" of experiments. In the 1960s and 1970s this occurred through the common practice of academics' spending a year or two in government agencies and later participating in large experiments conducted by the major research firms.[19] Stack explains OMB's leadership thus: "The ultimate answer . . . is that it is all about relationships." Singer in part concurs: "The way in which ideas travel around and create revolutions, it happens in waves and it happens through chance or facilitated encounters, and it happens with money."

Some of the same interpersonal exchanges and serendipity spread the contagion internationally. In the 1980s, a European visitor to MDRC remarked, "What you are doing with random assignment is fascinating [long pause], but thank God we don't have to do that. We can just legislate reform; we don't have to test it first." Now, with tight budgets, attitudes have changed, and evidence-based social policy has gone global, aided by the "internationalization of graduate education in economics" (Cook 2010, 27), conferences, the Campbell Collaboration, the Abdul Latif Jameel Poverty Action Lab, international organizations, and the Internet.[20]

HAS RANDOM ASSIGNMENT WON THE WAR?

Over the period covered in this book, experiments have moved from a fringe activity to the work—and passion—of an astonishing array of scholars, groups, and government officials across the globe. Even in education, where enormous opposition remains, experiments have "won the hearts and minds" of young scholars (Howard Bloom), creating the hope that, as they move into senior positions, "these changes in the field will be irreversible" (Hedges).

In response to my query about the transformation, Cook says that, though it is not true across all the social sciences, in applied microeconomics and public policy schools "the battle has been won."

> But it is reversible, it is bound to be reversible, because random assignment doesn't speak to the kind of questions you get Nobel prizes for. You don't get Nobel prizes for saying if you vary x, y will happen. You get Nobel prizes for identifying new theories, and random assignment experiments can speak to theory but most of them don't very clearly or very directly.
>
> Science is about why things happen and not whether things happen. So the theory of causation . . . [the welfare and employment experiments] operated from . . . [is] a very important theory of causation but not the [one] that science most aspires to and admires, which is explanatory causation, identifying mechanisms, finding causal pathways, and the like. Random assignment is now being turned to that, but it is not an end in itself, it is a means. . . . And so there is a lot of creative work being done with multiple [instrumental variables] or using random assignment or site variation or some subpopulation variation to look at why things work not whether they work. And that is what I consider the next evolutionary step after the battle to get a better handle on identification through random assignment.

Others are also cautious because, as Angrist (2004, 210) has stated, "it is premature to declare victory," and poorly executed experiments could discredit the scientific integrity that makes random assignment so unique.[21]

Bloom adds that in some fields—notably education—experiments have yet to deliver the same kind of consistent and important findings as the welfare studies or, as we note throughout this book, explain why programs do or do not work.[22] Singer agrees, but for different reasons: "Money is important. In education, if the money goes away, it will go back. . . . You can't do these things without money." Maynard emphasizes leadership: "The most critical factor [in institutionalizing experiments] seems to be a strong commitment on the part of agency leadership to random assignment evaluations for studies of intervention effectiveness. If there is any ambivalence on the part of the agency leadership, staff and their contractors will slip into substituting fancy statistical modeling or qualitative research when there is any resistance to experimental design research by the practitioner community or when the available staff to carry out the project are not well-trained in experimental methods."

Hedges casts the fight for random assignment in the context of other struggles:

> I believe that, at least superficially, fights over methodology often have a similar character. . . . When the term "meta-analysis" was invented and the activity was proposed in 1976, the reaction of most established scientists was to dismiss it (atheoretical, misuse of statistics, even voodoo statistics). Some thoughtful critics said this might be good in principle, but impossible to do well in practice. Not every scholar dismissed it, but most good statisticians (whose own work concerned remarkably similar problems) said meta-analysis wasn't a real statistical problem. . . . Then, suddenly, the tide turned and everybody knew they had always seen meta-analysis as a core area of statistics. . . . I think that there are parallels in the acceptance of experimentation. . . .

> Methodological innovations (as we know them today) emerge out of a history of a methodological problem that troubles a field for a while before it is "solved." Usually the solution isn't completely novel. There is opposition to the innovation from many in the field, including many of the most established. The opposition dismisses the innovation as not being a real scientific method and being unimportant. Young people are often easier to capture, but some senior support is probably necessary to keep the innovators persisting. At some point, the vast field of critics melts away, often rather quickly.

This book tells of the fight, in one policy area, to show that experiments are a feasible and uniquely powerful method for answering a central evaluation question: Does a social program cause a change in behavior? The views shared in this coda suggest that the welfare story is not an aberration. During these forty years, and in some cases in interaction with our story, experiments moved out of the back room to take a starring role. However, this book also tells a cautionary tale: random assignment has not provided, and cannot alone provide, all the answers policy makers seek to make progress against tough problems. It is not enough to know whether programs produce results. Decision makers need to know why and how programs succeed or fail if they are to design more effective approaches. Although increasingly sophisticated experiments get part way inside the black box, many challenges remain for tomorrow's researchers.

APPENDIX

INDIVIDUALS CONTACTED FOR THE BOOK

(*Note*: Interviewees are identified by the titles they held at the time about which they were questioned, except for individuals whose most recent affiliation is also relevant and for MDRC staff who had multiple titles over the period of the book.)

Interviewed in Person or by Telephone

Mary Jo Bane (Howard, 2010): Former Assistant Secretary for Children and Families, U.S. Department of Health and Human Services

Jo Anne Barnhart (Howard, 2010, 2011): Former Associate Commissioner for Family Assistance, Social Security Administration, U.S. Department of Health and Human Services; Former Assistant Secretary for Children and Families, U.S. Department of Health and Human Services; Former Commissioner, Social Security Administration

Jon Baron (Howard, Judy, 2012)*: President, Coalition for Evidence-Based Policy

Michael Barth (Judy, 2009): Former Deputy Assistant Secretary for Income Security Policy, Office of the Assistant Secretary for Planning and Evaluation, U.S. Department of Health, Education, and Welfare

Gordon Berlin (Judy, 2007, 2009, 2011): Former Project Officer and Program Analyst, Office of Research and Development, Employment and Training Administration, U.S. Department of Labor; Former Deputy Director, Urban Poverty Program, Ford Foundation; Former Senior Vice President, MDRC; President, MDRC

*Individuals contacted for the coda to this book, "Random Assignment Takes Center Stage."

Susan Berresford (Judy, 2007): Former Vice President and President, Ford Foundation

Howard Bloom (Judy, 2012)*: Chief Social Scientist, MDRC

Thomas Brock (Judy, 2010): Director, Young Adults and Postsecondary Education, MDRC

Prudence Brown (Judy, 2007): Former Program Officer, Urban Poverty, Ford Foundation

David Butler (Judy, 2010): Vice President, Director, Health and Barriers to Employment, MDRC

Nancye Campbell (Howard, 2010): Research Analyst, Office of Planning, Research, and Evaluation, Administration for Children and Families, U.S. Department of Health and Human Services

Thomas Cook (Judy, 2012)*: Joan and Sarepta Harrison Chair of Ethics and Justice, Professor of Sociology, Psychology, Education, and Social Policy, Northwestern University

Mike Fishman (Howard, 2010): Former Director, Division of Income Security Policy, Office of the Assistant Secretary for Planning and Evaluation, U.S. Department of Health and Human Services

Keith Fontenot (Howard, 2012): Former Chief, Income Maintenance Branch, U.S. Office of Management and Budget

Peter Germanis (Howard, 2010): Former Senior Policy Analyst, Office of Policy Development, The White House

Olivia Golden (Howard, 2011): Former Commissioner for Children, Youth, and Families, Administration for Children and Families, U.S. Department of Health and Human Services; Former Assistant Secretary for Children and Families, U.S. Department of Health and Human Services

Barbara Goldman (Judy, 2006, 2009, 2010; Howard, 2010): Vice President, MDRC

Naomi Goldstein (Howard, 2012): Director, Office of Planning, Research, and Evaluation, Administration for Children and Families, U.S. Department of Health and Human Services

Robert Granger (Judy, 2010): Former Senior Vice President, MDRC; President, William T. Grant Foundation

John Greenwood (Judy, 2010): Former Director of Research, Innovations Program, Human Resources Development Canada; Former Executive Director, Social Research and Demonstration Corporation

William Grinker (Judy, 2009, and by email): Former President, MDRC

Jean Grossman (Howard, 2012): Former Chief Evaluation Officer, U.S. Department of Labor

Gayle Hamilton (Howard, 2010): Senior Fellow, MDRC

Ron Haskins (Howard, 2010): Former Welfare Counsel to the Republican Staff and Staff Director, Subcommittee on Human Resources, Committee on Ways and Means, U.S. House of Representatives

Martin Hirsch (Judy, 2011)*: Former High Commissioner Against Poverty and High Commissioner for Youth Policy, France

Robinson Hollister (Judy, 2009; Howard, Judy, 2012):* Former Chief of Research and Plans Division, U.S. Office of Economic Opportunity; Former Principal Investigator, National Supported Work Demonstration and Research Director, Mathematica Policy Research; Joseph Wharton Professor of Economics, Swarthmore College

Wade Horn (Howard, 2010): Former Commissioner for Children, Youth, and Families, Administration for Children and Families, U.S. Department of Health and Human Services; Former Assistant Secretary for Children and Families, U.S. Department of Health and Human Services

Robert Ivry (Judy, 2010, 2012, and by email)*: Senior Vice President, Development and External Affairs, MDRC

Julie Kerksick (Judy, 2010): Former Executive Director, New Hope Project

David Kleinberg (Howard, 2010): Former Deputy Associate Director, Health and Income Maintenance Division, U.S. Office of Management and Budget

Virginia Knox (Judy, 2010): Director, Family Well-Being and Child Development, MDRC

Karl Koerper (Howard, 2010): Former Director, Division of Economic Independence, Office of Planning, Research, and Evaluation, Administration for Children and Families, U.S. Department of Health and Human Services

Frederick (Fritz) Kramer (Judy, 2009): Former Program Officer and Division Chief, Office of Research and Development, Employment and Training Administration, U.S. Department of Labor

Michael Laracy (Howard, 2010): Former Assistant Commissioner for Policy, Program Development, and Evaluation, New Jersey Department of Human Services

Joan Leiman (Judy, 2009): Former Vice President, MDRC

Julia Lopez (Judy, 2010): Former Chief Consultant to the California Legislature's GAIN Joint Oversight Committee; Former Senior Vice President, Rockefeller Foundation

Richard Nathan (Judy, 2010): Former Chairman of the Board of Directors, MDRC

John Petraborg (Judy, 2010): Former Deputy Commissioner, Minnesota Department of Human Services

James Riccio (Judy, 2010, 2012)*: Director, Low-Wage Workers and Communities, MDRC

William Roper (Howard, 2010): Former Deputy Assistant to the President for Domestic Policy and Former Director of the Office of Policy Development, The White House

Ann Segal (Howard, 2010): Former Deputy to the Deputy Assistant Secretary for Human Services Policy, Office of the Assistant Secretary for Planning and Evaluation, U.S. Department of Health and Human Services

Judith Singer (Judy, 2012)*: Senior Vice Provost for Faculty Development and Diversity and James Bryant Conant Professor of Education, Harvard University

Robert Solow (Judy, 2009): Chairman of the Board of Directors, MDRC; Institute Professor, Massachusetts Institute of Technology

Kathryn Stack (Howard, Judy, 2012)*: Deputy Associate Director, Education and Human Resources, U.S. Office of Management and Budget

Franklin Thomas (Judy, 2010): Former President, Ford Foundation

John Wallace (Judy, 2010): Former Vice President, MDRC

Gail Wilensky (Howard, 2010): Former Administrator, Health Care Finance Administration, U.S. Department of Health and Human Services; Former Deputy Assistant to the President for Policy Development, The White House

Carl Williams (Judy, 2010): Former Deputy Director, California State Department of Social Services

Don Winstead (Judy, 2010): Former Assistant Secretary for Economic Services, Florida Department of Health and Rehabilitative Services

Responded in Writing to Questions (via email or letter)

Henry Aaron (Judy, 2012): Former Assistant Secretary for Planning and Evaluation, U.S. Department of Health and Human Services.

Joshua Angrist (Judy, 2012)*: Ford Professor of Economics, Massachusetts Institute of Technology

Richard Bavier (Howard, 2011): Former Policy Analyst, U.S. Office of Management and Budget

Dan Bloom (Judy, 2011): Director, Health and Barriers to Employment, MDRC

Barbara Blum (Judy, 2010): Former Commissioner, New York State Department of Social Services; Former President, MDRC

David Card (Judy, 2012)*: Class of 1950 Professor of Economics, University of California, Berkeley

Esther Duflo (Judy, 2012)*: Abdul Latif Jameel Professor of Poverty Alleviation and Development Economics, Massachusetts Institute of Technology; Cofounder and Director of Abdul Latif Jameel Poverty Action Lab

David Ellwood (Judy, 2012)*: Former Assistant Secretary for Planning and Evaluation, U.S. Department of Health and Human Services; Dean of the John F. Kennedy School of Government and Scott M. Black Professor of Political Economy, Harvard University

David Greenberg (Judy, 2011, 2012)*: Professor Emeritus of Economics, University of Maryland, Baltimore County

Virginia Hamilton (Judy, 2011): Former Research Manager, Employment Data and Research Division, California State Employment Development Department

James Healy (Judy, 2006): Senior Operations Associate and Director of Administration, MDRC

James Heckman (Judy, 2012)*: Henry Schultz Distinguished Service Professor of Economics, University of Chicago

Larry Hedges (Judy, 2012)*: Board of Trustees Professor of Statistics, Northwestern University

Aletha Huston (Judy, 2011): Endowed Professor, Department of Human Ecology, University of Texas at Austin

Rebecca Maynard (Howard, Judy, 2012)*: University Trustee Professor of Education and Social Policy, University of Pennsylvania; Former Commissioner of the National Center for Education Evaluation and Regional Assistance, Institute of Education Sciences, U.S. Department of Education

Larry Orr (Judy, 2012)*: Former Director, Office of Income Security Policy Research, Office of the Assistant Secretary for Planning and Evaluation, U.S. Department of Health, Education, and Welfare; Former Chief Economist, Abt Associates

Janice Peskin (Howard, 2011): Former Principal Analyst, Budget Analysis Division, Congressional Budget Office

Grover (Russ) Whitehurst (Judy, 2012)*: Founding Director, Institute of Education Sciences, U.S. Department of Education

Joan Zinzer (Judy, 2010): Former chief of the Workfare Division of the San Diego County Department of Social Services.

ABBREVIATIONS

ACF	Administration for Children and Families
AFDC	Aid to Families with Dependent Children
AFDC-UP	Aid to Families with Dependent Children-Unemployed Parent
ASPE	Office of the Assistant Secretary for Planning and Evaluation
CBO	Congressional Budget Office
CETA	Comprehensive Employment and Training Act (1973)
CWEP	Community Work Experience Program
DOL	U.S. Department of Labor
EITC	Earned Income Tax Credit program
ERA	Employment Retention and Advancement demonstration
FSA	Family Support Act of 1988
GAIN	Greater Avenues for Independence program (California)
HHS	U.S. Department of Health and Human Services
HRDC	Human Resources Development Canada
HRS	Department of Health and Rehabilitative Services (Florida)
IES	Institute of Education Sciences in U.S. Department of Education
ILIOAB	Interagency Low Income Opportunity Advisory Board
JOBS	Job Opportunities and Basic Skills Training program in the FSA (1988)
JTPA	Job Training Partnership Act (1982)
LEAP	Learning, Earning, and Parenting program (Ohio)
LIOB	Low Income Opportunity Board
MDRC	Until 2003, Manpower Demonstration Research Corporation
MFIP	Minnesota Family Investment Program

NIT	negative income tax
NLSY	National Longitudinal Survey of Youth
OBRA	Omnibus Budget Reconciliation Act of 1981
OFA	Office of Family Assistance
OMB	U.S. Office of Management and Budget
OPD	Office of Policy Development in the White House
OPRE	Office of Planning, Research, and Evaluation
PESD	Post-Employment Services demonstration
PRWORA	Personal Responsibility and Work Opportunity Reconciliation Act (1996)
REACH	Realizing Economic Achievement program (New Jersey)
RFP	request for proposals
SDSS	State Department of Social Services (California)
Section 1115	Section 1115(a) of the Social Security Act
SRDC	Social Research and Demonstration Corporation
SSA	Social Security Administration
SSP	Self-Sufficiency Project, Canada
SWIM	Saturation Work Initiative Model (San Diego)
TANF	Temporary Assistance for Needy Families in PRWORA (1996)
TPD	Teen Parent demonstration
WIN	Work Incentive program (1967)
WIN Labs	WIN Laboratory Project
Work/Welfare Demonstration	Demonstration of State Work/Welfare Initiatives (MDRC demonstration)
YIEPP	Youth Entitlement or Youth Incentive Entitlement Pilot Projects (1977)

NOTES

PREFACE

1. *The New York Times,* January 1, 2007.

CHAPTER 1

1. Rivlin (1971, 118–119).
2. Orr (1999, xi).
3. The number of families on welfare increased from 160,000 in 1936 to 270,000 in 1945; to 600,000 in 1955; 1,000,000 in 1965; 3,400,000 in 1975; 3,700,000 in 1985; and 4,900,000 in 1995. Another often unspoken change was that the program evolved from one that overwhelming supported white families to one that by 1995 was 36 percent non-Hispanic whites and 58 percent African Americans and Hispanics.
4. Milton Friedman (1962), from the political right, first developed the concept of an NIT in his famous book, *Capitalism and Freedom.* James Tobin (1966), from the left, advocated the idea in a seminal article in *The Public Interest.*
5. Louise Forsetlund, Iain Chalmers, and Arild Bjørndal (2007) find that random assignment was also used at least as early as 1928 in a study of social or education interventions.
6. Simple comparisons of means for treatment and control groups show an average decline in hours of work of about 7 percent for husbands and 17 percent for wives and single mothers (on a lower base for the women). Although these reductions may seem modest, the associated decline in earnings for married couples would result in an increase in total income that was less than half the benefit paid by the NIT (Burtless 1986).

CHAPTER 2

1. Member of MDRC's founding Board of Directors, as recalled in a 2009 interview.

2. MRDC Board of Directors (1980, 4).

3. California's Community Work Experience Program (known as workfare) was a three-year demonstration operating from 1972 to 1975.

4. The Vera Institute of Justice, a private, nonprofit corporation in New York City, was established in 1961 to develop ways to improve the criminal justice system. The Vera program, called the Wildcat Service Corporation, initially employed former addicts but soon expanded to include former offenders. Starting in 1971, Vera ran a similar but smaller program, the Pioneer Messenger Service.

5. For more on Sturz's style, see Roberts (2009).

6. As Richard Nathan, a member of the original Supported Work Advisory Committee, recalls.

7. The rest of the $32.9 million was raised by Supported Work local program operators from the sale of goods and services produced by supported workers and from locally generated grants. Of the $82.1 million total, $66.4 million was spent on local program operations, $3.6 million went for MDRC oversight, technical assistance, and research activities, and $12.4 million for contracted impact, benefit-cost analysis, and data collection work.

8. Section 1115, added to the Social Security Act in 1962, allows the relevant federal agency to "waive" (that is, permit states to ignore) provisions of the act in order to test, on a demonstration basis, new approaches to advancing the goals of the AFDC program. In Supported Work, the states sought seven waivers so that the programs could use some or all of the AFDC participants' welfare grants to pay wages, operate the program in only part of the state, equalize work incentives for experimentals and controls, ensure similar incentives across sites, and treat Supported Work participants as volunteers and thereby not subject to WIN sanctions. The existence and style of the planned research were not important factors in HHS's decision to approve the Supported Work waivers (unlike the later generations of waivers). A more explicit appeal was the idea of using AFDC funds to pay people to work, which some saw as an alternative, and voluntary, vision of workfare. Previously, AFDC waivers had also been used to divert funds in the Emergency Employment Act welfare demonstration project. (For full discussion of waivers, see chapter 7 in this volume.)

9. Grinker recalls that the building-block philosophy—in which one develops strategies, builds, tests, learns, and builds further—particularly appealed to the management styles of the assistant secretaries in the Nixon and Ford administrations, as did the fact that the demonstration "was sold on the basis of target groups." You put in your money, and you got your group.

10. For example, from the beginning, DOL made it clear that there had to be a credible and strong research component. As Michael Barth, then a research analyst in the Office of the Assistant Secretary of Planning and Evaluation recalls, HHS thought Supported Work might offer a way to move people from welfare to work without cutting off their benefits and would thereby help fend off the pressure from Russell Long, the powerful chairman of the Senate Finance Committee, and the White House to get tougher on welfare recipients. Furthermore, it could increase the quality and visibility of their own research operation. He remembers saying to John Palmer, his boss at the time, "This just seemed like a natural. Then you got people like Eli [Ginzberg] and Bob Solow involved in it and we said 'Wow, this is a good group for us to be associated with.'"

11. As an early chronicler noted, "Of the utmost importance from Sviridoff's point of view, [Ginzberg] was chairman of the National Manpower Advisory Committee, a post he retained through the Kennedy, Johnson, and Nixon administrations . . . which gave him a direct voice in the policies of DOL's Manpower Administration" (Brecher 1976, 54–55).

12. Among later examples is this comment from Grinker, as quoted in the *Wall Street Journal*, April 1, 1976: "We're not going to change the world with this concept. But maybe we can get a substantial number of people to function in a work setting so they can get jobs and hold them and begin to break the cycle of dependency and destructiveness. And that's not such a small accomplishment." MDRC's board of directors (1980, 2) made a similar statement at the project's conclusion: "Given the severe handicaps of the groups to whom it addressed itself, the Supported Work program was not expected to be successful with all or even a majority of its target groups."

13. In response to my query as to why he had favored random assignment, Solow sounds almost indignant: "My first job was as a professor of statistics! I favored it because I wanted to have a defensible response. I couldn't see just saying 'Well, we did this and so many of them got jobs or did whatever.' That's not adequate to an academic like me."

14. Ginzberg, Nathan, and Solow (1984, 313), writing about Supported Work in

1984, distinguish three primary roles for social experiments and science in general: "to refine estimates of numerical parameters; to choose between serious competing hypotheses; to test new ideas." The NITs fit the first category, Supported Work the third.

15. As Barth describes it looking back, the NITs were an intellectual landmark, but operationally simple, compared with Supported Work, because they were a completely stand-alone parallel welfare system.

16. This action fit with Sviridoff's and Ford's tradition of creating and sustaining institutions, prior and subsequent examples including the Urban Institute and the Local Initiatives Support Corporation. Kramer recalls Rosen stating that creating MDRC and having a federal funding consortium turn funds over to a nonprofit group was the biggest thing that DOL had done and something that had never been done before.

17. As to how MDRC got its first off-putting and oft-misstated original name (the Manpower Demonstration Research Corporation), Grinker says he "wanted something that would accurately represent what we were doing and did not have a catchy name or acronym. This goes to my vision of the organization. . . . I didn't want to scare off the feds or other potential interest groups with a name that would telegraph big ambitions and so we carefully orchestrated a low key approach . . . and the name was part of it."

18. I worked for Grinker from 1974 to early 1981, and Gordon Berlin did from 1988 to 1989 at New York City's Human Resources Administration, when Grinker was administrator-commissioner.

19. An example of how the tough guy also had a sense of humor was when Grinker once reported to staff that a job-aptitude diagnostic test he had taken at one of our demonstration sites indicated that he should become a florist.

20. I had spent two years in the research office at New York City's Human Resources Administration in teams studying welfare employment programs, caseload dynamics, and multiple city and federal reforms. In the process I learned from my colleagues in the agency and at the New York City RAND Institute and gained a healthy respect for the complexity of the AFDC program and an appreciation of effective ways to communicate with welfare administrators.

21. To focus the demonstration on people particularly in need of assistance and not typically served by other programs, supported workers had to be currently unemployed and have limited recent work experience. Furthermore, the welfare group had to be women on AFDC currently and for thirty out of the preceding thirty-six months (they actually averaged almost nine years on welfare) and

have no children under the age of six; former addicts had to be recently enrolled in a drug treatment program; former offenders had to be recently incarcerated; youth had to be seventeen to twenty years old, have dropped out of school, and (for at least half) have a criminal record or a history of delinquency.

22. Hollister (1984, 34), the architect of the statistical process study, describes it as "a multivariate analysis which related the character of the participants' Supported Work experience to such outcome variables as attendance and length of stay in Supported Work and the type of termination (whether the participant left to a job, was fired, or withdrew for other reasons such as health), and to postprogram outcomes such as hours of work and earnings. Variables which reflected the participants' work experience were developed for the type of work, the work environment (size of crew, characteristics of the crew members), the sector of supervision, and whether the work was for private or public sector clients." Many years later, Hollister notes, "I knew even then . . . that when you went inside the black box, you learned something but you can't attach any causality to that so it's exploratory always."

23. See chapters 4, 8, 9, and 10 for later examples of experimental designs with random assignment to multiple treatments and components, as Mathematica Policy Research had pushed for in Supported Work (and as had been done in the NIT experiments).

24. An exception was the variation in program duration (either twelve or eighteen months) among sites, but this was only weakly implemented.

25. In the case of the AFDC group, the Supported Work eligibility criteria meant both experimentals and controls were required to enroll in the WIN program. At the time, however, most were likely to be placed in what was called the unassigned pool and not likely to receive WIN services.

26. In the final Seattle-Denver NIT, for example, there were forty-eight different treatment groups.

27. According to Nathan (2000, 65), Lampman's concern was that the program had to "be large enough and last long enough so that it could reasonably be expected to have a significant impact. Lampman wanted to be sure we did not load the deck in favor of the null—or no effect—hypothesis. Lampman said: 'When persons with severe employment handicaps and disabilities are singled out for remediation, positive and lasting effects are not likely. In the case of supported work, the odds in favor of the null hypothesis were even greater . . . since the four groups chosen were from among those least likely to succeed in the labor market.'"

28.   On the null-hypothesis risk, according to an early account, Solow had pointed to why the challenge was tougher in Supported Work than in the earlier NIT experiments, where the projects would be deemed successful if the null hypothesis was affirmed. "In the New Jersey Negative Income Tax Experiment, for example, the concern was that participants might have less incentive to work and might even quit work altogether to enjoy to the full the benefits of the negative income tax. If the evaluation failed to secure evidence of a change in their job-seeking and work behavior, the null hypothesis would prevail and the sponsors would be pleased. But the Supported Work demonstration, it was hoped, *would* produce significant behavioral changes—a much more difficult hypothesis to prove" (Brecher 1978, 44).

29.   There was a consensus among funders and advisers that, if the national unemployment rate reached 6 percent or higher, the demonstration should be postponed. Ultimately it was not, despite an unemployment rate that reached 8 percent, its highest level since World War II, when most sites began in early 1975.

30.   In contrast to experiments discussed in later chapters, we expected some short-term impacts, when supported workers were employed in the program, but that this would decline when they left. This is somewhat different from the "decay" in impacts from unpaid programs, which came from a combination of experimental decay and control catch up. Our main question in Supported Work was: Did the up-front expense have a long-term payoff, after people left the program?

31.   In Mathematica Policy Research's original Supported Work proposal to MDRC, Charles Metcalf contrasted this aspect of Supported Work to the NITs, "which applied a treatment to each household for the full duration of the experiment."

32.   These are samples scheduled for baseline interviews. This strategy produced the most interviews at the least cost but led to a cohort problem, in that the subsamples for which we had outcome data for the longest period (follow-up) were those enrolled earliest and at particular sites, generating some uncertainty on whether changes in impacts over time for the combined sample reflected real trends or changes in sample composition. The resulting analysis problems prompted MDRC to steer clear of this and analyze what came to be called rectangular samples (where the analysis sample had uniform length of follow-up) in later studies.

33.   In Supported Work, there was substantial evidence of an operational learning curve, as reflected in indicators as diverse as attendance rates, postprogram job placements, and unit costs. The hope was that two factors—site selection that

sought strong sites and technical assistance—might yield a fair test of the program model.

34. Barbara Blum (with Blank 1990, 7), who was commissioner of the New York State Department of Social Services and later president of MDRC, points to this in explaining why welfare administrators did not pay much attention to the project. "Local sites were programs either developed specifically for the demonstration or operated by community social service agencies; the demonstration had no explicit connections to AFDC programs."

35. The full list of actions needed to ensure a quality experiment is too long to enumerate here. Important additional factors that Supported Work paid particular attention to include securing high survey completion rates, handling data meticulously, checking for biases (by comparing the survey data with various administrative records sources, conducting the baseline before and after random assignment, and examining sample attrition), and counting the right people in the various analyses.

36. I elaborate further on this "art" in Gueron (2002).

37. They raised warning flags on diverse issues: for example, be sure the researchers control the random assignment process; impose and rigorously defend the confidentiality procedures, including possibly moving the data to Canada if prosecutors sought access to survey data on self-reported drug use and arrests; beware of the premature release of findings.

38. Because every supported worker was tracked in the management information and time sheet systems, we could also ensure that no controls slipped by. Other steps to reduce burden include those already mentioned: how decisions about systematic variation, standardization, and sequential design explicitly weighed program interference against research yield.

39. Between 80 and 94 percent of people in the other three groups were male. For former addicts, the program did produce a substantial drop in illegal activities and, for the earliest cohort of enrollees, an increase in long-term earnings. There were no postprogram impacts for youth or former offenders.

40. Treatment-control differences that exceed certain thresholds are called statistically significant at the 1, 5, or 10 percent level, which means that one can be 99, 95, or 90 percent sure that the impact is greater than zero (that is, confident to that extent about rejecting the null hypothesis that the program had an impact of zero or less, not confident about affirming a specific impact number).

41. Estimates are for months nineteen to twenty-seven after random assignment and are all statistically significant at the 5 percent level.

42. The social perspective does not count changes in welfare and other transfer

payments that redistribute income among different groups in society because they involve no change in overall resources. However, welfare savings do show up as benefits in the nonparticipant and budget perspectives. For the AFDC group, the study found that nonparticipants came out ahead under most assumptions. Under the narrower budget perspective (which does not count the value of the output produced by the supported workers while in the program), the findings suggested that the government ultimately might save money, but this conclusion was very sensitive to the rather generous assumptions about how long the beneficial impacts lasted. Participants came out ahead or behind depending on similar assumptions (Kemper, Long, and Thornton 1981).

43. During the time people were getting paid by their program jobs, there was a dramatic reduction in the percentage in poverty (12 percent for experimentals versus 53 percent for controls), but this fell to a small, nonsignificant difference by the end of the follow-up.

44. Women on welfare volunteered for Supported Work jobs, stayed the longest, and often had to be forced to leave.

45. In-depth interviews with participants would not have solved the problem, since they could not have known whether their favorable results were attributable to the program.

46. The cohort phenomenon, as described earlier in this chapter, resulted from the design decision to create a sample in which early enrollees had longer follow-up. Because the economy and, arguably, the programs improved over time, it is not surprising that impacts varied by cohorts of people (experimentals and controls) defined by the length of follow-up.

47. Two early studies, LaLonde (1986) and Fraker and Maynard (1987) were particularly influential. Bloom, Michalopoulos, and Hill (2005) provide an eloquent summary of this literature.

48. Completion rates for the twenty-seven-month interviews were 63 to 79 percent (depending on the target group) of those randomly assigned and scheduled for the interview.

49. This included the quality of leadership and the strategies and techniques used to implement each aspect of the program: recruiting people, raising money, creating work sites, structuring the program, and placing people in unsubsidized jobs.

50. Lee Friedman (1977, 170), who conducted the benefit-cost analysis of the Vera supported work program, had urged that researchers use the subsequent national demonstration to try to identify which aspects of the program contrib-

ute to its results: "A good social program in one area is of little national value unless it can be replicated. Preliminary success is relative only to having no program at all, not to what might be. Unless we go beyond simply measuring inputs and outputs in the hope of learning about the alternative technologies available for operations, we are likely to reduce unnecessarily our chances of successfully implementing complex social programs."

51. Ginzberg shared this view: "I seriously doubt on the basis of my three and a half decades of continuing involvement in the activities of the federal government that it would have been possible to design, launch, and make operational such an ambitious multi-site experiment with an elaborate research component except through an independent management arm" (Gueron, Rubinger, and Walker 1976, x).

52. This contrasts sharply with our later strategy, described in chapters 4, 6, 8, and 10.

53. The 1973 Comprehensive Employment and Training Act provided block grants to states and localities to support job training and related programs. States were given more control of federally funded programs, one step in the process of increasing devolution of authority.

54. Although it was not clear that those approaches would help the same group of women on welfare (who were very long-term recipients, but nonetheless volunteers), their greater apparent cost effectiveness turned policy makers away from Supported Work.

CHAPTER 3

1. DOL Program Officer for WIN Labs, as recalled in a 2009 interview.

2. Elmore (1985, 312).

3. Both projects were sole-source contracts with the Department of Labor. This may sound strange in the current era of virtually universal competitive bidding. MDRC did have to submit a detailed written proposal in each case, however, and the proposals did have to go through DOL's formal evaluation and approval process.

4. Berlin went on to become deputy director of the Urban Poverty Program at the Ford Foundation and eventually president of MDRC. In the WIN Labs project, the research funds came from Rosen and the operating funds from Hans. Ford also provided a small grant, which fit William Grinker's style of using Ford funds to give MDRC some independence.

5. Grinker proposed six criteria that MDRC should use in assessing new projects.

Four were relatively straightforward: the project should be susceptible to reliable evaluation, have an institution interested in using the results, be within our capacity, and both build on our experience and not jeopardize existing work. However, the last two—the program would deal with a significant national concern with a philosophy consistent with that of MDRC's board and staff and MDRC would be invited by sponsoring agencies that made an adequate commitment to guarantee our independence, flexibility, and control—would be discarded when MDRC launched evaluations of controversial Reagan-era workfare programs without any "invitation" and under state contracts (see chapter 4).

6. This was Nathan Azrin's study of mandatory job-finding clubs conducted between 1976 and 1978, which involved the random assignment of 1,000 people (half women and half men) in five WIN offices. The job clubs included daily group meetings to teach methods to look for a job and to develop positive job-search attitudes through group reinforcement, supervised job search, help in preparing resumes, and access to a telephone bank (Greenberg and Shroder 2004).

7. Only eleven states and the District of Columbia expressed initial interest.

8. Ultimately, for reasons given later in this chapter, WIN Labs ended after two projects at three of the sites and after only one at the fourth site. In an early experimental attempt to measure the impact of separate aspects of a multicomponent program, the first Denver project actually included two experiments, in which groups received different combinations of recruitment activities and services.

9. There was also a field observation study to understand client-staff interactions and decision making.

10. Random assignment was not used in St. Louis, where the study focused on the feasibility and potential of establishing the link between WIN and a business organization.

11. We subsequently learned that the Colorado Monthly Reporting Experiment, started in 1976, had used AFDC records to track the effect of changes in administrative procedures on payments.

12. To do this, we reordered the administrative records into longitudinal data files on each person in the sample. In the end, reflecting in part our inexperience and in part the state of computerized records, this was far more labor intensive than anticipated, requiring that extensive data be copied by hand from case files. As a result, the cost and time needed to gain access to these data and ensure their quality were unexpectedly high.

13. The normal intake process was altered to give staff the opportunity to explain the study, to get people's informed consent (indicating awareness of the random assignment procedure and consent for researchers to view program records), and to collect some minimal background characteristics on each person in the sample.

14. Net cost is the average additional cost WIN incurred for the experimentals above the costs incurred for the control group.

15. During its much shorter follow-up, Louisville's second test (the group job-search experiment) had surprisingly similar employment impacts.

16. For example, in Louisville, interviews with about five hundred clients six months after random assignment were used to collect minimal information on wage levels, hours worked, and type of jobs.

17. We developed a participation "funnel" explaining the fall-off from the number of youths eligible for the program to the number of those who heard of it, applied, enrolled, and ultimately participated.

18. The impact study compared the behavior of eligible youth in four YIEPP sites (Baltimore, Denver, Cincinnati, and eight rural counties in Mississippi) with that of similar youth in four comparison sites (Cleveland, Phoenix, Louisville, and six neighboring counties in Mississippi). While the program was operating, roughly 40 percent of African American youth in program sites were working, compared with around 20 percent in comparison sites. In the months after the demonstration ended, the difference fell to 5 percentage points (Gueron 1984a, 14–17).

19. As a result, we avoided what Henry Aaron (1978, 158–59), in an oft-quoted passage, describes as the relationship between scholarship and policy during the Great Society and its aftermath. Pointing to the conservative effect on policy makers of disputes among experts, he asks, "What is an ordinary member of the tribe [that is, the public] to do when the witch doctors [the scientists and scholars] disagree?" He goes further, arguing that such conflict not only paralyzes policy but also undercuts the "simple faiths" that often make action possible.

CHAPTER 4

1. September 1981.

2. April 1982.

3. In this book, we use the term *workfare* narrowly, to describe a mandatory work-for-benefits program; some others, at the time, used the term to cover programs requiring participation in any work-related activity.

4. Previously, states needed federal waivers or could require participation in WIN

work experience for up to thirteen weeks and up to full time in positions intended not as work for benefits but as a way to develop basic work habits and acquire work experience.

5. Years later, Barbara Blum, New York State's welfare commissioner at the time, notes the significance of the shift to single agency administration for both the WIN program and MDRC. "I can't overemphasize how important this change was. It contributed greatly to the implementation of MDRC's work-welfare experiments."

6. Looking back years later, Grinker recalls initially thinking that what MDRC did would be right up Reagan's alley because "it's experimenting, it's using data and information about what works and what doesn't." But at DOL, he remembers, "They couldn't care less. They just wanted out, they didn't want to do anything. It was the end, at least for a while."

7. Under the public service employment program (funded under the 1973 Comprehensive Employment and Training Act), state and local governments provided subsidized jobs in public and nonprofit agencies to economically disadvantaged and unemployed people.

8. In chapter 5, Howard Rolston, who was at OFA at the time, recounts this story from the government's perspective.

9. More than thirty years later, reacting to a draft of this chapter, Grinker commented that it overstated the threat of MDRC's extinction: "Sure, I might have set it up as a straw man in a memo or two, but it was not seriously on the table during my tenure." I can imagine that it might not have been real for him (possibly because of his perspective on the Ford Foundation), but after he left I certainly experienced it that way and felt that pulling off the project described in this chapter was a do-or-die challenge.

10. In a January 19, 1982, internal memo, Gary Walker, MDRC's senior vice president, reasoned that staff should not agonize too much about improving workfare, since our ability to influence the outcome of large-scale state initiatives was modest at best. He argued, moreover, that if it was central to current social policy, then "the origin of the idea—be it Karl Marx or Attila the Hun—should influence us only to the extent that it impacts our ability to do our developmental, evaluation, and reporting tasks in a competent and honest manner."

11. However, our ambiguity about our mission lingered. Some staff remained restive with the concept of MDRC as just a research firm with a purely academic interest in securing valid results rather than an organization institutionally committed to helping the disadvantaged. Over the years, I chose not to force resolu-

tion of this issue, since different staff were clearly motivated by each formulation. As discussed in chapters 6, 8, and 10, this played itself out in our decision to present and actively communicate the findings and trade-offs but not to make recommendations on what we viewed as primarily political questions. This was a departure from our position in Supported Work and YIEPP, when we had recommended expanded funding.

12. Because of these constraints, we called these projects unfunded demonstrations (in contrast to funded demonstrations, such as Supported Work). Although this was the original vision of the project, over time most of the states were able to obtain some supplemental operating funds either from a foundation (in two states) or through special federal section 1115 demonstrations that included such resources.

13. Although some (for example, Moffitt and Ver Ploeg 2001, 30) characterize the early 1980s experiments as small scale, neither the studies nor the programs were small. For example, in addition to the study areas shown in table 4.2, Virginia and West Virginia implemented the WIN demonstration program statewide, and Arkansas, Illinois, and Maryland in selected other areas. In San Diego, additional people were assigned to a nonresearch group that also received the experimental treatment. Thus in most cases the programs were substantially larger than the local Supported Work sites, although smaller than the full-scale studies described in chapter 8.

14. The allure of grant diversion comes from the mathematical formula that drives any means-tested program (see chapter 2). Under the rules of AFDC, when a single mother went to work, her grant was reduced or eliminated based on a formula that took into consideration the amount she earned and the prevailing rules on whether some of those earnings could be ignored to provide a work incentive and to cover some of her child care and other work-related expenses. Under normal procedures, the grant reduction was simply returned as welfare savings to the federal and state or local agencies that paid for AFDC benefits. The idea behind grant diversion was to use this potential savings (that is, to divert it) to fund programs intended to employ welfare recipients. The attraction was both financial and rhetorical. From the program's perspective, grant diversion seems like a way to print money: you can suddenly tap open-ended entitlement funds to pay for a new service. But from the government's perspective, it is a productive investment only if the program succeeds in getting more people to work—or to work sooner. If that is not the case, the process diverts from the treasury money that would come from normal welfare turnover, without

achieving any additional savings. Sorting this out is one rationale for an impact study, as Howard discusses in some detail in chapter 7. It is also the reason for targeting grant diversion–funded programs at people unlikely to leave the rolls on their own, as was the case in Supported Work.

15. In addition to this design for states with mandatory programs, we had a parallel study for voluntary grant-diversion programs.

16. In WIN demonstration programs, as was true before OBRA, staff could impose sanctions—reducing the welfare grant for single-parent AFDC cases and ending support for two-parent AFDC-UP cases—on persons who refused to participate without good cause.

17. This lack of saturation also prompted us to abandon a planned study of whether the mandates deterred people from applying for welfare, a phenomenon sometimes called "entry effects," since it seemed less likely that the general population would be affected by a new message. We decided that the first-order question was to get a reliable estimate of whether the programs had an impact on people who actually heard the message and got the services (to determine whether they were deterred from completing the application process or were prompted to exit the rolls more quickly). If the programs affected those measures, it would suggest that our estimates were conservative and there might be some further deterrence from an expanded program.

18. For reasons discussed in chapter 6, in contrast to Supported Work, the WIN Labs, and other prior studies of voluntary programs, the Work/Welfare demonstration did not give people the opportunity to opt out of the program or the random assignment study.

19. Virginia Hamilton, the state's contract officer for the evaluation, recalls two reasons for this decision: a prior study comparing Employment Preparation Program and nonprogram sites had been discredited, and the state knew of and valued earlier random assignment studies.

20. Two examples illustrate this. In early July 1982, we won a state competition to evaluate San Diego's program and by early August had to finalize the random assignment procedures, develop the intake and other forms, specify the data needs, develop the training materials, and begin random assignment so that the San Diego program could start on schedule. Ford fronted the funds to support all of this, since we did not get a signed contract from California until November 1982. In West Virginia, we devised a way to tap federal funds to support the expansion of the evaluation to include single mothers, but it involved Ford's taking back $170,000 it had previously awarded MDRC and regranting these funds to the state, which could then draw down an equal

amount in federal matching funds and use the $340,000 for the evaluation. Not only did this create an administrative burden, but it carried some risk, since under federal rules there could be no up-front guarantee that the funds Ford gave the state would be used for MDRC's evaluation. Although Brown later agreed that keeping track of this was complex (recalling a spaghetti diagram of funding flows), her memory is that MDRC had more to lose than Ford, so her view was that if MDRC was willing to take the risk of giving back the money, so was she.

21. This was before a highly acclaimed report by two Harvard professors, Mary Jo Bane and David Ellwood (1983), popularized the concept.

22. It was only later that waiver approval was conditioned on the state's conducting a random assignment study; see chapter 7. For a full discussion of section 1115 waivers, see chapter 5.

23. See the discussion in chapter 6 of ethics and gaining cooperation.

24. See chapter 8 for states' and foundations' increased support of later evaluations.

25. Thus when OFA's RFP for the Saturation Work Initiative Model came out in 1984 (see chapter 5), the San Diego leadership applied and invited us to conduct the random assignment evaluation. Also see the discussion in chapter 8 of California's Greater Avenues for Independence and Florida's Project Independence.

26. The wisdom of Bopp's reaction was suggested by the Illinois commissioner Gregory Coler's comment the day before the conference that improvement in impacts of 5 to 8 percent[age points] would be "disappointing" and that if this was all that could be expected, he probably would not be in the MDRC study.

27. Two studies of the Massachusetts program's impacts, neither of which used random assignment, subsequently reported conflicting results.

28. Here I describe the federal actions from MDRC's perspective. In the next chapter, Howard recounts how the same events looked from the federal point of view.

29. The meeting included Anthony Pollechio, the deputy assistant secretary for income maintenance, and others in the Office of the Assistant Secretary for Planning and Evaluation, and Michael deMaar, the director of policy and evaluation, and others in OFA.

CHAPTER 5

1. Department of Health and Human Services Associate Commissioner from 1983 to 1986, as recalled in a 2011 interview.

2. The Health Insurance Experiment, initiated in 1971 and completed in 1982,

randomly assigned 2,750 families to one of five health insurance plans. It addressed the question of the effects of cost sharing on service use, quality of care, and health. For a brief summary, see RAND (2006).

3. For the federal role in early social experiments, see chapter 1; for MDRC and the Work/Welfare demonstration, see chapter 4.

4. Microsimulation was the basis for the administration proposals to change the disregard structure and several others. Although later there would be disagreement with CBO about whether the proposals would result in a labor supply reduction, later assessment of the effects of changes to law that actually occurred supported the administration's position.

5. Given that the estimates are specific numbers already set, such an exercise is not a scientific search for new knowledge, wherever it may lead, but rather the more intellectually questionable search for the strongest numbers to support a case already made. A truly objective investigation, in contrast, always runs the risk of finding new evidence that at least casts doubt on, and may outright disprove, the original estimates.

6. There can be circumstances in which crossing an immediate political superior is necessary, for example, when asked a factual question by the secretary who has been given misinformation by the assistant secretary of one's own agency.

7. It is peculiar that the Administration on Children, Youth, and Families is a subagency in ACF, since its name implies a more expansive set of responsibilities. However, the former existed before the latter and was established by federal statute.

8. For me this usually meant presenting an annual research plan, which reflected the budget appropriated by Congress, to an assistant secretary, meeting with him or her, and getting feedback and approval. Usually the assistant secretary would have ideas to contribute, in which case we would modify the plan, but not in major ways. After plan approval, my staff and I would execute it, with flexibility to modify it operationally as needed. In the course of a year, events would typically arise that required a larger midcourse correction; these would require the assistant secretary's approval.

9. In addition, labor unions opposed workfare as potentially endangering the jobs of regular workers, although CWEP had provisions that prohibited displacement of current workers and positions.

10. Statutory language asserted that CWEP was not to be regarded as employment nor would requiring an individual to participate in it "convert" her welfare benefit into earnings.

11. "Medicaid notch" describes the fact that, with limited, temporary exceptions, the additional dollar of income that led to AFDC ineligibility also resulted in Medicaid ineligibility, creating a "marginal tax rate" in excess of 100 percent.

12. The tone of the memorandum is a prelude to the fact that OFA would become responsible for the AFDC research function by the end of 1982.

13. It is common for federal grants and contracts to be awarded late in September as the close of the federal fiscal year is September 30, and in almost all cases unobligated funds cannot be carried over into the next year and, thus, are lost to the program. In a transition year, such as 1981, this is even more pronounced as the new political officials' late arrival pushes events even closer to the end of the fiscal year.

14. Unless required for clarity, from here on I refer to subsection 1115(a) simply as section 1115.

15. The following discussion is based on the legal framework under which HHS has operated for nearly fifty years and which was set forth by HHS general counsel Joel Cohen in a March 13, 1964, draft memorandum to the files entitled "Scope of Section 1115 of the Social Security Act." Although subsequent legal interpretations were made regarding specific issues, the general framework remains unchanged.

16. For a fuller discussion of JOBS, see chapter 9.

17. Joel Cohen, March 13, 1964, draft memorandum, "Scope of Section 1115 of the Social Security Act."

18. At various times there were other rates for special purposes, for example, for the JOBS program and for state computer systems development.

19. This argument primarily pertains to CWEP. In fact, the disregard changes had substantial empirical support, and subsequent research on OBRA policies strongly suggested they produced large savings. However, there was no rigorous evaluation of whether, over the long run, the restriction in the disregards reduced employment, particularly the uptake of work by those not currently working.

20. Barnow (1987) reviews in detail analyses by five groups of organization/authors, some of which themselves involve multiple analyses, along with briefly describing a number of additional studies.

21. Then Jo Anne Ross.

22. At the time, grant diversion in the form contemplated in the announcement required section 1115 waivers; in the course of the funded projects, the Deficit Reduction Act of 1984 made it statutorily permissible without waivers.

23. The American Recovery and Reinvestment Act of 2009 (ARRA) provided generous federal funding of subsidized employment that generated much larger numbers of such positions than was true for such regular programs under AFDC or Temporary Assistance for Needy Families (TANF). It is plausible that the particularly difficult economic times of the 2008–2009 recession, plus the fact that the act targeted many laid-off workers who had higher skills than the more disadvantaged welfare recipients previously targeted, made the subsidy more attractive to employers.

24. Staff who work for congressional committees or members of Congress are virtually always affiliated with the party of the members for whom they work. In contrast, most staff of the three congressional agencies—CBO, the Congressional Research Service, and the General Accountability Office (until 2004, the Government Accounting Office)—are career appointments. In the case of CBO, only the director and the deputy director are not civil servants. The Speaker of the House and the president pro tempore of the Senate jointly appoint the director, who under law is to be selected "without regard to political affiliation and solely on the basis of his fitness to perform his duties." The director appoints the deputy (Lynch 2010).

25. Appropriate experimental designs can be used to capture effects on entry, for example, those of the negative income tax, but these designs were not realistic in this case.

26. Another important predecessor that operated from mid-1980 to 1983 was Project Redirection, a matched comparison study, conducted by MDRC, of whether a voluntary program of services for teen parents improved their employment outcomes. The two-year findings were primarily negative, suggesting that the program had been ineffective for the average participant. Five-year findings, which became available later, were more positive in a number of dimensions (Polit, Quint, and Riccio 1988).

27. In HHS, operating divisions are agencies that operate programs (as opposed to staff agencies), for example, the Center for Medicare and Medicaid Services, the National Institutes of Health, and, before it became an independent agency in 1994, the Social Security Administration.

28. Since this planning took place before the reorganization that created the Family Support Administration, it did not hurt that the ASPE contracts office was much more amenable to acting positively than their SSA counterparts.

29. The contract was awarded to Mathematica Policy Research in September 1986.

CHAPTER 6

1. The *Congressional Record,* September 12, 1995, S13327.

2. Editorial, March 7, 1986.

3. House Ways and Means Committee staff 1986–2000, as recalled in a 2010 interview.

4. This chapter focuses on the years preceding passage of the Family Support Act and thus on MDRC's Work/Welfare demonstration, not on SWIM. However, MDRC's first SWIM report was published in August 1988, and some findings on participation were shared in April 1988, while Congress was still debating the final shape of the legislation. Thus for completeness, the next few pages include findings from the saturation work initiative model and some longer follow-up that became available after passage of the act. These do not change the lessons; but in the case of SWIM, the findings were somewhat more positive than for the six original demonstration sites. Lessons from the two grant diversion studies are summarized in chapter 5.

5. This is the rate at which people ever took part in some required activity. In the two programs with adequate funds to saturate the caseload for as long as people were on welfare (West Virginia for fathers, in two-parent cases, and SWIM), we used a tougher measure (the monthly participation rate) and again found a maximum of about 50 percent, suggesting that the constraint was not money but operational feasibility.

6. In three of the sites, we implemented a three-group random assignment design to determine whether adding workfare had an incremental effect over and above that of job search. The most reliable results, from San Diego, suggested possible gains in earnings (but not reductions in welfare); however, the lack of consistent results for people enrolling at different times in that site, and the lack of impacts in the other two sites (where the program was weaker), suggested that, at most, the impact was small.

7. Our mistakes were agreeing to do random assignment by using social security numbers in a second site in California (San Mateo, which fortunately was never part of the core study) and by using the welfare rolls in Cook County (where we subsequently restarted random assignment under our own rules).

8. San Diego was included in the work-site surveys and a small six-month follow-up survey.

9. MDRC had convened institutional review boards and sought informed con-

sent in its studies of voluntary programs, including those discussed in chapters 2 and 3.

10. In terms of the taxonomy in List 2011, these tests of mandatory welfare-to-work programs are more akin to natural field experiments (where people are not given a choice about whether to participate in the study) than to framed field experiments (where people self-select by volunteering for the study) and thereby produce more generalizable results.

11. This was the case because, in the absence of the study, people in the experimental group could not refuse to be in the new program (since it was mandatory) and because some people would ordinarily be denied services (since funds were limited); thus controls were not unduly disadvantaged. Moreover, all people in the study would continue to receive basic entitlements.

12. The AFDC and unemployment insurance earnings data come from systems that have strong incentives to be accurate: the former records actual checks paid and the latter comes from employers and is tied to unemployment insurance benefits. There may be data entry errors or, for unemployment insurance, underreporting (if people moved out of state or worked in jobs not covered by the system). But there is no reason to believe such factors would differentially affect people in the experimental and control groups.

13. Because they documented their views at the time, Moynihan, Baum, and Haskins get central billing in this chapter; however, other senators and representatives (most notably Thomas Downey) played major roles crafting the legislation, as did senior staff, including Sheila Burke, Margaret Malone, Joseph Humphreys, and Deborah Colton.

14. See chapter 8 for criticism of this strategy as a kind of minimal common denominator.

15. Early in the Work/Welfare demonstration, we set up a committee of board members and outside experts to review the research design and every major report. The committee (always chaired by Robert Solow and later renamed the Welfare Studies Committee) went on to play this role for MDRC welfare work for the next twenty years. (Other initial members included Henry Aaron, Gary Burtless, David Ellwood, Frank Levy, Richard Nathan, Robert Reischauer, and Harold Richman.) In contrast to many such committees—where the contribution is not obvious and the role withers away over time—this one provided value that vastly exceeded our initial vision. From the beginning, it provided critical review of methodological and design issues, analysis strategy, and the many reports; it also served as a sounding board for staff ideas on issues as di-

verse as the priorities among questions and our interpretation of results. We had started the Work/Welfare project with a relatively green staff. That they were by the end savvy veterans was mainly a result of their own efforts but also to our internal review process and to the critiques, coaching, and inspiration from members of that committee.

16. One somewhat helpful approach was to present how the experimentals and controls were distributed by earnings levels, or by the four possible combinations of employment and welfare status (receiving no earnings and no welfare, receiving some earnings and no welfare, and so on) or by different income levels (as measured by the sum of welfare and earnings). Producing these distributions held some surprises, as we discovered a large group of people with no welfare benefits and no reported earnings, which raised questions that were addressed in later studies.

17. As a result, unit costs and average impacts for broad-coverage programs might almost by definition be expected to be lower than for selective-voluntary programs, unless (as some people hoped and as was suggested ten years later by the two-stage random assignment conducted in some Job Opportunities and Basic Skills Training program evaluation sites) the mandatory message and sanctions per se had an important effect. For this reason, I warned against using comparisons of average impacts from these two types of studies to reach a conclusion on whether specific activities (for example, mandatory job clubs versus voluntary skills training) are more successful, without considering the differences in participation and average unit cost, and I pointed to benefit-cost analysis as a way to level the playing field for assessing relative effectiveness. I do not think many people were convinced by this argument.

18. Our experience with the first set of reports prompted a structured review process that ultimately proved critical to maintaining state cooperation and support. We would produce a draft and meet with state and at times county staff to explain the results and diffuse tensions. This led to detailed written comments that helped us avoid errors of fact or tone but did not change the bottom-line story.

19. My guess is that another aspect of the Work/Welfare demonstration also contributed to its impact in Congress. Blum or I would sometimes testify in a hearing at which an official from the participating state or county would describe the program and share his or her view of the achievements and lessons. This amplified the message, adding authenticity and political heft to the research findings.

CHAPTER 7

1. United We Stand American Conference, August 12, 1995.

2. Former OMB Policy Analyst.

3. This was unlike the Wisconsin waiver request after passage of the Omnibus Budget Reconciliation Act, in which the state asked to be allowed to continue to apply the thirty-and-one-third disregard indefinitely, as had been provided for under prior law. Under the thirty-and-one-third provision, welfare recipients could supplement their benefits package with earnings from work. The first $30 of earnings could be kept in its entirety; for each additional $3 in earnings, $1 could be kept.

4. Why some HHS staff had doubts about the authority to alter disregards is not clear, since AFDC disregard rules were in section 402 and thus subject to waiver.

5. Although I have not found the term "federal cost neutrality" in documents dated before the summer of that year, certainly from the time of Wisconsin's initial request, both HHS and the state were talking in terms of a counterfactual baseline for federal costs.

6. Since this was totally unexpected, I called back to Washington to ask for approval to do so. Procedures in most federal agencies require staff to have clearance from the public affairs office before talking with the media.

7. Steven Teles (1996, 127) writes that "one of the board's first actions was to approve two waivers—for New Jersey and Wisconsin—for which rejection letters had been signed by HHS Secretary Otis Bowen." In this statement he makes three errors in addition to a misleading suggestion. First, there was only a single letter for Wisconsin. Second, it was an unsigned draft. Third, as implied by its name, the board's role was advisory; authority to approve or disapprove state waiver demonstrations resided with the department secretaries. Finally, Teles's description wrongly suggests that HHS had made a firm decision that was subsequently reversed.

8. When Congress appropriates funds to departments, the dollars are not immediately available to them. Rather there is a process, called apportionment, by which OMB makes the funds available.

9. There was no strong evidence that adding a child care benefit or a longer Medicaid extension for those leaving welfare for work would be effective in increasing the number who did so. And given the many recipients who already left welfare for work, any likely increase would be much smaller than the current

number, so "buying out the base" would more than offset any savings (probably by a very large margin).

10. Federal cost neutrality was a policy position, not a legal requirement as Teles incorrectly states. It is an easy mistake to make if one is not familiar with reading statutes. Section 1115(b) of the Social Security Act, a special demonstration authority enacted in 1977 and no longer available to states after October 1980, did require cost neutrality, but all the waiver demonstrations approved were under section 1115(a). Rogers-Dillon (2004) and R. Kent Weaver (2000) follow Teles and repeat his error.

11. Barnhart tells me that Hobbs also expressed ethical concerns in conversation with her, but he did not do so within my earshot until his final board meeting.

12. Plager had responsibility at OMB for a broad range of social and health programs, including all programs under HHS.

13. The Roosevelt Room was so named by President Nixon to commemorate the work of both Roosevelt presidents: Theodore, who built the West Wing, and Franklin, who remodeled it, moving the president's office from that room in the center of the building, where it had resided, to the current Oval Office because he wanted a window (a sentiment any office worker can appreciate).

14. Over time, the drafts would typically be in the forty-page range, as proposals became more complex and we learned more and more about the multiple bases that needed to be covered. Lawyers for HHS reviewed all approved section 1115 waiver demonstrations for legal clearance. I know of only one case in which their views were overruled (on a later decision by Secretary Louis Sullivan to approve Wisconsin's Two-Tier proposal), and in this case the attorney general provided the secretary with an oral opinion that contradicted that of the HHS lawyers. Ultimately, the Supreme Court ruled unanimously that the approved waiver was unconstitutional, reaffirming the HHS lawyers' original position. Thus I found it surprising that Teles (1996, 124), based on his confusion of section 1115(b) with 1115(a), could assert that "the language in the law has been virtually irrelevant with respect to how the waiver authority has been used—most of its provisions have been ignored" Rogers-Dillon (2004, 36), citing Teles, repeats this falsity. What I find most surprising is not that someone could misread the statute but that otherwise competent researchers could have such a misunderstanding of how the federal government operates that they would not have looked more deeply into the matter when they reached that conclusion.

15. The Washington and Alabama designs were what are now described as cluster

random assignment designs. At the time, at least in social policy, these designs were less common, and certainly we did not understand the problems they create in reducing power or how to properly adjust standard errors to account for the clustering.

16. Ohio and MDRC had been in discussions about including the state's Learning, Earning and Parenting initiative, a program for teen parents that required school attendance and included both sanctions and positive incentives, as part of its second Ford challenge grant studies (described in chapter 8). In the summer, after Ohio agreed with HHS to use random assignment, MDRC and the state made a commitment to move forward.

17. I can find no record of a denial, and it would have been inconsistent with our approach; we would only fail to act or to approve with conditions.

18. Stanton left almost immediately after the inauguration, and Roper moved to OPD.

19. The meeting agenda says April 19, but the minutes are dated April 20; the meeting was likely delayed a day.

20. Germanis recalls arriving at his views in ways very similar to mine. He says he was influenced by "reading . . . quasi-experimental and nonexperimental evaluations of training programs and seeing the potential for selection bias and the big differences in findings," specifically identifying his "reading about the evaluations from the [Comprehensive Employment and Training Act] days and the lack of consistency of the findings." He contrasted "the demonstrated credibility of the MDRC evaluations with the lack of consensus surrounding other methods."

21. In a 2010 interview with Roper, I shared the relevant materials with him. Unsurprisingly, he has no recollection of the events that occurred more than twenty years earlier and cannot shed light on why no further steps were taken. Although I have no direct evidence for the speculation, the sequence of events suggests that Hobbs had a role in Sununu's recommendation but that after Hobbs left the White House no senior staff person really cared about the issue. Given the immense number of its own initiatives that occupy any new administration, it seems plausible that nobody was sufficiently invested in relaxing the standard to expend the energy necessary to implement the recommendation.

22. None of us were in any way penalized for our position, and we all continued to have the same senior roles.

23. When the initial results of the original (nonexperimental) Learnfare evaluation became public, they contradicted the governor's assertion.

24. Between Stanton's departure in January 1989 and Barnhart's arrival in May 1990, a series of individuals acted in this position. Although the absence of a confirmed assistant secretary over such a long period limited what I could do in some cases, it gave me unusual flexibility in others (see chapter 9).

25. For a detailed discussion of the Minnesota Family Investment Plan, see chapter 10.

26. The Carolina Abecedarian Project was a random assignment study of early childhood education for poor infants born between 1972 and 1977 (www.fpg .unc.edu/~abc/ [accessed April 28, 2013]).

27. As recalled by Richard Bavier.

28. It is not entirely clear when Clinton's phrase began to garner attention. According to Jason DeParle (2004), candidate Clinton first used it on October 23, 1991, and at that time he was in the pack of several candidates and certainly not the leading one. Another factor that informed the budget proposal may have been the lack of significant antipoverty or welfare reform initiatives in the previous three years of the administration.

29. The Food and Nutrition Service in the Department of Agriculture would also become a key participant, although the initial state waiver requests were more focused on HHS programs.

30. See chapter 8 for further discussion.

31. On the GAIN program, see chapter 8; and for JOBS, chapter 9.

32. An experiment requires identification of a population to be randomly assigned before any behavioral effects of the intervention that the evaluation is designed to estimate. Randomly assigning individuals to differential benefits after they were in Wisconsin would capture any effects on their subsequent behavior, including emigration from the state. But it would miss the main hypothesized effect of the policy to be tested, namely, that the state's benefits attracted individuals into the state. To determine the latter, who would be randomly assigned, and where would it occur?

33. Ellwood is currently the dean of Harvard's Kennedy School of Government and is on the Abt Associates board of directors.

34. The original ILIOAB standard was that the proposed program had some chance to reduce dependency, which in practice meant full flexibility; in the Bush years even this thin criterion was dropped in favor of explicit full flexibility.

35. The Clinton administration approved seventy-eight applications from forty-three states. The state total of forty-five includes two additional states with

demonstrations approved from September 1987 forward in the Reagan and Bush administrations.

36. That is, section 415 allowed states to continue their policies, independent of continuing their section 1115 projects (which would have implied continuing their federally approved evaluation designs).

37. See also the discussion in chapter 4.

38. As discussed in more detail in chapter 9, with respect to the JOBS evaluation, and chapter 10, with respect to the Minnesota Family Investment Plan.

39. See, for example, the JOBS evaluation discussed in chapter 9.

CHAPTER 8

1. February 4, 1990.

2. Florida Department of Health and Rehabilitative Services, as recalled in a 2010 interview.

3. Answers to the first two questions would inform the key choice states faced in redesigning programs after passage of FSA. With limited funds, should they provide low-cost services and extend mandates to many people; impose more expensive, longer-term requirements on a smaller number; or some combination by targeting different services to different groups? Could mandates be extended to the full caseload without compromising quality, encountering political or administrative resistance, or reducing cost-effectiveness? As early as mid-1987 we suggested addressing the first question by randomly assigning people to more or less intensive services, and we began making plans for such a test. See Howard's chapter 9 discussion of the April 1989 meeting about shaping the evaluation of the federal JOBS program.

4. The study by David Ellwood (1986), which Howard discusses in chapter 5, had shown that teen mothers were at particularly high risk of long-term dependency.

5. Betsey, Hollister, and Papageorgiou (1985) and Job Training Longitudinal Survey Research Advisory Panel (1985).

6. Among the early funders, in addition to Ford, were the Charles Stewart Mott, William and Flora Hewlett, and Rockefeller Foundations, all of which supported experiments that targeted disadvantaged youth.

7. Twenty years later I was stunned to read in an article about this dispute the following statement from an unnamed source, denigrating both research firms (including prominently, by name, MDRC) and federal agency staff: "The contract shops, according to this view, have substituted skill in working the bureaucracy for respect for scientific method. They have absolutely no respect for

data. They have absolutely no respect for knowledge. They're beltway bandits, pure and simple, just a bullshit operation. They have absolute contempt for anything. What they're good at is sort of greasing the palms of Labor Department bureaucrats with low IQs. And that's basically what they've got in the pocket right now'" (quoted in Breslau 1997, 377–78).

8.   I remember thinking, when Heckman was awarded the Nobel Prize in Economics in 2000, at a time when he was still an outspoken critic of random assignment, "How can I possibly defend MDRC against someone with his reputation?" My only hope was that people in the states would not hear about or understand what he was saying. I also recall how relieved I was later when Heckman, through his experience working with us on the Job Training Partnership Act of 1982 evaluation (see later in the chapter), expressed his appreciation for the integrity of our work. In the coda to this book, I discuss others' views on the reality of and reasons for the lack of academic support for experiments and for the gradual turnaround over the past twenty years.

9.   I did not fully appreciate at the time that the accusation that we treated programs like "black boxes" was not an attack on experiments per se but on our use of experiments to answer questions of interest to state or federal funders— does a particular policy or program work?—rather than to estimate behavioral parameters in theoretical models.

10.   In the early years, there was validity to this critique. We not only believed in random assignment's unique strength but also knew that it was our comparative advantage. We lacked the deep expertise in quantitative methods that we developed later, particularly after Howard Bloom joined MDRC as its chief social scientist in 1999.

11.   An extreme example: when MDRC's principal investigator on a pathbreaking four-year, 4,600-person, $8 million experiment testing a welfare-to-work innovation in one major U.S. city submitted the project as part of a dissertation proposal at an Ivy League school, only to have one of the committee members suggest that she repeat the experiment in another location.

12.   See chapter 6.

13.   Here is the view of Charles Manski and Irwin Garfinkel (1992, 20): "Present contractual funding encourages assembly-line evaluations, executed with conventional procedures, reported in standardized format. It discourages innovation in methods, efforts to understand the complex set of processes that define a program, evaluation of long-term program impacts, and creative thinking about program design."

14.   In the same communication, Solow defines a natural experiment as "an occa-

sion when Nature produces a random assignment to some treatment A and to treatment B. For instance, everyone born before 1/2011 gets A and everyone after gets B; so those born in 12/2010 and those born in 1/2011 are statistically alike except for A/B." Bruce Meyer (1995) discusses the strengths and weaknesses of natural experiments—that use changes in state law, government draft mechanisms, or other plausibly exogenous actions to generate research designs patterned after randomized experiments—and proposes ways to increase the validity of inferences from such studies.

15.   See chapters 7 and 9.

16.   Discussed in chapter 10.

17.   See chapter 4.

18.   The GAIN program laid out specific tracks for people according to their education and skills levels. Those without a high school diploma (or its equivalent) or who lacked basic reading and math skills or were not proficient in English were deemed to be in need of basic education. They could choose to attend a basic education class or job search activity first. But if they chose the latter and failed to get a job, they had to go to basic education. Other registrants generally had to start with job search, unless they were already enrolled in approved education and training. People in any of these sequences who did not get a job after completing their first activities were assessed and offered a choice among a range of further activities. This sequence was formalized in various agreements and contracts between the staff and recipients. The decision to target more expensive services on the most disadvantaged drew on MDRC lessons from earlier experiments.

19.   As an example of the diversity, Los Angeles, the largest county in the nation as well as the state, had 8.2 million people; the smallest county in the state had only 1,180.

20.   Except for two minor provisions, neither having to do with the evaluation design itself, GAIN could be implemented under regular welfare rules.

21.   Richard Nathan (2000, 112) recounts Swoap's view: "Shortly after the California GAIN law was enacted, Swoap described the delicate political balancing act involved in its enactment by saying the program 'incorporates a unique blend of what have traditionally been considered "liberal" and "conservative" attitudes toward caring for the poor.'" Nathan also noted that Swoap credited MDRC's earlier study. Linda McMahon (who ran the welfare agency under Swoap) pointed to a deeper connection: "I suppose you might say that when we saw that the San Diego program had pretty limited results, it convinced us in a

negative way that perhaps we do need to look at education and training" (quoted in Blum with Blank 1990, 11).

22. Nathan (1988, 141) described the San Diego and GAIN studies as two stages in a process, with the former a relatively small-scale demonstration "to decide what should and, indeed, what could be done to reform California's welfare system" and the latter an evaluation of the resulting large-scale program.

23. SDSS is now the California Department of Social Services.

24. As Lopez describes it, "GAIN was literally built on the best evidence available at the time. It's a nifty little case study about how intelligent policy can be done. And then the question was, how will we know if it works?" She points to three findings from San Diego as particularly influential: the limits of job search alone, that workfare was not as bad as the liberals thought, and that the biggest impacts did not occur for the job ready, which led to the provision to give priority to single-parent over two-parent families if funding ran short.

25. In GAIN, the state put up roughly half of the $11 million budget, with the rest coming from the federal government's 50-50 matching of AFDC administrative costs. This was the first time a state put up substantial funds for a random assignment study. In later years, more states funded such studies, but at a much smaller scale and usually because this type of research had become the quid pro quo for obtaining federal waivers (see chapter 7).

26. We insisted that the contract specify no censorship, no undue delays in report release, and no MDRC liability for problems created by county intransigence or unrealistic state demands. We were particularly concerned about financial risk because, at the beginning, SDSS wanted us to develop a statewide GAIN tracking system, a mammoth undertaking which was quickly abandoned.

27. In answer to my retrospective question about why Lopez and Williams persevered against the critics of random assignment, Wallace reflects that it was a different era, when good government types were steadfast because they thought it was the right thing to do.

28. Lopez recalls that the evidence was thin and nobody else supported GAIN's emphasis on up-front, basic education, but Senator Greene's insistence was decisive.

29. This ruled out selecting the counties by lottery.

30. This decision, rather than random assignment in the abstract, is what provoked some counties to object.

31. Nathan (1988, 124–28) has argued that researchers have more control in demonstrations than in evaluations of ongoing government programs because the

purpose of the former is to learn something, whereas the primary purpose of the latter is to do something. From this, he draws two conclusions: first, for an ongoing program, research becomes a lower-order objective and random assignment is likely to be strongly resisted; second, demonstration research should focus more on individual outcomes, and evaluation research more on changes in the behavior of institutions. One explanation for why we ultimately prevailed in using random assignment in GAIN may come from the fact that, to Lopez and others involved in the legislation, finding out whether the program succeeded was not a lower-order objective but part and parcel of the original package.

32. Our response to GAIN was influenced by the simultaneous and in some ways even tougher challenge we and our partners at Abt Associates faced launching the Department of Labor–sponsored random assignment evaluation of the Job Training Partnership Act (JTPA) of 1982. These were the first two experimental evaluations of permanent, large-scale employment and training systems: GAIN for welfare recipients in California, and the JTPA for multiple economically disadvantaged groups nationwide. Although JTPA had the advantage that no one claimed it was a universal entitlement, it had the added burdens that it was an established program, was a voluntary system facing recruitment challenges, operated under an extensive system of performance standards and incentives, and was even more decentralized and diverse than GAIN promised to be and that the evaluation sought to recruit a statistically representative sample of sites (which it ultimately failed to do) and to obtain the impacts of specific treatments (for example, classroom occupational training). In an unusual report on the reconnaissance preceding the start of a major evaluation, Fred Doolittle and Linda Traeger (1990) recount the challenges, adjustments, and trade-offs in recruiting sites for the JTPA study.

33. It took until early 1988 to get San Diego to sign on as one of the impact counties.

34. Williams recalls being so adamant about random assignment that he would have recommended against passage of the legislation without it. "I remember being anxious about the fact that we might somehow lose [random assignment], but being the kind of person that I am, my feeling was, well, if I lose it, let's say in a court action, I am still going to go back with this to the administration and back to the legislature and say, 'You wanted us to do this, you've got to permit this.'"

35. Wallace views Lopez as "the grease that greased the wheels of the evaluation. . . .

Without her, I doubt it would have happened. . . . It would have been a very different evaluation." He particularly credits her with keeping the legislature interested and, through that, keeping SDSS staff on their toes.

36. This process could be viewed as a high-octane, collaborative version of the "sequential" design process (Hollister's term) that gave euphemistic order to the need to continually rethink the parameters of the Supported Work evaluation (see chapter 2).

37. For example, after the election of Pete Wilson as governor, Boyle and Lewis orchestrated a briefing for the transition team that ended with the Health and Welfare Agency secretary's summarizing the message as "hang in there for the returns on the evaluation; cut elsewhere if you have to."

38. They also could protest, using the normal state fair-hearing process. Although controls would not receive GAIN services, they might have absorbed some of the GAIN message, which might lead to some underestimate of program impacts.

39. Over the following years, as participation became a hot-button issue in congressional welfare reform debates, we used similar charts to explain why rates could never get close to 100 percent and that falling substantially below this level need not mean that program operators were not being tough or were letting clients slip through the cracks. Instead, much of the explanation flowed from the appropriate enforcement of program rules and normal welfare turnover.

40. In anticipation of just such a situation, the original GAIN legislation had included specific directions regarding how counties should target resources if they were unable to serve all eligible people.

41. Riverside also chose to implement a substudy involving the random assignment of welfare recipients and staff to more or less intensive GAIN case management.

42. All findings reported here are for AFDC applicants or recipients (mostly single mothers) who were followed for five years after random assignment. The study also included heads of two-parent welfare families (mostly fathers), for whom we again found higher outcomes but lower impacts.

43. In an op-ed in the *Washington Post* on September 12, 1995, I described the unusual tone and message in the Riverside offices: "When you walk in the door of a high-performance, employment-focused program, it is clear that you are there for one purpose—to get a job. Staff continually announce job openings and convey an upbeat message about the value of work and people's potential to succeed. You—and everyone else subject to the mandate—are required to

search for a job, and if you don't find one, to participate in short-term education, training or community work experience. You cannot just mark time; if you do not make progress in the education program, for example, the staff will insist that you look for a job. Attendance is tightly monitored and recipients who miss activities without a good reason face swift penalties."

44. Riccio (1997, 249) adds the following refinement to the Riverside message: "None of our results demonstrate that basic education or other education and training *can't* work in some circumstances or for some people. Even Riverside placed some recipients in basic education. . . . However, the findings clearly cast doubt on the value of pushing recipients en masse into education as their first activity and assuming that for most recipients education and training must precede any efforts to find work."

45. Riccio notes that because of the staff opposition and our own faith that the human capital investment strategy would pay off, we thought Riverside would cycle people off and back on welfare but ultimately would not perform well. The results reaffirmed the value of a control group to protect even experienced observers (and analysts) from their own biases.

46. In a study that extended the follow-up to nine years, Joseph Hotz, Guido Imbens, and Jacob Klerman (2006, 31, 38) conclude that the other counties eventually caught up with Riverside in final employment and earnings impacts (their study did not look at costs or welfare impacts). However, they caution that the results might have been affected by the fact that, at the end of MDRC's evaluation, members of the control group were allowed and then required to be in GAIN, which might have reduced the experimental-control difference.

47. All dollar values in table 8.3 are averages that include zero earnings for the substantial number of people who did not work at all during the five years. Since this applied to around 40 percent of controls and 30 percent of experimentals (in the full sample in the two counties), those who worked earned substantially more than shown.

48. On the Louisville program, see chapter 3; and on the San Diego demonstration, chapter 4. Of course, it remains possible that, in testing a full-scale program, controls are more likely to think they will be subject to program mandates. As noted earlier, if this had occurred in GAIN, the experimental-control comparison would have underestimated impacts.

49. We were aware that, though this could generate plausible hypotheses on what drove impacts, competing explanations would exist, and ultimate proof would

depend on either replication of success or random assignment to different treatments within the program group.

50. Similarly, in his book about the making of the 1996 law, Haskins (2006, 11) states, "Seldom has social science presented a clearer case to policymakers. . . . Conservatives adopted the mantra 'What works is work.' Here was a message that resonated with both policymakers and the American public."

51. MDRC created a public-use data file that allowed other researchers to replicate the results.

52. Sometimes we got pressure to issue reports in time for a budget debate, at other times to avoid the politically charged budget discussions.

53. The high stakes did not stop in Sacramento. County directors also felt on the block and wanted an opportunity to have input on reports. An extreme example was Townsend's telling us, early in our relationship, that he had been prepared to duplicate MDRC's data collection activities so he could rebut us, but that after checking with welfare directors across the country he had decided he could trust us to handle the counties fairly.

54. Joan Zinzer, a senior official in San Diego during the three experiments, recalls the impact on the county, state, and herself from participating in the experiments: "Without the MDRC studies, San Diego would not have had a seat at the state policy table. With them, we became an influential force. MDRC's studies and dissemination increased the role that evidence played in state policy making, giving greater credibility to the design of the state's Temporary Assistance for Needy Families program, Calworks. Without that, given the polarization with Republican governors and a Democratic legislature, it would have been driven more by ideology and politics."

55. Donald Kennedy, editor of *Science,* quoted in the *New York Times,* January 31, 2006.

56. Although DeParle understood that Riverside's "work first" did not mean "work only," others did not, and we often found ourselves playing catch-up, trying to correct that impression. (The MDRC report issued in May 1993 contained the two-year follow-up results.) Greenberg, Linksz, and Mandell (2003, 278–301) agree that the GAIN findings were "common knowledge" among welfare administrators and that they "did directly contribute to the decision in many states to adopt the work-first approach," but that other factors probably played a more important role. The authors contrast the direct effect on national policy with the more indirect effect on state policy, where the findings served more to

support existing trends than to change them. Thus, they argue, the Riverside approach reinforced an existing conservative shift in state policy and was used to help sell this policy. They also note that states valued information on how GAIN was implemented and how Riverside changed the culture in welfare offices.

57. Similarly, in their examination of whether social experiments affected public policy, Greenberg, Linksz, and Mandell (2003, 249, 301) contrast 1988, when the welfare-to-work findings had a "strong influence" on the design of FSA, to 1996, when politics drove the outcome and research "played only a minor role."

58. Weaver (2000, 160, 164), summing up conservatives' reaction: "Welfare-to-work programs, even if they involved substantial new paternalist mandatoriness and sanctions, were unlikely to make a major dent in welfare dependency. More dramatic changes in incentives, involving both program entry and hard time limits, would be required to produce a significant change in behavior. . . . Welfare-to-work programs were not a solution to what they saw as the social catastrophe of welfare dependence."

59. Weaver (2000, 161) argues that policy research was used mainly as "ammunition to defend existing value-based and coalition-based policy positions."

60. During the period when Congress was debating PRWORA, a number of states (under waivers) had begun implementing time limits, and MDRC was conducting random assignment evaluations of three of them. However, impact and cost findings were not yet available, although an early report on implementation (Bloom and Butler 1995) highlights the diversity of approaches and the importance of complementary pre-time-limit activities (particularly strong welfare-to-work programs) if states were to minimize the number of people reaching the cutoff. After PRWORA's passage, in their conforming legislation states drew heavily on GAIN and other experiments in reshaping their welfare-to-work programs to meet that goal.

61. In addition, FSA required teen mothers on welfare to be in an education program (the Learnfare provision), promoted vigorous child support collections, and required all states to provide cash assistance to two-parent families and other provisions.

62. Winstead's conversion to random assignment is an example of the continuity across experiments and the key role played by the small number of supporters: Coler suggested that Winstead call me; I sent him to Hollister (who had been in the Office of Economic Opportunity, the federal office that sponsored the

first negative-income-tax studies, and was later principal investigator in Supported Work, see chapter 2); and Winstead later became deputy assistant secretary in the Office of the Assistant Secretary for Policy and Evaluation in HHS, where he helped sustain the same tradition.

63.   The result was a contract whereby the Ford Foundation, the state, and the federal government would each fund a third of the cost. The contract, originally for $2.4 million, was subsequently expanded to include a child care study. Winstead recalls that, given the controversy and the importance of the program, he would have made this recommendation even if there had been no Ford dollars. Federal waivers played no role in the random assignment decision, although the state did need waivers for the core program.   ·

64.   The final design included nine counties randomly chosen from among the state's twenty-five largest and a sample of more than 18,000 people, since the state wanted to be able to detect impacts on key subgroups (Kemple and Haimson 1994, v, xv, 7).

65.   The Tuskegee study followed a group of poor, rural African American men known to have syphilis, without ever telling them they had the disease or treating them for it.

66.   The editorial ends by asking HRS to find an alternative approach: "Any well-trained social scientist—no doubt including many who already work for HRS—is capable of constructing a research project that protects the dignity of those chosen to participate in it." Coler did not flinch. The *St. Petersburg Times* reported on January 27, 1990, that "Coler defended the study Friday, saying control groups are vital to proving scientifically whether the program works and have been used in research studies for years. 'The truth of the matter is that in the history of social welfare programs, these kinds of studies have made a critical difference in the policy of this country,' he said. 'It is not the only type [of study] but it is the best type.'"

67.   Reporting on the context in an internal memo, Ivry observed that the issue was not really about control groups but about politics, with both sides exploiting the controversy to serve their own political purposes making, according to Winstead, the moral high ground the most popular spot in Florida.

68.   Specifically, we said that we were not interested in defeating Graber's proposed amendment and proceeding with the study if there was not broad-based support and trust; we were not willing to come back with an alternative to random assignment as a way to keep the contract alive because we did not think it

would provide defensible findings; we thought a quality study had been proposed and that it would answer important questions; and we thought the expressed ethical concerns were the right ones and could be dealt with.

69. That is, whether there would be any difference in in-program child care. We never proposed that there be any difference in access to transitional child care (that is child care provided after people left welfare).

70. He later became a member of MDRC's Welfare Studies Committee.

71. The statewide Human Rights Advocacy Committee, based in Tampa, had just voted unanimously against the use of control groups, calling them unconstitutional.

72. HRS and HHS refused to compromise on the advocates' other issue, informed consent, arguing that denying service is a routine state activity in any JOBS program and random assignment was fairer than the regular administrative procedures.

73. Letters from two state officials involved in random assignment evaluations—Lopez, one of the people so valuable in negotiating the GAIN evaluation, and Paul Offner, a Wisconsin state legislator turned Ohio state welfare administrator—were particularly effective. Lopez's letter stated, in part, "I am well aware of people's initial hesitation to establish a control group. The GAIN program is being evaluated using random assignment after lengthy discussion with members of the Legislature. In California, the consensus was that control groups did not inappropriately or unethically deny anyone service. By the simple fact that resources are limited we cannot serve everyone who requests services. We concluded that random assignment was another legitimate selection criteria for the program. Having a designed control group will help the Legislature and the Governor decide whether the $450 million being spent on the GAIN program in California will actually make a difference for those who participate. Given competing priorities for funding, it is critical that we have more than 'conventional wisdom' or poignant anecdotes to justify the level of funding required by a comprehensive program like GAIN." Offner's letter pointed out that administrators routinely experiment with elements of people's lives as they test out different program approaches and argued that when resources are inadequate to serve all eligibles, it is "the essence of fairness to allocate the services on the basis of random selection." Of the letters from researchers, the one from a local academic (the University of Miami's Philip Robins, who had been the research director for the Seattle/Denver Income Maintenance Experiment negative-income-tax study) was especially useful.

74. See chapter 9. There was mixed success in the three GAIN counties enrolling this group.

75. Every month MDRC sent HRS a list identifying the experimentals and controls, which Winstead agreed not to share with his field staff, and an analyst constructed a data base matching monthly welfare, food stamps, and Medicaid records—and quarterly unemployment insurance earnings data—that Winstead then used to see how things were going and to produce quarterly reports for the feds on cost neutrality.

76. That study was awarded competitively. Winstead recalls feeling that by 1993 other firms had conducted such studies, overturning a central criterion for sole-source procurement.

CHAPTER 9

1. Director of the Income Security Policy Division, HHS/ASPE, during the JOBS evaluation, as recalled in a 2011 interview.

2. After passage of the Personal Responsibility and Work Opportunity Reconciliation Act in 1996 and its elimination of the JOBS program, the JOBS evaluation was renamed the National Evaluation of Welfare to Work Strategies. Since this chapter is historical, I refer to it by its original name.

3. As Amy Brown (1997, 2) observes, what defines a work-first program is not a single model but rather "[its] overall philosophy: that any job is a good job and that the best way to succeed in the labor market is to join it, developing work habits and skills on the job rather than in a classroom." In most of this chapter, I describe specific program models, but when I turn to describing what was learned across evaluations at its end, I return to using "work first."

4. Some categories of spending do not require annual appropriation of funds, for example, Social Security Retirement and Disability benefits, or payments to states under TANF (or previously under AFDC).

5. FSA required that proposed rules be published within six months of its passage and final rules to be published within one year. At the time, given the transition in administrations, these were regarded as impossible deadlines, although we did meet both.

6. Earlier in the 1980s I had served on a group that provided input to the Department of Labor on performance standards for the Job Training Partnership Act program and had been negatively impressed that the department had proceeded in the absence of any reliable information on the impacts of the program. By the time of the JOBS request for proposals, we knew outcomes bore

no relationship to impacts, and could even be counterintuitive, thanks to MDRC's work. We also believed, but did not survey the evidence, that Job Training Partnership Act's performance standards promoted "creaming" (that is, selection of the most, not the least, work-ready applicants), thus tending to leave out many welfare recipients. Later research supported our perspective (Barnow and Smith 2004).

7. In her notes on the meeting described in the next section, for example, Judy wrote that HHS was "trying to interpret the effectiveness studies in a way quite different from the bill: don't give the money to states, use random assignment, evaluate JOBS, use it to develop performance standards. There may be a potential conflict here as their plan to use the effectiveness study funds for a super JOBS evaluation has nothing to do with the legislation's description." Although we did not have her notes at the time, of course, we assumed that MDRC, having established strong relationships with a number of states, would have preferred to deal directly with them and not have to compete with others at the federal level.

8. The ability to call on the substantive strengths of both staffs was also an important factor. But I should add that, collegiality notwithstanding, if both partners had not contributed major funding, the primary contributor would have been highly unlikely to cede ownership, and with it control, of the project.

9. I discuss the most important syntheses of multiple studies at the end of this chapter.

10. Offner would later serve as Senator Moynihan's chief aide on welfare issues.

11. The requirement to submit a report to Congress, of course, remained. Later in this chapter I discuss it.

12. Given that much social policy programming in the United States is designed and administered in a highly decentralized manner, nationally representative findings, and hence rigorous evidence on the first question, are seldom feasible (I am aware of five such evaluations, along with a handful that are state representative, including Florida's Project Independence, discussed in chapter 8, and Ohio's Learning, Earning, and Parenting program evaluation, included in table 8.1).

13. MDRC, facing a similar problem in the GAIN evaluation, reached a similar conclusion (see chapter 8).

14. Another, related consideration was that we were seeking to identify and enroll a variety of mature sites, and we believed it was necessary to visit them in person to determine their maturity.

15. Later, the model would become even more flexible by replacing the grant mechanism with a process through which the evaluation contractor would fund sites directly through memorandums of understanding and subcontracts.

16. Canta Pian and later Audrey Mirsky-Ashby were ASPE project officers, and Alan Yaffe was the project officer for my office. From the early 1980s Yaffe and his supervisor, Paul Bordes, were both strong supporters of random assignment, as was Leonard Sternbach, who joined the staff later.

17. A fourth site in Columbus, Ohio, also included a three-stream design that compared integration of income maintenance and employment services in a single caseworker with more traditional separation using two workers, as well as to a control group.

18. Pre/post designs and their more sophisticated cousins, difference-in-difference designs and matched-comparison group designs, are some obvious examples.

19. Determining whether there are differences in effects among subgroups will yield even less precise estimates. For more on the issue of reduced power for subgroup analyses, which too often undermines their utility, see, for example, Klerman (2009) and Bloom and Michalopoulos (2010).

20. We would have liked to use the Private Opinion Survey in all sites, but we were limited to those in which an orientation occurred before random assignment, as that was necessary for administering it.

21. MDRC used the same Private Opinion Survey in Florida's Project Independence evaluation (see chapter 8) and the Minnesota Family Investment Program (see chapter 10).

22. An exception was the head-to-head test of a more integrated program against a standard program and a control group in Columbus, Ohio, referenced earlier.

23. The study was identified in the original contract as "Analysis of Impact of JOBS in Participants' Children," but it has also been referenced in other ways. I refer to it here as the "JOBS Child Impact study."

24. By design, the effects of JOBS would not be confounded with the effects of child care, because access to child care subsidies was equally available to treatment and control groups, although the JOBS mandate was expected to lead to greater child care use by those in the treatment groups. This decision was largely driven by the firestorm over random assignment in Florida, and indirectly in Texas, which Judy describes in chapter 8.

25. ASPE ultimately covered 80 percent of the Child Impact Study add-on, so our contribution was only 20 percent.

26.   Section 203(c)(4) of FSA called for the secretary to establish an advisory panel to oversee implementation and evaluation studies. The Department of Health and Human Services convened the panel, and on November 7, 1990, it reviewed the design of the JOBS evaluation, which, by this point, was quite fully developed.

27.   California's GAIN (see chapter 8), which became the nation's largest JOBS program as noted, was based on the same hypothesis. As described in the next section, this gave great synergy to the findings from the two studies.

28.   See chapter 4.

29.   Head-to-head tests were not new to welfare-to-work experiments. MDRC had used them in the early 1980s experiments, but less systematically and with less clear policy impact.

30.   Later in this chapter I discuss the findings of welfare-to-work experiments more generally with respect to subgroup analyses.

31.   It is notable that three other MDRC experiments, Florida's Family Transition Program, Milwaukee's New Hope, and Canada's Self-Sufficiency Program also identified some negative impacts on adolescents, so there is some consistency to the overall pattern, even if it is not well understood (Hamilton et al. 2001).

32.   See chapter 8.

33.   It is important to note that the Riverside GAIN and JOBS interventions were not the same in that the former, despite its emphasis on rapid job entry, did not require individuals determined to be in need of education to look for jobs first, unlike the Labor Force treatment in JOBS. In addition, the effects of the GAIN treatment were larger and more persistent that the JOBS treatment (briefly discussed later in the chapter).

34.   Haskins is speaking hypothetically with respect to the pre-PRWORA debate, as the JOBS Child Impact study and other findings did not become available until after PRWORA became law.

35.   In the Employment Retention and Advancement demonstration (see chapter 11), one of the sites in Los Angeles tested a replication of the job search element of the model that Portland implemented in the JOBS evaluation. In the latter study, the "enhanced" job club did not result in improved outcomes when compared with the standard job club that Los Angeles operated (Hendra et al. 2010).

36.   Although the two programs do have common features, in most respects they were very different program models.

37.   Despite my skepticism about the performance standards movement, I do think

it is important and useful for program operators to track outcomes locally, even if they cannot answer questions of impact without using the techniques of evaluation. But I am skeptical about the ability of federal or state level observers, or philanthropic funders, to interpret outcomes in ways that reflect performance.

38. The diversity of the studies is notable and represents a strength. Although efforts were made to coordinate many of them, the studies grew organically, were initiated by a variety of organizations, and, although the federal government was the primary funder, were also provided financial support by others at key times, enriching the range of subject matter. "The strength of the thread does not reside in the fact that some one fibre runs though its whole length, but in the overlapping of many fibres" (Wittgenstein 1953, #67).

39. On JOBS, GAIN, and the Florida Family Transition Program evaluations, see chapter 8; on the Saturation Work Initiative Model, see chapters 5 and 6; and on the Minnesota Family Investment Program, see chapter 10.

40. The one exception is Supported Work, for which the midpoint (1976) was roughly a decade earlier.

41. The model results are the same for both 2003 and 2005, but management practice was the focus of the former and methods the focus of the latter. In the welfare-to-work research, Howard Bloom and his colleagues have been the major force for advancing more powerful methods for analyzing experimental data. His edited volume (2005) is a much-referenced source for those designing major social experiments. Others have also made important methods advances in conducting social experiments that we do not discuss, because they did not grow directly out of the welfare experiments.

42. The data for Michalopoulos and Schwartz (2001) and Bloom, Hill, and Riccio (2003, 2005) overlap substantially, which in part accounts for the similarity of findings when they address common questions.

43. Finding statistically significant difference in impacts across subgroups requires much larger samples than finding them for a subgroup. Two exceptions to the pattern of modest variation in earnings impacts across subgroups were the much higher impacts for individuals entering welfare for the first time (less than 10 percent of the sample) and no impacts for those who scored at high risk of depression (about one-seventh of the smaller Private Opinion Survey sample).

44. The study reached a similar conclusion on reducing welfare.

45. Syntheses of the findings for financial incentive programs show greater hetero-

geneity of earnings impacts, with stronger effects for the more disadvantaged (which is consistent with theory). See chapter 10.

46. Impacts were also significantly positively correlated with individualized attention, but less strongly.

47. In chapter 2, Judy points to this fear at the start of the Supported Work demonstration.

CHAPTER 10

1. Kuttner (2008, 182).

2. Lawrence Mead (1997) dubbed this the "new paternalism."

3. Under AFDC, people leaving welfare to work not only saw their grants reduced at quite high tax rates but also might have to cut further into their new earnings to pay for child care, transportation, and health insurance.

4. David Ellwood, as a Harvard professor and Clinton's assistant secretary for planning and evaluation at HHS, was an eloquent voice arguing that "long-term cash-based welfare for the healthy is inherently flawed" (Ellwood 1988, 237) and should be replaced by a combination of approaches that encourage and reward work. Among his recommendations were replacing the indefinite guaranteed income of AFDC with an income supplement for the working poor, temporary cash welfare for those who are not working, public jobs as a last resort for those who cannot find work, and a uniform child support "assurance" system.

5. During the same years, we were also conducting random assignment studies of different versions of time limits in Vermont, Connecticut, and Florida.

6. Entitlement in this context did not mean the program was open to all eligibles who applied, as I used the term in chapter 8 when discussing California GAIN and Florida Project Independence. The Self-Sufficiency Project subsidies would be offered to a fixed number of people for the duration of the demonstration, as long as they met the work and other eligibility requirements. The budget was uncertain because, at the start, the factors that would drive cost (participation rate, number of months, and amount claimed) were unknown.

7. One concern was that the project not revoke the existing entitlement to welfare. This condition was met: the program was voluntary, and people could opt out of the subsidy and retain eligibility for all social assistance programs. We also wanted to be sure that we had the funds to pay the supplement on demand to all program eligibles. Rather than rely on theory or guesswork, we estimated the costs from actual take-up and phase-in rates during the early period of the project.

8. We considered three alternatives (a negative income tax with a work requirement, a wage rate subsidy, and an EITC) under various levels of generosity and
targeting.

9. Restricting eligibility for benefits to people who meet certain criteria always
raises the specter of unintended negative consequences: that is, that people
would change their behavior—for example, work less or have children out of
wedlock—in order to qualify. In the case of SSP, the concern was that this generous program limited to long-term recipients would create an incentive for
new people to apply for aid or to stay on the rolls longer in order to "enter" the
program (Berlin et al. 1998). Aaron argued that, because entry effects could
offset any positive results the program might have in increasing employment
for people already on welfare, we should not go forward if we could not get a
reliable measure of their magnitude. Robert Moffitt (1992) criticized prior experiments for neglecting this issue.

10. The SSP supplement was calculated as half the difference between a participant's gross earnings and a province-specific earnings benchmark, which in
1993 was C$37,000 in British Columbia and C$30,000 in New Brunswick.
For example, a British Columbian participant who worked thirty-five hours a
week at C$7 an hour could earn C$12,740 and in addition collect an earnings
supplement of C$12,130 per year, for a total pretax income from these two
sources of C$24,870 (Liu-Gurr, Vernon, and Mijanovich 1994, 3). When we
started the project, we were told that the subsidies were so generous that they
were far outside the realistic U.S. policy envelope. We went ahead anyway,
thinking that such a test would provide a valuable upper-bound estimate of
potential impacts.

11. Memos at the time show that Greenwood attributed support at the top of the
agency to SSP's explicit reversal of their usual approach of spending billions and
then conducting ambiguous evaluations. He added three other factors. They
would not be withholding an entitlement. There was a growing conviction that
money for social programs would be limited, and HRDC would have to make
choices based on evidence, thus the need to determine program effectiveness.
Finally, there was strong interest in the subsidy approach but no evidence on
impacts. SSP was designed to change that.

12. Spiegelman had directed the Seattle-Denver negative-income-tax experiment.

13. Berlin puts it this way: "They began with the noble goal of doing this right,
programmatically and scientifically. As in the U.S. Supported Work experience
twenty years earlier, they had program people who said they could run it and

researchers who said they could study it but no organization or entity that could manage the two sides of the project simultaneously—program design and research design done together in an integrated, holistic way, with neither driving the other. They had to create such an entity." In line with this, from the beginning HRDC staff made it clear that they had two objectives in SSP: to learn whether an earnings subsidy would prompt more welfare recipients to take and retain jobs and also to build their own experience and expertise in doing large-scale random assignment studies.

14. The SSP study was unusual in having two types of random assignment. First, Statistics Canada selected the study sample at random from the pool of all welfare recipients who met SSP's eligibility criteria. Second, after Statistics Canada had collected baseline data, explained the study (and a welfare recipient's 50 percent chance of being eligible for the supplement), and asked recipients to join the study, participants were randomly assigned to the program or the control group.

15. Early memos record the warning that advocates would "scream bloody murder" if the project enticed women into taking jobs and putting their children in inadequate child care. "You are offering women an impossible choice: take a job and neglect your child." As Berlin recalls, "The advocates and many in the government believed that 'lone parents' could not and should not work. It was almost a time warp for us—we had had that debate one or two decades earlier in the U.S."

16. SRDC in turn contracted with MDRC and several academics to conduct the research and provide other expertise, with local agencies to run the program, Statistics Canada to collect survey and administrative data, and SHL Systemhouse in Nova Scotia to develop and maintain the program's automated management information and supplement payroll systems.

17. To protect against the obvious potential conflict of interest in having Berlin and Granger in management roles in both SRDC and MDRC, SRDC had a majority-Canadian board of directors, and it was agreed that HRDC would approve all SRDC subcontracts and major modifications.

18. In addition to Hollister, the original panel members were Michael Wiseman, Gary Burtless, Lawrence Mead, Phoebe Cottingham, Robert Haveman, and William Prosser. The panel tempered its enthusiasm with a concern that the sample size was small and included widely varied groups of people, which meant that the study might not be able to discern important policy-relevant findings for key subgroups, such as single mothers on welfare.

19. For example, someone working twenty hours a week at $6 an hour would receive $237 per month more in benefits if they were in MFIP than someone working the same amount of time at the same wage in the control group (that is, on AFDC); the difference would be an additional $148 more per month if they worked forty hours.

20. Ultimately, fearing that the Reagan administration might not provide waivers (Petraborg described a meeting in which Charles Hobbs said he favored waivers to reduce caseload but not to combat poverty), Minnesota sought and got federal legislation that specifically directed the two departments to grant the waivers. (See chapter 7 for Howard's description of Hobbs's role.)

21. The final MFIP sample was increased to more than 14,000 families.

22. Lopez was a key advocate for using random assignment to assess GAIN; see chapter 8.

23. See chapter 9.

24. Huston notes that both her training in psychology and her experience with laboratory experiments and later field experiments studying mass media and children led her to value random assignment as a method allowing clear causal inference. "Hence, no one had to persuade me that experimental tests have great value."

25. Bloom (1997) and David Greenberg, Victoria Deitch, and Gayle Hamilton (2009) provide useful summaries of the relative success of different approaches in reaching these different goals within a specific time horizon, including how some mandatory employment programs were more successful at increasing earnings and others at cutting costs. As Howard describes in chapter 9, the JOBS evaluation showed that welfare-to-work mandates, whether starting with job search or basic education, had few if any effects on young children.

26. Rebecca Blank, David Card, and Philip Robins (2000) discuss the theory behind these programs and point to three differences from the earlier income maintenance experiments that explain their greater success: their targeting on welfare recipients (and sometimes only long-term recipients) and not the broader low-income population; the combination of financial incentives with mandatory welfare-to-work programs; and the fact that in two cases (SSP and New Hope) the incentives were paid only if people worked full time.

27. See Michalopoulos (2005); Morris, Gennetian, and Duncan (2005); and Morris, Gennetian, and Knox (2002).

28. For example, for people receiving the full MFIP program (single-parent, long-term welfare recipients), quarterly employment rates during the first ten quar-

ters after random assignment averaged 50 percent versus 37 percent for controls on AFDC. By the end of the three years, poverty rates were a full 12 percentage points lower for the same group in MFIP than under the old AFDC program. (For example, 78 percent of controls remained poor at the end of the three years, compared with 65 percent of those who had been in MFIP.)

29.   Although this is simply a built-in result, the distinction has political significance for those who view welfare negatively and programs such as the EITC or SSP (seen as providing cash assistance to low-income working families) positively.

30.   Michalopoulos (2005, 21n5) finds no systematic explanation for why subgroup results differ by program or from his earlier synthesis of welfare-to-work programs, which Howard discusses in chapter 9.

31.   Despite its high supplements, costs were lowest for SSP because it required full-time work and collected income taxes on SSP payments. The most encouraging results came from the SSP Applicant experiment, which was explicitly designed to determine the effects of an ongoing program (including one form of unintended entry effects). This study found impacts on employment, welfare receipt, and poverty rates that continued through the fifth year of follow-up, after supplement payments had long since ended. Moreover, the Canadian government recovered (in taxes and reduced welfare payments) almost the entire cost of the program. It also found that entry effects were small and barely statistically significant, suggesting that targeted work incentive programs can be designed to limit the magnitude of such effects (Ford et al. 2003; Berlin et al. 1998). A synthesis of benefit-cost research from twenty-eight welfare reform programs (Greenberg, Deitch, and Hamilton 2009) concludes that earnings supplements were an economically efficient mechanism for transferring income to low-income families (using the social benefit-cost perspective) because participants gained more than a dollar for every dollar the government spent.

32.   For adolescents, in contrast, there were either no or small negative (sometimes temporary) effects from their parents' participation in both mandatory JOBS and earnings supplement programs.

33.   Research syntheses include monographs by Bloom (1997), Berlin (2000), Bloom and Michalopoulos (2001), Morris et al. (2001), and Lisa Gennetian et al. (2002). Policy briefs and summary articles include Morris, Gennetian, and Knox (2002); Morris, Gennetian, and Duncan (2005); and Morris and Duncan (2001).

34.   This contrast between readily understood employment and welfare measures

and opaque measures of effect size prompted Bloom et al. (2008) to look more deeply at the interpretation of effect sizes. Their work suggested that the widely used rule of thumb for what effect sizes are small, medium, or large was misleading.

35. Knox recalls that, as states got new flexibility to restructure welfare under TANF, advocates used results from these studies to urge them to keep earnings supplements in place. "Organizations that might want to argue for more supports for children felt on very firm ground because they could point to experiments. They felt free to say that poverty was bad for kids anyway, but now they could point to this as another piece of evidence that bolstered what they were saying."

36. Petraborg recalls that "every governor in the country was vying for attention on the topic of welfare reform and by that time we had a Republican, Arnie Carlson, and he was in quite a bit of competition with Tommy Thompson, so being able to trumpet those results and make that part of the statewide plan, it all came together well, right at that time."

37. For a summary of the results, see Bloom and Michalopoulos (2001) and Farrell et al. (2008).

38. Blank describes this labor market as "the longest period of continuous economic growth in U.S. history . . . a job-rich economy that offered more job availability and better wages to low-skilled workers than at any time in the previous two or three decades," and she estimates that the increases in the EITC, other programs, and the minimum wage combined to raise the real income from a full-time minimum wage job by 34 percent, enough to move single mothers with one or two children above the poverty line. She also charts the "enormous" 42 percent increase in employment among low-skilled single mothers between 1993 and 2000 (Blank 2006, 40–41, 45).

39. Berlin also recalls, "My skepticism about the effect of time limits per se is fueled by the reality that many states (including California, New York, and Michigan) did not implement a real time limit, and others had not even passed conforming legislation, much less put in place new policies, when their caseloads began falling in lockstep with every other state. It seems to me that a likely reason caseloads fell is that states began closing the front door, making it harder and harder to establish eligibility. This would also explain mechanically why the rolls have not gone up substantially in the Great Recession."

40. Jeffrey Grogger and Lynn Karoly (2005) discuss the various reasons why random assignment evaluations are best suited for evaluating particular reforms

and programs and less useful for evaluating sweeping policy changes such as PRWORA.

41. This contrasts with the majority of states that, as Howard describes in chapter 7, agreed to random assignment only because it was the quid pro quo for the waivers they sought.

42. There were also trade-offs among the different types of welfare-to-work programs discussed in chapters 4, 8, and 9: those that primarily required individuals to look for jobs immediately tended to reduce government budgets but not to raise participants' income; those that offered a mix of first activities sometimes both saved money and benefited participants; those that required basic education first cost more and did not increase participants' income. See the synthesis by Greenberg, Deitch, and Hamilton (2009). See Grogger and Karoly (2005) for the trade-offs as seen from a large number of experiments conducted during the 1990s.

43. In community colleges, MDRC conducted the first random assignment studies and (with funding from the Lumina, Bill and Melinda Gates, Robin Hood, and other foundations) is pushing for reliable evidence, much as we had initially in welfare-to-work evaluations.

44. Reflecting and driving this shift, we implemented a strategic plan in 1999 that rapidly reduced welfare reform studies from 50 percent of our budget in 1998 to less than 20 percent by 2003.

CHAPTER 11

1. HHS Assistant Secretary for Children and Families from 2001 to 2007, as recalled in a 2010 interview.

2. Even without the requirement of random assignment, the existence of the waiver approval process with a requirement of some evaluation was useful in improving evaluation standards, as Judy describes in chapter 4.

3. The major evaluation research firms were important parts of this strategy. Although MDRC was responsible for pioneering this partnership role, by the 1990s direct relationships between states and evaluation firms had become standard.

4. In addition to the random assignment projects described in this chapter, the Administration for Children and Families also sponsored the Rural Welfare-to-Work (WtW) Strategies Demonstration Evaluation, which was conducted by Mathematica Policy Research. It yielded an evaluation of one important pro-

gram, Building Nebraska Families. Because it is an isolated single-site evaluation, I have not included it in my discussion here.

5. The survey did begin collecting monthly information in 1984.

6. Although a world with time limits come did not actually become federal law
until 1996, time limits were important in candidate Clinton's 1992 election
campaign and prominent in the post-election flow of state waiver requests (see
next section).

7. It was also a time, as Judy discusses in chapters 8 and 10, when some demonstrations were testing more expansionary approaches, such as increasing the
generosity of earned income disregards and allowing families to keep more savings and better cars while on welfare. But in most state policy environments,
these were definitely not the major focus.

8. Running for president, Dole resigned from the Senate about two months before President Clinton signed the welfare reform legislation. We were concerned that this would leave the research funding vulnerable, but that proved
not to be the case.

9. The study had two stages: the Project on State-Level Child Outcomes and the
Child Outcomes Synthesis Project. Since the study came to include experiments in five states, I refer to it here as the Five-State Child Impact study or
simply the Five-State study.

10. See chapter 10 for a fuller discussion of the MDRC states.

11. The original synthesis work for this book was funded by ACF through a contract
with the RAND Corporation, and issued as a report titled "Consequences of
Welfare Reform: A Research Synthesis" (Grogger, Karoly, and Klerman 2002).

12. The final report (Rangarajan and Novak 1999) was as discouraging as the preliminary results.

13. The ACF project officers were John Maniha, Patrice Richards, Tim Baker,
Brendan Kelly, and Michael Dubinsky.

14. The populations targeted by the remaining four programs were very disadvantaged individuals, the analysis of which was included in a separate report, along
with analysis of four other programs in a separate project that also targeted
hard-to-employ individuals (see next section).

15. The final report points out that, unlike the PESD programs, this program was
operated by community-based organizations, not welfare agencies; but given
that it is a single site, the evidence that this was indeed the differentiating cause
is very weak.

16.   The model can represent expected local variation of a program approach as long as the underlying causal assumptions are the same (for example, that remediation is the causal lever in improving employment prospects for low-skilled welfare recipients).

17.   The Administration for Children and Families project officer for the Hard-to-Employ was Girley Wright. The ASPE project officers were Audrey Mirsky-Ashby, Elizabeth Lower-Basch, Peggy Helgren, Kristen Joyce, and Amy Madigan. After the award, the Department of Labor also made a substantial investment in the study. The Department of Labor project officer was Roxie Nicholson.

18.   OPRE created a strong research agenda on healthy marriage, including two large-scale, multisite experiments, Building Strong Families and Supporting Healthy Marriage.

19.   Various problems prevented a fourth ERA program from being implemented as designed and it was terminated before analysis.

20.   In Philadelphia, only about half of those assigned to the treatment group participated in a subsidized job; hence the average length of stay for those who did was thirty days.

21.   The latter is based on the author's calculation, with a simplifying assumption, to Jacobs and Bloom (2011, table 1.1).

22.   The two transitional jobs evaluations cited in notes 27 and 28 below are currently investigating whether enhanced programs may yield greater success.

23.   Higher cost does not always mean better outcomes, as the Labor Force Versus Human Capital findings of the JOBS evaluation (chapter 9) demonstrate.

24.   The OPRE project officers for ISIS are Brendan Kelly and Emily Schmitt.

25.   In several welfare-to-work programs, occupational skills training did play a role, although for a much smaller proportion of the population than basic skills remediation or job search. Notable examples in the experimental research were in Baltimore (in the Work/Welfare demonstration), the Saturation Work Initiative Model in San Diego, and Portland's JOBS evaluation site. In addition, even in the period of the JOBS program, various smaller-scale efforts to improve welfare recipients' access to occupational skills training were under way.

26.   Of first-time community college entrants, only 15 percent obtain a degree or credential within three years, and 45 percent never do (Scott-Clayton 2011). Outcomes are considerably worse for low-income adults, who often enter requiring remediation (Bettinger and Long 2007; Goldrick-Rab and Sorenson 2010).

27. Certainly elements of career pathways programs are not new. For example, in the 1980s, the Center for Employment (CET) program in San Jose integrated basic and occupational skills and in random assignment evaluations showed strong impacts on earnings (Zambrowski, Gordon, and Berenson 1993).

28. The Worker Investment Act Adult and Dislocated Worker Programs Gold Standard evaluation, the Young Parents Demonstration Program, the Green Jobs and Health Care Impact evaluation, the YouthBuild evaluation, and the Enhanced Transitional Jobs demonstration.

29. The Subsidized and Transitional Employment demonstration, the TANF/SSI (Supplemental Security Income) Disability Transition Project, Behavioral Interventions to Advance Self-Sufficiency, Design Options of the Search for Employment, and Health Profession Opportunity Grants Impact Studies.

30. To some extent this was foreshadowed in ERA and Hard-to-Employ; in the former, the research samples for several sites included former TANF recipients, and in the latter only one of the four sites targeted current or even former recipients.

CHAPTER 12

1. This was the case, for example, in many experimental tests of employment programs for disadvantaged youth conducted during the same years.

2. These factors were sometimes also relevant at the county level, but it was important there to make sure that special funds offset added agency cost.

3. Hollister and Hill (1995, 134) captured this spirit: "random assignment designs are a bit like the nectar of the gods: once you've had a taste of the pure stuff it is hard to settle for the flawed alternatives."

4. These include Betsey, Hollister, and Papageorgiou (1985); Job Training Longitudinal Survey Research Advisory Panel (1985); LaLonde (1986); and Fraker and Maynard (1987).

5. One reason for the high federal concern about the fiscal neutrality of the waiver requests (particularly on the part of OMB, see chapter 7) was that some states sought changes that would disrupt this alignment of fiscal interests by shifting costs to the federal government, for example, through federal matching for activities that would otherwise have been 100 percent paid for with state dollars.

6. Because they are not truly universal, unemployment insurance records have their own limitations. There have been multiple studies comparing survey data with administrative records, including unemployment insurance records, as

sources for earnings information. A useful summary of studies is Hotz and Scholz (2001).

7. The recent explosion in studies that randomly assign groups or clusters (for example, schools or communities), used in only a few of the studies mentioned in this book, has opened up new domains.

8. For discussion and examples, see Bloom (2005).

9. Adapted from Doolittle, Hasselbring, and Traeger (1990).

10. "Effect size" is used to compare results across studies that use different outcome measures or when there is no easily transparent outcome measure. A common effect size measure is the standardized mean difference, defined as the difference between the means for experimentals and controls expressed in standard deviation units (that is, divided by either the pooled standard deviations of the two groups or the standard deviation of the control group).

11. As a paper by Gwyn Bevan and Christopher Hood (quoted in Heckman et al. 2011, 3) aptly put it, they may succeed in "hitting the target and missing the point."

12. This has not been the case in all areas of social policy, however. For example, Congress canceled a random assignment evaluation of Upward Bound and required that any future evaluation of it use nonexperimental methods. An earlier experimental evaluation of Upward Bound found that it had no significant effect on college enrollment.

CODA

1. See discussion in chapter 2.

2. Orr offers his view on why academics did not embrace experiments. "Experiments are totally antithetical to the rhythms and exigencies of academic life. At least as conducted in the early years, they required an enormous investment of the principal investigator's time and their results had a very long gestation period. It would have been hard to teach the obligatory course per semester and write several journal articles a year while running an experiment. They also required the kind of organization that few academic institutions had—one that could house (and manage!) a team of researchers and direct a large, multiyear field effort. More fundamentally, they did not involve the kind of methodological complexity for which academics were rewarded. The statisticians had worked out all the interesting questions involved in designing experiments by 1950. All that was left for the social experimenters was the grubby task of fielding the enterprise and then, after 5 or 6 years, computing some mean differ-

ences and t-statistics. In contrast, Heckman's method and statistical matching and instrumental variables—THERE was some stuff that could get you publications in top journals!"

3. As an example of support from at least some statisticians, Singer points to the clear message of her mid-1980s course: if you really want to draw causal inferences, do a randomized trial, with her tag line "You can't fix by analysis what you bungled by design" (Light, Singer, Willet 1990, viii).

4. For example, *Randomized Social Experiments eJournal*, edited by David H. Greenberg and Mark D. Shroder.

5. The number of completed experiments grew from twenty-one during 1962–1974, to fifty-two in 1975–1982, to seventy in 1983–1996 (Greenberg, Shroder, and Onstott 1999, 161), and the percentage outside the United States grew from about 15 percent of the total in 1991–1996 to 29 percent in 1997–2002 (Greenberg and Shroder 2004, 473). The latter article also shows that experiments decreased immediately after the 1996 welfare legislation, as we had anticipated (see chapters 10 and 11).

6. Baron states that he also found the combination of the evidence that nonrandomized studies got the wrong answer and that experiments worked to be particularly persuasive with nonresearchers.

7. Orr agrees that change "really picked up steam in the 90s. . . . Really good, smart, highly respected academics began to question—and improve upon—nonexperimental methods and to hold experiments up as the most reliable (if not the only) way to eliminate selection bias. Their writings not only swayed a number of their academic colleagues, but perhaps more importantly, framed the experimental method within a continuum of methods addressing a long-standing problem in econometrics: the so-called 'identification problem.' Suddenly, experiments had a natural place in academic lectures and it became de rigueur for thesis-writing students to explain how they had solved the identification problem in their own research."

8. Because the welfare studies almost always randomized individuals, our book does not highlight this trend.

9. The IES replaced the Office of Educational Research and Improvement as the research arm of the U.S. Department of Education.

10. As Whitehurst (2012, 115–16) puts it, "How is strong research to trump weak research in a marketplace that is unsophisticated with regard to research quality? There has to be an entity that vets research on program effectiveness . . . using rigorous scientific standards. And it has to become the preeminent source

for such information, effectively muting the cacophony of conflicting claims and assertions that arise from those who advocate with numbers or draw conclusions based on methods that cannot support causal conclusions. The Food and Drug Administration serves this function . . . and has had a transforming effect on health outcomes . . . by elevating science over quackery, opinion, and professional best (and often wrong) guess."

11. Angrist and Pischke (2010, 6) point out that, although Donald Campbell and Julian Stanley (1963) and Thomas Cook and Campbell (1979) "were well known in some disciplines, [they were] distinctly outside the econometric canon."

12. Robert Ivry calls the shift phenomenal. "In recent years, OMB has taken a very strong position that we are going to sustain or scale up what is proven to work and discontinue what doesn't work. And we are also going to subject long-standing federal programs that haven't been subjected to rigorous scrutiny to evaluation. . . . There was a greater recognition, with Peter Orszag being incredibly visible on this point, about the importance of evidence to making choices in a tough budget environment." An early Orszag blog (2009) makes the case for smarter investments based on evidence of effectiveness.

13. Both Stack and Baron affirm, as Howard and I note in earlier chapters, that interest in evidence varied among people, not parties. As Stack puts it, "I see so much similarity between Republicans and Democrats in leadership roles so that if you present the same evidence and data to them and it is strong, regardless of what party they are from, they will agree 85 percent of the time and where they don't agree it is because the data aren't there or it's fuzzy, so they have to rely on ideology."

14. See the Poverty Action Lab website at: www.povertyactionlab.org/ (accessed March 6, 2012).

15. As a signal that experiments had moved from a sideshow to center stage in economics, the American Economic Association in 2010 awarded Duflo its John Bates Clark Medal, given to an American economist under the age of forty who is judged to have made the most significant contribution to economic thought and knowledge. A year later, in a very different symbol of recognition, *Time* magazine named her one of the one hundred most influential people in the world.

16. The Coalition for Evidence-Based Policy website can be found at coalition4evidence.org. Quotes in chapter text come from website accessed March 14, 2012. Howard and I serve on the Coalition's Advisory Board, and Howard does consulting work for them.

17. The website www.campbellcollaboration.org (accessed March 6, 2012) lists its mission as helping people make informed decisions by preparing, maintaining, and disseminating systematic reviews of the effects of social programs.

18. Ivry also flags the Robin Hood foundation, as moving from an exclusive focus on direct service to valuing and supporting experiments, the Joyce Foundation for recognizing that null findings from an experiment can reflect a good investment in learning by a foundation in the business of taking risks, and the Growth Philanthropy Network, which seeks to use evidence to guide venture philanthropists and individual donors toward reputable nonprofits. Howard Bloom points to the role of the William T. Grant Foundation in advancing research methodology and training.

19. Orr singles out the importance of happenstance, that certain academics got involved in experiments early in their careers "in professional environments that were not constrained by the prevailing academic norms."

20. At MDRC, I watched the virus travel systematically to Canada (chapter 10) and informally to the UK (where James Riccio's repeated message about random assignment shared during a six-month fellowship contributed to that government's enthusiasm for launching its own large-scale social policy experiments) and to France (where Martin Hirsch, the high commissioner against poverty from 2007 to 2010 and the key person responsible for bringing experiments to that country, happened to be my cousin). As Hirsch writes, "Whenever she came on vacation, she would tell me about the [experiments] they were implementing. . . . For years I half-listened to her until I realized that such methods might be the means to unblock our French sclerosis" (Hirsch 2010, 223–24). When Hirsch was given responsibility to overhaul the French welfare system to reward work, he put his conviction into action, launching a program of social experimentation, emphasizing random assignment, in partnership with local authorities. The vision and rationale were very similar to that in the United States thirty years earlier but new in France: test promising ideas at small to moderate scale, get rigorous evidence of effectiveness and costs, and then use the findings to make more rational choices and decisions.

21. Baron calls a remaining challenge: convincing nonresearchers that experiments are really needed. "While people might understand that findings from random assignment provide the strongest evidence and accept that, there is not an understanding of the unreliability of either small, partly flawed random assignment studies or quasi-experiments. There is still too much of a tendency to jump to the silver and bronze standard, of saying, 'Well . . . it's still pretty good

evidence,' when there is reason to believe that these studies, in most cases, are not confirmed in more definitive evaluations."

22. Bloom continues: "I think that it will become more difficult to keep doing educational experiments unless we can find things that work more consistently and produce bigger effects and unless we can test things that we are better able to describe, to [tell] people what they are and how they can implement them. . . . We have to get inside the black box more. I think we won a war that says we can identify when things work, but we still need to be able to show we are valuable because we are also going to help figure out what it was that made that happen." Richard Murnane and Richard Nelson (2007) raise a different caution: that experiments in education may be more useful in evaluating routinized practices than in assessing the more complex and continually evolving practices that produce high-performing schools. For a recent critique of random assignment, see Deaton (2010).

NOTE ON SOURCES

GENERAL

Except for the sources cited specifically in the text and notes, which are included in the reference list at the back of the book, and the other important source documents listed below by chapter, the narrative is based on MDRC annual reports; memorandums, meeting minutes, and project reports from MDRC files and from Judith M. Gueron's and Howard Rolston's (or their colleagues') personal files; and retrospective author interviews with the major actors in the story, conducted between 2006 and 2012.

Sources for all direct quotes are cited, with page numbers in text and full publication information in the reference list, with the following exceptions:

- Quotes from MDRC annual reports are noted as such, by year, in the text.
- Quotes introduced in the present tense and identified as the speaker "recalling," "remembering," "now seeing it this way," and similar language are from the 2006 to 2012 personal interviews by the authors, as noted above (see the appendix for complete alphabetical listing by interviewee and method of interview—in person, by telephone, or by email).
- Quotes from newspaper articles are noted by date in the text.

SPECIAL SOURCE NOTES, BY CHAPTER

Chapter 2 (Judith M. Gueron) is based in part on Gueron (1980) and Gueron (1984b).

Chapter 3 (Judith M. Gueron) draws on Gueron (1984a) and particularly on Leiman (with Seessel 1982).

Chapter 4 (Judith M. Gueron) draws on Gueron (1983); Gueron (1985); and Gueron (1987).

Chapter 5 (Howard Rolston) relies on copies of the grant announcements for the relevant projects that OFA sponsored.

Chapter 6 (Judith M. Gueron) draws on Gueron (1985); Gueron (1987); Gueron (2002); Gueron and Pauly (1991); and MDRC 1987.

Chapter 7 (Howard Rolston) draws heavily on the states' waiver applications, original and revised as relevant, and the respective written responses from HHS.

Chapter 8 (Judith M. Gueron) draws on Riccio (1997); Freedman et al. (1996); and Bloom (1997).

Chapter 9 (Howard Rolston) relies on Institute for Research on Poverty (1989); Knab et al. (2001); and Hamilton (2000).

Chapter 10 (Judith M. Gueron) is informed by Berlin (2000); Gueron (2002); Michalopoulos (2005); and the other citations in the text. It also benefits from the projects' final reports: Miller et al. (2000); Gennetian and Miller (2000); Huston et al. (2003); Michalopoulos et al. (2002); and Ford et al. (2003).

Chapter 12 (Judith M. Gueron and Howard Rolston) draws on Gueron (2003); Gueron (2002); and Gueron (2007).

REFERENCES

Aaron, Henry J. 1978. *Politics and the Professors: The Great Society in Perspective.* Washington, D.C.: Brookings Institution Press.

———. 1990. "Review Essay." In "Social Science Research and Policy." *Journal of Human Resources* 25(2): 276–80.

Angrist, Joshua D. 2004. "American Education Research Changes Tack." *Oxford Review of Economic Policy* 20(2): 198–212.

Angrist, Joshua D., and Jorn-Steffen Pischke. 2010. "The Credibility Revolution in Empirical Economics: How Better Research Design Is Taking the Con out of Econometrics." *Journal of Economic Perspectives* 24(2): 3–30.

Ashenfelter, Orly, and David Card. 1985. "Using the Longitudinal Structure of Earnings to Estimate the Effects of Training Programs." *Review of Economics and Statistics* 67(4): 648–60.

Atkins, Charles M. 1986. "20,000 Choose Paycheck over Welfare Check." *Public Welfare* 44(1): 20–22.

Auspos, Patricia, George Cave, and David Long. 1988. *Maine: Final Report on the Training Opportunities in the Private Sector Program.* New York, N.Y.: MDRC (April).

Bane, Mary Jo, and David Ellwood. 1983. *The Dynamics of Dependence: The Routes to Self-Sufficiency.* Report to the U.S. Department of Health and Human Services. Cambridge, Mass.: Urban Systems Research and Engineering.

Bangser, Michael, James Healy, and Robert Ivry. 1985. *Grant Diversion: Early Observations from Programs in Six States.* New York, N.Y.: MDRC (March).

Barnow, Burt S. 1987. "The Impact of CETA Programs on Earnings: A Review of the Literature." *Journal of Human Resources* 22(2): 157–93.

Barnow, Burt S., and Jeffrey A. Smith. 2004. "Performance Management of U.S. Top Training Programs: Lessons from the Job Training Partnership Act." *Public Finance and Management* 4(3): 247–87.

Barr, N. A., and R. E. Hall. 1981. "The Probability of Dependence on Public Assistance." *Economica* 49(190): 109–23.

Baum, Erica B. 1991. "When the Witch Doctors Agree: The Family Support Act and Social Science Research." *Journal of Policy Analysis and Management* 10(4): 603–15.

Bavier, Richard. 2003. "Conditions Limiting Work Among TANF Entries, Stayers, and Leavers." Paper presented to the APPAM Panel on TANF Hard to Serve. Washington, D.C. (November 5, 2003).

Bell, Stephen H., Nancy R. Burstein, and Larry L. Orr. 1987. *Overview of Evaluation Results: Evaluation of the AFDC Homemaker-Home Health Aide Demonstrations.* Cambridge, Mass.: Abt Associates (December).

Berlin, Gordon L. 2000. *Encouraging Work and Reducing Poverty: The Impact of Work Incentive Programs.* New York, N.Y.: MDRC (March).

Berlin, Gordon L., et al. 1998. *Do Work Incentives Have Unintended Consequences? Measuring "Entry Effects" in the Self-Sufficiency Project.* Ottawa, Ont.: Social Research and Demonstration Corporation (March).

Betsey, Charles L., Robinson G. Hollister Jr., and Mary R. Papageorgiou. 1985. *Youth Employment and Training Programs: The YEDPA Years.* Washington, D.C.: National Academy Press.

Bettinger, Eric, and B. T. Long. 2007. "Institutional Responses to Reduce Inequalities in College Outcomes: Remedial and Developmental Courses in Higher Education." In *Economic Inequality and Higher Education: Access, Persistence, and Success,* edited by Stacy Dickert-Conlon and Ross Rubenstein. New York, N.Y.: Russell Sage Foundation.

Blank, Rebecca M. 2006. "What Did the 1990s Welfare Reforms Accomplish?" In *Public Policy and the Income Distribution,* edited by Alan J. Auerbach, David Card, and John M. Quigley. New York, N.Y.: Russell Sage Foundation.

Blank, Rebecca M., David E. Card, and Philip K. Robins. 2000. "Financial Incentives for Increasing Work and Income among Low-Income Families." In *Finding Jobs: Work and Welfare Reform,* edited by David E. Card and Rebecca M. Blank. New York, N.Y.: Russell Sage Foundation.

Bloom, Dan. 1997. *After AFDC: Welfare-to-Work Choices and Challenges for States.* New York, N.Y.: MDRC.

Bloom, Dan, and David Butler. 1995. *Implementing Time-Limited Welfare: Early Experiences in Three States.* New York, N.Y.: MDRC (November).

Bloom, Dan, and Charles Michalopoulos. 2001. *How Welfare and Work Policies Affect Employment and Income: A Synthesis of Research.* New York, N.Y.: MDRC (May).

Bloom, Howard S., ed. 2005. *Learning More from Social Experiments: Evolving Analytic Approaches.* New York, N.Y.: Russell Sage Foundation.

Bloom, Howard S., Carolyn J. Hill, and James A. Riccio. 2003. "Linking Program Implementation and Effectiveness: Lessons from a Pooled Sample of Welfare-to-Work Experiments." *Journal of Policy Analysis and Management* 22(4): 551–75.

———. 2005. "Modeling Cross-Site Experimental Differences to Find Out Why Program Effectiveness Varies." In *Learning More from Social Experiments: Evolving Analytic Approaches,* edited by Howard S. Bloom. New York, N.Y.: Russell Sage Foundation.

Bloom, Howard S., and Charles Michalopoulos. 2010. "When Is the Story in the Subgroups? Strategies for Interpreting and Reporting Intervention Effects on Subgroups." Working paper. New York, N.Y.: MDRC.

Bloom, Howard S., Charles Michalopoulos, and Carolyn J. Hill. 2005. "Using Experiments to Assess Nonexperimental Comparison-Group Methods for Measuring Program Effects." In *Learning More from Social Experiments: Evolving Analytic Approaches,* edited by Howard S. Bloom. New York, N.Y.: Russell Sage Foundation.

Bloom, Howard S., et al. 2008. "Performance Trajectories and Performance Gaps as Achievement Effect-Size Benchmarks for Educational Interventions." *Journal of Research on Educational Effectiveness* 1(4): 289–328.

Blum, Barbara B., with Susan Blank. 1990. "Bringing Administrators into the Process." *Public Welfare* 48(4): 4–12.

Brecher, Edward M. 1976. "Supported Work: A Social, Economic, and Administrative History Through December 31, 1974." Unpublished paper. New York, N.Y.: Ford Foundation (July).

———. 1978. *The Manpower Demonstration Research Corporation: Origins and Early Operations.* New York, N.Y.: Ford Foundation (February).

Breslau, Daniel. 1997. "Contract Shop Epistemology: Credibility and Problem Construction in Applied Social Science." *Social Studies of Science* 27(3): 363–94.

Brown, Amy. 1997. *Work First: How to Implement an Employment-Focused Approach to Welfare Reform.* New York, N.Y.: MDRC (January).

Burtless, Gary. 1986. "The Work Response to a Guaranteed Income: A Survey of Experimental Evidence." In *Lessons from the Income Maintenance Experiments: Pro-*

ceedings of a Conference, edited by Alicia Munnell. Conference Series 30. Boston, Mass.: Federal Reserve Bank of Boston (September 1986).

Butler, David, et al. 2012. *What Strategies Work for the Hard-to-Employ? Final Results of the Hard-to-Employ Demonstration and Evaluation Project and Selected Sites from the Employment Retention and Advancement Project.* OPRE report 2012-08. Washington: U.S. Department of Health and Human Services, Administration for Children and Families, Office of Planning and Evaluation (March).

Campbell, Donald T., and Julian C. Stanley. 1963. *Experimental and Quasi-Experimental Designs for Research.* Chicago, Ill.: Rand McNally.

Card, David E., Stefano DellaVigna, and Ulrike Malmendier 2011. "The Role of Theory in Field Experiments." *Journal of Economic Perspectives* 25(3): 39–62.

Congressional Budget Office. 1987. *Work-Related Programs for Welfare Recipients.* Washington: Congressional Budget Office (April).

Cook, Thomas D. 2010. "An Alien Parachutes into Economic Research on Low-Income Populations." *Focus* 27(2): 27–32.

Cook, Thomas D., and Donald T. Campbell. 1979. *Quasi-Experimentation: Design and Analysis Issues for Field Settings.* Chicago, Ill.: Rand McNally.

Coyle, Dennis J., and Aaron Wildavsky. 1986. "Social Experimentation in the Face of Formidable Fables." In *Lessons from the Income Maintenance Experiments: Proceedings of a Conference,* edited by Alicia Munnell. Conference Series 30. Boston, Mass.: Federal Reserve Bank of Boston (September 1986).

Deaton, Angus. 2010. "Instruments, Randomization, and Learning About Development." *Journal of Economic Literature* 48(2): 424–55.

Decker, Paul. 1991. *REACH Welfare Initiative Program Evaluation: Estimating the Effects of the REACH Program on AFDC Receipt.* Princeton, N.J.: Mathematica Policy Research (August).

DeParle, Jason. 2004. *American Dream: Three Women, Ten Kids, and a Nation's Drive to End Welfare.* New York, N.Y.: Viking Press.

Domestic Policy Council Low Income Opportunity Working Group. 1986. *Up from Dependency: A New National Public Assistance Strategy.* Report to the President. Washington, D.C.: Domestic Policy Council (December).

Doolittle, Fred, Darlene Hasselbring, and Linda Traeger. 1990. "Lessons on Site Relations from the JTPA Team: Test Pilots for Random Assignment." Internal Paper. New York, N.Y.: MDRC.

Doolittle, Fred, and Linda Traeger. 1990. *Implementing the National JTPA Study.* New York, N.Y.: MDRC (April).

Duflo, Esther, *and* Michael Kremer. 2008. "Use of Randomization in the Evaluation of Development Effectiveness." In *Reinventing Foreign Aid,* edited by William R. Easterly. Cambridge, Mass.: MIT Press.

Duncan, Greg J., Aletha C. Huston, and Thomas S. Weisner. 2007. *Higher Ground: New Hope for the Working Poor and Their Children.* New York, N.Y.: Russell Sage Foundation.

Edelman, Jonah M. 1995. "The Passage of the Family Support Act of 1988 and the Politics of Welfare Reform in the United States." Ph.D. diss., Oxford University.

Ellwood, David T. 1986. *Targeting "Would-Be" Long-Term Recipients of AFDC: Who Should Be Served.* Princeton, N.J.: Mathematica Policy Research.

———. 1988. *Poor Support: Poverty in the American Family.* New York, N.Y.: Basic Books.

Elmore, Richard F. 1985. "Knowledge Development Under the Youth Employment and Demonstration Projects Act, 1977–1981." In *Youth Employment and Training Programs: The YEDPA Years,* edited by Charles L. Betsey, Robinson G. Hollister Jr., and Mary R. Papageorgiou. Washington, D.C.: National Academy Press.

Farrell, Mary, et al. 2008. *Welfare Time Limits: An Update on State Policies, Implementation, and Effects on Families.* New York, N.Y.: Lewin Group and MDRC (April).

Federal Register. 1981. Vol. 46, No. 112. Notices (June 11).

Finney, Graham S. 1974. *Supported Work: Present Operations, Future Prospects.* New York, N.Y.: Ford Foundation (February).

Ford, Reuben, et al. 2003. *Can Work Incentives Pay for Themselves? Final Report on the Self-Sufficiency Project for Welfare Applicants.* Ottawa, Can.: Social Research and Demonstration Corporation (October).

Forsetlund, Louise, Iain Chalmers, and Arild Bjørndal. 2007. "When Was Random Allocation First Used to Generate Comparison Groups in Experiments to Assess the Effects of Social Interventions?" *Economics of Innovation and New Technology* 16(5): 371–84.

Fraker, Thomas M., and Rebecca A. Maynard. 1987. "The Adequacy of Comparison Group Designs for Evaluations of Employment-Related Programs." *Journal of Human Resources* 22(2): 194–227.

Freedman, Stephen, Jan Bryant, and George Cave. 1988. *New Jersey: Final Report on the Grant Diversion Project.* New York, N.Y.: MDRC (November).

Freedman, Stephen, et al. 1996. "The GAIN Evaluation: Five-Year Impacts on Employment, Earnings, and AFDC Receipt." Working paper. New York, N.Y.: MDRC (September).

Friedlander, Daniel. 1988. *Subgroup Impacts and Performance Indicators for Selected Welfare Employment Programs.* New York, N.Y.: MDRC (August).

Friedlander, Daniel, and Gayle Hamilton. 1993. *The Saturation Work Initiative Model (SWIM) in San Diego: A Five-Year Follow-Up Study.* New York, N.Y.: MDRC (July).

Friedman, Lee S. 1977. "An Interim Evaluation of the Supported Work Experiment." *Policy Analysis* 3(2): 147–70.

Friedman, Milton. 1962. *Capitalism and Freedom.* Chicago, Ill.: University of Chicago Press.

Garfinkel, Irwin. 1988. "Child Support Assurance: A New Tool for Achieving Social Security." In *Child Support: From Debt Collection to Social Policy,* edited by Alfred J. Kahn and Sheila B. Kamerman. Newbury Park, Calif.: Sage Publications.

Gennetian, Lisa A., and Cynthia Miller. 2000. *Reforming Welfare and Rewarding Work: Final Report on the Minnesota Family Investment Program.* Vol. 2, *Effects on Children.* New York, N.Y.: MDRC (September).

Gennetian, Lisa A., et al. 2002. *How Welfare and Work Policies for Parents Affect Adolescents: A Synthesis of Research.* New York, N.Y.: MDRC (May).

Ginzberg, Eli, Richard P. Nathan, and Robert M. Solow. 1984. "The Lessons from the Supported Work Demonstration." In *The National Supported Work Demonstration,* edited by Robinson G. Hollister, Peter Kemper, and Rebecca Maynard. Madison, Wisc.: University of Wisconsin Press.

Ginzberg, Eli, and Robert M. Solow. 1974. "Some Lessons of the 1960s." Special issue, *The Public Interest* 34(Winter): 211–20.

Goldman, Barbara S. 1980. *Immediate Job Search Assistance: Preliminary Results from the Louisville WIN Research Laboratory Project.* New York, N.Y.: MDRC (February).

Goldrick-Rab, Sara, and Kia Sorenson. 2010. "Unmarried Parents in College." *The Future of Children* 20(2): 179–203.

Gramlich, Edward M. 1990. "Review Essay." In "Social Science Research and Policy." *Journal of Human Resources* 25(2): 281–89.

Greenberg, David H., and Andreas Cebulla. 2005. *Report on a Meta-Analysis of Welfare-to-Work Programs.* Washington: U.S. Department of Health and Human Services (June).

Greenberg, David H., Victoria Deitch, and Gayle Hamilton. 2009. *Welfare-to-Work Program Benefits and Costs: A Synthesis of Research.* New York, N.Y.: MDRC (February).

Greenberg, David H., Donna Linksz, and Marvin Mandell. 2003. *Social Experimentation and Public Policymaking.* Washington, D.C.: Urban Institute Press.

Greenberg, David H., and Marvin B. Mandell. 1991. "Research Utilization in Policymaking: A Tale of Two Series (of Social Experiments)." *Journal of Policy Analysis and Management* 10(4): 633–56.

Greenberg, David H., and Mark Shroder. 2004. *The Digest of Social Experiments*. 3rd ed. Washington, D.C.: Urban Institute Press.

Greenberg, David H., Mark Shroder, and Matthew Onstott. 1999. "The Social Experiment Market." *Journal of Economic Perspectives* 13(3): 157–72.

Greenberg, David H., et al. 2001. "Explaining Variation in the Effects of Welfare-to-Work Programs." Discussion Paper 1225-01. Madison, Wisc.: University of Wisconsin, Institute for Research on Poverty.

Grogger, Jeffrey, and Lynn A. Karoly. 2005. *Welfare Reform: Effects of a Decade of Change*. Cambridge, Mass.: Harvard University Press.

Grogger, Jeffrey, Lynn A. Karoly, and Jacob Alex Klerman. 2002. *Consequences of Welfare Reform: A Research Synthesis*. Santa Monica Calif.: RAND (June).

Gueron, Judith M. 1980. "The Supported Work Experiment." In *Employing the Unemployed*, edited by Eli Ginzberg. New York, N.Y.: Basic Books.

———. 1982. "A Demonstration of State Welfare/Employment Initiatives." Paper presented at the Evaluation Research Society meetings. Baltimore (October 28, 1982).

———. 1983. "Remarks." In *Workfare: The Impact of the Reagan Program on Employment and Training*. New York, N.Y.: MDRC (June).

———. 1984a. *Lessons from a Job Guarantee: The Youth Incentive Entitlement Pilot Projects*. New York, N.Y.: MDRC (June).

———. 1984b. "Lessons from Managing the Supported Work Demonstration." In *The National Supported Work Demonstration*, edited by Robinson G. Hollister, Peter Kemper, and Rebecca Maynard. Madison, Wisc.: University of Wisconsin Press.

———. 1985. "The Demonstration of State Work/Welfare Initiatives." In *Randomization and Field Experimentation*, edited by Robert F. Boruch and Werner Wotke. New Directions for Program Evaluation 28. San Francisco: Jossey-Bass (December).

———. 1987. "Reforming Welfare with Work." Occasional Paper 2. Ford Foundation Project on Social Welfare and the American Future. New York, N.Y.: Ford Foundation.

———. 1997. "Learning About Welfare Reform: Lessons from State-Based Evaluations." In *Progress and Future Directions in Evaluation: Perspectives on Theory, Practice, and Methods*, edited by Debra J. Rog and Deborah Fournier, New Directions for Evaluation, 76. San Francisco, Calif.: Jossey-Bass (Winter).

———. 2002. "The Politics of Random Assignment: Implementing Studies and Affecting Policy." In *Evidence Matters: Randomized Trials in Education Research,* edited by Frederick Mosteller and Robert Boruch. Washington, D.C.: Brookings Institution Press.

———. 2003. "Presidential Address—Fostering Research Excellence and Impacting Policy and Practice: The Welfare Story." *Journal of Policy Analysis and Management* 22(2): 163–74.

———. 2007. "Building Evidence: What It Takes and What It Yields." *Research on Social Work Practice* 17(1): 134–42.

———. 2008. "Failing Well: Foundations Need to Make More of the Right Kind of Mistakes." *Stanford Social Innovation Review* 6(1): 25.

Gueron, Judith M., and Richard P. Nathan. 1985. "The MDRC Work/Welfare Project." *Policy Studies Review* 4(3): 417–32.

Gueron, Judith M., and Edward Pauly. 1991. *From Welfare to Work.* New York, N.Y.: Russell Sage Foundation.

Gueron, Judith M., Michael Rubinger, and Gary Walker. 1976. *First Annual Report on the National Supported Work Demonstration.* New York, N.Y.: MDRC (December).

Hamilton, Gayle. 2000. *Do Mandatory Welfare-to-Work Programs Affect the Well-Being of Children? A Synthesis of Child Research Conducted as Part of the National Evaluation of Welfare-to-Work Strategies.* Washington: U.S. Department of Health and Human Services and the U.S. Department of Education (June).

Hamilton, Gayle, et al. 2001. *How Effective Are Different Welfare-to-Work Approaches? Five-Year Adult and Child Impacts for Eleven Programs.* Washington: U.S. Department of Health and Human Services and the U.S. Department of Education (December).

Haskins, Ron. 1991. "Congress Writes a Law: Research and Welfare Reform." *Journal of Policy Analysis and Management* 10(4): 616–32.

———. 2006. *Work over Welfare: The Inside Story of the 1996 Welfare Reform Law.* Washington, D.C.: Brookings Institution Press.

Haskins, Ron, and Jon Baron. 2011. "Building the Connection Between Policy and Evidence: The Obama Evidence-Based Initiatives." Paper commissioned by the UK National Endowment for Science, Technology, and the Arts. September. Available at: http://coalition4evidence.org/wordpress/wp-content/uploads/Haskins-Baron-paper-on-fed-evid-based-initiatives-2011.pdf (accessed March 14, 2012).

Heckman, James J. 1992a. "Randomization and Social Policy Evaluation." In *Evalu-*

ating Welfare and Training Programs, edited by Charles F. Manski and Irwin Garfinkel. Cambridge, Mass.: Harvard University Press.

———. 1992b. "Basic Knowledge—Not Black Box Evaluations."*Focus* 14(1): 24–25.

Heckman, James J., et al., eds. 2011. *The Performance of Performance Standards.* Kalamazoo, Mich.: W. E. Upjohn Institute for Employment Research.

Hendra, Richard, et al. 2010. *How Effective Are Different Approaches Aiming to Increase Employment Retention and Advancement? Final Impacts for Twelve Models.* New York, N.Y.: MDRC (April).

Herr, Toby, and Robert Halpern. 1991. *Changing What Counts: Rethinking the Journey out of Welfare.* Evanston, Ill.: Northwestern University, Project Match and Center for Urban Affairs and Policy Research.

Hirsch, Martin. 2010. *Secrets de Fabrication: Chroniques d'une politique expérimentale.* Paris, France: Bernard Grasset.

Hobbs, Charles D. 1978. *The Welfare Industry.* Washington, D.C.: Heritage Foundation.

Hollister, Robinson G. 1984. "The Design and Implementation of the Supported Work Evaluation." In *The National Supported Work Demonstration,* edited by Robinson G. Hollister, Peter Kemper, and Rebecca Maynard. Madison, Wisc.: University of Wisconsin Press.

Hollister, Robinson G., Peter Kemper, and Rebecca A. Maynard (eds.). 1984. *The National Supported Work Demonstration.* Madison, Wisc.: University of Wisconsin Press.

Hollister, Robinson G., and Jennifer Hill. 1995. "Problems in the Evaluation of Community-Wide Initiatives." In *New Approaches to Community Initiatives: Concepts, Methods, and Contexts,* edited by James P. Connell et al. Roundtable on Comprehensive Community Initiatives for Children and Families. Aspen, Colo.: Aspen Institute.

Hotz, V. Joseph, Guido Imbens, and Jacob A. Klerman. 2006. "Evaluating the Differential Effects of Alternative Welfare-to-Work Training Components: A Re-Analysis of the California GAIN Program." Working Paper 11939. Cambridge, Mass.: National Bureau of Economic Research (January).

Hotz, V. Joseph, and John K. Scholz. 2001. "Measuring Employment and Income for Low-Income Populations with Survey and Administrative Data." Discussion Paper 1224-01. Madison, Wisc.: Institute for Research on Poverty.

Huston, Aletha C., et al. 2003. *New Hope for Families and Children: Five Year Results of a Program to Reduce Poverty and Reform Welfare.* New York, N.Y.: MDRC (June).

Jacobs, Erin, and Dan Bloom. 2011. *Alternative Employment Strategies for Hard-to-Employ TANF Recipients: Final Results from a Test of Transitional Jobs and Preemployment Services in Philadelphia.* OPRE Report 2011–19. Washington: U.S. Department of Health and Human Services, Administration for Children and Families, Office of Planning, Research, and Evaluation (December).

Job Training Longitudinal Survey Research Advisory Panel. 1985. *Recommendations: Report Prepared for the Office of Strategic Planning and Policy Development, Employment and Training Administration.* Washington: U.S. Department of Labor.

Kemper, Peter, David A. Long, and Craig Thornton. 1981. *The Supported Work Evaluation: Final Benefit-Cost Analysis.* New York, N.Y.: MDRC (September).

Kemple, James J., and Joshua Haimson. 1994. *Florida's Project Independence: Program Implementation Participation Patterns and First-Year Impacts.* New York, N.Y.: MDRC (January).

Kershaw, David, and Jerilyn Fair. 1976. *New Jersey Income Maintenance Experiment.* Vol. 1, *Operations, Surveys, and Administration.* New York, N.Y.: Academic Press.

Klerman, J. A. 2009. "'The Good, the Bad, and the Ugly' of Subgroup Analysis of Interventions and Some Suggestions for Improvement." Paper presented to the Interagency Federal Methodological Meeting, Subgroup Analysis in Prevention and Intervention Research. Washington, D.C. (September 30, 2009).

Knab, Jean Tansey, et al. 2001. *Do Mandates Matter? The Effects of a Mandate to Enter a Welfare-to-Work Program.* Washington: U.S. Department of Health and Human Services and U.S. Department of Education (November).

Kuttner, Robert. 2008. *Obama's Challenge: America's Economic Crisis and the Power of a Transformative Presidency.* White River Junction, Vt.: Chelsea Green Publishing.

LaLonde, Robert. 1986. "Evaluating the Econometric Evaluations of Training Programs with Experimental Data." *American Economic Review* 76(4): 604–20.

Leiman, Joan M., with Thomas Seessel. 1982. *The WIN Labs: A Federal/Local Partnership in Social Research.* New York, N.Y.: MDRC (July).

Levy, Frank. 1978. "Labor Supply of Female Household Heads, or AFDC Work Incentives Don't Work Too Well." *Journal of Human Resources* 14(1): 76–98.

Light, Richard J., Judith D. Singer, and John B. Willett. 1990. *By Design: Planning Research on Higher Education.* Cambridge, Mass.: Harvard University Press.

List, John A. 2011. "Why Economists Should Conduct Field Experiments and 14 Tips for Pulling One Off." *Journal of Economic Perspectives* 25(3): 3–16.

Lui-Gurr, Susanna, Sheila Currie Vernon, and Tod Mijanovich. 1994. *Making Work Pay Better Than Welfare: An Early Look at the Self-Sufficiency Project.* Ottawa, Ont.: Social Research and Demonstration Corporation (October).

Lynch, M. S. 2010. "Congressional Budget Office: Appointment and Tenure of the Director and Deputy Director." Washington, D.C.: Congressional Research Service (September 2).

Manski, Charles F., and Irwin Garfinkel, eds. 1992. *Evaluating Welfare and Training Programs.* Cambridge, Mass.: Harvard University Press.

MDRC. 1987. *Findings on State Welfare Employment Programs.* New York, N.Y.: MDRC (January).

MDRC Board of Directors. 1980. *Summary and Findings of the National Supported Work Demonstration.* Cambridge, Mass.: Ballinger.

Mead, Lawrence M., ed. 1997. *The New Paternalism.* Washington: Brookings Institution Press.

Meyer, Bruce D. 1995. "Natural and Quasi-Experiments in Economics." *Journal of Business & Economic Statistics* 13(2): 151–61.

Michalopoulos, Charles. 2005. *Does Making Work Pay Still Pay? An Update on the Effects of Four Earnings Supplement Programs on Employment, Earnings, and Income.* New York, N.Y.: MDRC (August).

Michalopoulos, Charles, and Christine Schwartz. 2001. *What Works Best for Whom? Impacts of 20 Welfare-to-Work Programs by Subgroup.* Washington: U.S. Department of Health and Human Services and the U.S. Department of Education (January).

Michalopoulos, Charles, et al. 2002. *Making Work Pay: Final Report on the Self-Sufficiency Project for Long-Term Welfare Recipients.* Ottawa, Ont.: Social Research and Demonstration Corporation (July).

Miller, Cynthia, et al. 2000. *Reforming Welfare and Rewarding Work: Final Report on the Minnesota Family Investment Program.* Vol. 1, *Effect on Adults.* New York, N.Y.: MDRC (September).

Moffitt, Robert A. 1992. "Evaluation Methods for Program Entry Effects." In *Evaluating Welfare and Training Programs,* edited by Charles F. Manski and Irwin Garfinkel. Cambridge, Mass.: Harvard University Press.

Moffitt, Robert A., and Michele Ver Ploeg, eds. 2001. *Evaluating Welfare Reform in an Era of Transition.* Washington, D.C.: National Academy Press.

Morris, Pamela A., and Greg J. Duncan. 2001. "Which Reforms Are Best for Children?" *Brookings Policy Brief* 6 (September): 1–7.

Morris, Pamela A., Lisa A. Gennetian, and Greg J. Duncan. 2005. "Effects of Welfare and Employment Policies on Young Children: New Findings on Policy Experiments Conducted in the Early 1990s." *Social Policy Report* 19(11): 3–18.

Morris, Pamela A., Lisa A. Gennetian, and Virginia Knox. 2002. "Welfare Policies Matter for Children and Youth." Policy brief. New York, N.Y.: MDRC (March).

Morris, Pamela A., et al. 2001. *How Welfare and Work Policies Affect Children: A Synthesis of Research.* New York, N.Y.: MDRC (March).

Moynihan, Daniel Patrick. 1987. *Welfare Reform, First Session on S869, S.1001, S.1511: Hearings before the Committee on Finance,* October 14 and 28.

———. 1992. *Congressional Record,* July 31, 1992.

———. 1995. Speaking before the Senate, August 7, 1995. 141 *Congressional Record,* August 7, 1995.

Murnane, Richard J., and Richard R. Nelson. 2007. "Improving the Performance of the Education Sector: The Valuable, Challenging, and Limited Role of Random Assignment Evaluations." *Economics of Innovation and New Technology* 16(5): 307–22.

Murray, Charles. 1994. "What to Do About Welfare." *Commentary* 98(6): 26–34.

Nathan, Richard P. 1988. *Social Science in Government: Uses and Misuses.* New York, N.Y.: Basic Books.

———. 2000. *Social Science in Government: The Role of Policy Researchers.* New York, N.Y.: Rockefeller Institute Press.

O'Neill, June A., et al. 1984. *An Analysis of Time on Welfare.* Washington, D.C.: Urban Institute.

Orr, Larry L. 1999. *Social Experiments: Evaluating Public Programs with Experimental Methods.* Thousand Oaks, Calif.: Sage Publications.

Orszag, Peter R. 2009. "Building Rigorous Evidence to Drive Policy." *OMBlog,* June 8. Available at: www.whitehouse.gov/omb/blog/09/06/08/BuildingRigorousEvidence toDrivePolicy (accessed May 25, 2010).

Peskin, Janice. 1983. "The Budgetary Effects of Work Requirements in AFDC." Internal document. Washington: Congressional Budget Office (June 3).

Polit, Denise F., Janet C. Quint, and James A. Riccio. 1988. *The Challenge of Serving Teenage Mothers: Lessons from Project Redirection.* New York, N.Y.: MDRC (October).

RAND. 2006. "The Health Insurance Experiment: A Classic RAND Study Speaks to the Current Health Care Reform Debate." RAND Research Brief. Santa Monica, Calif.: RAND Corporation.

Rangarajan, Anu, and Tim Novak. 1999. *The Struggle to Sustain Employment: The Effectiveness of the Post-Employment Services Demonstration.* Princeton, N.J.: Mathematica Policy Research (April).

Rangarajan, Anu, Peter Schochet, and Dexter Chu. 1998. *Employment Experiences of Welfare Recipients Who Find Jobs: Is Targeting Possible?* Princeton, N.J.: Mathematica Policy Research (August).

Redcross, Cindy, et al. 2010. *Work After Prison: One-Year Findings from the Transitional Jobs Reentry Demonstration.* New York, N.Y.: MDRC (October).

Research Triangle Institute. 1983. *Final Report: Evaluation of the 1981 AFDC Amendments.* Research Triangle Park, N.C.: Research Triangle Institute (April 15).

Riccio, James. 1997. "MDRC's Evaluation of GAIN: A Summary." *Evaluation Practice* 18(3): 241–52.

Riccio, James, and Daniel Friedlander. 1992. *GAIN: Program Strategies, Participation Patterns, and First-Year Impacts in Six Counties.* New York, N.Y.: MDRC (May).

Riccio, James, Daniel Friedlander, and Stephen Freedman. 1994. *GAIN: Benefits, Costs, and Three-Year Impacts of a Welfare-to-Work Program.* New York, N.Y.: MDRC (September).

Riemer, David R. 1988. *The Prisoners of Welfare.* Westport, Conn.: Greenwood (October).

Rivlin, Alice M. 1971. *Systematic Thinking for Social Action.* Washington, D.C.: Brookings Institution Press.

Roberts, Sam. 2009. *A Kind of Genius.* New York, N.Y.: Public Affairs.

Rogers-Dillon, Robin H. 2004. *The Welfare Experiments: Politics and Policy Evaluation.* Stanford, Calif.: Stanford University Press.

Rossi, Peter H. 1987. "The Iron Law of Evaluation and Other Metallic Rules." In *Research in Social Problems and Public Policy,* edited by Joann L. Miller and Michael Lewis. Vol. 4. Greenwich, Conn.: JAI Press.

Scott-Clayton, Judith. 2011. "The Shapeless River: Does Lack of Structure Inhibit Students' Progress at Community Colleges?" CCRC Working Paper 25. New York, N.Y.: Columbia University, Teachers College, Community College Research Center (January).

Solow, Robert M. 1980. "The Story of a Social Experiment and Some Reflections." Thirteenth Geary Lecture. Dublin, Ire.: Economic and Social Research Institute.

State of California. 1976. *Third Year and Final Report on the Community Work Experience Program.* Sacramento, Calif.: Employment Development Department (January).

Stromsdorfer, Ernst W. 1987. "Economic Evaluation of the Comprehensive Employment and Training Act: An Overview of Recent Findings and Advances in Evaluation Methods." *Evaluation Review* 11(4): 387–94.

Szanton, Peter L. 1991. "The Remarkable 'Quango': Knowledge, Politics, and Welfare Reform." *Journal of Policy Analysis and Management* 10(4): 590–602.

Teles, Steven M. 1996. *Whose Welfare: AFDC and Elite Politics*. Lawrence, Kans.: University of Kansas Press.

Tobin, James. 1966. "The Case for a Guaranteed Income." *The Public Interest* 4(4): 31–41.

Tout, Kathryn, et al. 2004. *Welfare Reform and Children: A Synthesis of Impacts in Five States; The Project on State-Level Child Outcomes*. Washington: U.S. Department of Health and Human Services (March).

Wallace, John W. 2011. "Review of the Coalition for Evidence-Based Policy." March 16. Available at: http://coalition4evidence.org/wordpress/wp-content/uploads/Report-on-the-Coalition-for-Evidence-Based-Policy-March-2011.pdf (accessed March 14, 2012).

Watts, Harold W., and Albert Rees, eds. 1977a. *New Jersey Income Maintenance Experiment*. Vol. 2, *Labor-Supply Responses*. New York, N.Y.: Academic Press.

———.1977b. *New Jersey Income Maintenance Experiment*. Vol. 3, *Expenditures, Health, and Social Behavior; and the Quality of the Evidence*. New York, N.Y.: Academic Press.

Weaver, R. Kent. 2000. *Ending Welfare as We Know It*. Washington, D.C.: Brookings Institution Press.

Whitehurst, Grover J. 2012. "The Value of Experiments in Education." *Education Finance and Policy* 7(2): 107–23.

Wiseman, Michael. 1991. "Research and Policy: An Afterword for the Symposium on the Family Support Act of 1988." *Journal of Policy Analysis and Management* 10(4): 657–66.

Wittgenstein, Ludwig. 1953. *Philosophical Investigations*. Translated by G. E. M. Anscombe. New York, N.Y.: Macmillan.

Zambrowski, Amy, Anne Gordon, and Laura Berenson. 1993. *Evaluation of the Minority Female Single Parent Demonstration: Fifth-Year Impacts at CET*. Princeton, N.J.: Mathematica Policy Research (December).

Zedlewski, Sheila R., and Donald W. Alderson. 2001. "Before and After Welfare Reform: How Have Families on Welfare Changed?" In *Assessing the New Federalism*. Policy Brief B-32. Washington, D.C.: Urban Institute.

INDEX

Boldface numbers refer to figures and tables.